Peterson's

MASTER THE

SAT

2011

Phil Pine
Margaret Moran, Editor

PETERSON'S

A **nelnet** COMPANY

About Peterson's

To succeed on your lifelong educational journey, you will need accurate, dependable, and practical tools and resources. That is why Peterson's is everywhere education happens. Because whenever and however you need education content delivered, you can rely on Peterson's to provide the information, know-how, and guidance to help you reach your goals. Tools to match the right students with the right school. It's here. Personalized resources and expert guidance. It's here. Comprehensive and dependable education content— delivered whenever and however you need it. It's all here.

For more information, contact Peterson's, 2000 Lenox Drive, Lawrenceville, NJ 08648; 800-338-3282 Ext. 54229.

Stephen Clemente, Managing Director, Publishing and Institutional Research; Bernadette Webster, Director of Publishing; Jill C. Schwartz, Editor; Ray Golaszewski, Manufacturing Manager; Linda M. Williams, Composition Manager; Carol Aickley, CD producer; Jeff Pagano, Jared Stein, CD Quality Assurance Analysts

ISBN-13: 978-0-7689-2881-5
ISBN-10: 0-7689-2881-1

Printed in the United States of America

10 9 8 7 6 5 4 3 2 1   12 11 10

Eleventh Edition

Petersons.com/publishing

Check out our Web site at www.petersons.com/publishing to see if there is any new information regarding the test and any revisions or corrections to the content of this book. We've made sure the information in this book is accurate and up-to-date; however, the test format or content may have changed since the time of publication.

Certified Chain of Custody

60% Certified Fiber Sourcing and
40% Post-Consumer Recycled

www.sfiprogram.org

*This label applies to the text stock.

Sustainability—Its Importance to Peterson's, a Nelnet company

What does sustainability mean to Peterson's? As a leading publisher, we are aware that our business has a direct impact on vital resources—most especially the trees that are used to make our books. Peterson's is proud that its products are certified by the Sustainable Forestry Initiative (SFI) and that all of its books are printed on paper that is 40 percent post-consumer waste.

Being a part of the Sustainable Forestry Initiative (SFI) means that all of our vendors—from paper suppliers to printers—have undergone rigorous audits to demonstrate that they are maintaining a sustainable environment.

Peterson's continually strives to find new ways to incorporate sustainability throughout all aspects of its business.

OTHER RECOMMENDED TITLES

Peterson's Master Critical Reading for the SAT
Peterson's Master Math for the SAT
Peterson's Master Writing for the SAT

Contents

PART I: SAT BASICS

PART II: DIAGNOSING STRENGTHS AND WEAKNESSES

PART III: SAT CRITICAL READING STRATEGIES

PART IV: SAT WRITING STRATEGIES

PART V: SAT MATH REVIEW

Contents

PART VI: FIVE PRACTICE TESTS

APPENDIX

Contents xi

Before You Begin

HOW THIS BOOK IS ORGANIZED

Whether you have three long months or just four short weeks to prepare for the exam, Peterson's *Master the SAT* will help you develop a study plan that caters to your individual needs and timetable. These step-by-step plans are easy to follow and remarkably effective. No matter which plan you select, begin by taking a diagnostic practice test.

THE DIAGNOSTIC PRACTICE TEST AND PROCESS

The diagnostic practice test does more than give you testing experience. Easy-to-use diagnostic tables help you track your performance, identify your strengths, and pinpoint areas for improvement. At the end of the diagnostic testing process, you will know what question formats are giving you the most difficulty: multiple-choice math or grid-ins, sentence completions, identifying sentence errors, or improving paragraphs. You will also know which topics to review in depth and which you can spend less time on, whether they are algebra or geometry, essay writing, or subject-verb agreement. By understanding your testing profile, you can immediately address your weak areas by working through the relevant review chapters, learning the important test-taking tips, and completing the additional practice exercises.

Alternate Uses of the Practice Tests

When you have completed your formal review, take the practice tests to sharpen your skills further. Even if you understand the SAT perfectly, you still need to practice applying the methods you have learned in Peterson's *Master the SAT*. Take the practice tests under simulated test conditions. Find a quiet place where you won't be interrupted, set a timer for the required time for each section, and work through each test as though it were test day. This will help you to get used to the time limits and to learn to pace yourself. If you don't have time to take full-length practice tests, Peterson's *Master the SAT* explains how to use timing drills to take shorter sections of the exams to combat your weaknesses, work on your pacing, and increase your level of confidence.

COMPREHENSIVE ANSWER EXPLANATIONS

At the end of each practice session, read all the answers and explanations, even for the questions that you answered correctly. There are comprehensive explanations for every one of the book's 1,000+ questions! By reading the answer explanations, you can learn from your mistakes.

You'll also find that Peterson's *Master the SAT* discusses all of the "big picture issues" other books ignore. For example, it addresses questions such as:

- How is the SAT really used for college admission?
- When should you take the test?
- How many times should you plan to take the SAT?
- Do all SAT scores "count" in the college admissions game?

By addressing these questions, Peterson's *Master the SAT* debunks prevailing myths and helps you put the SAT into its proper perspective. It also serves as your "college guidance counselor," giving you the expert advice you need to apply to college. And when you think about it, that's our number-one goal here. Our objective is to help you dramatically raise your scores so that you can maximize the likelihood of getting into the college of your choice.

SPECIAL STUDY FEATURES

Peterson's *Master the SAT* was designed to be as user friendly as it is complete. It includes several features to make your preparation easier. By taking full advantage of all features presented in Peterson's *Master the SAT,* you will become much more comfortable with the SAT and considerably more confident about getting a good score.

Overview

Each chapter begins with a bulleted overview listing the topics that will be covered in the chapter. You know immediately where to look for a topic that you need to work on.

Summing It Up

Each strategy chapter ends with a point-by-point summary that captures the most important points. The summaries are a convenient way to review the content of these strategy chapters.

Bonus Information

In addition, be sure to look in the page margins of your book for the following test-prep tools:

Note

Notes highlight critical information about the SAT format—for example, that the answers in the multiple-choice math section always go from smaller to larger.

Tip

Tips draw your attention to valuable concepts, advice, and shortcuts for tackling the SAT. By reading the tips, you will learn how to approach different question types, use process-of-elimination techniques, pace yourself, and guess most effectively.

Alert!

Wherever you need to be careful of a common pitfall or test-taker trap, you'll find an *Alert!* This information reveals and eliminates the misperceptions and wrong turns many people take on the exam.

ABOUT THE CD

If you have the CD edition of this book, you have additional SAT preparation available to you. The CD links you to 3 online practice tests. We suggest that you begin by taking the diagnostic test at the beginning of the book. Once you have an idea of how you did and where to focus your preparation, review the material in the book. As the final part of your preparation, take the other tests in the book and online, via the CD.

The CD also provides access to StudentEdge.com, Peterson's personalized online resource center that helps students prepare for life after high school. StudentEdge.com combines test preparation (a free online course for SAT prep), college search, financial aid planning, scholarship information, and career exploration in one convenient location.

The SAT isn't the only important part of your college application. Today more than ever, colleges are also putting substantial weight on your admissions essays. The experienced editors at EssayEdge can help you ensure that your essays are as good as they can be, whether you need a thorough proofread or one-on-one guidance from the start of the writing process. You will find a link to EssayEdge.com on the CD.

LINKS TO HIPPOCAMPUS™

Need additional subject review in math? Throughout the algebra and geometry review chapters, you'll see links to HippoCampus.org, a great new way to get the extra subject help you need. HippoCampus brings learning to life by providing multimedia lessons and course materials to students and teachers via the Web. Follow the links to the HippoCampus Web site, and you'll instantly have access to information on all aspects of algebra—from basic algebra principles to graphs of linear equations.

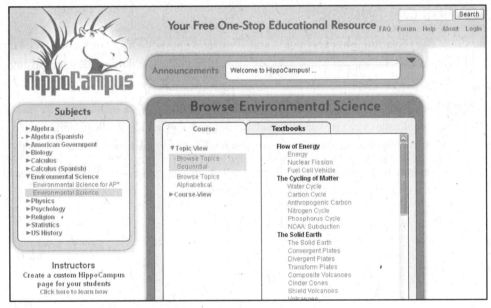

Throughout the Math chapters you'll see links that look like this:

 http://bit.ly/hippo_math2

Each link will take you to the specific subject you want to review. You can also use HippoCampus to take an actual refresher course. Either way, you'll not only have fun while learning, you'll also gain the extra knowledge and confidence you need to score high on your SAT.

A technical note: The HippoCampus Web site uses Adobe Flash. It's recommended that you have Adobe Flash Player 7.0 or higher installed on your system. In addition, some of the content requires Apple QuickTime version 6 or higher. Be sure to have QuickTime set to enable embedded flash content (you will find this option in the QuickTime control panel under advanced settings). Finally, because HippoCampus contains multimedia instructional content, it is also recommended that you have a high-speed Internet connection, such as DSL or Cable Modem.

HippoCampus is a project of the Monterey Institute for Technology and Education (MITE). Its goal is to provide high-quality, multimedia content on general education subjects to high school and college students free of charge. HippoCampus is supported by The William and Flora Hewlett Foundation and was designed as part of Open Education Resources (OER). The continually growing content on HippoCampus has been created by colleges and universities worldwide.

Peterson's is proud to join forces with HippoCampus to offer students like you access to the finest—and most innovative—educational content and resources.

YOU'RE WELL ON YOUR WAY TO SUCCESS

Remember that knowledge is power. By using Peterson's *Master the SAT,* you will be studying the most comprehensive SAT preparation guide available and you will become extremely knowledgeable about the SAT. We look forward to helping you raise your SAT scores and improve your college prospects. Good luck!

FIND US ON FACEBOOK®
FOLLOW US ON TWITTER™

Join the SAT conversation on Facebook® and Twitter™ at www.facebook.com/prep4sat and www.twitter.com/prep4sat. Peterson's resources are available to help you do your best on this important exam—and others in your future.

Peterson's publishes a full line of books—test prep, education exploration, financial aid, and career preparation. Peterson's publications can be found at high school guidance offices, college libraries and career centers, and your local bookstore and library. Peterson's books are now also available as eBooks.

We welcome any comments or suggestions you may have about this publication. Your feedback will help us make educational dreams possible for you—and others like you.

TOP 10 STRATEGIES TO RAISE YOUR SCORE

When it comes to taking the SAT, some test-taking skills will do you more good than others. There are concepts you can learn and techniques you can follow that will help you do your best. Here's our pick for the top 10 strategies to raise your score:

1. **Create a study plan and follow it.** The right SAT study plan will help you get the most out of this book in whatever time you have.

2. **Don't get stuck on any one question.** Since you have a specific amount of time to answer questions, you can't afford to spend too much time on any one problem.

3. **Learn the directions in advance.** If you already know the directions, you won't have to waste your time reading them. You'll be able to jump right in and start answering questions as soon as the testing clock begins.

4. **For the essay, it's important to develop your ideas and express them clearly, using examples to back them up.** Your essay doesn't have to be grammatically perfect, but it does have to be focused and organized.

5. **For the writing multiple-choice questions, think about the simplest, clearest way to express an idea.** If an answer choice sounds awkward or overly complicated, chances are good that it's wrong.

6. **For sentence completions, as you read, try to predict what word should go in each blank.** Sometimes you can guess the meaning of one blank, but not the other. In that case, scan the answer choices, look for a word that's similar to the one you've predicted, and then eliminate the answer choices that don't match up.

7. **For reading comprehension questions, skim the passage to see what it's about.** Don't worry about the details; you can always look them up later if you need to. Look for the main ideas, then tackle the questions that direct you straight to the answer by referring you to a specific line in the passage. If you have time afterward, you can try solving the harder questions.

8. **For the math multiple-choice questions, you're allowed to use a calculator, but it won't help you unless you know how to approach the problems.** If you're stuck, try substituting numbers for variables. You can also try plugging in numbers from the answer choices. Start with the middle number. That way, if it doesn't work, you can strategically choose one that's higher or lower.

9. **For the math grid-ins, you come up with the answer and fill it into a grid.** Unlike the multiple-choice questions, you won't be penalized for wrong answers, so make your best guess even if you're not sure.

10. **Finally, relax the night before the test.** Don't cram. Studying at the last minute will only stress you out. Go to a movie or hang out with a friend—anything to get your mind off the test!

PART I

SAT BASICS

All About the SAT

HOW THE SAT IS USED FOR COLLEGE ADMISSIONS

One explicitly stated purpose of the SAT is to predict how students will perform academically as first-year college students. But the more practical purpose of the SAT is to help college admissions officers make acceptance decisions. When you think about it, admissions officers have a difficult job, particularly when they are asked to compare the academic records of students from different high schools in different parts of the country taking different classes. It's not easy to figure out how one student's grade point average (GPA) in New Mexico correlates with that of another student in Florida. Even though admissions officers can do a good deal of detective work to fairly evaluate candidates, they benefit a great deal from the SAT. The SAT provides a single, standardized means of comparison. After all, virtually every student takes the SAT, and the SAT is the same for everyone. It doesn't matter whether you hail from Maine, Maryland, or Montana.

chapter 1

So the SAT is an important test. But it is not the be-all, end-all. Keep it in perspective! It is only one of several important pieces of the college admissions puzzle. Other factors that weigh heavily into the admission process include GPA, difficulty of course load, level of extracurricular involvement, and the strength of the college application itself.

WHEN YOU SHOULD TAKE THE SAT (AND SAT SUBJECT TESTS)

When you decide which schools you're going to apply to, find out if they require the SAT. Most do! Your next step is to determine when they need your SAT scores. Write that date down. That's the one you *really* don't want to miss.

You do have some leeway in choosing your test date. The SAT is offered on one Saturday morning in October, November, December, January, March, May, and June. Check the exact dates to see which ones meet your deadlines. To do this, count back six weeks from each deadline, because that's how long it takes ETS to score your test and send out the results.

What if you don't know which schools you want to apply to? Don't panic! Even if you take the exam in December or January of your senior year, you'll probably have plenty of time to send your scores to most schools.

When you plan to take the SAT, there is something even more important than the application deadlines of particular schools. You need to select a test date that works best with your schedule. Ideally, you should allow yourself at least two to three months to use this book to prepare. Many students like to take the test in March of their junior year. That way, they take the SAT several months before final exams, proms, and end-of-the-year distractions. Taking the test in March also gives students early feedback as to how they are scoring. If they are dissatisfied with their scores, there is ample opportunity to take the test again in the spring or following fall. But your schedule might not easily accommodate a March testing. Maybe you're involved in a winter sport or school play that will take too much time away from SAT studying. Maybe you have a family reunion planned over spring break in March. Or maybe you simply prefer to prepare during a different time of year. If that's the case, just pick another date.

If the schools you've decided on also require SAT Subject Tests, here's one good piece of advice: try to take SAT Subject Tests immediately after you finish the subject(s) in school. For most of you, this means taking the SAT Subject Tests in June. By taking the exam then, you'll save an awful lot of review work. Remember this, too: you have to register for the SAT Subject Tests separately, and you can't take the Subject Tests on the same day as the SAT. So check the dates, think ahead, and plan it out. It's worth it in the end.

HOW YOUR SCORES ARE REPORTED

After you have taken the SAT, ETS scores your test and creates a score report. We will discuss in detail how the SAT is scored later in this chapter. You and your high school receive score reports from each SAT and SAT Subject Test that you decide to take.

At the time of registration, you can pick four colleges or universities to also receive your score report. ETS will send your scores to these four schools for free. Within nine days of taking the test, you can change your school selection. If you want to send more than four reports or change your mind more than nine days after your test date, you will have to pay for it.

If you decide to take the SAT, or any SAT Subject Test, more than once, ETS offers you the option to decide which scores to send to the schools you've picked—scores from one, several, or all test dates. You may only designate the test date or dates for your score reports; you cannot designate individual test sections. In other words, if you take the SAT in October, December, and March, you cannot pick the Verbal score from October, Math score from December, and Essay score from March and tell ETS to send those results to the schools of your choice. You can only choose whether ETS should send your complete results from one, two, or all three test dates.

If you choose not to take advantage of this option, ETS will send all of your scores to the schools you've selected. However, no score reports will ever be sent without your specific consent. ETS will send e-mail reminders to you and your counselor, asking which scores you want to send, so you have time to make a decision at the time you take the SAT. You can find more information about this and how colleges and universities use your score reports on the Web site www.collegeboard.com.

HOW MANY TIMES SHOULD YOU TAKE THE SAT?

Different colleges evaluate the SAT in different ways. Some take your highest math, critical reading, and writing scores, even if they were earned on different test days. So if you nailed the math portion in March, the verbal portion in October, and the writing in December, the colleges will combine those three numbers to maximize your overall score. However, many other colleges won't do that. Some pay most attention to your highest combined score from a single day. Many others will average all of your scores or lend equal weight to all of them.

So what does this mean? It means that you should only take the SAT when you are truly prepared. There is nothing wrong with taking the SAT two or three times, as long as you are confident that your scores will improve substantially each time. Let's say that you scored a 1720 on your first SAT. If you would have been thrilled to have hit 1740, it's probably not worth taking the test again. Most colleges look at SAT scores in ranges and will not hold 20 points against you. They understand that scoring 1720 means that you were only one or two questions away from 1740. But if you scored 1720 and expected to score closer to 1900 or 2000 based on practice testing, then you should probably retake the exam. In other words, it is of little value to take the SAT multiple times if you expect to earn roughly the same score. But it is worthwhile if you expect to score significantly higher on a second or third try. For more advice about this, see your high school guidance counselor.

HOW TO REGISTER FOR THE SAT

You should register for the SAT at least six weeks before your testing date. That way you will avoid late registration fees and increase your chances of taking the exam at your first-choice testing center. You can register through the mail by completing the SAT registration form found inside the annual SAT bulletin. Your high school guidance office should have plenty of extra copies of the SAT bulletin. If you'd like, you can also register online or by telephone. Be sure to have a credit card handy to charge the fee. Check out the CollegeBoard Web site, www.collegeboard.com, for more information.

TIP

The questions in a set usually go from the easiest to the hardest. Try to go through the easy ones quickly but carefully. The exception to the easiest-to-hardest rule is the critical reading questions. These follow the development of the passage.

GET TO KNOW THE SAT FORMAT

The SAT consists of sections on mathematical reasoning, critical reading, and writing. There are eight sections that count toward your accumulated score and one—the wild card—that does not. The wild card, formally known as the experimental, section can be math, critical reading, or writing. This is the part of the test where ETS—the company that writes the SAT—tries out questions that might be used on future tests. Even though the wild card section doesn't count toward your score, you won't know which section it is. ETS does this on purpose. It knows that if you knew which section didn't count, you probably wouldn't try your hardest on it. So you'll have to do your best on all the sections.

The sections are timed to range from 20 to 35 minutes. The whole test, including the experimental section, takes 3 hours and 45 minutes. Don't worry. There are breaks. The following chart gives you an idea of what to expect. Note that the order of the sections will vary and are mixed so that you may have a math section followed by a critical reading section followed by a writing section. You won't have all the math sections grouped together and then both writing sections.

FORMAT OF A TYPICAL SAT

Critical Reading

Time	Total: 70 minutes • Two 25-minute sections • One 20-minute section
Content	Reading Comprehension: Questions based on • Single paragraphs • Longer passages • Paired paragraphs • Paired longer passages • Sentence-level reading
Question Types	• Multiple-choice with 5 answer choices • Critical reading • Sentence completions
Score	200–800

Writing

Time	Total: 60 minutes • 25-minute essay • One 25-minute multiple-choice section • One 10-minute multiple-choice section
Content	• Grammar and usage • Word choice (diction)
Question Types	• Multiple-choice with 5 answer choices • Identifying sentence errors • Improving sentences • Improving paragraphs • Student-written essay
Score	200–800; essay subscore 2–12

Math

Time	Total: 70 minutes • Two 25-minute sections • One 20-minute section
Content	• Algebra I • Algebra II • Geometry • Data analysis, statistics, probability
Question Types	• Multiple-choice with 5 answer choices • Student-produced responses (grid-ins)
Score	200–800

TIP

On the SAT, all questions count the same. You won't get more points for answering a really difficult math question than you will get for answering a very simple sentence completion question. Remember that when you're moving through the test. The more time you spend wrestling with the answer to one "stumper," the less time you have to whip through several easier questions.

www.twitter.com/prep4sat

GET TO KNOW THE SAT QUESTION TYPES

The question types in the SAT don't cover a wide variety of topics. They are very limited—no science, no world languages, no social studies. You'll find only questions testing reading comprehension, writing skills, and math skills—skills that you've been working on since kindergarten.

Most of the questions are multiple choice. That's good because it means the correct answer is right there on the page for you. You just have to find it—easier said than done sometimes, but true. Only the math grid-ins and the essay are student-produced answers. For the grid-ins, you'll need to do the calculations and then fill in bubbles on the answer sheet to show your answers. (More about the bubbles later in this chapter.) The following pages provide you with a closer look at the question types and question formats that you will find in each section on the SAT.

SAT CRITICAL READING SECTION

The critical reading section tests your reading comprehension, critical reading skills, and vocabulary. All the questions are multiple choice. The critical reading section may be a mix of sets of sentence completion questions and sets of questions relating to paragraphs and/or longer passages.

Sentence Completions

Just as the name implies, sentence completions are fill-in-the-blank questions. They may have one or two blanks. Your job is to analyze the answer choices and choose the word or words that best fit each blank. The questions test how well you can use context clues and word meanings to complete a sentence.

The directions for SAT sentence completion questions look like this:

Directions: Each of the following sentences contains one or two blank spaces to be filled in by one of the five choices listed below each sentence. Select the word or words that best complete the meaning of the sentence.

Here are three sample SAT sentence completion questions. Try each one on your own, before you read the explanation that accompanies it.

Many hours of practice are required of a successful musician, so it is often not so much _____ as _____ that distinguishes the professional from the amateur.

(A) genius .. understanding

(B) money .. education

(C) talent .. discipline

(D) fortitude .. mediocrity

(E) technique .. pomposity

The sentence gives you a clue about the correct answer. The "not so much . . . as . . ." lets you know that there is some kind of contrast here. Choices (B) and (C) both show a contrast, but choice (C) is the only one that makes sense in the sentence. **The correct answer is (C).**

The sudden death of the world-renowned leader _____ his followers, but it _____ his former opponents.

(A) saddened .. devastated

(B) shocked .. encouraged

(C) depressed .. tempered

(D) satisfied .. aided

(E) prostrated .. depressed

The word *but* is your clue that the word in the second blank will contrast with the word in the first blank. Only the words *shocked* and *encouraged* offer the logical contrast that is expected between the feelings of followers and opponents on the death of a leader. **The correct answer is (B).**

Despite his valor on the football field, the star athlete _____ when forced to take a flu shot.

(A) relaxed

(B) trembled

(C) hustled

(D) sidled

(E) embellished

The word *despite* is your clue that the athlete will do something less than heroic when confronted with the flu shot. *Trembled* completes the sentence and continues the strong tone of irony. **The correct answer is (B).**

Reading Comprehension

SAT reading comprehension questions present a passage about which you'll read and answer questions. The passage may be a single paragraph, paired paragraphs, one long passage, or paired long passages. The questions follow the order in which the information appears in the passage. The passage can be about almost anything, and the questions test how well you understand the passage and the information in it. The answer to every question is either directly stated or implied in the reading selection.

The directions for reading comprehension questions look like the following:

Directions: The passage below is followed by a set of questions. Read the passage and answer the accompanying questions, basing your answer on what is stated or implied in the passage.

Here is a sample of what to expect in the way of passages. This is about the length of a single paragraph passage.

The following passage discusses the mythical island of Atlantis.

A legendary island in the Atlantic Ocean beyond the Pillars of Hercules was first mentioned by Plato in the Timaeus. Atlantis was a fabulously beautiful and prosperous land, the seat of an empire 9,000 years before Solon. Its inhabitants overran part of Europe and Africa, Athens alone being able to defy them. Because of the impiety of its people, the island was destroyed by an earthquake and inundation. The legend may have existed before Plato and may have sprung from the concept of Homer's Elysium. The possibility that such an island once existed has caused much speculation, resulting in a theory that pre-Columbian civilizations in America were established by colonists from the lost island.

NOTE

In SAT critical reading questions, the answers will always be directly stated or implied in the passage.

The main purpose of the passage is to discuss

(A) the legend of Atlantis.

(B) Plato's description of Atlantis in the Timaeus.

(C) the conquests made by citizens of Atlantis.

(D) the possibility that the Americas were settled by colonists from Atlantis.

(E) the destruction of Atlantis.

The main purpose should be represented by an overall statement. While the details in choices (B), (C), (D), and (E) are all mentioned in the text, choice (A) is the only overall statement. **The correct answer is (A).**

According to the passage, we may safely conclude that the inhabitants of Atlantis

(A) were known personally to Homer.

(B) were a peace-loving people who stayed close to home.

(C) were a religious and superstitious people.

(D) used the name Columbus for America.

(E) were never visited by Plato.

At the time Plato mentioned Atlantis, it was already legendary. Therefore, Plato could not have visited the island. **The correct answer is (E).**

According to the legend, Atlantis was destroyed because the inhabitants

(A) failed to obtain an adequate food supply.

(B) failed to conquer Greece.

(C) failed to respect their gods.

(D) believed in Homer's Elysium.

(E) had become too prosperous.

The only cause that's mentioned in the passage is the impiety of the people of Atlantis. **The correct answer is (C).**

SAT WRITING SECTION

The SAT writing test consists of multiple-choice questions and one student-produced essay. The multiple-choice questions test how well you understand and use Standard Written English. The questions are divided into the following topics:

- Identifying sentence errors
- Improving sentences
- Improving paragraphs

Identifying Sentence Errors

Identifying sentence error questions provide you with four possible errors in a single sentence to correct. You must decide which underlined portion, if any, is incorrect. The directions for identifying sentence errors look something like the following:

Directions: The sentences below contain errors in grammar, usage, word choice, and idiom. Parts of each sentence are underlined and lettered. Decide which underlined part contains the error and circle its letter. If the sentence is correct as it stands, circle E under "No error." No sentence contains more than one error.

Here are some examples.

Our blue team competed <u>with</u> our white team <u>for</u> five years, but the white
                     A   B   C

team was <u>best</u> every time. <u>No error</u>
        D   E

In cases of comparison of two things, the comparative form of the adjective must be used. The comparative form of the word *good* is *better*. Only where there are three or more things being compared should the superlative form be used. **The correct answer is (D).**

From the <u>shards</u> of glass <u>laying all</u> <u>over</u> the living room, we hastily <u>inferred</u>
        A   B   C   D

that there had been an implosion brought on by the cyclone. <u>No error</u>
                                           E

Laying is the present participle of *lay* ("to put in place," "to set, as a table"). *Lying* is the present participle of *lie* ("to recline," "to remain in position," "to remain motionless"), which should be used here. **The correct answer is (B).**

<u>According to</u> Thoreau, Walden was the <u>deepest</u> pond in the area and the last
   A   B

<u>to freeze</u> every <u>winter.</u> <u>No error</u>
   C   D   E

The sentence is correct as written. Be careful on the real SAT: Answer choice (E) does not come up more than a couple of times. If you pick that answer choice more than that, go back and reconsider your choices. **The correct answer is (E).**

Improving Sentences

Improving sentence questions test how well you know and use standard punctuation and grammar. Some questions also assess your ability to spot and revise wordiness. The directions look something like the following:

NOTE

Remember that choice (E) is always "No error" in identifying sentence error questions. You can save yourself some time by not reading answer (E)—but only for identifying sentence error questions.

Directions: The sentences below contain problems in grammar, sentence construction, word choice, and punctuation. Part or all of each sentence is underlined. Select the lettered answer that contains the best version of the underlined section. Answer (A) always repeats the original underlined section exactly. If the sentence is correct as it stands, select choice (A). Circle the letter that appears before your answer.

The reason we stopped fishing was <u>because the fish had already stopped biting</u>.

(A) because the fish had already stopped biting

(B) because the fish had all ready stopped biting

(C) that the fish had already stopped biting

(D) that the fish had all ready stopped biting

(E) because the fish had stopped biting already

The conjunction "because" makes no sense following "reason." A subordinate conjunction like "that" or "why" makes better logic. Choice (D) is wrong because "all ready" is not an adverb. **The correct answer is (C).**

Ignorance of the law does not <u>preclude you from being arrested</u> for a misdemeanor.

(A) preclude you from being arrested

(B) prevent you from being innocent

(C) preclude you from being innocent

(D) prevent your being acquitted

(E) preclude your being arrested

"Preclude" should not be confused with "prevent." The idea of preventing something from happening *in advance* differs from mere prevention "on the spot." Choice (D) is correct usage since the genitive *your* precedes the participle *being,* but it changes the meaning of the original sentence. **The correct answer is (E).**

The textbook was poorly written, outdated, and <u>with errors</u>.

(A) with errors

(B) with mistakes

(C) factually incorrect

(D) showing errors

(E) being erroneous

Factually incorrect is needed to parallel *poorly written, outdated.* **The correct answer is (C).**

Improving Paragraphs

For this set of questions, you will be given passages about which you'll read and answer questions. The passages are supposed to imitate a first draft, and your job is to revise and improve it. Questions may relate to individual sentences, paragraphs, or the essay as a whole. The directions are similar to the following:

Directions: Questions 1–3 are based on a passage that might be an early draft of a student's essay. Some sentences in this draft need to be revised or rewritten to make them both clear and correct. Read the passage carefully, then answer the questions that follow it. Some questions require decisions about diction, usage, tone, or sentence structure in particular sentences or parts of sentences. Other questions require decisions about organization, development, or appropriateness of language in the essay as a whole. For each question, choose the answer that makes the intended meaning clearer and more precise and that follows the conventions of Standard Written English.

(1) Is television an enhancer of or a deterrent to education? (2) Some educators feel that, properly managed, television can open up educational vistas to children and expose them to ideas; others say that television stifles activity and turns children into passive creatures. (3) Certainly most people will agree that television is here to stay and that parents must accept the fact that their children are going to watch programs and they will have to deal with it. (4) By this, they must learn first of all what kind of programs are available and also the time schedule. (5) Perhaps they will have to preview programs. (6) Then parents must decide which programs will be beneficial for children.

In relation to the entire passage, which of the following best describes the writer's intention in sentence (2).

(A) To evaluate an opinion set forth in paragraph two

(B) To point out a difference of opinion regarding the opening sentence

(C) To restate the opening sentence

(D) To provide examples

(E) To summarize contradictory evidence

The first sentence, phrased as a question, presents the two opposing views of television vis-à-vis education. The second sentence rephrases this by using the two camps of educators, the first viewing it as an enhancer and the second viewing it as a deterrent to education. Thus, sentence (2) restates the first sentence. **The correct answer is (C).**

Which of the following is the best revision of the underlined portion of sentence (3) below?

Certainly most people will agree that television is here to stay and that parents must accept the fact that their children are going to watch programs and they will have to deal with it.

(A) will have to deal with their children's television watching

(B) will as a result be forced to accept their children as they watch television

(C) must accept and deal with their children if they watch television

(D) must accept this, children will watch television and this must be handled

(E) will have to deal with their children since they will watch television

The underlined portion is awkward and wordy, and it ends with a pronoun whose antecedent is not clear. Choice (A) corrects these weaknesses. Choices (B), (C), and (E) change the meaning of the sentence, and choice (D) is grammatically incorrect. **The correct answer is (A).**

Which of the following is the best way to combine sentences (4), (5), and (6)?

(A) Parents will have to learn time schedules, programs, and how to evaluate television.

(B) The availability of programs as well as the time schedule will help parents to evaluate programs beneficial to children.

(C) Subject matter of programs, time scheduling, and even actual previewing are factors that help parents decide on the suitability of television for children.

(D) In order to decide on what programs are beneficial for their children, parents will have to develop criteria.

(E) It is up to parents to evaluate programs for their children.

Only choice (C) takes in all the ideas expressed in sentences (4), (5), and (6)—kinds of programs available, time schedules, previewing, and deciding which programs are beneficial—and combines them in a grammatically correct sentence. Choice (A) is awkward and changes the intended meaning. Choices (B), (D), and (E) omit much of the original meaning. **The correct answer is (C).**

The Essay

You will be given one essay prompt and asked to write a persuasive essay in response to it. You don't need any specific subject-area knowledge to write your essay. The objective is to show the readers that you can develop a thesis, support it with examples, and come to a conclusion that accurately describes your point of view on the topic. The directions and essay prompt will be similar to the following:

Directions: Think carefully about the statement below and the assignment that follows it.

Topic: Some people criticize city life for being dangerous, expensive, and noisy. Others describe country life as dull, culturally empty, and narrow-minded.

Assignment: What is your opinion of the city versus country living argument? Plan and write an essay that develops your ideas logically. Support your opinion with specific evidence taken from your personal experience, your observations of others, or your reading.

To write an essay in response to this prompt, you would need first to determine what you think about the issue and why. The "why" would then become your argument. The next step would be deciding on at least three examples to present to support your "why's." This planning step is the most important part of your essay.

SAT MATH SECTION

The questions in the math section are about problem solving in arithmetic, basic and intermediate algebra, geometry, data analysis, statistics, and probability. There are two question formats for math questions: multiple-choice and grid-ins (student-produced responses).

Multiple-Choice Math

SAT multiple-choice math questions look like all the other standard multiple-choice math questions you've ever seen. A problem is given in arithmetic, algebra, geometry, or statistics, and five answers are presented from which you must choose the correct answer. The major concepts that you might need in order to solve math problems are given in the test section. You don't need to worry about memorizing these facts, but you do need to know when to use each one. The directions are similar to the following:

> **Directions:** Solve the following problems using any available space on the page for scratchwork. On your answer sheet, fill in the choice that best corresponds to the correct answer.
>
> **Notes:** The figures accompanying the problems are drawn as accurately as possible unless otherwise stated in specific problems. Again, unless otherwise stated, all figures lie in the same plane. All numbers used in these problems are real numbers. Calculators are permitted for this test.

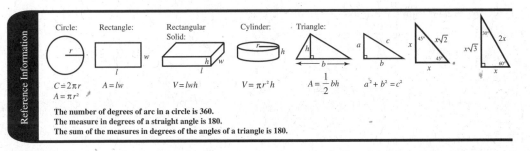

Here are some sample multiple-choice math questions. Try them yourself before looking at the solutions that are given.

> A certain triangle has sides that are, respectively, 6 inches, 8 inches, and 10 inches long. A rectangle with an area equal to that of the triangle has a width of 3 inches. What is the perimeter of the rectangle, in inches?
>
> **(A)** 11
>
> **(B)** 16
>
> **(C)** 22
>
> **(D)** 24
>
> **(E)** 30

The area of the triangle is $\frac{1}{2}bh$, which in this case is $\frac{1}{2} \times 6 \times 8 = 24$. The area of a rectangle is $A = l \times w$. We know the width and area, $24 = l \times 3$; therefore, $l = 8$. The perimeter of the rectangle is $P = 2l + 2w$, which we find to be $(2 \times 8) + (2 \times 3) = 16 + 6 = 22$. **The correct answer is (C).**

TIP

While a calculator may be helpful in solving some SAT math questions, it isn't *absolutely* necessary for any problem—and in some cases it won't help you at all. In this book, we show you where we think a calculator may be helpful. On test day, use your judgment in choosing whether—and when—to use a calculator.

The closest approximation to the correct answer for $5 - \sqrt{32.076} + 1.00017^3$ is

(A) 9.

(B) 7.

(C) 5.

(D) 3.

(E) 0.

$\sqrt{32.076}$ is slightly more than halfway between 5 and 6, say 5.6. Also, 1.00017^3 is slightly over $1^3 = 1$. Therefore, $5 - 5.6 + 1 = 0.40$. The closest answer given is 0. **The correct answer is (E).**

If the numerator and denominator of a proper fraction are increased by the same quantity, the resulting fraction is

(A) always greater than the original fraction.

(B) always less than the original fraction.

(C) always equal to the original fraction.

(D) one half the original fraction.

(E) not determinable.

If the numerator and denominator of the fraction $\dfrac{n}{d}$ are increased by a quantity q, the new fraction is $\dfrac{(n+q)}{(d+q)}$. Compare this to the old fraction by finding a common denominator $d(d+q)$. The old fraction is $\dfrac{n(d+q)}{d(d+q)} = \dfrac{(nd+nq)}{d(d+q)}$; the new fraction is $\dfrac{d(n+q)}{d(d+q)} = \dfrac{(nd+dq)}{d(d+q)}$. Comparing the old numerator $(nd+nq)$ with the new, the new fraction is larger, since $d > n$. The fraction in this example must be a proper fraction. **The correct answer is (A).**

Grid-Ins

Unlike multiple-choice math, the grid-in section of the SAT does not give you the answers. You have to compute the answer and then fill in your answer in the bubbles on your answer sheet. You may use the Reference Information table for these problems also. The directions for the grid-ins are similar to the following:

Directions: Solve each of the following problems and write the arithmetic value of your answer in the open spaces at the top of the correspondingly numbered grid on your answer sheet. Then grid your answer by blackening the ovals that correspond to the decimal point, fraction line, and numbers in your answer.

Notes: If a question has more than one correct answer, grid only one of them.

To grid $4\frac{1}{4}$, use 4.25 or $\frac{17}{4}$. Do not use $4\frac{1}{4}$ as it will be read as $\frac{41}{4}$.

None of these answers requires a minus sign.

Answers may begin in any grid column.

Decimal answers should be entered with the greatest accuracy allowed by the grid.

The circumference of a circle is 20π. If the area of the circle is $a\pi$, what is the value of a?

$C = 2\pi r = 20\pi$

$r = 10$

$A = \pi r^2 = \pi(10)^2 = 100\pi = a\pi$

$a = 100$

If 35% of a number is 70, what is the number?

$\frac{35}{100} \bullet x = 70$

$\frac{35x}{100} = 70$

$x = 200$

Find the mode of the following group of numbers: 8, 8, 9, 10, 11

The mode is the number that occurs most frequently. The mode = 8.

THE SAT ANSWER SHEET

On the day of the test when you are given your test booklet, you'll also be given a separate answer sheet. For each multiple-choice question, you'll see a corresponding set of answer ovals, also known as bubbles. The ovals are labeled A to E. Remember the following about the answer sheet:

- Answer sheets are read by machines—and machines can't think. That means it's up to you to make sure you're in the right place on the answer sheet every time you record an answer. The machine won't know that you really meant to answer Question 25 when you marked the space for Question 26.

- Don't be a wimp with that pencil. Fill in your chosen answer ovals completely and boldly so that there can be no mistake about which answers you chose.

Take a look at this sample answer sheet. You can just imagine what the machine will do with it.

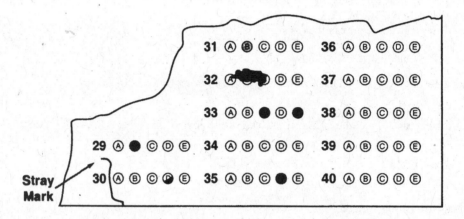

In the answer-sheet example we show you here, the only answers that will be registered correctly are 29 and 35. Question 30 isn't filled in completely, and Question 31 isn't dark enough, so the machine might miss it. Question 32 is a total mess—will the machine choose A, B, or C?

Since Question 33 has two ovals filled in, they cancel each other out and this is registered as an omitted question. There's no penalty, but there's no credit either. The same will happen with Question 34; no answer, no credit.

Let's move on to the student-produced responses. You'll still be filling in ovals, but they will look a little different from the multiple-choice ovals. Here's a sample of the special grid you will use.

TIP

Make sure you're in the right place! Always check to see that the answer space you fill in corresponds to the question you are answering.

← *boxes to write your numerical answer*
← *fraction lines—use at most one per answer*
← *decimal points—use at most one per answer*

At the top of the grid, you'll write in the actual numerical answer. The slashes are used for answers with fractions. If you need one of these fraction lines in your answer, darken one of the ovals. The ovals with the dots are for answers with decimal points—use these ovals just as you do the fraction line ovals. Then you use the number ovals to represent the actual numbers in your answer.

HOW THE SAT IS SCORED

OK, you've filled in all your ovals, written your essay, the 3 hours and 45 minutes are up (not a minute too soon), and you've turned in your answer sheet and your essay sheet. What next? Off your answers go to the machines at ETS and to the high school and college teachers who have been trained to read and score the essays. The machines can scan the bubble sheets in seconds and calculate a score for most of your test. Two readers will score your essay and return their scores to ETS.

In scoring the multiple-choice and grid-in sections of the SAT, the machines give one point for each correct answer and deduct one-quarter point for each incorrect answer. Incorrect answers to grid-in questions have no effect on your score. Each reader of your essay uses a rubric against which he or she reads your essay. Each reader then gives your essay a score from 1 to 6. The two scores will be combined by ETS to give you an essay subscore. You will also receive a subscore ranging from 20 to 80 for the multiple-choice section of the writing test.

The result of these calculations for each part of the SAT—critical reading, mathematics, and writing—is your raw score. This is then converted to a scaled score between 200 and 800. This is the score that is reported to you and to the colleges you have chosen.

Remember, if you take the SAT more than once, you can choose whether the school you are applying to receives the scores from each test date or just some of them.

STRATEGIES FOR SAT SUCCESS

What makes some people better test-takers than others? The secret isn't just knowing the subject; it's knowing specific test-taking strategies that can add up to extra points. This means psyching out the test, knowing how the test-makers think and what they're looking for, and using this knowledge to your advantage. Smart test-takers know how to use pacing and guessing to add points to their score.

Pace Yourself

Suppose there are 20 questions in one of the math sections and they need to be answered in 25 minutes. That means that you have 1 minute and 15 seconds to answer each question. But smart test-takers know that's not the best way to use their time. If you use less than a minute to answer the easier questions, you'll have extra time to help you answer the more difficult ones. That's why learning to pace yourself is so important.

NOTE

Because the SAT can vary in format, scaled scores allow the test-maker to account for differences from one version of the SAT to another. Using scaled scores ensures that a score of 500 on one SAT is equivalent to 500 on another.

Question Sets Usually Go from Easiest to Most Difficult— You Should, Too

A question set is one set of similar questions within the larger math, critical reading, or writing sections. Except for the reading passages in the critical reading section, SAT questions follow the pattern of easiest to hardest. Work your way through the earlier, easier questions as quickly as you can. That way you'll have more time for the later, more difficult ones.

But two words of caution. What may be easy to the test-writer may not be to you. Don't panic if Question 3 seems hard. Try to work through it, but don't spend too much time on it if it's a topic such as factoring that has just never been easy for you to understand. Second, work quickly but carefully. Don't work so fast that you make a silly mistake and lose a point that you should have aced.

You Can Set Your Own Speed Limit

All right, how will you know what your speed limit is? Use the practice tests to check your timing and see how it affects your answers. If you've answered most of the questions in the time limit but have a lot of incorrect answers, you'd better slow down. On the other hand, if you are very accurate in your answers but aren't answering every question in a section, you can probably pick up the pace a bit.

It's Smart to Keep Moving

It's hard to let go, but sometimes you have to. Don't spend too much time on any one question before you've tried all the questions in a section. There may be questions later on in the test that you can answer easily, and you don't want to lose points just because you didn't get to them.

The Easy Answer Isn't Always Best

Are you at the end of a section? Remember, that's where you'll find the hardest questions, which means that the answers are more complex. Look carefully at the choices and really think about what the question is asking.

You Don't Have to Read the Directions

What? Yes, you read it correctly the first time—you don't have to read the directions. Look, by the time you actually sit down to take the SAT, you've read this book, you've taken all the practice tests you could find, and you've read enough SAT directions to fill a library. So when the exam clock starts ticking, don't waste time rereading directions you already know. Instead, go directly to Question 1.

You're Going to Need a Watch

If you're going to pace yourself, you need to keep track of the time—and what if there is no clock in your room or if the only clock is out of your line of vision? That's why it's a good idea to bring a watch to the test. A word of warning: Don't use a watch alarm or your watch will end up on the proctor's desk.

EDUCATED GUESSING WILL BOOST YOUR SCORE!

The fractional deduction for wrong answers makes random guessing a wash—statistically speaking, you're unlikely to change your score. This means that if you come to a question that you have absolutely no idea how to answer, you're probably better off skipping it and moving on, rather than just choosing an answer at random.

Although random guessing won't help you, anything better than random guessing will. On most questions, you should be able to guess better than randomly by using common sense and the process-of-elimination techniques that are developed throughout this book. Even if you aren't certain which answer is correct, you might be certain that one or more of the answer choices is definitely *wrong*. If you can knock out one choice out of five, you have a 25 percent chance of guessing correctly. If you can knock out two choices, the odds go up to $33\frac{1}{3}$ percent. If you can knock out three, you have a 50/50 chance of guessing the right answer. With odds like this, it makes sense to guess, especially when you realize that a single correct guess can raise your scaled score as much as 10 points.

How Educated Guessing Can Help

Let's take a sample situation to demonstrate the effectiveness of educated guessing. Let's say that on the entire SAT there were 40 questions you were unsure of. Now, we know what you're thinking. Forty questions seem like an awful lot of questions with which to have difficulty. But think about it: If you answered every other one of the SAT's questions correctly, you'd already be scoring over 1800! So to have trouble with 40 questions is not only possible, it's likely.

Now remember how the SAT is scored. Every question you answer correctly is worth 1 raw score point, which corresponds to roughly 10 scaled score points. For every question you leave blank, you gain nothing and lose nothing. And for every incorrect answer you mark down, you lose $\frac{1}{4}$ of a raw score point, which corresponds to approximately 2.5 scaled score points. When students first learn this, they usually get nervous about guessing. After all, who wants to lose points on questions you're unsure of? However, a more careful look demonstrates the exact opposite: educated guessing can dramatically improve your score even if you make many incorrect guesses along the way.

Let's get back to those 40 difficult questions. You basically have three choices: you can leave them all blank in fear of losing points; you can guess randomly; or you can use process-of-elimination techniques to make educated guesses. Let's examine the outcome of each approach:

The *fearful student* takes the first approach and leaves all 40 questions blank. For his effort, he receives no points and loses no points. So he breaks even.

The *random guesser* picks the answers for random reasons. Maybe he picks choice (C) for every one. Or maybe he fills his answer sheet in such a way as to make a visually appealing pattern. What will happen to the random guesser? Well, statistically speaking, he will answer 1 out of every 5 questions correctly, since most questions have five answer choices. That means he will answer 8 questions correctly out of 40 ($\frac{1}{5}$ of 40). For his effort, the random guesser will pick up 80 points for the questions he got right (8 × 10 points)

ALERT!
Don't spin yuor wheels by spending too much time on any one question. Give it some thought, take your best shot, and move along.

NOTE

You may be wondering how you can possibly wade through all this information in time for the test. Don't be discouraged! We wrote this book knowing that some of you would be on very condensed schedules. The information in this section will help you construct a study plan that works for you—one that will help you boost your score no matter how limited your time may be. Remember, though, that practice and targeted study are essential elements of that score boosting, so invest as much time as possible in your SAT preparation.

and lose 80 points for the 32 questions he got wrong (32 × 2.5 pts.). So the random guesser ends up in the exact same position as the fearful student.

The *smart test-taker* will take advantage of what she *does* know to make educated guesses. You will become the smart test-taker! You will use the process-of-elimination techniques that we develop in this book. On virtually every question, you will eliminate one, two, or three poor choices. Let's say that you answer 16 questions correctly out of the 40 you're unsure of. Even though that's a pretty low percentage, you will do considerably better than the fearful student or the random guesser. For the 16 questions you answer correctly, you will receive 160 points (16 × 10 pts.), and for the 24 questions you answer incorrectly, you will lose 60 points (24 × 2.5 pts.). So by doing nothing more than answering questions you've already thought about, you pick up 100 scaled score points. Here's a table that might make more sense of these numbers:

GUESSING ON 40 DIFFICULT QUESTIONS

	#Right	#Wrong	#Blank	Total Pts.
The Fearful Student	0	0	40	0 pts
The Random Guesser	8 (+80)	32 (−80)	0	0 pts
The Smart Test-Taker	16 (+160)	24 (−60)	0	100 pts

Obviously, the better you get at eliminating implausible choices, the more points you will pick up from educated guessing. But no matter what, if you have time to read through a question and eliminate at least one choice, it is always to your benefit to guess. Don't worry about the fact that you will probably get the question wrong, because you don't need to guess correctly on too many questions to gain points. As long as you are guessing better than randomly, you will do considerably better.

MAKE AN SAT STUDY PLAN

As with almost any form of learning, preparing for the SAT is an investment of time. The more you have, the better your chances of boosting your score significantly. Next, we'll walk you through two different study plans, each tailored to a specific amount of preparation time. Choose the plan that fits your circumstances and adapt it to your needs.

Regardless of how much time you have before the actual exam, your first step should be to take the Diagnostic Test in Part II of this book. After you score it, compute your category percentages to assess your relative strengths and weaknesses. Hang on to the scoring sheet so you know where to get started.

The Complete Course

If you have three or more months to prepare, you should congratulate yourself! This will give you sufficient time to familiarize yourself with the test, learn critical strategies, review grammar and math fundamentals, practice writing, and take full-length tests.

You'll get the most out of your SAT preparation if you:
- Reread this chapter to ensure that you understand the format, structure, and scoring of the SAT.
- Take the Diagnostic Test and identify your areas that need improvement.

- Read each and every strategy and review chapter.
- Work through all the examples, exercises, and practice exams.
- Read all the answer explanations.
- Focus on the chapters where your scores show you need to improve.

The Accelerated Course

If you have one month or less to prepare for the SAT or if you cannot devote a lot of time to studying for any other reason, follow the accelerated course. You'll get the most out of this course if you:

- Reread this chapter to ensure that you understand the format, structure, and scoring of the SAT.
- Take the Diagnostic Test and identify your areas that need improvement.
- Focus on the chapters that cover material that is most problematic for you and work through all the examples and exercises in these chapters.
- Work through as many practice exams as you can.
- Read all the answer explanations.

MEASURING YOUR PROGRESS

It does seem like you're on a treadmill sometimes, doesn't it? Question after question after question—are you really getting anywhere? Is all of this studying really working?

The way to find out is to monitor your progress throughout the preparation period, whether it's three months or four weeks. By taking a diagnostic examination at the beginning, you'll establish your home base of skills, and you'll be able to craft the study plan that's right for you. Then, you can either start to read the entire book (if you are taking the complete course) or go directly to the chapters that address your weaknesses (if you are taking the accelerated course). At the end of each chapter, complete the exercises and compare your percentages to your original diagnostic percentages. How have you improved? Where do you still need work? Even if you haven't reached your ultimate performance goal, are you at least applying new test-taking methods?

One Third of the Way Through Your Study

When you are approximately one third of the way through your course of study—this can be after ten days or a month—it's time to take one of the practice tests. When you have finished scoring and reading the answer explanations, compare your scores with your original diagnostic scores. Hopefully, you're doing better. But if you're not, don't panic. At this point in test preparation, it's not unusual to score about the same as you did at the beginning.

What's more important than *what* you scored is *how* you took the practice test. Did you really use the test-taking strategies to which you've been introduced? If you didn't, go back to the strategy chapters and either reread them, if you are doing the complete course, or at least reread the summaries, if you are on the accelerated course. Then continue your review. Read more review chapters, and complete the exercises.

TIP

Here's an important point: You don't have to go through the book in order. You might want to start with the topic that you find most difficult, such as functions or grammar, or the question type that you're most unsure about, such as grid-ins. Then move to the next most difficult and so on down the line, saving the easiest topics or question types until the end. If you take the accelerated course, you should definitely take this approach.

Two Thirds of the Way Through Your Study

After you have worked through most of the review chapters (under the complete course plan) or all of the material relating to your areas of weakness (under the accelerated course), it's time to take another practice test. By now you should be seeing some real improvement in your scores. If you are still having trouble with certain topics, review the problematic material again.

The Home Stretch

For the most part, the last phase of study should involve *less learning* and *more practice.* Take more practice tests! By now, you probably understand how to take the SAT. What you need is more practice taking the test under simulated test-day conditions to work on your pacing and test-taking strategies.

When you take additional practice exams, be sure to do so in a near-test environment. Keep analyzing your scores to ensure that all of this practice is working. Determine which areas need additional work. Now is probably the perfect time to take timing drills whether you are following the complete course or the accelerated course. Because you have already reviewed the chapters, work on your weaknesses by doing timing drills.

The Final Week

One last word of advice: no matter which study plan you select, you should probably take one full, timed practice SAT the week before you take the actual SAT. This will get you ready for the big day. But don't take the test the day before the real SAT. That's a time when you should be relaxing, not cramming.

GETTING READY: THE NIGHT BEFORE AND THE DAY OF THE TEST

If you follow the guidelines in this book, you will be extremely well prepared for the SAT. You will know the format inside and out; you will know how to approach every type of question; you will have worked hard to strengthen your weak areas, and you will have taken multiple practice tests under simulated testing conditions. The last 24 hours before the SAT is not the time to cram—it's actually the time to relax. Remember that the SAT is primarily a test of how you think, not what you know. So last-minute cramming can be more confusing than illuminating.

That said, there are plenty of steps you can take over the final 24 hours to get ready. For one thing, don't do anything too stressful. On the night before the big day, find a diversion to keep yourself from obsessing about the SAT. Maybe stay home and watch some of your favorite television shows. Or go out to an early movie. Or talk for hours and hours on the phone about a subject other than the SAT. Do whatever is best for you. Just make sure you get plenty of sleep.

You should also lay out the following items before you go to bed:
- **Registration ticket:** Unless you are taking the test as a standby tester, you should have received one of these in the mail.
- **Identification:** A driver's license is preferable, but anything with a picture will do.
- **Pencils:** Make sure you bring at least three number 2 pencils; those are the only pencils that the machines can read.

- **Calculator:** Bring the calculator with which you're most comfortable. Don't pack a scientific or graphing calculator if you're unfamiliar with how it works. And don't take any calculator that beeps, produces a paper tape, makes any noise at all, or that is a part of a computer or other device. You won't be allowed to use such a calculator on the SAT.
- **Layered clothing:** You never know what the test-taking temperature will be. By dressing in layers, you can adapt to either a warm or a cold room.
- **Wristwatch:** Your classroom should have an operational clock, but if it doesn't, you want to be prepared. Again, don't wear a watch that beeps, unless you can turn off the alarm function. You won't be allowed to wear a noise-making watch during the exam.
- **Snack:** You're not allowed to eat during the test administration in your test room, but you are given a 5- to 10-minute break. So be armed with a fortifying snack that you can eat quickly in the hallway.

Make sure you allow enough time to arrive at the test site at least 15 minutes before the 8 a.m. start time. You don't want to raise your level of anxiety by having to rush to get there.

In the morning, take a shower to wake up and then eat a sensible breakfast. If you are a person who usually eats breakfast, you should probably eat your customary meal. If you don't usually eat breakfast, don't gorge yourself on test day, because it will be a shock to your system. Eat something light (like a granola bar and a piece of fruit) and pack that snack.

SUMMING IT UP

- Learning the seven SAT question types is the best way to prepare for the SAT. Knowing the test format and question types will relieve test anxiety because you'll know exactly what to expect on test day.

  ❶ Essay: You will have 25 minutes to write a first draft of a persuasive essay. The readers are trained to evaluate the essays as first drafts, not polished final products.

  ❷ Sentence completions: Each question asks you to find the answer choice with the word or words that make the most sense in each blank.

  ❸ Reading comprehension: The answer to every question will be either directly stated or implied in the passage.

  ❹ Identifying sentence errors: Choice (E) is always "No error." Save yourself some time and don't bother reading choice (E).

  ❺ Improving sentences and improving paragraphs: These question sets test your ability to spot and correct grammatical errors, usage problems, and wordiness.

  ❻ Multiple-choice math: A set of reference formulas is given at the beginning of each math section, so you don't have to worry about forgetting an important formula.

  ❼ Grid-ins: You have to calculate the answer and then fill in ovals on the grids provided on the answer sheet. Only the ovals count, so fill in each one correctly.

- You may use a calculator on the SAT, but while it may be helpful for some problems, it isn't absolutely necessary for any of them. So use your calculator, but don't rely on it too much.

- Except for reading passages, questions are arranged from easiest to most difficult. Where a question falls in a set provides an instant indication of how difficult it is.

- Every SAT question is worth 1 point, whether it is an easy question or a difficult one. So nail the easier questions—and quickly accumulate points.

- Fill in the answer bubbles cleanly and completely. Otherwise you won't get credit for your answers.

- Random guessing will have no effect on your score, but educated guessing can boost your score. So if you've read through a question and can eliminate at least one answer, guess!

- Pace yourself and move through the test relatively quickly.

- Relax the evening before the SAT, but also be sure you're prepared.
  —Assemble the supplies you will need for the test.
  —Pick out what you'll wear and remember to layer your clothes.
  —Be sure your calculator has fresh batteries.

- On the morning of the test, eat breakfast, pack your snack, and leave for the test site in plenty of time to get there 15 minutes before the start time.

PART II
DIAGNOSING STRENGTHS AND WEAKNESSES

CHAPTER 2   Practice Test 1: Diagnostics

Practice Test 1: Diagnostic

Before you begin preparing for the SAT, it's important to know your strengths and the areas where you need improvement. If you find sentence completion questions easy, for example, it would be a mistake to dedicate hours practicing them. Taking the Diagnostic Test in this chapter and then working out your scores will help you determine how you should apportion your study time.

PREPARING TO TAKE THE DIAGNOSTIC TEST

If possible, take the test in one sitting. Give yourself 3 hours and 20 minutes to complete the Diagnostic Test. (The actual test is 3 hours and 45 minutes; the experimental section of the actual test is 25 minutes.) Doing this will give you an idea of how long the sections are and how it feels to take the test. You will also get a sense of how long you can spend on each question in each section, so you can begin to work out a pacing schedule for yourself.

First, assemble all the things you will need to take the test. These include:
- Lined paper for the essay, at least two sheets
- Number 2 pencils, at least three
- A calculator with fresh batteries
- A timer
- The answer sheet, provided on the following pages

Set a timer for the time specified for each section. Stick to the time, so you are simulating the real test. At this point, it's as important to know how many questions you can answer in the time allotted as it is to answer questions correctly.

ANSWER SHEET PRACTICE TEST 1: DIAGNOSTIC

SECTION 1: Essay

_____

_____

_____

_____

_____

_____

_____

_____

_____

_____

_____

_____

_____

_____

_____

_____

_____

_____

_____

_____

_____

_____

_____

_____

_____

answer sheet

If a section has fewer questions than answer ovals, leave the extra ovals blank.

SECTION 2

1 (A) (B) (C) (D) (E)   11 (A) (B) (C) (D) (E)   21 (A) (B) (C) (D) (E)   31 (A) (B) (C) (D) (E)
2 (A) (B) (C) (D) (E)   12 (A) (B) (C) (D) (E)   22 (A) (B) (C) (D) (E)   32 (A) (B) (C) (D) (E)
3 (A) (B) (C) (D) (E)   13 (A) (B) (C) (D) (E)   23 (A) (B) (C) (D) (E)   33 (A) (B) (C) (D) (E)
4 (A) (B) (C) (D) (E)   14 (A) (B) (C) (D) (E)   24 (A) (B) (C) (D) (E)   34 (A) (B) (C) (D) (E)
5 (A) (B) (C) (D) (E)   15 (A) (B) (C) (D) (E)   25 (A) (B) (C) (D) (E)   35 (A) (B) (C) (D) (E)
6 (A) (B) (C) (D) (E)   16 (A) (B) (C) (D) (E)   26 (A) (B) (C) (D) (E)   36 (A) (B) (C) (D) (E)
7 (A) (B) (C) (D) (E)   17 (A) (B) (C) (D) (E)   27 (A) (B) (C) (D) (E)   37 (A) (B) (C) (D) (E)
8 (A) (B) (C) (D) (E)   18 (A) (B) (C) (D) (E)   28 (A) (B) (C) (D) (E)   38 (A) (B) (C) (D) (E)
9 (A) (B) (C) (D) (E)   19 (A) (B) (C) (D) (E)   29 (A) (B) (C) (D) (E)   39 (A) (B) (C) (D) (E)
10 (A) (B) (C) (D) (E)   20 (A) (B) (C) (D) (E)   30 (A) (B) (C) (D) (E)   40 (A) (B) (C) (D) (E)

SECTION 3

1 (A) (B) (C) (D) (E)   11 (A) (B) (C) (D) (E)   21 (A) (B) (C) (D) (E)   31 (A) (B) (C) (D) (E)
2 (A) (B) (C) (D) (E)   12 (A) (B) (C) (D) (E)   22 (A) (B) (C) (D) (E)   32 (A) (B) (C) (D) (E)
3 (A) (B) (C) (D) (E)   13 (A) (B) (C) (D) (E)   23 (A) (B) (C) (D) (E)   33 (A) (B) (C) (D) (E)
4 (A) (B) (C) (D) (E)   14 (A) (B) (C) (D) (E)   24 (A) (B) (C) (D) (E)   34 (A) (B) (C) (D) (E)
5 (A) (B) (C) (D) (E)   15 (A) (B) (C) (D) (E)   25 (A) (B) (C) (D) (E)   35 (A) (B) (C) (D) (E)
6 (A) (B) (C) (D) (E)   16 (A) (B) (C) (D) (E)   26 (A) (B) (C) (D) (E)   36 (A) (B) (C) (D) (E)
7 (A) (B) (C) (D) (E)   17 (A) (B) (C) (D) (E)   27 (A) (B) (C) (D) (E)   37 (A) (B) (C) (D) (E)
8 (A) (B) (C) (D) (E)   18 (A) (B) (C) (D) (E)   28 (A) (B) (C) (D) (E)   38 (A) (B) (C) (D) (E)
9 (A) (B) (C) (D) (E)   19 (A) (B) (C) (D) (E)   29 (A) (B) (C) (D) (E)   39 (A) (B) (C) (D) (E)
10 (A) (B) (C) (D) (E)   20 (A) (B) (C) (D) (E)   30 (A) (B) (C) (D) (E)   40 (A) (B) (C) (D) (E)

SECTION 4

1 (A) (B) (C) (D) (E)   14 (A) (B) (C) (D) (E)   27 (A) (B) (C) (D) (E)
2 (A) (B) (C) (D) (E)   15 (A) (B) (C) (D) (E)   28 (A) (B) (C) (D) (E)
3 (A) (B) (C) (D) (E)   16 (A) (B) (C) (D) (E)   29 (A) (B) (C) (D) (E)
4 (A) (B) (C) (D) (E)   17 (A) (B) (C) (D) (E)   30 (A) (B) (C) (D) (E)
5 (A) (B) (C) (D) (E)   18 (A) (B) (C) (D) (E)   31 (A) (B) (C) (D) (E)
6 (A) (B) (C) (D) (E)   19 (A) (B) (C) (D) (E)   32 (A) (B) (C) (D) (E)
7 (A) (B) (C) (D) (E)   20 (A) (B) (C) (D) (E)   33 (A) (B) (C) (D) (E)
8 (A) (B) (C) (D) (E)   21 (A) (B) (C) (D) (E)   34 (A) (B) (C) (D) (E)
9 (A) (B) (C) (D) (E)   22 (A) (B) (C) (D) (E)   35 (A) (B) (C) (D) (E)
10 (A) (B) (C) (D) (E)   23 (A) (B) (C) (D) (E)
11 (A) (B) (C) (D) (E)   24 (A) (B) (C) (D) (E)
12 (A) (B) (C) (D) (E)   25 (A) (B) (C) (D) (E)
13 (A) (B) (C) (D) (E)   26 (A) (B) (C) (D) (E)

SECTION 5

1 Ⓐ Ⓑ Ⓒ Ⓓ Ⓔ   6 Ⓐ Ⓑ Ⓒ Ⓓ Ⓔ
2 Ⓐ Ⓑ Ⓒ Ⓓ Ⓔ   7 Ⓐ Ⓑ Ⓒ Ⓓ Ⓔ
3 Ⓐ Ⓑ Ⓒ Ⓓ Ⓔ   8 Ⓐ Ⓑ Ⓒ Ⓓ Ⓔ
4 Ⓐ Ⓑ Ⓒ Ⓓ Ⓔ   9 Ⓐ Ⓑ Ⓒ Ⓓ Ⓔ
5 Ⓐ Ⓑ Ⓒ Ⓓ Ⓔ   10 Ⓐ Ⓑ Ⓒ Ⓓ Ⓔ

Note: ONLY the answers entered on the grid are scored.

Handwritten answers at the top of the column are NOT scored.

11. 12. 13. 14. 15.

16. 17. 18. 19. 20.

answer sheet

SECTION 6

1 Ⓐ Ⓑ Ⓒ Ⓓ Ⓔ	11 Ⓐ Ⓑ Ⓒ Ⓓ Ⓔ	21 Ⓐ Ⓑ Ⓒ Ⓓ Ⓔ	31 Ⓐ Ⓑ Ⓒ Ⓓ Ⓔ
2 Ⓐ Ⓑ Ⓒ Ⓓ Ⓔ	12 Ⓐ Ⓑ Ⓒ Ⓓ Ⓔ	22 Ⓐ Ⓑ Ⓒ Ⓓ Ⓔ	32 Ⓐ Ⓑ Ⓒ Ⓓ Ⓔ
3 Ⓐ Ⓑ Ⓒ Ⓓ Ⓔ	13 Ⓐ Ⓑ Ⓒ Ⓓ Ⓔ	23 Ⓐ Ⓑ Ⓒ Ⓓ Ⓔ	33 Ⓐ Ⓑ Ⓒ Ⓓ Ⓔ
4 Ⓐ Ⓑ Ⓒ Ⓓ Ⓔ	14 Ⓐ Ⓑ Ⓒ Ⓓ Ⓔ	24 Ⓐ Ⓑ Ⓒ Ⓓ Ⓔ	34 Ⓐ Ⓑ Ⓒ Ⓓ Ⓔ
5 Ⓐ Ⓑ Ⓒ Ⓓ Ⓔ	15 Ⓐ Ⓑ Ⓒ Ⓓ Ⓔ	25 Ⓐ Ⓑ Ⓒ Ⓓ Ⓔ	35 Ⓐ Ⓑ Ⓒ Ⓓ Ⓔ
6 Ⓐ Ⓑ Ⓒ Ⓓ Ⓔ	16 Ⓐ Ⓑ Ⓒ Ⓓ Ⓔ	26 Ⓐ Ⓑ Ⓒ Ⓓ Ⓔ	36 Ⓐ Ⓑ Ⓒ Ⓓ Ⓔ
7 Ⓐ Ⓑ Ⓒ Ⓓ Ⓔ	17 Ⓐ Ⓑ Ⓒ Ⓓ Ⓔ	27 Ⓐ Ⓑ Ⓒ Ⓓ Ⓔ	37 Ⓐ Ⓑ Ⓒ Ⓓ Ⓔ
8 Ⓐ Ⓑ Ⓒ Ⓓ Ⓔ	18 Ⓐ Ⓑ Ⓒ Ⓓ Ⓔ	28 Ⓐ Ⓑ Ⓒ Ⓓ Ⓔ	38 Ⓐ Ⓑ Ⓒ Ⓓ Ⓔ
9 Ⓐ Ⓑ Ⓒ Ⓓ Ⓔ	19 Ⓐ Ⓑ Ⓒ Ⓓ Ⓔ	29 Ⓐ Ⓑ Ⓒ Ⓓ Ⓔ	39 Ⓐ Ⓑ Ⓒ Ⓓ Ⓔ
10 Ⓐ Ⓑ Ⓒ Ⓓ Ⓔ	20 Ⓐ Ⓑ Ⓒ Ⓓ Ⓔ	30 Ⓐ Ⓑ Ⓒ Ⓓ Ⓔ	40 Ⓐ Ⓑ Ⓒ Ⓓ Ⓔ

SECTION 7

1 Ⓐ Ⓑ Ⓒ Ⓓ Ⓔ	6 Ⓐ Ⓑ Ⓒ Ⓓ Ⓔ	11 Ⓐ Ⓑ Ⓒ Ⓓ Ⓔ
2 Ⓐ Ⓑ Ⓒ Ⓓ Ⓔ	7 Ⓐ Ⓑ Ⓒ Ⓓ Ⓔ	12 Ⓐ Ⓑ Ⓒ Ⓓ Ⓔ
3 Ⓐ Ⓑ Ⓒ Ⓓ Ⓔ	8 Ⓐ Ⓑ Ⓒ Ⓓ Ⓔ	13 Ⓐ Ⓑ Ⓒ Ⓓ Ⓔ
4 Ⓐ Ⓑ Ⓒ Ⓓ Ⓔ	9 Ⓐ Ⓑ Ⓒ Ⓓ Ⓔ	14 Ⓐ Ⓑ Ⓒ Ⓓ Ⓔ
5 Ⓐ Ⓑ Ⓒ Ⓓ Ⓔ	10 Ⓐ Ⓑ Ⓒ Ⓓ Ⓔ	15 Ⓐ Ⓑ Ⓒ Ⓓ Ⓔ

SECTION 8

1 Ⓐ Ⓑ Ⓒ Ⓓ Ⓔ	6 Ⓐ Ⓑ Ⓒ Ⓓ Ⓔ	11 Ⓐ Ⓑ Ⓒ Ⓓ Ⓔ	16 Ⓐ Ⓑ Ⓒ Ⓓ Ⓔ
2 Ⓐ Ⓑ Ⓒ Ⓓ Ⓔ	7 Ⓐ Ⓑ Ⓒ Ⓓ Ⓔ	12 Ⓐ Ⓑ Ⓒ Ⓓ Ⓔ	17 Ⓐ Ⓑ Ⓒ Ⓓ Ⓔ
3 Ⓐ Ⓑ Ⓒ Ⓓ Ⓔ	8 Ⓐ Ⓑ Ⓒ Ⓓ Ⓔ	13 Ⓐ Ⓑ Ⓒ Ⓓ Ⓔ	18 Ⓐ Ⓑ Ⓒ Ⓓ Ⓔ
4 Ⓐ Ⓑ Ⓒ Ⓓ Ⓔ	9 Ⓐ Ⓑ Ⓒ Ⓓ Ⓔ	14 Ⓐ Ⓑ Ⓒ Ⓓ Ⓔ	19 Ⓐ Ⓑ Ⓒ Ⓓ Ⓔ
5 Ⓐ Ⓑ Ⓒ Ⓓ Ⓔ	10 Ⓐ Ⓑ Ⓒ Ⓓ Ⓔ	15 Ⓐ Ⓑ Ⓒ Ⓓ Ⓔ	20 Ⓐ Ⓑ Ⓒ Ⓓ Ⓔ

SECTION 9

1 Ⓐ Ⓑ Ⓒ Ⓓ Ⓔ	6 Ⓐ Ⓑ Ⓒ Ⓓ Ⓔ	11 Ⓐ Ⓑ Ⓒ Ⓓ Ⓔ
2 Ⓐ Ⓑ Ⓒ Ⓓ Ⓔ	7 Ⓐ Ⓑ Ⓒ Ⓓ Ⓔ	12 Ⓐ Ⓑ Ⓒ Ⓓ Ⓔ
3 Ⓐ Ⓑ Ⓒ Ⓓ Ⓔ	8 Ⓐ Ⓑ Ⓒ Ⓓ Ⓔ	13 Ⓐ Ⓑ Ⓒ Ⓓ Ⓔ
4 Ⓐ Ⓑ Ⓒ Ⓓ Ⓔ	9 Ⓐ Ⓑ Ⓒ Ⓓ Ⓔ	14 Ⓐ Ⓑ Ⓒ Ⓓ Ⓔ
5 Ⓐ Ⓑ Ⓒ Ⓓ Ⓔ	10 Ⓐ Ⓑ Ⓒ Ⓓ Ⓔ	15 Ⓐ Ⓑ Ⓒ Ⓓ Ⓔ

PRACTICE TEST 1: DIAGNOSTIC

Section 1

Essay • 25 Minutes

Directions: Think carefully about the statement below and the assignment that follows it.

It seems as though more and more people are interested only in results, not in how the results are achieved. If the results are what they want, people don't care who is hurt or what is done to get them. These people seem to believe that the end justifies the means.

—Author unknown

Assignment: What is your opinion of the idea that the end justifies the means? Plan and write an essay that develops your ideas logically. Support your opinion with specific evidence taken from your personal experience, your observations of others, or your reading.

STOP

END OF SECTION 1. IF YOU HAVE ANY TIME LEFT, GO OVER YOUR WORK IN THIS SECTION ONLY. DO NOT WORK IN ANY OTHER SECTION OF THE TEST.

diagnostic test

Section 2

26 Questions • 25 Minutes

Directions: Each of the following questions consists of an incomplete sentence followed by five words or pairs of words. Choose that word or pair of words that, when substituted for the blank space or spaces, best completes the meaning of the sentence and mark the letter of your choice on your answer sheet.

In view of the extenuating circumstances and the defendant's youth, the judge recommended ___.

(A) conviction

(B) a defense

(C) a mistrial

(D) leniency

(E) life imprisonment

The correct answer is (D).

1. Her position in the agency authorized her to award contracts and to ___ obligations for payment of expenses.
   (A) rescind
   (B) incur
   (C) procure
   (D) recur
   (E) resume

2. Despite all his courtroom experience, the attorney was able to pry very little information out of the ___ witness.
   (A) cooperative
   (B) recalcitrant
   (C) reactionary
   (D) presumptive
   (E) credulous

3. Although over the years ___ resources had been devoted to alleviating the problem, a satisfactory solution remained ___.
   (A) natural .. costly
   (B) adequate .. probable
   (C) substantial .. elusive
   (D) capital .. decisive
   (E) conventional .. abstract

4. The team attributes its ___ season to a number of ___ factors.
   (A) losing .. propitious
   (B) long .. irrelevant
   (C) remarkable .. derogatory
   (D) embarrassing .. optimistic
   (E) winning .. favorable

5. While fewer documents are being kept, the usefulness of those ___ is now ___ by an improved cataloging system.
   (A) printed .. documented
   (B) discarded .. concurred
   (C) read .. emblazoned
   (D) retained .. insured
   (E) received .. negated

6. The ___ with which the agent calmed the anxieties and soothed the tempers of the travelers ___ by the delay was a mark of frequent experience with similar crises.
   (A) evasiveness .. angered
   (B) reverence .. pleased
   (C) facility .. inconvenienced
   (D) mannerism .. destroyed
   (E) acuity .. accommodated

7. The lover of democracy has an ___ toward totalitarianism.
   (A) antipathy
   (B) empathy
   (C) equanimity
   (D) idolatry
   (E) obstinacy

8. A ___ of employment opportunities ___ prospective employees entering the job market.
   (A) surfeit .. impedes
   (B) paucity .. discourages
   (C) plethora .. deters
   (D) dearth .. inspires
   (E) deluge .. enervates

9. In truth, ___ has a cost; for every free person we pay with the ___ of fifty others.

   (A) liberty .. subjection
   (B) liberalism .. environmentalism
   (C) capitalism .. punishment
   (D) independence .. individualism
   (E) authority .. autonomy

Directions: Each passage below is followed by a set of questions. Read each passage; then answer the accompanying questions, basing your answers on what is stated or implied in the passage and in any introductory material provided. Mark the letter of your choice on your answer sheet.

QUESTIONS 10 AND 11 ARE BASED ON THE FOLLOWING PASSAGE.

Gustav Mahler's Symphony No. 1 is universally applauded today, but when it was premiered in 1900, the public, including music critics, were divided in their response. As one music historian
5 has noted, "[the work] was truly a bone of contention .... A large majority of the audience applauded, and Mahler was repeatedly called out. But there were also startled faces all around, and some hissing was heard." One problem
10 apparently was that Mahler did not provide any explanatory notes for his music. The audience was left on their own to figure it out.

10. The phrase "bone of contention" (lines 5–6) means

   (A) strife.
   (B) struggle.
   (C) matter for argument.
   (D) competitive.
   (E) contest.

11. Based on the audience's response, an accurate way to describe the work might be as

   (A) an instant success.
   (B) a complete failure.
   (C) mediocre.
   (D) superficially a success.
   (E) a flop.

QUESTIONS 12 AND 13 ARE BASED ON THE FOLLOWING PASSAGE.

The 1990s saw a remarkable increase in labor productivity. Investment in new technology is usually credited with the boost in productivity. However, some economists who have looked at
5 the data have come up with a surprising finding. These economists think that the rise in productivity is not only the result of new technology but also of innovative workplace practices. Rotating workers through jobs and allowing workers to
10 share jobs are two such practices. Connecting pay to job performance is another and asking workers for their suggestions on how to get jobs done efficiently are two other innovations that some companies have introduced into the
15 workplace.

12. The main idea of this passage is that

   (A) workers have ideas for boosting productivity and they should be asked to share those ideas.
   (B) technology is not the only reason that productivity has risen.
   (C) innovative workplace practices have boosted productivity.
   (D) companies that use innovative workplace practices have boosted their productivity.
   (E) innovative workplace practices and technology together have boosted productivity.

13. All of the following new workplace practices are noted in this passage EXCEPT

(A) tying pay to performance.

(B) job rotation.

(C) using workers' suggestions for improvements.

(D) investing in new technology.

(E) job sharing.

QUESTIONS 14–20 ARE BASED ON THE FOLLOWING PASSAGE.

The principles of classical architecture have endured over time. Modern buildings built in the classical style still adhere to architectural principles established during the times of the ancient Romans. The following passage considers some of those principles.

Classical architecture, the origins of which can be traced to ancient Rome, was the type of architecture embraced by the very highest social levels of that ancient civilization. As
5 such, classical architecture was characterized by a rigorous adherence to the principles of coherence, exactness, and detail.

The basis of the classical style was the manner in which a building's space was divided so as
10 to create a coherent whole. An example of a plan for the division of a building's space was the *tripartite* plan, which would divide the space in a particular building into three equal parts. Such a plan would be followed no matter
15 what the purpose of the building—churches, homes, or public government buildings could all be designed with such a plan. Even gardens, designed in the classical style, might have a three-part plan. It is interesting, too, that the clas-
20 sical tripartite plan spilled over from architecture to other arts—music, poetry, and dance—so that it is not uncommon to have a three-part hierarchy within those artistic areas as well.

Once the framework of a building designed in
25 the classical style was established, architectural elements were added. Columns are fairly typical architectural elements, with the five most common column types being the *Doric, Ionic, Corinthian, Tuscan,* and *Composite.* Each
30 column was distinctive and of a certain specified proportion, base to top. Just as the building itself might embody a tripartite plan, so did the

columns themselves have a three-part organization. Above the column is a horizontal piece,
35 called the *entablature,* then comes the column itself, which is tall and cylindrical, and finally comes the three-step platform upon which the column rests, called the *crepidoma.* The top piece is further divided into three parts—the cornice,
40 the frieze, and the architrave. The column breaks down into three parts—the capital, the shaft, and the base. The crepidoma maintains the three-part division with its three steps.

Symmetry was also an important element in
45 classical architecture. The relationship between architectural elements and the whole edifice was conceived, studied, and implemented with a great deal of attention paid at each stage of the plan to assuring that balance was achieved.
50 Proportion and parallelism were critical in the achievement of the plan's coherence as well.

Classical architecture was filled with conventions, scrupulously adhered to, which although perhaps not obvious to the viewer become
55 apparent upon closer analysis. For example, classical buildings must stand free; they cannot touch the sides of other buildings. This is so because in the view of the classicist, the building was a world within a world of its own. Thus,
60 the building had to stand alone, an example of its singular world. Consequently, groups of classical buildings became problematic because of perceived violations of spatial conventions that troubled rule-based classical architects. The
65 classical mode required an adherence to formal patterns and symmetry sometimes not possible to impose on groups of buildings.

Classical architects longed to bring order to the world through designs that struggled for con-
70 sistency and completeness. The classical plan was a disciplined plan requiring the ability to divide, relate, and align elements. The resulting building was thus created in a way pleasing to the eye and appropriate to the time and place
75 in which it was placed.

14. The origins of classical architecture date back to the time of ancient

(A) Egypt.

(B) Greece.

(C) Sumeria.

(D) Rome.

(E) Mesopotamia.

15. Classical architecture is characterized by all of the following EXCEPT
    (A) attention to detail.
    (B) rigorous exactness.
    (C) different spatial divisions for different types of buildings.
    (D) attention to a coherent whole.
    (E) use of a *tripartite* division of spaces.

16. The word *tripartite* in line 12 most nearly means
    (A) geometric.
    (B) three-part.
    (C) political.
    (D) spatial.
    (E) mathematical.

17. All of the following are column types EXCEPT
    (A) Egyptian.
    (B) Doric.
    (C) Ionic.
    (D) Tuscan.
    (E) Corinthian.

18. Which of the following is one of the three parts of the column proper?
    (A) The cornice
    (B) The capital
    (C) The frieze
    (D) The architrave
    (E) The detail

19. The word *symmetry* in line 44 most nearly means
    (A) absence of proportion.
    (B) lack of parallelism.
    (C) spatial qualities.
    (D) architectural element.
    (E) balance.

20. The main idea of this passage is that
    (A) classical architecture is out of fashion.
    (B) the classical approach to architecture allows for much freedom of expression.
    (C) there is no place for architectural elements in the classical scheme.
    (D) the Ionic column is the most perfect example of a classical element.
    (E) the conventions of classical architecture are scrupulously followed.

QUESTIONS 21–26 ARE BASED ON THE FOLLOWING PASSAGE.

Angel Decora was born Hinookmahiwikilinaka on the Winnebago Reservation in Nebraska in 1871. She worked as a book illustrator, particularly on books by and about Native Americans, and lectured and wrote about Indian art. The story from which this excerpt is taken, "The Sick Child," may be autobiographical.

It was about sunset when I, a little child, was sent with a handful of powdered tobacco leaves and red feathers to make an offering to the spirit who had caused the sickness of my little sister. It had
5　been a long, hard winter, and the snow lay deep on the prairie as far as the eye could reach. The medicine-woman's directions had been that the offering must be laid upon the naked earth, and that to find it I must face toward the setting sun.

10　I was taught the prayer: "Spirit grandfather, I offer this to thee. I pray thee restore my little sister to health." Full of reverence and a strong faith that I could appease the anger of the spirit, I started out to plead for the life of our little one.

15　But now where was a spot of earth to be found in all that white monotony? They had talked of death at the house. I hoped that my little sister would live, but I was afraid of nature.

I reached a little spring. I looked down to its
20　pebbly bottom, wondering whether I should leave my offering there, or keep on in search of a spot of earth. If I put my offering in the water, would it reach the bottom and touch the earth, or would it float away, as it had always done
25　when I made my offering to the water spirit?

Once more I started on in my search of the bare ground.

The surface was crusted in some places, and walking was easy; in other places I would wade
30　through a foot or more of snow. Often I paused, thinking to clear the snow away in some place and there lay my offering. But no, my faith must be in nature, and I must trust to it to lay bare the earth. It was a hard struggle for so small a child.

35　I went on and on; the reeds were waving their tasselled ends in the wind. I stopped and looked at them. A reed, whirling in the wind, had formed a space round its stem, making a loose socket. I stood looking into the opening. The reed must be

40 rooted in the ground, and the hole must follow
the stem to the earth. If I poured my offerings
into the hole, surely they must reach the ground;
so I said the prayer that I had been taught, and
dropped my tobacco and red feathers into the
45 opening that nature itself had created.

No sooner was the sacrifice accomplished than
a feeling of doubt and fear thrilled me. What if
my offering should never reach the earth? Would
my little sister die?

50 Not till I turned homeward did I realize how
cold I was. When at last I reached the house
they took me in and warmed me, but did not
question me, and I said nothing. Everyone was
sad, for the little one had grown worse.

55 The next day the medicine-woman said my little
sister was beyond hope; she could not live. Then
bitter remorse was mine, for I thought I had been
unfaithful, and therefore my little sister was to
be called to the spirit land. I was a silent child,
60 and did not utter my feelings; my remorse was
intense. . . .

21. The word *offering* (line 3) means

(A) proposal.

(B) bid.

(C) advance.

(D) tribute.

(E) suggestion.

22. The narrator's journey could be called a

(A) reverie.

(B) retreat.

(C) junket.

(D) quest.

(E) jaunt.

23. Line 34 ("It was a hard struggle for so small a child.") are

(A) an aside by an omniscient narrator.

(B) the adult narrator's realization that saving her sick sister was too big a task for the child.

(C) an ironic statement by an outside observer.

(D) the adult narrator's excuse for placing the feathers and tobacco in a poor spot.

(E) the adult narrator's explanation for the young girl's silent remorse.

24. The narrator's remorse is due to her

(A) uncaring attitude toward her sister.

(B) mixed feelings toward her own religion.

(C) secret longing for attention.

(D) perceived failure at following instructions.

(E) mistrust of the medicine-woman.

25. If her sister died, you would expect the narrator to feel

(A) relieved.

(B) elated.

(C) surprised.

(D) confused.

(E) guilty.

26. What feeling does the narrator have toward the child?

(A) Shame

(B) Bewilderment

(C) Forgiveness

(D) Irritation

(E) Anxiety

STOP

END OF SECTION 2. IF YOU HAVE ANY TIME LEFT, GO OVER YOUR WORK IN THIS SECTION ONLY. DO NOT WORK IN ANY OTHER SECTION OF THE TEST.

Section 3

20 Questions • 25 Minutes

Directions: Solve the following problems using any available space on the page for scratchwork. On your answer sheet fill in the choice that best corresponds to the correct answer.

Notes: The figures accompanying the problems are drawn as accurately as possible unless otherwise stated in specific problems. Again, unless otherwise stated, all figures lie in the same plane. All numbers used in these problems are real numbers. Calculators are permitted for this test.

Reference Information

Circle:
$C = 2\pi r$
$A = \pi r^2$

Rectangle:
$A = lw$

Rectangular Solid:
$V = lwh$

Cylinder:
$V = \pi r^2 h$

Triangle:
$A = \frac{1}{2}bh$

$a^2 + b^2 = c^2$

The number of degrees of arc in a circle is 360.
The measure in degrees of a straight angle is 180.
The sum of the measures in degrees of the angles of a triangle is 180.

1. Which of the following fractions is more than $\frac{3}{4}$?

   (A) $\frac{35}{71}$

   (B) $\frac{13}{20}$

   (C) $\frac{71}{101}$

   (D) $\frac{19}{24}$

   (E) $\frac{15}{20}$

2. If $820 + R + S - 610 = 342$, and if $R = 2S$, then $S =$

   (A) 44
   (B) 48
   (C) 132
   (D) 184
   (E) 192

3. What is the cost, in dollars, to carpet a room x yards long and y yards wide, if the carpet costs five dollars per square foot?

   (A) xy
   (B) $5xy$
   (C) $25xy$
   (D) $30xy$
   (E) $45xy$

4. If $7M = 3M - 20$, then $M + 7 =$

   (A) 0
   (B) 2
   (C) 5
   (D) 12
   (E) 17

5. In circle O below, AB is the diameter, angle BOD contains 15°, and angle EOA contains 85°. Find the number of degrees in angle ECA.

   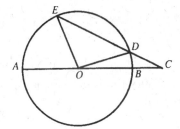

   (A) 15
   (B) 35
   (C) 50
   (D) 70
   (E) 85

6. What is the smallest positive number, other than 2, which, when it is divided by 3, 4, or 5, will leave a remainder of 2?

    (A) 22
    (B) 42
    (C) 62
    (D) 122
    (E) 182

7. A taxi charges 75 cents for the first quarter of a mile and 15 cents for each additional quarter of a mile. The charge, in cents, for a trip of d miles is

    (A) $75 + 15d$
    (B) $75 + 15(4d - 1)$
    (C) $75 + 75d$
    (D) $75 + 4(d - 1)$
    (E) $75 + 75(d - 1)$

8. In a certain army post, 30% of the enlistees are from New York State, and 10% of these are from New York City. What percentage of the enlistees in the post are from New York City?

    (A) 0.03
    (B) 0.3
    (C) 3
    (D) 13
    (E) 20

9. The diagonal of a rectangle is 10. What is the area of the rectangle?

    (A) 24
    (B) 48
    (C) 50
    (D) 100
    (E) It cannot be determined from the information given.

10. In triangle PQR below, angle RPQ is greater than angle RQP, and the bisectors of angle P and angle Q meet in S.

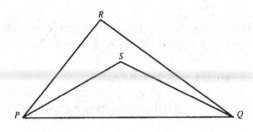

Note: Figure not drawn to scale.

    Therefore,
    (A) $SQ > SP$
    (B) $SQ = SP$
    (C) $SQ < SP$
    (D) $SQ \geq SP$
    (E) It cannot be determined from the information given.

11. Which of the following is equal to 3.14×10^6?

    (A) 314
    (B) 3140
    (C) 31,400
    (D) 314,000
    (E) 3,140,000

12. $\dfrac{36}{29 - \dfrac{4}{0.2}} =$

    (A) $\dfrac{3}{4}$
    (B) $\dfrac{4}{3}$
    (C) 2
    (D) 4
    (E) 18

13. In terms of the square units in the figure below, what is the area of the semicircle?

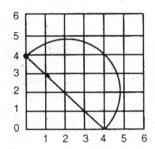

(A) 32π

(B) 16π

(C) 8π

(D) 4π

(E) 2π

14. The sum of three consecutive odd numbers is always divisible by

   I. 2.

   II. 3.

   III. 5.

   IV. 6.

(A) I only

(B) II only

(C) I and II only

(D) I and III only

(E) II and IV only

15. In the diagram, triangle *ABC* is inscribed in a circle and *CD* is tangent to the circle. If angle *BCD* is 40°, how many degrees are there in angle *A*?

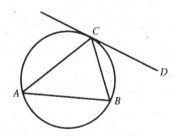

(A) 20

(B) 30

(C) 40

(D) 50

(E) 60

16. If a discount of 20% off the marked price of a jacket results in a savings of $15, what is the discounted price of the jacket?

(A) $35

(B) $60

(C) $75

(D) $150

(E) $300

17. While researching a term paper, a student read pages 7 through 49 and pages 101 through 157 of a particular source book. Altogether, how many pages from this book did this student read?

(A) 98

(B) 99

(C) 100

(D) 101

(E) 102

18. If $f(x) = x^2 - 2x$, what is the value of $f(y + 2)$?

(A) $y^2 + 2y$

(B) $y^2 + 8$

(C) $y^2 - 8$

(D) $y^2 + 2y + 8$

(E) y^2

19. Which of the following is equal to $(27c^9)^{\frac{1}{3}}$?

(A) $3c^3$

(B) $3c^6$

(C) $9c^3$

(D) $9c^6$

(E) $27c^3$

20. What is the slope of a line that is perpendicular to $3y + x = 21$?

(A) -3

(B) $-\dfrac{1}{3}$

(C) 0

(D) $\dfrac{1}{3}$

(E) 3

STOP

END OF SECTION 3. IF YOU HAVE ANY TIME LEFT, GO OVER YOUR WORK IN THIS SECTION ONLY. DO NOT WORK IN ANY OTHER SECTION OF THE TEST.

Section 4

35 Questions • 25 Minutes

Directions: Some of the sentences below contain an error in grammar, usage, word choice, or idiom. Other sentences are correct. Parts of each sentence are underlined and lettered. The error, if there is one, is contained in one of the underlined parts of the sentence. Assume that all other parts of the sentence are correct and cannot be changed. For each sentence, select the one underlined part that must be changed to make the sentence correct and mark its letter on your answer sheet. If there is no error in a sentence, mark answer space (E). No sentence contains more than one error.

Being that it's such a lovely day, we are having
  A   B   C
a difficult time concentrating on our
                      D
assignment. No error
                E
The correct answer is (A).

1. Trouble developed at the power plant
   when a number of fuses blew; I don't know
        A   B   C
   how it happened but it certainly didn't seem
   to phase the workers. No error
   D   E

2. The amount of people who have registered
           A   B
   for this course is so high that two sections
                    C   D
   will be created. No error
                    E

3. I thought the books were their's, but I see
                         A   B   C
   now that was mistaken. No error
       D   E

4. In order to protect themselves when writing
   A   B
   a research paper, students should be certain
                              C
   they know the meaning of the word
   "plagiarism." No error
   D   E

5. The police officer claims that you drunk
                       A   B
   too much liquor before you drove home
   C   D
   last night. No error
              E

6. I would much rather be outside playing
              A
   football then inside studying for the math
            B
   test, but I know I will never pass the course
   C
   unless I learn the material thoroughly.
   D
   No error
   E

7. This evening when I went outside to feed
                   A   B
   my cat, the animal was nowheres to be
                      C   D
   found. No error
          E

8. The most exciting part of the novel was when
             A   B
   Matilda rejected Count Vladimir and accepted
                    C
   the proposal of the peasant, Hugo. No error
                        D   E

9. We were constantly arguing with John and
            A   B
   her concerning their support of our
   C
   government's policies. No error
   D   E

10. I can hardly believe that you drank all
      A   B
    the coffee and didn't leave none for the
                    C
    other workers. No error
    D   E

11. You are <u>liable</u> <u>to be selected</u> to be the next
          A   B
    <u>chairperson</u> of the <u>department</u> since
        C   D
    you possess the necessary skills. <u>No error</u>
                                   E

12. We are not pleased with <u>him</u> being <u>chosen</u>
                         A   B
    as our new <u>president</u>, but we know that we
            C
    have to become <u>reconciled to</u> the decision
                 D
    made by our peers. <u>No error</u>
                   E

13. Because all the reviews <u>claimed</u> that the
                      A
    novel <u>was</u> very well written, I hoped
        B
    <u>to have read</u> <u>it</u>. <u>No error</u>
       C   D   E

14. <u>Whatever</u> problem the players face,
        A
    <u>the coach</u> is the one person <u>who</u> <u>they</u>
        B   C D
    always consult. <u>No error</u>
                E

15. <u>The mayor</u> is a woman <u>with great integrity</u>
       A   B
    and <u>who</u> should <u>receive</u> our financial
       C   D
    support. <u>No error</u>
            E

16. <u>Having won</u> the divisional final, our high
       A
    school team <u>are</u> <u>getting</u> ready <u>to play</u> for the
            B   C   D
    state championship next week. <u>No error</u>
                        E

17. The early morning delivery <u>did not</u> add to
                              A
    traffic <u>congestion,</u> <u>he</u> was pleased <u>to note</u>.
         B   C   D
    <u>No error</u>
     E

18. Isolated on a remote island, with <u>little work</u>
                                     A
    to <u>occupy them</u>, the soldiers <u>suffered from</u>
        B   C
    boredom and <u>low moral</u>. <u>No error</u>
             D   E

19. The child's <u>forthrightness</u> <u>could not but</u>
               A   B
    <u>disconcert</u> the old man, who expected
       C
    children to be <u>cowed</u> by authority. <u>No error</u>
               D   E

Directions: The sentences below may contain problems in grammar, usage, word choice, sentence construction, or punctuation. Part or all of each sentence is underlined. Following each sentence you will find five ways of expressing the underlined part. Choice (A) always repeats the original underlined section. The other four answer choices are all different. You are to select the lettered answer that produces the most effective sentence. If you think the original sentence is best, choose (A) as your answer. If one of the other choices makes a better sentence, mark your answer sheet for the letter of that choice. Do not choose an answer that changes the meaning of the original sentence.

I have always enjoyed <u>singing as well as to dance.</u>

(A) singing as well as to dance

(B) singing as well as dancing

(C) to sing as well as dancing

(D) singing in addition to dance

(E) to sing in addition to dancing

The correct answer is (B).

20. <u>Neither the boys nor their teacher are</u> responsible for causing the situation.
    (A) Neither the boys nor their teacher are
    (B) Neither the boys nor their teacher is
    (C) Neither the boys or their teacher are
    (D) Neither the boys or their teacher is
    (E) Neither the boys nor there teacher is

21. Over the loudspeaker, <u>the principle announced that the school was going to change its attendance policy</u>.
    (A) the principle announced that the school was going to change its attendance policy
    (B) the principle announced that the school was going to change their attendance policy
    (C) the principal announced that the school was going to change it's attendance policy
    (D) the principal announcing that the school was going to change its attendance policy
    (E) the principal announced that the school was going to change its attendance policy

22. If we had left the house earlier, we <u>might of been on time</u> for the plane.
    (A) might of been on time
    (B) could of been on time
    (C) should of been in time
    (D) might have been on time
    (E) might of made in time

23. They <u>arrived on time and were able</u> to witness the entire graduation ceremony.
    (A) arrived on time and were able
    (B) have arrived on time and were able
    (C) were arriving on time in order
    (D) arrived in time
    (E) arrived on time being able

24. He was more <u>aggravated than us</u> by the boy's behavior.
    (A) aggravated than us
    (B) aggravated than we
    (C) annoyed then us
    (D) annoyed than we
    (E) annoyed than us

25. Playing ball, swimming in the pool, and <u>a diet without starchy foods help</u> keep his weight down.
    (A) a diet without starchy foods help
    (B) avoiding starchy foods help
    (C) dieting without starchy foods helps
    (D) avoiding starchy foods helps
    (E) a diet without starchy foods helped

26. According to the *Farmer's Almanac,* <u>it looks like this will be the coldest winter in many years</u>.
    (A) it looks like this will be the coldest winter in many years
    (B) it looks like this winter will be colder than many other years
    (C) it looks like a cold winter is coming this year
    (D) this may be the coldest winter in many years
    (E) this year will be a cold winter

27. To decipher the instructions for assembling this tuner <u>it demands the clairvoyance of genius</u>.
   (A) it demands the clairvoyance of genius
   (B) the clairvoyance of genius are demanded
   (C) the clairvoyance of genius is demanded
   (D) it demands genius clairvoyance
   (E) demands the clairvoyance of genius

28. If <u>the stage sets were to be designed by him</u>, I would have more confidence in the production.
   (A) the stage sets were to be designed by him
   (B) he were designing the stage sets
   (C) he were to be designing the stage sets
   (D) the stage sets are designed by him
   (E) the stage sets by him were to be designed

29. Jennifer lined the walls of her room with shelves, <u>making them straight by means of using a level</u>.
   (A) making them straight by means of using a level
   (B) straightening them up by means of using a level
   (C) using a level to make them straight
   (D) making them, by means of a level, straight
   (E) using the means of a level to make them straight

Directions: Questions 30–35 are based on a passage that might be an early draft of a student's essay. Some sentences in this draft need to be revised or rewritten to make them both clear and correct. Read the passage carefully; then answer the questions that follow it. Some questions require decisions about diction, usage, tone, or sentence structure in particular sentences or parts of sentences. Other questions require decisions about organization, development, or appropriateness of language in the essay as a whole. For each question, choose the answer that makes the intended meaning clearer and more precise and that follows the conventions of Standard Written English.

(1) Today more and more people are losing their respect for authority. (2) A reason for this may be because there is corruption in high places. (3) Those whom we have put our trust in and who should have faith in our society have not earned it. (4) As a result, our society is in a turmoil.

(5) In many cities, violence has broken out. (6) What has precipitated this you may ask. (7) Sometimes this has resulted from arrests of people. (8) Groups then complain that they are being disenfranchised and that justice is not equal for all. (9) They, then, in their anger and frustration, seek to break the fabric of our society apart. (10) Because they feel that they have nothing to lose, they seek to destroy.

(11) We may agree or disagree with the methods being used by those who feel neglected and shut out. (12) Whatever our opinion, we must agree that there is a real problem. (13) Young people are taking matters into their own hands. (14) They feel that they cannot trust their elders and so they lash out against society.

30. Which of the following is the best revision of the underlined portion of sentence (2) below?

   A reason for this <u>may be because there is</u> corruption in high places.
   (A) may be that there is
   (B) is because there may be
   (C) may be possibly there is
   (D) may possibly be there is
   (E) may be because possibly there is

31. Which of the following is the best revision of the underlined portion of sentence (3) below?

   Those whom we have put our trust in and who should have faith in our society <u>have not earned it.</u>
   (A) are not and have not deserved it.
   (B) are losing it.
   (C) have not earned our trust.
   (D) do not have it.
   (E) are not and have not earned our trust.

32. Which is the best way to combine sentences (6) and (7)?

(A) Has this been precipitated by arrests?

(B) Sometimes arrests have precipitated this.

(C) You may well ask if arrests have precipitated this.

(D) Have arrests precipitated this?

(E) You may ask if arrests that precipitated this were unjust.

33. Which of the following is the best revision of the underlined portion of sentence (9) below?

They, then, in their anger and frustration, seek <u>to break the fabric of our society apart.</u>

(A) breaking the fabric of our society apart.

(B) the breaking of the fabric of our society.

(C) to destroy the fabric of our society apart.

(D) to break apart the fabric of our society.

(E) to rend the fabric of our society.

34. In relation to the passage as a whole, which of the following is the best description of the writer's intention in the third paragraph?

(A) To change the position of the reader

(B) To indicate that a problem exists and should be addressed

(C) To present contradictory viewpoints

(D) To provide additional examples or illustrations

(E) To suggest a solution to a serious situation

35. Which is the best way to combine sentences (13) and (14)?

(A) Young people are taking matters into their own hands, they lash out against society, feeling they cannot trust their elders.

(B) They take matters into their own hands when they lash out against society, feeling they can put no trust in their elders.

(C) Because they feel that they cannot trust their elders, they take matters into their own hands and lash out against society.

(D) Feeling that they cannot trust their elders, young people take matters into their own hands and lash out against society.

(E) When they feel that they cannot trust their elders or society and take matters into their own hands.

STOP

END OF SECTION 4. IF YOU HAVE ANY TIME LEFT, GO OVER YOUR WORK IN THIS SEC-TION ONLY. DO NOT WORK IN ANY OTHER SECTION OF THE TEST.

Section 5

20 Questions • 25 Minutes

Directions: Solve the following problems using any available space on the page for scratchwork. On your answer sheet fill in the choice that best corresponds to the correct answer.

Notes: The figures accompanying the problems are drawn as accurately as possible unless otherwise stated in specific problems. Again, unless otherwise stated, all figures he in the same plane. All numbers used in these problems are real numbers. Calculators are permitted for this test.

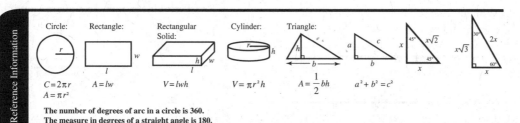

Reference Information

Circle: $C = 2\pi r$ $A = \pi r^2$

Rectangle: $A = lw$

Rectangular Solid: $V = lwh$

Cylinder: $V = \pi r^2 h$

Triangle: $A = \frac{1}{2}bh$ $a^2 + b^2 = c^2$

The number of degrees of arc in a circle is 360.
The measure in degrees of a straight angle is 180.
The sum of the measures in degrees of the angles of a triangle is 180.

1. In the figure below, l_1 is parallel to l_2. If the measure of $\angle x$ is 70°, and the measure of $\angle y$ is 105°, what is the measure of $\angle r$?

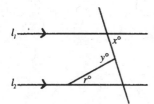

   (A) 35°
   (B) 70°
   (C) 75°
   (D) 105°
   (E) 110°

2. What is the value of $-x^2 - 2x^3$ when $x = -1$?
   (A) −2
   (B) −1
   (C) 0
   (D) 1
   (E) 2

3. If $\frac{1}{7} - \frac{1}{8} = \frac{1}{x}$, what is the value of x?

   (A) 6
   (B) 9
   (C) 52
   (D) 54
   (E) 56

4. $|-4| - |-8| + |-2||-3| =$
   (A) −2
   (B) 2
   (C) 4
   (D) 6
   (E) 10

5. The number of bacteria in a colony starts at 200 and doubles every 6 hours. The formula for the number of bacteria in the colony is $200 \times 2^{\frac{t}{6}}$, where t is the number of hours that have elapsed. How many bacteria are there in the colony after 30 hours?
   (A) 1200
   (B) 2400
   (C) 3600
   (D) 4800
   (E) 6400

6. If $x(p + 1) = M$, then $p =$
   (A) $M - 1$
   (B) $-M$
   (C) $\dfrac{M - 1}{x}$
   (D) $M - x - 1$
   (E) $\dfrac{M}{x} - 1$

7. If T tons of snow fall in 1 second, how many tons fall in M minutes?

   (A) $60MT$

   (B) $MT + 60$

   (C) MT

   (D) $\dfrac{60M}{T}$

   (E) $\dfrac{MT}{60}$

8. Which of the following is the graph of $x \geq -2$ and $x \leq 3$?

   (A)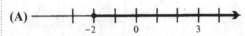

   (B)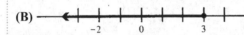

   (C)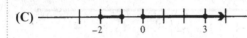

   (D)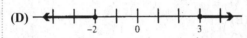

   (E)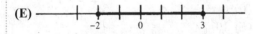

9. From 9 a.m. to 2 p.m., the temperature rose at a constant rate from $-14°F$ to $+36°F$. What was the temperature at noon?

   (A) $-4°$

   (B) $+6°$

   (C) $+16°$

   (D) $+26°$

   (E) $+31°$

10. What is the sum of $\angle EBA + \angle DCF$?

    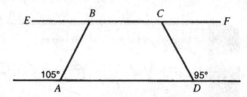

    (A) $160°$

    (B) $180°$

    (C) $195°$

    (D) $200°$

    (E) It cannot be determined from the information given.

Student-Produced Response Questions

Directions: Solve each of these problems. Write the answer in the corresponding grid on the answer sheet and fill in the ovals beneath each answer you write. Here are some examples.

Answer: $\frac{3}{4} = .75$; show answer either way   **Answer: 325**

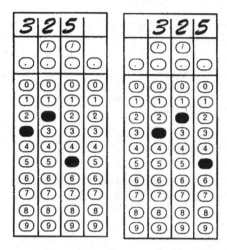

Note: A mixed number such as $3\frac{1}{2}$ must be gridded as 7/2 or as 3.5. If gridded as "3 1/2," it will be read as "thirty-one halves."

Note: Either position is correct.

11. Jessica received marks of 87, 93, and 86 on three successive tests. What grade must she receive on a fourth test in order to have an average of 90?

12. In a circle with radius 6, what is the measure (in degrees) of an arc whose length is 2π? (Disregard the degree symbol when you grid your answer.)

13. If $\frac{2x}{3\sqrt{2}} = \frac{3\sqrt{2}}{x}$, what is the positive value of x?

14. Using the table below, what is the median of the following data?

Score	Frequency
20	4
30	4
50	7

15. If A * B is defined as $\frac{AB - B}{-B}$, what is the value of $-2 * 2$?

16. A man travels 320 miles in 8 hours. If he continues at the same rate, how many miles will he travel in the next 2 hours?

17. A booklet contains 30 pages. If 9 pages in the booklet have drawings, what percent of the pages in the booklet have drawings? (Disregard the percent symbol when you grid your answer.)

18. If 3 copier machines can copy 300 sheets in 3 hours, assuming the same rate, how long (in hours) will it take 6 such copiers to copy 600 sheets?

QUESTIONS 19 AND 20 ARE BASED ON THE INFORMATION IN THE TABLES BELOW.

During a sale, the Sound Studio offers special discounts to customers who purchase more than one item. The regular prices and discount amounts for multiple purchases are shown in the tables below.

THE SOUND STUDIO

Regular Prices	
CD Player	$120
DVD Player	$80
Stereo Receiver	$340
Speakers	$260

Discount Amounts for Multiple Purchases	
CD Player and Speakers	15% off Total Regular Price
DVD Player and Stereo Receiver	25% off Total Regular Price
CD Player, Speakers, and DVD Player	20% off Total Regular Price

19. If Sean purchases both a DVD player and a stereo receiver during the sale, how many dollars will he save?

20. During the sale, Brian plans to buy a CD player and speakers. How many dollars more would it cost him if he decides to also purchase a DVD player?

STOP

END OF SECTION 5. IF YOU HAVE ANY TIME LEFT, GO OVER YOUR WORK IN THIS SECTION ONLY. DO NOT WORK IN ANY OTHER SECTION OF THE TEST.

Section 6

26 Questions • 25 Minutes

Directions: Each of the following questions consists of an incomplete sentence followed by five words or pairs of words. Choose that word or pair of words that, when substituted for the blank space or spaces, best completes the meaning of the sentence and mark the letter of your choice on your answer sheet

In view of the extenuating circumstances and the defendant's youth, the judge recommended ___.

(A) conviction

(B) a defense

(C) a mistrial

(D) leniency

(E) life imprisonment

The correct answer is (D).

1. Human survival is a result of mutual assistance, since people are essentially ___ rather than ___.
   (A) superior .. inferior
   (B) cooperative .. competitive
   (C) individualistic .. gregarious
   (D) physical .. mental
   (E) dependent .. insensate

2. For centuries, malnutrition has been ___ in the drought-stricken areas of Africa.
   (A) impalpable
   (B) evasive
   (C) endemic
   (D) divisive
   (E) redundant

3. Even as they ___ their pledges of support, they secretly planned a betrayal; their actions ___ their words.
   (A) demonstrated .. echoed
   (B) confirmed .. reinforced
   (C) compromised .. precluded
   (D) reiterated .. belied
   (E) submitted .. emphasized

4. The day will come when our ___ will look back upon us and our time with a sense of superiority.
   (A) antecedents
   (B) descendants
   (C) predecessors
   (D) ancestors
   (E) contemporaries

5. Their ___ debate, billed as a(n) ___ of their opinions, was only needless repetition.
   (A) senseless .. exoneration
   (B) national .. travesty
   (C) incessant .. distillation
   (D) primary .. renunciation
   (E) final .. clarification

6. With the ___ of winter storms, all drivers should take extra ___ while on the road.
   (A) demise .. caution
   (B) approach .. precautions
   (C) waning .. care
   (D) proximity .. leisure
   (E) duration .. heed

7. Despite our ___, Eva ___ the stranger for directions.
   (A) compliance .. harrassed
   (B) encouragement .. questioned
   (C) entreaties .. pinioned
   (D) intentions .. assailed
   (E) warnings .. approached

8. The young man was very unlikely to be hired; his appearance was disheveled, slovenly, and ___.
   (A) tousled
   (B) harried
   (C) beleaguered
   (D) mortified
   (E) despondent

What happened to the sunshine? Scientists are asking this question because the amount of sunshine that reaches the Earth dropped by 10 percent between the early 1950s and the early
5 1990s. The problem is not the sun. No instruments have recorded any dimming of the sun's rays. The problem appears to be between the Earth and the Sun. Pollution has gotten in the way. Particulates in pollution reflect sun back
10 into outer space. Pollution also causes increased condensation in the air. This condensation forms thicker, darker clouds. To verify their theory, scientists point to areas with little or no pollution. Instruments in those places have shown
15 sunshine as bright as ever.

9. All of the following could be used as titles for this passage EXCEPT
   (A) "The Sun Dims"
   (B) "Sunshine: Where Are You?"
   (C) "Who Needs Sunglasses with Pollution?"
   (D) "SPF: Sunshine Pollution Factor"
   (E) "Pollution: An Unnatural Sunshade"

10. The theory referred to in line 12 is that
   (A) the amount of sunlight reaching the Earth decreased by 10 percent between the 1950s and the 1990s.
   (B) pollution causes condensation.
   (C) condensation causes darker clouds.
   (D) pollution is the reason for a decrease in sunlight reaching the Earth.
   (E) particulates in the air and condensation cause pollution.

Beginning in the 1850s, various Plains nations had signed treaties with the United States government that set aside certain lands for the Native Americans. In return, the army would
5 keep whites out of Native American lands. However, when gold was discovered in Colorado on lands belonging to Native Americans, the local militia under Colonel John Chivington attacked a peaceful camp of Indians and killed
10 some 300. The attack became known as the Sand Creek Massacre. Chivington had hoped to ride this supposed victory into the new Colorado statehouse as governor. However, the massacre was met with general opprobrium across the
15 country. Any political ambitions that Chivington held were dashed forever.

11. Based on the passage, the use of the term "supposed victory" (line 12) indicates that
   (A) Chivington saw it as a victory.
   (B) Chivington thought that Americans would not care how Native Americans died.
   (C) Chivington told everyone it was a battle and his militia had won.
   (D) Chivington saw any opportunity to kill Native Americans as a victory.
   (E) the writer is being ironic.

12. The word *opprobrium* (line 14) means
   (A) approval.
   (B) dismay.
   (C) hate.
   (D) contempt.
   (E) disregard.

QUESTIONS 13 AND 14 ARE BASED ON THE FOLLOWING PASSAGE.

What's new around your house? In 1990, there were few home computers, no DVDs, no hand-held computers, and no plasma televisions. Most people had never heard of the World Wide Web or the Internet, so who needed wi-fi. MP3 players? No one needed a digital music player because digitized music did not exist. The consumer electronics business in those days consisted of CD players and answering machines. By 2004, the market for consumer electronics had reached $100 billion. Two of the fastest-growing areas are DVD devices, MP3 players, and HD-TV. Interest in DVD recorders soared when companies introduced recorders that could burn movies, television programs, and photos onto recordable disks.

13. According to the passage, the consumer electronics market includes all of the following EXCEPT
    (A) home computers.
    (B) electric cars.
    (C) MP3 players.
    (D) plasma televisions.
    (E) CD players.

14. A good word to describe DVD recorders would be
    (A) multiplex.
    (B) multipurpose.
    (C) multiple.
    (D) multivariate.
    (E) multitudinous.

Directions: The reading passage below is followed by a set of questions. Read the passage and answer the accompanying questions, basing your answers on what is stated or implied in the passage. Mark the letter of your choice on your answer sheet.

QUESTIONS 15–26 ARE BASED ON THE FOLLOWING PASSAGE.

Stephen Crane (1871–1900) wrote a number of novels, short stories, and poems in his short life, as well as working as a war correspondent overseas. "The Bride Comes to Yellow Sky" (1898) is the story of a small-town sheriff who brings home a bride, changing his frontier home forever. It opens with this scene.

The great Pullman was whirling onward with such dignity of motion that a glance from the window seemed simply to prove that the plains of Texas were pouring eastward. Vast flats of
5 green grass, dull-hued spaces of mesquite and cactus, little groups of frame houses, woods of light and tender trees, all were sweeping into the east, sweeping over the horizon, a precipice.

A newly married pair had boarded this coach
10 at San Antonio. The man's face was reddened from many days in the wind and sun, and a direct result of his new black clothes was that his brick-colored hands were constantly performing in a most conscious fashion. From time to time
15 he looked down respectfully at his attire. He sat with a hand on each knee, like a man waiting in a barber's shop. The glances he devoted to other passengers were furtive and shy.

The bride was not pretty, nor was she very young.
20 She wore a dress of blue cashmere, with small reservations of velvet here and there, and with steel buttons abounding. She continually twisted her head to regard her puff sleeves, very stiff, straight, and high. They embarrassed her. It was
25 quite apparent that she had cooked, and that she expected to cook, dutifully. The blushes caused by the careless scrutiny of some passengers as she had entered the car were strange to see upon this plain, under-class countenance, which was
30 drawn in placid, almost emotionless lines.

They were evidently very happy. "Ever been in a parlor-car before?" he asked, smiling with delight.

"No," she answered; "I never was. It's fine, ain't it?"

35

"Great! And then after a while we'll go forward to the diner, and get a big layout. Finest meal in the world. Charge a dollar."

"Oh, do they?" cried the bride. "Charge a dollar? Why, that's too much—for us—ain't it Jack?"

40

"Not this trip, anyhow," he answered bravely. "We're going to go the whole thing."

Later he explained to her about the trains. "You see, it's a thousand miles from one end of Texas to the other; and this train runs right across it, and never stops but for four times." He had the pride of an owner. He pointed out to her the dazzling fittings of the coach; and in truth her eyes opened wider as she contemplated the sea-green figured velvet, the shining brass, silver, and glass, the wood that gleamed as darkly brilliant as the surface of a pool of oil. At one end a bronze figure sturdily held a support for a separated chamber, and at convenient places on the ceiling were frescoes in olive and silver.

45

50

55

To the minds of the pair, their surroundings reflected the glory of their marriage that morning in San Antonio; this was the environment of their new estate; and the man's face in particular beamed with an elation that made him appear ridiculous to the negro porter. This individual at times surveyed them from afar with an amused and superior grin. On other occasions he bullied them with skill in ways that did not make it exactly plain to them that they were being bullied. He subtly used all the manners of the most unconquerable kind of snobbery. He oppressed them; but of this oppression they had small knowledge, and they speedily forgot that infrequently a number of travelers covered them with stares of derisive enjoyment. Historically there was supposed to be something infinitely humorous in their situation.

60

65

70

15. Crane highlights the newlyweds'
   (A) tactlessness.
   (B) unsophistication.
   (C) wealth.
   (D) merriment.
   (E) fear.

16. The bride's dress is clearly
   (A) beautiful.
   (B) torn.
   (C) red.
   (D) comfortable.
   (E) unfamiliar.

17. The sentence "It was quite apparent that she had cooked, and that she expected to cook, dutifully." (lines 24–26) shows the bride's
   (A) natural talent.
   (B) submissiveness.
   (C) commonness.
   (D) Both (A) and (B)
   (E) Both (B) and (C)

18. When the bridegroom answers his bride "bravely" (line 41), the implication is that
   (A) he has overcome his fear of her.
   (B) his usual posture is weak and sniveling.
   (C) gallantry is his natural mode.
   (D) he will conquer his anxiety about money for her sake.
   (E) it takes courage to speak forthrightly.

19. The line "He had the pride of an owner" (lines 46–47) is ironic because
   (A) the bride has no sense of style.
   (B) the bridegroom could never own anything so fine.
   (C) Crane prefers workers to owners.
   (D) the owners of the train take no pride in it.
   (E) the bridegroom is not proud of his own belongings.

20. The word *estate* (line 60) is used to mean
   (A) property.
   (B) inheritance.
   (C) status.
   (D) statement.
   (E) manor.

21. The figure of the porter is used to indicate
    - (A) a parallel between slavery and marriage.
    - (B) where the line between worker and owner is drawn.
    - (C) the absurdity of young love.
    - (D) that the newlyweds are not alone in the world.
    - (E) just how unworldly and lower class the newlyweds are.

22. The last sentence of the passage refers to
    - (A) the fact that newlyweds are figures of fun.
    - (B) Crane's amusement at the behavior of the travelers.
    - (C) people's delight at others' misfortunes.
    - (D) the joy of the newlyweds despite their surroundings.
    - (E) readers' sympathy with the characters.

23. Crane uses the word *historically* (line 72) to mean
    - (A) importantly.
    - (B) famously.
    - (C) customarily.
    - (D) prominently.
    - (E) ritually.

24. Crane's feeling toward the newlyweds is one of
    - (A) amused sympathy.
    - (B) disgusted revulsion.
    - (C) weary resignation.
    - (D) scornful derision.
    - (E) honest hatred.

25. Crane probably does not name the newlyweds in this part of the story
    - (A) because he does not know who they are.
    - (B) to make them seem ordinary and universal.
    - (C) because he wants to surprise the reader.
    - (D) to prove that they are worthless in his eyes.
    - (E) to focus attention on the peripheral characters.

26. The main goal of this passage is to
    - (A) introduce characters and setting.
    - (B) illustrate a conflict between two characters.
    - (C) resolve a crisis.
    - (D) express an opinion.
    - (E) instruct the reader.

STOP

END OF SECTION 6. IF YOU HAVE ANY TIME LEFT, GO OVER YOUR WORK IN THIS SECTION ONLY. DO NOT WORK IN ANY OTHER SECTION OF THE TEST.

Section 7

15 Questions • 20 Minutes

Directions: Solve the following problems using any available space on the page for scratchwork. On your answer sheet fill in the choice that best corresponds to the correct answer.

Notes: The figures accompanying the problems are drawn as accurately as possible unless otherwise stated in specific problems. Again, unless otherwise stated, all figures lie in the same plane. All numbers used in these problems are real numbers. Calculators are permitted for this test.

Reference Information

Circle:
$C = 2\pi r$
$A = \pi r^2$

Rectangle:
$A = lw$

Rectangular Solid:
$V = lwh$

Cylinder:
$V = \pi r^2 h$

Triangle:
$A = \frac{1}{2}bh$

$a^2 + b^2 = c^2$

The number of degrees of arc in a circle is 360.
The measure in degrees of a straight angle is 180.
The sum of the measures in degrees of the angles of a triangle is 180.

1. The coordinates of vertices X and Y of an equilateral triangle XYZ are $(-4,0)$ and $(4,0)$, respectively. The coordinates of Z may be
   (A) $(0, 2\sqrt{3})$.
   (B) $(0, 4\sqrt{3})$.
   (C) $(4, 4\sqrt{3})$.
   (D) $(0,4)$.
   (E) $(4\sqrt{3}, 0)$.

2. There are just two ways in which 5 may be expressed as the sum of two different positive (nonzero) integers, namely, $5 = 4 + 1 = 3 + 2$. In how many ways may 9 be expressed as the sum of two different positive (nonzero) integers?
   (A) 3
   (B) 4
   (C) 5
   (D) 6
   (E) 7

3. A board 7 feet 9 inches long is divided into three equal parts. What is the length of each part?
   (A) 2 ft. $6\frac{1}{3}$ in.
   (B) 2 ft. 7 in.
   (C) 2 ft. 8 in.
   (D) 2 ft. $8\frac{1}{3}$ in.
   (E) 2 ft. 9 in.

4. What is the smallest possible integer $K > 1$ such that $R^2 = S^3 = K$, for some integers R and S?
   (A) 4
   (B) 8
   (C) 27
   (D) 64
   (E) 81

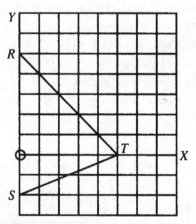

5. The number of square units in the area of triangle *RST* is
   (A) 10
   (B) 12.5
   (C) 15.5
   (D) 17.5
   (E) 20

6. Which of the following has the same value as $\dfrac{P}{Q}$?

   (A) $\dfrac{P-2}{Q-2}$

   (B) $\dfrac{1+P}{1+Q}$

   (C) $\dfrac{P^2}{Q^2}$

   (D) $\dfrac{3P}{3Q}$

   (E) $\dfrac{P+3}{Q+3}$

7. In the accompanying figure, $\angle ACB$ is a straight angle and $\overline{DC}$ is perpendicular to $\overline{CE}$. If the number of degrees in angle ACD is represented by x, the number of degrees in angle BCE is represented by

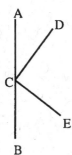

   (A) $90 - x$
   (B) $x - 90$
   (C) $90 + x$
   (D) $180 - x$
   (E) $45 + x$

QUESTIONS 8 AND 9 REFER TO THE FOLLOWING DRAWING.

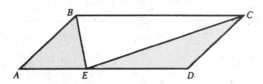

8. In parallelogram $ABCD$, what is the ratio of the shaded area to the unshaded area?

   (A) 1:2
   (B) 1:1
   (C) 4:3
   (D) 2:1
   (E) It cannot be determined from the information given.

9. If the ratio of AB to BC is 4:9, what is the area of parallelogram $ABCD$?

   (A) 36
   (B) 26
   (C) 18
   (D) 13
   (E) It cannot be determined from the information given.

10. A store owner buys eggs for M cents per dozen and sells them for $\dfrac{M}{6}$ cents apiece. At this rate, what is the profit on a dozen eggs?

   (A) $\dfrac{M}{12}$ cents

   (B) $\dfrac{M}{6}$ cents

   (C) $\dfrac{M}{2}$ cents

   (D) M cents

   (E) $2M$ cents

11. If $\dfrac{P}{Q} = \dfrac{4}{5}$, what is the value of $2P + Q$?

   (A) 14
   (B) 13
   (C) 3
   (D) −1
   (E) It cannot be determined from the information given.

12. A 15-gallon mixture of 20% alcohol has 5 gallons of water added to it. The strength of the mixture, as a percent, is approximately

(A) $12\frac{1}{2}$.

(B) $13\frac{1}{3}$.

(C) 15.

(D) $16\frac{2}{3}$.

(E) 20.

13. In the figure below, *QXRS* is a parallelogram and *P* is any point on side *QS*. What is the ratio of the area of triangle *PXR* to the area of *QXRS*?

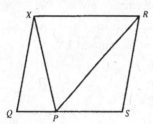

(A) 1:4

(B) 1:3

(C) 1:2

(D) 2:3

(E) 3:4

14. A high school club with 10 members meets to elect four officers: president, vice president, secretary, and treasurer. How many different election results are possible if no student can hold more than one position?

(A) 24

(B) 34

(C) 3024

(D) 5040

(E) 10,000

15. If $X = \{10, 20, 30\}$, $Y = \{15, 25, 35\}$, and $Z = \{10, 15, 20\}$, which of the following sets represents $X \cup Y \cup Z$?

(A) {15}

(B) {10, 15, 20}

(C) {10, 15, 20, 25}

(D) {10, 15, 20, 25, 35}

(E) {10, 15, 20, 25, 30, 35}

STOP

END OF SECTION 7. IF YOU HAVE ANY TIME LEFT, GO OVER YOUR WORK IN THIS SECTION ONLY. DO NOT WORK IN ANY OTHER SECTION OF THE TEST.

Section 8

16 Questions • 20 Minutes

Directions: The two passages given below deal with a related topic. Following the passages are questions about the content of each passage or about the relationship between the two passages. Answer the questions based upon what is stated or implied in the passages and in any introductory material provided. Mark the letter of your choice on your answer sheet.

QUESTIONS 1–4 ARE BASED ON THE FOLLOWING PASSAGES.

After the successful mission to Mars in 2003, there was an initiative announced to put humans on Mars by 2019. The following are two viewpoints on the topic.

Passage 1

The Mars mission to land humans on the red planet will take $600 billion in current dollars. The cost will be even higher by 2019. The trip to Mars from Earth takes 14 months. How can
5 enough supplies be loaded onto a spaceship for that amount of time for one or two or three or more scientists? A ship big enough to haul all that material and people would be too heavy for any of our current technology to thrust into space. In
10 addition, the cost of the mission is prohibitive. Draconian cuts would be required across the board in government-financed programs.

Passage 2

Right now, we cannot say that NASA and aircraft manufacturers cannot build a rocket engine big enough to power a Mars-bound ship into space. Their research scientists have years to work on
5 this. But in reality, a huge spaceship carrying two years of supplies may not be necessary. The probes on Mars have found ice below its surface. If this ice could be purified and used as a source of water, the astronauts could grow
10 their own food. It is too soon to consider the Mars initiative unworkable.

1. Which of the following correctly states the arguments that the writer of Passage 1 uses?
   (A) Scientific problems
   (B) The human costs of the mission
   (C) Scientific problems and the human costs of the mission
   (D) The cost of the mission and scientific problems
   (E) The impossibility of the mission

2. The word *Draconian* (Passage 1, line 11) means
   (A) dragonlike.
   (B) huge.
   (C) exaggerated.
   (D) severe.
   (E) cutting.

3. Which of the following best describes the tone of Passage 2?
   (A) Emotional
   (B) Rational
   (C) Optimistic
   (D) Dismissive of critics
   (E) Cautious

4. Which argument described in Passage 1 does the author of Passage 2 NOT address?
   (A) The way the Mars mission will be paid for
   (B) The difficulties of carrying enough supplies on the spaceship
   (C) The possibility of growing food on Mars
   (D) The size of the spacecraft required for the mission
   (E) The cost of the Mars mission

QUESTIONS 5–16 ARE BASED ON THE FOLLOWING PASSAGES.

Matthew Henson was born in 1866 of free black parents in Maryland. He met Commander Robert Peary in 1888 and became first his servant, and then his assistant, on Peary's major expeditions to the Arctic. In these two passages, Henson and Peary describe the same area in Greenland, a place known as Karnah.

Passage 1—from Henson's Account of the 1908 Expedition

We stopped at Kookan, the most prosperous of the Esquimo settlements, a village of five tupiks (skin tents), housing twenty-four people, and from there we sailed to the ideal community
5   of Karnah.

Karnah is the most delightful spot on the Greenland coast. Situated on a gently southward sloping knoll are the igloos and tupiks, where I have spent many pleasant days with my Esquimo
10 friends and learned much of the folklore and history. Lofty mountains, sublime in their grandeur, overtower and surround this place, and its only exposure is southward toward the sun. In winter its climate is not severe, as
15 compared with other portions of this country, and in the perpetual daylight of summer, life here is ideal. Rivulets of clear, cold water, the beds of which are grass- and flower-covered, run down the sides of the mountain and, but for
20 the lack of trees, the landscape is as delightful as anywhere on Earth.

Passage 2—from Peary's Account of the 1891 Expedition

From the eastern point of Academy Bay the main shore of the gulf extends, due east, to the face of the great Heilprin Glacier, and then on beside the great ice-stream, until the crests of
5   the cliffs disappear under the white shroud of the "Great Ice." From here on, the eastern and northern sides of the head of the gulf are an almost continuous glacier face, six great ice-streams, separated by as many precipitous nunataks,
10 flowing down from the interior ice-cap to discharge an enormous fleet of bergs. As a result of this free discharge, the great white viscosity of the interior has settled down into a huge, and

in clear weather easily discernible, semi-circular
15 basin, similar to those of Tossukatek, Great Kariak, and Jacobshavn. In this head of the gulf, situated some in the face of the glaciers, and others a short distance beyond them, are seven or eight islands, most of which bear proof of
20 former glaciation. Along the north-western shore of the gulf, the vertical cliffs resume their sway, back of which rise the trio of striking peaks, Mounts Daly, Adams, and Putname. The cliffs continue westward for some little distance, then
25 gradually merge into a gentle slope, which is in turn succeeded by the face of the Hubbard Glacier. West of the glacier, cliffs of a different character (red and grey sandstone) occur, and extend to the grand and picturesque red-brown
30 Castle Cliffs at the entrance to Bowdoin Bay. At these cliffs, the shore takes an abrupt turn to the northward, into the now familiar but previously unknown Bowdoin Bay, in which was located the headquarters of my last Expedition.

35 This bay has an extreme length of eleven miles, and an average width of between three and four miles. What with its southern exposure, the protection from the wind afforded by the cliffs and bluffs which enclose it, and the warmth
40 of colouring of its shores, it presents one of the most desirable locations for a house. The scenery is also varied and attractive, offering to the eye greater contrasts, with less change of position, than any other locality occurring to me.
45 Around the circuit of the bay are seven glaciers with exposures to all points of the compass, and varying in size from a few hundred feet to over two miles in width.

The ice-cap itself is also in evidence here, its
50 vertical face in one place capping and forming a continuation of a vertical cliff which rises direct from the bay. From the western point of the bay, a line of grey sandstone cliffs—the Sculptured Cliffs of Karnah—interrupted by
55 a single glacier in a distance of eight miles, and carved by the restless arctic elements into turrets, bastions, huge amphitheatres, and colossal statues of men and animals, extends to Cape Ackland, the Karnah of the natives. Here
60 the cliffs end abruptly, and the shore trending north-westward to Cape Cleveland, eighteen miles distant, consists of an almost continuous succession of fan-shaped, rocky deltas formed by glacier streams. Back of the shoreline is a

65 gradually sloping foreshore, rising to the foot
of an irregular series of hills, which rise more
steeply to the ice-cap lying upon their summits.
In almost every depression between these hills,
the face of a glacier may be seen, and it is the
70 streams from these that have made the shore
what it is, and formed the wide shoals off it, on
which every year a numerous fleet of icebergs
becomes stranded.

5. Henson uses the word *exposure* (line 13) to
   mean
   (A) denunciation.
   (B) unmasking.
   (C) emptiness.
   (D) danger.
   (E) openness.

6. Henson's main impression of Karnah is
   one of
   (A) apprehension.
   (B) dismay.
   (C) indifference.
   (D) pleasure.
   (E) tolerance.

7. Henson might prefer that Karnah
   (A) were not so far north.
   (B) were warmer.
   (C) were uninhabited.
   (D) lay further inland.
   (E) had more trees.

8. Peary admires Bowdoin Bay for its
   (A) diverse vistas.
   (B) incredible length.
   (C) calm waters.
   (D) impressive tides.
   (E) great ice-streams.

9. Peary compares the arctic elements to
   (A) avenging Furies.
   (B) athletic challenges.
   (C) stonecarvers.
   (D) wild horses.
   (E) ice palaces.

10. Future explorers might use Peary's
    description to
    (A) locate their ships in Karnah's harbor.
    (B) find their way around Greenland's
        shoreline.
    (C) decide the future of native settlements.
    (D) identify trees and vegetation on the
        island.
    (E) reenact Peary's discovery of the North
        Pole.

11. In general, Peary's description is in
    (A) chronological order, according to his
        various trips.
    (B) spatial order, proceeding along the
        coastline.
    (C) chronological order, moving from past to
        present.
    (D) spatial order, moving from west to east.
    (E) spatial order, moving in a circle around
        the ship.

12. The "lofty mountains" described by Henson
    (line 11) are probably Peary's
    (A) Heilprin Glacier (line 3).
    (B) Great Kariak (lines 15–16).
    (C) Mount Daly (line 23).
    (D) Sculptured Cliffs (line 54).
    (E) Cape Cleveland (line 61).

13. Unlike Henson, Peary seems intent on
    (A) snubbing the natives.
    (B) discussing flora and fauna.
    (C) focusing on geology.
    (D) raising political issues.
    (E) extolling the delights of Karnah.

14. Peary and Henson seem to agree on
    (A) the severity of Greenland's weather.
    (B) the area's attractiveness.
    (C) the need for future exploration.
    (D) both (A) and (B).
    (E) both (B) and (C).

15. Unlike Peary's account, Henson's tone is primarily

(A) humorous.

(B) objective.

(C) scientific.

(D) appreciative.

(E) technical.

16. Unlike Henson's account of his 1908 expedition, Peary pays considerable attention to

(A) Esquimo settlements.

(B) Esquimo folklore.

(C) Esquimo dietary restrictions.

(D) glaciers and ice formations.

(E) Karnah's overall physical characteristics.

STOP

END OF SECTION 8. IF YOU HAVE ANY TIME LEFT, GO OVER YOUR WORK IN THIS SECTION ONLY. DO NOT WORK IN ANY OTHER SECTION OF THE TEST.

Section 9
15 Questions • 10 Minutes

Directions: The sentences below may contain problems in grammar, usage, word choice, sentence construction, or punctuation. Part or all of each sentence is underlined. Following each sentence you will find five ways of expressing the underlined part. Choice (A) always repeats the original underlined section. The other four answer choices are all different. You are to select the lettered answer that produces the most effective sentence. If you think the original sentence is best, choose (A) as your answer. If one of the other choices makes a better sentence, mark your answer sheet for the letter of that choice. Do not choose an answer that changes the meaning of the original sentence.

1. Because the drug had been proved to cause cancer in mice, the FDA banned its use as a food additive.
   - (A) Because the drug had been proved to cause
   - (B) Since the drug had been proved to cause
   - (C) Seeing as how the drug was proved to cause
   - (D) Because the drug had been proved to be a cause of
   - (E) Because the drug, as it proved, was a cause of

2. Some gardeners put dead leaves or straw between the rows of seedlings so that the ground doesn't dry out and you don't have to weed as much.
   - (A) you don't have to weed as much
   - (B) they don't have to weed as much
   - (C) they don't have weeding as much as before
   - (D) your weeding is less
   - (E) you don't have as much weeding to do

3. If all of this bickering were to be stopped by you children, we might be able to reach an equitable solution.
   - (A) all of this bickering were to be stopped by you children
   - (B) all this bickering were stopped by you children
   - (C) all of you children had stopped this bickering
   - (D) all of this bickering stopped you children
   - (E) you children stopped all of this bickering

4. Perched on the roof like a fantastic mechanical bird, electricity is generated by the windmill to light the classroom building.
   - (A) electricity is generated by the windmill to light the classroom building
   - (B) the classroom building is lit by electricity generated by the windmill
   - (C) the windmill's electricity is generated to light the classroom building
   - (D) the windmill generates electricity and lights the classroom building
   - (E) the windmill generates electricity to light the classroom building

5. I am in the market for a comfortable for long trips and inexpensive to operate car.
   - (A) a comfortable for long trips and inexpensive to operate car
   - (B) a car that will be comfortable for long trips and inexpensive to operate
   - (C) a car that will be comfortable and inexpensive for long trips and to operate
   - (D) an inexpensively comfortable for long trips car
   - (E) a car to operate inexpensively and comfortably on long trips

6. After starting to attend the art class, Edward's sketches were more lifelike.
   - (A) After starting to attend the art class
   - (B) Since starting to attend the art class
   - (C) After the art class began to be attended
   - (D) After he started attending the art class
   - (E) After starting and attending the art class

7. The world seems to grow smaller as <u>they devise faster means of communication</u>.
   - (A) they devise faster means of communication
   - (B) they device faster means of communication
   - (C) means of communication are devised faster
   - (D) they devise faster communication means
   - (E) faster means of communication are devised

8. The April weather was so invigorating that we did not realize until we came to the signpost how far <u>it was that we had walked</u>.
   - (A) it was that we had walked
   - (B) we had walked
   - (C) we walked
   - (D) it was that we walked
   - (E) we walked to

9. The only ones <u>who opposed the consolidation of the clubs are</u> Gerald Rasmussen and he.
   - (A) who opposed the consolidation of the clubs are
   - (B) that opposed the consolidation of the clubs are
   - (C) that oppose the consolidation of the clubs are
   - (D) who oppose the consolidation of the clubs are
   - (E) who oppose the consolidation of the clubs were

10. Someone <u>has taken the book off of</u> the shelf.
    - (A) has taken the book off of
    - (B) has took the book off
    - (C) took the book off of
    - (D) has taken the book off
    - (E) has taken the book off from

11. <u>Unlike football</u>, baseball fields can vary some-what in size and shape.
    - (A) Unlike football
    - (B) Not like in football
    - (C) Contrary to football fields
    - (D) Unlike football fields
    - (E) Contrary to football

12. In the six months since the truce was declared, <u>several minor skirmishes occuring along the border</u>.
    - (A) several minor skirmishes occurring along the border
    - (B) several minor skirmishes breaking out along the border
    - (C) there have been several minor skirmishes along the border
    - (D) along the border there has been several minor skirmishes
    - (E) the several akirmishes along the border have been minor

13. Sunshine, good soil, and <u>caring continually</u> will almost always result in beautiful house plants.
    - (A) caring continually
    - (B) caring on a continual basis
    - (C) continual care
    - (D) care that is continuing
    - (E) care which can be continuous

14. <u>The pump having been repaired,</u> my cousin could turn on the heating system once again.
    - (A) The pump having been repaired,
    - (B) Because the pump is repaired,
    - (C) The pump's having been repaired,
    - (D) The pump has been repaired so that
    - (E) Having the pump repaired,

15. She jumped out of the bed as soon as the alarm rang <u>and races to be the first in the shower</u>.
    - (A) and races to be the first in the shower
    - (B) and she races to be the first in the shower
    - (C) and raced to be first in the shower
    - (D) and raced first to the shower
    - (E) then she raced to be first in the shower

STOP

END OF SECTION 9. IF YOU HAVE ANY TIME LEFT, GO OVER YOUR WORK IN THIS SECTION ONLY. DO NOT WORK IN ANY OTHER SECTION OF THE TEST.

ANSWER KEY AND EXPLANATIONS

Section 1: Essay

Sample Essay 1

Some people really believe that "the end justifies the means." They say it doesn't matter what you do or who you hurt along the way as long as you get what you desire in the end.

I couldn't disagree more with this idea. No one should be so anxious to obtain something that he will do anything just to achieve that thing. Like lying or stealing or acting immorally.

Just think if someone wanted to become the mayor or the governor or even our president and felt that he would do almost anything to achieve that goal. He would hurt people, tell lies about his opponents, say things he didn't really believe just to get votes. And then, just think of how horrible it would be if he did get elected. What kind of a president or governor or mayor would he make? He would be power hungry and probably just continue lying and cheating to keep himself in office. The people would be the ones who would suffer.

We once read a play about Faust. He sold his soul to the devil in order to get what he wanted. But once he got what he thought would make himself happy, it really didn't. And in the end he had to give up everything.

It is more important to do the right thing and to behave in the correct way in order to achieve your goal. If you do everything right and you do not get what you are striving for at least you will be able to live with yourself. If you do get your heart's desire then you will be even happier because you will know that you earned your reward.

Analysis of Sample Essay 1

The writer of this essay develops the thesis in an organized essay that stays on the topic and presents a clear point of view. The examples from politics are appropriate and serve as effective supporting material. The conclusion provides a summary.

The essay could be improved by eliminating some technical flaws and strengthening word choice and clarity. In paragraph two, the last sentence is a fragment (it might be joined to the sentence that precedes it), and *like* should be changed to *such as*. To improve clarity and diction, a number of words should be changed. In paragraph one, *who* should be changed to *whom*. In paragraph two, *will* should be changed to *would*, and *thing* should be changed to *goal*. In paragraph three, "the mayor," "the governor," "our president" would be better phrased as "a mayor," "a governor," "the president"; "felt that" should be deleted; and in the hypothetical examples "would hurt people" and "would be power hungry," *might* should replace *would*. In paragraph four, the pronoun *We* is not clear and should be *I*, and *himself* is awkward and should be *him*. And in paragraph five, since the writer starts out with the third person *people*, it would be preferable not to change to the second person *your*, *you*, and *yourself*. Removing the inconsistency would improve the tone. Also, the first sentence of the second paragraph is better phrased as "I strongly disagree with this idea."

Sample Essay 2

In a movie about the world of finance, a wall street tycoon insists that whatever he does in order to make more and more money is correct and acceptable. That it is okay to do whatever is necessary in order to be successful in business and make as much money as possible. These two works are typical of the prevailing philosophy that, "The ends justify the means." You can do anything you want as long as it gets you what you want.

You can throw a spitball if it will result in a strikeout. You can cheat on a test if it will result in a higher score. You can use an inferior part in a piece of equipment if it will result in a greater margin of profit.

What a terrible philosophy! How sad it is to think of all the people who are influenced by films, books, TV, and unscrupulous people in the news to believe in selfish, illegal ways in order to acquire possessions or make money or become famous for a brief time. The journalist who makes up sources for a story, the doctor who prepares phony medicare bills, the lawyer who charges for more time than he spends on a case, the businessman who fixes up his home and charges stockholders for the work. All these are common examples of too many people today.

Nobody wants to be a good guy who finishes last. And society seems to condone this attitude. What ever happened to the old-fashioned view of morality and ethics?

Analysis of Sample Essay 2

There are several serious errors in technical English that detract from the rather good content of this essay. In the first paragraph, the third sentence (beginning with "That it is...") is a fragment, as is the third sentence of paragraph three (beginning with "The journalist . . ."). An error in capitalization appears in the first sentence of the essay; *Wall Street* should be capitalized. *Medicare* should also be capitalized. Although points are not taken off for errors like these, they do detract from the general impression of the writer as competent and in command of Standard Written English.

The style is rather informal, and this is certainly acceptable. However, certain devices should be avoided; it is better to use a third-person approach (*people*) rather than a second-person approach (*you*). The last sentence of the first paragraph would be stylistically improved in this way, as would the second paragraph. Also, words such as *okay* should be changed to *acceptable* or *permissible*.

The content is clear and the writer addresses the central issue throughout the essay. Good examples are provided in the third paragraph. The first sentence of the third paragraph captures the attention of the reader, as does the final sentence of the essay.

Section 2

1. B	7. A	12. E	17. A	22. D
2. B	8. B	13. D	18. B	23. B
3. C	9. A	14. D	19. E	24. D
4. E	10. C	15. C	20. E	25. E
5. D	11. D	16. B	21. D	26. C
6. C				

1. **The correct answer is (B).** A position that provides authority to award contracts is also likely to allow the holder to *incur* (take on) obligations to pay bills.

2. **The correct answer is (B).** A witness who reveals very little information, even when questioned by an experienced attorney, is *recalcitrant* (stubborn).

3. **The correct answer is (C).** The word *although* signifies a shift in meaning. Even though *substantial* (large) resources had been applied, the solution was still *elusive* (hard to determine).

4. **The correct answer is (E).** The only logical choice is the one in which both words have the same connotation; both must be either positive or negative. Only choice (E) satisfies this condition with two positive words.

5. **The correct answer is (D).** The word in the first blank must be a synonym for *kept. Retained* and *received* both might satisfy this condition, but only *insured* makes sense in the second blank.

6. **The correct answer is (C).** The first blank needs a positive word to describe the way the agent calmed the travelers; the second blank needs a negative word to describe the delayed travelers. Only choice (C) meets both conditions.

7. **The correct answer is (A).** The lover of democracy has an aversion or *antipathy* toward totalitarianism.

8. **The correct answer is (B).** This answer needs either two negative or two positive words. The other four choices have a com-

bination of positive and negative words. Since choice (B) has two negative words describing the situation, it is the only correct response.

9. **The correct answer is (A).** The words need to be opposites. One word needs to be supportive of free individuals and the other needs to be negative.

10. **The correct answer is (C).** Substitute the answer choices into the sentence and also check the context in which the phrase is used. *Matter for argument* makes the most sense.

11. **The correct answer is (D).** Although most people applauded, there were people who did not understand it and some who displayed their displeasure by hissing.

12. **The correct answer is (E).** The passage describes the productivity increases as the result of both technology and innovation in the workplace.

13. **The correct answer is (D).** Investing in technology was not included as an innovative workplace practice.

14. **The correct answer is (D).** The roots of classical architecture date back to ancient Rome, when people of the highest social orders embraced its style.

15. **The correct answer is (C).** This answer is the exception because just the opposite is true—the same spatial divisions were applied no matter what the type of building.

16. **The correct answer is (B).** The context of the sentence indicates that *three-part* is the only possible answer.

17. **The correct answer is (A).** The passage mentions all of the columns by name with the exception of Egyptian.

18. **The correct answer is (B).** *Capital* is the answer. Lines 40–42 define the parts of the column as the capital, the shaft, and the base.

19. **The correct answer is (E).** The context of the sentence indicates that *balance* is the only possible answer.

20. **The correct answer is (E).** Throughout the passage the idea that classical architecture is filled with rules that must be followed is stressed.

21. **The correct answer is (D).** The word is used several times to refer to the feathers and leaves with which the narrator will appease the spirit. It is thus a *tribute* rather than any of the other synonyms.

22. **The correct answer is (D).** It is a *quest*, because she is looking for a patch of bare ground where she can perform a religious rite.

23. **The correct answer is (B).** Looking back on the events, the adult narrator feels sorry for the small child she was. She now sees that the task was too great for someone so small—that a child could not hope or be expected to save her sister's life.

24. **The correct answer is (D).** The child is afraid that the offering did not reach the ground, and therefore, her sister will not be saved. If it did not reach the ground, perhaps it is because she did not have faith in nature to show her a bare patch of ground and did not follow the medicine-woman's instructions.

25. **The correct answer is (E).** If you understand Question 24, you probably answered this question correctly. The small child blames herself for her lack of faith, which she sees as causing her sister's turn for the worse.

26. **The correct answer is (C).** This evaluation question is a restatement of interpretation of Question 25. Throughout the passage, the reader is made aware of the child's struggle and her essential decency. The author wants us to like the child and forgive her as she herself has done.

Section 3

(Code: A = Arithmetic; AL = Basic Algebra; G = Geometry; IA = Intermediate Algebra;
O = Data, Statistics, and Probability)

1. D (A)	5. B (G)	9. E (G)	13. D (G)	17. C (O)
2. A (AL)	6. C (O)	10. A (G)	14. B (O)	18. A (IA)
3. E (G)	7. B (AL)	11. E (A)	15. C (G)	19. A (IA)
4. B (AL)	8. C (A)	12. D (A)	16. B (A)	20. E (G)

Note: A 🖩 following a math answer explanation indicates that a calculator could be helpful in solving that particular problem.

1. The correct answer is (D).

$$\frac{3}{4} = 0.75$$

$\frac{35}{71}$ is slightly less than $\frac{35}{70} = 0.5$

$$\frac{13}{20} = \frac{13 \times 5}{20 \times 5} = \frac{65}{100} = 0.65$$

$\frac{71}{101}$ is very close to $\frac{7}{10}$, or 0.7

$$\frac{15}{20} = \frac{15 \times 5}{20 \times 5} = \frac{75}{100} = 0.75$$

$\frac{19}{24} = 24\overline{)19.00}$ which is more than $\frac{3}{4}$

$$\begin{array}{r} 0.79 \\ 168 \\ \hline 200 \\ 216 \end{array}$$

🖩

2. The correct answer is (A).

$$820 + R + S - 610 = 342$$
$$R + S + 210 = 342$$
$$R + S = 132$$
$$2S + S = 132$$
$$3S = 132$$

If $R = 2S$, then $S = 44$ 🖩

3. The correct answer is (E).

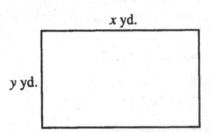

x yd.

y yd.

Area = xy sq. yd. = $9xy$ sq. yd.
$9xy \cdot 5 = 45xy$

4. The correct answer is (B).

$$+7M = 3M - 20$$
$$+4M = -20$$
$$+M = -5$$
$$M + 7 = -5 + 7 = 2$$

5. The correct answer is (B). Arc $EA = 85°$ and arc $BD = 15°$, since a central angle is measured by its arc. Then

$$\text{angle } ECA = \frac{1}{2}\left(\widehat{AE} - \widehat{BD}\right)$$
$$= \frac{1}{2}(85 - 15)$$
$$= \frac{1}{2} \cdot 70$$
$$= 35°$$ 🖩

6. The correct answer is (C). The smallest positive number divisible by 3, 4, or 5 is $3 \cdot 4 \cdot 5 = 60$. Hence, the desired number is $60 + 2 = 62$.

7. **The correct answer is (B).** Since there are $4d$ quarter miles in d miles, the charge = $75 + 15(4d - 1)$.

8. **The correct answer is (C).** Assume that there are 100 enlistees on the post; then 30 are from New York State and $\frac{1}{10} \times 30$ are from New York City. $0.10 \times 30 = 3\%$. 🖩

9. **The correct answer is (E).** If you know only the hypotenuse of a right triangle, you cannot determine its legs. Hence, the area of the rectangle cannot be determined from the data given.

10. **The correct answer is (A).** If angle $RPQ >$ angle RQP, then $\frac{1}{2}$ angle $P > \frac{1}{2}$ angle Q; then angle $SPQ >$ angle SQP. Since the larger side lies opposite the larger angle, it follows that $SQ > SP$.

11. **The correct answer is (E).**
$$3.14 \times 10^6 = 3.14 \times 1,000,000$$
$$= 3,140,000$$ 🖩

12. **The correct answer is (D).**
$$\frac{36}{29 - \dfrac{4}{0.2}} = \frac{36}{29 - 20} = \frac{36}{9} = 4$$

13. **The correct answer is (D).** Diameter = $4\sqrt{2}$, since it is the hypotenuse of a right isosceles triangle of leg 4.

Then the radius = $2\sqrt{2}$.

Area of semicircle $= \frac{1}{2} \times \pi \times \left(2\sqrt{2}\right)^2$
$$= \frac{1}{2} \times \pi 8 = 4\pi$$

14. **The correct answer is (B).** Consecutive odd numbers may be represented as
$$2n + 1$$
$$2n + 3$$
$$\underline{2n + 5}$$
$$\text{Sum} = 6n + 9$$

Divide by 3. Thus, only II is correct.

15. **The correct answer is (C).** Angle BCD is formed by tangent and chord and is equal to one half of arc BC. Angle A is an inscribed angle and is also equal to one half of arc BC. Hence, angle $A =$ angle $BCD = 40°$.

16. **The correct answer is (B).** Let $x =$ amount of marked price. Then:
$$\frac{1}{5}x = 15$$
$$x = 75$$
$$75 - 15 = \$60$$ 🖩

17. **The correct answer is (C).** This problem cannot be solved by simply doing subtraction. To give an example: if you read pages 1 and 2 of a book, how many pages have you read? The answer is obviously 2; we can conclude then that we do not obtain the answer by subtracting 1 from 2. Instead we subtract 1 from 2 and add 1.
$$49 - 7 + 1 \quad = \quad 43$$
$$157 - 101 + 1 \quad = \quad 57$$
$$43 + 57 \quad = \quad 100$$ 🖩

18. **The correct answer is (A).** Substitute $y + 2$ for x in the formula $f(x) = x^2 - 2x$. Thus, $f(y + 2) = (y + 2)^2 - 2(y + 2) = y^2 + 4y + 4 - 2y - 4 = y^2 + 2y$.

19. **The correct answer is (A).**
$$\left(27c^9\right)^{\frac{1}{3}} = (27)^{\frac{1}{3}}\left(c^9\right)^{\frac{1}{3}} = 3c^{\frac{9}{3}} = 3c^3$$

20. **The correct answer is (E).** Begin by finding the slope of the given line by writing the equation in slope-intercept form.
$$3y + x = 21$$
$$3y = -x + 21$$
$$y = -\frac{1}{3}x + 7$$

Therefore, the slope of the given line is $-\frac{1}{3}$.

The slope of a line perpendicular to this would be the "negative reciprocal" of $-\frac{1}{3}$, which is 3.

Section 4

1. D	8. B	15. B	22. D	29. C
2. A	9. E	16. B	23. A	30. A
3. B	10. C	17. E	24. D	31. C
4. E	11. A	18. D	25. B	32. B
5. B	12. A	19. B	26. D	33. E
6. B	13. C	20. B	27. E	34. B
7. D	14. C	21. E	28. B	35. D

1. **The correct answer is (D).** *Phase*, meaning "an aspect," is incorrect; substitute *faze*, meaning "to disturb."

2. **The correct answer is (A).** The correct word for countable items is *number*.

3. **The correct answer is (B).** The correct word is *theirs*.

4. **The correct answer is (E).** The sentence is correct.

5. **The correct answer is (B).** The correct word is *drank*.

6. **The correct answer is (B).** The correct word to indicate a comparison is *than*.

7. **The correct answer is (D).** The standard form is *nowhere*.

8. **The correct answer is (B).** The correct phrase is *occurred when*.

9. **The correct answer is (E).** The sentence is correct.

10. **The correct answer is (C).** The correct phrase is *didn't leave any* since the double negative must be eliminated.

11. **The correct answer is (A).** The correct word is *likely*, suggesting "probable behavior"; *liable* means "responsible according to law."

12. **The correct answer is (A).** The participle *being* should be preceded by the possessive *his*.

13. **The correct answer is (C).** The correct verb is *hoped to read* since the action has not yet occurred.

14. **The correct answer is (C).** The objective form *whom* is required.

15. **The correct answer is (B).** For parallel structure, the sentence should be rephrased: a woman *who has great integrity*.

16. **The correct answer is (B).** The singular verb form *is* is required since *team* is a collective noun that should be considered singular.

17. **The correct answer is (E).** The sentence is correct.

18. **The correct answer is (D).** Substitute *morale*, a noun denoting the state of the spirits of a person or group, for *moral*, an adjective meaning ethical.

19. **The correct answer is (B).** The expression *not but* is a double negative. Use *could but* or *could only*.

20. **The correct answer is (B).** In a neither-nor construction, the verb agrees with the closest subject. In this example, the singular *is* should agree with *teacher*.

21. **The correct answer is (E).** The correct word for the head of a school is *principal*; therefore, choices (A) and (B) are wrong. Choice (C) uses the contraction for *it is* instead of the possessive *its*. Choice (D) has no verb in the main clause.

22. **The correct answer is (D).** *Might of, could of,* and *should of* are nonstandard English. The correct form is might *have* (or, informally, might've).

23. **The correct answer is (A).** The sentence is correct. Both verbs should be in the past tense.

24. **The correct answer is (D).** The correct word is *annoyed*, meaning made angry; *aggravated* means made worse. The completed comparison is *than we (were)*. Only choice (D) meets both of these requirements.

25. **The correct answer is (B).** To maintain parallel structure, the participle *avoiding* is required. The verb must be the plural *help* to agree with the compound subject.

26. **The correct answer is (D).** The original sentence uses *like* where *as if is* required. Choices (B) and (C) have the same problem. Choice (E) is not idiomatic. Choice (D) is both correct and concise.

27. **The correct answer is (E).** The use of *it* in the original sentence is awkward and unnecessary.

28. **The correct answer is (B).** Avoid the awkward use of the passive.

29. **The correct answer is (C).** *By means of* means the same as *using*: the use of the two together is redundant.

30. **The correct answer is (A).** Idiomatic construction requires that the word *that*—not *because*—should be used. Therefore, choices (B) and (E) are poor. Choices (C) and (D) are awkward since the word *possibly* following *may* is not necessary. Choice (A) is best.

31. **The correct answer is (C).** As it stands, the sentence is awkward since the antecedent for the pronoun *it* appears to be *society* and not *trust,* as was intended. Choice (C) corrects this error.

32. **The correct answer is (B).** Asking a question is contrived and providing an answer makes the essay unnecessarily wordy. To add strength to the paragraph, a simple declarative sentence, choice (B), is best.

33. **The correct answer is (E).** The metaphor *fabric of our society* should be consistent with its accompanying verb. The verb *break* is not appropriate because one does not *break fabric* as stated in the original sentence as well as in choices (A), (B), and (D). Choice (C) is incorrect because the preposition *apart* at the end of the sentence is wrong. The correct choice is (E).

34. **The correct answer is (B).** Sentence (12) states that a problem exists, and the two sentences that follow present this problem, which requires a solution.

35. **The correct answer is (D).** Choice (A) contains a comma splice error. Choices (B) and (C) are poor since the antecedent of *they* is not clear in either sentence. Choice (E) is a fragment and is incorrect. Choice (D) is best.

Section 5

(Code: A = Arithmetic; AL = Basic Algebra; G = Geometry; IA = Intermediate Algebra; O = Data, Statistics, and Probability)

1. A (G)	5. E (IA)	9. C (A)	13. 3 (IA)	17. 30 (A)
2. D (AL)	6. E (AL)	10. A (G)	14. 30 (O)	18. 3 (A)
3. E (IA)	7. A (A)	11. 94 (AL)	15. 3 (AL)	19. 105 (O)
4. B (AL)	8. E (O)	12. 60 (G)	16. 80 (A)	20. 45 (O)

Note: A 🔲 following a math answer explanation indicates that a calculator could be helpful in solving that particular problem.

1. The correct answer is (A).

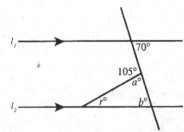

The measure of $\angle b$ is $70°$ since it is an alternate interior angle with $\angle x$. The measure of $\angle a = 75°$ since it is supplementary to $\angle y$. Since there are $180°$ in a triangle, $r° + a° + b° = 180°$.

$$r° + 75° + 70° = 180°$$
$$r° = 35°$$

2. The correct answer is (D). Substitute the value -1 for x:

$$-(-1)^2 - 2(-1)^3 = -(1) - 2(-1) = -1 + 2 = 1$$

3. The correct answer is (E). Begin by multiplying all terms of the equation by the LCD of $56x$.

$$56x\left(\frac{1}{7}\right) - 56x\left(\frac{1}{8}\right) = 56x\left(\frac{1}{x}\right)$$
$$8x - 7x = 56$$
$$x = 56$$

4. The correct answer is (B).

$$|-4| - |-8| + |-2||-3| = 4 - 8 + (2)(3) = -4 + 6 = 2$$

5. The correct answer is (E). To solve this problem, you simply need to determine the value of $200 \times 2^{\frac{t}{6}}$, with $t = 30$. Simply compute

$$200 \times 2^{\frac{t}{6}} = 200 \times 2^{\frac{30}{6}} = 200 \times 2^5$$
$$= 200 \times 32 = 6400.$$

6. The correct answer is (E). $x(p + 1) = M$

Divide both sides by x.

$$p + 1 = \frac{M}{x} \quad \text{or} \quad p = \frac{M}{x} - 1$$

7. The correct answer is (A).

$$\frac{T}{1} = \frac{x}{60M}$$
$$x = 60MT$$

8. The correct answer is (E). It can be helpful to graph each of the inequalities and then put the two graphs together to find the overlapping area.

9. The correct answer is (C). Rise in temperature $= 36 - (-14) = 36 + 14 = 50°$. $\frac{50}{5} = 10°$ (hourly rise). Hence, at noon,

temperature $= -14 + 3(10) = -14 + 30 = +16°$. 🔲

10. The correct answer is (A). When we are asked for the sum of two items, we often *cannot* state the values of the individual items. This is the case in this problem. We can say $\angle BAD$ is $75°$ and $\angle CDA$ is $85°$. We also know that *ABCD* is a quadrilateral and must contain 360°. Therefore:

$$\angle ABC + \angle BCD = 200°$$

$$\angle EBA + \angle ABC = 180°$$

$$\angle BCD + \angle DCF = 180°$$

$$\angle EBA + \angle ABC + \angle BCD + \angle DCF = 360°$$

$$\angle EBA + 200° + \angle DCF = 360°$$

$$\angle EBA + \angle DCF = 160°$$

11. The correct answer is 94.

$$\text{Average} = \frac{\text{Sum of the test scores}}{\text{Quantity of tests}}$$

$$90 = \frac{87 + 93 + 86 + x}{4}$$

By cross-multiplication:

$$4(90) = 87 + 93 + 86 + x$$

$$360 = 266 + x$$

$$x = 94$$

12. The correct answer is 60. Circumference = $2\pi r = 2\pi(6) = 12\pi$. 2π is $\frac{2\pi}{12\pi} = \frac{1}{6}$ of the circumference. In turn, the central angle is:

$$\frac{1}{6}(360°) = 60°, \text{ or } \frac{\text{arc length}}{\text{circumference}} = \frac{x°}{360°}$$

$$\frac{2\pi}{12\pi} = \frac{x}{360}$$

$$\frac{1}{6} = \frac{x}{360}$$

$$6x = 360$$

$$x = 60$$

13. The correct answer is 3.

$$\frac{2x}{3\sqrt{2}} = \frac{3\sqrt{2}}{x}$$

By cross-multiplication:

$$2x(x) = \left(3\sqrt{2}\right)\left(3\sqrt{2}\right)$$

$$2x^2 = 9(2) = 18$$

$$x^2 = 9$$

$$x = \pm 3$$

The positive value of *x* is 3.

14. The correct answer is 30. The median is the "middle" data element when the data are arranged in numerical order.

$$20, 20, 20, 20, 30, 30, 30, 30, 50, 50, 50, 50, 50, 50, 50$$
$$\uparrow$$

The "middle" data element is 30.

15. The correct answer is 3.

$$A * B = \frac{AB - B}{-B}$$

$$-2 * 2 = \frac{(-2)(2) - 2}{-2} = \frac{-4 - 2}{-2} = \frac{-6}{-2} = 3$$

16. The correct answer is 80.

$$\text{distance} = \text{rate} \times \text{time} \rightarrow \text{rate} = \frac{\text{distance}}{\text{time}}$$

$$\frac{320 \text{ miles}}{8 \text{ hrs.}} = 40 \text{ miles /hour}$$

$$40 \text{ mph} \times 2 \text{ hrs.} = 80 \text{ miles}$$

17. The correct answer is 30.

$$\frac{\text{part}}{\text{whole}} \times 100 = \frac{9}{30} \times 100 = 30\%$$

18. The correct answer is 3. The number of sheets is directly proportional to the number of machines and also directly proportional to the amount of time. Mathematically this can be expressed as:

$$\frac{\text{sheets}}{(\text{number of machines})(\text{time})} = \frac{\text{sheets}}{(\text{number of machines})(\text{time})}$$

$$\frac{300}{3(3)} = \frac{600}{6(t)}$$

$$\frac{300}{9} = \frac{600}{6t}$$

Simplify the fractions and then cross-multiply:

$$\frac{100}{3} = \frac{100}{t}$$

$$100t = 300$$

$$t = 3$$

19. **The correct answer is 105.** The regular price for a DVD player and stereo receiver is $80 + $340 = $420. During the sale, Sean would receive a 25% discount, so he would save 25% of $420 = 0.25 × $420 = $105. Thus, the number of dollars he would save is 105.

20. **The correct answer is 45.** The regular price for a CD player and speakers is $120 + $260 = $380. During a sale, Brian would receive a 15% discount, so he would save

0.15 × $380 = $57, and therefore pay $380 − $57 = $323. If he also decides to buy the DVD player, he qualifies for the larger 20% discount. The regular price for a CD player, speakers, and DVD player is $120 + $260 + $80 = $460. Since 20% of this amount is 0.20 × $460 = $92, Brian would pay $460 − $92 = $368 for all three items. $368 − $323 = $45.

Section 6

1. B	7. E	12. D	17. E	22. A
2. C	8. A	13. B	18. D	23. C
3. D	9. A	14. B	19. B	24. A
4. B	10. D	15. B	20. C	25. B
5. E	11. B	16. E	21. E	26. A
6. B				

1. **The correct answer is (B).** "Mutual assistance" implies that people are *cooperative.* Since "rather than" indicates a shift in meaning, the word in the second blank must have an opposing connotation; only *competitive* satisfies this condition.

2. **The correct answer is (C).** A condition that has existed for a long time in a particular place is said to be *endemic* to that location.

3. **The correct answer is (D).** The first blank could logically be filled by any of the choices. However, the secret betrayal implies that the actions *belied* (showed to be untrue) the words of the *reiterated* (repeated) pledges of support.

4. **The correct answer is (B).** Of the choices, the only one that could "look back upon us and our time" is our *descendants.*

5. **The correct answer is (E).** Choices (B), (D), and (E) are possibilities for the first blank. However, the second words in choices (B)

and (D) make no logical sense. A *final* debate is likely to offer *clarification* of opinions.

6. **The correct answer is (B).** This is the only logical answer. "With the *duration*" is poor diction.

7. **The correct answer is (E).** The sentence establishes an opposition between "our" wishes and Eva's action. Only choice (E) satisfies this requirement.

8. **The correct answer is (A).** A key word in this sentence is *appearance.* The words following all tell how a person physically looks. Choices (B), (C), (D), and (E) describe feelings or behaviors. The only word describing physical appearance is *tousled,* choice (A), which means "unkempt."

9. **The correct answer is (A).** The passage specifically states that there has been no recording of the sun's dimming.

10. **The correct answer is (D).** That the amount of sunlight reaching the Earth has decreased

is not a theory since instruments have tracked this phenomenon. The other answers are either statements of facts or misstatements, as in choice (E).

11. **The correct answer is (B).** Chivington's viewpoint is revealed in the sentence about his hoping to use this assault as a way to become governor. He expected the electorate to be approving. There is nothing in the passage to confirm choice (C). Choice (A) can't be correct because if Chivington considered it a victory, there would be no reason to use the word *supposed.*

12. **The correct answer is (D).** Context indicates that choices (A) and (E) can't be correct. Choice (B) isn't strong enough.

13. **The correct answer is (B).** This choice is not mentioned in the passage.

14. **The correct answer is (B).** The prefix *multi* means "many," so you need to decide which of the root words applies. Based on the passage, only the word that indicates multiple uses makes sense.

15. **The correct answer is (B).** Their preoccupation with their stiff, new clothing, their awe at the train's typical conveniences, and their blushes at the glances of travelers—all of these combine to paint the picture of an innocent, unworldly pair.

16. **The correct answer is (E).** The bride constantly "twisted her head to regard her puff sleeves" and is embarrassed by them. Her dress is probably brand new, and she is certainly unused to such finery.

17. **The correct answer is (E).** With this single line, Crane paints a life of hard work and resignation.

18. **The correct answer is (D).** The bridegroom is putting on a brave face for the sake of his bride, who is even more unsophisticated than he.

19. **The correct answer is (B).** The bridegroom's pride is part of his delight in his "new estate" of marriage. He can show off for his bride, but there is no doubt that such elegance is rare for him.

20. **The correct answer is (C).** The charmingly decorated train is thought by the newlyweds to be indicative of their new status in life. Because they feel exalted by their new marriage, they imagine that they deserve such luxury.

21. **The correct answer is (E).** The porter is a lower-class working man and is probably looked down upon by travelers, but he welcomes this opportunity to sneer at those lower on the ladder than himself.

22. **The correct answer is (A).** Travelers look at the newlyweds with "derisive enjoyment." It is clear that they are just married, and there is something amusing about this.

23. **The correct answer is (C).** Customarily, people in the position of the newlyweds are amusing to others. None of the other synonyms makes sense in this context.

24. **The correct answer is (A).** Crane is not derisive, choice (D); he leaves that to the other travelers and the porter. On the contrary, his attitude seems to be a slightly detached air of sympathy at the newlyweds' embarrassment and innocence.

25. **The correct answer is (B).** Their names are unimportant; what is vital is their provincialism and ordinariness. The reader can thus identify a type without feeling overly empathetic.

26. **The correct answer is (A).** This is, in fact, the beginning of the story, and, as with most short stories, its object is to introduce characters and setting. No opinion is expressed, choice (D); the passage is simply descriptive.

Section 7

(Code: A = Arithmetic; AL = Basic Algebra; G = Geometry; IA = Intermediate Algebra; O = Data, Statistics, and Probability)

1. B (G)	4. D (A)	7. A (G)	10. D (AL)	13. C (G)
2. B (O)	5. D (G)	8. B (G)	11. E (A)	14. D (O)
3. B (G)	6. D (AL)	9. E (G)	12. C (A)	15. E (A)

Note: A ▦ following a math answer explanation indicates that a calculator could be helpful in solving that particular problem.

1. **The correct answer is (B).** Since Z is equidistant from X and Y, it must lie on the y-axis. Then $\triangle OZY$ is a 30°-60°-90° triangle with $YZ = 8$. Hence, $OZ = \dfrac{8}{2}\sqrt{3} = 4\sqrt{3}$. Coordinates of Z are $(0, 4\sqrt{3})$. ▦

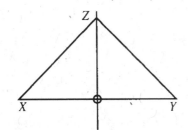

2. **The correct answer is (B).** $9 = 8 + 1 = 7 + 2 = 6 + 3 = 5 + 4$.

   Thus, 4 ways. ▦

3. **The correct answer is (B).**

   $\dfrac{7 \text{ ft. } 9 \text{ in.}}{3} = \dfrac{6 \text{ ft. } 21 \text{ in.}}{3} = 2 \text{ ft. } 7 \text{ in.}$ ▦

4. **The correct answer is (D).** Since K is an integer and R and S are integers, K must be a perfect square and perfect cube. The smallest such number listed is $64 = 8^2 = 4^3$. ▦

5. **The correct answer is (D).** The $\triangle RST$ has a base of 7 and an altitude of 5.

   Hence, the area $\dfrac{1}{2} \bullet 7 \bullet 5 = 17\dfrac{1}{2}$. ▦

6. **The correct answer is (D).** $\dfrac{3P}{3Q}$ is obviously reducible to $\dfrac{P}{Q}$. The others cannot be reduced.

7. **The correct answer is (A).** If ACB is a straight angle and angle DCE is a right angle, then angle ACD and angle BCE are complementary. Hence, $BCE = 90 - x$.

8. **The correct answer is (B).** When a triangle is inscribed in a parallelogram or a rectangle, the area inside the inscribed triangle will always be the same as the area outside the inscribed triangle. All three triangles have the same altitude. Since AE plus ED equals BC, the two shaded triangles combined have the same base as the unshaded triangle. If the base and the altitude are the same, then the area is the same.

9. **The correct answer is (E).** The most important point here is that we do not know the altitude of the parallelogram; the area of a parallelogram is altitude times base. A secondary point would be that we do not know the lengths of AB and BC; we only know the ratio of the two sides. The actual lengths of the sides could be, for example, 8 and 18.

10. **The correct answer is (D).** If a dozen eggs cost M cents, then 1 egg costs $\dfrac{M}{12}$ cents (there are 12 items in a dozen). The profit per egg would be Selling Price − Cost, or $\dfrac{M}{6} - \dfrac{M}{12}$. Using a common denominator of 12, the profit per egg would be $\dfrac{M}{12}$ cents. Then the profit on a dozen eggs would be $\dfrac{M}{12} \times 12$, which is M cents.

11. **The correct answer is (E).** If $\dfrac{P}{Q} = \dfrac{4}{5}$, then $5P = 4Q$. However, there is no way of determining from this the value of $2P + Q$.

12. **The correct answer is (C).** The new solution is $\dfrac{3}{20}$ pure alcohol, or 15%.

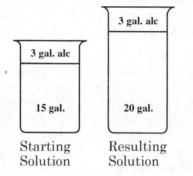

Starting   Resulting
Solution   Solution

13. **The correct answer is (C).** Area of $QXRS$ $= XR \times$ altitude from P to XR. Area of $\triangle PXR = \dfrac{1}{2}XR \times$ altitude from P to XR. Hence, ratio of area of $\triangle$ to $QXRS = 1{:}2$.

14. **The correct answer is (D).** There are 10 possible choices for president, which means there are only 9 remaining choices for vice president. After the vice president is elected, there are 8 choices for secretary, and then 7 choices for treasurer. Overall, then, there are $10 \times 9 \times 8 \times 7 = 5040$ different possible election results.

15. **The correct answer is (E).** The union of the three sets will contain all of the elements of the three sets. The set $\{10, 15, 20, 25, 30, 35\}$ contains all of the elements in the sets X, Y, and Z.

Section 8

1. D	5. E	9. C	13. C
2. D	6. D	10. B	14. D
3. C	7. E	11. B	15. D
4. E	8. A	12. D	16. D

1. **The correct answer is (D).** The writer talks about the costs of the mission in terms of money. Only choice (D) includes both the costs and the problems.

2. **The correct answer is (D).** Choice (A) is too cute for the SAT test-writers. There is nothing to indicate that cuts would be exaggerated, because the cost of the mission is very high.

3. **The correct answer is (C).** While the passage could be considered rational, choice (C) better fits the tone. The last sentence helps to support this choice.

4. **The correct answer is (E).** The writer never talks about the costs of the project, just how and why it may work.

5. **The correct answer is (E).** The town's only exposure is southward toward the sun; it is open only on the south side.

6. **The correct answer is (D).** Henson calls Karnah "pleasant," "delightful," even "ideal."

7. **The correct answer is (E).** The lack of trees is the only thing that keeps Karnah from having a landscape "as delightful as anywhere on earth."

8. **The correct answer is (A).** "The scenery is also varied and attractive, offering to the eye greater contrasts. . . .," writes Peary. This diversity is one of the attractions of the bay.

9. **The correct answer is (C).** Lines 56–58 describe the "restless arctic elements" carving the cliffs into "turrets, bastions, huge amphitheatres, and colossal statues. . . ."

10. **The correct answer is (B).** Peary does not talk about vegetation, choice (D), nor is this a passage about the North Pole, choice (E). The passage follows the coast of Greenland with enough specific detail that a reader could use it as a map.

11. **The correct answer is (B).** The description of the geology and scenery of Greenland seems to be from the vantage point of a ship traveling along the coastline. Everything that is mentioned is along the shore.

12. **The correct answer is (D).** Henson's "lofty mountains" surround Karnah; the only mention of landmarks around Karnah in Peary's description is the "Sculptured Cliffs of Karnah."

13. **The correct answer is (C).** Peary's descriptions are much more technical than Henson's; his purpose is not to write a simple travelogue, but to detail an expedition for future explorers.

14. **The correct answer is (D).** Both writers mention the severity of most of the arctic, Henson in comparing it to Karnah's more moderate climate, and Peary in his description of the restless arctic elements. Both, too, remark on the unusual attractiveness of Karnah and the bay.

15. **The correct answer is (D).** As was previously mentioned, Peary's descriptions are more objective and technical than those of Henson. Henson's sound more like the appreciative words of a casual traveler.

16. **The correct answer is (D).** Although Henson's account discusses the "rivulets of clear, cold water," he does not focus on the impact of glacial and iceberg activity, as does his counterpart.

Section 9

1. A	4. E	7. E	10. D	13. C
2. B	5. B	8. B	11. D	14. A
3. E	6. D	9. D	12. C	15. C

1. **The correct answer is (A).** The sentence is correct.

2. **The correct answer is (B).** Do not switch from the third person *(gardeners)* to the second person *(you)* in the middle of a sentence.

3. **The correct answer is (E).** Avoid the awkward use of the passive as in choices (A) and (B) and unnecessary shifts in tense as in choice (C).

4. **The correct answer is (E).** The original sentence contains a dangling phrase. Since *perched* must refer to *windmill, windmill* should be made the subject of the sentence.

5. **The correct answer is (B).** Avoid placing too many modifiers in front of a noun.

6. **The correct answer is (D).** Since *starting* cannot refer to *Edward's sketches,* the original phrase must be rewritten as a clause containing its own subject.

7. **The correct answer is (E).** Avoid using *they* without a clear antecedent.

8. **The correct answer is (B).** The original version is wordy.

9. **The correct answer is (D).** The verb tense of the two clauses needs to be the same; in this case, present tense.

10. **The correct answer is (D).** The correct phrase is *taken off,* not *taken off of.*

11. **The correct answer is (D).** Choices (A), (B), and (E) improperly contrast an entire sport *(football)* with one aspect of another sport *(baseball fields).* Choices (B), (C), and (E) are also unidiomatic. Only choice (D) corrects the sentence logically and idiomatically.

12. **The correct answer is (C).** The original sentence lacks a complete verb in the main clause. Both choices (C) and (E) provide a verb that agrees with the subject, but choice (E) changes the meaning of the original sentence.

13. **The correct answer is (C).** In order to maintain parallelism, the third item must also be a noun.

14. **The correct answer is (A).** The sentence is correct.

15. **The correct answer is (C).** The original choice (A) is inconsistent in tense, starting in the past *(jumped, rang)* and then switching to the present *(races).* Choice (B) exhibits the same problem. Choices (C), (D), and (E) all supply the required past tense, but choice (D) changes the meaning of the original sentence, and choice (E) is a run-on sentence.

COMPUTING YOUR SCORES

How did you do on the Diagnostic Test? To get a sense of where you did well and where you need to improve, figure out your raw scores for each section.

Multiple-Choice Writing Section	Total Number of Questions	Number of Questions Correct	Number of Questions Incorrect
4	35	_____	_____
9	15	_____	_____
	Total 50	_____	_____

Critical Reading Section

2	26	_____	_____
6	26	_____	_____
8	16	_____	_____
	Total 68	_____	_____

Math Section

3	20	_____	_____
5	20	_____	_____
7	15	_____	_____
	Total 55	_____	_____

Essay score (from 1 to 6):   _____

To score your essay, turn to the scoring rubric and self-evaluation table starting on page 187. Assess your essay on each point on the rubric. Write each score in the table, work out your raw score, and enter it above.

PINPOINTING RELATIVE STRENGTHS AND WEAKNESSES

You can pinpoint how to focus your review time by calculating the percentage of each type of question you answered correctly. For each question type, divide the number of correct questions by the total number of questions.

Writing Section	Number of Questions Correct	Total Number of Questions	Percent Correct (Number Correct ÷ Total)
Identifying sentence errors	_____	19	_____
Improving sentences	_____	25	_____
Improving paragraphs	_____	6	_____
Critical Reading Section			
Sentence completions	_____	17	_____
Reading comprehension	_____	51	_____
Math Section			
Multiple-choice	_____	45	_____
Grid-ins	_____	10	_____

Compare the percentages for each type of question within a test. If any individual percentage was considerably lower than the others, say identifying sentence errors relative to improving sentences and paragraphs, then you should concentrate your study of writing on becoming very familiar with this format and the kinds of errors that are tested in it. Do this by reading the appropriate strategy chapter and completing the exercises.

Math Topics

To get an in-depth look at your performance on the math topics on the Diagnostic Test, look back at the math sections' answer keys. You'll notice that each answer in the math sections has a letter code next to it. By using this code and the table below, you can pinpoint math topics that need improvement.

Math Topic	Number of Questions Correct	Total Number of Questions	Percent Correct (Number Correct ÷ Total)
Arithmetic (A)	_____	14	_____
Basic Algebra (AL)	_____	10	_____
Geometry (G)	_____	17	_____
Intermediate Algebra (IA)	_____	5	_____
Data, Statistics, Probability (O)	_____	9	_____

If you have any score that is considerably lower than the others, this indicates a topic that you need to spend some time reviewing.

CONVERSION SCALES

CRITICAL READING

Raw Score	Scaled Score	Raw Score	Scaled Score
68	800	30	480
65	760	25	440
60	710	20	410
55	670	15	370
50	620	10	340
45	590	5	290
40	550	0	230
35	520		

MATH

Raw Score	Scaled Score	Raw Score	Scaled Score
55	800	20	510
50	760	15	480
45	690	10	440
40	650	5	340
35	610	0	200
30	580		
25	550		

MULTIPLE-CHOICE WRITING

Raw Score	Scaled Score	Raw Score	Scaled Score
50	800	20	470
45	760	15	420
40	680	10	370
35	620	5	320
30	580	0	270
25	520		

SELF-EVALUATION CHARTS

Critical Reading:	Raw Score
Excellent	60–68
Good	50–59
Average	30–49
Fair	20–29
Poor	0–19

Math:	Raw Score
Excellent	50–55
Good	40–49
Average	20–39
Fair	10–19
Poor	0–9

MEASURING YOUR PROGRESS

As you read the chapters and work through the exercises, don't forget to compare your performance on those exercises with the verbal and mathematical percentages you calculated here. Down the road, you can also measure your progress very easily by comparing how you did on this test with how you do on other practice examinations.

Take note of whether you had difficulty finishing any particular part of the test. It might be that you are spending too long on certain questions and not allotting enough time for others. This should improve as you work through the strategy sections of this book and increase your familiarity with the test and question format.

PART III

SAT CRITICAL READING STRATEGIES

Sentence Completion Strategies

OVERVIEW

- A closer look at sentence completions
- Basic steps for solving sentence completions
- Strategies for tackling the most difficult sentence completions
- Summing it up

A CLOSER LOOK AT SENTENCE COMPLETIONS

Are you drawing a blank? Get used to it, because you'll see a lot of them in the sentence completion questions on the SAT. In this kind of question, you are given a sentence that has one or more blanks. A number of words or pairs of words are suggested to fill in the blank spaces. It's up to you to select the word or pair of words that will best complete the meaning of the sentence. In a typical sentence completion question, several of the choices could be inserted into the blank spaces. However, only one answer will make sense and carry out the full meaning of the sentence.

Sentence completion questions test two main attributes:

1 The strength of your vocabulary

2 Your general verbal ability, especially your ability to understand the logic of sentences

To improve your vocabulary, you should *read* as widely as you can between now and the time of the test, looking up words you do not recognize. Read newspapers, novels, short stories, magazine articles—you name it! To improve your general verbal ability, you should *practice* by using the exercises in this book. If you do both of these things, you will substantially improve your score on the SAT.

chapter 3

Sentence Completion Questions and Their Format

Every section of questions will be preceded by a set of directions and an example for your reference, like the following example:

Directions: Each of the following questions consists of an incomplete sentence followed by five words or pairs of words. Choose the word or pair of words that, when substituted for the blank space or spaces, best completes the meaning of the sentence. Circle the letter that appears before your answer.

Medieval kingdoms did not become constitutional republics overnight; on the contrary, the change was ____.

(A) unpopular

(B) unexpected

(C) advantageous

(D) sufficient

(E) gradual

The correct answer is (E).

NOTE

Don't forget that you're being tested on your ability to find the *best* answer. Though more than one answer may seem to work, only one is correct; be sure to make your choice very carefully.

BASIC STEPS FOR SOLVING SENTENCE COMPLETIONS

Are you ready to start filling in some of those blanks? The following six steps will help you answer sentence completion questions:

1 Read the sentence carefully.

2 Think of a word or words that will fit the blank(s) appropriately.

3 Look through the five answer choices for the word(s). If it's not there, move on to step 4.

4 Examine the sentence for clues to the missing word.

5 Eliminate any answer choices that are ruled out by the clues.

6 Try the ones that are left and pick whichever is best.

Now that you know how to approach these questions most effectively, try these sample SAT sentence completion questions:

Those who feel that environmental regulations are intrusions on industry and unnecessary think that the federal financing of research on alternative fuels is ____.

(A) courageous

(B) expensive

(C) wasteful

(D) useful

(E) unwarranted

Now, follow the six steps to find the correct answer:

1 Read the sentence.

2 Think of your own word to fill in the blank. You're looking for a word that completes the logic of the sentence. You might come up with something like "illegal" or "unlawful."

3 Look for either word among the answer choices. Neither is there, but "unwarranted" is. That's pretty close, so mark it and go to step 5.

4 If you couldn't guess the word, take your clue from the words *intrusions* and *unnecessary* in the sentence. They point toward some negative-sounding word.

5 The clues immediately eliminate choice (A), *courageous,* and choice (D), *useful,* which are both positive words.

6 Try the remaining choices in the sentence, and you'll see that *unwarranted* fits best, that is, it completes the sense of the sentence best. Choice (B), *expensive,* and choice (C), *wasteful,* don't have the strongly negative sense that *intrusions* has. **The correct answer is (E).**

Here's another question:

Unruly people may well become _____ if they are treated with _____ by those around them.

(A) angry .. kindness

(B) calm .. respect

(C) peaceful .. abuse

(D) interested .. medicine

(E) dangerous .. love

Now, here are your six steps for finding the right answer:

1 Read the sentence. This time there are two blanks, and the missing words need to have some logical connection.

2 Think of your own words to fill in the blanks. You might guess that the unruly people will become "well-behaved" if they are treated with "consideration."

3 Now look for your guesses in the answer choices. They're not there, but there are some possibilities.

4 Go back to the sentence and look for clues. "Become" signals that the unruly people will change their behavior. How that behavior changes will depend on how they are treated.

5 You can eliminate choices (A) and (E) because a negative behavior change (*angry* and *dangerous*) doesn't logically follow a positive treatment (*kindness* and *love*). Likewise, you can eliminate choice (C) because a *peaceful* behavior change is not likely to follow from *abuse*. Finally, you can eliminate choice (D) because *interested* and *medicine* have no logical connection.

6 The only remaining choice is (B), which fits the sentence and must be the correct answer.

ALERT!

Don't let sentence completions hold you up. Allow yourself about 45 to 50 seconds to answer each one.

STRATEGIES FOR TACKLING THE MOST DIFFICULT SENTENCE COMPLETIONS

The six-step method for solving sentence completion questions is a tried-and-true approach to solving these questions on the SAT. But, because you want to move through these questions as quickly as you can (while choosing the right answers, of course), you also need to arm yourself with some basic strategies for tackling even the most difficult sentence completion questions. The following strategies and their explanations offer some very simple—and effective—ways to quickly and accurately answer even the hardest sentence completion questions.

Thinking Up Your Own Answer Is the Way to Start

If you've thought up the best answer before you even look at the choices, you've started solving the problem in advance and have saved time. To test this theory, look at this typical SAT sentence completion question:

Robert was extremely _____ when he received a B on the exam, for he was almost certain he had gotten an A.

(A) elated

(B) dissatisfied

(C) fulfilled

(D) harmful

(E) victorious

In this example, it is obvious that Robert would be "dissatisfied" with the grade he received. You may have come up with a different word, such as "discouraged" or "frustrated," but you can quickly deduce that choice (B) is the correct answer by the relationship of the answer choice to the word you guessed. **The correct answer is (B).**

The Surrounding Words in the Sentence Offer Clues to the Missing Word

When it comes to sentence completion questions, the word that does *not* appear is the key to the meaning of the sentence. But by thinking about the words that *do* appear, we can see the connection between the two parts of the sentence. Most sentences contain not only a collection of words but also a number of *ideas* that are connected to one another in various ways. When you understand how these ideas are connected, you can say that you really understand the sentence. The following strategies show you how to use the ideas in a sentence to help you choose the correct answer.

Some Blanks Go with the Flow

The missing word may be one that supports another thought in the sentence, so you need to look for an answer that goes with the flow.

> The service at the restaurant was so slow that by the time the salad had arrived we were ____.
>
> **(A)** ravenous
> **(B)** excited
> **(C)** incredible
> **(D)** forlorn
> **(E)** victorious

Where is this sentence going? The restaurant service is very slow. That means you have to wait a long time for your food, and the longer you wait, the hungrier you'll get. So the word in the blank should be something that completes this train of thought. Choice (A), "ravenous," which means very hungry, is the best answer. It works because it goes with the flow. **The correct answer is (A).**

Here's another example:

> As a teenager, John was withdrawn, preferring the company of books to that of people; consequently, as a young adult John was socially ____.
>
> **(A)** successful
> **(B)** uninhibited
> **(C)** intoxicating
> **(D)** inept
> **(E)** tranquil

The word *consequently* signals that the second idea is an outcome of the first, so again, you are looking for a word that completes the train of thought. What might happen if you spent too much time with your nose stuck in a book (except for this one, of course)? Most likely you would be more comfortable with books than with people. Choice (D), "inept," meaning awkward, is a good description of someone who lacks social graces, making this the right answer. **The correct answer is (D).**

Here's yet another example:

> A decision that is made before all of the relevant data are collected can only be called ____.
>
> **(A)** calculated
> **(B)** insincere
> **(C)** laudable
> **(D)** unbiased
> **(E)** premature

The word *called* tells you that the blank is the word that the rest of the sentence describes. A decision that is made before all the facts are collected can only be described as "premature." **The correct answer is (E).**

Some Blanks Shift Gears

The missing word may be one that reverses a thought in the sentence, so you need to look for an answer that shifts gears. Try this technique in the following example:

> The advance of science has demonstrated that a fact that appears to contradict a certain theory may actually be _____ a more advanced formulation of that theory.
>
> (A) incompatible with
> (B) in opposition to
> (C) consistent with
> (D) eliminated by
> (E) foreclosed by

Look at the logical structure of the sentence. The sentence has set up a contrast between what appears to be and what is actually true. This indicates that the correct answer will shift gears and be the opposite of "contradict." The choice "consistent with" provides this meaning. The other choices do not. **The correct answer is (C).**

Here's another example:

> Although she knew that the artist's work was considered by some critics to be ____, the curator of the museum was eager to acquire several of the artist's paintings for the museum's collection.
>
> (A) insignificant
> (B) important
> (C) desirable
> (D) successful
> (E) retroactive

The very first word of the sentence, "although," signals that the sentence is setting up a contrast between the critics and the curator. The critics had one opinion, but the curator had a different one. Since the curator liked the artworks well enough to acquire them, you can anticipate that the critics disliked the artworks. So the blank requires a word with negative connotations, and choice (A), "insignificant," is the only one that works. **The correct answer is (A).**

Here's another example of this type of contrast in a sentence completion question:

> After witnessing several violent interactions between the animals, the anthropologist was forced to revise her earlier opinion that the monkeys were ____.
>
> (A) peaceable
> (B) quarrelsome
> (C) insensitive
> (D) prosperous
> (E) unfriendly

Where do you begin? The words "forced to revise" clearly signal a shift in the anthropologist's ideas. Her discovery that the monkeys were violent made her abandon an earlier contrasting opinion. Among the answer choices, the only contrast to "violent" is choice (A), "peaceable." **The correct answer is (A).**

The Right Answer Must Be Both Logical and Grammatically Correct

When answering sentence completion questions, you can always simply toss out any answer choices that do not make sense in the sentence or that would not be grammatically correct. Try this technique in the following example:

> An advocate of consumer rights, Ralph Nader has spent much of his professional career attempting to ____ the fraudulent claims of American business.
>
> **(A)** expose
> **(B)** immortalize
> **(C)** reprove
> **(D)** construe
> **(E)** import

What would you do with a fraudulent claim? Immortalize it? Import it? Not likely. These choices are not logical. The only logical answer is choice (A). You would expose a fraudulent claim. **The correct answer is (A).**

Two-Blank Questions Give You Two Ways to Get It Right

Most SAT sentence completions—about two thirds—have two blanks rather than one. This provides another way of working by elimination. Sometimes you can guess the meaning of one blank, but not the other. Good! Scan the answer choices, looking only for the word you've guessed. Eliminate the answers that *don't* include it (or a near-synonym). Cross them out with your pencil if you like (this saves time if you look back at the question later). Then guess from what remains.

Difficult Questions Generally Have Difficult Answers

Easier sentence completions typically have easier answers and harder sentence completions typically have harder answers. This does not mean that you should always guess the hardest words on the hardest questions. However, if you have absolutely no idea which of the remaining choices is correct, it is to your benefit to select the choice with the most difficult vocabulary.

NOTE

Why do difficult questions typically have difficult answers? Because the test-writers know what they're doing. They know that students prefer to pick answer choices that contain familiar vocabulary. After all, it's human nature to be afraid of words we don't know. So don't fall into their trap. Have courage and guess the hardest words when all else fails!

EXERCISES: SENTENCE COMPLETIONS

Exercise 1

35 Questions • 25 Minutes

Directions: Each of the following questions consists of an incomplete sentence followed by five words or pairs of words. Choose the word or pair of words that, when substituted for the blank space or spaces, best completes the meaning of the sentence. Circle the letter that appears before your answer.

In view of the extenuating circumstances and the defendant's youth, the judge recommended___.

(A) conviction

(B) a defense

(C) a mistrial

(D) leniency

(E) life imprisonment

The correct answer is (D).

1. The ___ workroom had not been used in years.
   (A) derelict
   (B) bustling
   (C) bereft
   (D) bereaved
   (E) stricken

2. Tempers ran hot among the old-timers, who ___ the young mayor and his ___ city council.
   (A) despised .. attractive
   (B) admired .. elite
   (C) resented .. reforming
   (D) forgave .. activist
   (E) feared .. apathetic

3. With the discovery of a(n)___alternative fuel source, oil prices dropped significantly.
   (A) potential
   (B) feasible
   (C) possible
   (D) variant
   (E) inexpensive

4. The product of a ___ religious home, he often found ___ in prayer.
   (A) zealously .. distraction
   (B) devoutly .. solace
   (C) vigorously .. comfort
   (D) fanatically .. misgivings
   (E) pious .. answers

5. Our ___ objections finally got us thrown out of the stadium.
   (A) hurled
   (B) modest
   (C) wary
   (D) vocal
   (E) pliant

6. We should have ___ trouble ahead when the road ___ into a gravel path.
   (A) interrogated .. shrank
   (B) anticipated .. dwindled
   (C) expected .. grew
   (D) enjoyed .. transformed
   (E) seen .. collapsed

7. The ___ of the house, fresh lobster, was all gone, so we ___ ourselves with crab.
   (A) suggestion .. resolved
   (B) embarrassment .. consoled
   (C) recommendation .. contented
   (D) specialty .. pelted
   (E) regret .. relieved

8. ___ mob began to form, full of angry men ___ incoherent threats.
    (A) An excited .. whispering
    (B) A listless .. shouting
    (C) An ugly .. gesturing
    (D) A lynch .. muttering
    (E) A huge .. waving

9. In the ___ downpour, the women managed to ___ us and disappear.
    (A) ensuing .. evade
    (B) incessant .. pervade
    (C) uncouth .. escape
    (D) torrential .. provoke
    (E) insipid .. avoid

10. As a staunch ___ of our right to leisure time, Ken had few ___.
    (A) proponent .. friends
    (B) advocate .. defenders
    (C) disciple .. rivals
    (D) defender .. equals
    (E) opponent .. duties

11. A single wall still stood in mute ___ to Nature's force.
    (A) evidence
    (B) tribute
    (C) remainder
    (D) memory
    (E) testimony

12. With the current wave of crime, tourists are ___ to make sure their passports are secure.
    (A) required
    (B) invited
    (C) permitted
    (D) forbidden
    (E) urged

13. Over the ___ of the sirens, you could still hear the hoarse ___ of his voice.
    (A) babble .. roar
    (B) drone .. power
    (C) gibbering .. cries
    (D) wail .. sound
    (E) groaning .. whisper

14. Working ___ under the pressure of time, Edmond didn't notice his ___ mistake.
    (A) leisurely .. stupid
    (B) frantically .. inevitable
    (C) rapidly .. careless
    (D) sporadically .. simple
    (E) continually .. redundant

15. Held up only by a ___ steel cable, the chairlift was ___ to carry only two people.
    (A) slender .. instructed
    (B) single .. intended
    (C) sturdy .. obliged
    (D) massive .. designed
    (E) narrow .. appointed

16. After completing her usual morning chores, Linda found herself ___ tired.
    (A) surprisingly
    (B) erratically
    (C) buoyantly
    (D) forcibly
    (E) unceasingly

17. With a ___ roar, the jet took off from New York on its ___ flight to Europe.
    (A) deafening .. subterranean
    (B) thunderous .. transoceanic
    (C) sickening .. transcontinental
    (D) frightening .. perennial
    (E) supersonic .. eventual

18. The cheerful, lively sound of dance music ___ almost everyone.
    (A) accosted
    (B) drained
    (C) flaunted
    (D) revived
    (E) expired

19. With a(n) ___ grin, Mark quickly ___ his way through the crowd toward us.
    (A) infectious .. demolished
    (B) sappy .. devoured
    (C) irrepressible .. maneuvered
    (D) surly .. crawled
    (E) hapless .. lost

20. Though a ___ of four campaigns, he had never seen action on the front lines.
    (A) veteran
    (B) victim
    (C) volunteer
    (D) reveler
    (E) recruit

21. The ___ of the early morning light ___ the room, making it larger and cozier at once.
    (A) brilliance .. shattered
    (B) softness .. transformed
    (C) harshness .. transfigured
    (D) warmth .. disfigured
    (E) glare .. annihilated

22. As a(n) ___ of the original team, Mickey had free ___ for all their games.
    (A) survivor .. advice
    (B) scholar .. passage
    (C) institution .. admission
    (D) organizer .. submission
    (E) member .. entrance

23. From his ___ manner, we could all tell that he was of ___ birth.
    (A) boorish .. noble
    (B) aristocratic .. humble
    (C) regal .. royal
    (D) refined .. common
    (E) courteous .. illegitimate

24. The presence of armed guards ___ us from doing anything disruptive.
    (A) defeated
    (B) excited
    (C) irritated
    (D) prevented
    (E) encouraged

25. A careful ___ of the house revealed no clues.
    (A) dissemination
    (B) incineration
    (C) autopsy
    (D) dereliction
    (E) examination

26. For his diligent work in astronomy, Professor Wilson was ___ at the banquet as ___ of the Year.
    (A) taunted .. Teacher
    (B) praised .. Lobotomist
    (C) lauded .. Scientist
    (D) honored .. Astrologer
    (E) welcomed .. Administrator

27. Because of his ___ sense of his own importance, Larry often tried to ___ our activities.
    (A) exaggerated .. monopolize
    (B) inflated .. autonomize
    (C) insecure .. violate
    (D) modest .. dominate
    (E) egotistic .. diffuse

28. After such a(n) ___ meal, we were all quick to ___ Arlene for her delicious cooking.
    (A) fearful .. congratulate
    (B) enormous .. console
    (C) delightful .. avoid
    (D) heavy .. thank
    (E) wonderful .. applaud

29. If you hear the ___ of a gun, don't worry; it's only my car backfiring.
    (A) burst
    (B) report
    (C) retort
    (D) flash
    (E) volume

30. He demanded ___ obedience from us, and was always telling us we must be ___ subjects.
    (A) total .. foolish
    (B) partial .. cringing
    (C) formal .. rigorous
    (D) complete .. compliant
    (E) marginal .. loyal

31. The ___ of the *Titanic* could have been avoided if more safety ___ had been taken.
    (A) tragedy .. precautions
    (B) embargo .. preservers
    (C) disaster .. reservations
    (D) crew .. measures
    (E) fiasco .. inspectors

32. We are ___ going to have to face the reality that the resources of Earth are ___.
   (A) finally .. worthless
   (B) gradually .. limitless
   (C) eventually .. finite
   (D) quickly .. unavailable
   (E) seldom .. vanished

33. A native wit, Angela never ___ for her words.
   (A) groaned
   (B) breathed
   (C) asked
   (D) groped
   (E) worried

34. With ___ a thought for his own safety, Gene ___ dashed back across the courtyard.
   (A) even .. quickly
   (B) scarcely .. nimbly
   (C) barely .. cautiously
   (D) seldom .. swiftly
   (E) hardly .. randomly

35. As she ___ retirement, Laura became more thoughtful and withdrawn.
   (A) circled
   (B) sighted
   (C) withdrew
   (D) neared
   (E) derived

Exercise 2

15 Questions • 10 Minutes

Directions: Each of the following questions consists of an incomplete sentence followed by five words or pairs of words. Choose the word or pair of words that, when substituted for the blank space or spaces, best completes the meaning of the sentence. Circle the letter that appears before your answer.

In view of the extenuating circumstances and the defendant's youth, the judge recommended ___.

(A) conviction

(B) a defense

(C) a mistrial

(D) leniency

(E) life imprisonment

The correct answer is (D).

1. Though many thought him a tedious old man, he had a ___ spirit that delighted his friends.
   (A) perverse
   (B) juvenile
   (C) meek
   (D) leaden
   (E) youthful

2. ___, the factories had not closed, and those who needed work most were given a chance to survive during the economic disaster.
   (A) Unintentionally
   (B) Mercifully
   (C) Blithely
   (D) Importunately
   (E) Tragically

3. There was a ___ all about the estate, and the ___ concerned the guards.
   (A) pall .. shroud
   (B) focus .. scrutiny
   (C) hush .. quiet
   (D) coolness .. temper
   (E) talent .. genius

4. The stubborn families feuded for generations, and ___ feelings are still fixed in their ___.
   (A) begrudging .. acceptance
   (B) bitter .. generosity
   (C) inimical .. antagonism
   (D) suspicious .. relief
   (E) chary .. helplessness

5. As the archaeologist expected, living conditions in the ancient culture were ___ worse than those of today.
   (A) awfully
   (B) surprisingly
   (C) significantly
   (D) begrudgingly
   (E) boldly

6. Our reunion was completely ___; who'd have guessed we would have booked the same flight?
   (A) illogical
   (B) fortuitous
   (C) expected
   (D) abandoned
   (E) usurped

7. There is one ___ thing about them: they have nothing in common and never will have.
   (A) immutable
   (B) atypical
   (C) indiscriminate
   (D) indigenous
   (E) alliterative

8. Always one for a long, pleasant talk, Nancy went on ___ for hours.
   (A) volubly
   (B) tiresomely
   (C) incessantly
   (D) relentlessly
   (E) articulately

9. He should be ___ to complain, since his salary is ___ with his productivity.
   - (A) right .. proportionate
   - (B) brought .. balanced
   - (C) foolish .. gratuitous
   - (D) loath .. commensurate
   - (E) entitled .. alleviated

10. Paul's ___ at work is a natural product of his ___ nature.
   - (A) wastefulness .. unpleasant
   - (B) thoughtfulness .. rarefied
   - (C) diligence .. sedulous
   - (D) candor .. familial
   - (E) stubbornness .. intrepid

11. Blustery winds knocked off hats and rattled windows, and the adventurous children were ___.
   - (A) frightened
   - (B) terrified
   - (C) improved
   - (D) anxious
   - (E) delighted

12. The ___ youngster thought old people should be polite to him!
   - (A) impertinent
   - (B) classless
   - (C) cultured
   - (D) submissive
   - (E) alternate

13. Wild beasts roamed the deserted country, which had not been ___ for hundreds of years.
   - (A) temperate
   - (B) active
   - (C) winnowed
   - (D) lived in
   - (E) civilized

14. At night, the inn turned into a theater, not one of actors and actresses, but one of the ___ of real people.
   - (A) sciences
   - (B) psychologies
   - (C) dramas
   - (D) jokes
   - (E) novels

15. "He who laughs last laughs ___."
   - (A) least
   - (B) fast
   - (C) best
   - (D) never
   - (E) softest

ANSWER KEY AND EXPLANATIONS

Exercise 1

1. A	8. D	15. B	22. E	29. B
2. C	9. A	16. A	23. C	30. D
3. E	10. D	17. B	24. D	31. A
4. B	11. E	18. D	25. E	32. C
5. D	12. E	19. C	26. C	33. D
6. B	13. D	20. A	27. A	34. B
7. C	14. C	21. B	28. E	35. D

1. **The correct answer is (A).** *Derelict* in this sense means "empty," or "abandoned." Only people are bereaved or bereft.

2. **The correct answer is (C).** This sentence implies discord between the old-timers and the young mayor. Old-timers are likely to *resent* those officials who are trying to change, or *reform,* things.

3. **The correct answer is (E).** There may be many possible alternative fuel sources, but unless they are *inexpensive,* they won't affect the price of oil.

4. **The correct answer is (B).** To say *a pious religious home* is redundant. Only choice (B) completes the thought and intent of the sentence.

5. **The correct answer is (D).** The objections mentioned must have been *vocal* to get them thrown out.

6. **The correct answer is (B).** Most people do not enjoy trouble, and you can't interrogate it, but you may logically conclude that they foresaw, or *anticipated,* trouble. A road doesn't grow into a path nor does it collapse into one.

7. **The correct answer is (C).** No restaurant would advertise an *embarrassment* of the house, but you may logically conclude that lobster was their *recommendation.*

8. **The correct answer is (D).** In this item, the final two words are the key. It is impossible to gesture or wave incoherent threats. An excited mob wouldn't whisper and a listless mob wouldn't shout.

9. **The correct answer is (A).** In this question, only choice (A) logically completes the thought of the sentence.

10. **The correct answer is (D).** This sentence assumes that most people support having leisure time, ruling out choices (A) and (B). A *staunch disciple* is bad usage. That an opponent of leisure would have few duties is illogical.

11. **The correct answer is (E).** "A single wall" implies that, formerly, there were other walls. That only one wall still stood is *testimony,* not a *tribute,* to Nature's power. *Evidence to* is poor diction.

12. **The correct answer is (E).** Checking your passport can only be a suggestion, not an order. As losing a passport can pose serious problems to a tourist, *urged* is a better choice than *invited.*

13. **The correct answer is (D).** Sirens may drone or wail, but they don't babble, gibber, or groan. *Hoarse sound* is a better choice than *hoarse power.*

14. **The correct answer is (C).** The pressure of time indicates a need to work quickly. Assuming that mistakes are not inevitable or redundant, choice (C) is the only logical answer.

15. **The correct answer is (B).** This sentence is concerned with the design of the lift. As it says "held up only by," you may assume that the cable is not large, which eliminates choices (C)

and (D). Of the three remaining options, only *intended,* choice (B), completes the sentence logically.

16. **The correct answer is (A).** Assuming that routine activity is not exhausting, it would be surprising to find yourself exhausted by it one day.

17. **The correct answer is (B).** A transoceanic flight is one that goes over an ocean, in this case, the Atlantic.

18. **The correct answer is (D).** This sentence assumes that cheerful, lively music has a positive effect on people.

19. **The correct answer is (C).** As there is no such thing as a *surly,* or sullen, grin, choice (C) is the only answer that supplies the appropriate words for Mark's expression as well as for the manner in which he made his way through the crowd.

20. **The correct answer is (A).** One may be a veteran without ever having seen action, but a *victim* has to have seen it.

21. **The correct answer is (B).** For the light to make the room cozier, it must be soft, not harsh. This implies that the light enhanced the room, rather than disfigured it.

22. **The correct answer is (E).** A person may be an institution, but not an institution of a team. It is more likely that a *member* of the original team rather than a scholar would have a free pass.

23. **The correct answer is (C).** This is the only answer in which the first and second words are consistent.

24. **The correct answer is (D).** Armed guards are intended to prevent any kind of disruption. Choice (D) is the only logical and grammatical option.

25. **The correct answer is (E).** The sentence implies that the house was being searched, and since you don't perform an autopsy on a house, choice (E) is the best answer.

26. **The correct answer is (C).** An astronomer would not be honored as an astrologer, much less as an administrator.

27. **The correct answer is (A).** Someone with a high opinion of his own importance tends to try to run others' activities. Choice (A) best reflects this attitude.

28. **The correct answer is (E).** One doesn't generally avoid or console someone else for a tasty meal. Thus, choice (E) is the only logical answer.

29. **The correct answer is (B).** The sound of an explosion, whether from a gun or a car, is called a *report.*

30. **The correct answer is (D).** You may assume that no one demands partial or marginal obedience. *Compliant* is the best adjective for *subjects.*

31. **The correct answer is (A).** The loss of the *Titanic* is best described as a tragedy or a disaster. *Precautions,* not *reservations,* is the second word that is required, making choice (A) the correct response.

32. **The correct answer is (C).** As the Earth's resources are not limitless, worthless, or unavailable, only choice (C) logically completes this sentence.

33. **The correct answer is (D).** A person may *grope* for words; to say that he or she worries for them is bad usage.

34. **The correct answer is (B).** If Gene dashed across the courtyard, he must have run swiftly or *nimbly.* He couldn't have taken time to think of himself.

35. **The correct answer is (D).** Retirement has no physical presence, so it can't be either circled or sighted. One approaches, or *nears,* retirement.

Exercise 2

1. E	4. C	7. A	10. C	13. E
2. B	5. C	8. A	11. E	14. C
3. C	6. B	9. D	12. A	15. C

1. **The correct answer is (E).** A meek spirit may comfort or console people, but it won't delight them. A juvenile spirit is immature and thus is also inappropriate. A *youthful* spirit, however, may be mature as well as vigorous.

2. **The correct answer is (B).** According to the sense of this sentence, it was *merciful,* not unintentional, blithe, importunate, or tragic, that the factories remained open.

3. **The correct answer is (C).** It follows that a *hush* or a quiet about an estate would concern the guards, not a pall, focus, coolness, or talent.

4. **The correct answer is (C).** This sentence describes enmity and a persistence of ill will. Choice (C) best completes the thought of this sentence.

5. **The correct answer is (C).** The archaeologist would expect conditions to be *significantly* worse, not surprisingly, awfully, begrudgingly, or boldly worse.

6. **The correct answer is (B).** The sentence implies that the reunion occurred by chance, so it was *fortuitous.*

7. **The correct answer is (A).** *Immutable* means "unchanging." The second part of the sentence concerns finality; therefore, the other choices are not appropriate.

8. **The correct answer is (A).** According to the sentence, Nancy is "one for a long, pleasant talk." *Voluble* means "garrulous," but does not necessarily imply unpleasantness, while tiresome, incessant, and relentless all imply offense. *Articulate* is simply speaking clearly.

9. **The correct answer is (D).** He should be *loath* (or reluctant) to complain if his salary is *commensurate* with (or equal to) his productivity.

10. **The correct answer is (C).** "Natural product" in this sentence means "logical extension or outgrowth of" and joins like characteristics. *Diligence* and *sedulousness* are synonyms.

11. **The correct answer is (E).** Adventurous children will be *delighted* by blustery winds and rattling windows.

12. **The correct answer is (A).** This sentence describes a rebellious attitude. *Impertinence* means "insolence."

13. **The correct answer is (E).** This sentence concerns a wilderness and an absence of people, or civilization. *Lived in* has a meaning similar to *civilized,* but it implies a home or a town and not a countryside.

14. **The correct answer is (C).** The concept of theater is satisfied by *dramas,* not sciences, psychologies, jokes, or novels.

15. **The correct answer is (C).** The last (i.e., "end-of-line") position in certain activities connotes a positive result or a favored position. Some examples are having the last word, being assigned the last (closing) spot in a show, being up last in baseball, or having a last (final) rebuttal in a debate. Laughing last, then, could not imply laughing *least, fast, never,* or *softest,* because these are not positive terms. The person who laughs last laughs *best,* because being last by definition precludes any possibility of someone else laughing back.

SUMMING IT UP

- The sentence completion questions are arranged in order from easiest to most difficult.

- Sentence completion questions test your vocabulary and your reading comprehension skills by presenting sentences with one or two blanks and asking you to choose the best words to fill the blanks.

- In general, you follow these six steps to answer sentence completion questions:

  1 Read the sentence carefully.

  2 Think of a word or words that will fit the blank(s) appropriately.

  3 Look through the five answer choices for that word(s). If it's not there, move on to step 4.

  4 Examine the sentence for clues to the missing word.

  5 Eliminate any answer choices that are ruled out by the clues.

  6 Try the ones that are left and pick whichever is best.

- Eliminate choices that are illogical or grammatically incorrect, and use both words within a two-word choice to test for the best response.

- Try to spend no more than 45 to 50 seconds on any one sentence completion question.

Reading Strategies

OVERVIEW

- **A closer look at critical reading**
- **Basic steps for answering critical reading questions**
- **The most important critical reading tips**
- **Strategies for answering specific question types**
- **Summing it up**

A CLOSER LOOK AT CRITICAL READING

The reading comprehension questions in the critical reading section are based on reading passages. Each one begins with a short introduction that gives you some idea of where the passage came from and, often, when it was written. Each passage contains all the information you need to answer the questions about it. Some of the readings are single paragraphs and some are longer passages of several paragraphs. A typical SAT may include the following passage lengths and number of questions:

- Short passage of a single paragraph of about 100 words followed by 2 questions
- Paired *short* passages of about 100 words each followed by 4 questions relating to the individual readings and to the relationship between the readings
- Long passages of 400 to 850 words followed by 5 to 13 questions
- Paired *long* passages of 400 to 850 words each followed by 5 to 13 questions relating to the individual passages and to the relationship between the passages

The topics of the readings are drawn from fiction, the humanities, social studies, and science. However, you don't need to know anything about the subject matter to be able to answer the questions correctly. The answer to every question is either directly stated or implied in the reading passage. The purpose of the reading comprehension questions is to assess how well you read and understand information. The questions don't test what you have learned in your course work.

chapter 4

NOTE

Note that the critical reading questions are not arranged in order of difficulty. The questions for each passage are arranged in the order in which the information is presented in the passage. In other words, the first questions deal with the early parts of the passage, and later questions deal with the later parts of the passage.

Question Format

On the SAT, each critical reading passage and question set starts with directions that look like this:

> **Directions:** Each passage below is followed by a set of questions. Read each passage and then answer the accompanying questions, basing your answers on what is stated or implied in the passage and in any introductory material provided. Mark the letter of your choice on your answer sheet.

or

> **Directions:** The two passages given below deal with a related topic. Following the passages are questions about the content of each passage or about the relationship between the two passages. Answer the questions based upon what is stated or implied in the passages and in any introductory material provided. Mark the letter of your choice on your answer sheet.

The questions that follow each passage are in the standard multiple-choice format with five answer choices each. Most often, these questions ask you to do one of the following:
- Identify the main idea or the author's purpose.
- Define a word based on its meaning in the passage.
- Choose a phrase that best restates an idea in the passage.
- Draw inferences from ideas in the passage.
- Identify the author's tone or mood.

BASIC STEPS FOR ANSWERING CRITICAL READING QUESTIONS

To answer critical reading questions, follow these four steps:
1. Read the introduction, if one is provided.
2. Read the passage.
3. Read the questions and their answer choices. Go back into the passage to find answers.
4. For any question you're not sure of, eliminate obviously wrong answers and take your best guess.

Let's look at the four steps in more detail.
1. You don't want to blow past the introductory paragraph because it can be very helpful to you. It might provide some important background information about the passage or it might set the stage so you know what you're reading about.
2. Now read the passage pretty quickly. Try to pick up main ideas, but don't get bogged down in the factual trivia. After all, you won't even be asked about most of the material in the passage!
3. Read the questions with their answer choices, and answer every question you can. Remember, all the answers are somewhere in the passage, so go back and reread any sections that will help you!
4. Here's the process of elimination again. If you're still not sure of an answer, toss the ones that are obviously wrong and take your best guess from the choices that are left.

Now that you're familiar with how to approach critical reading passages and questions, let's try a few.

Sample Long Reading Passage

The following is an excerpt from a short story, "Miss Tempy's Watchers," by Sarah Orne Jewett, a novelist and short-story writer who lived from 1849–1909. In the story, two women watch over their deceased friend on the evening before her funeral and share their memories of her.

The time of year was April; the place was a small farming town in New Hampshire, remote from any railroad. One by one the lights had been blown out in the scattered houses near Miss Tempy Dent's, but as her neighbors took a last look out of doors, their eyes turned with instinctive curiosity toward the old house where a lamp burned steadily. They gave a little sigh. "Poor Miss Tempy!" said more

5 than one bereft acquaintance; for the good woman lay dead in her north chamber, and the lamp was a watcher's light. The funeral was set for the next day at one o'clock.

The watchers were two of her oldest friends. Mrs. Crowe and Sarah Ann Binson. They were sitting in the kitchen because it seemed less awesome than the unused best room, and they beguiled the long hours by steady conversation. One would think that neither topics nor opinions would hold out, at that

10 rate, all through the long spring night, but there was a certain degree of excitement just then, and the two women had risen to an unusual level of expressiveness and confidence. Each had already told the other more than one fact that she had determined to keep secret; they were again and again tempted into statements that either would have found impossible by daylight. Mrs. Crowe was knitting a blue yarn stocking for her husband; the foot was already so long that it seemed as if she must have forgotten

15 to narrow it at the proper time. Mrs. Crowe knew exactly what she was about, however; she was of a much cooler disposition than Sister Binson, who made futile attempts at some sewing, only to drop her work into her lap whenever the talk was most engaging.

Their faces were interesting—of the dry, shrewd, quick-witted New England type, and thin hair twisted neatly back out of the way. Mrs. Crowe could look vague and benignant, and Miss Binson was, to

20 quote her neighbors, a little too sharp-set, but the world knew that she had need to be, with the load she must carry supporting an inefficient widowed sister and six unpromising and unwilling nieces and nephews. The eldest boy was at last placed with a good man to learn the mason's trade. Sarah Ann Binson, for all her sharp, anxious aspect never defended herself, when her sister whined and fretted. She was told every week of her life that the poor children would never have had to lift a finger if their

25 father had lived, and yet she had kept her steadfast way with the little farm, and patiently taught the young people many useful things for which, as everybody said, they would live to thank her. However pleasureless her life appeared to outward view, it was brimful of pleasure to herself.

Mrs. Crowe, on the contrary, was well-to-do, her husband being a rich farmer and an easy-going man. She was a stingy woman, but for all of that she looked kindly; and when she gave away anything, or

30 lifted a finger to help anybody, it was thought a great piece of beneficence, and a compliment, indeed, which the recipient accepted with twice as much gratitude as double the gift that came from a poorer and more generous acquaintance. Everybody liked to be on good terms with Mrs. Crowe. Socially, she stood much higher than Sarah Ann Binson.

NOTE

Just to give you an idea of the breadth of the subject areas covered within the critical reading portion of the SAT, here are some of the topics that have been the subject of reading passages on previous exams: Chinese American women writers, the classification of species, pioneer life on the Great Plains, the relationship between plants and their environment, the meaning of *Robinson Crusoe,* and the philosophy of science.

TIP

Never skip the introduction as it is likely to contain some important information about both the passage and the types of questions that accompany it. The introduction will identify the type of passage being presented, the source or author of the passage, the era in which the passage was written, or the event that the passage describes. All of this information will help you focus your reading and find the correct answers to the questions.

The word *bereft* (line 5) means

(A) without hope.

(B) greedy.

(C) anxious.

(D) sad.

(E) lonesome.

The introduction and the rest of the sentence talk about the death of a well-liked person. Sadness would probably be the first thing you'd feel after someone died. **The correct answer is (D).**

The author implies that the two women have divulged secrets to each other because

(A) they are lonely.

(B) it is nighttime.

(C) it is a sad occasion.

(D) they trust each other.

(E) it is the only time they talk to each other.

We already know that folks are sad, but the author doesn't say anything about the women being trusting or lonely, or only talking because of the situation. The author does make a specific reference to the time of day. Reread those sentences (lines 7–13) and you'll see why the best answer is choice (B). **The correct answer is (B).**

If Mrs. Crowe were confronted with an emergency, you would expect her to

(A) remain calm.

(B) ask Miss Binson for help.

(C) become distracted.

(D) panic.

(E) run away.

The passage has clues to Mrs. Crowe's character, talking about her knowing "exactly what she was about" (line 15) and her "cooler disposition" (line 16). Choice (A) is clearly the best answer. **The correct answer is (A).**

The phrase "a little too sharp-set" (line 20) means

(A) thin.

(B) stern and anxious-looking.

(C) strong-featured.

(D) angular.

(E) well-defined.

The description of Miss Binson's everyday life with her nieces and nephews illustrates that she runs a tight ship and keeps them all in line. So, choice (B) is the best answer. **The correct answer is (B).**

Sarah Ann Binson seems to be a woman who is

(A) terribly unhappy.

(B) jealous of Mrs. Crowe.

(C) disloyal.

(D) quite wealthy.

(E) self-contented.

To all outward appearances, Miss Binson seemed to have an especially hard life. However, the author ends that sentence saying that "it was brimful of pleasure to herself." Since Miss Binson was pretty happy with her life, choice (E) is the best answer. **The correct answer is (E).**

Sample Short Reading Passage

World War II was the result of both long-term and short-term events. In the short-term, Hitler's craving for territory caused Great Britain and France to declare war on Germany when Hitler invaded Poland in 1939. The long-term causes go back to the Treaty of Versailles and 1919. Although Woodrow Wilson had worked tirelessly at the Paris Peace Conference for a just peace, he was not able to convince the
5 Allies that punishing Germany would create new problems. Instead, the Allies forced Germany to admit sole responsibility for World War I. They also insisted on the payment of millions of dollars in reparations by Germany.

The word *craving* (line 1) means

(A) inspiration.

(B) appetite.

(C) excitement.

(D) natural attraction.

(E) agitation.

Craving means a strong desire or appetite, choice (B). Try substituting the other answers in the sentence, and they don't make sense. For example, Hitler didn't agitate for territory; according to the passage, he took it. There is no such thing as a natural attraction for territory. **The correct answer is (B).**

According to the author, a "just peace" (line 4)

(A) would have lessened the possibility of future war.

(B) would have been impossible to attain at the conference.

(C) would not have held Germany liable for any guilt.

(D) would not have forced Germany to give back Poland.

(E) was Wilson's ultimate hope for the conference.

This question is a good example of why you should read all the answers before making your choice. You might have chosen choice (A) because it seems like what the passage is saying and skipped reading the other answers, only to be marked wrong. The passage doesn't say that Wilson hoped to avoid future wars; it just says that punishment would create problems. Choice (E) is the author's view of what Wilson's hope for the conference was, and thus the answer to the question. **The correct answer is (E).**

Sample Paired Long Reading Passages

Among the great loves in history are those of the composer Robert Schumann for his wife, Clara, and of Napoleon Bonaparte for his wife, Josephine. Their love is public knowledge due to the hundreds of love letters they left behind. The excerpts that follow are from letters. The first one is from Schumann to his then-fiancee, and the second is from Napoleon on the battlefield to his wife at home.

Passage 1—Robert Schumann to Clara Wieck (1838)

I have a hundred things to write to you, great and small, if only I could do it neatly, but my writing grows more and more indistinct, a sign, I fear, of heart weakness. There are terrible hours when your image forsakes me, when I wonder anxiously whether I have ordered my life as wisely as I might, whether I had any right to bind you to me, my angel, or can really make you as happy as I should wish.

5 These doubts all arise, I am inclined to think, from your father's attitude towards me. It is so easy to accept other people's estimate of oneself. Your father's behaviour makes me ask myself if I am really so bad—of such humble standing—as to invite such treatment from anyone. Accustomed to easy victory over difficulties, to the smiles of fortune, and to affection, I have been spoiled by having things made too easy for me, and now I have to face refusal, insult, and calumny. I have read of many such things

10 in novels, but I thought too highly of myself to imagine I could ever be the hero of a family tragedy of the Kotzebue sort myself. If I had ever done your father an injury, he might well hate me; but I cannot see why he should despise me and, as you say, hate me without any reason. But my turn will come, and I will then show him how I love you and himself; for I will tell you, as a secret, that I really love and respect your father for his many great and fine qualities, as no one but yourself can do. I have a

15 natural inborn devotion and reverence for him, as for all strong characters, and it makes his antipathy for me doubly painful. Well, he may some time declare peace, and say to us, "Take each other, then."

You cannot think how your letter has raised and strengthened me . . . You are splendid, and I have much more reason to be proud of you than of me. I have made up my mind, though, to read all your wishes in your face. Then you will think, even though you don't say it, that your Robert is a really good sort,

20 that he is entirely yours, and loves you more than words can say. You shall indeed have cause to think so in the happy future. I still see you as you looked in your little cap that last evening. I still hear you call me *du*. Clara, I heard nothing of what you said but that *du*. Don't you remember?

Passage 2—Napoleon Bonaparte to Josephine Bonaparte (1796)

I have not spent a day without loving you; I have not spent a night without embracing you; I have not so much as drunk a single cup of tea without cursing the pride and ambition which force me to remain separated from the moving spirit of my life. In the midst of my duties, whether I am at the head of my army or inspecting the camps, my beloved Josephine stands alone in my heart, occupies my mind, fills

5 my thoughts. If I am moving away from you with the speed of the Rhône torrent, it is only that I may see you again more quickly. If I rise to work in the middle of the night, it is because this may hasten by a matter of days the arrival of my sweet love. Yet in your letter of the 23rd and 26th Ventôse, you call me *vous*. *Vous* yourself! Ah! wretch, how could you have written this letter? How cold it is! And then there are those four days between the 23rd and the 26th; what were you doing that you failed

10 to write to your husband? . . . Ah, my love, that *vous*, those four days make me long for my former indifference. Woe to the person responsible! May he, as punishment and penalty, experience what my convictions and the evidence (which is in your friend's favour) would make me experience! Hell has no torments great enough! *Vous! Vous!* Ah! How will things stand in two weeks? . . . My spirit is heavy; my heart is fettered and I am terrified by my fantasies . . . You love me less; but you will get

15 over the loss. One day you will love me no longer; at least tell me; then I shall know how I have come to deserve this misfortune. . . .

In Passage 1, the word *calumny* (line 9) means

(A) remorse.

(B) chance.

(C) victory.

(D) kindness.

(E) slander.

Here's a prime example of context to the rescue. Take a look at the sentence and then test each choice in place of *calumny*. Basically, Schumann is talking about the hard time he is having with Clara's father, so you would not choose a positive word; eliminate choices (C) and (D). Out goes choice (B) because it makes no sense in the sentence. Choice (A) technically makes sense, but it is not a roadblock to success like insults and refusals are. Therefore, the remaining answer is the best one—choice (E). **The correct answer is (E).**

To what does Napoleon refer in Passage 2 when he writes of "the moving spirit of my life" (line 3)?

(A) France

(B) ambition

(C) the army

(D) his wife

(E) the Rhone River

Now you have to do some interpretation using the information in the passage. To do this you must know the author's intent. After you find the phrase, read the sentences around it. They all deal with Napoleon's love for Josephine. Since he curses his pride and ambition, choice (B) is out. He is with his army in France, so you can toss out choices (A) and (C). Choice (E) doesn't make sense, so the only choice is (D), his beloved wife. **The correct answer is (D).**

How do the authors feel about being separated from their lovers?

(A) Separation raises doubts and fears.

(B) Separation is due to parental disapproval.

(C) Separations never last long.

(D) Separations improve a relationship.

(E) Separations between lovers are inevitable.

This is where the comparison comes into play. The question asks about both authors, so you have to think about both passages and find the similarities. Let's start eliminating choices. The first to go are (D) and (E), since neither author mentions these at all. Choice (C) goes out because the authors don't tell us anything about the length of their separations. We know that while Robert Schumann has a big problem with Clara's dad, Napoleon doesn't seem to have a parental problem; choice (B) is gone. Why is choice (A) the best answer? Take a look back at both passages. Schumann mentions his doubts, and Napoleon tells Josephine that he is "terrified." Choice (A) is the only answer that fits both authors' thoughts. **The correct answer is (A).**

ALERT!

Don't choose answers that only work for one of a pair of passages. When you're working with paired passages, some questions ask you to identify a common idea. When that happens, you can immediately reject any answer choice that only applies to one of the passages.

Why do the writers refer to the words *du* and *vous*?

(A) To remind their readers of their rank

(B) To refer to their lovers' intimacy or formality

(C) To ask their lovers to be faithful

(D) To demonstrate their knowledge of languages

(E) To address their unborn children

NOTE

The short paired passages have the same types of questions as the long passages. The only difference is that you have less to reread to find your answers.

This is the kind of question that can send you into a panic. Calm down—you don't really have to know what the two words mean, you just have to figure out why the authors put them in. Reread the sentences in which the authors mention these special words. Are both authors happy about hearing the words? Are they both upset? Do they feel differently about hearing their sweethearts use these words? Aha! That's the key; Schumann is pleased that Clara used the word *du* (which is an informal word in German), but Napoleon is insulted and worried because Josephine used *vous* (a formal French word). Only choice (B) indicates that the authors might feel differently; the other choices aren't supported at all by a rereading of the information. **The correct answer is (B).**

THE MOST IMPORTANT CRITICAL READING TIPS

Critical reading questions can eat up a lot of your time. But you can use some specific strategies and techniques to move through this portion of the SAT efficiently. Check out these tips for smarter solutions to solving critical reading questions quickly and accurately.

Do the Critical Reading Questions Last

In addition to the critical reading questions, the verbal section of the SAT also contains sentence completions. Because the critical reading questions require the most time to complete, you should save these questions for last. You've already learned time-saving tips for the sentence completions, so do those questions first. That way, you'll save extra time for critical reading.

Answer All of the Questions Before You Move on to the Next Passage

There won't be time to go back to these passages at the end of this section, so you'll want to answer every question that you can about the passage before moving on. If you skip a question and try to come back to it later, you might have to reread the whole passage to find the answer—and you'll be out of time. Guess if you have to, but finish all the questions that you can before you move on to the next passage.

Remember That the Questions Follow the Order of the Passage

The questions are like a map to the passage. The order of the questions follows the order of the information in the passage. For a long passage, the first questions refer to the early part of the passage, and later questions refer to later parts of the passage. If there are two long passages, the first questions are for Passage 1, the next for Passage 2, and the last questions refer to both.

This arrangement is true for short passages as well. In a single short passage, the questions will follow the order of the information in the passage. For paired short passages there will be four questions. Each passage may have one or two questions, and the final one or two questions will ask about the relationship between the two short passages. Regardless of how the four questions are apportioned between the two passages, any questions about an individual passage will ask for information in the order in which it was discussed.

Do Double Passages One Passage at a Time

Since the questions are arranged like a map, take advantage! Read Passage 1 and answer the questions that relate to Passage 1. Then read Passage 2 and answer the questions that relate to Passage 2. Finally, answer the comparative questions. In this way, you won't have to read too much at once and you won't confuse the message of Passage 1 with that of Passage 2.

Don't Panic When You Read an Unfamiliar Passage

The passages are supposed to be unfamiliar. In their attempt to be fair, the test-makers purposely choose passages that are from the darkest recesses of the library. This helps make sure that no test-taker has ever seen them before. Remember, you're not being tested on your knowledge of the topic, but on how well you:

- Figure out the meaning of an unfamiliar word from its context
- Determine what an author means by noting certain words and phrases
- Understand the author's assumptions, point of view, and main idea
- Analyze the logical structure of a piece of writing

Remember That Everything You Need to Know Is Right There in Front of You

The introductory paragraph and the passage have all the information you'll need to answer the questions. Even if the passage is about the price of beans in Bulgaria or the genetic makeup of a wombat, don't worry. It's all right there on the page.

Start with the Short Passages and with the Passages That Interest You

A point is a point. It doesn't matter if the point comes from answering correctly a question about the longest passage or the shortest. Check the short passages and the paired short passages first. If the topics seem familiar, or at least not mind-numbing, start with them.

Then try the long passages. If you can find some long passages that interest you, whether they're fiction, science, or whatever, start with those and work your way down to the ones that you think will be hardest for you. If the style and subject matter appeal to you, you will probably go through a passage more quickly and find the questions easier to deal with.

Highlight Important Information as You Read the Passages

It pays to be an active reader. When you read, actively use your pencil to underline important names, dates, and facts. Bracket the main idea. Circle the supporting details. The questions are likely to be about the most important information in a passage. If you've highlighted those pieces of information, you'll be able to find them easily when you need them to answer the questions.

Don't Get Bogged Down in the Details

Remember, you don't have to understand every bit of information. You just have to find the information you need to answer the questions. Don't waste your time trying to analyze technical details or information not related to a question.

Don't Confuse a "True" Answer with a "Correct" Answer

The fact that an answer choice is true doesn't mean it's right. What does that mean? It means that a certain answer choice may be perfectly true—in fact, all of the answer choices may be true. But the *right* answer must be the correct answer to the question that's being asked. Only one of the answer choices will be correct and, therefore, the right choice. Read carefully—and don't be fooled!

STRATEGIES FOR ANSWERING SPECIFIC QUESTION TYPES

As you learned earlier, critical reading questions ask you to do one of five things:

1. Identify the main idea or the author's purpose.
2. Define a word based on its meaning in the passage.
3. Choose a phrase that best restates an idea in the passage.
4. Draw inferences from ideas in the passage.
5. Identify the author's tone or mood.

The next six tips present strategies for dealing with specific types of SAT critical reading questions. You should use these six tips in combination with the basic steps you just learned. They don't take the place of the basic steps but are extra tools to help you with certain types of questions. These tools work as well with short passages as with long ones.

1. Remember that the answer to a main idea question is neither too general nor too specific.
2. Check the introductory and concluding paragraphs for the main idea of the passage.
3. Plug in choices to solve vocabulary-in-context questions.
4. Find the right restatement by first restating an author's phrase in your own words.
5. Read between the lines to draw inferences from the passage.
6. Look for descriptive words to clue you in to the tone or mood of the passage.

To help you see how the six tips work, read the following introductory paragraph and the passage. Then read each tip and try to use it to help you answer each question before you read the answer explanation.

John Dewey, an American educator and philosopher of education, was a prolific writer on the subject. He was particularly interested in the place of education in a democratic republic.

The place of public education within a democratic society has been widely discussed and debated through the years. Perhaps no one has written more widely on the subject in the United States than John Dewey, sometimes called "the father of public education," whose theories of education have a large social component, that is, an emphasis on education as a social act and the classroom or learning
5   environment as a replica of society.

Dewey defined various aspects or characteristics of education. First, it was a necessity of life inasmuch as living beings needed to maintain themselves through a process of renewal. Therefore, just as humans needed sleep, food, water, and shelter for physiological renewal, they also needed education to renew their minds, assuring that their socialization kept pace with physiological growth.

10 A second aspect of education was its social component, which was to be accomplished by providing the young with an environment that would provide a nurturing atmosphere to encourage the growth of their as yet undeveloped social customs.

A third aspect of public education was the provision of direction to youngsters, who might otherwise be left in uncontrolled situations without the steadying and organizing influences of school. Direction
15 was not to be of an overt nature, but rather indirect through the selection of the school situations in which the youngster participated.

Finally, Dewey saw public education as a catalyst for growth. Since the young came to school capable of growth, it was the role of education to provide opportunities for that growth to occur. The successful school environment is one in which a desire for continued growth is created—a desire that extends
20 throughout one's life beyond the end of formal education. In Dewey's model, the role of education in a democratic society is not seen as a preparation for some later stage in life, such as adulthood. Rather, education is seen as a process of growth that never ends, with human beings continuously expanding their capacity for growth. Neither did Dewey's model see education as a means by which the past was recapitulated. Instead education was a continuous reconstruction of experiences, grounded very much
25 in the present environment.

Since Dewey's model places a heavy emphasis on the social component, the nature of the larger society that supports the educational system is of paramount importance. The ideal larger society, according to Dewey, is one in which the interests of a group are all shared by all of its members and in which interactions with other groups are free and full. According to Dewey, education in such a society should
30 provide members of the group a stake or interest in social relationships and the ability to negotiate change without compromising the order and stability of the society.

Thus, Dewey's basic concept of education in a democratic society is based on the notion that education contains a large social component designed to provide direction and assure children's development through their participation in the group to which they belong.

Remember That the Answer to a Main Idea Question Is Neither Too General Nor Too Specific

The main idea of this passage can best be stated as:

(A) The role of education is extremely complex.

(B) Dewey's notion of education contains a significant social component.

(C) Dewey's model of education is not relevant today.

(D) Direction provided in education must not be overt.

(E) Public education should be a catalyst for growth.

Choices (A) and (C) are very general; you'd be hard-pressed to find any supporting information in the passage for those main ideas. Choices (D) and (E) seem as if they were single sentences plucked right out of the passage; too specific! Choice (B)—the correct choice—gives an overall statement, and you could find supporting details for it as a main idea. **The correct answer is (B).**

Check the Introductory and Concluding Paragraphs for the Main Idea of the Passage

Look in the first or last (or both) paragraphs of the passage for answers to main idea/ author's purpose questions. Choice (B) above is stated in the last sentence of the first paragraph and restated in the last paragraph. Remember to mark stuff like this as you read. Though the main idea may occur elsewhere in the passage, most often you'll find it in the first or last paragraph. In a short passage, you may well find the main idea—if it is directly stated—as the first or last sentence of the paragraph.

Plug In Choices to Solve Vocabulary-in-Context Questions

For vocabulary-in-context questions, plug the choices into the original sentence and don't be fooled by the obvious synonym.

The word *nurturing* (line 11) means

(A) nourishing.

(B) educational.

(C) critical.

(D) supportive.

(E) motivational.

Take a look at the sentence in the passage—". . . nurturing atmosphere to encourage the growth. . ." —and then try each of the answer choices. You might be tempted to just pick *nourishing*, but choice (D) is the answer that makes sense and supports the idea of the sentence. **The correct answer is (D).**

Find the Right Restatement by First Restating an Author's Phrase in Your Own Words

The phrase "a continuous reconstruction of experiences" (line 24) used in reference to education means that education is

(A) based in life experiences.

(B) a never-ending process.

(C) a meaning-based endeavor.

(D) an individual pursuit.

(E) something unattainable.

Not to put words in your mouth, but if you had stated this phrase in your own words you might have used *ongoing* as a substitute for *continuous*. If you take it one more step, you come to choice (B), "a never-ending process." **The correct answer is (B).**

Read Between the Lines to Draw Inferences from the Passage

While not directly stated, the passage suggests that

(A) true education fosters the desire for lifelong learning.

(B) a truly educated person has an understanding of physics.

(C) Dewey was a radical philosopher.

(D) education must cease at some point.

(E) Dewey's model has been embraced by all.

When a critical reading question asks for something the author has suggested, implied, or not stated directly, you have to use the information in the passage and draw your own conclusions. Read between the lines to see if the author has given any hints that would lead you to the correct answer. In this question, the correct answer is choice (A) because the author's stated positions, taken together, logically lead to this statement. Choice (B) is a pretty far-fetched conclusion to make, and choices (C), (D), and (E) are not logical extensions of the information in the passage. **The correct answer is (A).**

Look for Descriptive Words to Clue You in to the Tone or Mood of the Passage

The tone of this passage can best be described as

(A) humorous.

(B) serious.

(C) dramatic.

(D) informal.

(E) frivolous.

This passage probably did not make you even chuckle, so choice (A) can be eliminated right off the bat. The topic is not frivolous, and the language was quite formal, so you can drop choices (D) and (E). There were no episodes or scenes that could be considered dramatic, choice (C). Take a minute to go back and scan the passage, look at the kind of language you find, and see how it sets the tone. **The correct answer is (B).**

EXERCISES: CRITICAL READING

Exercise 1

22 Questions • 25 Minutes

Directions: The passage below is followed by questions based on its content. Answer the questions on the basis of what is *stated* or *implied* in the passage and in any introductory material that may be provided.

QUESTIONS 1–10 ARE BASED ON THE FOLLOWING PASSAGE.

"The Goodman Who Saved Another from Drowning" is a French tale from the Middle Ages. In today's litigious times, the lesson it teaches remains relevant.

It happened one day that a fisherman putting out to sea in a boat was just about to cast a net, when right in front of him he saw a man on the point of drowning. Being a stout-hearted and at
5 the same time an agile man, he jumped up and, seizing a boathook, thrust it towards the man's face. It caught him right in the eye and pierced it. The fisherman hauled the man into the boat and made for the shore without casting any of
10 his nets. He had the man carried to his house and given the best possible attention and treatment, until he had got over his ordeal.

For a long time, that man thought about the loss of his eye, considering it a great misfortune. "That
15 wretched fellow put my eye out, but I didn't do him any harm. I'll go and lodge a complaint against him—why, I'll make things really hot for him!" Accordingly he went and complained to the magistrate, who fixed a day for the hearing.
20 They both waited till the day came round, and then went to the court. The one who had lost an eye spoke first, as was appropriate. "Gentlemen," he said, "I'm bringing a complaint against this worthy, who, only the other day, savagely struck
25 me with a boathook and knocked my eye out. Now I'm handicapped. Give me justice, that's all I ask. I've nothing more to say."

The other promptly spoke up and said, "Gentlemen, I cannot deny that I knocked his eye out,
30 but if what I did was wrong, I'd like to explain how it all happened. This man was in mortal danger in the sea, in fact he was on the point of drowning. I went to his aid. I won't deny I struck him with my boathook, but I did it for
35 his own good: I saved his life on that occasion.

I don't know what more I can say. For God's sake, give me justice!"

The court was quite at a loss when it came to deciding the rights of the case, but a fool who
40 was present at the time said to them, "Why this hesitation? Let the first speaker be thrown back into the sea on the spot where the other man hit him in the face, and if he can get out again, the defendant shall compensate him for the loss of
45 his eye. That I think, is a fair judgment." Then they all cried out as one man, "You're absolutely right! That's exactly what we'll do!" Judgment was then pronounced to that effect. When the man heard that he was to be thrown into the sea,
50 just where he had endured all that cold water before, he wouldn't have gone back there for all the world. He released the goodman from any liability, and his earlier attitude came in for much criticism.

55 In the light of this incident, you can take it from me that it's a waste of time to help a scoundrel. Release a guilty thief from the gallows, and he will never like you for it. A wicked man will never be grateful to anyone who does him a
60 good turn: He'll forget all about it; it will mean nothing to him. On the contrary, he would be only too glad to make trouble for his benefactor if he ever saw him at a disadvantage.

1. The word *cast* (line 2) is used to mean
   (A) tint.
   (B) perform.
   (C) hurl.
   (D) mold.
   (E) copy.

2. Paragraph 1 makes it clear that the fisherman is
   (A) essentially well-meaning.
   (B) clumsy and foolish.
   (C) fat but nimble.
   (D) hard-working and honest.
   (E) basically unlucky.

3. The word *fixed* (line 19) is used to mean
   (A) corrected.
   (B) secured.
   (C) set.
   (D) mended.
   (E) attached.

4. The word *worthy* (line 24) is used to mean
   (A) caliber.
   (B) significance.
   (C) morality.
   (D) gentleman.
   (E) prize.

5. Paragraph 3 concerns the
   (A) narrator's beliefs.
   (B) court's wishes.
   (C) one-eyed man's complaint.
   (D) fisherman's plea.
   (E) magistrate's judgment.

6. The fool's suggested solution to the case was
   (A) pitiless and spiteful.
   (B) absurd but lawful.
   (C) harsh but fair.
   (D) just and merciful.
   (E) sensible but unjust.

7. The phrase "as one man" (line 46) means
   (A) manfully.
   (B) as someone once said.
   (C) one by one.
   (D) together.
   (E) as he believed.

8. "In the light of this incident" (line 55) means
   (A) "thanks to that event."
   (B) "because of this tale."
   (C) "without further ado."
   (D) "as darkness falls."
   (E) "as you can see from this story."

9. The narrator clearly believes that the one-eyed man
   (A) showed good sense.
   (B) had bad luck.
   (C) deserved better.
   (D) was a scoundrel.
   (E) did the right thing.

10. The moral of this story might be
   (A) "Do unto others as you would have them do unto you."
   (B) "A wicked man is never satisfied."
   (C) "You can only be good so long."
   (D) "There is no such thing as justice."
   (E) "The one-eyed man is king."

QUESTIONS 11–20 ARE BASED ON THE FOLLOWING PASSAGE.

Because of its enormous size, the United States is a country of contrasts. Nowhere are the differences between the eastern and western United States so profound as in terms of climate and availability of water.

The eastern and western United States differ in many ways, but perhaps the most significant difference between the two regions is climate. The East receives enough rainfall to sustain
5 agriculture, while the West does not receive adequate rainfall to do so. Additionally, there are widely disparate climatic variations within smaller regions in the West than there are in the East. The mountains, the Sierra Nevadas and
10 the Cascades, that impede the Pacific Ocean's ability to cool in the summer and warm in the winter, as well as the fronts that bring moisture in the form of rain and snow, have much to do with the extremes of climate found in the West.
15 Elevations in the interior West also affect climate because even the mountainous flatlands have elevations higher than a mile.

Because of these extremes, particularly in the area of rainfall (there can be as much as 150
20 inches of precipitation annually on the western side of the Sierra-Cascade range as contrasted with as little as four inches annually on the eastern side), irrigation becomes critical if the area is to remain viable for human habitation.
25 Actually, it is so hot in some portions of the

western desert that even when rain clouds form, it does not rain because the earth's reflected heat dissipates the moisture before it can reach the ground. Any drops that actually
30 reach the ground quickly evaporate. While the arid Central Plains of the United States can use water for irrigation from the Ogallala Aquifer, a closed-basin aquifer discovered after World War I, the western regions are too far away to
35 benefit from this trapped run-off from several Ice Ages that is confined in gravel beds, stretching from South Dakota to west Texas. No wonder then that water is so precious to the people and farmlands of this area and that the population
40 of this area presses for national, state, and local funding for irrigation projects that will store and reroute water for them.

The Colorado River, with its various tributaries, including, for example, the Gunnison, the Green,
45 and the Gila, has long been the source of most irrigation projects in the desert areas of the West. Much of the water from the Colorado River goes into the state of California to irrigate the Imperial and San Joaquin Valleys. On its
50 route from high in the Rockies to the Gulf of California, the river is diverted in many areas to irrigate fields. Unfortunately, when it returns after having passed through deposits of mineral salts in the soil that was irrigated, the salinity
55 content of the water has increased dramatically. The amount of salt in the water can then have a detrimental effect on the crops if proper drainage systems are not built. Not only is a proper drainage system exorbitantly expensive,
60 but drainage systems also create a run-off, which must be handled in some efficient way. By the time the water is drained, this run-off would not only contain salt, but probably pesticides as well, and the question of what to do with the
65 run-off becomes an issue.

Despite the years of better than average rainfall in the late 70s and early to mid-80s that even caused the Great Salt Lake in Utah to flood, the situation in the western desert areas, particularly
70 California, remains critical. It is not uncommon for droughts in the state to last several years. Consequently, water, not only for crops, but for human consumption itself, is at stake. Thus, it becomes a serious mandate to solve the water
75 problem in this area if the area is to survive.

11. The word *disparate* (line 7) means
   (A) distinct.
   (B) different.
   (C) unusual.
   (D) analogous.
   (E) similar.

12. According to the passage, one of the mountain ranges that affects rainfall in the West is the
   (A) Rockies.
   (B) Appalachian.
   (C) Colorado.
   (D) Blue Ridge.
   (E) Sierra Nevadas.

13. According to the passage, another factor influencing climate in the West is
   (A) desert plants.
   (B) the Pacific Ocean.
   (C) elevation.
   (D) the Colorado River.
   (E) plateaus.

14. According to the passage, what has become critical on the eastern side of the Sierra-Cascade range?
   (A) Crop rotation
   (B) Truck farming
   (C) Crop dusting
   (D) Irrigation
   (E) Drainage

15. In some areas of the arid western desert, the formation of rain clouds doesn't assure rain because
   (A) the earth's reflected heat dissipates moisture.
   (B) mountains are too high.
   (C) desert winds blow clouds away.
   (D) plateaus are too dry.
   (E) riverbeds are too deep.

16. The arid Central Plains are able to irrigate with water from the
   (A) Ogallala Aquifer.
   (B) Colorado River.
   (C) Rio Grande River.
   (D) Dakota River.
   (E) Green River.

17. Which of the following is a tributary of the Colorado River?

(A) San Joaquin River

(B) Aspen River

(C) Gila River

(D) Cascade River

(E) Dakota River

18. Most of the water from the Colorado River goes into the state of

(A) Nevada.

(B) New Mexico.

(C) Arizona.

(D) California.

(E) Utah.

19. The word *salinity* (line 54) means

(A) mineral.

(B) pesticide.

(C) oxide.

(D) salt.

(E) vegetable.

20. Which of the following statements expresses an opinion the author of this passage might have?

(A) Irrigation projects are an unnecessary expense.

(B) The situation in the desert of the West is hopeless.

(C) If this area is to survive as a viable place of habitation, the water problem must be solved.

(D) The water supply from the Colorado River is completely adequate to take care of the irrigation needs of the area.

(E) Only the Imperial and San Joaquin Valleys should be irrigated.

QUESTIONS 21–22 ARE BASED ON THE FOLLOWING PASSAGE.

Some people proclaimed the death of the mainframe computer with the advent of desktop computers. The mainframe was the original work-horse of data entry and processing. However,
5 the mainframe has not gone away. It is still the predominant host for data in government and industry. In addition, the mainframe concept provided the model for the current system of using central servers to store, sort, and process
10 data. The data may be processing an online ticket purchase for a concert, a Medicare payment to a doctor, or an inventory check on the number of jeans in a manufacturer's warehouse. All these functions run through a central server—the
15 concept behind the mainframe.

21. The main idea of this passage is the

(A) continuing influence of mainframes.

(B) continuing importance of mainframe computing.

(C) importance of data to business.

(D) many uses of the mainframe.

(E) many uses of central servers.

22. The word *functions* (line 14) means

(A) duty.

(B) algorithm.

(C) business.

(D) capacity.

(E) activity.

Exercise 2

20 Questions • 22 Minutes

Directions: The passage below is followed by questions based on its content. Answer the questions on the basis of what is *stated* or *implied* in the passage and in any introductory material that may be provided.

QUESTIONS 1–10 ARE BASED ON THE FOLLOWING PASSAGE.

The Library of Congress in Washington, D.C., is noteworthy in many ways. In this passage, the history of the Library is traced, and the manner in which the Library evolved is considered.

The Library of Congress is the world's largest and most open library. With collections numbering more than 97 million items, it includes materials in 460 languages; the basic manuscript

5   collections of 23 Presidents of the United States; maps and atlases that have aided explorers and navigators in charting both the world and outer space; and the earliest motion pictures and examples of recorded sound, as well as the latest

10   databases and software packages. The Library's services extend not only to members and committees of Congress, but to the executive and judicial branches of government, to libraries throughout the nation and the world, and to

15   scholars, researchers, artists, and scientists who use its resources.

This was not always the case. When President John Adams signed the bill that provided for the removal of the seat of government to the

20   new capital city of Washington in 1800, he created a reference library for Congress only. The bill provided, among other items, $5,000 "for the purchase of such books as may be necessary for the use of Congress—and for

25   putting up a suitable apartment for containing them therein . . . ."

After this small congressional library was destroyed by fire along with the Capitol building in 1814, former President Thomas Jefferson

30   offered therein ". . . as a replacement his personal library, accumulated over a span of fifty years." It was considered to be one of the finest in the United States. Congress accepted Jefferson's offer. Thus the foundation was laid for a great

35   national library.

By the close of the Civil War, the collections of the Library of Congress had grown to 82,000 volumes and were still principally used by members of Congress and committees. In

40   1864, President Lincoln appointed as Librarian of Congress a man who was to transform the Library: Ainsworth Rand Spofford, who opened the Library to the public and greatly expanded its collections. Spofford successfully advocated

45   a change in the copyright law so that the Library would receive two free copies of every book, map, chart, dramatic or musical composition, engraving, cut, print, or photograph submitted for copyright. Predictably, Spofford soon filled

50   all the Capitol's library rooms, attics, and hallways. In 1873, he then won another lobbying effort, for a new building to permanently house the nation's growing collection and reading rooms to serve scholars and the reading public.

55   The result was the Thomas Jefferson Building, completed in 1897. Since then, two more buildings have been constructed to house the Library's ever-expanding collection.

The first Librarian in the new building was a

60   newspaperman with no previous library experience, John Russell Young. He quickly realized that the Library had to get control of the collections that had been overflowing the rooms in the Capitol. Young set up organizational units

65   and devised programs that changed the Library from essentially an acquisitions operation into an efficient processing factory that organized the materials and made them useful.

Young was succeeded after only two years by

70   Herbert Putnam, formerly head of the Boston Public Library, who served as Librarian of Congress for 40 years. While Librarian Spofford had collected the materials, and Young had organized them, Putnam set out to insure that

75   they would be used. He took the Library of Congress directly into the national library scene and made its holdings known and available to the smallest community library in the most distant part of the country.

80 About 1912, both Librarian Putnam and members of Congress became concerned about the distance that was widening between the Library and its employer, the Congress. Various states had begun to set up "legislative reference 85 bureaus," which brought together skilled teams of librarians, economists, and political scientists whose purpose was to respond quickly to questions that arose in the legislative process. Congress wanted the same kind of service for 90 itself, so Putnam designed such a unit for the Library of Congress. Called the Legislative Reference Service, it went into operation in 1914 to prepare indexes, digests, and compilations of law that the Congress might need, but it 95 quickly became a specialized reference unit for information transfer and research. This service was the forerunner of the Library's current Congressional Research Service.

1. By saying that the Library of Congress is the world's "most open library" (line 2), the author means that

(A) the Library has branches all over the world.

(B) anyone who wants to can use any of the resources of the Library.

(C) the Library maintains hours from very early in the morning to very late at night.

(D) the Library's services are available to a wide variety of institutions and individuals.

(E) the Thomas Jefferson Building contains several reading rooms for public use.

2. Which of the following kind of materials is NOT mentioned in the passage as being part of the collection of the Library of Congress?

(A) Computer software

(B) Every book published in English

(C) Musical recordings

(D) Congressional research

(E) Every photograph copyrighted in the United States

3. Thomas Jefferson's donation of his personal library to Congress can be seen as

(A) an attempt to outdo John Adams.

(B) an indication of Jefferson's disenchantment with the library.

(C) a well-meant but inadequate effort to replace what had been lost.

(D) the largest single contribution by an individual to the Library of Congress.

(E) the seed from which the present Library of Congress grew.

4. Which of the following made the collections of the Library of Congress available to the public?

(A) Thomas Jefferson

(B) Ainsworth Rand Spofford

(C) John Adams

(D) Herbert Putnam

(E) John Russell Young

5. Ainsworth Rand Spofford wanted to build a new building for the Library of Congress because

(A) his efforts to expand the collection were so successful that there was no longer room for it in the Capitol.

(B) he wanted to leave a lasting legacy of his tenure as Librarian of Congress.

(C) housing the collection in the Capitol made the Library inaccessible to the public.

(D) there were no reading rooms in the Capitol.

(E) there was an overwhelming request from the populace for such a building.

6. According to the passage, the Library of Congress now uses how many buildings?

(A) Three

(B) Two

(C) One

(D) Five

(E) Four

7. A comparison between Ainsworth Rand Spofford and John Russell Young, as they are described in the passage, shows that

(A) Young made a greater effort to expand the collection of the Library of Congress than Spofford did.

(B) Spofford had more library experience at the time of his appointment as Librarian of Congress than Young did.

(C) Spofford served as Librarian of Congress longer than Young did.

(D) Young was more concerned with housing the collection of the Library of Congress than Spofford was.

(E) Spofford was more interested in building a memorial to himself.

8. Herbert Putnam's contributions to the Library of Congress included which of the following?

  I. Giving other libraries access to the Library of Congress's resources

  II. Creating distinct organizational units within the Library

  III. Instigating the Legislative Reference Service

(A) II only
(B) III only
(C) I and II only
(D) II and III only
(E) I and III only

9. One difference between John Russell Young and Herbert Putnam is

(A) their level of personal wealth.
(B) the extent to which they focused on expanding the Library's collection.
(C) their ability to lobby Congress on the Library's behalf.
(D) their interest in making the Library's resources available to the public.
(E) the kind of experience they brought to the post of Librarian of Congress.

10. The purpose of the Legislative Reference Service was

(A) to encourage members of Congress to use the Library's collection more fully.
(B) to replace the states' legislative reference bureaus.
(C) more broadly defined than that of any other unit of the Library.
(D) similar to the purpose for which the Library was originally established.
(E) to assist lawyers in preparing trial briefs.

QUESTIONS 11–12 ARE BASED ON THE FOLLOWING PASSAGE.

The following is from an eleventh-century book on government written by Nizam al-Mulik, a Seljuk Turk.

It should be realized that when kings send ambassadors to one another, their purpose is not merely the message or the letter which they communicate, but secretly they have a hundred other points and objects in view. In fact they want to know about the state of roads, mountain passes, rivers and grazing grounds, to see whether an army can pass or not; where fodder is available and where not; what is the size of the king's army and how well it is armed and equipped; what is the standard of his table and company; what is the organization and etiquette of his court and audience hall . . .

11. The word *fodder* (line 8) means
(A) light.
(B) animal food.
(C) armaments.
(D) trees.
(E) tobacco.

12. The phrase "standard of his table and company" (line 11) refers to the king's
(A) flag.
(B) requirements.
(C) hospitality.
(D) performance.
(E) language.

Directions: The two passages below deal with a related topic. Following the passages are questions about the content of each passage or about the relationship between the two passages. Answer the questions based upon what is stated or implied in the passages and in any introductory material provided.

QUESTIONS 13–16 ARE BASED ON THE FOLLOWING PASSAGES.

Fanny Wright was a reformer, author, and orator, unusual occupations for a woman in the early nineteenth century. Young Robert Emmet was condemned to death for treason after organizing a rebellion against the English in Ireland. He, too, had achieved fame as an orator, with speeches decrying tyranny.

Passage 1—Fanny Wright to a Fourth-of-July Audience at New Harmony, Indiana (1828)

In continental Europe, of late years, the words patriotism and patriot have been used in a more enlarged sense than it is usual here to attribute to them, or than is attached to them in Great
5 Britain. Since the political struggles of France, Italy, Spain, and Greece, the word patriotism has been employed, throughout continental Europe, to express a love of the public good; a preference for the interests of the many to those
10 of the few; a desire for the emancipation of the human race from the thrall of despotism, religious and civil: in short, patriotism there is used rather to express the interest felt in the human race in general than that felt for any country,
15 or inhabitants of a country, in particular. And patriot, in like manner, is employed to signify a lover of human liberty and human improvement rather than a mere lover of the country in which he lives, or the tribe to which he belongs. Used
20 in this sense, patriotism is a virtue, and a patriot is a virtuous man. With such an interpretation, a patriot is a useful member of society capable of enlarging all minds and bettering all hearts with which he comes in contact; a useful member
25 of the human family, capable of establishing fundamental principles and of merging his own interests, those of his associates, and those of his nation in the interests of the human race. Laurels and statues are vain things, and mischievous as
30 they are childish; but could we imagine them of use, on such a patriot alone could they be with any reason bestowed. . . .

Passage 2—Robert Emmet to the Court That Condemned Him to Death (1803)

I am charged with being an emissary of France. An emissary of France! and for what end? It is alleged that I wish to sell the independence of my country; and for what
5 end? Was this the object of my ambition? . . . No; I am no emissary; and my ambition was to hold a place among the deliverers of my country, not in power nor in profit, but in the glory of the achievement. Sell my country's
10 independence to France! and for what? Was it a change of masters? No, but for ambition. Oh, my country! Was it personal ambition that could influence me? Had it been the soul of my actions, could I not, by my education and
15 fortune, by the rank and consideration of my family, have placed myself amongst the proudest of your oppressors? My country was my idol! To it I sacrificed every selfish, every endearing sentiment; and for it I now offer up myself, O
20 God! No, my lords; I acted as an Irishman, determined on delivering my country from the yoke of a foreign and unrelenting tyranny, and the more galling yoke of a domestic faction, which is its joint partner and perpetrator in the
25 patricide, from the ignominy existing with an exterior of splendor and a conscious depravity. It was the wish of my heart to extricate my country from this double riveted despotism—I wished to place her independence beyond the reach
30 of any power on earth. I wished to exalt her to that proud station in the world. Connection with France was, indeed, intended, but only as far as mutual interest would sanction or require. Were the French to assume any authority inconsistent
35 with the purest independence, it would be the signal for their destruction. . . .

Let no man dare, when I am dead, to charge me with dishonor; let no man attaint my memory by believing that I could have engaged in any
40 cause but that of my country's liberty and independence; or that I could have become the pliant minion of power in the oppression and misery of my country. The proclamation of the provisional government speaks for our views; no

inference can be tortured from it to countenance barbarity or debasement at home, or subjection, humiliation, or treachery from abroad. I would not have submitted to a foreign oppressor, for the
45 same reason that I would resist the foreign and domestic oppressor. In the dignity of freedom,
50 I would have fought upon the threshold of my country, and its enemy should enter only by passing over my lifeless corpse. And am I, who lived but for my country, and who have
55 subjected myself to the dangers of the jealous and watchful oppressor, and the bondage of the grave, only to give my countrymen their rights, and my country its independence—am I to be loaded with calumny, and not suffered to resent
60 it? No; God forbid!

13. In Passage 1, the word *thrall* (line 11) is used to mean
   (A) freedom.
   (B) bondage.
   (C) tremor.
   (D) excitement.
   (E) stimulation.

14. How could you restate Wright's last sentence?
   (A) Laurels and statues are silly, but if they had any meaning at all, a patriot like the one I describe might deserve them.
   (B) Tributes make men vain, but such a man could wear them wisely.
   (C) We decorate men in vain, but a useful man could be called a patriot.
   (D) A patriot such as the one I have mentioned will have no need for statues and laurels.
   (E) In vain do we search for appropriate laurels and statues with which to reward such a patriot.

15. Emmet's speech moves from
   (A) a plea for mercy to acceptance.
   (B) interpretation to description.
   (C) polite refusal to calm denial.
   (D) impassioned denial to angry challenge.
   (E) expressions of remorse to expressions of fear.

16. In what way does Emmet fail to fit Wright's definition of a patriot?
   (A) He prefers the despotism of France to that of England.
   (B) He wants to free his people.
   (C) He idolizes his own country over all.
   (D) He declares the court's sentence to be unjust.
   (E) He sees no dishonor in his actions.

exercises

Directions: The two passages below deal with a related topic. Following the passages are questions about the content of each passage or about the relationship between the two passages. Answer the questions based upon what is stated or implied in the passages and in any introductory material provided.

QUESTIONS 17–20 ARE BASED ON THE FOLLOWING PASSAGES.

Passage 1

According to some researchers, the main culprit in Alzheimer's disease is the formation of plaques in the brain. Plaque appears to be formed by the amyloid gene. Amyloid occurs naturally
5 in nerve cells in the brain. When mutant genes keep amyloid from functioning properly, it forms sticky clumps that kill neurons. The immune system then kicks into action by setting up an inflammatory reaction to the death of neurons.
10 Additional damage to the neurons results from this inflammatory response. Tangles, another identifying characteristic of Alzheimer's, are then caused by a chemical reaction to the activity within the brain. The whole is known as the
15 amyloid cascade hypothesis.

Passage 2

Some researchers have conducted studies that show that tangles in the brain are a major determinant in Alzheimer's disease. These researchers believe that a protein called tau is
5 responsible for the tangles that are one characteristic of Alzheimer's. Tau occurs normally in neurons and consists of microtubules that look like ropes. These become the tangled masses of Alzheimer's when abnormal formations
10 of tau occur. A specific gene is thought to be responsible for inhibiting the formation of tangles. When this gene is not present, the tau goes unchecked and tangles result. The gene that replaces the tau inhibitor gene is thought
15 to be responsible for the formation of plaque, the other physiological brain abnormality seen in those with Alzheimer's.

17. The purpose of Passage 1 is to
    (A) explain why neurons die.
    (B) set up the difference between tangles and plaques.
    (C) explain the place of the immune system in Alzheimer's disease.
    (D) explain the amyloid cascade hypothesis.
    (E) explain the cause of Alzheimer's disease.

18. In Passage 1, the word *culprit* (line 1) means
    (A) malefactor.
    (B) felon.
    (C) criminal.
    (D) villain.
    (E) trespasser.

19. If one "physiological brain abnormality" is plaque, the other discussed in Passage 2 is
    (A) neurons.
    (B) tau.
    (C) tangles.
    (D) a missing gene.
    (E) microtubules.

20. Based on the information in Passages 1 and 2, the cause of Alzheimer's is
    (A) proven by the amyloid cascade hypothesis.
    (B) plaques.
    (C) tangles.
    (D) tangles and plaques.
    (E) still under debate.

ANSWER KEY AND EXPLANATIONS
Exercise 1

1. C	6. C	11. B	16. A	21. A
2. A	7. D	12. E	17. C	22. E
3. C	8. E	13. C	18. D	
4. D	9. D	14. D	19. D	
5. D	10. B	15. A	20. C	

1. **The correct answer is (C).** It is used in relation to nets, so the only appropriate synonym for *cast* is *hurl,* choice (C).

2. **The correct answer is (A).** The fisherman may be choice (D), but that is never made clear. He is certainly not choice (B), and he is stout-hearted, not stout, choice (C). There is no support for choice (E). The only answer possible is choice (A), and, in fact, the narrator makes it clear that the fisherman has done everything possible to help the drowning man.

3. **The correct answer is (C).** *Fixed* has many meanings, and each choice is a possible synonym. However, in the context of "[fixing] a day for the hearing," only choice (C) makes sense.

4. **The correct answer is (D).** This archaic term means "man of worth," or gentleman. Testing the choices in context should lead you to this conclusion.

5. **The correct answer is (D).** All of paragraph 3 is given over to the fisherman's tale of what happened.

6. **The correct answer is (C).** The fool's suggestion to throw the one-eyed man back into the sea may have been harsh, but it offered a certain rough justice.

7. **The correct answer is (D).** Try the choices in context, and you will find that *together* is the only meaningful substitute.

8. **The correct answer is (E).** Choice (B) is incorrect—the narrator did not draw this conclusion because of the incident, but rather uses the incident to illustrate a moral.

9. **The correct answer is (D).** The *scoundrel* mentioned in line 62 is a reference to the man helped in the story—the one-eyed man.

10. **The correct answer is (B).** This is a reasonable paraphrase of the final paragraph. When you see the word *moral,* you know that you need to draw conclusions about the theme of what you have read. It may help to look back at the end of the story to see whether the author has done that for you, as in this case.

11. **The correct answer is (B).** The context of the sentence, particularly the use of the word *variations,* supports choice (B).

12. **The correct answer is (E).** The two mountain ranges mentioned in the passage are the Sierra Nevadas and the Cascades.

13. **The correct answer is (C).** While the Pacific Ocean, choice (B), is mentioned as a potential source of moisture for the area, *elevation* is the critical factor influencing climate.

14. **The correct answer is (D).** Because of the virtual absence of rainfall on the eastern side, *irrigation,* choice (D), is critical.

15. **The correct answer is (A).** The passage specifically states that moisture is dissipated by the earth's heat.

16. **The correct answer is (A).** The underground aquifer is the source of much of the water used for irrigation in the Central Plains.

17. **The correct answer is (C).** Only the *Gila* is a tributary of the Colorado River, according to the passage.

18. The correct answer is (D). The passage specifically states that most of the water for irrigation from the Colorado River is used by the state of *California.*

19. The correct answer is (D). The context of the sentence, which indicates that the water passes through deposits of mineral salts, supports the choice of (D), *salt.*

20. The correct answer is (C). If you have understood the main idea of the passage, you will know that the author believes that the water problem in the area must be solved if the area is to survive.

21. The correct answer is (A). Remember the strategy: The answer to the main idea question is neither too general nor too specific. Only choice (A) hits the right balance. It's not the general importance of mainframes but specifically their influence on how computing is done that this is the main idea of the paragraph.

22. The correct answer is (E). If you were caught up in the science of computing, you might have jumped at choice (B), but in the context of the sentence, the list of uses relate to *activities* that are performed by servers.

Exercise 2

1. D	5. A	9. E	13. B	17. D
2. B	6. A	10. D	14. C	18. D
3. E	7. C	11. B	15. D	19. C
4. B	8. E	12. C	16. C	20. E

1. The correct answer is (D). In the last sentence of the first paragraph, the author explains what is meant by an "open library" by describing who can use the Library of Congress's resources.

2. The correct answer is (B). Computer software is mentioned in line 10, musical recordings in line 9 combined with line 47, Congressional research in line 98, and copyrighted photographs in line 48. Every book *copyrighted in the United States* is put into the Library's collection, but many books published in English are not copyrighted in the United States.

3. The correct answer is (E). This answer uses a different metaphor to say what the author says in lines 34–35: "Thus the foundation was laid for a great national library."

4. The correct answer is (B). See lines 42–49.

5. The correct answer is (A). This answer can be inferred from lines 43–44, which says that Spofford "greatly expanded [the Library's] collections," and lines 49–51, which say that all the Capitol's space had been filled.

6. The correct answer is (A). The three buildings are the Thomas Jefferson Building (line 55) and "two more" constructed "since then" (lines 56–57).

7. The correct answer is (C). Young served as Librarian of Congress for two years (line 69). The length of Spofford's tenure is not mentioned, but he served at least from 1864 (line 40) to 1873 (line 51).

8. The correct answer is (E). Answer I is supported in lines 74–79 and answer III in the last paragraph. Creating distinct organizational units was the work of John Russell Young (lines 64–68).

9. The correct answer is (E). Young was a newspaperman (lines 59–61), and Putnam was a librarian (lines 70–72).

10. The correct answer is (D). According to the second paragraph, the Library's original purpose was to provide Congress with information necessary to its work. The purpose of the Legislative Reference Service, as described in lines 91–96, is also to provide Congress with reference information.

11. **The correct answer is (B).** If this is a familiar word, you had no trouble answering it. If not, substitute the choices into the sentence to find the one that makes the most sense.

12. **The correct answer is (C).** The phrase uses *standard* to mean "measure." The ambassador is interested in gauging the measure of the king's table (food) and company—the size of his hospitality and the quality of his companions.

13. **The correct answer is (B).** If this is a familiar word, you had no trouble answering it. If not, substitute the choices into the sentence to find the one that makes the most sense.

14. **The correct answer is (C).** This is the best way to restate Wright's last sentence.

15. **The correct answer is (D).** This kind of synthesis/analysis question asks you to look at the flow of a passage and analyze the author's intent in light of the structure of the work. Skim the passage and look for a point where the tone or intent of the passage changes. Usually this will happen between paragraphs, so the paragraphing of the passage is a definite clue. Paragraph 1 of Passage 2 begins with a statement of the charge against Emmet and his denial of that charge. The tone is impassioned rather than polite, choice (C). He never asks for mercy, choice (A), or expresses remorse, choice (E). Nor could this paragraph be termed "interpretation," choice (B). To test whether choice (D) is correct, go on to paragraph 2. Here, Emmet begins with the words "Let no man dare," angrily challenging those who might call him a dishonorable man. Choice (D) is the only possible answer.

16. **The correct answer is (C).** This evaluation question requires you to use Passage 1 to evaluate Passage 2—in this case, to apply a definition from one passage to something in the other passage. In a science selection, you might be asked to apply one writer's hypothesis to another writer's results or to compare two theories. Here, first you must look at Wright's definition of a patriot. She believes that a patriot is a lover of human

liberty in general rather than a lover of country in particular. Next, you must look at the choices in light of what you recall about Passage 2. Choice (A) has nothing to do with Wright's definition, and in terms of Emmet's speech, it is simply wrong. He does not prefer one type of tyranny; he hates all tyranny. Choice (B) is certainly true of Emmet, but it does not contradict Wright's definition, and you are looking for some aspect of Emmet's speech that does. The answer is choice (C)—Wright does not believe in blind chauvinism, but Emmet continually repeats the point that everything he has done, he has done for his country alone. In fact, Emmet supported the French Revolution and probably would have been admired by Fanny Wright, but you must base your answer solely on the material given in the passages. Neither choice (D) nor choice (E) discusses actions or attitudes that are part of Wright's definition of patriotism.

17. **The correct answer is (D).** This is a main idea question in disguise. It asks you what the passage is about.

18. **The correct answer is (D).** The word with the closest meaning to *culprit* is *villain,* "someone or something regarded as the cause of a problem."

19. **The correct answer is (C).** This question tests how well you read for information. If you underlined important information as you read the passage, it should have been easy to find this stated fact.

20. **The correct answer is (E).** In comparing the two passages, you saw that there are two competing theories being advanced for the cause of brain abnormalities present in Alzheimer's. Two competing theories implies that there is still ongoing debate.

SUMMING IT UP

- All of the information you need is right in the passage.
- Read the introduction, if one is provided.
- Read the passage without getting bogged down in details.
- Read the questions and their answer choices. Go back into the passage to find answers.
- Critical reading questions follow the order of information in the passage. They are not arranged in order of difficulty.
- Answer every question for a passage before starting the next passage.
- For any question you're not sure of, eliminate obviously wrong answers and take your best guess.

PART IV
SAT WRITING STRATEGIES

Multiple-Choice Writing Strategies

chapter 5

OVERVIEW

- A closer look at the multiple-choice writing section
- Basic strategies for answering the multiple-choice writing questions
- The format of identifying sentence errors questions
- Strategies for answering identifying sentence errors questions
- The format of improving sentences questions
- Strategies for answering improving sentences questions
- The format of improving paragraph questions
- Strategies for answering improving paragraph questions
- Summing it up

A CLOSER LOOK AT THE MULTIPLE-CHOICE WRITING SECTION

The SAT writing section consists of three types of multiple-choice questions; identifying sentence errors, improving sentences, and improving paragraphs. The format of each type of question is slightly different, but the purpose underlying all three is the same—to find out how well you can recognize what is and is not Standard Written English. The questions that ask about sentence errors are more likely to focus on grammar and punctuation. The improving sentences section has questions about grammar and punctuation, and it also asks you to identify and correct awkwardness and wordiness. In the improving paragraphs section, you will most likely find questions about sentence structure, diction, and usage.

The most important piece of information to remember about the multiple-choice sections is that the answer is right there on the page for you. You just have to find it, which will be easy in some cases, a little difficult in others, and hard work for a few questions. The rest of this chapter and Chapter 7 will help you. This chapter will teach you some important strategies for answering multiple-choice writing questions; Chapter 7 reviews grammar, usage, and punctuation.

BASIC STRATEGIES FOR ANSWERING THE MULTIPLE-CHOICE WRITING QUESTIONS

The different multiple-choice question types will be in separate sections. You won't find improving paragraph questions mixed in with identifying sentence errors, but here are a few basic strategies that will help with any of the three question types.

For identifying sentence errors and improving sentences, read each sentence twice before you do anything else.

Try to find the error or improve the sentence yourself before looking at the answer choices.

Look for errors based on level of difficulty. Check for errors in:
* Capitalization and punctuation
* Grammar
* Tenses, usage, parallel structure, redundancy

Pace yourself. If you have no idea how to answer a question within a few seconds, circle it in your test booklet and move on.

If you have some idea about an answer but aren't sure enough to fill in an answer oval, put an "X" next to the question and move on.

Don't expect to be able to go back to a lot of questions once you've been through the section, so if you know something about a question and can eliminate at least one answer, GUESS.

Remember to Use Educated Guessing

If you follow the process of eliminating answers that you know are wrong, you won't be guessing at random. You will be making an educated guess. There is a big difference between guessing wildly and making an educated guess. Remember what you read in Chapter 1 about making an educated guess? This one strategy can raise your score, whereas guessing for the sake of filling in ovals won't make any difference.

THE FORMAT OF IDENTIFYING SENTENCE ERRORS QUESTIONS

In the identifying sentence errors section, you are given a sentence that may or may not contain an "error"—that is, a part not expressed in Standard Written English. Four different portions of the sentence are underlined; each underlined segment is labeled with a letter, A–D. You are to find which underlined segment contains an error and mark its letter on your answer sheet. Or, if there is no error—if all underlined parts are Standard Written English—then you mark choice (E) on your answer sheet.

The directions on the test will look something like the following. Save yourself time on test day by becoming familiar with the directions now.

Directions: The sentences below contain errors in grammar, usage, word choice, and idiom. Parts of each sentence are underlined and lettered. Decide which underlined part contains the error and circle its letter. If the sentence is correct as it stands, circle (E) under "No error." No sentence contains more than one error.

STRATEGIES FOR ANSWERING IDENTIFYING SENTENCE ERRORS QUESTIONS

Unlike most of the SAT, you are looking for what's wrong in these sentences, not what's right. Use the following six strategies to help you find the error:

1 Read the sentence carefully—twice.

2 As you read, listen for any awkward or strange-sounding word or phrase.

3 If you can't hear the mistake, check to see what kinds of words and phrases are underlined. Sentence errors often involve wrong tenses, incorrect subject-verb agreement, and incorrect agreement between pronoun and antecedent.

4 Cross out any answer choices that you know are correct. Remember you are looking for what's wrong.

5 Check the remaining choices to see if they are correct.

6 If you have ruled out all the answer choices except (E), *No error,* choose it.

Let's try applying these rules to a question.

Philadelphia is an interesting city to visit because of its great museums and

     A   B   C

their other cultural attractions. No error.

          D   E

Ⓐ Ⓑ Ⓒ Ⓓ Ⓔ

Now follow these five steps to find the correct answer, that is, what's wrong in the sentence:

1 Read the sentence twice.

2 Could you hear the error as you read the sentence? Did the word "their" stick out as wrong? If so, great. That's the answer.

3 If you didn't hear it, look at the kinds of errors that are underlined. Choice (A) is a subject-verb agreement answer, but it's correct. The subject and the verb are both singular. Choice (C) is a possessive pronoun that refers back to Philadelphia. Both are singular and neither is a person, so choice (C) is correct. Choice (D) is another agreement answer. This time the possessive pronoun is plural, but it refers to Philadelphia, which is singular. Here's the error.

4 To be sure, check choice (B).

5 Choice (B) is a preposition that begins a prepositional phrase. There's no error there.

The identifying sentence error questions are relatively easy. You don't have to correct the error; you just have to find it—if there is one. Of course, to find the error, you have to know what's wrong. That's where Chapter 7 will help you. Be sure to spend time studying the grammar, punctuation, and usage reviews and working through those exercises.

THE FORMAT OF IMPROVING SENTENCES QUESTIONS

The second type of question on the Writing Test is the improving sentences question. Here, the task is to rewrite the underlined portion of a sentence so that it is as representative as possible of correct Standard Written English: The punctuation must be right, the rules of grammar must be followed, and awkwardness or long-windedness must be avoided. You are writing awkwardly when your reader knows what you mean, but wishes you had said it more simply and directly. You are long-winded if you take fifty words to state what you could have said in ten.

The directions on the real test are similar to the following:

> **Directions:** The sentences below contain problems in grammar, sentence construction, word choice, and punctuation. Part or all of each sentence is underlined. Select the lettered answer that contains the best version of the underlined section. Answer (A) always repeats the original underlined section exactly. If the sentence is correct as it stands, select (A).

Like the rest of the SAT, these questions ask you to find the best answer. Note that choice (A) is always the same as the underlined portion in the sentence. Remember this and save yourself some time on the test. Don't bother reading choice (A).

STRATEGIES FOR ANSWERING IMPROVING SENTENCES QUESTIONS

TIP

Always cross out answer choices that you are eliminating. If you find that you can't decide on an answer and have to move on, you won't have to waste time reading all the answer choices again if you have time to come back.

Use the following six basic steps to answer improving sentences items:

1. Read the entire sentence. Don't try to save time by reading only the underlined part. You may think that it sounds correct until you fit it into the rest of the sentence.
2. Errors in this section often involve verbs, incorrect comparisons, pronoun reference mistakes, and errors in standard English usage.
3. If the underlined portion sounds incorrect to you, substitute answers (B) through (E) into the sentence. Don't just substitute choice (B), decide it's correct, fill in the oval, and move on. Try all the answer choices—unless you read an answer choice and find that it has an error in it.
4. Cross out each answer choice that has an error in it.
5. Cross out each answer choice that is not the best substitution in the sentence. An answer may be correctly written but not fit the answer very well. You are looking for the best answer.
6. If the sentence sounds correct to you, then choose answer choice (A), which repeats the underlined portion.

Let's try the following example:

> Roberto is a new employee, and he is from Mexico City.
>
> **(A)** Roberto is a new employee, and he is from Mexico City.
> **(B)** Roberto, a new employee and from Mexico City.
> **(C)** Being from Mexico City, Roberto is a new employee.
> **(D)** Roberto, a new employee, comes from Mexico City.
> **(E)** From Mexico City, Roberto is a new employee.

- In this case, the entire sentence is the test item. You have to read it carefully to determine if there is an error.
- Reading the sentence over, you should have decided that there is no error in the sentence as such. But there is probably a better way to give the information than a dull compound sentence. Subordinating one idea to the other would make the sentence more interesting.
- Read each answer choice and see if it relates the information in a better—more interesting and less awkward—way.
- Do any of the answer choices have an error? Yes, choice (B) is not a complete sentence. Cross it off.
- Choices (C) and (E) use subordination, which makes for a more interesting way of relating the information, but both change the meaning of the sentence. Coming from Mexico City becomes the reason that Roberto is a new employee. This is not true. The fact that Roberto is from Mexico City is additional information about him. Also, choice (C) is awkward. Only choice (D) is grammatically correct and uses subordination properly.

Remember that improving sentences questions may ask you to revise a sentence to make it read more smoothly or have a more interesting style. You may not necessarily be asked to revise a sentence to correct an error.

THE FORMAT OF IMPROVING PARAGRAPH QUESTIONS

The third type of multiple-choice question is called improving paragraphs. This section consists of a passage that is an early draft of a student's essay followed by questions about revising and improving the draft. The questions may relate to individual sentences or to the essay as a whole. You may be asked to examine sentence structure, diction, usage, or organization and development of the essay as a whole. Your task is to choose the answer that makes the meaning clear and that follows the conventions of Standard Written English.

Save yourself some time on test day and become familiar with the directions ahead of time. They will be similar to the following:

Directions: Questions 1–3 are based on a passage that might be an early draft of a student's essay. Some sentences in this draft need to be revised or rewritten to make them both clear and correct. Read the passage carefully; then answer the questions that follow it. Some questions require decisions about diction, usage, tone, or sentence structure in particular sentences or parts of sentences. Other questions require decisions about organization, development, or appropriateness of language in the essay as a whole. For each question, choose the answer that makes the intended meaning clearer and more precise and that follows the conventions of Standard Written English.

STRATEGIES FOR ANSWERING IMPROVING PARAGRAPH QUESTIONS

There are two ways to approach improving paragraph questions. One way is to read the questions first and then the paragraph. The other way is to read the paragraph first and then the questions. You can try out both techniques as you work through the practice tests. This will help you decide which technique better suits you.

Reading the Essay First

Reading is really not the right word. You will be skimming the essay for general meaning. You won't be looking for errors, awkwardness, or redundancies, but for what the essay is about, how it's organized, and what its purpose is. Then you can either reread the essay more slowly looking for problems before you begin to answer questions, or you can go right to answering questions and reread parts of the essay only as needed to find an answer.

Reading the Questions First

When you read the questions, read just the questions. Don't spend time on the answers at this point. You want to find out how many questions you have to answer for this passage, what kind of questions they are (main idea, revision, sentence combining, sentence purpose, and so on), and which paragraph has the most questions. You will want to read that paragraph with particular care.

Once you have read the questions, skim the essay to get an overall idea of what it is about and how it is organized. Jot question numbers in the margin next to information that will help you answer particular questions. If you can't remember question numbers, make notes such as "chrono" for type of organization and "to persuade" for author's intent. Once you've read through the essay, go back and answer the questions.

Finding the Right Answer

This is where working through Chapter 7 will help you; so will reading good writing. You need to tune your ear to what sounds right and smooth—no jarring incorrect subject-verb or noun-pronoun agreements, no inconsistent parallel constructions, no irregular verb forms.

In terms of attacking each question:
- Read the question.
- Depending on what you have to do, try to answer the question on your own, or go right to the answers. If you must revise a sentence, try it yourself first. If you have to combine sentences, you might save time by going right to the answers.

TIP

Don't rely on your memory. Go back to the essay to check your answer.

EXERCISES: MULTIPLE-CHOICE WRITING

Exercise 1

Identifying Sentence Errors

Directions: Some of the sentences below contain an error in grammar usage, word choice, or idiom. Other sentences are correct. Parts of each sentence are underlined and lettered. The error, if there is one, is contained in one of the underlined parts of the sentence. Assume that all other parts of the sentence are correct and cannot be changed. For each sentence, select the one underlined part that must be changed to make the sentence correct and mark its corresponding letter oval. If there is no error in a sentence, select answer E. No sentence contains more than one error.

1. <u>Being that</u> <u>it's</u> such a lovely day, we
     A   B
   <u>are having</u> a difficult time <u>concentrating</u>
     C   D
   on our assignment. <u>No error.</u>
                  E
   Ⓐ Ⓑ Ⓒ Ⓓ Ⓔ

2. He was <u>shocked</u> by the <u>students</u>
            A   B
   outburst when the professor reprimanded the
   boys <u>who</u> <u>had arrived</u> a few minutes before
        C   D
   the test was over. <u>No error.</u>
                 E
   Ⓐ Ⓑ Ⓒ Ⓓ Ⓔ

3. <u>I'm</u> not surprised that my brother
    A
   <u>always eats twice as much as I do since</u>
                  B
   he is so much bigger <u>than</u> <u>me.</u> <u>No error.</u>
                 C D   E
   Ⓐ Ⓑ Ⓒ Ⓓ Ⓔ

4. You <u>would of been</u> able to go to the
        A
   theater with <u>us</u> <u>if</u> you had purchased
            B C
   <u>your</u> ticket in advance. <u>No error.</u>
    D   E
   Ⓐ Ⓑ Ⓒ Ⓓ Ⓔ

5. Everyone in both groups <u>except</u>
                 A
   for John and <u>me</u> <u>were</u> amazed when
             B C
   the <u>contest's</u> results were announced.
        D
   <u>No error.</u>
     E
   Ⓐ Ⓑ Ⓒ Ⓓ Ⓔ

6. <u>There was</u> scarcely <u>no</u> possibility that
    A   B
   we would be able <u>to go</u> to the beach
               C
   with <u>them.</u> <u>No error.</u>
       D   E
   Ⓐ Ⓑ Ⓒ Ⓓ Ⓔ

7. The <u>assent</u> of Mount Everest <u>brought</u>
       A   B
   <u>lasting</u> fame <u>to</u> Sir Edmund Hillary.
     C   D
   <u>No error.</u>
     E
   Ⓐ Ⓑ Ⓒ Ⓓ Ⓔ

8. Because the moon rotates on <u>its</u>
                        A
   axis <u>at the same rate</u> as <u>revolving</u>
       B   C
   around the earth, only one side of the lunar
   surface <u>is ever visible</u> to us. <u>No error.</u>
           D   E
   Ⓐ Ⓑ Ⓒ Ⓓ Ⓔ

Improving Sentences

> **Directions:** The sentences below may contain problems in grammar, usage, word choice, sentence construction, or punctuation. Part or all of each sentence is underlined. Following each sentence you will find five ways of expressing the underlined part. Answer choice (A) always repeats the original underlined section. The other four answer choices are all different. You are to select the lettered answer that produces the most effective sentence. If you think the original sentence is best, choose (A) as your answer. If one of the other choices makes a better sentence, select the letter of that choice. Do not choose an answer that changes the meaning of the original sentence. Circle the letter next to your answer.

9. Her first novel having been published, the author began to take notes for her second.

   (A) Her first novel having been published
   (B) Having been her most recent novel published
   (C) Her first novel, having been published
   (D) When having had her first novel published
   (E) Having published her first novel

10. Van Gogh's early work has often been described as being in sharp contrast with his later work, despite there is a fundamental continuity between the two.

   (A) with his later work, despite
   (B) with his later work; despite the fact that
   (C) with his later work, rather,
   (D) with his later work, but
   (E) with his later work, notwithstanding

11. After working on his serve for several days, rumors circulated that the challenger would win the rematch.

   (A) After working on his serve for several days, rumors circulated that the challenger would win the rematch.
   (B) After working on his serve for several days, the challenger circulated rumors that he would win the rematch.
   (C) Rumors circulated that the challenger, after working on his serve for several days, would win the rematch.
   (D) After having worked on his serve for several days, the rematch was rumored to be won by the challenger.
   (E) After working on his serve for several days, rumors circulated, the challenger would win the rematch.

12. The artist thought that it was important both to portray the subject truthfully, no matter the difficulty, and revealing something new about the subject.

   (A) and revealing something new about the subject.
   (B) and so he revealed something new about the subject.
   (C) and to reveal something new about the subject.
   (D) having thereby revealed something new about the subject.
   (E) and revealing something about the subject that is new.

13. Max Planck was not only one of the founders of quantum mechanics, but an accomplished pianist.

   (A) mechanics, but an accomplished pianist.
   (B) mechanics, but he was also an accomplished pianist.
   (C) mechanics; and he was also an accomplished pianist.
   (D) mechanics, and an accomplished pianist.
   (E) mechanics, but also an accomplished piano.

14. Coffee shops, which were formerly found only in urban settings and near college campuses, have been expanding in the last few years outside these circumspect domains.

   (A) which were formerly found only in urban settings and near college campuses
   (B) being formerly found only in urban settings and near college campuses
   (C) which have been found formerly only in urban settings and near college campuses
   (D) which were formerly found only in urban settings or near college campuses
   (E) that were formerly found only in urban settings and near college campuses

15. Until the Chin dynasty changed this practice, most Chinese intellectuals did not travel to the imperial court <u>but remained in their native provincial centers.</u>

    (A) but remained in their native provincial centers.

    (B) and remained in their native provincial centers.

    (C) but rather they remained in the native provinces.

    (D) yet they remained in their native provincial centers.

    (E) but remained in the provinces to which they were native.

16. The artwork of the late Renaissance was characterized by a deep sympathy for the human subject, <u>often portraying human frailties and failings</u>.

    (A) often portraying human frailties and failings.

    (B) and it often portrayed human frailties and failings.

    (C) human frailties and human failings being often portrayed.

    (D) although it often portrayed human frailties and failings.

    (E) though portraying human frailties and failings.

Improving Paragraphs

Directions: Questions 17–20 are based on a passage that might be an early draft of a student's essay. Some sentences in this draft need to be revised or rewritten to make them both clear and correct. Read the passage carefully; then answer the questions that follow it. Some questions require decisions about diction, usage, tone, or sentence structure in particular sentences or parts of sentences. Other questions require decisions about organization, development, or appropriateness of language in the essay as a whole. For each question, choose the answer that makes the intended meaning clearer and more precise and that follows the conventions of Standard Written English. Circle the letter next to your answer.

(1) Reconstruction failed former slaves in many ways. (2) It set them up with hope and then abandoned them. (3) First, Congress established the Freedmen's Bureau. (4) But it didn't give it enough money to work effectively. (5) It did help freed African Americans by giving them food and clothing and helped them find housing and negotiating for work with landowners. (6) The greatest success of the Freedmen's Bureau was in education. (7) It set up schools and taught not only children but also adults. (8) Former slaves clamored to be taught to read and write. (9) They had been forbidden to go to school under slavery.

(10) Second, backed by the determination of the Radical Republicans, the nation adopted the Fourteenth Amendment, which guaranteed the rights of citizenship to African Americans. (11) The states also ratified the Fifteenth Amendment giving African Americans the right to vote. (12) The vote was only guaranteed for men, not women—white or black. (13) The Southern states found ways around the amendments. (14) They instituted a reign of terror against African Americans to keep them from voting. (15) Secret organizations like the Ku Klux Klan and the White Camellias dragged African Americans out of their homes and beat them. (16) Several hundred African Americans a year were lynched.

(17) Third, by the 1870s, most Northerners had lost patience with the Radical Republicans' desire to right the injustices of slavery. (18) Northern businessmen and bankers saw economic opportunities in the South, but military rule was a problem. (19) In the Compromise of 1877, Northern Republicans and white Southern Democrats reached an understanding. (20) In exchange for a Republican president, the Republicans removed the last of the troops from the South. (21) The Democrats took control of the governments in all the Southern states and began almost 100 years of Jim Crow segregation and discrimination against African Americans.

17. The writer used which of the following types of development in this essay?
    (A) Order of importance
    (B) Chronological order
    (C) Spatial order
    (D) Comparison and contrast
    (E) Cause and effect

18. Which of the following is the best revision of sentences (1) and (2)?
    (A) Reconstruction failed former slaves by setting them up and then abandoning them.
    (B) Reconstruction failed former slaves by setting up their hopes and then abandoning these people.
    (C) Former slaves were failed by Reconstruction when it abandoned them.
    (D) Former slaves looked upon Reconstruction with hope but were failed by it.
    (E) The hopes of former slaves were abandoned by Reconstruction.

19. Which of the following sentences could be deleted without damaging the flow of the paragraph?
    (A) Sentence 7
    (B) Sentence 8
    (C) Sentence 9
    (D) Sentence 15
    (E) Sentence 18

20. Which of the following is the best revision of the underlined portion of sentence (5) below?

    It did help freed African Americans <u>by giving them food and clothing and helped them find housing and negotiating</u> for work with landowners.
    (A) by giving them food and clothing and housing and negotiating
    (B) by giving them food, clothing, and housing and negotiating
    (C) by giving them food and clothing, helping them find housing, and negotiating
    (D) gave them food and clothing, helped them find housing, and negotiated
    (E) by giving them food, clothing, housing, and negotiations

Exercise 2

Identifying Sentence Errors

Directions: Some of the sentences below contain an error in grammar usage, word choice, or idiom. Other sentences are correct. Parts of each sentence are underlined and lettered. The error, if there is one, is contained in one of the underlined parts of the sentence. Assume that all other parts of the sentence are correct and cannot be changed. For each sentence, select the one underlined part that must be changed to make the sentence correct and mark its corresponding letter oval. If there is no error in a sentence, select answer E. No sentence contains more than one error.

1. Except for Amit and I no one expects
                        A   B
    the results of the election to be
                                   C
    very close. No error.
        D   E
    Ⓐ Ⓑ Ⓒ Ⓓ Ⓔ

2. Eating only foods lower in
        A   B
    carbohydrates means that people
                   C
    lose the important nutrients in fruits.
    D
    No error.
        E
    Ⓐ Ⓑ Ⓒ Ⓓ Ⓔ

3. The boys team had left for its game
        A   B   C
    before the debate team had left.
                            D
    No error.
        E
    Ⓐ Ⓑ Ⓒ Ⓓ Ⓔ

4. Christine, Tara, and Amanda are
                                A
    all graceful dancers, but Christine
        B
    has the better technique. No error.
    C   D   E
    Ⓐ Ⓑ Ⓒ Ⓓ Ⓔ

5. Students seem to believe that if teachers
    expected more of them they
        A   B   C
    would do better. No error.
            D   E
    Ⓐ Ⓑ Ⓒ Ⓓ Ⓔ

6. The hybrid cars, which costs around
                        A   B
    $20,000, are extremely fuel efficient
                    C
    and environmentally friendly.
            D
    No error.
        E
    Ⓐ Ⓑ Ⓒ Ⓓ Ⓔ

7. The company who owns the old mill
                    A   B
    wants to tear it down and build a mall
                            C
    with 100 stores and parking for
                        D
    5,000 cars. No error.
                    E
    Ⓐ Ⓑ Ⓒ Ⓓ Ⓔ

8. The problem of entangling overseas
                    A
    alliances are a consideration in the
            B
    president's foreign policy
        C   D
    deliberations. No error.
                    E
    Ⓐ Ⓑ Ⓒ Ⓓ Ⓔ

9. The ten new members of the European Union
   <u>were</u> <u>formerly</u> <u>recognized</u> on
    A   B   C
   May 1 in a <u>colorful</u> ceremony. <u>No error.</u>
             D   E
   Ⓐ Ⓑ Ⓒ Ⓓ Ⓔ

10. The students <u>were</u> very disappointed when
                A
    <u>fewer</u> <u>then</u> <u>were expected</u> came to the play.
      B   C   D
    <u>No error.</u>
      E
    Ⓐ Ⓑ Ⓒ Ⓓ Ⓔ

Improving Sentences

Directions: The sentences below may contain problems in grammar, usage, word choice, sentence construction, or punctuation. Part or all of each sentence is underlined. Following each sentence you will find five ways of expressing the underlined part. Answer choice (A) always repeats the original underlined section. The other four answer choices are all different. You are to select the lettered answer that produces the most effective sentence. If you think the original sentence is best, choose (A) as your answer. If one of the other choices makes a better sentence, select the letter of that choice. Do not choose an answer that changes the meaning of the original sentence. Circle the letter next to your answer.

11. <u>The students were excited to read the prom announcement while waiting for the cafeteria to open.</u>
    (A) The students were excited to read the prom announcement while waiting for the cafeteria to open.
    (B) The excited students read the prom announcement while waiting for the cafeteria to open.
    (C) The students excitedly read the prom announcement while waiting for the cafeteria to open.
    (D) While waiting for the cafeteria to open, the students excitedly read the prom announcement.
    (E) The prom announcement was read by the excited students waiting for the cafeteria to open.

12. Keisha reacted <u>with quickness and skill to her teammate's fumbled ball</u>.
    (A) with quickness and skill to her teammate's fumbled ball
    (B) with quickness and skillfulness to her teammate's fumbled ball
    (C) quickly and skillfully to her teammate's fumbled ball
    (D) quickly and with skillfulness to her teammates' fumbled ball
    (E) with quickness and with skillfulness to her teammates' fumbled ball

13. A fearless player, Chris <u>participating in rugby for a number of years suffering</u> few injuries for much of his career.
    (A) participating in rugby for a number of years suffering
    (B) participating in rugby for a number of years and suffering
    (C) participated in rugby for a number of years; he suffered
    (D) participated in rugby for a number of years and suffered
    (E) participated in rugby for a number of years, yet he suffered

14. A recent study found that <u>watching television 2 hours a day can affect children's</u> attention span.

(A) watching television 2 hours a day can affect children's

(B) watching television 2 hours' a day can affect children's

(C) watching television 2 hours a day can affect childrens

(D) to watch television 2 hours a day affects children's

(E) by watching television 2 hours a day children's attention span can be affected.

15. Gardening for an hour provides as much exercise <u>as if a person walked</u> at a moderate pace for 20 minutes.

(A) as if a person walked

(B) as walking

(C) if a person walked

(D) as if a person walks

(E) as if you walked

16. Mary is an avid runner competing in marathons at least three times a year, <u>but she finds training in the winter more difficult.</u>

(A) but she finds training in the winter more difficult.

(B) but training in the winter is more difficult.

(C) but training in the winter is difficult.

(D) but she finds training in the winter difficult.

(E) because she trains in the winter, which is difficult.

Improving Paragraphs

Directions: Questions 17–20 are based on a passage that might be an early draft of a student's essay. Some sentences in this draft need to be revised or rewritten to make them both clear and correct. Read the passage carefully; then answer the questions that follow it. Some questions require decisions about diction, usage, tone, or sentence structure in particular sentences or parts of sentences. Other questions require decisions about organization, development, or appropriateness of language in the essay as a whole. For each question, choose the answer that makes the intended meaning clearer and more precise and that follows the conventions of Standard Written English. Circle the letter next to your answer.

(1) Reconstruction failed former slaves in many ways. (2) It set them up with hope and then abandoned them. (3) First, Congress established the Freedmen's Bureau. (4) But it didn't give it enough money to work effectively. (5) It did help freed African Americans by giving them food and clothing and helped them find housing and negotiating for work with landowners. (6) The greatest success of the Freedmen's Bureau was in education. (7) It set up schools and taught not only children but also adults. (8) Former slaves clamored to be taught to read and write. (9) They had been forbidden to go to school under slavery.

(10) Second, backed by the determination of the Radical Republicans, the nation adopted the Fourteenth Amendment, which guaranteed the rights of citizenship to African Americans. (11) The states also ratified the Fifteenth Amendment giving African Americans the right to vote. (12) The vote was only guaranteed for men, not women—white or black. (13) The Southern states found ways around the amendments. (14) They instituted a reign of terror against African Americans to keep them from voting. (15) Secret organizations like the Ku Klux Klan and the White Camellias dragged African Americans out of their homes and beat them. (16) Several hundred African Americans a year were lynched.

(17) Third, by the 1870s, most Northerners had lost patience with the Radical Republicans' desire to right the injustices of slavery. (18) Northern businessmen and bankers saw economic opportunities in the South, but military rule was a problem. (19) In the Compromise of 1877, Northern Republicans and white Southern Democrats reached an understanding. (20) In exchange for a Republican president, the Republicans removed the last of the troops from the South. (21) The Democrats took control of the governments in all the Southern states and began almost 100 years of Jim Crow segregation and discrimination against African Americans.

17. Which of the following is the best revision of sentences (3) and (4)?

(3) First, Congress established the Freedmen's Bureau. (4) But it didn't give it enough money to work effectively.

(A) First, Congress established the Freedmen's Bureau, which it didn't give enough money to.

(B) First, Congress established the Freedmen's Bureau, but Congress did not give the Bureau enough money to work effectively.

(C) First, the Freedmen's Bureau was established by Congress without enough money to work effectively.

(D) First, Congress established the Freedmen's Bureau, which was not given enough money to work effectively.

(E) First, Congress established the Freedmen's Bureau but did not give it enough money to work effectively.

18. Which of the following would be the best conclusion to this passage?

(A) Reconstruction had indeed failed for many reasons.

(B) As Northerners abandoned Reconstruction, they also abandoned freed African Americans.

(C) Reconstruction that had begun with such hope ended with such hopelessness.

(D) Former slaves had indeed been abandoned by Reconstruction.

(E) After 12 years of Reconstruction, former slaves had little to show for it.

19. Which of the following is the best revision of sentence 18?

Northern businessmen and bankers saw economic opportunities in the South, but military rule was a problem.

(A) Northern businessmen and bankers saw economic opportunities in the South, but not as long as it was under military rule.

(B) Economic opportunities were possible for Northern businessmen and bankers, but the problem was military rule.

(C) There was the problem of military rule for Northern businesses and bankers.

(D) Military rule was a problem for realizing the economic opportunities that Northern businessmen and bankers saw.

(E) The economic opportunities in the South that businessmen and bankers saw in the South were off limits by military rule.

20. Which of the following is the best condensation of sentences 10, 11, and 12?

(10) Second, backed by the determination of the Radical Republicans, the nation adopted the Fourteenth Amendment, which guaranteed the rights of citizenship to African Americans. (11) The states also ratified the Fifteenth Amendment giving African Americans the right to vote. (12) The vote was only guaranteed for men, not women—white or black.

(A) Second, Radical Republicans got the states to ratify the Fourteenth and Fifteenth Amendments, granting the rights of citizenship and voting rights to African American men.

(B) Second, the nation adopted the Fourteenth and Fifteenth Amendments that gave citizenship rights and voting rights to American African men, but not to women.

(C) Second, with Radical Republican support, the nation adopted the Fourteenth Amendment, which guaranteed citizenship to African Americans, and the Fifteenth Amendment, which granted the right to vote to African American men, but not to women—white or black.

(D) Second, with the determined support of the Radical Republicans, the nation adopted the Fourteenth and Fifteenth Amendments. The Fourteenth Amendment granted the rights of citizenship to African Americans and the Fifteenth Amendment guaranteed them the right to vote.

(E) Second, Radical Republicans adopted the Fourteenth and Fifteenth Amendments, which guaranteed certain rights of citizens to African American men but not women—white or black.

ANSWER KEY AND EXPLANATIONS

Exercise 1

1. A	6. B	11. C	16. D
2. B	7. A	12. C	17. B
3. D	8. C	13. B	18. B
4. A	9. E	14. A	19. C
5. C	10. D	15. A	20. C

1. **The correct answer is (A).** A subordinate conjunction is needed to begin the subordinate clause, not a participle.

2. **The correct answer is (B).** The correct word is *students'* or *student's* since the possessive form is required.

3. **The correct answer is (D).** The nominative *I* following the comparative *bigger than* is required.

4. **The correct answer is (A).** The correct verb form is *would have been.*

5. **The correct answer is (C).** The singular was, agreeing with the singular subject *everyone,* is required.

6. **The correct answer is (B).** *Scarcely no* is a double negative, the correct phrase is *scarcely any.*

7. **The correct answer is (A).** *Assent* means agreement. The word needed here is *ascent,* meaning climbing or scaling.

8. **The correct answer is (C).** The idea calls for parallel structure: "Because the moon rotates on its axis at the same rate as *it revolves* around the Earth. . ."

9. **The correct answer is (E).** This sentence is unnecessarily wordy. *Having published her first novel, the author* is a lot snappier and more direct. The answer is choice (E).

10. **The correct answer is (D).** Here, *despite* is not used in a grammatically correct way. *Despite the fact that* is grammatically correct, but it is unnecessarily wordy and it is not appropriately

joined with a semicolon. How about just *but*? That's choice (D).

11. **The correct answer is (C).** This sentence might have sounded okay to you, but it has a misplaced modifier. These are very popular mistakes in the sentence correction questions. The phrase *after he had worked on his serve for a few days* modifies the noun *player,* so *player* must be right next to it. Only (B) and (C) accomplish this. Choice (B), however, changes the sense of the original sentence. The answer is choice (C).

12. **The correct answer is (C).** In sentence construction, parallel parts of a sentence should have parallel forms. In this sentence the verbs *portray* and *reveal are* parallel, but in the original sentence construction they are not in parallel form. Choice (C) corrects this mistake.

13. **The correct answer is (B).** This is another favorite of the test-writers: Any time you have "not only" you need to signal the contrasting phrase with "but also." The answer here is therefore choice (B).

14. **The correct answer is (A).** There is no error here. The sentence is correct as written.

15. **The correct answer is (A).** There is not a grammatical error in the underlined portion, and none of the alternatives improve upon the original. Because you do not repeat the subject, there is no comma needed before the underlined portion. Were you to choose answer (C), you would need to add a comma. Choice (A) is the best answer.

16. **The correct answer is (D).** Here the error is logical rather than grammatical per se. The first part of the sentence emphasizes sympathy, but the second part focuses on negative human qualities. You need a contrasting coordinator. That leaves choices (D) and (E). Choice (D) is the better option.

17. **The correct answer is (B).** The words *first, second,* and *third* signal that the author used chronological order to develop this passage.

18. **The correct answer is (B).** This answer clearly indicates that Reconstruction abandoned the freed slaves. In choices (A) and (E), Reconstruction abandoned the hopes of African Americans and this is incorrect. Choices (C) and (D) change the focus of the sentence from Reconstruction to former slaves, making the transition into sentence 2 awkward.

19. **The correct answer is (C).** The fact that slaves were forbidden to learn to read and write is overkill. It is implied in the preceding sentences.

20. **The correct answer is (C).** Only choice (C) corrects the structure of the phrases to make them parallel. Choices (A) and (E) change the meaning of the sentence.

Exercise 2

1. A	6. B	11. D	16. D
2. B	7. A	12. C	17. E
3. D	8. B	13. E	18. B
4. D	9. B	14. A	19. A
5. B	10. C	15. B	20. C

1. **The correct answer is (A).** *Except for* is a preposition, and prepositions require an objective form of a pronoun. *I* is the subjective form and is, therefore, incorrect.

2. **The correct answer is (B).** There is no reason to have a comparative form of the adjective.

3. **The correct answer is (D).** The use of the past perfect verb *had left in* the second clause is incorrect. The debate team left later and, therefore, simple past tense is needed.

4. **The correct answer is (D).** Three dancers are being compared, so the superlative *best* is required.

5. **The correct answer is (B).** The antecedent of *they* is unclear. Replacing *them* with *students* improves the clarity of the sentence.

6. **The correct answer is (B).** *Which* refers back to the plural subject *cars*. The predicate then should be plural, *cost,* not *costs*.

7. **The correct answer is (A).** *Company* is a thing, not a person. Use *who* only to refer to people.

8. **The correct answer is (B).** Don't be confused by the word *alliances* just before the verb. The subject is the singular *problem,* so the verb must be singular.

9. **The correct answer is (B).** *Formerly* means *before* or *earlier.* The word that should be used here is *formally.*

answers exercises

10. **The correct answer is (C).** This is a common error. Don't confuse *then* meaning time with *than*, which is used in comparisons.

11. **The correct answer is (D).** Choices (B) and (C) have misplaced modifiers. It appears that the cafeteria is reading the announcement. Although choice (E) correctly places the phrase, the sentence uses passive voice. Active voice is always preferable.

12. **The correct answer is (C).** Although choice (B) corrects the parallel structure problem by using two nouns, the sentence is awkward. The same is true of choice (E), which also introduces an error in the possessive noun. Choice (D) creates a new error in parallelism.

13. **The correct answer is (E).** As written, the test item has no verb. Choice (E) adds a verb and a coordinating conjunction that fits the sense of the sentence better than choice (D), which simply joins the two ideas. The use of *yet* indicates that it's unusual or surprising that Chris suffered few injuries. Choice (C) adds a semicolon rather than develop the relationship between the two clauses. Choice (B) repeats the error in the sentence and compounds it by using another participle.

14. **The correct answer is (A).** The sentence is correct.

15. **The correct answer is (B).** The sentence lacks parallel structure. Only choice (B) corrects this problem. Choices (C), (D), and (E) shift the focus to the incorrect subordinate clause.

16. **The correct answer is (D).** There is no comparison, so there is no need for the word *more*. That eliminates choice (B). Choice (C) makes no sense nor does choice (E). That's why it's important to read the answers in relation to the whole sentence.

17. **The correct answer is (E).** Choice (A) is awkward. Choice (B) is wordy. Choice (C) is in the passive voice, and it is unclear which word the phrase "without enough money to work effectively" modifies. Expressing the idea of the lack of money in a subordinate clause, choice (D), does not convey its importance.

18. **The correct answer is (B).** Choice (A) sums up the passage but not in a very interesting way. Choice (C) sounds good, but what does it really say? Be careful of these kinds of sentences. Choice (D) only deals with part of the story; choice (B) includes who abandoned Reconstruction and African Americans and relates better to the beginning of the passage. Choice (E) describes the situation accurately but doesn't relate back to the beginning of the passage by using the same words.

19. **The correct answer is (A).** Choice (B) is not very interesting and uses passive voice. Choice (C) doesn't include all the information in the original sentence. Choice (D) is wordy as is choice (E). Choice (E) also uses the informal "off limits."

20. **The correct answer is (C).** Choice (C) creates parallel clauses and includes all the information in the original sentences. Choice (A) is awkward and doesn't contain all the information in the original sentences. Choices (B), (D), and (E) do not include all the information.

SUMMING IT UP

- The right answer is always there on the page.
- Try to identify the sentence error or improve the sentence on your own before you read the answer choices.
- Listen for the error as you read the sentence to yourself. A word or phrase that doesn't sound right to you is more than likely the error. You can use the same technique in answering revision questions in the improving paragraphs section of the SAT.
- Look for errors based on level of difficulty:

  — Capitalization and punctuation

  — Grammar

  — Tenses, usage, parallel structure, redundancy
- Pace yourself. If you are not sure about an answer but can eliminate at least one answer, guess.

The Writing Process and the SAT Essay

OVERVIEW

- **A closer look at the essay question**
- **Prewriting**
- **Writing the introduction**
- **Developing your ideas**
- **Writing the conclusion**
- **The scoring rubric for the SAT essay**
- **Summing it up**

The essay section of the SAT is 25 minutes long. In this time, you need to read the essay prompt, choose a position, and plan and write your essay. It doesn't need to be—and isn't supposed to be—a final, polished version. The high school and college English teachers who will score your essay are trained to view the essays as first drafts. They will be assessing your essay and hundreds of others against a rubric that guides them to look at the essays holistically. They are reading for an overall general impression of your writing abilities. Later in this chapter you will analyze a rubric that is similar to the one the scorers will use.

A CLOSER LOOK AT THE ESSAY QUESTION

You will be given one essay prompt and asked to write a persuasive essay in response to it. You won't have a choice of questions to answer. This is good because it saves you time, as you don't have to decide which one to choose. The essay section is made up of a prompt, which sets out an issue, and a question, which asks whether you agree or disagree with the issue as stated.

Once you have figured out your response, then you can begin your planning. You don't need any specific subject-area knowledge to write your essay. The purpose of the essay is to demonstrate for the readers that you can develop a thesis, support it with examples, and present a conclusion that accurately describes your point of view on the topic.

chapter 6

Pacing Your Writing

You want to use everything you've been taught in English class about the writing process—but sped up to fit within 25 minutes. Pacing yourself is important so that you are able to get your ideas down on paper in a complete, coherent, and unified essay with at least three strong supporting arguments. As you practice writing essays in this chapter and in the practice tests in this book, work out a pacing schedule for yourself. Begin by trying out the following timetable and see how it works for you. If necessary, adjust it as you practice, but be sure to give yourself enough time to finish a complete draft.

- Prewriting: 2 to 3 minutes
- Writing the introduction: 4 to 5 minutes
- Writing the body of the essay: 10 to 13 minutes
- Writing the conclusion: 3 to 4 minutes
- Revising: 1 to 2 minutes
- Proofing: 1 to 2 minutes

NOTE

Remember that the readers do not take off points for specific errors in grammar, usage, and mechanics, but they will take note of a pattern of errors. These can contribute to a lower score. Check the rubric (later in this chapter).

PREWRITING

Before you begin to write your essay, read the prompt and the question several times so you are sure you understand it and are familiar with the issue. Underline key words or phrases to help you.

You want to spend no more than 2 to 3 minutes on prewriting. Your goals in this planning stage are the following:

- To gain familiarity with the essay question
- To develop a point of view, either agreeing or disagreeing with the statement given
- To develop a thesis statement that is the essential idea of your essay

Developing a Thesis

The first step in planning an essay is to decide on a *thesis,* the point you intend to make in your essay. It is often of great value to try to state the thesis of your composition in a single sentence during the prewriting time. When developing a thesis, keep the following ideas in mind:

- The thesis must be neither too broad nor too narrow.
- The thesis must be clear to you and to the reader of your essay.
- Everything in the essay must support the thesis. To introduce material that drifts away might well result in a confusing essay and a low score.
- Use specific details rather than vague generalizations to support your thesis.

These four tips are very important to keep in mind when planning and writing your essay. You have only 25 minutes. By the nature of the question, your thesis should be narrow. You need to keep your writing tightly focused on your thesis. You can't use very complicated supporting ideas or a great number of them. You can't drift off the subject by letting your ideas get away from you as you write.

Organizing Your Essay

Decide how many paragraphs you need to write to develop your idea. Remember that length is not a valid substitute for strength. Your answer booklet provides a certain number of pages for your essay. You can't write more than the lines provided, but you can write fewer. The idea is not the number of lines you fill, but what you have to say. However, an essay of five sentences won't earn you a high score.

A safe number of paragraphs is five. Use the first paragraph for the introduction and the last one for the conclusion. That gives you three paragraphs to develop your ideas. That doesn't mean that you can't write a fourth or even fifth paragraph in the body of your essay to develop your ideas. But it's more important to have a tightly written and well-developed shorter essay than a longer, rambling, repetitious one that you didn't have time to revise or proofread. There is a limit to what you can write in 25 minutes. Use the opportunity that you have for practice in this book to work on your pacing and see how much you can plan and write well in 25 minutes.

WRITING THE INTRODUCTION

Now it's time to write. You've analyzed the question in your prewriting step and decided what your position is. You've also developed your thesis statement. Now, begin writing your introduction.

In your introduction, you want to indicate your position to the readers. You also want to point out the general direction that your essay is going to take. You may also want to give some background that relates to why you hold your particular view. Three to six sentences should accomplish these tasks.

As you practice writing essays in this book and as you write the real one on test day, keep the following five ideas in mind:

1. In writing your introduction, keep the key words of the question in mind.
2. Avoid being cute, funny, ironic, satiric, overly emotional, or too dramatic. Set the tone or attitude in your first sentence. You want to be sincere, clear, and straightforward.
3. Don't bother repeating the question word for word. A paraphrase in your own words is far better than just copying the words of the exam question.
4. Try in your first paragraph to let the reader know what your essay is going to deal with and what your controlling idea is. This can be accomplished in a clear topic sentence.
5. Each sentence should advance your topic and be interesting to your reader.

Skill Builder: Topic Sentence

Directions: Which of the following is the best topic sentence?

1. I have an aunt who is quite old, past 80, and she lives alone in a very run-down neighborhood.
2. Old age can be a real problem.
3. I am going to do my best in the next 25 minutes to try to let you know what I really and truly believe about this problem that was stated in the essay question assigned to us.
4. Since people are living to a more advanced age, we might do well to examine how we can utilize the wisdom and experience that our senior citizens have to offer instead of just disregarding them.

Answers and Explanations

Sentence four is the best opening sentence since it states the topic clearly, limits the scope of the essay, and even presents the attitude of the writer.

Recognizing Effective Introductions

An *effective* introduction often refers to the subject of the essay, explains the value of the topic, or attracts the attention of the reader by giving a pertinent illustration. Ineffective beginnings often contain unrelated material, ramble, and lack clarity.

Skill Builder: Effective Introductions

Directions: Examine the following five introductory paragraphs and decide whether each is effective or ineffective. Be able to defend your decision.

1. I agree that older people have many problems just as young people do. Adolescents often say that it's tough being young and I guess I agree.

2. Today more than ever before child abuse is coming under careful scrutiny. Although it is true that children have been abused in the past, the focus has never been clearer and that is all for the better.

3. It's really very important to think about and discuss such things. I know many people are very concerned about it.

4. Corruption in government must be everyone's concern. We can no longer hide behind the old saying, "You can't fight City Hall." Actually we can and we must.

5. I'm tired of hearing about dirty politics. It was always there just like sickness and other problems only now we read more about it. Sometimes I get disgusted because with all my schoolwork I can't pay attention to taking care of other matters. And then I'm criticized.

Answers and Explanations

1. *Ineffective.* The conclusion is not clear. The writer confuses the reader by discussing young people, older people, and adolescents.

2. *Effective.* The writer presents a strong statement on the need for writing the essay and addressing the topic.

3. *Ineffective.* The paragraph is not clear. The use of the phrase "such things" and the pronoun "it" without an appropriate antecedent to confuse the reader.

4. *Effective.* The initial sentence contains a strong and valid thesis. The use of a quotation tends to reinforce the subject under discussion. The paragraph is clear and the tone is strong.

5. *Ineffective.* The paragraph is rambling and muddled. The writer never presents a clear thesis statement.

DEVELOPING YOUR IDEAS

The heart of your essay is the development, or middle paragraphs. In these paragraphs, you must use explanations, details, and examples to support the main idea of your essay. The developmental paragraphs must serve as a link in the chain of your ideas and must contribute directly to your essay's thesis. All the sentences of the development must explain and support your position on the issue and must not digress.

In the limited time you have on the essay section of the SAT, you can take only 10 to 13 minutes to write the body of your essay. In this time, you need to support your main idea and prove the validity of your point of view on the issue. Your writing must be coherent, logical, unified, and organized.

Avoid the following three pitfalls in the development of your essay:

1 Using sentences that are irrelevant and contain extraneous material

2 Using sentences that have no sequence of thought but seem to jump from one idea to another

3 Using sentences that do not relate to the topic sentence or do not flow from the preceding sentence

Using Transitions

The successful writer uses transitional words and phrases to connect thoughts and provide a logical sequence of ideas. Become familiar with the following list of transitions and use them in your practice essays. They will help make your writing smoother.

therefore	for example	nevertheless
first of all	in any case	but
then	consequently	still
moreover	for instance	yet
secondly	on the other hand	also
indeed	of course	in addition
however	finally	furthermore

Skill Builder: Using Transitions

Directions: In the following three samples, the transition is missing. Supply a transitional word or phrase that will allow the second sentence to follow smoothly or logically from the first.

1. He is an excellent piano player. There are times when his technique seems weak.

2. In the view of the critic, there was so much wrong with the painting. The colors were too bright and the figures were too realistic.

3. He arrived late to take the examination. He dropped his pen and book when he finally got to his seat.

Answers and Explanations

1. The sentences require a transition that indicates contrast, such as *yet, but, however, still,* or *nevertheless.*

   He is an excellent piano player, but there are times when his technique seems weak.

2. These sentences require a transition that indicates an example is to follow.

   In the view of the critic, there was so much wrong with the painting; for example, the colors were too bright and the figures were too realistic.

3. These sentences require a transition that indicates the idea of addition.

   He arrived late to take the test. Furthermore, he dropped his pen and book when the finally got to his seat.

Writing Effectively

There are three important factors that should be considered in writing an essay:

1 Unity

2 Coherence

3 Support

Essays are judged by how well they meet these three basic requirements. To improve an essay you are writing, ask yourself these questions:

Unity

- Do all the details in the essay support and develop the main thesis?
- Do all the examples relate to the main point and add to the general effectiveness of the essay?
- Have irrelevant ideas been deleted?

Coherence

- Does the essay show a sense of organization?
- Is the material presented logically?
- Does the essay include transitional words or phrases that allow the reader to move easily from one idea to the next?

Support

- Does the essay use details that make it interesting and vivid?
- Is the main idea supported with concrete and specific examples?
- Does the essay contain sufficient supporting details to clarify and persuade?

WRITING THE CONCLUSION

Lewis Carroll, the author *of Alice in Wonderland,* once gave some very good advice for writers. He said, "When you come to the end, stop!"

When you come to the end of your ideas, stop writing the development—and begin writing your conclusion. You can't just end your essay with your last supporting detail. You need to draw your comments together in a strong, clear concluding paragraph.

A good concluding paragraph for your SAT essay should assure your reader that you have successfully established and explained your position on the issue. You should be able to do this in three to six sentences written in 3 to 4 minutes. The following are three possible ways to end your essay:

1. Through a *restatement* of the main idea
2. Through a *summary* of the material covered in the essay
3. Through a *clear statement of the writer's opinion* of the issue(s) involved

Of course, if you had a good deal of time, there would be many additional techniques that you could use for your conclusion. But since the SAT essay is limited to 25 minutes, one of these three techniques will give you a structure and allow you enough time to write a strong conclusion.

Keep in mind that a good conclusion is related to the thesis of the essay and is an integral part of the essay. It may be a review or a restatement, or it may lead the reader to do thinking on his or her own, but the conclusion must be strong, clear, and effective.

What Not to Say in Your Conclusion

Just as there are good techniques, there are also some very ineffective methods that students are tempted to use in drawing a composition to a close. Try to avoid falling into the following three traps:

1. Apologizing for your inability to discuss all the issues in the allotted time
2. Complaining that the topics did not interest you or that you don't think it was fair to be asked to write on so broad a topic
3. Introducing material that you will not develop, rambling on about nonpertinent matters, or using material that is trite or unrelated

Recognizing Effective Conclusions

Remember that an *effective* concluding paragraph may restate the thesis statement, summarize the main idea of the essay, draw a logical conclusion, or offer a strong opinion of what the future holds. An *ineffective* final paragraph often introduces new material in a scanty fashion, apologizes for the ineffectiveness of the material presented, or is illogical or unclear. Use the following skill-builder exercises to test yourself.

Skill Builder: Effective Conclusions

Directions: Why are the following sentences ineffective in a concluding paragraph?

1. I wish I had more time to write a more convincing paper, but I find that in the allotted time this is all that I could do.

2. Although I have not mentioned this before, many senior citizens centers are being set up all over the country.

3. I urge each and everyone to make good use of their leisure time and spend their free hours wisely.

Directions: Examine the following five conclusions and decide whether each is effective or ineffective.

4. That's all I have to say about the topic. I know I'm not an expert, but at least this is my opinion and what I believe.

5. Certainly we can conclude that we are affected by the media. The advertisers are beginning to control our thinking and our decision making. The alert consumer must recognize this and act accordingly.

6. We must find other solutions to this problem. I know in England they have developed hospices to handle the terminally ill. But we can't discuss that here because of lack of time.

7. From all the evidence we have, smoking presents a clear and present danger to the young person. The best cure for the habit appears to be to stop before beginning.

8. So be careful not to skip school. You must realize that a good education is important for you and so you should take advantage of your teachers when you are young. You won't be sorry.

Answers and Explanations

1. Avoid using a complaining or apologetic tone in your conclusion. This detracts from the strength of your conclusion and serves to point out your inability to communicate ideas.

2. Do not add an idea that is completely new in your conclusion unless you are prepared to justify its inclusion and to develop it before you end your essay.

3. This call to action is unrealistic in the context of the essay. It would be better stated as a conclusion on the part of the writer. Note also the grammatical error (each and everyone . . . their).

4. *Ineffective.* This statement is a repetitious apology.

5. *Effective.* The paragraph is strong and clear. The conclusion is logical and the writer's opinion is well stated.

6. *Ineffective.* New material is presented but not developed.

7. *Effective.* The conclusion drawn appears to be logical. The phrasing is concise and to the point.

8. *Ineffective.* The tone is preachy; it is preferable to avoid addressing the reader directly or giving commands. It would be better to use the third person.

THE SCORING RUBRIC FOR THE SAT ESSAY

The SAT essay is scored from 1 to 6, with 6 being the highest score. Two readers will assess your essay and the scores will be combined, so your final score will range somewhere between 2 and 12. If the scores from the two readers differ by more than one point, a third scorer will read the essay. The two closest scores will then be used.

All the scorers read the essays against the same rubric developed by the College Board and the Educational Testing Service, which administers the SAT. This rubric guides the scorers in considering overall impression, development, organization, diction, sentence structure, grammar, usage, and mechanics. The score guidelines are similar to the following:

Essay Scoring 6 (Outstanding)
- *Overall impression:* develops a point of view with clarity and insight; uses excellent critical thinking in presenting the viewpoint; uses appropriate supporting examples, reasoning, and details
- *Organization:* is well organized with a clear focus; coherent; clear and orderly progression of ideas
- *Diction:* uses appropriate, varied, and accurate vocabulary for interest and clarity
- *Sentence structure:* varies sentence structure
- *Grammar, usage, mechanics:* is almost free of grammar, usage, and mechanics errors

Essay Scoring 5 (Effective)
- *Overall impression:* develops viewpoint effectively; uses strong critical thinking in presenting viewpoint; most examples, reasons, and details are appropriate
- *Organization:* is well organized and focused; coherent; progression of ideas present
- *Diction:* demonstrates skill in the use of appropriate language
- *Sentence structure:* varies sentence structure
- *Grammar, usage, mechanics:* is mostly free of grammar, usage, and mechanics errors

Essay Scoring 4 (Competent)
- *Overall impression:* develops viewpoint; shows competent critical thinking; provides adequate support through the use of examples, reasons, and details
- *Organization:* is mostly organized and focused; coherent for the most part; has some clear progression of ideas
- *Diction:* is inconsistent in the use of appropriate vocabulary; is generally adequate
- *Sentence structure:* uses some varied sentence structure
- *Grammar, usage, mechanics:* makes some grammar, usage, and mechanics errors

Essay Scoring 3 (Inadequate)
- *Overall impression:* develops a point of view; shows some use of critical thinking; may be inconsistent in reasoning; may provide insufficient support
- *Organization:* shows limited organization or some lack of focus; some lack of coherence or progression of ideas
- *Diction:* shows some facility in language use; uses weak or inappropriate vocabulary
- *Sentence structure:* uses little sentence variety; may have problems in use of sentence structures
- *Grammar, usage, mechanics:* shows a number of grammar, usage, and mechanics errors

Essay Scoring 2 (Limited)

- *Overall impression:* develops a vague or limited viewpoint; weak critical thinking; uses inappropriate supporting evidence or too few examples to make the points
- *Organization:* poor or unfocused; serious weaknesses in coherence or progression of ideas
- *Diction:* shows little facility with language; limited word choice; inappropriate vocabulary
- *Sentence structure:* has numerous errors in sentence structure
- *Grammar, usage, mechanics:* has numerous errors in grammar, usage, and mechanics that interfere with meaning

Essay Scoring 1 (Fundamentally Flawed)

- *Overall impression:* has no point of view on the issue or offers little or no support for the point of view
- *Organization:* lacks organization or focus; incoherent; no progression of ideas
- *Diction:* has basic errors in the use of vocabulary
- *Sentence structure:* has serious problems with sentence structure
- *Grammar, usage, mechanics:* has numerous errors in grammar, usage, and mechanics interfering with meaning

Note that a score of 0 will be given if an essay is not based on the writing prompt.

Read the rubric several times. As you practice writing essays for the SAT, keep this rubric in mind. When you write each essay, try to focus on one or two qualities of good writing as measured by the rubric. After you have finished writing your essay, come back to the rubric and see how your essay measures up.

Use the following tables to help you. Give yourself anywhere from 1 to 6 points for each quality of good writing. Then divide the total by 5 to get your score.

PRACTICE TEST 2

Overall impression   _____
Organization   _____
Diction   _____
Sentence structure   _____
Grammar, usage, mechanics _____
Total points: _____
Divide by 5 for final score: _____

PRACTICE TEST 3

Overall impression   _____
Organization   _____
Diction   _____
Sentence structure   _____
Grammar, usage, mechanics _____
Total points: _____
Divide by 5 for final score: _____

PRACTICE TEST 4

Overall impression   _____
Organization   _____
Diction   _____
Sentence structure   _____
Grammar, usage, mechanics _____
Total points: _____
Divide by 5 for final score: _____

PRACTICE TEST 5

Overall impression   _____
Organization   _____
Diction   _____
Sentence structure   _____
Grammar, usage, mechanics _____
Total points: _____
Divide by 5 for final score: _____

PRACTICE TEST 6

Overall impression   _____
Organization   _____
Diction   _____
Sentence structure   _____
Grammar, usage, mechanics _____
Total points: _____
Divide by 5 for final score: _____

EXERCISES: PRACTICING YOUR ESSAY SKILLS

Use the following two essays as practice and as a guide to writing an effective essay. First, read the writing prompt and then write an essay to answer it. Simulate the actual test and give yourself 25 minutes to read the question, plan, and write your essay. Then read the sample responses for each essay and the critique of each.

Essay 1

Directions: Think carefully about the statement below and the assignment that follows it.

Topic: Were the good old days actually all that good? We must remember that people living in the nineteenth century did not have all the modern conveniences that make our lives easier. There were no airplanes or cars, no washing machines, no television, and no computers. Therefore, it is better to live today, in the modern world, than it was to live in the days of horse-drawn carriages.

Assignment: What is your opinion of the idea that it is better to live today than it was to live in the nineteenth century? Plan and write an essay that develops your ideas logically. Support your opinion with specific evidence taken from your personal experience, your observations of others, or your reading.

Answers and Explanations

Sample Essay 1A

I prefer to be living today rather than when my grandparents were born in the last century or before that even. Today young people can really enjoy themselves they have TV and movies and all sorts of entertainment. Not like long ago when all you did all day was work and then at night you were to tired to do anything accept sleep.

Today we have greater opportunities to do things and to get ahead. There is less prejudism against people because of there race or color or religion. You can go to more kinds of colleges like a two year school or a four year school and there are even many programs to help you if you are financially unable to pay the tuition costs and payments.

I don't believe that the good old days were really that good. I'm very happy to be living today in today world. These are the good days.

Analysis of Sample Essay 1A

1. There is a sense of organization. The essay is divided into three paragraphs—an introduction, a development, and a conclusion.

2. The author attempts to stick to the topic and provide examples.

3. Although there are technical errors in the third paragraph, the conclusion provides an interesting summary.

4. There are some problems with sentence structure, but the writer attempts to vary the sentences.

5. There are serious errors with grammar, usage, and punctuation.

Suggestions for Improvement

1. The essay lacks clarity and is wordy. The opening sentence could have been concluded after "born." In the second paragraph, the first sentence is vague; "to do things" and "to get ahead" should be explained and clarified. The third sentence of the second paragraph needs to be tightened: "There are two- and four-year colleges with various programs to assist those in financial need."

2. There are sentence structure problems. The second sentence of the first paragraph is a run-on sentence. A period should follow "themselves." The sentence that follows is a fragment. "Not like long ago" could be changed to add clarity and also to provide a subject for the sentence: "This is different from times past when all people did. . . ."

3. There are several errors in word choice. In the last sentence of the first paragraph, *to tired* should be changed to *too tired,* and *accept* should be *except.* In the second sentence of the second paragraph, *prejudism* should be *prejudice,* and *there* should be *their.*

4. There is an error in the use of the possessive form. In the second sentence of the third paragraph, *today world* should be *today's world.*

5. The ideas could have been better developed had the writer used one paragraph for each idea that he or she introduced in the second paragraph.

Sample Essay 1B

Someone once said that for everything you gain you have to give up something. I agree. We gained the subway, but we have to put up with being crowded like sardines and herded like cattle, being pushed and shoved. We gained large buildings and big cities, but we lost our privacy and we are forced to live in little cubby holes. We gained airplanes and automobiles and with it comes all the dirty air and pollution.

People in the nineteenth century worked hard and didn't have time to relax but maybe they got real pleasure from their work. At least they ate the food that they grew and weren't concerned about all the chemicals and sprays and sickness that came from the fruit and vegetables. Maybe they developed a real feeling of accomplishment too.

They didn't have TV or radios but they had good neighbors and they would enjoy visiting with friends and family. We gained television but we lost the ability to have a good conversation and to enjoy the company of other people.

Every century has its good points and its problems. I don't want to go back to living in the 1800s but I do feel that we could learn from the way they lived. Maybe we could adopt some of their customs and bring some of the good old days into today's world.

Analysis of Sample Essay 1B

1. There is an excellent four-paragraph organization. The introduction is fully developed with several pertinent illustrations. The body provides several additional points that support the writer's contention. The conclusion is a thought-provoking summary of the essay.

2. The use of contrast between past and present provides a fine frame for the essay. The theme of "gain and loss" is carried through with appropriate illustrations and a mature vocabulary.

3. There are no errors in sentence structure. The writer uses both simple and complex sentences effectively.

4. There is a consistent comma error but no other mechanics errors.

Suggestions for Improvements

1. The second sentence of the opening paragraph seems ineffective in the context of so many mature comments. It could be rewritten: "This is especially true in comparing our world with the world of our grandparents."

2. There is a problem with pronouns and antecedents; this results in a lack of clarity. In the last sentence of the first paragraph, the singular pronoun "it" is incorrect since it does not agree with the plural "airplanes and automobiles." It would be better to write: "We gained airplanes and automobiles, but with modern means of travel we must suffer dirty air and pollution." In addition, the second sentence of the concluding paragraph could be rewritten to clarify the pronoun, "they": ". . . but I do feel that we could learn from the way our grandparents lived." This change clarifies the use of the pronoun "their" in the subsequent sentence.

Essay 2

Directions: Think carefully about the statement below and the assignment that follows it.

Topic: Our government is spending millions of dollars in the area of space exploration. This expenditure represents a misdirection of funds. It would be far better to use these funds to improve our own society and to upgrade our living conditions.

Assignment: What is your opinion of the idea that government funds should not be spent on space exploration but used for domestic purposes? Plan and write an essay that develops your ideas logically. Support your opinion with specific evidence taken from your personal experience, your observations of others, or your reading.

Answers and Explanations

Sample Essay 2A

I can see the point of those who say that "this expenditure represents a misdirecting of funds." However, I feel it is necessary for humans to explore the stars and outer space in order to acquire more knowledge of the universe. Humans have always tried to learn more, even when it gets them in trouble. Wouldn't it be terrible if we bother some aliens and get destroyed by strange creatures who don't want us bothering them?

Anyhow, it is still important to send up rockets and space capsules to explore. The pictures we got to see and rock samples that come back are also fascinating. Someday maybe people will travel to far off countries and set up new civilizations. This would be a good chance to eliminate some of the overcrowded life on earth. We could also learn alot about what kind of gas or air, or surface other places have. This might help us back on earth too. The space program is also good for people's egos. It also may take their minds off of problems in our own world, which is not so bad.

We are spending far too much money on space travel and space exploration. As the question points out it would be far better to use these funds to help improve our own society and better our living conditions here on earth.

Analysis of Sample Essay 2A

1. There are several weaknesses in the essay. First, the writer does not take a clear stand. Does this student support or reject the thesis that space travel is of value and should be funded by the government? The first paragraph presents both views. The second paragraph basically supports the need for space exploration. The third paragraph, the concluding one, rejects this view, pointing out that too much money is needlessly spent on "space travel and space exploration." The essay ends up being confusing and disorganized.

2. The essay also contains many weaknesses in technical English. Problems in spelling and diction appear throughout *(humans* instead of *human beings* in the third sentence of the first paragraph; *alot* instead of *a lot* in the fifth sentence of the second paragraph; *off of* instead of *off* in the eighth sentence of the second paragraph). There are several awkward and ill-phrased sentences.

3. The writer appears to understand the basic elements of essay organization, and the essay contains an introduction referring to the question, a development of supporting details, and a summarizing conclusion. Unfortunately, the lack of coherence strongly detracts from the value of the piece.

Suggestions for Improvement

In the second paragraph, the first sentence ends with the infinitive "to explore," but it lacks an object of the infinitive. The second sentence of the second paragraph has a poorly ended verb clause. A better sentence would be, "The pictures and rock samples that came back to use . . . ." The word *good* is used three times in the second paragraph and should be replaced by more specific words, such as *valuable* or *important*.

Sample Essay 2B

In our own country we have so many people who are unemployed and without jobs. Their families are without proper shelter and often don't have the money to buy the necessary food and clothing. If we took a portion of this money and provided employment for the jobless and homes for the homeless we would be doing our citizens a service. We could also use this money to develop research in medicine and find the cures for fatal diseases like cancer and HIV. Then we would be using our money correctly. What good is it to read about a flight to the moon when you are hungry or out of work.

I know that many people say that we have to be first in everything. That our national pride demands it. If we spend millions of dollars, we should be proud of the achievements of our scientists. Also we learn so many things about our vast universe and the world in which we live in.

Does this make good sense. I think that Charity begins at home. Lets not worry about what's happening on the moon. Let's be more concerned about what's happening here on the earth.

Analysis of Sample Essay 2B

1. The writer has a point of view that is clear and consistent.
2. Paragraph one provides excellent examples to support what is evidently the writer's position: that the money for space exploration should be used on earth to help society.
3. The conclusion provides a summary and reinforces the writer's point of view.

Suggestions for Improvement

1. The author of this essay appears to have begun the essay in the middle. There is no introductory paragraph stating the issue or the writer's position. In the middle of the first paragraph the writer refers to "this money," but the reader doesn't know what "this money" is. While you don't need to restate the question word for word, you do need to include it in your introduction to provide the reader with a frame of reference.
2. Unfortunately, the many errors in punctuation, grammar, and usage seriously reduce the effectiveness of the essay and would no doubt lower the grade considerably. The writer should try to eliminate redundancies such as "unemployed and without jobs." End-stop punctuation is weak. The author uses periods instead of question marks to conclude the interrogative sentence in the last sen-

tence of the first paragraph and the first sentence of the concluding paragraph. There is no reason to capitalize "Charity" (in the second sentence of the third paragraph), and although "Let's" is spelled correctly in the fourth sentence of the third paragraph, the necessary apostrophe is omitted in the same word in the preceding sentence. A careful proofreading of the essay might have helped the writer to locate and correct many of these errors.

SUMMING IT UP

Don't forget to:

- Set a timer for 25 minutes.
- Read the prompt.
- Decide whether you agree or disagree with it.
- Plan and write an essay within the 25 minutes.
- Score it against the rubric.

For more practice, use the following quotations as writing prompts.

"Life is not a spectacle or a feast; it is a predicament."

"There is only one thing age can give you, and that is wisdom."

"Not to know is bad; not to wish to know is worse."

"Public employees should not have the right to strike."

"Every young American should serve the nation, either in the armed forces or in community service."

Guide to Good Writing

OVERVIEW

- Agreement
- Principal parts of verbs
- Verb tense
- The subjunctive mood
- Pronouns
- Comparisons
- Modifiers
- Sentence fragments
- Run-on sentences
- Levels of usage
- Confusing words
- Capitalization
- Punctuation
- Summing it up

In Chapter 6 you reviewed the steps in the writing process and learned how the essay graders will be using a rubric to score your essay. Although the readers are trained to take a holistic approach to scoring, they will consider grammar, usage, and mechanics. Points won't be subtracted for errors in these areas, but the readers will take note of them. Why? Because as the College Board says "pervasive errors in grammar, usage, or mechanics [can] persistently interfere with meaning." It's not that the reader is looking to see if you forget to use a comma or that you use a cliché, but how this affects meaning.

This chapter reviews many of the rules of standard English grammar and punctuation. While we're not attempting to teach you all the rules of punctuation and grammar, we do want you to review those rules that may be tested or that you may need to call on for your own writing.

This chapter also teaches you to identify and correct sloppy language—both in your own essay and in improving sentences and paragraphs on the test. These are clichés, incorrectly used idioms, mixed metaphors, and wordiness. Remember that this review can also help you with the multiple-choice questions on the SAT's writing section.

The review for each element of the chapter—grammar, usage, and punctuation—is broken up into manageable sections. The sections are followed by exercises with answer explanations. Be sure to read all the answer explanations, even for the questions you answered correctly. Repetition is an important part of your SAT preparation.

AGREEMENT

Basic Rule

A verb agrees in number with its subject. A singular subject takes a singular verb. A plural subject takes a plural verb.

Examples: The <u>boy</u> <u>is</u> studying.

                      S   V

The <u>teacher</u> <u>was</u> dozing while his <u>students</u> <u>were</u> studying.

      S   V   S   V

Choose the *correct verb:* (is, am, are) John, Mary, Bill, and I _____ going to spend the summer together.

Explanation: Remember that the verb must agree with the subject. Since the subject is plural—subjects joined by *and* are plural—a plural verb is needed. The correct response therefore should be:

John, Mary, Bill, and I *are* going to spend the summer together.

Caution

Sometimes the subject comes after the verb, but the rule still applies.

Choose the correct verb: (is, are) There _____ three more items on the agenda.

Explanation: Are is correct since the subject *items* is plural and requires a plural verb.

Caution

There is one major exception to this rule. When the sentence is introduced by the word "there" and the verb is followed by a compound (double) subject, the first part of the subject dictates whether the verb should be singular or plural.

Example: There *is one woman* in the living room and four women in the kitchen.

When compound subjects are joined by *either-or* or *neither-nor,* the verb agrees with the subject closest to the verb.

Examples: Neither the young man nor *his friends have had* much practice.

           Neither you nor *I am* willing to serve as chairperson.

Explanation: In the first example, *friends* (plural) is closest to the verb; in the second example, *I* (singular) is closest to the verb.

Caution

Sometimes a word or a group of words may come between the subject and the verb. The verb still must agree with the simple subject, and the *simple subject is never part of a prepositional phrase.*

Example: The author of the three books *is* well known.

The simple subject is *author,* a singular noun. The verb must be *is.*

Choose the correct verb: (was, were) The causes of the war ___ not known.

Explanation: The simple subject is *causes; of the war* is a prepositional phrase. Since the subject is plural, the plural verb *were* is required.

Correct: The *causes* of the war *were* not known.

Basic Rule

A pronoun agrees with the word it refers to (the *antecedent)* in both person and number.

> *Example:* They deposited their money in the bank since they were afraid they might lose *it.*
>
> *Explanation:* The pronoun *it* refers to *money,* the antecedent.

Caution

Remember to use a singular pronoun when you refer to words such as *everyone, everybody, each, every, anyone, anybody, nobody, no one, one, each, either,* and *neither.*

> *Examples: Everyone* should take *his* coat (not *their).*
>
> Each *woman* brought *her* child (not *their).*
>
> We heard that *none* of the men neglected to bring *his* ticket (not *their).*

Caution

Collective words present special problems. A *collective* names a group of people or things. Although usually singular in form, it is treated as either singular or plural according to the sense of the sentence:

Singular when members of the group act, or are considered, as a *unit:*

> The junior *class is sponsoring* the fund drive.

Plural when the members act, or are considered, *individually:*

> The *Boston Red Sox have* finally won a World Series.

Common collectives include:

> assembly, association, audience, board, cabinet, class, commission, committee, company, corporation, council, counsel, couple, crowd, department, family, firm, group, jury, majority, minority, number, pair, press, public, staff, United States

The following short words—though seldom listed as collectives—are governed by the rule for collectives. They are singular or plural according to the intended meaning of the sentence.

> all, any, more, most, some, who, which

TIP

The third person singular of most verbs ends in "s."
First person *I, we speak;*
Second person *you speak;*
Third person *he, she, it speaks.*
Examples:
He runs.
She jogs.
It jumps.
The man sees.
Mary laughs.
The child walks.

Skill Builder: Principles of Agreement

Directions: Try the following skill builder to see if you understand the basic principles of agreement. Then choose the correct word for each blank.

1. (is, are) Bill and Jean ___ going to the game tomorrow.
2. (have, has) Either Jay or his friends ___ the answer key.
3. (was, were) There ___ several students absent last week.
4. (his, their) I hope that no one has left ___ homework at home.
5. (her, their) Each of the sisters celebrated ___ birthday at the Plaza.
6. (is, are) The music of Verdi's operas ___ filled with dramatic sweep.
7. (his, their) All the musicians tuned ___ instruments.
8. (know, knows) Neither Mark nor the twins ___ the correct answer.
9. (go, goes) Either Mrs. Martinez or Carlos ___ to church each week.
10. (is, are) However, neither the seller nor the buyers ___ satisfied with the arrangement.

Answers and Explanations

1. **are**   The subject, *Bill and Jean,* is plural.
2. **have**   The verb must agree with the word closest to it, in this case a plural, *friends.*
3. **were**   The subject, *students,* is plural.
4. **his**   The antecedent is *no one,* which requires the singular, *his.*
5. **her**   The antecedent, *each,* requires the singular pronoun.
6. **is**   The subject of the verb is singular, *music.*
7. **their**   The antecedent of the pronoun is *musicians,* a plural.
8. **know**   In a *neither-nor* construction, the verb is governed by the closest subject, *twins.*
9. **goes**   The verb is governed by *Carlos,* a singular noun.
10. **are**   In a *neither-nor* construction, the verb is governed by the closest subject, *buyers.*

Skill Builder: Subject-Verb Agreement

Directions: In the following paragraph, there are ten words underlined. If the word is grammatically correct, write C in the margin; if a change is necessary, indicate the change and give a grammatical reason for it. Do not make unnecessary changes.

Joseph, one of my best friends, are planning to be a doctor. He and I feel that medicine,
                                        1   2

of all the professions, are one of the most exciting. He has asked each of his friends to
                         3

give their opinion and everyone stated what they thought was most valid. Then Joseph
     4   5

asked his parents what they think he should do. It seems that his friends and his mother
                      6

is in agreement but his father do not agree. His father strongly feels that the medical
7   8

profession, unlike other professions, requires too much study and will be too taxing.
                             9

There is always several considerations that must be examined before making a choice.
    10

Answers and Explanations

1. **is** The subject, *Joseph,* is singular.
2. **C** The subject, *He and I,* is plural.
3. **is** The subject, *medicine,* is singular.
4. **his** The antecedent *each* governs the singular pronoun *his.*
5. **he** The antecedent *everyone* governs the singular pronoun *his.*
6. **C**
7. **are** The plural subject *his friends and his mother* governs the plural verb *are.*
8. **does** Since the subject, *father,* is singular, a singular verb is required.
9. **C**
10. **are** The subject, *considerations,* a plural, requires a plural verb.

PRINCIPAL PARTS OF VERBS

We indicate tense by changing the verb itself or by combining certain forms of the verb with auxiliary verbs. The verb tenses from which we derive every form of a verb are called the *principal parts*. The three principal parts of a verb are:

1. Present Tense: *talk, write*
2. Past Tense: *talked, wrote*
3. Present Perfect Tense: *have talked, has written*

Principal Parts of Regular Verbs

Verbs are classified as *regular* (or weak) and *irregular* (or strong), according to the way in which their principal parts are formed. Regular verbs form their past tense and present perfect tense by the addition of *-ed* to the infinitive:

Present Tense	Past Tense	Present Perfect Tense
talk	talked	has (have) talked
help	helped	has (have) helped
walk	walked	has (have) walked

The principal parts of irregular verbs are formed by changes in the verb itself:

Present Tense	Past Tense	Present Perfect Tense
see	saw	has (have) seen
say	said	has (have) said
go	went	has (have) gone

Principal Parts of Common Irregular Verbs

Present	Past	Past Participle
arise	arose	arisen
be	was, were	been
bear	bore	borne
become	became	become
begin	began	begun
bid	bade	bid, bidden
blow	blew	blown
break	broke	broken
bring	brought	brought
build	built	built
buy	bought	bought
catch	caught	caught
choose	chose	chosen
cling	clung	clung
come	came	come
cut	cut	cut
do	did	done
draw	drew	drawn
drink	drank	drunk
drive	drove	driven
eat	ate	eaten
fall	fell	fallen
feed	fed	fed
feel	felt	felt
fight	fought	fought
find	found	found
flee	fled	fled
fling	flung	flung
fly	flew	flown
forget	forgot	forgotten
forgive	forgave	forgiven
freeze	froze	frozen
get	got	gotten
give	gave	given
go	went	gone
grow	grew	grown
hang (a person)	hanged	hanged
hang (an object)	hung	hung
hear	heard	heard
hide	hid	hidden
hold	held	held
hurt	hurt	hurt
keep	kept	kept
know	knew	known
lay	laid	laid

Present	Past	Past Participle
lead	led	led
leave	left	left
lend	lent	lent
lie	lay	lain
light	lit, lighted	lit, lighted
lose	lost	lost
make	made	made
meet	met	met
ride	rode	ridden
ring	rang	rung
rise	rose	risen
run	ran	run
see	saw	seen
send	sent	sent
shake	shook	shaken
shoot	shot	shot
shrink	shrank, shrunk	shrunk, shrunken
sit	sat	sat
slay	slew	slain
sleep	slept	slept
slide	slid	slid
speak	spoke	spoken
spend	spent	spent
spin	spun	spun
spring	sprang, sprung	sprung
stand	stood	stood
steal	stole	stolen
sting	stung	stung
strive	strove	striven
swear	swore	sworn
swim	swam	swum
swing	swung	swung
take	took	taken
teach	taught	taught
tear	tore	torn
tell	told	told
think	thought	thought
throw	threw	thrown
wake	waked, woke	waked, woken
wear	wore	worn
weave	wove	woven
win	won	won
wring	wrung	wrung
write	wrote	written

Skill Builder: Verb Form

Directions: Choose the correct form of the verb.

1. (hanged, hung) The picture was ___ on the wall nearest the bay window.
2. (sewn, sewed) She has ___ the hem on the skirt perfectly.
3. (frozen, freezed, froze) The water has not ___ on the pond sufficiently.
4. (lent, loaned) The bank ___ him the required money.
5. (drank, drunk) He ___ all the poison from the vial.
6. (flang, flinged, flung) He ___ the papers on the desk and ran out of the room.
7. (lieing, lying, laying) You have been ___ on the beach for over 2 hours.
8. (losed, lost) He had to pay a fine because he ___ the book.
9. (hanged, hung) The outlaw was ___ in the town square.
10. (rang, rung) They ___ the bell so softly that we did not hear it.

Answers
1. hung
2. sewed
3. frozen
4. lent
5. drank
6. flung
7. lying
8. lost
9. hanged
10. rang

Skill Builder: Verb Agreement

Directions: Write the correct form of the verb on the blank provided.

1. (come) A gentleman has _____ to see you.
2. (suppose) Bill was _____ to telephone you last night.
3. (begin) My friend has _____ to get impatient.
4. (catch) He has _____ a serious cold.
5. (sing) He could _____ before large groups, if asked.
6. (sing) She has _____ before large groups several times.
7. (go) They have already _____ to the theater.
8. (give) He has _____ me excellent advice.
9. (devote) He is _____ to his parents.
10. (build) The engineer has designed and _____ his own home.

Answers

1. come
2. supposed
3. begun
4. caught
5. sing
6. sung
7. gone
8. given
9. devoted
10. built

VERB TENSE

Basic Rule

Use the same verb tense whenever possible within a sentence or paragraph. Do not shift from one tense to another unless there is a valid reason.

Incorrect: Joan *came* home last week and *goes* to her home in the country where she *spends* the last weekend of her vacation.

Correct: Joan *came* home last week and *went* to her home in the country where she *spent* the last weekend of her vacation.

When to Use the Perfect Tenses

Basic Rule

Use *present perfect* for an action begun in the past and extended to the present.

Example: I am glad you are here at last; I *have waited* an hour for you to arrive.

Explanation: In this case, *I waited* would be incorrect. The action *have waited* (present perfect) began in the past and extends to the present.

Basic Rule

Use *past perfect* for an action begun and completed in the past before some other past action.

Example: The foreman asked what *had happened* to my eye.

Explanation: In this case, *what happened* would be incorrect. The action *asked* and the action *had happened* (past perfect) are used because one action (regarding the speaker's eye) is "more past" than the other (the foreman's asking).

Basic Rule

Use *future perfect* for an action begun at any time and completed in the future.

Example: When I reach Chicago tonight, my uncle *will have left* for Los Angeles.

Explanation: In this case the action *will have left* is going to take place before the action *reaches,* although both actions will occur in the future. When there are two future actions, the action completed first is expressed in the future perfect tense.

Skill Builder: Verb Tense

Directions: In the following sentences, select the correct verb tense.

1. (cheer, have cheered, cheered) When he spoke, all the people _____ him.
2. (is, was, be) Since he _____ late, he didn't receive a gift.
3. (had completed, have completed) I am told that you _____ the job.
4. (had completed, have completed) I was told that you _____ the job.
5. (are, were) We were taught that vitamins _____ important for our well-being.

Answers

1. cheered
2. was
3. have completed
4. had completed
5. are (When you are expressing a permanent fact, the *present tense* is used.)

THE SUBJUNCTIVE MOOD

Basic Rule

The *subjunctive mood* expresses a condition contrary to fact, a wish, a supposition, or an indirect command. Although it is going out of use in English, the subjunctive can still be seen in the following forms:

- To express a wish not likely to be fulfilled or impossible to be realized.

  I wish it *were* possible for us to approve his transfer at this time. (It is *not* possible.)

- In a subordinate clause after a verb that expresses a command, a request, or a suggestion.

  He asked *that* the report *be* submitted in duplicate.

  It is recommended *that* this office *be* responsible for preparing the statements.

  We suggest *that* he *be* relieved of the assignment.

- To express a condition known or supposed to be contrary to fact.

  If I *were* in St. Louis, I should be glad to attend.

  If this *were* a simple case, we would easily agree on a solution.

  If I *were* you, I should not mind the assignment.

- After *as if* or *as though.* In formal writing and speech, *as if* and *as though* are followed by the subjunctive, since they introduce as supposition something not factual. In informal writing and speaking, the indicative is sometimes used.

  He talked *as if* he *were* an expert on taxation. (He's not.)

  This report looks *as though* it *were* the work of a college freshman.

Caution

Avoid shifts in mood. Once you have decided on the mood that properly expresses your message, use that mood throughout the sentence or the paragraph. A shift in mood is confusing to the listener or reader; it indicates that the speaker or writer himself has changed his way of looking at the conditions.

Not: It is requested that a report of the proceedings *be* prepared and copies *should be* distributed to all members. (*Be* is subjunctive; *should be,* indicative.)

But: It is requested that a report of the proceedings *be* prepared and that copies *be* distributed to all members.

Skill Builder: Mood

Directions: In the following sentences, fill in the correct mood.

1. (was, were)   If Mark _____ to win the student council presidency, the entire school would be surprised.

2. (was, were)   If he _____ to go to the party, he would be welcome.

3. (be, should be)   The principal asked that the coach _____ present when the award was given.

4. (was, were)   The team played as if the game _____ the final game in the playoffs.

Answers and Explanations

1. were   The sense of the sentence tells you that Mark is unlikely to win, so the subjunctive is correct.

2. was   There is nothing conditional about the construction. It is a simple statement.

3. be   The statement expresses a request, so the conditional is correct.

4. were   The phrase *as if* signals the need for the subjunctive mood.

PRONOUNS

Pronouns substitute for nouns.

Examples: Helen is my sister; *she* is older than my brother.

Bill just purchased a new wristwatch; *it* keeps perfect time.

The following pronoun chart may prove helpful:

Number	Person	Subjective Case	Objective Case	Possessive Case
Singular	1st person	I	me	mine
	2nd person	you	you	yours
	3rd person	he, she, it, who	him, her, it, whom	his, hers, whose
Plural	1st person	we	us	ours
	2nd person	you	you	yours
	3rd person	they, who	them, whom	theirs, whose

Basic Rule

The subject of the sentence is in the subjective case. The subject of each verb is in the subjective case. If the pronoun is used as an appositive to the subject or as a predicate nominative, the pronoun is kept in the subjective case.

Incorrect: John and *him* were chosen.

Correct: John and *he* were chosen. *(He is the subject of the verb; we certainly would not say that him was chosen.)*

Incorrect: It was *her* who was chosen.

Correct: It was *she* who was chosen.

Incorrect: *Us* students were chosen.

Correct: *We* students were chosen.

Incorrect: He is as witty *as her.*

Correct: He is as witty *as she.*

Incorrect: I will give the book to *whomever* comes first.

Correct: I will give the book to *whoever* comes first. (Don't be fooled by the preposition *to;* we would say *who comes* since *who* [or *whoever*] is the subject of the verb *comes.*)

Basic Rule

If a pronoun is the object of a verb or preposition, it is placed in the objective case.

Incorrect: They accused Tom and *he* of stealing.

Correct: They accused Tom and *him* of stealing.

(*Him* is the object of the verb *accused;* they *accused him*, not *he.*)

Incorrect: The tickets were given to the instructor and *I.*

Correct: The tickets were given to the instructor and *me.*

(*Me* is the object of the preposition *to;* the tickets were given *to me*, not to *I.*)

Incorrect: *Who* did you see?

Correct: *Whom* did you see?

(*Hint:* Make this a declarative sentence: You saw *him.*)

Basic Rule

A pronoun that expresses ownership is in the possessive case.

Personal pronouns that express ownership never require an apostrophe.

Incorrect: This book is *your's*, not *her's.*

Correct: This book is *yours*, not *hers.*

A pronoun that precedes a gerund is usually in the possessive case.

Incorrect: He rejoiced at *him* going to the party.

Correct: He rejoiced at *his* going to the party.

(In this sentence, *going* is a *gerund*, a verb ending in *-ing* used as a noun.)

Basic Rule

Do not use forms of the same pronoun to refer to different antecedents.

Not: The teacher told John that *he* thought *his* work was improving. (Does the teacher think that his own work is improving, or that John's work is improving?)

But: John was told by *his* teacher that *his* work was improving.

Basic Rule

Place the pronoun as close as possible to its antecedent to avoid ambiguity or confusion.

Not: The letter is on the desk *that* we received yesterday.

But: The *letter that* we received yesterday is on the desk.

Caution

Be sure that the reference to an antecedent is specific.

Not: *When* you have finished the book and written your summary, please return it to the library. (What are you returning? The book or the summary?)

But: When you have finished the book and written your summary, please return *the book* to the library.

Caution

The impersonal use of *it, they,* and *you* tends to produce vague, wordy sentences.

Not: In the manual *it* says to make three copies.

But: The manual says to make three copies.

Not: They say we are in for a cold, wet winter.

But: The *almanac* predicts a cold, wet winter.

Skill Builder: Pronouns

Directions: Some of the following sentences contain misused pronouns. Make all corrections. If the sentence is correct, indicate by marking it with a C.

1. We are happy that Bob, Bill, and he are going to be there.

   _____

2. I know that us men will be able to complete the job by next week.

   _____

3. Whoever is here will see Mr. Smythe and me.

   _____

4. They objected to them taking the exam late.

   _____

5. He is more intelligent than her.

   _____

6. He is not as good a runner as Mary or her.

   _____

7. He will change the sweater for her.

   _____

8. He laughed at me addressing such a prestigious group.

   _____

9. If you get here before John or me, please tell the director that the poor roads may have caused John and me to drive slowly.

   _____

10. Who are you thinking about, John or me?

    _____

Answers and Explanations

1. C
2. I know that *we* men will be able to complete the job by next week.
3. C
4. They objected to *their* taking the exam late.
5. He is more intelligent than *she.*
6. He is not as good a runner as Mary or *she.*
7. C
8. He laughed at *my* addressing such a prestigious group.
9. C
10. *Whom* are you thinking about, John or me? (*Hint:* You are thinking about *me*; both pronouns require the objective case.)

COMPARISONS

Basic Rule

When two things are being compared, the comparative form of the adjective is used. The comparative is formed in one of two ways: (1) Adding *-er* to the adjective; (2) placing *more* before the adjective.

Examples: He is *more* educated than his brother.

She is *prettier* than her sister.

Note

Do not use *both* of the above methods.

Not: Jeremy is *more wiser* than we know.

But: Jeremy is *wiser* (or *more wise)* than we know.

Basic Rule

When three or more things are compared, the superlative form of the adjective is used. The superlative is formed in one of two ways: (1) adding *-est* to the adjective; (2) placing *most* before the adjective.

Examples: Of all the books, this one is the *most* difficult.

Which is the *shortest* of all Shakespeare's plays?

Incorrect: Mary is the *shorter* of all her friends.

Correct: Mary is the *shortest* of all of her friends.

Note

Do not use both of the above methods.

Not: This is the *most sharpest* knife I have.

But: This is the *sharpest* knife I have.

Note

Some modifiers are compared by changes in the words themselves. A few of these irregular comparisons are given below; consult your dictionary whenever you are in doubt about the comparisons of any adjective or adverb.

Positive	Comparative	Superlative
good	better	best
well	better	best
bad (evil, ill)	worse	worst
badly (ill)	worse	worst
far	farther, further	farthest, furthest
late	later, latter	latest, last
little	less, lesser	least
many, much	more	most

Caution

Some adjectives and adverbs express qualities that go beyond comparison. They represent the highest degree of a quality and, as a result, cannot be improved. Some of these words are listed below:

complete	deadly	immortally
correct	exact	infinitely
dead	horizontally	perfect
perfectly	secondly	totally
perpendicularly	square	unique
preferable	squarely	uniquely
round	supreme	universally

Note

The use of the comparative in such an expression as *This thing is better than any other* implies that *this thing* is separate from the group or class to which it is being compared. In these expressions a word such as *other* or *else* is required to separate the thing being compared from the rest of the group of which it is a part.

Not: Our house is cooler than any house on the block. (The mistake here is not separating the item being compared—*house*—from the group to which it is being compared.)

But: Our house is cooler than any *other* house on the block. (Our house is one of the houses on the block.)

Not: He has a better record than any salesman in our group.

But: He has a better record than any *other* salesman in our group. (*He* himself is one of the salesmen in the group.)

Caution

Be careful of incomplete comparisons. The result is illogical and confusing.

Incorrect: The plays of Shakespeare are as good as Marlowe.

Correct: The plays of Shakespeare are as good as *those* of Marlowe.

Incorrect: His skill in tennis is far better than other athletes his age.

Correct: His skill in tennis is far better than *that* of other athletes his age.

Incorrect: His poetry is as exciting, if not more exciting than, the poetry of his instructor.

Correct: His poetry is as exciting *as,* if not more exciting than, the poetry of his instructor.

Skill Builder: Comparisons

Directions: Some of the following sentences have incorrect comparisons. Correct the mistake on the lines provided.

1. Ashlyn played better basketball than anyone on her team.

   _____

2. I thought that *Mill on the Floss* was deadly, but *The Mayor of Casterbridge* was deadlier.

   _____

3. Cleveland is far from New York than Philadelphia.

   _____

4. Sekou is taller than Liam and Liam is taller than Jake, so Jake must be the smaller.

   _____

5. Writing that research paper was the worse assignment I ever had.

   _____

Answers and Explanations

1. Add *else,* so that the sentence reads "than anyone else on her team." Ashlyn needs to be separated from the category of players.

2. *Deadly* is one of those words that cannot be used in a comparison. A rewrite might be "was deadly, too." Or "I thought that *Mill on the Floss* was very boring, but *The Mayor of Casterbridge* was deadly."

3. **farther**   The word *than* signals that this is a comparison. Because only two cities are being compared, only the comparative is needed.

4. **smallest**   Three people are being compared, so the correct form is the superlative.

5. **worst**   The sense of the sentence tells you that the speaker is comparing this assignment with all others, so the superlative is needed.

MODIFIERS

Basic Rule

Modifiers should be placed as close as possible to the words they modify. This is true whether the modifier is a single word, a phrase, or a clause.

Incorrect: I bought a piano from an old lady with intricate carvings.

Correct: Who or what had the carvings? It would be better to write: I bought a piano with intricate carvings from an old lady.

Incorrect: I read about the destruction of Rome in my history class.

Correct: In my history class, I read about the destruction of Rome.

Caution

The word *only* often causes confusion. Examine the following sentences.

Only he kissed her.

He *only* kissed her.

He kissed *only* her.

All three sentences are possible, but a different meaning is conveyed in each, depending on the positioning of the word *only.*

Caution

Sometimes a problem is created by the placement of a participle phrase.

Incorrect: *Answering* the doorbell, the cake remained in the oven. (The *cake* answered the *doorbell*?)

Correct this sentence by adding a subject to which the phrase can refer:

Correct: Answering the doorbell, *we* forgot to take the cake from the oven.

Incorrect: Falling on the roof, *we* heard the sound of the rain.

Correct: *We* heard the sound of the rain falling on the roof.

Skill Builder: Modifiers

Directions: Rewrite the following sentences so that the word being modified is clear.

1. He tripped on a crack in the pavement going to school.

   _____

2. Mary only failed the test.

   _____

3. Did you see the film about the five on the boat on television?

   _____

4. The police officer ordered the man to stop in his patrol car.

   _____

5. Upon picking up the phone, the noise became muted.

   _____

6. While swimming, a fish nibbled on my toe.

   _____

7. He went to the old church to pray for the people on Cemetery Hill.

   _____

8. Of all his admirers, his wife only loved him.

   _____

9. Upon entering the class, the chalkboard came into view.

   _____

10. The baby was pushed by his mother in a stroller.

   _____

Answers

1. Going to school, he tripped on a crack in the pavement.
2. Only Mary failed the test.
3. Did you see the film on television about the five on the boat?
4. The police officer in his patrol car ordered the man to stop.
5. When we picked up the phone, the noise became muted.
6. While I was swimming, a fish nibbled on my toe.
7. He went to the old church on Cemetery Hill to pray for the people.
8. Of all his admirers, only his wife loved him.
9. When we entered the class, the chalkboard came into view.
10. The baby was in a stroller pushed by his mother.

SENTENCE FRAGMENTS

Basic Rule

Every sentence must have a complete subject and verb and express a full idea. There are three ways to correct incomplete sentences:

① Add the fragment to the sentence that precedes it.

② Add the fragment to the sentence that follows it.

③ Add a subject and verb to the fragment.

Incorrect: My uncle is a very unusual person. A man fluent in several languages.

Correct: My uncle is a very unusual person, a man fluent in several languages.

Explanation: The fragment is added to the sentence that precedes it.

Incorrect: Worrying about how to prepare for the examination. I finally decided to set up a conference with my instructor to ask for advice.

Correct: Worrying about how to prepare for the examination, I finally decided to set up a conference with my instructor to ask for advice.

Explanation: The fragment is added to the sentence that follows it.

Incorrect: Slipping on the ice.

Correct: Slipping on the ice, the elderly woman lost her balance and fell.

Explanation: A subject and verb are added to the fragment.

Caution

Do not use a phrase as a sentence.

Incorrect: To walk down the street.

Incorrect: Walking down the street.

Incorrect: By walking down the street.

Correct: By walking down the street, you will pass many places of interest.

Incorrect: In the afternoon.

Incorrect: By mid-day.

Correct: We will see you sometime in the afternoon.

Caution

If a sentence begins with a subordinating conjunction such as *If, When, Since, Because,* or *Although,* a comma usually comes after the dependent clause and is followed by a main clause.

Incorrect: Although she is young. She is weary and aimless.

Incorrect: Although she is young she is weary and aimless.

Correct: Although she is young, she is weary and aimless.

Skill Builder: Sentence Correction

Directions: Read the following pairs of sentences carefully. Circle the letter of the answer next to the correctly written sentence in each pair.

1. **(A)** Late registration, at best, is always a difficult experience; especially since so many sections are no longer available.

   (B) Late registration, at best, is always a difficult experience, especially since so many sections are no longer available.

2. **(A)** We try to arrive on time, feeling this is crucial to the whole process.

   (B) We try to arrive on time. Feeling this is crucial to the whole process.

3. **(A)** Usually, the night before we review all the courses we should like to take. Making out a schedule that we feel would be desirable.

   (B) Usually, the night before, we review all the courses we should like to take, making out a schedule that we feel would be desirable.

4. **(A)** If we are fortunate. We move through the lines quickly; if not, we see what changes must be made to avoid conflicts.

   (B) If we are fortunate, we move through the lines quickly; if not, we see what changes must be made to avoid conflicts.

5. **(A)** It is helpful to keep a sense of humor and two aspirins with you on the day of registration. I certainly do.

   (B) It is helpful to keep a sense of humor and two aspirins with you on the day of registration. As I do.

Answers

1. B
2. A
3. B
4. B
5. A

RUN-ON SENTENCES

To confirm what I have now said and further to show the miserable effects of a confined education I shall here insert a passage which will hardly obtain belief in hopes to ingratiate myself farther into his Majesty's favour I told him of an invention discovered between three and four hundred years ago to make a certain powder into an heap of which the smallest spark of fire would kindle the whole in a moment although it were as big as a mountain and make it all fly up in the air together with a noise and agitation greater than thunder that a proper quantity of this powder rammed into an hollow tube of brass or iron according to its bigness would drive a ball of iron or lead with such violence and speed as nothing was able to sustain its force.

—From *Gulliver's Travels* by Jonathan Swift

The paragraph cited above appears to be a jumble of ideas because there are no punctuation marks to help set off thoughts. Indeed, all ideas run into each other. In order to make sense out of the paragraph, we need to use end-stop punctuation to divide complete thoughts or suitable connectors (conjunctions) to join two ideas.

Basic Rule

Do not carelessly run main clauses together without appropriate punctuation or connectors. Run-on sentences can be corrected in several ways.

METHOD 1

The most common way to correct a run-on sentence is to divide the sentence using end-stop punctuation.

Incorrect: The lecture was dull you almost fell asleep.

Correct: The lecture was dull. You almost fell asleep.

Incorrect: Was the lecture dull you almost fell asleep.

Correct: Was the lecture dull? You almost fell asleep.

Incorrect: The lecture was incredibly dull you almost fell asleep.

Correct: The lecture was incredibly dull! You almost fell asleep.

Note

When end-stop punctuation is used, the new thought begins with a capital letter.

In the above three corrections, three different end-stop marks were used:

1. The period (.)
2. The question mark (?)
3. The exclamation point (!)

Caution

The comma is not an end-mark. It cannot be used by itself to separate two sentences.

Incorrect: Close the window, there is a draft in the room.

Correct: Close the window. There is a draft in the room.

METHOD 2

Sometimes, two sentences are very closely related in meaning and full end-stop punctuation may seem too strong. A semicolon can then be used to divide the two sentences. If a semicolon is used, do not use a capital letter to begin the word following the semicolon, unless the word normally begins with a capital letter.

Incorrect: It was a beautiful day there was not a cloud in the sky.

Correct: It was a beautiful day; there was not a cloud in the sky.

METHOD 3

A third way to correct the run-on is to use a connector (conjunction) such as *and, but, for, or,* and *nor,* if the two sentences are equal in importance. It is usually advisable to place a comma before these connectors.

Incorrect: I like to ski, my friend prefers to sit by the fire.

Correct: I like to ski, but my friend prefers to sit by the fire.

Note

Some problem words that may cause run-ons are *however, therefore, consequently,* and *moreover.* These words are not sentence connectors, and when they follow a complete thought, they should be preceded by either a period or semicolon.

Skill Builder: Punctuation

Directions: Examine the following word groups. Wherever you believe a sentence ends, put in the correct punctuation mark and capitalize the next word. Do this only where you feel that punctuation is necessary. Indicate a correct sentence with the letter C. Sometimes it is helpful to read the word groups aloud.

1. It was an exhausting day we could hardly wait to get home.
2. The house was completely empty, no one came to the door.
3. Where had everyone gone all the lights were off.
4. We entered slowly, almost afraid.
5. Suddenly I felt that something was going to happen my heart began to beat furiously.

Answers

1. It was an exhausting day. We could hardly wait to get home.
2. The house was completely empty. No one came to the door.
3. Where had everyone gone? All the lights were off.
4. C
5. Suddenly, I felt that something was going to happen. My heart began to beat furiously. (You might have inserted an exclamation point in place of the final period.)

Skill Builder: Sentence Correction

Directions: Read each sentence below. If you think there is a mistake in a sentence, rewrite the mistake correctly on the blank provided.

1. Playing basketball was Jack's favorite sport, while softball was Sofia's.

   _____

2. School, work, practicing the guitar, homework—Amit never felt he had any free time.

   _____

3. Unhappy about the program, she resigned her job and beginning a new company.

   _____

4. Hoping to regain his former physical health, the retired football player worked out three hours a day, doing push-ups and sit-ups, running on a treadmill, and pumping iron.

   _____

5. Confident of her abilities and sure of her research, the lawyer approached the trial with excitement.

   _____

Answers and Explanations

1. **playing softball** In spoken English most people might have said simply "softball," but in Standard Written English the parallel construction is needed.

2. There are two possibilities for correcting this sentence. One is to replace "practicing the guitar" with "guitar practice," and the other is to add gerunds. The sentence would then read: "Going to school, working, practicing the guitar, and doing homework. . ."

3. **began** The verbs in this compound sentence need to be parallel.

4. **No error.** The phrases are all parallel. The predicate is *worked* and the words *doing, running,* and *pumping* are gerunds.

5. **No error.** The words *confident* and *sure* are both adjectives modifying *lawyer.*

LEVELS OF USAGE

Successful writers select words that are appropriate and correct for the purpose. It is important for a writer to know the difference between standard and nonstandard English. Your awareness of this difference will be tested on the writing section of the SAT.

Standard English is the language of instruction, scholarship, and public speaking. It is used to convey precise, exact meaning. This is the level of writing that a college student is expected to master. It is the level of writing that is being tested on the SAT.

Nonstandard English includes colloquialisms, such as ungrammatical constructions, slang, obsolete words, and jargon. While colloquialisms may be appropriate in informal conversation, they should be avoided in formal speaking and writing, including your SAT essay.

Effective expression is more than just using words correctly. It also means avoiding clichés, using idioms properly, creating images that are both logical and appropriate, and eliminating unnecessary words.

Clichés

A *cliché* is an expression that seems dull and unimaginative because of overuse. The effectiveness and originality that such expressions once possessed are no longer present. Perhaps the first time someone wrote "busy as a bee," the expression was clever. By now, however, readers are so used to seeing it that all the sparkle is gone and it has become a cliché. The careful writer will try very hard to avoid using trite phrases, including the following:

abreast of the times	budding genius
acid test	burning the midnight oil
after all is said and done	busy as a bee
agony of suspense	by and large
all in all	by leaps and bounds
all work and no play	center of attention
along these lines	checkered career
as luck would have it	clear as crystal
at a loss for words	clinging vine
at the tender age of	cold as ice
bathed in tears	conspicuous by (in) its absence
beat a hasty retreat	cool as a cucumber
beauties of nature	covers a multitude of sins
better half (husband or wife)	deadly earnest
better late than never	deep, dark secret
bitter end	die laughing
blood is thicker than water	doomed to disappointment
blushing bride	drastic action
bolt from the blue	easier said than done
brave as a lion	equal to the occasion
bright and early	eyes like stars
brown as a berry	fair sex

favor with a selection

few and far between

fiber of his (my) being

footprints on the sands of time

force of circumstances

generous to a fault

goes without saying

goodly number

good points

green with envy

hanging in the balance

heartfelt thanks

heated argument

heavy as lead

Herculean efforts

hungry as bears

ignorance is bliss

in great profusion

in one fell swoop

in the final analysis

institution of higher learning

it stands to reason

last but not least

last straw

life's little ironies

lion's share

mantle of snow

meets the eye

method to his madness

neat as a pin

needs no introduction

never got to first base

nipped in the bud

none the worse for wear

on the ball

paramount issue

partake of refreshment

poor but honest

powers that be

promising future

pure and simple

quick as a flash

rear its ugly head

reigns supreme

riot of color

rotten to the core

sad to relate

sadder but wiser

sea of faces

self-made man

short but sweet

sigh of relief

simple life

skeleton in the closet

slow but sure

snow-capped mountains

soul of honor

steady as a rock

straight from the shoulder

strong as a lion

strong, silent type

struggle for existence

sturdy as an oak

sweat of his brow

take my word for it

thereby hangs a tale

this day and age

thunderous applause

time marches on

time of my life

tiny tots

tired but happy

too funny for words

untiring efforts

view with alarm

walk of life

the weaker sex

wee, small hours

wheel of fortune

white as a sheet

white as snow

with bated breath

words fail me

work like a dog

the worse for wear

wreathed in smiles

Prepositional Idioms

Prepositional idioms are among the most confusing word-choice issues for writers. Which prepositions go with which words? For example, "you replace something *with* something else," but you "substitute something *for* something else." Or, "since that *implies* something, you can *infer from* it." It can be very confusing. Here is a list of words that often give writers trouble:

abounds in (or *with*) This letter *abounds in* mistakes.

accompanied by (a person) The salesman was *accompanied by* the buyer.

accompanied with (a present) He *accompanied* the closing of the contract *with* a gift.

acquiesce in The executives were compelled to *acquiesce in* the director's policy.

acquit of The manager was *acquitted of* the charges against him.

adept in (or *at*) He is *adept in* typing.

agree to (an offer) The firm *agrees to* your payment in settlement of the claim.

agree upon (or *on*) (a plan) We must *agree upon* the best method.

agree with (a person) I *agree with* the doctor.

angry about (an event, situation) I am very *angry about* the high unemployment rate.

angry at (a thing, an animal) The child is *angry at* his stuffed animals.

angry with (a person) We were *angry with* the careless attendant. (Mad is used informally to mean *angry,* but, more properly, it means *insane.*)

appropriate for (meaning *suitable to*) The gown is also *appropriate for* a dinner dance.

available for (a purpose) The specialist is *available for* a consultation now.

available to (a person) What course of action is *available to* you at this time?

averse to The President is *averse to* increasing his staff.

cognizant of He was not *cognizant of* dissension among the workers.

coincide with Your wishes *coincide with* mine in this situation.

commensurate with What you earn will be *commensurate with* the amount of effort you apply to your task.

compare to (shows similarity between things that have different forms) In one sonnet, Shakespeare *compares* a woman's hair *to* wire.

compare with (shows similarity or difference between things of like form) The assignment was to *compare* Thoreau's essays *with* Emerson's.

compatible with The ideas of the section manager should be *compatible with* those of the buyer.

comply with If you do not wish to *comply with* his request, please notify him at once.

conducive to The employer's kindness is *conducive to* good work.

conform to (or *with*) The average person *conforms to* the vote of the majority.

conversant with We need a salesman who is fully *conversant with* what he is selling.

desirous of We are not *desirous of* a price increase.

different from This new machine is *different from* the old one.

differ from (a thing in appearance) A coat *differs from* a cape.

differ with (an opinion) I *differ with* your views on public affairs.

dissuade from She will *dissuade* him *from* making that investment.

employed at (a definite salary) The student aide is *employed at* the minimum wage.

employed in (certain work) His brother is *employed in* reading blueprints.

envious of Some of the employees are *envious of* his good fortune.

identical to (or *with*) These stockings are *identical to* those I showed you last week.

in accordance with Act *in accordance with* the regulations.

infer from I *infer from* his remarks that he is dissatisfied.

in search of He set out *in search of* fame and fortune.

necessary to Your help is *necessary to* the success of the project.

oblivious of (or to) The typist is *oblivious of* the construction noise outside.

opposite to (or *from*) (meaning contrary) Your viewpoint is *opposite to* mine.

pertinent to Your comment is not really *pertinent to* the discussion.

plan to Do you *plan to* go to the play tonight?

prefer to She *prefers* silk *to* polyester.

prior to You will receive a deposit *prior to* the final settlement.

required of The letter states what is *required of* you.

stay at He wants to *stay at* home this evening.

vie with The salesmen are *vying with* one another for this week's prize.

Mixed Metaphors

A *metaphor* is a figure of speech that makes an implied comparison. Unlike a simile, which is a comparison using *like* or *as* as indicators, the metaphor does not make use of indicators. If used correctly, metaphors and similes may add vividness and color to writing, but if used incorrectly, the opposite effect may result and the writing can become trite and even silly. You should be careful to use metaphors that are appropriate to the style of your essay and logical in construction. If the logic is faulty, a *mixed metaphor* may result.

Good: James Joyce once wrote, "My body was like a harp and her words and gestures like fingers running upon wires."

Poor: The lovely ocean beat against the shore with its strident voice clawing at the sands.

Good: The ballet dancer floated through space, her feet tracing graceful circles in the air.

Poor: The ballet dancer's feet moved with hushed grace, flapping their wings with flowery movements.

Wordiness

Wordiness involves needless repetition of words or phrases that do not add meaning or give called-for emphasis to the sentence. Very often a sentence can be made more effective by eliminating needless repetitions, or redundancies, and expressing the thought in a more compact way.

Repeating Meaning

Instead of:	Say:
the honest truth	the truth
blue in color	blue
same exact	same
the month of June	June
new innovation	innovation
consensus of opinion	consensus
repeat again	repeat

Repeating Words

Instead of:	Say:
In which pool did he swim *in*?	In which pool did he swim?
From what school did you graduate *from*?	From what school did you graduate?
At which position are you working *at*?	At which position are you working?

Unnecessary Use of Pronouns After a Noun

Instead of:	Say:
My aunt *she* is a social worker.	My aunt is a social worker.
The boy and girl *they* will both be here.	The boy and girl will both be here.
The teacher *he* gave a difficult assignment.	The teacher gave a difficult assignment.

Unnecessary Expressions

Instead of:	Say:
In my opinion, I believe that	I believe that
In the event of an emergency	In an emergency
On the possibility that it may	Since it may

Wordy Phrases

Instead of:	Say:
close to the point of	close to
have need for	need
with a view to	to
in view of the fact that	because
give consideration to	consider
mean to imply	imply
disappear from view	disappear
in this day and age	today
the issue in question	issue
come in contact with	meet

Skill Builder: Usage and Grammar

Directions: In the space provided, indicate:

(A) If the sentence contains language that is not idiomatic.

(B) If the sentence contains wordy or repetitious elements.

(C) If the sentence contains a cliché or mixed metaphor.

(D) If the sentence is correct.

1. He prepared very thoroughly for the interview, because his job was hanging in the balance. _____

2. He is the kindest, happiest person I have ever met. _____

3. Please try not to be too mad at your sister, since your parents are very worried about her health. _____

4. It is amazing and incredible how doctors and physicians are able to replace various and sundry elements of the human body with synthetic plastic parts. _____

5. She wanted to arrive early, but, as luck would have it, the car broke down on the highway almost immediately. _____

6. He launched the program like a rocket but then couldn't keep its momentum above water. _____

7. We need a campaign that is different than the one our adversary is employing in this election year. _____

8. The newly elected member of the forum who was just given membership status was not eager to meet with and be presented to the governing body. _____

9. I am afraid that he was deadly earnest when he told you that story yesterday. _____

10. Did the board of trustees agree with your offer to negotiate the contract after the first of the month? _____

11. They are envious at our family's many close friends and associates. _____

12. Please stop making such a nuisance of yourself. _____

13. When she ran around the corner and collided with the postman, all the wind was taken from her sails and her speed disintegrated. _____

14. I try to see every film that is shown in the movie theater across the street from my office. _____

15. Neither Sue or/nor Mary is going to start to proceed with the test experiment until and unless we are all together in a group again. _____

16. I sent him out in search for a good pastrami sandwich on rye bread. _____

17. My brother Ben, my sibling, is incapable of and unable to accept the position he was offered last night. _____

18. The director stated that the final round of auditions would be held on Monday. _____

19. I may be allowed to attend the concert, perhaps, but yet I shall need to get permission obtained from my mother. _____

20. She was a brilliant child who entered college at the tender age of 15. _____

Answers and Explanations

1. **The correct answer is (C).** The cliché "was hanging in the balance" should be eliminated. Better: "because his job depended on it."

2. **The correct answer is (D).** This sentence is correct.

3. **The correct answer is (A).** *Mad at* should be changed to *angry with*.

4. **The correct answer is (B).** The sentence contains wordy and repetitious elements *(amazing and incredible, doctors and physicians, various and sundry, synthetic plastic)* that should be condensed.

5. **The correct answer is (C).** The cliché "as luck would have it" should be eliminated.

6. **The correct answer is (C).** Since *rockets* don't operate in *water*, the sentence contains a mixed metaphor.

7. **The correct answer is (A).** *Different than* should be changed to *different from*.

8. **The correct answer is (B).** The sentence contains wordy and repetitious elements *(who was just given membership status, and be presented to)* that should be eliminated.

9. **The correct answer is (C).** The cliché "deadly earnest" should be eliminated. Better: "he was serious."

10. **The correct answer is (A).** *Agree with* should be changed to *agree to*.

11. **The correct answer is (A).** *Envious at* should be changed to *envious of*.

12. **The correct answer is (D).** This sentence is correct.

13. **The correct answer is (C).** The combination of *she ran, wind was taken from her sails,* and *speed disintegrated* results in a mixed metaphor in the sentence.

14. **The correct answer is (D).** This sentence is correct.

15. **The correct answer is (B).** The sentence contains wordy and repetitious elements *(or/nor, start to proceed, test experiment, until and unless)* that should be revised or eliminated.

16. **The correct answer is (A).** *In search for* should be changed to *in search of*.

17. **The correct answer is (B).** The sentence contains wordy and repetitious elements *(my sibling, incapable of and)* that should be eliminated.

18. **The correct answer is (D).** This sentence is correct.

19. **The correct answer is (B).** The sentence contains wordy and repetitious elements *(perhaps, yet; obtained)* that should be eliminated.

20. **The correct answer is (C).** The cliché "the tender age of" should be eliminated. Better: ". . . when she was only 15 years of age."

CONFUSING WORDS

The following pages review groups of words that are similar in sound and/or meaning and are generally found to be confusing to students and adults alike. Misunderstanding what they mean or how they are used results in various usage problems. The word groups have been broken down into manageable sections to help you learn them more easily. Do not try to master all the information at once. Study one section at a time. At the end of each section there is a practice exercise. See how well you do on the exercise by checking your answers against the answers and explanations given. If you do well, go on to the next section. If you find that you have made a number of errors, review the section. It is important that you master each section before moving on to the next one.

Confusing Words: Group 1

a is used before words that start with a consonant sound
an is used before words that start with a vowel sound

> Please give the baby *a* toy.

> He is *an* only child. We put up *a* united front. *(United* begins with a consonant sound—*y*.)

> We spent *an* hour together. *(Hour* begins with a vowel sound, since the *h* is silent.)

and is used to join words or ideas

> We enjoy shopping *and* sightseeing.

> She is a very serious student, *and* her grades are the best in the class.

accept means *to receive* or *to agree* to something
except means *to exclude* or *excluding*

> I'll *accept* the gift from you.

> Everyone *except* my uncle went home.

> My uncle was *excepted* from the group of losers.

advice means *counsel* (noun), opinion
advise means *to offer advice* (verb)

> Let me give you some free *advice*.

> I'd *advise* you to see your doctor.

affect means *to influence* (verb)
effect means *to cause* or *bring about* (verb) or a *result* (noun)

> The pollution *affected* our health.

> Our lawsuit *effected* a change in the law.

> The *effect* of the storm could not be measured.

all ready means *everybody* or *everything ready*
already means *previously*

> They were *all ready* to write when the test began.

> They had *already* written the letter.

all together means *everybody* or *everything together*
altogether means *completely*

> The boys and girls stood *all together* in line.
>
> His action was *altogether* strange for a person of his type.

desert (DEZZ-ert) means an *arid area*
desert (di-ZERT) means *to abandon,* or *a reward or punishment* (usually plural)
dessert (di-ZERT) means the *final course of a meal*

> I have seen several movies set in the Sahara *desert.*
>
> The soldier was warned not to *desert* his company.
>
> We're certain that execution is a just *desert* for his crime.
>
> He received his just *deserts.*
>
> We had strawberry shortcake for *dessert.*

in is used to indicate *inclusion, location,* or *motion within limits*
into is used for *motion toward* one place *from* another

> The spoons are *in* the drawer.
>
> We were walking *in* the room.
>
> I put the spoons *into* the drawer.

it's is the contraction of *it is* or *it has*
its is a possessive pronoun meaning *belonging to it*

> *It's* a very difficult assignment.
>
> *It is* a very difficult assignment.
>
> We tried to analyze *its* meaning.

lay means *to put*
lie means *to recline*

> *To lay:*
>
> (present)   I lay
>
> (past)   I laid the gift on the table.
>
> (present perfect) I have laid
>
> *To lie:*
>
> (present)   I lie
>
> (past)   I lay on my blanket at the beach.
>
> (present perfect) I have lain

lets is third person singular present of *let*
let's is a contraction for *let us*

> He *lets* me park my car in his garage.
>
> *Let's* go home early today.

loose means *not fastened or restrained,* or *not tight-fitting*
lose means *to mislay, to be unable to keep, to be defeated*

> The dog got *loose* from the leash.
>
> Try not to *lose* your umbrella.

passed is the past tense of *to pass*

past means *just preceding* or *an earlier time*

> The week *passed* very quickly.

> The *past* week was a very exciting one.

principal means *chief* or *main* (adjective), or a *leader,* or a *sum of money* (noun)

principle means a *fundamental truth or belief*

> His *principal* support comes from the real estate industry.

> The *principal* of the school called a meeting of the faculty.

> He earned 10% interest on the *principal* he invested last year.

> As a matter *of principle,* he refused to register for the draft.

quiet means *silent, still*

quit means *to give up or discontinue*

quite means *very* or *exactly, to the greatest extent*

> My brother is very shy and *quiet.*

> I *quit* the team last week.

> His analysis is *quite* correct.

raise means *to lift, to erect*

raze means *to tear down*

rise means *to get up, to move from a lower to a higher position, to increase in value*

> The neighbors helped him *raise* a new barn.

> The demolition crew *razed* the old building.

> The price of silver will *rise* again this month.

set means *to place something down* (mainly)

sit means *to seat oneself* (mainly)

> *To set:*
> (present)   He sets
> (past)   He set the lamp on the table.
> (present perfect)   He has set
> *To sit:*
> (present)   He sits
> (past)   He sat on the chair.
> (present perfect)   He has sat

stationary means *standing still*

stationery means *writing material*

> In ancient times, people thought that the earth was *stationary.*

> We bought our school supplies at the *stationery* store.

suppose means *to assume* or *guess*
supposed is the *past tense* and also *past participle* of *suppose*
supposed also means *ought to* or *should* (when followed by *to*)

>   I *suppose* you will be home early.
>   I *supposed* you would be home early.
>   I had *supposed* you would be there.
>   I am *supposed to* be in school tomorrow.

than is used to express *comparison*
then is used to express *time* or *a result or consequence*

>   Jim ate more *than* we could put on the large plate.
>   I knocked on the door, and *then* I entered.
>   If you go, *then* I will go, too.

their means *belonging to them*
there means *in that place*
they're is the contraction for *they are*

>   We took *their* books home with us.
>   Your books are over *there* on the desk.
>   *They're* coming over for dinner.

though means *although* or *as if*
thought is the past tense of *to think*, or *an idea* (noun)
through means *in one side and out another, by way of, finished*

>   *Though* he is my friend, I can't recommend him for this job.
>   I *thought* you were serious!
>   We enjoyed running *through* the snow.

to means *in the direction of* (preposition); it is also used before a verb to indicate the *infinitive*
too means *very, also*
two is the numeral 2

>   We shall go *to* school.
>   It is *too* hot today.
>   We shall go, *too*.
>   I ate *two* sandwiches for lunch.

use means *to employ, put into service*
used is the past tense and the past participle of *use*

>   I want to *use* your chair.
>   I *used* your chair.

used meaning *in the habit of* or *accustomed to*, is followed by *to*
used is an adjective meaning *not new*

>   I am *used to* your comments.
>   I bought a *used* car.

weather refers to *atmospheric conditions*

whether introduces a *choice;* it should not be preceded by *of* or *as to*

    I don't like the *weather* in San Francisco.

    He inquired *whether* we were going to the dance.

were is a past tense of *be*

we're is a contraction of *we are*

where refers to *place* or *location*

    They *were* there yesterday.

    We're in charge of the decorations.

    Where are we meeting your brother?

who's is the contraction for *who is* (or *who has*)

whose means *of whom,* implying ownership

    Who's the next batter?

    Whose notebook is on the desk?

your is a possessive, showing ownership

you're is a contraction for *you are*

    Please give him *your* notebook.

    You're very sweet.

Skill Builder: Spelling

Directions: Underline the correct choice.

1. He is the (principal, principle) backer of the play.
2. I hope your company will (accept, except) our offer.
3. We hope to have good (weather, whether) when we are on vacation.
4. Put the rabbit back (in, into) the hat.
5. The attorney will (advice, advise) you of your rights.
6. She is far taller (than, then) I imagined.
7. Are they (all ready, already) to go?
8. She answered the letter on shocking pink (stationary, stationery).
9. What is the (affect, effect) you are trying to achieve?
10. I want to (set, sit) next to my grandfather.
11. He's going to (lay, lie) down for a nap.
12. I'm (all together, altogether) tired of his excuses.
13. He saluted when the flag (passed, past) by.
14. I'd like another portion of (desert, dessert).
15. Try not to (loose, lose) your good reputation.

Answers

1. principal
2. accept
3. weather
4. into
5. advise
6. than
7. all ready
8. stationery
9. effect
10. sit
11. lie
12. altogether
13. passed
14. dessert
15. lose

Skill Builder: Sentence Correction

Directions: Check ✓ the space provided if the sentence is correct; if there is an error, correct it.

1. How much will the final examination effect my grade? _____
2. What is it your trying to suggest? _____
3. If it's a clear day, let's go sailing. _____
4. I don't have too much money with me. _____
5. She's not use to such cold weather. _____
6. He ate a apple before lunch. _____
7. The cost of the coat will raise again. _____
8. They are all though with the task. _____
9. Who's basketball are we using? _____
10. We live in a clean and quite neighborhood. _____
11. You are suppose to be home at six o'clock. _____
12. Where are their bags? _____
13. Her cat ran straight for it's bowl of food. _____
14. Are they leaving when we're leaving? _____
15. Have their been any calls for me? _____

Answers

1. affect
2. you're
3. ✓
4. ✓
5. used
6. an
7. rise
8. through
9. Whose
10. quiet
11. supposed
12. ✓
13. its
14. ✓
15. there

Confusing Words: Group 2

abbreviate means *to shorten by omitting*
abridge means *to shorten by condensing*

New York is *abbreviated* to NY.
In order to save time in the reading, the report was *abridged*.

ad is used informally, but in formal usage *advertisement* is correct; similarly: exam (examination), auto (automobile), phone (telephone), gym (gymnasium)

advantage means *a superior position*
benefit means a *favor conferred or earned* (as a profit)

He had an *advantage* in experience over his opponent.
The rules were changed for his *benefit*.

aggravate means *to make worse*
annoy means *to bother* or *to irritate*

Your nasty comments *aggravated* a bad situation.
Your nasty comments *annoyed* him. (Not: Your nasty comments aggravated him.)

ain't is an unacceptable contraction for *am not, are not,* or *is not,* although *ain't* is sometimes heard in very informal speech

alibi is an *explanation on the basis of being in another place*

excuse is an *explanation on any basis*

> The accused man's *alibi* was that he was in another town when the robbery occurred.
>
> Whenever he is late, he makes up a new *excuse*.

all ways means *in every possible way*

always means *at all times*

> He was in *all ways* acceptable to the voters.
>
> He was *always* ready to help.

almost means *nearly, not quite*

most refers to the *greatest amount or number* or to the *largest part, a majority*

> We are *almost* finished writing the book.
>
> *Most* of the credit should be given to his uncle.

alongside of means *side by side with*

alongside means *parallel to the side*

> He stood *alongside of* her at the corner.
>
> Park the car *alongside* the curb.

allot means *to give* or *apportion*

> I will *allot* 3 hours for painting the table.

alot is a misspelling of *a lot*

> He earned *a lot* of money. (Better: He earned *a great deal* of money.)

alright is now often employed in common usage to mean *all right* (In formal usage, *all right* is still preferred by most authorities.)

all right means *satisfactory, very well, uninjured,* or *without doubt*

> I'm *alright,* thank you.
>
> It was his responsibility, *all right*.

alternate, as a noun, means a *substitute* or *second choice*

alternate, as a verb, means to *perform by turns*

alternative means a *choice between two things, only one of which may be accepted*

> She served as an *alternate* delegate to the convention.
>
> The cook *alternated* green beans and cauliflower on the menu.
>
> Is there an *alternative* to the proposition? (In less formal usage, *alternative* is not always limited to a choice between *two.)*

alumna means *a female graduate* (plural: alumnae; *ae* rhymes with key)

alumnus means *a male graduate* (plural; almuni; *ni* rhymes with high)

> She is an *alumna* of Mrs. Brown's School for Young Women.
>
> He is an *alumnus* of City College.

among is used to discuss *more than two* items
between is used to discuss *two* items only
> The work was divided *among* the four brothers.
> She divided the pie *between* Joe and Marie.

amount is used to refer to *a quantity not individually countable*
number is used to refer to *items that can be counted individually*
> A tremendous *amount* of work had piled up on my desk.
> We ate a great *number* of cookies at the party.

annual means *yearly*
biannual means *twice a year* (also semiannual)
biennial means *once in two years* or *every two years*
> Are you going to the *annual* holiday party?
> I received *biannual* car insurance statements in April and in October.
> He gets a new car *biennially*.

anxious means *worried*
eager means *keenly desirous*
> We were *anxious* about our first airplane flight.
> I am *eager* to see you again.

anyways is an incorrect form for *anyway*
anywheres is an incorrect form for *anywhere*
> I didn't want to go *anyway*.
> I couldn't locate her *anywhere*.

aren't I is used informally, but in formal usage *am I not* is correct
> *Am I not* entitled to an explanation?

as is not always as clear as *because, for,* or *since* (also see *like*)
> She wants to cry *because* she is very sad.

as, used as a *conjunction,* is followed by a verb
like, used as a *preposition,* is *not* followed by a verb
> Do as I do, not *as* I say.
> Try not to behave *like* a child.

as...as is used in an *affirmative* statement
so...as is used in a *negative* statement
> She is *as* talented *as* any other actress in the show.
> He is *not so* reliable *as* his older brother.

as good as is used for *comparisons,* not to mean *practically*
> This bicycle is *as good as* the other one.
> They *practically* promised us a place in the hall. (Not: They *as good as* promised us a place in the hall.)

astonish means *to strike with sudden wonder*
surprise means *to catch unaware*
>   The extreme violence of the hurricane *astonished* everybody.
>   A heat wave in April would *surprise* us.

at should be avoided when it does not contribute to the meaning of an idea
>   *Where do you live at?* may be heard in informal usage, but *Where do you live?* is the correct form.
>   The group will arrive *about* noon. (not *at about* noon)

awfully is sometimes heard in informal usage. In formal usage, *very* is correct.
>   This pie is very good. (not *awfully* good)

a while is used after a preposition (noun)
awhile is used in other cases (adverb)
>   I coached the team for *a while*.
>   I coached the team *awhile*.

backward and **backwards** both may be used as adverbs
>   We tried to skate *backward*. (Or: *We tried to skate backwards.*)

bad is used after verbs that refer to the senses, such as *look, feel* (adjective)
badly means *greatly, in a bad manner* (adverb)
>   He felt *bad* that he could not attend the meeting.
>   The young man needs a part-time job very *badly*.

been is the past participle of *to be*, used after helping verbs *have, has,* or *had*
being is the *-ing* form of *to be*, usually used after helping verbs *is, am, are, was,* and *were*
>   I have *been* living here for six years.
>   He was *being* a troublemaker, so we told him to stay away from us.

being as and **being that** should not be used in standard English. *Because* and *since* are preferable.
>   *Since* it was dark, we turned on the lights.
>   *Because* he is my friend, I give him a gift.

Skill Builder: Usage

Directions: Check ✓ the space provided if the sentence is correct; if there is an error in usage, correct it.

1. He shared the riches between Laura, Millie, and Ernestine. _____
2. We are all ways available to babysit for you during the week. _____
3. The housing law was rewritten for his advantage. _____ .
4. Alot of the time, he falls asleep at nine o'clock. _____
5. The colorful advertisement caught my attention as I skimmed through the magazine. _____
6. It was hard to keep track of the amount of people who visited him last week. _____
7. He claims that he ain't going to vote in the next election. _____
8. I see him in the park most every day. _____
9. The coach sent in the alternate quarterback. _____
10. Are you certain that he is alright now? _____
11. She is beginning to aggravate her mother. _____
12. He is the school's oldest living alumnus. _____
13. I read an abridged version of the novel. _____
14. He invents a new alibi whenever he forgets his keys. _____
15. He guided the canoe alongside of the riverbank. _____
16. Being as it is Wednesday, we are going to a Broadway matinee. _____
17. He is anxious to be finished with the dental treatment. _____
18. Let's surprise him with a party tomorrow. _____
19. I been looking for a good used car, but I haven't located one yet. _____
20. The club will hold its luncheon anywheres you decide. _____
21. Where do you want to meet at? _____
22. I feel very badly that I drank all the coffee. _____
23. His manners are terrible; he is eating just as a child. _____
24. I gave you as much as I can afford. _____
25. He is an awfully good instructor. _____
26. He responded in a loud voice: "Am I not capable of deciding for myself?" _____
27. My aunt just went inside to rest a while. _____
28. It was around noon when we met for lunch. _____

Answers

1. among
2. always
3. benefit
4. A lot
5. ✓
6. number
7. is not
8. almost
9. ✓
10. all right
11. annoy
12. ✓
13. ✓
14. excuse
15. alongside (delete *of*)
16. Since
17. eager
18. ✓
19. have been
20. anywhere
21. delete *at*
22. bad
23. like
24. ✓
25. a very
26. ✓
27. awhile
28. about

Confusing Words: Group 3

beside means *at the side of*

besides means *in addition to*

> In our tennis game, he played *beside* me at the net.
>
> We entertained Jim, Sue, and Louise, *besides* the members of the chorus.

better means *recovering*

well means *completely recovered*

better is used with the verb *had* to show desirability

> He is *better* now than he was a week ago.
>
> In a few more weeks, he will be *well*.
>
> He *had better* (not *he better*) follow instructions or pay the penalty.

between you and I is incorrect form, since the object of the preposition *between* should be the objective case *me*, not the subjective case *I*

> *Between you and me,* he has not been very helpful this week.

both means *two considered together*

each means *one of two or more*

> *Both* of the applicants qualified for the position.
>
> *Each* applicant was given a good reference.

bring means *to carry toward the speaker*

take means *to carry away from the speaker*

> *Bring* the coat to me.
>
> *Take* money for carfare when you leave.

bunch is used informally to describe a group of people, but in formal usage *group* is preferred

> When he returned to his office, he learned that a *group* of students was waiting for him.

burst is used in present and past tenses to mean *to explode* (or *to break*)

bust and **busted** are incorrect forms of *burst*

> I do hope the balloon will not *burst*.
>
> He cried when the balloon *burst*. (not *busted*)

but that is sometimes heard in informal usage, but in formal usage *that* is correct

> He never doubted *that* she would visit him.

can means *able*

may implies *permission* or *possibility*

> I *can* eat both desserts.
>
> *May I* eat both desserts?
>
> It *may* snow tonight.

cannot seem is sometimes used informally, but in formal usage *seems unable* is correct
> My elderly uncle *seems unable* to remember his own phone number.

complected should not be used for *complexioned*
> At the beach, the fair-*complexioned* boy stayed under an umbrella.

consistently means *in harmony*
constantly means *regularly, steadily*
> If you give me advice, you should act *consistently* with that advice.
> I *constantly* warned him about leaving the door unlocked.

continual means *happening again and again at short intervals*
continuous means *without interruption*
> The teacher gave the class *continual* warnings.
> Noah experienced *continuous* rain for forty days.

could of is an incorrect form of *could have,* which can be contracted to *could've* in speech or informal writing
> I wish that I *could've gone.* (Better: I wish that I *could have gone.*)

couple refers to *two; several* or *a few* refers to *more than two*
> Alex and Frieda are the most graceful *couple* on the dance floor.
> A *few* of my cousins—Mary, Margie, Alice, and Barbara—will be at the reunion tonight.

data is the Latin plural of *datum,* meaning *information* (*data* is preferred with plural verbs and pronouns, but is now acceptable in the singular)
> *These data* were very significant to the study. (Or: *This data* was very significant to the study.)

did is the past tense of *do*
done is the past participle of *do*
> I *did* whatever was required to complete the job.
> I have *done* what you requested.

different than is often used informally, but in formal usage *different from* is correct
> Jack is *different from* his brother.

disinterested means *impartial*
uninterested means *not interested*
> The judge must be a *disinterested* party in a trial.
> I'm an *uninterested* bystander, so I find the proceedings boring.

doesn't is a contraction of *does not* (third person singular)
don't is a contraction of *do not* and is not a substitute for *doesn't*
> She *doesn't* go to school.
> They *don't* go to school.

doubt whether is often heard in informal usage, but *doubt that* is the correct form
> I *doubt that* I will be home this evening.

due to is sometimes used informally at the beginning of a sentence, but in formal usage *because of, on account of,* or some similar expression is preferred
> *Because of* (not *due to*) the rain, the game was postponed. (But: The postponement was *due to* the rain.)

each other refers to *two persons*
one another refers to *more than two persons*
> Jane and Jessica have known *each other* for many years.
> Several of the girls have known *one another* for many years.

either...or is used to refer to choices
neither...nor is the negative form
> *Either* Lou *or* Jim will drive you home.
> *Neither* Alice *nor* Carol will be home tonight.

else than is sometimes heard in informal usage, but in formal usage *other than* is correct
> Shakespeare was rarely regarded by students as anything *other than* the writer of plays.

enthuse or **enthused** should be avoided; use *enthusiastic*
> We were *enthusiastic* when given the chance to travel abroad.

equally as good is an incorrect form; *equally good* or *just as good* is correct
> This bicycle is *just as good* as that one.

etc. is the abbreviation for the Latin term *et cetera,* meaning *and so forth, and other things.* In general, it is better to be specific and not use *etc.*
> I think that oranges, peaches, cherries, *etc.,* are healthful. (*Etc.* is not preceded by *and*)

everyone, written as one word, is a *pronoun*
every one, written as two words, is used to refer to each *individual*
> *Everyone* present voted for the proposal.
> *Every one* of the voters accepted the proposal.

every bit is incorrect usage for *just as*
> You are *just as* (not *every bit as*) clever as she is.

ever so often means *frequently* or *repeatedly*
every so often means *occasionally* or *now and again*
> He sees his brother *ever so often,* practically every day.
> Since tickets are so expensive, we only attend the theater *every so often.*

expect is sometimes used incorrectly to mean *assume* or *presume*
> I *assume* (not *expect*) that he won the race.

Skill Builder: Usage

Directions: Check ✓ the space provided if the sentence is correct; if there is an error in usage, correct it.

1. I expect a large bunch of visitors today. _____
2. We wish we could of been with you in Paris. _____
3. She better do what they say. _____
4. The boy got wet when the water balloon busted. _____
5. I brought a couple of books for you; both are historical novels. _____
6. Between you and I, I think that her hat is ugly. _____
7. The continual ticking of the clock was very disconcerting. _____
8. He is standing besides me in the picture. _____
9. We never doubted but that you would make a fine leader. _____
10. Can I have your permission to skip tonight's game? _____
11. Both women were willing to work the night shift. _____
12. Who is your light-complected friend? _____
13. Please take her report card to me at once. _____
14. She cannot seem to get up early enough to eat breakfast with him. _____
15. They are consistently hugging and kissing. _____
16. I expect that you really earned your salary today. _____
17. He said that he done that problem in class. _____
18. They are very enthused about going to the baseball game with you. _____
19. Neither Eleanor or Jan will be dancing in the show tonight, since they are both ill. _____
20. My sister is very different than your sister. _____
21. Because of my heavy work schedule, I can only go fishing every so often. _____
22. I'm truly disinterested in seeing that movie. _____
23. He don't want to cook dinner for us this week. _____
24. You must be every bit as sleepy as I am. _____
25. I doubt whether it will snow today. _____
26. Due to the star's illness, the understudy performed the role. _____
27. My car is equally as good as the one he wants to sell me. _____
28. Sam, Joe, Lou, and Artie have worked with each other before. _____
29. Every one of the soldiers had volunteered for the assignment. _____
30. I like to play racquet sports such as tennis, squash, paddleball, and etc. _____

Answers

1. group
2. could have
3. had better
4. burst
5. ✓
6. you and me
7. continuous
8. beside
9. delete *but*
10. May
11. ✓
12. light-complexioned
13. bring
14. seems unable
15. constantly
16. assume
17. did
18. enthusiastic
19. nor
20. from
21. ✓
22. uninterested
23. doesn't
24. just as
25. that
26. Because of
27. just as good
28. one another
29. ✓
30. delete *and*

Confusing Words: Group 4

fewer is used to refer to items that can be *counted*
less is used to refer to something viewed as *a mass,* not as a series of individual items
> I made *fewer* repairs on the new car than on the old one.
> After the scandal, the company enjoyed *less* prestige than it had the previous year.

finalized is used to mean *concluded* or *complete,* usually in informal usage; in formal usage, *completed* is preferred
> Labor and management *completed* arrangements for a settlement.

flaunt means *to make a display of*
flout means *to show contempt, scorn*
> He *flaunted* his new wealth in an ostentatious manner.
> She *flouted* the policeman's authority.

former means *the first of two*
latter means *the second of two*
> The *former* half of the story was in prose.
> The *latter* half of the story was in poetry.

good is an adjective; *good* is often used informally as an adverb, but the correct word is *well*
> She is a *good* singer.
> She sings *well.*

graduated is followed by the preposition *from* when it indicates completion of a course of study
graduated also means *divided into categories or marked intervals*
> He *graduated from* high school last year. (Or: He *was graduated from* high school last year.)
> A *graduated* test tube is one that has markings on it to indicate divisions.

guess is sometimes used informally to mean *think* or *suppose,* but it is incorrect in formal use
> I *think* (not *guess*) I'll go home now.

habit means an *individual tendency to repeat a thing*
custom means *group habit*
> He had a *habit* of breaking glasses before each recital.
> The *custom* of the country was to betroth girls at an early age.

had ought is an incorrect form for *ought* or *should*
hadn't ought is an incorrect form for *should not* or *ought not*
> The men *ought* (not *had ought*) to go to the game now.
> He *ought not* (not *hadn't ought*) to have spoken.
> He *should not* (not *hadn't ought*) have spoken.

hanged is used in reference to a *person*
hung is used in reference to a *thing*
> The prisoner was *hanged* in the town square.
> The drapes were *hung* unevenly.

have got is incorrect usage; *got* should be omitted
> I *have* an umbrella.

healthful is used to express whatever *gives* health
healthy is used to express whatever *has* health
> He follows a *healthful* diet.
> He is a *healthy* person.

hisself is a misspelling of *himself*
> Let him do it *himself*.

humans is used informally to refer to human beings, but in formal usage *human beings* is correct
> He says that love is a basic need of all *human beings*. (But, used as an adjective: He says that love is a basic *human* need.)

if introduces a *condition*
whether introduces a *choice*
> I shall go to Greece *if* I win the prize.
> He asked me *whether* I intended to go to Greece.

if it was implies that *something might have been true in the past*
if it were implies *doubt* or indicates *something that is contrary to fact*
> If your book *was* there last night, it is there now.
> *If it were* summer now, we would all go swimming.

imply means *to suggest* or *hint* at (the speaker *implies*)
infer means *to deduce* or *conclude* (the listener *infers*)
> Are you *implying* that I have disobeyed orders?
> From your carefree tone, what else are we *to infer*?

in back of means *behind*
in the back of (or *at the back of*) means *in the rear of*
> The shovel is *in back of* (behind) the barn.
> John is sitting *in the back of* the theater.

in regards to is an incorrect form for *in regard to*
> He called me *in regard to* your letter.

instance where is sometimes used informally, but the correct term is *instance in which*
> Can you tell me of one *instance in which* such a terrible thing occurred?

irregardless in an incorrect form for *regardless*

  I'll be your friend *regardless* of what people say, even if the people are accurate.

is when and ***is where*** are sometimes used informally, but in formal usage *occurs when* and *is a place where* are correct

  The best scene *occurs when* the audience least expects it.

  My favorite vacation spot *is a place where* there are no telephones.

kind of and ***sort of*** are informal expressions that should be rephrased in formal writing—for instance, *somewhat* or *rather* are preferable

  I am *rather* sorry he retired.

  He was *somewhat* late for the meeting.

kid is used informally to mean *child* (noun) or *to make fun of* (verb), but is incorrect in formal usage

  My cousin is a very sweet *child*.

  They always laugh when you *make fun of me*.

learn means *to acquire knowledge*
teach means *to give knowledge*

  We can *learn* many things just by observing carefully.

  He is one actor who likes to *teach* his craft to others.

least means the *smallest in degree* or *lowest rank*
less means the *smaller* or *lower of two*

  This is the *least* desirable of all the apartments we have seen.

  This apartment is *less* spacious than the one we saw yesterday.

leave means *to go away from* (a verb is NOT used with *leave*)
let means *to permit* (a verb IS used with *let*)

  Leave this house at once.

  Let me remain in peace in my own house.

lend is a verb meaning *to give to*
loan is a noun denoting *what is given*
borrow means *to take from*

  The bank was willing to *lend* him $500.

  He was granted a *loan* of $500.

  I'd like to *borrow* your electric drill for an hour.

liable means *responsible according to the law*
likely suggests *probable behavior*
> If he falls down the stairs, we may be *liable* for damages.
> A cat, if annoyed, is *likely* to scratch.

libel is a *written and published statement injurious to a person's character*
slander is a *spoken statement of the same sort*
> The unsubstantiated negative comments about me in your book constitute *libel*.
> When you say these vicious things about me, you are committing *slander*.

like is a preposition used to introduce a phrase
as if is used to introduce a clause (a subject and a verb)
as is a conjunction used to introduce a clause
like if is an incorrect form for *like, as,* or *as if*
> It seems *like* a sunny day.
> It seems *as if* it is going to be a sunny day.
> He acted *as* he was expected to act.

many refers to a *number*
much refers to a *quantity* or *amount*
> How *many* inches of rain fell last night?
> *Much* rain fell last night.

may of is an incorrect form for *may have*
might of is an incorrect form for *might have*

Note

Contractions of these terms are unacceptable in formal usage.

> He *may have* been there, but I didn't see him.

> I *might have* gone to the party if I hadn't been ill.

Skill Builder: Usage

Directions: Check ✓ the space provided if the sentence is correct; if there is an error in usage, correct it.

1. She asked him if he wanted to have lunch with her or with her sister. _____
2. There are less details to worry about in this project. _____
3. All humans need to take a certain amount of water into their bodies every week. _____
4. I guess he is a good person. _____
5. We hadn't ought to have shouted out the answer. _____
6. We hope to finalize the deal this month. _____
7. She had a custom of wearing the same necklace to every performance. _____
8. He wanted to arrange the flowers hisself, if that is acceptable to you. _____
9. We were upset when she flaunted her mother's orders. _____
10. I hung the heavy picture in the living room. _____
11. The family was extremely proud when she graduated college last week. _____
12. His girlfriend only eats healthy foods. _____
13. Actually, we thought that the latter comment was excellent. _____
14. He runs good. _____
15. I have got your phone number in my book. _____
16. I'm not certain, but she might of said she was going home. _____
17. Your remark leads me to imply that you are not satisfied. _____
18. He said he can learn you a few things. _____
19. Remember that she is less fortunate than you are. _____
20. How much pounds have you lost so far? _____
21. The swimming pool is in the back of those trees. _____
22. He said such terrible things about her that she is suing him for libel. _____
23. I would like to see you in regards to the apartment you plan to rent. _____
24. Do you intend to enroll your kid in the nursery school? _____
25. Please let me be alone. _____
26. She is always late for work, irregardless of how early she wakes up in the morning. _____
27. She treats her stuffed animal like if it were alive. _____
28. He'll loan you money for the cab. _____
29. He's not likely to be ready yet. _____
30. The most exciting part of the film is when he kills the dragon. _____

Answers

1. whether
2. fewer
3. human beings
4. suppose
5. should not have
6. conclude
7. habit
8. himself
9. flouted
10. ✓
11. graduated from
12. healthful
13. ✓
14. well
15. delete *got*
16. might have
17. infer
18. teach
19. ✓
20. many
21. in back of
22. slander
23. in regard to
24. child
25. ✓
26. regardless
27. as if
28. lend
29. ✓
30. occurs when

Confusing Words: Group 5

maybe means *perhaps, possibly* (adverb)
may be shows *possibility* (verb)
> *Maybe* he will meet us later.
> He *may be* here later.

mighty means *powerful* or *great;* it should not be used in formal writing to mean *very*
> He was *very* (not *mighty*) sleepy.

media is the Latin plural of *medium;* it refers to a means of mass communication or artistic expression and is used with a plural verb
> Most *media* that report the news realize their responsibility to the public.
> That artist's favorite *medium* is watercolor.

must of is incorrect form for *must have*
> I *must have* been sleeping when you called. (A contraction of this term is unacceptable in formal usage.)

myself is used as an *intensifier* if the subject of the verb is *I*
myself instead of *I* or *me,* is not correct
> Since I know *myself* better, let me try it my way.
> My daughter and *I* (not *myself)* will play.
> They gave my son and *me* (not *myself)* some food.

nice is used informally to mean *pleasing, good, fine,* but a more exact, less overused word is preferred
> This is *sunny* (or *good* or *fine*) weather (not *nice* weather).
> He is a *good* (or *kind*) person.

nowheres is incorrect usage for *nowhere*
> The dog was *nowhere* to be found.

off of is sometimes used informally, but *off* is correct in formal usage
> Joe was taken *off* the team.

okay (O.K.) is used informally but is to be avoided in formal writing
> *Informal:* His work is *okay.*
> *Formal:* His work is *acceptable* (or *good*).

on account of is an incorrect form for *because*
> We could not meet you *because* we did not receive your message in time.

oral means *spoken*
verbal means *expressed in words,* either spoken or written
> Instead of writing a note, she gave him an *oral* message.
> Shorthand must usually be transcribed into *verbal* form.

outdoor is an adjective
outdoors is an adverb
>   We spent the summer at an *outdoor* music camp.
>   We played string quartets *outdoors*.

owing to is used informally, but in formal usage *because* is preferred
>   *Because* of a change of management, his company cancelled the takeover attempt.

people comprise a *united or collective group of individuals*
persons are *individuals that are separate and unrelated*
>   The *people* of our city will vote next week.
>   Only ten *persons* remained in the theater after the first act.

per is a Latin term used mainly in business: *per diem* (by the day), *per hour* (by the hour). In formal writing, *according to* or *by the* is preferred
>   As *per* your instructions... (Better: *According* to your instructions...)

plan on is used informally, but in formal usage *plan to* is correct
>   Do you *plan to go* (not *plan on going*) to the lecture?

plenty means *abundance* (noun)
plenty is incorrect as an adverb or adjective
>   There is *plenty* of room in that compact car.
>   That compact car is *very* large (not *plenty* large).

prefer that than is the incorrect form for *prefer that to*
>   I *prefer that to* anything else you might suggest.

put in is incorrect for to *spend, make,* or *devote*
>   Every good student should *spend* (not *put in*) several hours a day doing homework.
>   Be sure *to make* (not *put in*) an appearance at the meeting.

quit is sometimes used informally to mean *stop,* but in formal usage *stop* is preferred
>   Please *stop* your complaining.

quite is used to mean *very* in informal usage, but in formal usage *very* is preferred
>   Your comment was *very* (not *quite)* intelligent.

quite a few is used to mean *many* in informal usage, but in formal usage *many* is preferred
>   My car has *many* (not *quite a few*) dents.

read where is heard in informal usage, but in formal usage *read that* is correct
>   I *read that* the troops were being reviewed today.

real is sometimes used informally instead of *really* or *very*, but in formal usage *really* is correct

    He's a *very* (not *real*) good ballplayer.

    He plays *really* (not *real*) well with the band.

reason is because is used informally in speech, but in formal usage *the reason is that* is correct

    The *reason* she calls *is that* (not *because*) she is lonely. (Or: She calls *because* she is lonely.)

refer back/report back: since *re* means *back* or *again,* the word *back* is redundant and should be omitted

    Please *refer* to your notes.

    Please *report* to the supervisor.

repeat again is redundant; *again* should be omitted

    Please *repeat* the instructions.

respectfully means *with respect and decency*

respectively means *as relating to each, in the order given*

    The students listened *respectfully* to the principal.

    Jane and Lena are the daughters *respectively* of Mrs. Smith and Mrs. Jones.

run is used informally to mean *conduct, manage,* but in formal usage *conduct* or a similar word is preferred

    He wants to *conduct* (not *run*) the operation on a profitable basis.

said is sometimes used in business or law to mean *the* or *this*; in formal usage, *the* or *this* is correct

said is also used incorrectly to mean *told someone*

    When *the* (not *said*) coat was returned, it was badly torn.

    The professor *told us* (not *said*) to study for the examination.

same as is an incorrect form for *in the same way as* or *just as*

    The owner's son was treated *in the same way as* any other worker.

says is present tense of *say*

said is past tense of *say*

    He *says* what he means.

    He *said* what he meant. (*Goes* or *went* should not be used instead of *says* or *said.*)

Skill Builder: Usage

Directions: Check ✓ the space provided if the sentence is correct; if there is an error in usage, correct it.

1. We had a very nice time at the museum. _____
2. She maybe one of the finalists in the contest. _____
3. He stayed indoors on account of the bad weather. _____
4. They are two of my favorite persons. _____
5. That was a mighty foolish thing to do. _____
6. My wife and myself wrote the cookbook together. _____
7. The children are playing outdoors. _____
8. The media is doing the job correctly. _____
9. Their oral presentation was excellent. _____
10. Owing to the high interest rates, she decided not to borrow from the bank. _____
11. There is nowhere for us to sit. _____
12. She may be able to bake fresh bread every week. _____
13. It must of been a beautiful house when it was first built. _____
14. The supervisor wrote that his assistant was doing an okay job so far. _____
15. The art director was taken off of the most profitable account. _____
16. He got quite bruised in a motorcycle accident. _____
17. I hope you'll be able to repeat your marvelous performance again. _____
18. I plan on going to college again next year. _____
19. He went, "Let's go to a movie together." _____
20. I hope that she will quit sending us the job applications. _____
21. The policeman waited his turn same as any other citizen. _____
22. His car is plenty expensive. _____
23. He treats his parents respectfully. _____
24. She's a real intelligent woman. _____
25. The reason the baby is crying is because she is hungry. _____
26. He claims to prefer that to any other idea. _____
27. In rehearsal, she never even referred back to the script. _____
28. He put in several months doing public relations work so that the business proposal would be accepted. _____
29. Does he run the department efficiently? _____
30. We read where your favorite program is being discontinued. _____

Answers

1. a very good (or enjoyable, or a similar word) time
2. may be
3. because of
4. people
5. very
6. I
7. ✓
8. are
9. ✓
10. Because of
11. ✓
12. ✓
13. must have
14. an acceptable (or a similar word) job
15. delete *of*
16. very
17. delete *again*
18. plan to go
19. said
20. stop sending
21. in the same way as
22. very
23. ✓
24. really
25. The reason the baby is crying *is that*..., or: The baby is crying *because* she is hungry.
26. ✓
27. delete *back*
28. spent
29. manage
30. read that

Confusing Words: Group 6

saw is the past tense of *see*
seen is the past participle of *see*
> We *saw* a play yesterday.
> I have never *seen* a Broadway show.

seem is used in informal speech and writing in the expressions *I couldn't seem to* and *I don't seem to,* but in formal usage:
> We *can't find* the address. (Not: We *can't seem to find* the address.)

seldom ever is used informally, but in formal usage *ever* is redundant and should be omitted, or *if* should be inserted
> I *seldom* swim in January.
> I *seldom if ever* swim in January.

shall is used with *I* and *we* in formal usage; informally, I *will (would)* may be used
will is used with *you, he, she, it, they*
> When an emphatic statement is intended, the rule is reversed
> I *shall* be there today.
> We *shall* pay the rent tomorrow.
> I certainly *will* be there.
> They *shall* not pass.

shape is incorrect when used to mean *state* or *condition*
> The refugees were in *serious condition* (not *shape*) when they arrived here.

should of is an incorrect form for *should have,* which can be contracted to *should've* in speech or informal writing
> You *should've* returned that sweater. (Better: You *should have* returned that sweater.)

sink down is sometimes heard in informal usage, but *down* is redundant and should be omitted
> You can *sink* into the mud if you are not careful.

some time means *a segment of time*
sometime means *at an indefinite time in the future*
sometimes means *occasionally*
> I'll need *some time* to make a decision.
> Let's meet *sometime* next week.
> *Sometimes* I have an urge to watch a late movie on television.

stayed means *remained*
stood means *took or remained in an upright position* or *erect*
> He *stayed* in bed for three days.
> The scouts *stood* at attention while the flag was lowered.

still more yet is redundant; *yet* should be omitted
> There is *still more* to be said.

sure is used informally to mean *surely* or *certainly,* but in formal usage *surely* or *certainly* is preferred
> She *certainly* (not *sure)* is pretty!
> We will *surely* be in trouble unless we get home soon.

testimony means *information given orally*
evidence means *information given orally or in writing; an object* that is presented as proof
> He gave *testimony* to the grand jury.
> He presented written *evidence* to the judge.

than any is used informally in a comparison, but in formal usage *than any other* is preferred
> He is smarter *than any other* boy in the class.

the both is used informally, but in formal usage *the* should be omitted
> I intend to treat *both* of you to lunch.

their, in informal usage, often appears in the construction "Anyone can lose their card," but since *anyone* takes a singular personal pronoun, *his* or *her* is the correct form
theirselves is an incorrect form for *themselves*
> They are able to care for *themselves* while their parents are at work.

them is the objective case of *they;* it is not used instead of *those* (the plural of *that)* before a noun
> Give me *those* (not *them)* books!

try and is sometimes used informally instead of *try to,* but in formal usage *try to* is correct
> My acting teacher is going to *try to* attend the opening of my play.

unbeknownst to is unacceptable for *without the knowledge of*
> The young couple decided to get married *without the knowledge of* (not *unbeknownst to)* their parents.

upwards of is an incorrect form for *more than*
> There are *more than* (not *upwards of)* 60,000 people at the football game.

valuable means *of great worth*
valued means *held in high regard*
invaluable means *priceless*
> This is a *valuable* manuscript.
> You are a *valued* friend.
> A good name is an *invaluable* possession.

wait on is sometimes used informally, but in formal usage *wait for* is correct
> We *waited for* (not *on)* him for over an hour.

which is sometimes used incorrectly to refer to people; it refers to things
who is used to refer to people
that is used to refer to people or things
> He decided to wear his orange striped tie, *which* had been a gift from his daughter.
> I am looking for the girl *who* made the call.
> He finally returned the books *that* he had borrowed.

while is unacceptable for *and, but, whereas,* or *though*

>   The library is situated on the south side, *whereas* (not *while)* the laboratory is on the north side.
>   *Though* (not *while)* I disagree with you, I shall not interfere with your right to express your opinion.

who is, who am—Note these constructions:

>   It is *I* who *am* the most experienced.
>   It is *he* who *is...*
>   It is *he or I* who *am...*
>   It is *I or he* who *is...*
>   It is *he and I* who *are...*

who, whom—To determine whether to use *who* or *whom* (without grammar rules): *(Who, Whom)* do you think should represent our company?

>   Step 1: Change the *who—whom* part of the sentence to its natural order:
>   >   Do you think *(who, whom)* should represent our company?
>   Step 2: Substitute *he* for *who,* and *him* for *whom:*
>   >   Do you think *(he, him)* should represent our company?
>   Step 3: Since *he* would be used in this case, the correct form is:
>   >   *Who* do you think should represent our company?

whoever, whomever (see *who, whom* above)

>   Give the chair to *whoever* wants it (subject of verb *wants).*
>   Speak to *whomever* you see (object of preposition *to).*

win—you *win* a game
beat—you *beat* another player; *beat* is incorrect usage for swindle

>   We *won* the contest.
>   We *beat* (not *won)* the other team.
>   The hustler *swindled* the gambler out of twenty dollars.

without is incorrect usage for *unless*

>   You will not receive the tickets *unless* (not *without)* you pay for them in advance.

worst kind and *worst way* are incorrect usages for terms such as *very badly* or *extremely*

>   The school is *greatly in need* of more teachers (not *needs teachers in the worst way).*

would of is an incorrect form for *would have,* which can be contracted to *would've* in informal usage

>   He *would've* treated you to the movies. (Better: He *would have* treated you to the movies.)

would have is *not* used instead of *had* in an *if* clause

>   If I *had* (not *would have)* gone, I would have helped him.

Skill Builder: Usage

Directions: Check ✓ the space provided if the sentence is correct; if there is an error in usage, correct it.

1. He sure did a good job repairing his car. _____
2. Since he had not exercised in three months, he was in very poor shape. _____
3. I seen that movie a long time ago. _____
4. He always takes sometime to concentrate before he shoots the foul shot. _____
5. Anyone who wants to have their conference with me today is invited to meet in my office at ten o'clock. _____
6. She can't seem to learn how to dance the tango. _____
7. There is still more ice cream yet to be eaten. _____
8. The truck rolled into the lake and began to sink to the bottom. _____
9. We should of purchased our tickets in advance. _____
10. The both of them will receive commendations for meritorious service. _____
11. He seldom eats breakfast. _____
12. She scored more points than any player on the team. _____
13. My sister shall pay the bill later. _____
14. Sometime when I am upset, I eat an entire box of cookies. _____
15. He presented his testimony in a soft voice. _____
16. His room is very neat while hers is very messy. _____
17. Joe's friends built the house by theirselves from a set of plans they had drawn up by an architect. _____
18. Of course, I would of taken you with me to California. _____
19. We're tired of seeing them dogs run through our garden. _____
20. Who will stay here with us? _____
21. He will try and be more pleasant to his sister. _____
22. I want to go to the concert in the worst way. _____
23. She wants to meet the boy which scored the winning goal. _____
24. That watch is extremely valuable. _____
25. Unbeknownst to the manager, the men in the shipping department decided to have a party today. _____
26. Upward of one hundred students attended the lecture this morning. _____
27. "I can't go without you pick me up at home," she said. _____
28. I shall give it to whoever arrives first. _____
29. Mike won Josh in the one-on-one basketball game. _____
30. This time, we will not wait on you for more than 10 minutes. _____

Answers

1. certainly, surely
2. condition
3. saw
4. some time
5. his
6. delete *seem to*
7. delete *yet*
8. ✓
9. should have
10. delete *The*
11. ✓
12. than any other player
13. will
14. Sometimes
15. ✓
16. *but,* not *while* (or add a semicolon and delete *while*)
17. themselves
18. would have
19. those dogs
20. ✓
21. try to
22. delete *in the worst way;* add *very badly*
23. who
24. ✓
25. Without the knowledge of
26. More than
27. *unless,* not *without*
28. ✓
29. beat
30. wait for you

CAPITALIZATION

The use of uppercase letters in certain situations is a convention of language and culture. There are languages that do not have capital letters, such as many Middle Eastern and Asian languages. There are many rules about capitalization in Standard Written English. The following are those that you might need in writing your essay. In Standard Written English, you must capitalize:

- The first word of a sentence.

  Example: With cooperation, a depression can be avoided.

- All proper names, as well as a word used as part of a proper noun.

  Examples: William Street is now called Morningside Terrace. (BUT: We have a terrace apartment.) America, General Motors, Abraham Lincoln

- The first, last, and all other important words in a title

  Example: The Art of Salesmanship

- Titles, when they refer to a particular official or family member.

  Examples: The report was read by Secretary Marshall. (BUT: Miss Shaw, our secretary, is ill.)

  Let's visit Uncle Harry. (BUT: I have three uncles.)

- The first word of a direct quotation.

  Example: It was Alexander Pope who wrote, "A little learning is a dangerous thing."

When a direct quotation is broken, the first word of the second half of the sentence is not capitalized.

  "Don't phone," Irene told me," because they're not in yet."

- Adjectives derived from the names of religions, countries, continents, languages.

  Examples: Jewish, British, South American, Spanish

Skill Builder: Capitalization

Directions: Circle any letter that should be capital rather than lowercase.

1. We took a trip to the city of tuscaloosa in alabama last June.
2. *"my brother was an only child* is a very catchy title and should interest people," said the talk show host.
3. The commentator was speaking outside the white house about the president's new budget request.
4. We heard dr. arnold speak at a modern language association conference in Washington.

Answers

1. We took a trip to the city of Tuscaloosa in Alabama last June.
2. *"My Brother Was an Only Child* is a very catchy title and should interest people," said the talk show host.
3. The commentator was speaking outside the White House about the president's new budget request.
4. We heard Dr. Arnold speak at a Modern Language Association conference in Washington.

PUNCTUATION

The Apostrophe

The apostrophe is usually either misused or omitted because of the writer's failure to proofread his paper or because he is not certain about its use. The apostrophe is used:

- To indicate the possessive case *of nouns*. It is not used with possessive pronouns, since such pronouns as *yours, hers, our, theirs*, and *whose* indicate possession already.

- To indicate a *contraction*—the omission of one or more letters.

- To indicate *plurals* of letters, abbreviations, and numbers.

To form the possessive of a noun: If the noun does not end in *s*—whether singular or plural—add an *'s*; if the noun ends in *s* simply add the '. Some writers like to add *'s* to all nouns, even those that already end in *s*.

> *Examples:*   the children's teacher
> the teacher's children
> Keats' poetry (or Keats's poetry)

To form a contraction: Place the apostrophe exactly where the missing letters occur.

> *Examples:*   can't = can not
> it's = it is

To form plurals of letters, abbreviations, and numbers: Usually the apostrophe is used to form the plurals of lowercase letters (a's, b's, c's, etc.), plurals of abbreviations with periods (Ph.D.'s, R.N.'s), and numbers (3's, 6's). With capital letters, abbreviations without periods, and even with numbers when no confusion results, you have a choice. In either case, the writer should be consistent in his or her style.

Skill Builder: Apostrophe Use

Directions: In each of the following sentences, decide if an apostrophe is needed in the italicized words.

1. The *boys* hand was injured.
2. He went to the *doctors* office.
3. The *rooms* were painted bright green.
4. The *colors* were muted by the *suns* rays.
5. The *teachers* had a meeting in the *principals* office.

Directions: Are the following italicized words contractions? If so, what letter(s) are missing? Decide whether or not an apostrophe is needed.

6. *Its* my book.
7. *What's* the matter?
8. I *won't* let him take the test.
9. The cat placed *its* paw in the milk.
10. This book is *hers,* not *yours.*

Answers

1. **boy's** (Since we are speaking of the hand of the boy, we add *'s* to boy.)
2. **doctor's** (We are speaking of the office of the doctor; therefore, we add *'s* to doctor.)
3. **rooms** (This is a simple plural, so no ' is needed.)
4. **sun's** Only *suns* requires the apostrophe since we are speaking of the rays (plural) of the sun; *colors* is a simple plural.
5. **principal's** Since *teachers* is a simple plural, no apostrophe is required; but it is the office of the principal, so we write principal's office.
6. **It's** = It is, so the apostrophe is needed.
7. **What's** = What is, so the apostrophe is correct.
8. **won't** = will not, so the apostrophe is needed. (You might look up wont in the dictionary and discover the meaning.)
9. No apostrophe is called for. This is a pronoun in the possessive case and no letters are missing.
10. No apostrophe is called for. Both *hers* and *yours* are in the possessive case, and no letters are missing.

NOTE
Formal writing tends to avoid the use of contractions. In a formal essay, it is preferable to spell out all words.

Skill Builder: Spelling

Directions: Circle the correct spelling in the following sentences.

1. The (boys, boys') books were stolen.
2. (Mary's, Marys', Marys) hat is new, but (its, it's) slightly soiled.
3. (Whose, Who's, Whoses's) class are you in?
4. There are two (M.B.A.S., M.B.A.'s) working for the firm.
5. He is a member of the (Diner's, Diners) Club.
6. The (ladies, ladies', ladie's) department is on the second floor.
7. The (instructor's, instructors) comments were worthwhile.
8. There are two 6's and three (sevens, 7s, 7's) on the paper.
9. Spell the word with two (t's, T S, Ts) and one r.
10. Is the hat (hers, her's, hers')?; (it's, its, its') certainly not (Joans, Joans', Joan's).

Answers

1. boys'
2. Mary's, it's
3. Whose
4. M.B.A.'s
5. Diner's
6. ladies'
7. instructor's
8. 7's (Be consistent!)
9. t's
10. hers, it's, Joan's

The Colon

The colon is used to precede a list of three or more items or a long quotation.

Examples: There are four different types of political systems:

The mayor made the following statements:

Caution

Avoid using the colon directly after a verb. Avoid using the colon to interrupt the natural flow of language.

Poor: We purchased: apples, pears, bananas, and grapes.

Better: We purchased apples, pears, bananas, and grapes.

The Semicolon

A semicolon may be used to separate two complete ideas (independent clauses) in a sentence when the two ideas have a close relationship and they are *not* connected with a coordinating conjunction.

Example: The setting sun caused the fields to take on a special glow; all were bathed in a pale light.

The semicolon is often used between independent clauses connected by conjunctive adverbs such as *consequently, therefore, also, furthermore, for example, however, nevertheless, still, yet, moreover,* and *otherwise.*

Example: He waited at the station for well over an hour; however, no one appeared.
(Note the use of the comma after the conjunctive adverb.)

Caution

Do *not* use the semicolon between an independent clause and a phrase or subordinate clause.

Skill Builder: Punctuation

Directions: Decide whether the colons and semicolons are correctly placed in the following sentences or whether another mark of punctuation would be better. Write the correct punctuation on the line provided.

1. He is an excellent student and a fine person; as a result, he has many friends.

   _____

2. Because he is such an industrious student; he has many friends.

   _____

3. We tried our best to purchase the books; but we were unsuccessful.

   _____

4. The students were required to pass the following exit tests: English, science, math, and social studies.

   _____

5. The rebuilt vacuum cleaner was in excellent condition; saving us a good deal of expense since we didn't have to purchase a new one.

   _____

6. Marie has a very soft voice; however, it is clear and distinct.

   _____

7. Don't open the door; the floor is still wet.

   _____

8. Don't open the door; because the floor is still wet.

   _____

9. To the campers from the city, every noise in the night sounded like a bear: a huge, ferocious, meat-eating bear.

   _____

10. We worked for three days painting the house; nevertheless, we still needed more time to complete the job.

    _____

11. The telephone rang several times, as a result; his sleep was interrupted.

    _____

12. Peter was chosen recently to be vice president of the business; and will take over his duties in a few days.

    _____

Answers

1. Correct.
2. Substitute a comma for the semicolon.
3. Substitute a comma for the semicolon.
4. Correct.
5. Substitute a comma for the semicolon.
6. Correct.
7. Correct.
8. Delete the semicolon.
9. Substitute a comma for the colon.
10. Correct.
11. The telephone rang several times; as a result, his sleep was interrupted. (Note the two punctuation changes. The semicolon is placed in front of the conjunctive adverb and the comma after it.)
12. Delete the semicolon; no punctuation is necessary in its place.

The Comma

The comma is used:

- To set off words in a series. Use a comma between words in a series when three or more elements are present. The elements may be words, phrases, or clauses. (Notice the use of the commas in this last sentence.)

    Examples: He hopped, skipped, and jumped.

    She is certainly a good student, a fine athlete, and a willing worker.

    I will not listen to, follow, or obey your instructions.

Note

It is acceptable to omit the comma before *and* or *or.* However, the writer should be consistent in his choice.

- Before coordinating conjunctions (*and, but, nor, or, for*) that join two independent clauses.

    Examples: Joe has been very diligent about completing his work, *but* he has had many problems concerning his punctuality.

    I sincerely hope that these exercises prove of assistance to you, *and* I believe that they will help you to make a better showing on your examinations.

Note

If the independent clauses are short, you may omit the separating comma.

    Example: I saw him and I spoke to him.

- To set off nonrestrictive, parenthetical, and appositive elements. A nonrestrictive element supplies material not essential to the sentence and, if removed, will not change the meaning of the original sentence.

  Example: Millie, who is a fine student, has a perfect attendance record.

A parenthetical element is one that is added to the sentence without changing the sentence's meaning. Some common parenthetical elements are: *to tell the truth, believe me, it appears to me, I am sure,* and *as a matter of fact.*

An appositive element describes a noun or pronoun but is not grammatically necessary for the sentence.

  Examples: Bob, an industrious and hard-working student, will run for class treasurer.

  Shrill and loud, her voice grated on our ears.

Note

In the first example, the appositive phrase follows the noun it describes *(Bob)*; in the second, the appositive phrase precedes the noun it describes *(voice).*

- To set off introductory clauses and phrases.

  Examples: When you come home, please ring the bell before opening the door.

  Forcing back his tears, he embraced her warmly.

- To separate two coordinate adjectives that precede the noun they describe. (Coordinate adjectives are adjectives of equal importance.)

  Examples: He is a wise, charming man.

  She is a slow, careful reader.

In both examples, *and* can be substituted for the comma. But if you cannot substitute *and* without changing the meaning, the adjectives are not coordinate, and no comma is needed.

  Example: He is a charming young man.

- To set off nouns in direct address. The name of the person addressed is separated from the rest of the sentence by commas.

  Examples: Bob, please close the door.

  I think, Jose, you are the one who was chosen.

- With dates and addresses: The different parts of a date and an address are separated by commas, including a comma after the last item.

  Examples: The train will arrive on Friday, January 18, 2011, if it is on schedule.

  My daughter traveled from Cambridge, Massachusetts, to Albany, New York, in 3 hours.

NOTE

Using a comma where it is not needed is as confusing as omitting one when it is required.

Skill Builder: Commas

Directions: Check the rules for using the comma and then insert commas as required in the following paragraph.

It was a cold blustery day and the temperature was hovering at twenty degrees. Although the calendar indicated that the month was October we felt that we were experiencing December weather. Bill Smith the newly appointed professor was arriving by plane from Seattle Washington and we had arranged to have a group welcome him at the airport. To tell the truth I was happy that I was not chosen to be part of the committee since I knew how windy the airport could be. But events that took place on that fateful day of October 15 1990 proved that I was more than lucky.

Answers

It was a cold, blustery day, and the temperature was hovering at twenty degrees. Although the calendar indicated that the month was October, we felt that we were experiencing December weather. Bill Smith, the newly appointed professor, was arriving by plane from Seattle, Washington, and we had arranged to have a group welcome him at the airport. To tell the truth, I was happy that I was not chosen to be part of the committee, since I knew how windy the airport could be. But events that took place on that fateful day of October 15, 1990, proved that I was more than lucky.

The Dash

A dash is used:

- Before a word or word group that indicates a summation or reversal of what preceded it.

  Examples: Patience, sensitivity, understanding, empathy—these are the marks of a friend.

  To lose weight, set yourself realistic goals, do not eat between meals, eat only in the kitchen or dining room, avoid restaurants—and then go out and binge.

Note

The material following the *dash* usually directs the attention of the reader to the content preceding it.

- Before and after abrupt material of a parenthetical nature.

  Example: He was not pleased with—in fact, he was completely hostile to—the take-over.

End-Stop Punctuation

There are three types of punctuation used to end a sentence: the period, the question mark, and the exclamation mark.

① A period is used at the end of a sentence that makes a statement.

   Examples: He is my best friend.

   There are thirty days in September.

② A question mark is used after a direct question. A period is used after an indirect question.

   Examples: *Direct Question*—Did you take the examination on Friday?

   Indirect Question—The instructor wanted to know if you took the examination on Friday.

③ An exclamation mark is used after an expression that shows strong emotion or issues a command. It may follow a word, a phrase, or a sentence.

   Examples: Wonderful! You won the lottery!

   Oh, no! I won't go!

   Do it!

Skill Builder: Punctuation

Directions: Add the necessary punctuation to these sentences.

1. He was not aware that you had lost your wallet
2. Did you report the loss to the proper authorities
3. I suppose you had to fill out many forms
4. What a nuisance
5. I hate doing so much paperwork
6. Did you ever discover where the wallet was
7. I imagine you wondered how it was misplaced
8. Good for you
9. At least you now have your money and your credit cards
10. What will you do if it happens again

Answers

1. He was not aware that you had lost your wallet.
2. Did you report the loss to the proper authorities?
3. I suppose you had to fill out many forms.
4. What a nuisance!
5. I hate doing so much paperwork!
6. Did you ever discover where the wallet was?
7. I imagine you wondered how it was misplaced.
8. Good for you!
9. At least you now have your money and your credit cards.
10. What will you do if it happens again?

The Hyphen

The hyphen is used with a compound modifier that precedes the noun.

> *Examples:* There was a sit-in demonstration at the office. (BUT: We will sit in the auditorium.)
>
> I purchased a four-cylinder car. (BUT: I purchased a car with four cylinders.)

The hyphen also is used with fractions that serve as adjectives or adverbs.

> *Example:* The optimist feels that his glass is one-half full; the pessimist feels that his glass is one-half empty.

Skill Builder: Punctuation

Directions: Rewrite the following sentences, inserting all <u>necessary</u> punctuation marks.

1. Bob read Tennyson's "Ulysses" to the class everyone seemed to enjoy the reading.
2. He ordered a set of books several magazines and a film.
3. He has $43,000 to spend however once that is gone he will be penniless.
4. The careless student may write dont in place of does not.
5. Before an examination do the following review your work get a good nights sleep eat a balanced breakfast and arrive on time to take the test.

Answers

1. Bob read Tennyson's "Ulysses" to the class; everyone seemed to enjoy the reading.
2. He ordered a set of books, several magazines, and a film.
3. He has $43,000 to spend; however, once that is gone, he will be penniless.
4. The careless student may write "don't" in place of "does not."
5. Before an examination, do the following: review your work, get a good night's sleep, eat a balanced breakfast, and arrive on time to take the test.

Quotation Marks

Quotation marks are used:

- To *enclose* the actual words of the speaker or writer.

- To *emphasize* words used in a special or unusual sense.

- To *set off titles* of short themes or parts of a larger work.

  Examples: Jane said, "There will be many people at the party."

                 He kept using the phrase "you know" throughout his conversation.

                 The first chapter of *The Scarlet Letter* is "The Custom House."

Caution

Do not use quotation marks for indirect quotations.

     Incorrect: He said that "he would be happy to attend the meeting."

     Correct: He said that he would be happy to attend the meeting.

     Correct: He said, "I would be happy to attend the meeting."

Caution

Do not use quotation marks to justify your own poor choice of words.

Note

The period and comma are placed inside the quotation marks; the colon and the semicolon are placed outside the quotation marks.

     Examples: My favorite poem is "My Last Duchess," a dramatic monologue written by Robert Browning.

                My favorite poem is "My Last Duchess"; this poem is a dramatic monologue written by Robert Browning.

Skill Builder: Quotation Marks

Directions: Add quotation marks in the following sentences as needed.

1. The guest said he was delighted to have been invited.
2. I think the party is great Alysha said.
3. Eduardo said he would come if he had his homework done.
4. I like Langston Hughes's poem The Negro Speaks of Rivers.
5. Becca was reading Nadine Gordimer's short story Comrades.

Answers

1. Correct
2. "I think the party is great," Alysha said.
3. Correct
4. I like Langston Hughes's poem "The Negro Speaks of Rivers."
5. Becca was reading Nadine Gordimer's short story "Comrades."

SUMMING IT UP

- If you have limited time, at least make sure you've mastered "Confusing Words: Group 1." The major problems appear in this list.

- Chances are you won't be using any dashes in your essay. Note that the rules don't indicate using dashes for emphasis.

- Pay particular attention to indirect questions. Using a question mark after an indirect question is a common error.

- If you cite a novel or a book of nonfiction in your essay, don't put it in quotations marks. Underline the title.

PART V

SAT MATH REVIEW

Multiple-Choice Math Strategies

OVERVIEW

- Why multiple-choice math is easier
- Question format
- Solving multiple-choice math questions
- Know when to use your calculator
- Learn the most important multiple-choice math tips
- Summing it up

WHY MULTIPLE-CHOICE MATH IS EASIER

How can one kind of math possibly be easier than another? SAT multiple-choice math is easier than the math tests you take in class because the answers are right there in front of you. As you know from other standardized tests, multiple-choice tests always give you the answer. You just have to figure out which answer is the correct one. So even if you aren't sure and have to guess, you can use estimating to narrow your choices and improve your odds.

The questions in each multiple-choice math section are arranged from easiest to most difficult. The questions don't stick to one content area. They jump around from algebra to geometry to arithmetic to data analysis to statistics and back to algebra in no particular pattern.

QUESTION FORMAT

On the SAT, each set of multiple-choice math questions starts with directions and a reference section that look like this:

Directions: Solve the following problems using any available space on the page for scratchwork. On your answer sheet, fill in the choice that best corresponds to the correct answer.

Notes: The figures accompanying the problems are drawn as accurately as possible unless otherwise stated in specific problems. Again, unless otherwise stated, all figures lie in the same plane. All numbers used in these problems are real numbers. Calculators are permitted for this test.

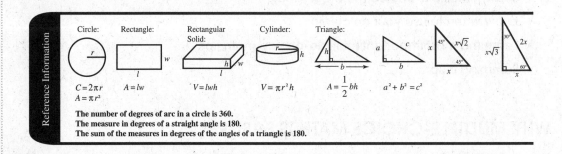

The number of degrees of arc in a circle is 360.
The measure in degrees of a straight angle is 180.
The sum of the measures in degrees of the angles of a triangle is 180.

NOTE

The answers line up by size. The quantities in math multiple-choice answer choices either go from largest to smallest or the other way around. Remember that when you're trying to eliminate or test answers.

The information in the reference section should all be familiar to you from your school-work. Know that it's there in case you need it. But remember: the formulas themselves aren't the answers to any problems. You have to know when to use them and how to apply them.

Some multiple-choice questions are straight calculations, while others are presented in the form of word problems. Some include graphs, charts, or tables that you will be asked to interpret. All of the questions have five answer choices. These choices are arranged in order by size from smallest to largest or occasionally from largest to smallest.

SOLVING MULTIPLE-CHOICE MATH QUESTIONS

These five steps will help you solve multiple-choice math questions:

1. Read the question carefully and determine what's being asked.
2. Decide which math principles apply and use them to solve the problem.
3. Look for your answer among the choices. If it's there, mark it and go on.
4. If the answer you found is not there, recheck the question and your calculations.
5. If you still can't solve the problem, eliminate obviously wrong answers and take your best guess.

Now let's try out these steps on a couple of SAT-type multiple-choice math questions.

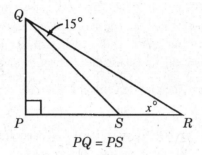

$PQ = PS$

In the figure above, $x =$

(A) 15°

(B) 30°

(C) 40°

(D) 60°

(E) 75°

1 The problem asks you to find the measure of one angle of right triangle PQR.

2 Two math principles apply: (1) the sum of the measures in degrees of the angles of a triangle is 180, and (2) 45-45-90 right triangles have certain special properties. Since $PQ = PS$, $\triangle PQS$ is a 45-45-90 right triangle. Therefore, angle $PQS = 45°$ and angle $PQR = 45 + 15 = 60°$. Therefore, angle $x = 180 - 90 - 60 = 30°$.

3 The correct answer, 30, is choice (B).

If x and y are negative numbers, which of the following is negative?

(A) xy

(B) $(xy)^2$

(C) $(x - y)^2$

(D) $x + y$

(E) $\dfrac{x}{y}$

1 The problem asks you to pick an answer choice that is a negative number.

2 The principles that apply are those governing operations with signed numbers. Since x and y are negative, both choices (A) and (E) must be positive. As for choices (B) and (C), so long as neither x nor y is zero, those expressions must be positive. (Any number other than zero squared gives a positive result.) Choice (D), however, is negative since it represents the sum of two negative numbers.

3 Therefore, the correct answer must be choice (D). If you have trouble working with letters, try substituting easy numbers for x and y in each choice.

KNOW WHEN TO USE YOUR CALCULATOR

Calculators are allowed on the SAT, but you won't *need* a calculator to solve any SAT math questions. Calculators can be helpful in doing basic arithmetic computations, square roots, and percentages and in comparing and converting fractions. But remember that your calculator is not some sort of magic brain. If you don't understand the questions in the first place, the calculator won't give you some magic solution.

Calculators don't have to be fancy. They just have to add, subtract, multiply, and divide. Actually, the simpler the better, because you're less likely to hit some wacky function key by mistake.

The most important thing to remember is to set up your work on paper first, and then plug the information into the calculator. For example, if you have a question that deals with an equation, set up the equation on your scratch paper. Then make your number substitutions on the calculator. This way, you always have something to refer to without having to think, "Oh, nuts, how did I set that up?" as the seconds tick by.

When you use your calculator, check the display each time you enter numbers to make sure you entered them correctly. And make sure to hit the Clear key after each finished operation, otherwise it could get ugly.

LEARN THE MOST IMPORTANT MULTIPLE-CHOICE MATH TIPS

Some of these you've heard before, some will be new to you. Whatever the case, read them, learn them, love them. They will help you.

The Question Number Tells You How Hard the Question Is

Just as in most of the other SAT sections, the questions go from easy to hard as you work toward the end. The first third of the questions is easy, the middle third is average but harder, and the final third gets more and more difficult. Take a look at these three examples. Don't solve them yet (you'll be doing that in a couple of minutes), just get an idea of how the level of difficulty changes from Question 1 to Question 12 to Question 25.

1. If $x - 2 = 5$, then $x =$
   (A) -10
   (B) -3
   (C) $\dfrac{5}{2}$
   (D) 3
   (E) 7

ALERT!

Don't automatically reach for your calculator. If it can't help you solve the problem, you'll just waste time fiddling with it. Save the calculator for what it does best, especially arithmetic calculations, percentages, and square roots.

12. For how many integers x is $-7 < 2x < -5$?

(A) None

(B) One

(C) Two

(D) Three

(E) Indefinite number

25. In a set of five books, no two of which have the same number of pages, the longest book has 150 pages and the shortest book has 130 pages. If x pages is the average (arithmetic mean) of the number of pages in the five-book set, which of the following best indicates all possible values of x and only possible values of x?

(A) $130 < x < 150$

(B) $131 < x < 149$

(C) $133 < x < 145$

(D) $134 < x < 145$

(E) $135 < x < 145$

Can you see the difference? You can probably do Question 1 with your eyes closed. For Question 12, you probably have to open your eyes and do some calculations on scratch paper. Question 25 may cause you to wince a little, and then get started on some heavy-duty thinking.

Easy Questions Have Easy Answers—Difficult Questions Don't

The easy questions are straightforward and don't have any hidden tricks. The obvious answer is almost always the correct answer. So for Question 1 the answer is indeed choice (E).

When you hit the difficult stuff, you have to think harder. The information is not straightforward and the answers aren't obvious. You can bet that your first-choice, easy answer will be wrong. If you don't believe it, let's take a look at the solution for difficult Question 25.

25. In a set of five books, no two of which have the same number of pages, the longest book has 150 pages and the shortest book has 130 pages. If x pages is the average (arithmetic mean) of the number of pages in the five-book set, which of the following best indicates all possible values of x and only possible values of x?

(A) $130 < x < 150$

(B) $131 < x < 149$

(C) $133 < x < 145$

(D) $134 < x < 145$

(E) $135 < x < 145$

TIP

Look for shortcuts. SAT math problems test your math reasoning, not your ability to make endless calculations. If you find yourself calculating too much, you've probably missed a shortcut that would have made your work easier.

Yes, it's difficult mostly because the process you have to use to find the solution is difficult. Let's start by eliminating answer choices. Choice (A) is for suckers. You see the same information that appears in the word problem, so you figure it's got to be right. Wrong. All it does is say that the shortest book is 130 pages, the longest book is 150 pages, and the average is between 130 and 150. Simple and wrong.

Choice (B) illustrates the reasoning that "no two books have the same number of pages, so the average must be one page more than the shortest book and one page less than the longest." Remember, it's a difficult question, so it's just not that easy an answer.

Let's skip to the correct answer, which is (E), and find out how we got there. First, you want to find the minimum value for x so you assume that the other three books contain 131, 132, and 133 pages. So the average would be:

$$\frac{130+131+132+133+150}{5} = \frac{676}{5} = 135.2$$

So x must be more than 135. Now assume that the other three books contain 149, 148, and 147 pages. Then the average length of all five books would be:

$$\frac{150+149+148+147+130}{5} = \frac{724}{5} = 144.8$$

Then x would be greater than 135 but less than 145.

Be Certain to Answer the Question Being Asked

Suppose that you were asked to solve the following problem:

> If $5x + 11 = 31$, what is the value of $x + 4$?
>
> **(A)** 4
> **(B)** 6
> **(C)** 8
> **(D)** 10
> **(E)** 12

The first step is to solve the equation $5x + 11 = 31$.

$5x + 11 = 31$ Subtract 11 from both sides.

$5x = 20$ Divide both sides by 5.

$x = 4$

Remember that the problem does not ask for the value of x, it asks for the value of $x + 4$, so the answer is actually choice (C). Make certain that the answer you select is the answer to the question that is being asked. **The correct answer is (C).**

When Guessing at Hard Questions, You Can Toss Out Easy Answers

Now that you know the difficult questions won't have easy or obvious answers, use a guessing strategy. (Use all the help you can get!) When you have less than a clue about a difficult question, scan the answer choices and eliminate the ones that seem easy or obvious, such as any that just restate the information in the question. Then take your best guess.

Questions of Average Difficulty Won't Have Trick Answers

Let's look again at Question 12:

12. For how many integers x is $-7 < 2x < -5$?

    (A) None

    (B) One

    (C) Two

    (D) Three

    (E) Indefinite number

This is a bit more difficult than Question 1, but it's still pretty straightforward. There is only one integer between -7 and -5, and that's -6. There's also only one value for integer x so that $2x$ equals -6, and that is -3. Get it? $2(-3) = -6$. So, choice (B) is the correct answer. Trust your judgment and your reasoning; no tricks here.

It's Smart to Work Backward

Every standard multiple-choice math problem includes five answer choices. One of them has to be correct; the other four are wrong. This means that it's always possible to solve a problem by testing each of the answer choices. Just plug each choice into the problem, and sooner or later you'll find the one that works! Testing answer choices can often be a much easier and surer way of solving a problem than attempting a lengthy calculation.

When Working Backward, Always Start from the Middle

When working on multiple-choice math questions, remember that all of the answer choices are presented in order—either smallest to largest, or vice versa. As a result, it's always best to begin with the middle option, or choice (C). This way, if you start with choice (C) and it's too large, you'll only have to concentrate on the smaller choices. There, you've just knocked off at least three choices in a heartbeat! Now let's give it a test run!

If a rectangle has sides of $2x$ and $3x$ and an area of 24, what is the value of x?

(A) 2

(B) 3

(C) 4

(D) 5

(E) 6

You know that one of these is right. Get started by testing choice (C), and assume that $x = 4$. Then the sides would have lengths $2(4) = 8$ and $3(4) = 12$ and the rectangle would have an area of $8 \cdot 12 = 96$. Since 96 is larger than 24 (the area in the question), start working with the smaller answer choices. (Which means, of course, that you can immediately forget about choices (D) and (E). Great!) When you plug 3 into the figuring, you get $2(3) = 6$ and $3(3)$ 9 and $6 \cdot 9 = 54$; still too large. The only choice left is (A), and it works. **The correct answer is (A).**

Now try this testing business with a more difficult question:

A farmer raises chickens and cows. If his animals have a total of 120 heads and a total of 300 feet, how many chickens does the farmer have?

(A) 50

(B) 60

(C) 70

(D) 80

(E) 90

Here goes—starting with choice (C). If the farmer has 70 chickens, he has 50 cows. (You know the farmer has 120 animals, because they each have only one head, right?) So now you're talking about $70 \cdot 2 = 140$ chicken feet and $50 \cdot 4 = 200$ cow feet, for a grand total of 340 animal feet. Well, that's more than the 300 animal feet in the question. How will you lose some of those feet? First, assume that the farmer has more chickens and fewer cows (cows have more feet than chickens do). Give choice (D)—80—a try. Test $80 \cdot 2 = 160$ and $40 \cdot 4 = 160$; your total is 320 feet, which is closer but not quite right. The only answer left is choice (E). Check it out: $90 \cdot 2 = 180$ and $30 \cdot 4 = 120$, and the total is . . . 300! **The correct answer is (E).**

It's Easier to Work with Numbers Than with Letters

Because numbers are more meaningful than letters, try plugging them into equations and formulas in place of variables. This technique can make problems much easier to solve. Here are some examples:

If $x - 4$ is 2 greater than y, then $x + 5$ is how much greater than y?

(A) 1

(B) 3

(C) 7

(D) 9

(E) 11

Choose any value for x. Let's say you decide to make $x = 4$. All right, $4 - 4 = 0$, and 0 is 2 greater than y. So $y = -2$. If $x = 4$, then $x + 5 = 4 + 5 = 9$, and so $x + 5$ is 11 more than y. **The correct answer is (E).**

The unit cost of pens is the same regardless of how many pens are purchased. If the cost of p pens is d dollars, what is the cost, in dollars, of x pens?

(A) xd

(B) xpd

(C) $\dfrac{xd}{p}$

(D) $\dfrac{xp}{d}$

(E) $\dfrac{pd}{x}$

Time to plug in some real numbers, since you need real money to buy anything, including pens. Say that four pens (p) cost \$2.00 (d), so each pen (x) would cost 50 cents. And say that you really only need one pen, so you're spending only \$0.50. Then $p = 4$, $d = 2$, and $x = 1$, and the right answer would be 0.5. Now, start using these numbers with the answer choices:

(A) $xd = (1)(2) = 2$ (Nope.)

(B) $xpd = (1)(4)(2) = 8$ (Nope, again.)

(C) $\dfrac{xd}{p} = \dfrac{(1)(2)}{4} = 0.5$ (Yes, there it is.)

(D) $\dfrac{xp}{d} = \dfrac{(1)(4)}{2} = 2$ (Nope.)

(E) $\dfrac{pd}{x} = \dfrac{(4)(2)}{1} = 8$ (Nope.)

The correct answer is (C).

If a question asks for an odd integer or an even integer, go ahead and pick any odd or even integer you like.

The test booklet is yours, so feel free to use it for your scratch-work. Also, go ahead and mark up any diagrams with length or angle information; it helps. But don't waste time try-ing to redraw diagrams; it's just not worth it.

In Problems Involving Variables, Pay Careful Attention to Any Restrictions on the Possible Values of the Variables

Consider the following question:

If a is a positive integer, $a > 1$, which of the following lists the numbers a, a^2, $\dfrac{1}{a}$, and $\dfrac{1}{a^2}$ in order from largest to smallest?

(A) $\dfrac{1}{a^2}, \dfrac{1}{a}, a, a^2$

(B) $\dfrac{1}{a}, \dfrac{1}{a^2}, a, a^2$

(C) $a^2, a, \dfrac{1}{a}, \dfrac{1}{a^2}$

(D) $a^2, a, \dfrac{1}{a^2}, \dfrac{1}{a}$

(E) The order cannot be determined.

This problem is fairly straightforward. To begin, since $a^2 = a \times a^2$, then $a^2 > a$. Now, since $a > 1$, the fraction $\dfrac{1}{a}$ is less than 1, and $\dfrac{1}{a^2}$ is smaller still. Therefore, the order, from largest to smallest, is a^2, a, $\dfrac{1}{a}$, $\dfrac{1}{a^2}$. **The correct answer is (C).**

Now, consider this slightly different version of the same problem.

If $0 < a < 1$, which of the following lists the numbers a, a^2, $\dfrac{1}{a}$ and $\dfrac{1}{a^2}$ in order from largest to smallest?

(A) $\dfrac{1}{a^2}, \dfrac{1}{a}, a, a^2$

(B) $\dfrac{1}{a}, \dfrac{1}{a^2}, a, a^2$

(C) $a^2, a, \dfrac{1}{a}, \dfrac{1}{a^2}$

(D) $a^2, a, \dfrac{1}{a^2}, \dfrac{1}{a}$

(E) The order cannot be determined.

The only difference between the two problems is that this time you are told that the value of a is between 0 and 1. Read too quickly and you might miss this fact entirely. Yet, this single difference changes the answer. When a number between 0 and 1 is squared, it actually gets smaller, so $a > a^2$. Now consider the fraction $\dfrac{1}{a}$. Since $a < 1$, the denominator of the fraction is smaller than the numerator, and so the value of $\dfrac{1}{a}$ is greater than 1, which makes it greater than a. The value of $\dfrac{1}{a^2}$ is larger still. The correct order is

$\dfrac{1}{a^2}, \dfrac{1}{a},$ a, a^2. **The correct answer is (A).**

Finally, consider this version of the problem.

> If a is a real number, which of the following lists the numbers a, a^2, $\dfrac{1}{a}$ and $\dfrac{1}{a^2}$ in order from largest to smallest?
>
> **(A)** $\dfrac{1}{a^2}, \dfrac{1}{a}, a, a^2$
>
> **(B)** $\dfrac{1}{a}, \dfrac{1}{a^2}, a, a^2$
>
> **(C)** $a^2, a, \dfrac{1}{a}, \dfrac{1}{a^2}$
>
> **(D)** $a^2, a, \dfrac{1}{a^2}, \dfrac{1}{a}$
>
> **(E)** The order cannot be determined.

Without the knowledge of the size of the a, you cannot tell what the correct order is. It's important to pay careful attention to any restrictions put on the values of a variable. **The correct answer is (E).**

Questions in the Three-Statement Format Can Be Solved by the Process of Elimination

You may find a three-statement format in certain questions in the multiple-choice math section. The best way to answer this kind of question is to tackle one statement at a time, marking it as either true or false. Here is an example:

> If $x - y$ is positive, which of the following statements could be true?
>
> **I.** $0 > x > y$
>
> **II.** $x > 0 > y$
>
> **III.** $y > x > 0$
>
> **(A)** I only
>
> **(B)** II only
>
> **(C)** III only
>
> **(D)** I and II only
>
> **(E)** II and III only

The answer choices all refer to the three statements. Let's start by checking statement I. If x and y are negative numbers so that x is greater than y, then y has a greater absolute value than x. Since both are negative numbers, $x - y$ is positive. For example, $-3 > -4$ and $-3 - (-4) = -3 + 4 = 1$, and $1 > 0$. Therefore, statement I will appear in the correct answer choice. Now, since choices (B), (C), and (E) don't contain statement I, you can eliminate them.

Now let's check out statement II. If x is positive and y is negative, then $x - y$ would be subtracting a negative number from a positive number, which will give you a positive number. (Subtracting a negative number is really adding a positive number.) Because statement II must appear in the correct answer, you can now eliminate answer choice (A). So, by the process of elimination, you know that choice (D) is correct, and you don't even have to test statement III. **The correct answer is (D).**

When Solving Equations Involving Square Roots or Algebraic Fractions, Make Certain to Check Your Answer

The procedure for solving such equations occasionally results in what are known as *extraneous solutions*. An extraneous solution is a number that is correctly obtained from the equation-solving process, but doesn't actually solve the equation.

Solve for x: $\sqrt{x+4} + 15 = 10$

(A) -29

(B) -21

(C) 12

(D) 21

(E) There are no solutions.

Let's solve the equation.

$$\sqrt{x+4} + 15 = 10 \qquad \text{Subtract 15 from both sides}$$
$$\sqrt{x+4} = -5 \qquad \text{Square both sides}$$
$$\left(\sqrt{x+4}\right)^2 = (-5)^2$$
$$x + 4 = 25$$
$$x = 21$$

It appears that the solution is choice (D). However, if you check the solution $x = 21$ in the original equation, you will see that it doesn't solve it.

$$\sqrt{x+4} + 15 = 10?$$
$$\sqrt{21+4} + 15 = 10?$$
$$\sqrt{25} + 15 = 10?$$
$$5 + 15 \neq 10.$$

The correct answer is (E).

The Area of an Unusual Shape Is Really the Difference Between the Areas of Two Regular Figures

Here's a visual example that might help:

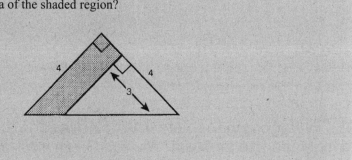

In the figure below, what is the area of the shaded region?

(A) $2\frac{1}{2}$

(B) 4

(C) $3\frac{1}{2}$

(D) 6

(E) 8

Try to isolate the shaded portion of the figure. When you do, you'll see it's a trapezoid. Now, you could try to remember the formula for the area of a trapezoid, but look at the figure you have left after you pull out the trapezoid. It's another, smaller triangle. What you really need to do is figure out the areas of the original large triangle and the smaller triangle and find the difference.

You know that the larger triangle has a right angle and two equal sides, so it's an isosceles right triangle. The smaller triangle has a right angle and its side is parallel to the side of the larger triangle, so it too is an isosceles triangle. Now use the information in the figure to find the areas and then subtract.

$$\text{Area of smaller triangle} = \frac{1}{2}(3)(3) = \frac{9}{2}$$

$$\text{Area of larger triangle} = \frac{1}{2}(4)(4) = 8$$

$$8 - \frac{9}{2} = 3\frac{1}{2}$$

The correct answer is (C).

Using the Measure of an Angle or a Side of Another Shape Can Help You Find a Measure You Need

In the figure, what is the length of *NP*?

(A) 3

(B) 8

(C) 9

(D) 12

(E) 15

TIP

Draw a diagram if none is supplied. Drawing a diagram is a great way to organize information. Mark it up with the information you're given, and you'll have a better idea of what you're looking for.

www.twitter.com/prep4sat

This figure is really two right triangles, *NMO* and *NMP*. Since *NM* is a side of both triangles, once you find the length of that, you can find the length of *NP*. The Pythagorean theorem is what you need:

$NM^2 + MO^2 = NO^2$

$NM^2 + (16)^2 = (20)^2$

Note that 16 and 20 are multiples of 4 and 5, respectively, so you now know that this is a 3-4-5 right triangle, which means that *NM* = 12.

Since you just found out that triangle *NMP* has sides of 9 and 12, it's also a 3-4-5 right triangle, so *NP* must be 15. **The correct answer is (E).**

The Pythagorean Theorem Is Usually Needed to Solve Problems Involving a Right Triangle for Which You Are Given the Lengths of Some of the Sides

The Pythagorean theorem enables you to compute the length of the third side of a right triangle if you know the lengths of the other two sides. It is one of the most useful and common SAT geometry facts. Consider the problem below.

Line segment $\overline{PQ}$ is tangent to the circle with center *O* at point *T*. If *T* is the midpoint of $\overline{PQ}$, *OQ* = 13, and the radius of the circle is 5, what is the length of $\overline{PQ}$?

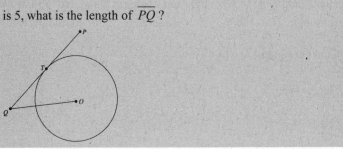

(A) 10
(B) 12
(C) 24
(D) 26
(E) 30

This is a tricky question since, at the moment, it doesn't appear to involve any triangles at all. However, you are told that the radius of the circle is 5, and if you draw in radius $\overline{OT}$, you will create triangle *OTQ*. Use the fact that a tangent line to a circle is perpendicular to the radius at the point of contact to deduce that $\angle OTQ$ is a right angle.

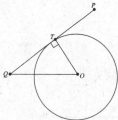

The diagram now depicts right triangle OTQ, and $OT = 5$ and $OQ = 13$. Now, use the Pythagorean theorem to determine that $TQ = 12$, as shown below.

$$\begin{aligned} OT^2 + TQ^2 &= OQ^2 \\ 5^2 + TQ^2 &= 13^2 \\ 25 + TQ^2 &= 169 \\ TQ^2 &= 144 \\ TQ &= 12 \end{aligned}$$

Finally, since T is the midpoint of line segment $\overline{PQ}$, the entire length of the line segment is 12 + 12 = 24. **The correct answer is (C).**

A Reality Check Can Help You Eliminate Answers That Can't Possibly Be Right

Knowing whether your calculations should produce a number that's larger or smaller than the quantity you started with can point you toward the right answer. It's also an effective way of eliminating wrong answers. Here's an example:

Using his bike, Daryl can complete a paper route in 20 minutes. Francisco, who walks the route, can complete it in 30 minutes. How long will it take the two boys to complete the route if they work together, one starting at each end of the route?

(A) 8 minutes

(B) 12 minutes

(C) 20 minutes

(D) 30 minutes

(E) 45 minutes

Immediately you can see that choices (C), (D), and (E) are impossible because the two boys working together will have to complete the job in less time than either one of them working alone.

	Daryl	Francisco
$\frac{\text{Time actual spent}}{\text{Time needed to do entire job alone}}$	$\frac{x}{20}$	$\frac{x}{30}$

$$\frac{x}{20} + \frac{x}{30} = 1$$

Multiply by 60 to clear fractions:

$$\begin{aligned} 3x + 2x &= 60 \\ 5x &= 60 \\ x &= 12 \end{aligned}$$

The correct answer is (B).

Your Eye Is a Good Estimator

Figures in the standard multiple-choice math section are always drawn to scale unless you see the warning "Note: Figure not drawn to scale." That means you can sometimes solve a problem just by looking at the picture and estimating the answer. Here's how this works:

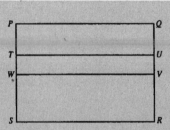

In the rectangle *PQRS* shown, *TU* and *WV* are parallel to *SR*. If *PS* = 6, *UV* = 1, and *PR* (not shown) = 10, what is the area of rectangle *TUVW*?

(A) 8

(B) 12

(C) 16

(D) 24

(E) 32

To solve the problem, you will need to find the length of *TU*. You can do this by using the Pythagorean theorem. The triangle *PSR* has sides of 6 and 10, so *SR* = 8. Since *TU* = *SR*, *TU* = 8, so the area of the small rectangle is equal to 1 • 8 = 8.

As an alternative, you could simply estimate the length of *TU*. *TU* appears to be longer than *PS* (6), and *TU* must be shorter than *PR* (10). Therefore, *TU* appears to be approximately 8. And the area must be approximately 1 • 8 = 8. Is that sufficiently accurate to get the right answer? Look at the choices. (A) is 8, and it's the only choice that is even close to 8. **The correct answer is (A).**

If Some Questions Always Give You Trouble, Save Them for Last

You know which little demons haunt your math skills. If you find questions that you know will give you nightmares, save them for last. They will take up a lot of your time, especially if you're panicking, and you can use that time to do more of the easier questions.

EXERCISES: MULTIPLE-CHOICE MATH

Exercise 1

15 Questions • 18 Minutes

Directions: Solve the following problems using any available space on the page for scratchwork. Circle the letter that appears before your answer.

Notes: The figures accompanying the problems are drawn as accurately as possible unless otherwise stated in specific problems. Again, unless otherwise stated, all figures lie in the same plane. All numbers used in these problems are real numbers. Calculators are permitted for this test.

Reference Information

Circle:
$C = 2\pi r$
$A = \pi r^2$

Rectangle:
$A = lw$

Rectangular Solid:
$V = lwh$

Cylinder:
$V = \pi r^2 h$

Triangle:
$A = \frac{1}{2}bh$

$a^2 + b^2 = c^2$

The number of degrees of arc in a circle is 360.
The measure in degrees of a straight angle is 180.
The sum of the measures in degrees of the angles of a triangle is 180.

1. If $8 \times 8 = 4^x$, what is x?

(A) 2
(B) 3
(C) 4
(D) 5
(E) 6

2. If $a > 2$, which of the following is the smallest?

(A) $\dfrac{2}{a}$

(B) $\dfrac{a}{2}$

(C) $a + \dfrac{1}{2}$

(D) $\dfrac{2}{a+1}$

(E) $\dfrac{2}{a-1}$

3. Which of the following has the greatest value?

(A) $\dfrac{1}{2}$

(B) $\sqrt{0.20}$

(C) 0.2

(D) $(0.2)^2$

(E) $(0.02)^3$

4. If $\dfrac{a}{b} = \dfrac{3}{4}$, then $12a =$

(A) b
(B) $3b$
(C) $9b$
(D) $12b$
(E) $16b$

5. If $a = b$ and $\dfrac{1}{c} = b$, then $c =$

(A) a
(B) $-a$
(C) b
(D) $\dfrac{1}{a}$
(E) $-b$

6. If a building B feet high casts a shadow F feet long, then at the same time of day, a tree T feet high will cast a shadow how many feet long?

(A) $\dfrac{FT}{B}$

(B) $\dfrac{FB}{T}$

(C) $\dfrac{B}{FT}$

(D) $\dfrac{TB}{F}$

(E) $\dfrac{T}{FB}$

7. The vertices of a triangle are (3,1), (8,1), and (8,3). What is the area of this triangle?

(A) 5
(B) 10
(C) 12
(D) 14
(E) 20

8. Of 60 employees at the Star Manufacturing Company, x employees are female. If $\dfrac{2}{3}$ of the remainder are married, how many unmarried men work for this company?

(A) $40-\dfrac{2}{3}x$

(B) $40-\dfrac{1}{3}x$

(C) $40+\dfrac{1}{3}x$

(D) $20-\dfrac{2}{3}x$

(E) $20-\dfrac{1}{3}x$

9. A circle whose center is at the origin passes through the point whose coordinates are (1,1). What is the area of this circle?

(A) π
(B) 2π
(C) $\sqrt{2\pi}$
(D) $2\sqrt{2\pi}$
(E) 4π

10. In triangle ABC, $AB=BC$ and $\overline{AC}$ is extended to D. If angle BCD contains $100°$, find the number of degrees in angle B.

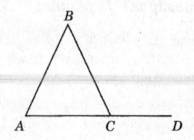

(A) 20
(B) 40
(C) 50
(D) 60
(E) 80

11. $\dfrac{4\frac{1}{2}}{10\frac{1}{8}}=$

(A) $\dfrac{2}{5}$

(B) $\dfrac{4}{9}$

(C) $\dfrac{4}{81}$

(D) $\dfrac{3}{7}$

(E) $\dfrac{15}{23}$

12. Which of the following is greater than $\dfrac{1}{3}$?

(A) 0.33

(B) $\left(\dfrac{1}{3}\right)^2$

(C) $\dfrac{1}{4}$

(D) $\dfrac{1}{0.3}$

(E) $\dfrac{3}{4}$

13. What percent of a half dollar is the total of a penny, a nickel, and a dime?

    (A) 8
    (B) 16
    (C) 20
    (D) 25
    (E) 32

14. If $\dfrac{1}{a} + \dfrac{1}{b} = \dfrac{1}{c}$ then $c =$

    (A) $a + b$

    (B) ab

    (C) $\dfrac{a+b}{ab}$

    (D) $\dfrac{ab}{b+a}$

    (E) $\dfrac{1}{2}ab$

15. What percent of a is b?

    (A) $\dfrac{100b}{a}$

    (B) $\dfrac{a}{b}$

    (C) $\dfrac{b}{100a}$

    (D) $\dfrac{b}{a}$

    (E) $\dfrac{100a}{b}$

Exercise 2

10 Questions • 12 Minutes

Directions: Solve the following problems using any available space on the page for scratchwork. Circle the letter that appears before your answer.

Notes: The figures accompanying the problems are drawn as accurately as possible unless otherwise stated in specific problems. Again, unless otherwise stated, all figures lie in the same plane. All numbers used in these problems are real numbers. Calculators are permitted for this test.

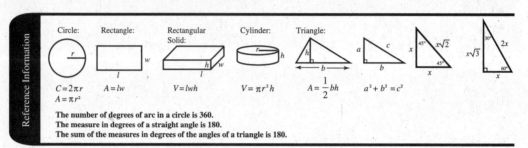

Circle: $C = 2\pi r$ $A = \pi r^2$

Rectangle: $A = lw$

Rectangular Solid: $V = lwh$

Cylinder: $V = \pi r^2 h$

Triangle: $A = \dfrac{1}{2}bh$ $a^2 + b^2 = c^2$

The number of degrees of arc in a circle is 360.
The measure in degrees of a straight angle is 180.
The sum of the measures in degrees of the angles of a triangle is 180.

1. The average of two numbers is A. If one of the numbers is x, what is the other number?

(A) $A - x$

(B) $\dfrac{A}{2} - x$

(C) $2A - x$

(D) $\dfrac{A + x}{2}$

(E) $x - A$

2. If $a = 5b$, then $\dfrac{3}{5}a =$

(A) $\dfrac{5b}{3}$

(B) $3b$

(C) $\dfrac{3b}{5}$

(D) $\dfrac{b}{3}$

(E) $\dfrac{b}{5}$

3. A rectangular door measures 5 feet by 6 feet 8 inches. What is the distance from one corner of the door to the diagonally opposite corner?

(A) 8 feet 2 inches

(B) 8 feet 4 inches

(C) 8 feet 8 inches

(D) 9 feet

(E) 9 feet 6 inches

4. Two ships leave from the same port at 11:30 a.m. If one sails due east at 20 miles per hour and the other due south at 15 miles per hour, how many miles apart are the ships at 2:30 p.m.?

(A) 25

(B) 50

(C) 75

(D) 80

(E) 85

5. If *m* men can paint a house in *d* days, how many days will it take *m* + 2 men to paint the same house?

   (A) $d + 2$

   (B) $d - 2$

   (C) $\dfrac{m+2}{md}$

   (D) $\dfrac{md}{m+2}$

   (E) $\dfrac{md+2d}{m}$

6. Ken received grades of 90, 88, and 75 on three tests. What grade must he receive on the next test so that his average for these four tests is 85?

   (A) 87

   (B) 89

   (C) 90

   (D) 92

   (E) 95

7. There is enough food at a picnic to feed 20 adults or 32 children. If there are 15 adults at the picnic, how many children can still be fed?

   (A) 6

   (B) 8

   (C) 12

   (D) 16

   (E) 18

8. In parallelogram *ABCD,* angle *A* contains 60°. What is the sum of angle *B* and angle *D*?

   (A) 60°

   (B) 180°

   (C) 240°

   (D) 280°

   (E) 300°

9. The area of circle *O* is 64π. What is the perimeter of square *ABCD*?

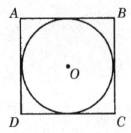

   (A) 32

   (B) 32π

   (C) 64

   (D) 16

   (E) 64π

10. If a train covers 14 miles in 10 minutes, what is the rate of the train in miles per hour?

   (A) 64

   (B) 76

   (C) 84

   (D) 90

   (E) 98

ANSWER KEY AND EXPLANATIONS
Exercise 1

1. B	4. C	7. A	10. A	13. E
2. D	5. D	8. E	11. B	14. D
3. A	6. A	9. B	12. D	15. A

1. **The correct answer is (B).**
   $64 = 4^x$
   $x = 3 \ (4 \times 4 \times 4 = 64)$

2. **The correct answer is (D).** Both choices (B) and (C) are greater than 1. Choices (A), (D), and (E) all have the same numerator. In this case, the one with the largest denominator will be the smallest fraction.

3. **The correct answer is (A).**
   $\dfrac{1}{2} = 0.5$
   $\sqrt{0.20} = 0.4^+$
   $(0.2)^2 = 0.04$
   $(0.2)^3 = 0.008$

4. **The correct answer is (C).** Cross-multiply.
   $4a = 3b$
   Multiply by 3.
   $12a = 9b$

5. **The correct answer is (D).**
   $a = b = \dfrac{1}{c}$
   $a = \dfrac{1}{c}$
   $ac = 1$
   $c = \dfrac{1}{a}$

6. **The correct answer is (A).** The ratio of height to shadow is constant.
   $\dfrac{B}{F} = \dfrac{T}{x}$
   $Bx = FT$
   $x = \dfrac{FT}{B}$

7. **The correct answer is (A).**

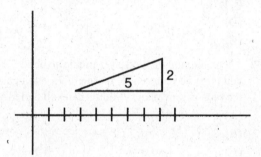

   $\text{Right triangle area} = \dfrac{1}{2} \times 5 \times 2 = 5$

8. **The correct answer is (E).**
   $60 - x$ employees are male.

   $\dfrac{1}{3}$ of these are unmarried.

   $\dfrac{1}{3}(60 - x) = 20 - \dfrac{1}{3}x$

9. **The correct answer is (B).**

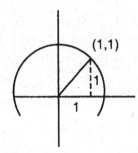

$$1^2 + 1^2 = r^2$$
$$2 = r^2$$
$$\text{Area} = \pi r^2 = 2\pi$$

10. **The correct answer is (A).**
Angle BCA = Angle BAC = 80°.
There are 20° left for angle B.

11. **The correct answer is (B).**
$$\frac{9}{2} \div \frac{81}{8} = \frac{9}{2} \times \frac{8}{81} = \frac{4}{9}$$

12. **The correct answer is (D).**
$$\frac{1}{0.3} = \frac{10}{3} = 3\frac{1}{3}$$

13. **The correct answer is (E).**
$$\frac{16}{50} = \frac{32}{100} = 32\%$$

14. **The correct answer is (D).** Multiply by abc.
$$bc + ac = ab$$
$$c(b+a) = ab$$
$$c = \frac{ab}{b+a}$$

15. **The correct answer is (A).**
$$\frac{b}{a} \times 100 = \frac{100b}{a}$$

Exercise 2

1. C	3. B	5. D	7. B	9. C
2. B	4. C	6. A	8. C	10. C

1. **The correct answer is (C).**
$$\frac{x+y}{2} = A$$
$$x+y = 2A$$
$$y = 2A - x$$

2. **The correct answer is (B).**
$$\frac{3}{\cancel{6}} = \cancel{6}b = 3b$$

3. **The correct answer is (B).**
5 feet = 60 inches
6 feet 8 inches = 80 inches
This is a 6-8-10 triangle, making the diagonal 100 inches, which is 8 feet 4 inches.

4. **The correct answer is (C).** In 3 hours, one ship went 60 miles, the other 45 miles. This is a 3-4-5 triangle as 45 = 3(15), 60 = 4(15). The hypotenuse will be 5(15), or 75.

5. **The correct answer is (D).** This is inverse variation.
$$m \times d = (m+2) \times x$$
$$\frac{md}{m+2} = x$$

6. **The correct answer is (A).** He must score as many points above 85 as below. So far he has 8 above and 10 below. He needs another 2 above.

7. **The correct answer is (B).** If 15 adults are fed, $\frac{3}{4}$ of the food is gone. $\frac{1}{4}$ of the food will feed $\frac{1}{4} \times 32$, or 8, children.

8. **The correct answer is (C).** If angle $A = 60°$, then angle $B = 120°$.

   Angle B = Angle D. Their sum is $240°$.

9. **The correct answer is (C).**

   Area of circle = $64\pi = \pi r^2$

   Radius of circle = 8

   Side of square = 16

   Perimeter of square = 64

10. **The correct answer is (C).**

    10 minutes = $\dfrac{1}{6}$ hour

    In one hour, the train will cover 6(14), or 84, miles.

SUMMING IT UP

- Follow the five-step plan for answering basic multiple-choice math questions:

  1 Read the question carefully and determine what's being asked.

  2 Decide which math principles apply and use them to solve the problem.

  3 Look for your answer among the choices. If it's there, mark it and go on.

  4 If the answer you found is not there, recheck the question and your calculations.

  5 If you still can't solve the problem, eliminate obviously wrong answers and take your best guess.

- Use a calculator where it can help the most: on basic arithmetic calculations, when calculating square roots and percentages, and in comparing and converting fractions.

- Always set up your work on paper, then enter the numbers in your calculator; that way, if your calculation becomes confused, you don't have to try to replicate your setup from memory.

- The question number tells you how hard the question will be (on a 1 to 25 scale).

- Work backward from the answer choices. When you do, start with choice (C).

- Try to work with numbers instead of letters. This will help you avoid unnecessary algebraic calculations.

- Figures in the math section are always drawn to scale unless you see a warning. So use your eye as an estimator if you need to.

Grid-In Strategies

chapter 9

OVERVIEW

- Why grid-ins are easier than you think
- How to record your answers
- Guessing on grid-ins can't hurt you
- Summing it up

WHY GRID-INS ARE EASIER THAN YOU THINK

You should be pretty good at filling in ovals by now, right? Here comes a new angle—grid-ins. These are officially named "student-produced responses," because you have to do the calculations and find the answer on your own; there are no multiple-choice answers to choose from.

Many students are intimidated by grid-ins. Don't be! Grid-in questions test the exact same mathematical concepts as the multiple-choice questions. The only difference is that there are no answer choices to work with.

The grid-in questions are in a section of their own and arranged in order of difficulty from easy to hard.

Take a Look at a Grid

The special answer grid has some very different sections. There are blank boxes at the top so you can actually write in your answer. Below the boxes are some ovals that have fraction slashes and decimal points. You fill these in if your answer needs them. The largest section has ovals with numbers in them. You have to fill in the ovals to correspond to the answer you have written in the boxes. Yes, it's a lot to think about, but once you understand how to use them it's not a big deal. Here is a sample grid:

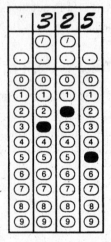

HOW TO RECORD YOUR ANSWERS

On the SAT, each set of grid-in questions starts with directions that look approximately like this:

Directions: Solve each of these problems. Write the answer in the corresponding grid on the answer sheet and fill in the ovals beneath each answer you write. Here are some examples.

Note: Either format is correct.   **Note:** Either position is correct.

Once you get the following six rules down pat, you can concentrate just on solving the math problems in this section.

1 Write your answer in the boxes at the top of the grid.

2 Mark the corresponding ovals, one per column.

3 Start in any column.

4 Work with decimals or fractions.

5 Express mixed numbers as decimals or improper fractions.

6 If more than one answer is possible, grid any one.

Now let's look at these rules in more detail:

1 Write your answer in the boxes at the top of the grid. Technically, this isn't required by the SAT. Realistically, it gives you something to follow as you fill in the ovals. Do it—it will help you.

2 Make sure to mark the ovals that correspond to the answer you entered in the boxes, one per column. The machine that scores the test can only read the ovals, so if you don't fill them in, you won't get credit. Just entering your answer in the boxes is not enough!

3 You can start entering your answer in any column, if space permits. Unused columns should be left blank; don't put in zeroes. Look at this example:

Here are two ways to enter an answer of "150."

NOTE

Don't use a comma in a number larger than 999. Just fill in the four digits and the corresponding ovals. You only have ovals for numbers, decimal points, and fraction slashes; there aren't any for commas.

4 You can write your answer as a decimal or as a fraction. For example, an answer can be expressed as $\frac{3}{4}$ or as .75. You don't have to put a zero in front of a decimal that is less than 1. Just remember that you have only four spaces to work with and that a decimal point or a fraction slash uses up one of the spaces.

For decimal answers, be as accurate as possible but keep it within four spaces. Say you get an answer of .1777; here are your options:

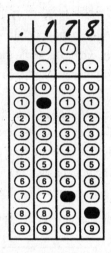

Answers .177 and .178 would both be marked as correct.

Answers .18 or .2 would be marked wrong because they could have been written more accurately in the space provided.

Fractions do not have to be simplified to simplest form unless they don't fit in the answer grid. For example, you can grid $\frac{4}{10}$, but you can't grid $\frac{12}{16}$ because you'd need five spaces. So, you would simplify it and grid $\frac{3}{4}$.

5 A mixed number has to be expressed as a decimal or as an improper fraction. If you tried to grid $1\frac{3}{4}$, it would be scored as $\frac{13}{4}$, which would give you a wrong answer. Instead, you could grid the answer as 1.75 or as $\frac{7}{4}$.

The above answers are acceptable.

The above answer is unacceptable.

6 Sometimes the problems in this section will have more than one correct answer. Choose one and grid it.

For example, if a question asks for a prime number between 5 and 13, the answer could be 7 or 11. Grid 7 or grid 11, but don't put in both answers.

Either answer is acceptable, but not both.

GUESSING ON GRID-INS CAN'T HURT YOU

Unfortunately, you cannot receive partial credit for grid-ins. Your answers are either completely correct or completely wrong. But no points are deducted for incorrect responses, so guessing is better than leaving a question blank.

EXERCISES: GRID-INS

Exercise 1

10 Questions • 15 Minutes

Directions: Solve each of these problems. Write the answer in the corresponding grid on the answer sheet and fill in the ovals beneath each answer you write. Here are some examples.

Answer: $\frac{3}{4} = .75$; show answer either way

Answer: 325

Note: A mixed number such as $3\frac{1}{2}$ must be gridded as 7/2 or as 3.5. If gridded as "3 1/2," it will be read as "thirty-one halves."

Note: Either position is correct.

1. Simplified to a simplest fraction, what part of a dime is a quarter?

2. Marion is paid $24 for 5 hours of work in the school office. Janet works 3 hours and makes $10.95. How much more per hour does Marion make than Janet? (Ignore the dollar sign in gridding your answer.)

3. If the outer diameter of a cylindrical oil tank is 54.28 inches and the inner diameter is 48.7 inches, what is the thickness of the wall of the tank, in inches?

4. What number added to 40% of itself is equal to 84?

5. If $r = 25 - s$, what is the value of $4(r + s)$?

6. What is the value of $\left(\dfrac{1}{16}\right)^{\frac{3}{2}}$?

7. If $f(x) = 5|3x| - 12$, what is the value of $f(-4)$?

8. How many different 3-digit *even* numbers can be formed from the digits 2, 3, 5, 7, and 9, if each digit can be used more than once?

9. In May, Carter's Appliances sold 40 washing machines. In June, because of a special promotion, the store sold 80 washing machines. What is the percent of increase in the number of washing machines sold?

10. Find the value of $\left(3\sqrt{2}\right)^2$.

Exercise 2

10 Questions • 15 Minutes

Directions: Solve each of these problems. Write the answer in the corresponding grid on the answer sheet and fill in the ovals beneath each answer you write. Here are some examples.

Answer: $\frac{3}{4}$ = .75 ; show answer either way   **Answer:** 325

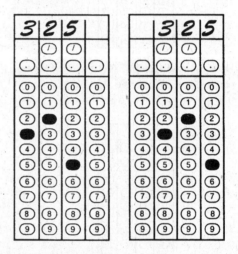

Note: A mixed number such as $3\frac{1}{2}$ must be gridded as 7/2 or as 3.5. If gridded as "3 1/2", it will be read as "thirty-one halves."

Note: Either position is correct.

1. 53% of the 1000 students at Jackson High are girls. How many boys are there in the school?

2. If $2^{n-3} = 32$, what is the value of n?

3. In a group of 40 students, 25 applied to Columbia and 30 applied to Cornell. If 3 students applied to neither Columbia nor Cornell, how many students applied to both schools?

4. If $x^2 - y^2 = 100$ and $x - y = 20$, what is the value of $x + y$?

5. A gallon of water is added to 6 quarts of a solution that is 50% acid. What percent of the new solution is acid?

6. A gasoline tank is $\frac{1}{4}$ full. After adding 10 gallons of gasoline, the gauge indicates that the tank is $\frac{2}{3}$ full. Find the capacity of the tank in gallons.

7. A plane flies over Denver at 11:20 a.m. It passes over Coolidge, 120 miles from Denver, at 11:32 a.m. Find the rate of the plane in miles per hour.

8. What is one of the real number values that must be excluded from the domain of the function $g(x) = \dfrac{3x - 6}{x^2 - 7x + 12}$?

9. What is the median of the set of numbers 2, 3, 4, 5, 6, 7, 8, and 9?

10. If $A = \{2, 4, 6, 8, 10, 12, 14\}$, $B = \{1, 3, 5, 7, 9, 11\}$, and $C = \{3, 6, 9, 12\}$, how many numbers are in the set $A \cup B \cup C$?

ANSWERS AND EXPLANATIONS

Exercise 1

1. $\dfrac{25}{10} = \dfrac{5}{2}$ **(answer)**

2. Marion's hourly wage is $\dfrac{\$24}{5}$, or \$4.80.

   Janet's hourly wage is $\dfrac{\$10.95}{3}$, or \$3.65.

   \$4.80 − \$3.65 = \$1.15 **(answer)**

3. The difference of 5.58 must be divided between both sides. The thickness on each side is 2.79 **(answer).**

4. $x + 0.40x = 84$ **(answer)**
   $$1.40x = 84$$
   $$14x = 840$$
   $$x = 60$$

5. $r + s = 25$

   $4(r + s) = 4(25) = 100$ **(answer)**

6. $\left(\dfrac{1}{16}\right)^{\frac{3}{2}} = (16)^{\frac{3}{2}} = \left(\sqrt{16}\right)^3 = 4^3 = 64$ **(answer)**

7. $f(x) = 5\,|3x| - 12$
   $$f(-4) = 5\,|3(-4)| - 12$$
   $$= 5\,|-12| - 12$$
   $$= 5(12) - 12$$
   $$= 48 \text{ \textbf{(answer)}}$$

8. Since the number has to be even, the only possible units digit is 2. Then, since digits can be used more than once, there are five different possible values for the tens digit, and five different possible values for the hundreds digit. Overall, there are $5 \times 5 \times 1 = 25$ possible even 3-digit numbers.

   25 **(answer)**

9. Increase of 40
   Percent of Increase =

   [Amount of Increase/Original] • 100%

   $\dfrac{40}{40} \cdot 100\% = 100\%$ **(answer)**

10. $\left(3\sqrt{2}\right)\left(3\sqrt{2}\right) = 9 \cdot 2 = 18$ **(answer)**

Exercise 2

1. 47% of 1000 are boys.

(0.47)(1000) = 470 boys **(answer)**

2. $2^{n-3} = 2^5$

$n - 3 = 5$

$n = 8$ **(answer)**

3.

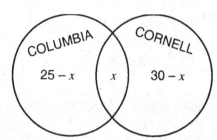

$25 - x + x + 30 - x = 37$

$55 - x = 37$

$18 = x$

18 **(answer)**

4. $x^2 - y^2 = (x - y)(x + y)$

$100 = 20(x + y)$

$5 = (x + y)$

5 **(answer)**

5.

	No. of quarts	% acid	Amount of acid
Original	6	0.50	3
Added	4	0	0
New	10		3

$\dfrac{3}{10} = 30\%$ **(answer)**

6. 10 gallons is $\dfrac{2}{3} - \dfrac{1}{4}$ of the tank.

$\dfrac{2}{3} - \dfrac{1}{4} = \dfrac{8-3}{12} = \dfrac{5}{12}$

$\dfrac{5}{12}x = 10$

$5x = 120$

$x = 24$ **(answer)**

7. The plane covers 120 miles in 12 minutes, or $\dfrac{1}{5}$ hour. In $\dfrac{5}{5}$, or 1 hour, it covers 5(120), or 600 miles. 600 **(answer)**

8. Any values that lead to division by 0 in the expression $\dfrac{3x - 6}{x^2 - 7x + 12}$ must be excluded from the domain. In order to determine these values, solve the quadratic equation $x^2 - 7x + 12 = 0$.

$x^2 - 7x + 12 = 0$ Factor the left side.

$(x - 4)(x - 3) = 0$ Set each factor equal to 0.

$x - 4 = 0$ $x - 3 = 0$

$x = 4, 3$ **(answers; both acceptable)**

9. The median is equal to the arithmetic mean of the two numbers in the middle, 5 and 6.

$\dfrac{5 + 6}{2} = \dfrac{11}{2} = 5.5$ **(answer)**

10. The union of the three sets will contain every element that appears in either A or B or C. That is, $A \cup B \cup C = \{1, 2, 3, 4, 5, 6, 7, 8, 9, 10, 11, 12, 14\}$. Therefore, there are 13 elements in $A \cup B \cup C$.

13 **(answer)**

SUMMING IT UP

- When you grid answers to student-produced response questions, follow these six rules:
  1. Write your answer in the boxes at the top of the grid.
  2. Mark the corresponding ovals, one per column.
  3. Start in any column.
  4. Work with decimals or fractions.
  5. Express mixed numbers as decimals or improper fractions.
  6. If more than one answer is possible, grid any one.

- Remember that grid-ins test the same concepts as multiple-choice math.

- The most important advice for grid-ins? Don't be intimidated.

Numbers and Operations Review

chapter 10

OVERVIEW

- Numbers and number systems
- Sets
- Operations with fractions
- Verbal problems involving fractions
- Direct and inverse variation
- Finding percents
- Verbal problems involving percent
- Arithmetic and geometric sequences
- Summing it up

NUMBERS AND NUMBER SYSTEMS

The numbers that are used for counting, that is, 1, 2, 3, 4, 5, 6, and so on, are called the *positive integers*. The positive integers, along with the number 0, are referred to as *whole numbers*. The negative integers, −1, −2, −3, −4, −5, −6, and so on, along with 0 and the positive integers, are called *integers*.

A *rational number* is defined as a number that can be written as the ratio of two integers, with the denominator not equal to 0. According to this definition, the following numbers are all rational:

$$-\frac{11}{12}, \ 0, \ 3\frac{2}{3}, \ 31, \ 9.25, \ 75\%$$

Note, for example, that 9.25 is rational since $9.25 = 9\frac{1}{4} = \frac{37}{4}$, and 75% is rational since it is equal to $\frac{3}{4}$. Thus, all integers, fractions, decimals, and percents are rational.

Numbers that cannot be expressed as ratios are called *irrational numbers*. The most common irrational numbers used on the SAT are certain square roots such as $\sqrt{2}$ or $\sqrt{3}$, and the number symbolized by the Greek letter π.

299

When rational and irrational numbers are combined, the result is *real numbers*. All numbers used on the SAT are real numbers.

> State each number system that the following numbers belong to:
>
> **A.** -13
>
> **B.** $9\dfrac{1}{5}$
>
> **C.** $\sqrt{7}$

The correct answers are:

A. Negative Integers, Integers, Rational Numbers, Real Numbers

B. Rational Numbers, Real Numbers

C. Irrational Numbers, Real Numbers

Properties of Integers

An integer is said to be *even* if it is *divisible by* 2, that is, if there is no remainder when the number is divided by 2. Note that the number 0, as well as negative numbers such as -2, -4, and -6, are considered even. An integer is *odd* if it is not divisible by 2.

A positive integer is said to be *prime* if it is greater than 1 and if its only positive divisors are 1 and the number itself. For example, 11 is prime since the only positive integers that divide into it evenly are 1 and 11. However, 12 is not prime. Note that 12 is not only divisible by 1 and 12, but also by 2, 3, 4, and 6. The numbers 1, 2, 3, 4, 6, and 12 are called the *factors,* or the *divisors,* of 12.

> What are the first 7 prime numbers?

Answer: 2, 3, 5, 7, 11, 13, and 17

Positive integers that are not prime can be *prime factored,* that is, expressed as a product of prime numbers, in only one way. For example, the number 30, which is not prime, can be prime factored as $2 \times 3 \times 5$.

> What is the prime factorization of the number 24?

To begin, note that 24 can be written as 2×12.

Then, $12 = 2 \times 6$, so that $24 = 2 \times 2 \times 6$.

Finally, since $6 = 2 \times 3$, $24 = 2 \times 2 \times 2 \times 3$.

Consecutive integers are integers that differ by 1. For example, the integers 5, 6, 7, and 8 are consecutive. A group of integers such as 4, 6, 8, and 10 are called *consecutive even integers*, and the group 3, 5, 7, and 9 are *consecutive odd integers*.

The *multiples* of a whole number are the numbers that can be obtained by multiplying that whole number by other whole numbers. For example, some of the multiples of 3 are 6, 9, 12, 15, and 18. The *least common multiple* of two whole numbers is the smallest whole number that is a multiple of both numbers. The *greatest common divisor* of two given whole numbers is the largest whole number that divides evenly into both of the given whole numbers.

The relative sizes of two numbers can be indicated by using the symbols "=" for *equals*, ">" for *greater than,* and "<" for *less than*. For example, the statement "5 > 3" is read "5 is greater than 3." The symbol "$\geq$" means *greater than or equal to,* and the symbol "$\leq$" means *less than or equal to.* Thus, the statement $x \geq 8$ means that the value of x is either equal to 8 or greater than 8.

> What is the least common multiple of 3 and 7?

Answer: The multiples of 3 are 3, 6, 9, 12, 15, 18, 21, 24, 27, and so on. The multiples of 7 are 7, 14, 21, 28, 35, and so on. The least common multiple of 3 and 7 is 21.

> What is the greatest common divisor of 12 and 18?

Answer: The largest whole number that divides evenly into both 12 and 18 is 6.

EXERCISES: NUMBERS AND NUMBER SYSTEMS

Directions: Work out each problem on scratch paper.

Name all of the number systems that the following numbers belong to:

1. $-67\dfrac{4}{5}$
2. 0
3. 5.25

Determine the prime factorization of the following numbers:

4. 60
5. 75

6. What is the least common multiple of 5 and 7?

7. What is the greatest common divisor of 24 and 36?

In the statements below, replace the "?" with the correct symbol, =, >, or <.

8. $3 \times 4 \,?\, 24 \div 2$
9. $4 + 5 \,?\, 12 - 4$
10. $27 \div 3 \,?\, 125 \div 5$

ANSWERS AND EXPLANATIONS

1. Rational numbers, real numbers

2. Whole numbers, integers, rational numbers, real numbers

3. Rational numbers, real numbers

4. $60 = 2 \times 2 \times 3 \times 5$

5. $75 = 3 \times 5 \times 5$

6. The multiples of 5 are 5, 10, 15, 20, 25, 30, 35, 40, 45, ...

   The multiples of 7 are 7, 14, 21, 28, 35, 42, ...

   It can be seen that the least common multiple is 35.

7. The largest number that divides evenly into both 24 and 36 is 12.

8. $3 \times 4 = 24 \div 2$, since $12 = 12$.

9. $4 + 5 > 12 - 4$, since $9 > 8$.

10. $27 \div 3 < 125 \div 5$, since $9 < 25$.

SETS

A *set* is a collection of objects. The objects that belong to a particular set are called its *members* or its *elements*. Typically, in math problems, the members of a set are numbers.

Sets are usually represented by capital letters. The elements of a set are written between braces, { and }. Thus, $A = \{6, 7, 8\}$ tells us that set A contains the elements 6, 7, and 8. The order in which the elements of a set are written is not important. The set $\{6, 7, 8\}$ is the same as the set $\{8, 7, 6\}$.

A set that contains a finite number of elements is called a *finite set,* and a set with an infinite number of elements is called an *infinite set.* When describing a set, three dots can be used to indicate "and so on." For example, the infinite set of all positive even integers can be written as $\{2, 4, 6, 8, 10, ...\}$. The set of all positive odd integers between 3 and 49 inclusive can be written as $\{3, 5, 7, ..., 45, 47, 49\}$.

> Write a set that represents all of the multiples of 3 between 3 and 51, inclusive.

Set A is a *subset* of set B if every element of set A is also in set B. For example, the set $A = \{2, 4, 6\}$ is a subset of the set $B = \{0, 2, 4, 6, 8, 10\}$. Every set is considered to be a subset of itself. The correct answer is $\{3, 6, 9, ...45, 48, 51\}$.

The set with no elements is called the *null set,* and can be represented either by { }, or by the symbol ϕ. The null set is considered to be a subset of every other set.

> Write all of the subsets of the set $G = \{2, 4, 6\}$

The *union* of the two sets A and B is the set that contains all of the elements that are in *either* A or B. The union of A and B is written $A \cup B$. Therefore, if $A = \{3, 4, 5, 6, 7\}$ and $B = \{4, 6, 8, 10\}$, then $A \cup B = \{3, 4, 5, 6, 7, 8, 10\}$. Note that, if an element is in both sets, it does not need to be listed twice when forming the union. The correct answer is ϕ, $\{2\}$, $\{4\}$, $\{6\}$, $\{2, 4\}$, $\{2, 6\}$, $\{4, 6\}$, $\{2, 4, 6\}$.

The *intersection* of two sets A and B is the set that contains all of the elements that are in *both* A and B. The intersection of A and B is written $A \cap B$. Thus, if $A = \{3, 4, 5, 6, 7\}$ and $B = \{4, 6, 8, 10\}$, then $A \cap B = \{4, 6\}$.

> If A = $\{-2, -1, 0, 1, 2\}$ and $B = \{1, 2, 3, 4, 5\}$, what is $A \cup B$? What is $A \cap B$?

$A \cup B = \{-2, -1, 0, 1, 2, 3, 4, 5\}$
$A \cap B = \{1, 2\}$

EXERCISES: SETS

Directions: Work out each problem. Circle the letter of your choice.

1. Which of the following is NOT an element of the set of integers?

    (A) -7

    (B) 0

    (C) $\dfrac{6}{3}$

    (D) 10^3

    (E) $\dfrac{6}{4}$

2. Which of the following is NOT an element of the set of rational numbers?

    (A) 57

    (B) -12

    (C) $\sqrt{2}$

    (D) $\dfrac{2}{7}$

    (E) $-\dfrac{7}{8}$

3. How many subsets does the set $P = \{-1, 0, 1, 2\}$ have?

    (A) 4

    (B) 6

    (C) 8

    (D) 12

    (E) 16

4. If $A = \{2, 4, 6\}$, $B = \{1, 3, 5\}$, and $C = \{1, 2, 3\}$, which of the following sets represents $A \cup B \cup C$?

    (A) $\{1, 3\}$

    (B) $\{2, 4, 5, 6\}$

    (C) $\{1, 2, 3\}$

    (D) $\{1, 2, 3, 4, 5, 6\}$

    (E) ϕ

5. If $A = \{2, 4, 6\}$, $B = \{1, 3, 5\}$, and $C = \{1, 2, 3\}$, which of the following sets represents $A \cap B \cap C$?

    (A) $\{1, 3\}$

    (B) $\{2, 4, 5, 6\}$

    (C) $\{1, 2, 3\}$

    (D) $\{1, 2, 3, 4, 5, 6\}$

    (E) ϕ

6. If A is the set containing all positive integers that are multiples of 2, and B is the set containing all positive integers that are multiples of 3, which of the following best describes the set $A \cap B$?

    (A) The set containing all positive integers that are multiples of 6

    (B) The set containing all positive integers that are multiples of either 2 or 3

    (C) The set containing all positive integers that are multiples of 5

    (D) The set containing all positive integers that are multiples of 12

    (E) ϕ

7. If A is the set containing all positive integers that are multiples of 2, and B is the set containing all positive integers that are multiples of 3, which of the following best describes the set $A \cup B$?

    (A) The set containing all positive integers that are multiples of 6

    (B) The set containing all positive integers that are multiples of either 2 or 3

    (C) The set containing all positive integers that are multiples of 5

    (D) The set containing all positive integers that are multiples of 12

    (E) ϕ

8. If $C = \{10, 20, 30, 40\}$, $D = \{5, 10, 15, 20, 25, 30\}$, and $E = \{15, 30, 45, 60\}$, which of the following represents the set $C \cap D \cap E$?

(A) $\{5, 10, 15, 20, 25, 30, 40, 45, 60\}$

(B) $\{30\}$

(C) $\{10, 15, 20, 30\}$

(D) $\{10, 20, 30\}$

(E) ϕ

9. If F is the set of all integers greater than or equal to 75, and G is the set of all integers less than 78, which of the following represents the set $F \cap G$?

(A) $\{75, 76, 77\}$

(B) $\{76, 77\}$

(C) $\{76, 77, 78\}$

(D) $\{75, 76, 77, 78\}$

(E) The set of all integers

10. If X is the set of all positive integers, and Y is the set of all negative integers, which of the following best describes $X \cup Y$?

(A) The set of all integers

(B) The set of all real numbers

(C) $\{0\}$

(D) ϕ

(E) The set of all integers except 0

ANSWER KEY AND EXPLANATIONS

1. E	3. E	5. E	7. B	9. A
2. C	4. D	6. A	8. B	10. E

1. **The correct answer is (E).** The number $\frac{6}{4}$ is equal to $1\frac{1}{2}$. This is a rational number, but not an integer.

2. **The correct answer is (C).** The number $\sqrt{2}$ is an irrational number.

3. **The correct answer is (E).** The sub-sets are ϕ, $\{-1\}$, $\{0\}$, $\{1\}$, $\{2\}$, $\{-1, 0\}$, $\{-1, 1\}$, $\{-1, 2\}$, $\{0, 1\}$, $\{0, 2\}$, $\{1, 2\}$, $\{-1, 0, 2\}$, $\{-1, 0, 1\}$, $\{0, 1, 2\}$, $\{-1, 1, 2\}$, $\{-1, 0, 1, 2\}$.

4. **The correct answer is (D).** The union of the three sets is the set that contains all of the elements of all three sets. The set $\{1, 2, 3, 4, 5, 6\}$ contains all of the elements of A, B, and C.

5. **The correct answer is (E).** The intersection of the three sets contains all of the elements that are in all three sets. However, there are no elements that are in all three sets.

6. **The correct answer is (A).** The easiest way to answer this question is to begin by writing down some of the elements in each of the sets.

   $A = \{2, 4, 6, 8, 10, 12, 14, 16, 18, \ldots\}$

   $B = \{3, 6, 9, 12, 15, 18,\ldots\}$. Then,

   $A \cap B = \{6, 12, 18,\ldots\}$. It is easy to see that the intersection contains the positive integers that are multiples of 6.

7. **The correct answer is (B).** Based on the work in question 6, $A \cup B = \{2, 3, 4, 6, 8, 9, 10, 12, 14, 15, 16, 18,\ldots\}$. This set contains all of the positive integers that are either multiples of 2 or 3.

8. **The correct answer is (B).** The only element in common in the three sets is 30.

9. **The correct answer is (A).** $F = \{75, 76, 77, 78, 79,\ldots\}$, and $G = \{77, 76, 75, 74, 73,\ldots\}$. The numbers that these sets have in common are 75, 76, and 77.

10. **The correct answer is (E).** The set of integers consists of the positive integers, the negative integers, and 0. If the two sets are combined, the result is a set with every integer except 0.

OPERATIONS WITH FRACTIONS

The four basic *arithmetic operations* are addition, subtraction, multiplication, and division. The results of these operations are called the *sum, difference, product,* and *quotient* respectively. These words are sometimes used in word problems, so you should be familiar with them.

You are permitted to use a calculator on the SAT. All computations involving whole numbers and decimals can therefore be done with your calculator. Some calculators also perform operations with fractions. If you do not own or are not familiar with the use of such a calculator, you can use this section to review the techniques for computing with fractions by hand.

Adding and Subtracting

In adding or subtracting fractions, you must remember that the numbers must have the same (common) denominator.

> Add $\dfrac{1}{3} + \dfrac{2}{5} + \dfrac{3}{4}$

The least number which is divisible by 3, 5, and 4 is 60. Therefore, use 60 as the common denominator. To add the fractions, divide 60 by each denominator and multiply the result by the given numerator.

$$\frac{20 + 24 + 45}{60} = \frac{89}{60}, \text{ or } 1\frac{29}{60}$$

$$\frac{a}{b} + \frac{c}{d} = \frac{ad + bc}{bd}$$

A similar shortcut applies to subtraction.

$$\frac{a}{b} - \frac{c}{d} = \frac{ad - bc}{bd}$$

$$\frac{3}{4} - \frac{5}{7} = \frac{21 - 20}{28} = \frac{1}{28}$$

All fractions should be left in their simplest form. That is, there should be no factor common to both numerator and denominator. Often, in multiple-choice questions, you may find that the answer you have correctly computed is not among the choices but an equivalent fraction is. Be careful!

In simplifying fractions involving large numbers, it is helpful to be able to tell whether a factor is common to both numerator and denominator before a lengthy trial division. Certain tests for divisibility help with this.

TIP

To add or subtract fractions quickly, remember that a sum can be found by adding the two cross-products and putting this answer over the denominator product.

TESTS FOR DIVISIBILITY

To test if a number is divisible by:	Check to see:
2	if it is even
3	if the sum of the digits is divisible by 3
4	if the number formed by the last two digits is divisible by 4
5	if its last digit is a 5 or 0
6	if it is even and the sum of the digits is divisible by 3
8	if the number formed by the last three digits is divisible by 8
9	if the sum of the digits is divisible by 9
10	if its last digit is 0

Simplify: $\dfrac{3525}{4341}$

This fraction can be simplified by dividing 3, since the sum of the digits of the numerator is 15 and those of the denominator add up to 12, both divisible by 3.

$$\frac{3525}{4341} = \frac{1175}{1447}$$

The resulting fraction meets no further divisibility tests and therefore has no common factor listed above. Larger divisors would be unlikely on the SAT.

To add or subtract mixed numbers, it is again important to remember common denominators. In subtraction, you must borrow in terms of the common denominator.

Addition:
$$43\frac{2}{5} = 43\frac{6}{15}$$
$$+8\frac{1}{3} = +8\frac{5}{15}$$
$$51\frac{11}{15}$$

Subtraction:
$$43\frac{2}{5} = 43\frac{6}{15} = 42\frac{21}{15}$$
$$-6\frac{2}{3} = -6\frac{10}{15} = -6\frac{10}{15}$$
$$36\frac{11}{15}$$

Multiplying

To multiply fractions, always try to divide common factors where possible before actually multiplying. In multiplying mixed numbers, always rename them as improper fractions first.

Multiply: $\dfrac{\cancel{2}}{\cancel{5}} \cdot \dfrac{\cancel{10}^{2}}{\cancel{11}} \cdot \dfrac{\cancel{99}^{9}}{\cancel{110}_{55}} = \dfrac{18}{55}$

Multiply: $4\dfrac{1}{2} \cdot 1\dfrac{2}{3} \cdot 5\dfrac{1}{5}$

$\dfrac{\cancel{9}^{3}}{\cancel{2}} \cdot \dfrac{\cancel{5}}{\cancel{3}} \cdot \dfrac{\cancel{26}^{13}}{\cancel{5}} = 39$

Dividing

To divide fractions or mixed numbers, remember to multiply by the reciprocal of the divisor (the number after the division sign).

Divide: $4\dfrac{1}{2} \div \dfrac{3}{4} = \dfrac{\cancel{9}^{3}}{\cancel{2}} \cdot \dfrac{\cancel{4}^{2}}{\cancel{3}} = 6$

Divide: $62\dfrac{1}{2} \div 5 = \dfrac{\cancel{125}^{25}}{2} \cdot \dfrac{1}{\cancel{5}} = 12\dfrac{1}{2}$

To simplify complex fractions (fractions within fractions), multiply every term by the least common multiple of all denominators in order to clear all fractions in the given numerator and denominator.

$$\dfrac{\dfrac{1}{2} + \dfrac{1}{3}}{\dfrac{1}{4} + \dfrac{1}{6}}$$

The least number that can be used to clear all fractions is 12. Multiplying each term by 12 yields:

$$\dfrac{6+4}{3+2} = \dfrac{10}{5} = 2$$

$$\dfrac{\dfrac{3}{4} + \dfrac{2}{3}}{1 - \dfrac{1}{2}}$$

Again, multiply by 12.

$$\dfrac{9+8}{12-6} = \dfrac{17}{6} = 2\dfrac{5}{6}$$

EXERCISES: OPERATIONS WITH FRACTIONS

Directions: Work out each problem in the space provided.

Add:

1. $12\dfrac{5}{6} + 2\dfrac{3}{8} + 21\dfrac{1}{4}$

2. $\dfrac{1}{2} + \dfrac{1}{3} + \dfrac{1}{4} + \dfrac{1}{5} + \dfrac{1}{6}$

Subtract:

3. $5\dfrac{3}{4}$ from $10\dfrac{1}{2}$

4. $17\dfrac{2}{3}$ from 50

5. $25\dfrac{3}{5}$ from $30\dfrac{9}{10}$

Multiply:

6. $5\dfrac{1}{4} \bullet 1\dfrac{5}{7}$

7. $\dfrac{3}{4} \bullet \dfrac{3}{4} \bullet \dfrac{3}{4}$

8. $12\dfrac{1}{2} \bullet 16$

Divide:

9. $\dfrac{1}{5} \div 5$

10. $5 \div \dfrac{1}{5}$

11. $3\dfrac{2}{3} \div 1\dfrac{5}{6}$

Simplify:

12. $\dfrac{\dfrac{5}{6} - \dfrac{1}{3}}{2 + \dfrac{1}{5}}$

13. $\dfrac{3 + \dfrac{1}{4}}{5 - \dfrac{1}{2}}$

ANSWERS AND EXPLANATIONS

1.

$$12\frac{5}{6} = 12\frac{20}{24}$$

$$2\frac{3}{8} = 2\frac{9}{24}$$

$$+21\frac{1}{4} = 21\frac{6}{24}$$

$$35\frac{35}{24} = 36\frac{11}{24}$$

2.

$$\frac{1}{2} = \frac{30}{60}$$

$$\frac{1}{3} = \frac{20}{60}$$

$$\frac{1}{4} = \frac{15}{60}$$

$$\frac{1}{5} = \frac{12}{60}$$

$$+\frac{1}{6} = \frac{10}{60}$$

$$\frac{87}{60} = 1\frac{27}{60} = 1\frac{9}{20}$$

3.

$$10\frac{1}{2} = 9\frac{3}{2} = 9\frac{6}{4}$$

$$-5\frac{3}{4}$$

$$4\frac{3}{4}$$

4.

$$\overset{49}{\cancel{50}}\frac{3}{3}$$

$$-17\frac{2}{3}$$

$$32\frac{1}{3}$$

5.

$$30\frac{9}{10} = 30\frac{9}{10}$$

$$25\frac{3}{5} = 25\frac{6}{10}$$

$$5\frac{3}{10}$$

6. $\dfrac{\overset{3}{\cancel{21}}}{\cancel{4}} \cdot \dfrac{\overset{3}{\cancel{12}}}{\cancel{7}} = 9$

7. $\dfrac{3}{4} \cdot \dfrac{3}{4} \cdot \dfrac{3}{4} = \dfrac{27}{64}$

8. $\dfrac{25}{\cancel{2}} \cdot \overset{8}{\cancel{16}} = 200$

9. $\dfrac{1}{5} \cdot \dfrac{1}{5} = \dfrac{1}{25}$

10. $5 \cdot 5 = 25$

11. $\dfrac{\cancel{4}}{\cancel{3}} \cdot \dfrac{\overset{2}{\cancel{6}}}{\cancel{4}} = 2$

12. $\dfrac{25 - 10}{60 + 6} = \dfrac{15}{66} = \dfrac{5}{22}$

Each term was multiplied by 30.

13. $\dfrac{12 + 1}{20 - 2} = \dfrac{13}{18}$

Each term was multiplied by 4.

VERBAL PROBLEMS INVOLVING FRACTIONS

Fraction problems deal with parts of a whole.

> If a class consists of 12 boys and 18 girls, what part of the class is boys?

12 out of 30 students, or $\frac{12}{30} = \frac{2}{5}$. So, boys represent $\frac{2}{5}$ of the class.

Read all the questions carefully. Often a problem may require more than one calculation.

> $\frac{1}{4}$ of this year's seniors have averages above 90. $\frac{1}{2}$ of the remainder have averages between 80 and 90 inclusive. What part of the senior class have averages below 80?

$\frac{1}{4}$ have averages above 90.

$\frac{1}{2}$ of $\frac{3}{4}$, or $\frac{3}{8}$, have averages between 80 and 90 inclusive.

$\frac{1}{4} + \frac{3}{8} = \frac{2}{8} + \frac{3}{8} = \frac{5}{8}$ have averages 80 and above.

Therefore, $\frac{3}{8}$ of the class have averages below 80.

> 14 is $\frac{2}{3}$ of what number?

$14 = \frac{2}{3}x$

Multiply each side by $\frac{3}{2}$.

$21 = x$

> If John has p hours of homework and has worked for r hours, what part of his homework is yet to be done?

If John had 5 hours of homework and had worked for 3 hours, you would first find he had $5 - 3$ hours, or 2 hours, yet to do. This represents $\frac{2}{5}$ of his work. Using letters, his remaining work is represented by $\frac{p-r}{p}$.

TIP

If a problem is given with letters in place of numbers, the same reasoning must be applied as for numbers. If you are not sure how to proceed, replace the letters with numbers to determine the steps that must be taken.

EXERCISES: VERBAL PROBLEMS INVOLVING FRACTIONS

Directions: Work out each problem. Circle the letter of your choice.

1. A team played 30 games, of which it won 24. What part of the games played did the team lose?

(A) $\dfrac{4}{5}$

(B) $\dfrac{1}{4}$

(C) $\dfrac{1}{5}$

(D) $\dfrac{3}{4}$

(E) $\dfrac{2}{3}$

2. If a man's weekly salary is X and he saves Y, what part of his weekly salary does he spend?

(A) $\dfrac{X}{Y}$

(B) $\dfrac{X-Y}{X}$

(C) $\dfrac{X-Y}{Y}$

(D) $\dfrac{Y-X}{X}$

(E) $\dfrac{Y-X}{Y}$

3. What part of an hour elapses between 11:50 a.m. and 12:14 p.m.?

(A) $\dfrac{2}{5}$

(B) $\dfrac{7}{30}$

(C) $\dfrac{17}{30}$

(D) $\dfrac{1}{6}$

(E) $\dfrac{1}{4}$

4. One half of the employees of Acme Co. earn salaries above $18,000 annually. One third of the remainder earn salaries between $15,000 and $18,000. What part of the staff earns below $15,000?

(A) $\dfrac{1}{6}$

(B) $\dfrac{2}{3}$

(C) $\dfrac{1}{2}$

(D) $\dfrac{1}{10}$

(E) $\dfrac{1}{3}$

5. David received his allowance on Sunday. He spends $\dfrac{1}{4}$ of his allowance on Monday and $\dfrac{2}{3}$ of the remainder on Tuesday. What part of his allowance is left for the rest of the week?

(A) $\dfrac{1}{3}$

(B) $\dfrac{1}{12}$

(C) $\dfrac{1}{4}$

(D) $\dfrac{1}{2}$

(E) $\dfrac{4}{7}$

6. 12 is $\dfrac{3}{4}$ of what number?

(A) 16

(B) 9

(C) 36

(D) 20

(E) 15

7. A piece of fabric is cut into three sections so that the first is three times as long as the second, and the second section is three times as long as the third. What part of the entire piece is the smallest section?

   (A) $\dfrac{1}{12}$

   (B) $\dfrac{1}{9}$

   (C) $\dfrac{1}{3}$

   (D) $\dfrac{1}{7}$

   (E) $\dfrac{1}{13}$

8. What part of a gallon is one quart?

   (A) $\dfrac{1}{2}$

   (B) $\dfrac{1}{4}$

   (C) $\dfrac{2}{3}$

   (D) $\dfrac{1}{3}$

   (E) $\dfrac{1}{5}$

9. A factory employs M men and W women. What part of its employees are women?

   (A) $\dfrac{W}{M}$

   (B) $\dfrac{M+W}{W}$

   (C) $\dfrac{W}{M-W}$

   (D) $\dfrac{W}{M+W}$

   (E) W

10. A motion was passed by a vote of 5:3. What part of the votes cast were in favor of the motion?

   (A) $\dfrac{5}{8}$

   (B) $\dfrac{5}{3}$

   (C) $\dfrac{3}{5}$

   (D) $\dfrac{2}{5}$

   (E) $\dfrac{3}{8}$

11. If the ratio of $x{:}y$ is 9:7, what is the value of $x+y$?

   (A) 2

   (B) 14

   (C) 16

   (D) 63

   (E) It cannot be determined from the information given.

12. In a certain class, the ratio of men to women is 3:5. If the class has 24 people in it, how many are women?

   (A) 9

   (B) 12

   (C) 15

   (D) 18

   (E) 21

13. If the ratio of men to women in a class is 3:5 and the class contains 24 people, how many additional men would have to enroll to make the ratio of men to women 1:1?

   (A) 3

   (B) 6

   (C) 9

   (D) 12

   (E) 15

14. If x is $\frac{2}{3}$ of y and y is $\frac{3}{4}$ of z, what is the ratio of $z:x$?

    (A) 1:2

    (B) 1:1

    (C) 2:1

    (D) 3:2

    (E) 4:3

15. What fraction of 8 tons is 1000 lbs.?

    (A) $\frac{1}{32}$

    (B) $\frac{1}{16}$

    (C) $\frac{1}{8}$

    (D) $\frac{8}{1}$

    (E) $\frac{16}{1}$

ANSWER KEY AND EXPLANATIONS

1. C	4. E	7. E	10. A	13. B
2. B	5. C	8. B	11. E	14. C
3. A	6. A	9. D	12. C	15. B

1. **The correct answer is (C).** The team lost 6 games out of 30. $\frac{6}{30} = \frac{1}{5}$

2. **The correct answer is (B).** The man spends $X - Y$ out of X. $\frac{X-Y}{X}$

3. **The correct answer is (A).** 10 minutes elapse by noon, and another 14 after noon, making a total of 24 minutes. There are 60 minutes in an hour. $\frac{24}{60} = \frac{2}{5}$

4. **The correct answer is (E).** One half earn over $18,000. One third of the other $\frac{1}{2}$ or $\frac{1}{6}$, earn between $15,000 and $18,000. This accounts for $\frac{1}{2} + \frac{1}{6}$, or $\frac{3}{6} + \frac{1}{6} + \frac{4}{6} = \frac{2}{3}$ of the staff, leaving $\frac{1}{3}$ to earn below $15,000.

5. **The correct answer is (C).** David spends $\frac{1}{4}$ on Monday and $\frac{2}{3}$ of the other $\frac{3}{4}$, or $\frac{1}{2}$, on Tuesday, leaving only $\frac{1}{4}$ for the rest of the week.

6. **The correct answer is (A).** $12 = \frac{3}{4}x$. Multiply each side by $\frac{4}{3}$. $16 = x$

7. **The correct answer is (E).** Let the third or shortest section $= x$. Then the second section $= 3x$, and the first section $= 9x$. The entire piece of fabric is then $13x$, and the shortest piece represents $\frac{x}{13x}$, or $\frac{1}{13}$, of the entire piece.

8. **The correct answer is (B).** There are four quarts in one gallon.

9. **The correct answer is (D).** The factory employs $M + W$ people, out of which W are women.

10. **The correct answer is (A).** For every 5 votes in favor, 3 were cast against. 5 out of every 8 votes cast were in favor of the motion.

11. **The correct answer is (E).** Remember, a ratio is a fraction. If x is 18 and y is 14, the ratio $x:y$ is 9:7, but $x + y$ is 32. The point of this problem is that x and y can take on *many* possible values, just as long as the ratio 9:7 is preserved. Given the multiplicity of possible values, it is not possible here to establish *one* definite value for the sum of x and y.

12. **The correct answer is (C).** The ratio of women to the total number of people is 5:8. We can set up a proportion. If $\frac{5}{8} = \frac{x}{24}$, then $x = 15$.

13. **The correct answer is (B).** From the previous problem we know that the class contains 15 women and 9 men. In order to have the same number of men and women, 6 additional men would have to enroll.

14. **The correct answer is (C).** There are several ways to attack this problem. If x is $\frac{2}{3}$ of y, then $x = \frac{2}{3} \cdot y$. If y is $\frac{3}{4}$ of z, then z is $\frac{4}{3}$ of y, or $z = \frac{4}{3} \cdot y$. Therefore, $z = 2x$. The ratio of $z:x$ is 2:1. You could also plug in a real number and solve. If x is 2, figure out what y and z would be. Therefore, y would be 3 and z would be 4, so the ratio of z to x is 2:1.

15. **The correct answer is (B).** A ton contains 2000 pounds. So the fraction would be $\frac{1000}{16,000}$, which is $\frac{1}{16}$.

answers exercises

DIRECT AND INVERSE VARIATION

Direct Variation

Two quantities are said to *vary directly* if as one increases, the other increases, and, as one decreases, the other decreases.

For example, the amount owed to the milkman varies directly with the number of quarts of milk purchased. The amount of sugar needed in a recipe varies directly with the amount of butter used. The number of inches between two cities on a map varies directly with the number of miles between the cities.

> If a two-ounce package of peanuts costs 20¢, what is the cost of a pound of peanuts?

Here you are comparing cents with ounces, so $\dfrac{20}{2} = \dfrac{x}{16}$.
In solving a proportion, it is easiest to cross-multiply, remembering that the product of the means (the second and third terms of a proportion) is equal to the product of the extremes (the first and last terms of a proportion).

$$2x = 320$$
$$x = 160$$

Remember that the original units were cents, so the cost is $1.60. When two fractions are equal, as in a proportion, it is sometimes easier to see what change has taken place in the given numerator or denominator and then to apply the same change to the missing term. In keeping fractions equal, the change will always involve multiplying or dividing by a constant. In the previous example, the denominator was changed from 2 to 16. This involved multiplication by 8; therefore, the numerator (20) must also be multiplied by 8, giving 160 as an answer without any written work necessary. Since time is a very important factor in this type of examination, shortcuts such as this can be critical.

> If a truck can carry m pounds of coal, how many trucks are needed to carry p pounds of coal?

You are comparing trucks with pounds. This again is a direct variation, because the number of trucks increases as the number of pounds increases.

$$\frac{1}{m} = \frac{x}{p}$$
$$mx = p$$
$$x = \frac{p}{m}$$

Inverse Variation

Two quantities are said to *vary inversely* if as one increases, the other decreases.

For example, the number of workers hired to paint a house varies inversely with the number of days the job will take. A doctor's stock of flu vaccine varies inversely with the number of patients injected. The number of days a given supply of cat food lasts varies inversely with the number of cats being fed.

> If a case of cat food can feed 5 cats for 4 days, how long would it feed 8 cats?

Since this is a case of inverse variation (the more cats, the fewer days), multiply the number of cats by the number of days in each instance and set them equal.

$$5 \times 4 = 8 \times x$$
$$20 = 8x$$
$$2\frac{1}{2} = x$$

> If M machines can complete a job in H hours, how many of these machines would be needed to complete the job in 2 fewer hours?

This is another case of inverse variation, since the more machines, the fewer hours it will take to complete the job. The question asks how many machines would be needed to complete the job in $H - 2$ hours. Multiply the number of machines times the number of hours in each case, and set them equal.

$$M \times H = (H - 2) \times x$$
$$MH = (H - 2)x$$
$$\frac{MH}{H - 2} = x$$

Therefore, we would need $\dfrac{MH}{H - 2}$ machines.

EXERCISES: DIRECT AND INVERSE VARIATION

Directions: Work out each problem. Circle the letter of your choice.

1. If 60 feet of uniform wire weigh 80 pounds, what is the weight of 2 yards of the same wire?

    (A) $2\frac{2}{3}$ pounds

    (B) 6 pounds

    (C) 8 pounds

    (D) 120 pounds

    (E) 2400 pounds

2. A gear 50 inches in diameter turns a smaller gear 30 inches in diameter. If the larger gear makes 15 revolutions, how many revolutions does the smaller gear make in that time?

    (A) 9

    (B) 12

    (C) 20

    (D) 25

    (E) 30

3. If x men can do a job in h days, how long would y men take to do the same job?

    (A) $\dfrac{x}{h}$

    (B) $\dfrac{xh}{y}$

    (C) $\dfrac{hy}{x}$

    (D) $\dfrac{xy}{h}$

    (E) $\dfrac{x}{y}$

4. If a furnace uses 40 gallons of oil in a week, how many gallons, to the nearest gallon, does it use in 10 days?

    (A) 4

    (B) 28

    (C) 57

    (D) 58

    (E) 400

5. A recipe requires 13 ounces of sugar and 18 ounces of flour. If only 10 ounces of sugar are used, how much flour, to the nearest ounce, should be used?

    (A) 24

    (B) 23

    (C) 15

    (D) 14

    (E) 13

6. If a car can drive 25 miles on two gallons of gasoline, how many gallons will be needed for a trip of 150 miles?

    (A) 3

    (B) 6

    (C) 7

    (D) 10

    (E) 12

7. A school has enough bread to feed 30 children for 4 days. If 10 more children are added, how many days will the bread last?

    (A) $1\frac{1}{3}$

    (B) $2\frac{2}{3}$

    (C) 3

    (D) $5\frac{1}{3}$

    (E) 12

8. At c cents per pound, what is the cost of a ounces of salami?

(A) $\dfrac{c}{a}$

(B) $\dfrac{a}{c}$

(C) ac

(D) $\dfrac{ac}{16}$

(E) $\dfrac{16c}{a}$

9. If 3 miles are equivalent to 4.83 kilometers, then 11.27 kilometers are equivalent to how many miles?

(A) $2\dfrac{1}{3}$

(B) 5

(C) $6\dfrac{1}{2}$

(D) 7

(E) $7\dfrac{1}{3}$

10. If p pencils cost d dollars, how many pencils can be bought for c cents?

(A) $\dfrac{100pc}{d}$

(B) $\dfrac{pc}{100d}$

(C) $\dfrac{pd}{c}$

(D) $\dfrac{pc}{d}$

(E) $\dfrac{cd}{p}$

ANSWER KEY AND EXPLANATIONS

1. C	3. B	5. D	7. C	9. D
2. D	4. C	6. E	8. D	10. B

1. **The correct answer is (C).** You are comparing feet with pounds. The more feet, the more pounds. This is DIRECT. Remember to rename yards as feet:

$$\frac{60}{80} = \frac{6}{x}$$
$$60x = 480$$
$$x = 8$$

2. **The correct answer is (D).** The larger a gear, the fewer times it revolves in a given period of time. This is INVERSE.

$$50 \bullet 15 = 30 \bullet x$$
$$750 = 30x$$
$$25 = x$$

3. **The correct answer is (B).** The more men, the fewer days. This is INVERSE.

$$x \bullet h = y \bullet ?$$
$$\frac{xh}{y} = ?$$

4. **The correct answer is (C).** The more days, the more oil. This is DIRECT. Remember to rename the week as 7 days.

$$\frac{40}{7} = \frac{x}{10}$$
$$7x = 400$$
$$x = 57\frac{1}{7}$$

5. **The correct answer is (D).** The more sugar, the more flour. This is DIRECT.

$$\frac{13}{18} = \frac{10}{x}$$
$$13x = 180$$
$$x = 13\frac{11}{13}$$

6. **The correct answer is (E).** The more miles, the more gasoline. This is DIRECT.

$$\frac{25}{2} = \frac{150}{x}$$
$$25x = 300$$
$$x = 12$$

7. **The correct answer is (C).** The more children, the fewer days. This is INVERSE.

$$30 \bullet 4 = 40 \bullet x$$
$$120 = 40x$$
$$3 = x$$

8. **The correct answer is (D).** The more salami, the more it will cost. This is DIRECT. Remember to rename the pound as 16 ounces.

$$\frac{c}{16} = \frac{x}{a}$$
$$x = \frac{ac}{16}$$

9. **The correct answer is (D).** The more miles, the more kilometers. This is DIRECT.

$$\frac{3}{4.83} = \frac{x}{11.27}$$
$$4.83x = 33.81$$
$$x = 7$$

10. **The correct answer is (B).** The more pencils, the more cost. This is DIRECT. Remember to rename dollars as cents.

$$\frac{p}{100d} = \frac{x}{c}$$
$$x = \frac{pc}{100d}$$

FINDING PERCENTS

Percent Equivalents

"Percent" means "out of 100." If you understand this concept, it becomes very easy to rename a percent as an equivalent decimal or fraction.

$$5\% \frac{5}{100} = 0.05$$

$$2.6\% = \frac{2.6}{100} = 0.026$$

$$c\% = \frac{c}{100} = \frac{1}{100} \bullet c = 0.01c$$

$$\frac{1}{2}\% = \frac{\frac{1}{2}}{100} = \frac{1}{100} \bullet \frac{1}{2} = \frac{1}{100} \bullet 0.5 = 0.005$$

Certain fractional equivalents of common percents occur frequently enough that they should be memorized. Learning the values in the following table will make your work with percent problems much easier.

Percent-Fraction Equivalent Table

$50\% = \frac{1}{2}$	$33\frac{1}{3}\% = \frac{1}{3}$	$12\frac{1}{2}\% = \frac{1}{8}$
$25\% = \frac{1}{4}$	$66\frac{2}{3}\% = \frac{2}{3}$	$37\frac{1}{2}\% = \frac{3}{8}$
$75\% = \frac{3}{4}$	$20\% = \frac{1}{5}$	$62\frac{1}{2}\% = \frac{5}{8}$
$10\% = \frac{1}{10}$	$40\% = \frac{2}{5}$	$87\frac{1}{2}\% = \frac{7}{8}$
$30\% = \frac{3}{10}$	$60\% = \frac{3}{5}$	$16\frac{2}{3}\% = \frac{1}{6}$
$70\% = \frac{7}{10}$	$80\% = \frac{4}{5}$	$83\frac{1}{3}\% = \frac{5}{6}$
$90\% = \frac{9}{10}$		

Most percentage problems can be solved by using the following proportion:

$$\frac{\%}{100} = \frac{\text{part}}{\text{whole}}$$

Although this method works, it often yields unnecessarily large numbers that are difficult to compute. Following are examples of the four basic types of percent problems and different methods for solving them.

TIP

To change a % to a decimal, remove the % sign and divide by 100. This has the effect of moving the decimal point two places to the LEFT.

TIP

To change a decimal to a %, add the % sign and multiply by 100. This has the effect of moving the decimal point two places to the RIGHT.

TIP

To change a % to a fraction, remove the % sign and divide by 100. This has the effect of putting the % over 100 and simplifying the resulting fraction.

To Find a Percent of a Number

Find 27% of 92.

PROPORTIONAL METHOD

$$\frac{27}{100} = \frac{x}{92}$$
$$100x = 2484$$
$$x = 24.84$$

SHORTER METHOD

Rename the percent as its decimal or fraction equivalent and multiply. Use fractions only when they are among the familiar ones given in the previous chart.

$$
\begin{array}{r}
92 \\
\times 0.27 \\
\hline
644 \\
184 \\
\hline
24.84
\end{array}
$$

Find $12\frac{1}{2}\%$ of 96.

TIP

To change a fraction to a %, add the % sign and multiply by 100.

PROPORTIONAL METHOD

$$\frac{12\frac{1}{2}}{100} = \frac{x}{96}$$
$$100x = 1200$$
$$x = 12$$

DECIMAL METHOD

$$
\begin{array}{r}
0.125 \\
\times 96 \\
\hline
750 \\
1125 \\
\hline
12.000
\end{array}
$$

FRACTIONAL METHOD

$$\frac{1}{8} \bullet 96 = 12$$

Which method is easiest? It really pays to memorize those fractional equivalents.

To Find a Number When a Percent of It Is Given

7 is 5% of what number?

PROPORTIONAL METHOD

$$\frac{5}{100} = \frac{7}{x}$$
$$5x = 700$$
$$x = 140$$

SHORTER METHOD

Translate the problem into an algebraic equation. In doing this, the percent must be written as a fraction or decimal.

$$7 = 0.05x$$
$$700 = 5x$$
$$140 = x$$

20 is $33\frac{1}{3}\%$ of what number?

PROPORTIONAL METHOD

$$\frac{33\frac{1}{3}}{100} = \frac{20}{x}$$
$$33\frac{1}{3}x = 2000$$
$$\frac{100}{3}x = 2000$$
$$100x = 6000$$
$$x = 60$$

SHORTER METHOD

$$20 = \frac{1}{3}x$$
$$60 = x$$

Just think of the time you will save and the number of extra problems you will solve if you know that $33\frac{1}{3}\% = \frac{1}{3}$.

To Find What Percent One Number Is of Another

90 is what percent of 1500?

PROPORTIONAL METHOD

$$\frac{x}{100} = \frac{90}{1500}$$
$$1500x = 9000$$
$$15x = 90$$
$$x = 6$$

SHORTER METHOD

Put the part over the whole. Simplify the fraction and multiply by 100.

$$\frac{90}{1500} = \frac{9}{150} = \frac{3}{50} \bullet 100 = 6$$

7 is what percent of 35?

PROPORTIONAL METHOD

$$\frac{x}{100} = \frac{7}{35}$$
$$35x = 700$$
$$x = 20$$

SHORTER METHOD

$$\frac{7}{35} = \frac{1}{5} = 20\%$$

18 is what percent of 108?

PROPORTIONAL METHOD

$$\frac{x}{100} = \frac{18}{108}$$
$$108x = 1800$$

Time-consuming long division is necessary to get:

$$x = 16\frac{2}{3}$$

SHORTER METHOD

$$\frac{18}{108} = \frac{9}{54} = \frac{1}{6} = 16\frac{2}{3}\%$$

Once again, if you know the fraction equivalents of common percents, computation can be done in a few seconds.

To Find a Percent Over 100

Find 125% of 64.

PROPORTIONAL METHOD	DECIMAL METHOD	FRACTIONAL METHOD

$$\frac{125}{100} = \frac{x}{64}$$

$$100x = 8000$$

$$x = 80$$

DECIMAL METHOD:

$$64$$
$$\times 1.25$$
$$320$$
$$128$$
$$\underline{64}$$
$$80.00$$

FRACTIONAL METHOD:

$$1\frac{1}{4} \cdot 64$$

$$\frac{5}{4} \cdot 64 = 80$$

36 is 150% of what number?

PROPORTIONAL METHOD	DECIMAL METHOD	FRACTIONAL METHOD

PROPORTIONAL METHOD:

$$\frac{150}{100} = \frac{36}{x}$$

$$150x = 3600$$

$$15x = 360$$

$$x = 24$$

DECIMAL METHOD:

$$36 = 1.50x$$

$$360 = 15x$$

$$24 = x$$

FRACTIONAL METHOD:

$$36 = 1\frac{1}{2}x$$

$$36 = \frac{3}{2}x$$

$$72 = 3x$$

$$24 = x$$

60 is what percent of 50?

PROPORTIONAL METHOD

$$\frac{x}{100} = \frac{60}{50}$$

$$50x = 6000$$

$$5x = 600$$

$$x = 120$$

FRACTIONAL METHOD

$$\frac{60}{50} = \frac{6}{5} = 1\frac{1}{5} = 120\%$$

EXERCISES: FINDING PERCENTS

Directions: Work out each problem. Circle the letter of your choice.

1. Write 0.2% as a decimal.
   (A) 0.002
   (B) 0.02
   (C) 0.2
   (D) 2
   (E) 20

2. Write 3.4% as a fraction.

   (A) $\dfrac{34}{1000}$

   (B) $\dfrac{34}{10}$

   (C) $\dfrac{34}{100}$

   (D) $\dfrac{340}{100}$

   (E) $\dfrac{34}{10,000}$

3. Write $\dfrac{3}{4}$% as a decimal.
   (A) 0.75
   (B) 0.075
   (C) 0.0075
   (D) 0.00075
   (E) 7.5

4. Find 60% of 70.
   (A) 420
   (B) 4.2
   (C) $116\dfrac{2}{3}$
   (D) 4200
   (E) 42

5. What is 175% of 16?
   (A) $9\dfrac{1}{7}$
   (B) 28
   (C) 24
   (D) 12
   (E) 22

6. What percent of 40 is 16?
   (A) 20
   (B) $2\dfrac{1}{2}$
   (C) $33\dfrac{1}{3}$
   (D) 250
   (E) 40

7. What percent of 16 is 40?
   (A) 20
   (B) $2\dfrac{1}{2}$
   (C) 200
   (D) 250
   (E) 40

8. $4 is 20% of what?
   (A) $5
   (B) $20
   (C) $200
   (D) $5
   (E) $10

9. 12 is 150% of what number?
   (A) 18
   (B) 15
   (C) 6
   (D) 9
   (E) 8

10. How many sixteenths are there in $87\dfrac{1}{2}$%?
    (A) 7
    (B) 14
    (C) 3.5
    (D) 13
    (E) 15

ANSWER KEY AND EXPLANATIONS

1. A	3. C	5. B	7. D	9. E
2. A	4. E	6. E	8. B	10. B

1. **The correct answer is (A).**
   0.2% = 0.002 The decimal point moves to the LEFT two places.

2. **The correct answer is (A).**
   $$3.4\% = \frac{3.4}{100} = \frac{34}{1000}$$

3. **The correct answer is (C).**
   $$\frac{3}{4}\% = 0.75\% = 0.0075$$

4. **The correct answer is (E).**
   $$60\% = \frac{3}{5} \qquad \frac{3}{5} \cdot 70 = 42$$

5. **The correct answer is (B).**
   $$175\% = 1\frac{3}{4} \qquad \frac{7}{4} \cdot 16 = 28$$

6. **The correct answer is (E).**
   $$\frac{16}{40} = \frac{2}{5} = 40\%$$

7. **The correct answer is (D).**
   $$\frac{40}{16} = \frac{5}{2} = 2\frac{1}{2} = 250\%$$

8. **The correct answer is (B).**
   $$20\% = \frac{1}{5}, \text{ so } 4 = \frac{1}{5}x$$
   $$20 = x$$

9. **The correct answer is (E).**
   $$150\% = 1\frac{1}{2}$$
   $$\frac{3}{2}x = 12$$
   $$3x = 24$$
   $$x = 8$$

10. **The correct answer is (B).**
    $$87\frac{1}{2}\% = \frac{7}{8} = \frac{14}{16}$$

VERBAL PROBLEMS INVOLVING PERCENT

Certain types of business situations are excellent applications of percent.

Percent of Increase or Decrease

TIP

In word problems, *of* can usually be interpreted to mean *times* (in other words, *multiply*).

The *percent of increase or decrease* is found by putting the amount of increase or decrease over the original amount and renaming this fraction as a percent.

> Over a five-year period the enrollment at South High dropped from 1000 students to 800. Find the percent of decrease.

Answer: $\dfrac{200}{1000} = \dfrac{20}{100} = 20\%$

> A company normally employs 100 people. During a slow spell, it fired 20% of its employees. By what percent must it now increase its staff to return to full capacity?

$$20\% = \frac{1}{5} \qquad \frac{1}{5} \bullet 100 = 20$$

The company now has $100 - 20 = 80$ employees. If it then increases by 20, the percent of increase is $\dfrac{20}{80} = \dfrac{1}{4}$, or 25%.

Discount

A *discount* is usually expressed as a percent of the marked price that will be deducted from the marked price to determine the sale price.

> Bill's Hardware offers a 20% discount on all appliances during a sale week. If they take advantage of the sale, how much must the Russells pay for a washing machine marked at $280?

LONG METHOD

$$20\% = \frac{1}{5}$$
$$\frac{1}{5} \bullet 280 = \$56 \text{ discount}$$
$$\$280 - \$56 = \$224 \text{ sale price}$$

The danger inherent in this method is that $56 is sure to be among the multiple-choice answers.

SHORTCUT METHOD

If there is a 20% discount, the Russells will pay 80% of the marked price.

$$80\% = \frac{4}{5}$$
$$\frac{4}{5} \bullet 280 = \$224 \text{ sale price}$$

A store offers a television set marked at $340 less discounts of 10% and 5%. Another store offers the same set with a single discount of 15%. How much does the buyer save by buying at the better price?

In the first store, the initial discount means the buyer pays 90%, or $\frac{9}{10}$, of $340, which is $306. The additional 5% discount means the buyer pays 95% of $306, or $290.70. Note that the second discount must be figured on the first sale price. Taking 5% off $306 is a smaller amount than taking the additional 5% off $340. The second store will therefore have a lower sale price. In the second store, the buyer will pay 85% of $340, or $289, making the price $1.70 less than in the first store.

Commission

Many salespeople earn money on a commission basis. In order to encourage sales, they are paid a percentage of the value of goods sold. This amount is called a *commission*.

A salesperson at Brown's Department Store is paid $80 per week in salary plus a 4% commission on all her sales. How much will that salesperson earn in a week in which she sells $4032 worth of merchandise?

Find 4% of $4032 and add this amount to $80.

4032
× 0.04
$161.28 + $80 = $241.28

Bill Olson delivers newspapers for a dealer and keeps 8% of all money collected. One month he was able to keep $16. How much did he forward to the newspaper?

First, determine how much he collected by finding the number that 16 is 8% of.

$$16 = 0.08x$$
$$1600 = 8x$$
$$200 = x$$

If Bill collected $200 and kept $16, he gave the dealer $200 − $16, or $184.

Taxes

Taxes are a percent of money spent or money earned.

> Noname County collects a 7% sales tax on automobiles. If the price of a car is $8532 before taxes, what will this car cost once sales tax is added in?

Find 7% of $8532 to determine tax and then add it to $8532. This can be done in one step by finding 107% of $8532.

$$
\begin{array}{r}
\$8532 \\
\times\ 1.07 \\
\hline
59724 \\
85320 \\
\hline
\$9129.24
\end{array}
$$

> If the tax rate in Anytown is $3.10 per $100, what is the annual real estate tax on a house assessed at $47,200?

Annual tax = Tax rate • Assessed value

$\qquad$ = ($3.10/$100)($47,200)

$\qquad$ = (0.031) (47,200)

$\qquad$ = $1463.20

EXERCISES: VERBAL PROBLEMS INVOLVING PERCENT

Directions: Work out each problem. Circle the letter of your choice.

1. A suit marked at $80 is sold for $68. What is the rate of discount?
   (A) 12%
   (B) 15%
   (C) $17\frac{11}{17}\%$
   (D) 20%
   (E) 24%

2. What was the original price of a radio that sold for $70 during a 20%-off sale?
   (A) $56
   (B) $84
   (C) $87.50
   (D) $90
   (E) $92

3. How many dollars does a salesperson earn on a sale of *s* dollars at a commission of *r*%?
   (A) rs
   (B) $\dfrac{r}{s}$
   (C) $100rs$
   (D) $\dfrac{r}{100s}$
   (E) $\dfrac{rs}{100}$

4. At a selling price of $273, a refrigerator yields a 30% profit on the cost. What selling price will yield a 10% profit on the cost?
   (A) $210
   (B) $221
   (C) $231
   (D) $235
   (E) $240

5. What single discount is equivalent to two successive discounts of 10% and 15%?
   (A) 25%
   (B) 24.5%
   (C) 24%
   (D) 23.5%
   (E) 22%

6. The net price of a certain article is $306 after successive discounts of 15% and 10% off the marked price. What is the marked price?
   (A) $234.09
   (B) $382.50
   (C) $400
   (D) $408
   (E) None of the above

7. If a merchant makes a profit of 20% based on the selling price of an article, what percent does the merchant make on the cost?
   (A) 20
   (B) 25
   (C) 40
   (D) 80
   (E) None of the above

8. A certain radio costs a merchant $72. At what price must the merchant sell this radio in order to make a profit of 20% of the selling price?
   (A) $86.40
   (B) $90
   (C) $92
   (D) $144
   (E) $148

9. A baseball team has won 40 games out of 60 played. It has 32 more games to play. How many of these must the team win to make its record 75% for the season?

    (A) 26
    (B) 28
    (C) 29
    (D) 30
    (E) 32

10. If prices are reduced 25% and sales increase 20%, what is the net effect on gross receipts?

    (A) They increase by 5%.
    (B) They decrease by 5%.
    (C) They remain the same.
    (D) They increase by 10%.
    (E) They decrease by 10%.

11. A salesperson earns 5% on all sales between $200 and $600, and 8% on the part of the sales over $600. What is her commission in a week in which her sales total $800?

    (A) $20
    (B) $36
    (C) $46
    (D) $78
    (E) $88

12. If the enrollment at State U. was 3000 in 1998 and 12,000 in 2008, what was the percent of increase in enrollment?

    (A) 400%
    (B) 300%
    (C) 125%
    (D) 25%
    (E) 3%

13. If 6 students, representing $16\frac{2}{3}$% of the class, failed algebra, how many students passed the course?

    (A) 48
    (B) 42
    (C) 36
    (D) 32
    (E) 30

14. If 95% of the residents of Coral Estates live in private homes and 40% of these live in air-conditioned homes, what percent of the residents of Coral Estates live in air-conditioned homes?

    (A) 3%
    (B) 3.8%
    (C) 30%
    (D) 38%
    (E) 40%

15. A salesperson receives a salary of $100 a week and a commission of 5% on all sales. What must be the amount of sales for a week in which the salesperson's total weekly income is $360?

    (A) $6200
    (B) $5200
    (C) $2600
    (D) $720
    (E) $560

ANSWER KEY AND EXPLANATIONS

1. B	4. C	7. B	10. E	13. E
2. C	5. D	8. B	11. C	14. D
3. E	6. C	9. C	12. B	15. B

1. **The correct answer is (B).** The amount of discount is $12. Rate of discount is figured on the original price.

$$\frac{12}{80} = \frac{3}{20} \qquad \frac{3}{20} \cdot 100 = 15\%$$

2. **The correct answer is (C).** $70 represents 80% of the original price.

$$70 = 0.80x$$
$$700 = 8x$$
$$\$87.50 = x$$

3. **The correct answer is (E).**

$$r\% = \frac{r}{100}$$

The commission is $\dfrac{r}{100} \cdot s = \dfrac{rs}{100}$

4. **The correct answer is (C).**

$$1.30x = 273$$
$$13x = 2730$$
$$x = \$210 = \text{cost}$$

$273 represents 130% of the cost.

The new price will add 10% of cost, or $21, for profit.

New price = $231

5. **The correct answer is (D).** Work with a simple figure, such as 100.

First sale price is 90% of $100, or $90

Final sale price is 85% of $90, or $76.50

Total discount is $100 − $76.50 = $23.50

Percent of discount = $\dfrac{23.50}{100} = 23.5\%$

6. **The correct answer is (C).** If marked price = m, first sale price = $0.85m$ and net price = $0.90(0.85m) = 0.765m$

$$0.765m = 306$$
$$m = 400$$

In this case, it would be easy to work from the answer choices.

15% of $400 is $60, making a first sale price of $340.

10% of this price is $34, making the net price $306.

Choices (A), (B), and (D) would not give a final answer in whole dollars.

7. **The correct answer is (B).** Use an easy amount of $100 for the selling price. If the profit is 20% of the selling price, or $20, the cost is $80. Profit based on cost is

$$\frac{20}{80} = \frac{1}{4} = 25\%$$

8. **The correct answer is (B).** If the profit is to be 20% of the selling price, the cost must be 80% of the selling price.

$$72 = 0.80x$$
$$720 = 8x$$
$$90 = x$$

9. **The correct answer is (C).** The team must win 75%, or $\dfrac{3}{4}$, of the games played during the entire season. With 60 games played and 32 more to play, the team must win $\dfrac{3}{4}$ of 92 games in all.

$\dfrac{3}{4} \cdot 92 = 69$. Since 40 games have already been won, the team must win 29 additional games.

10. **The correct answer is (E).** Let original price $= p$, and original sales $= s$. Therefore, original gross receipts $= ps$. Let new price $= 0.75p$, and new sales $= 1.20s$. Therefore, new gross receipts $= 0.90ps$. Gross receipts are only 90% of what they were.

11. **The correct answer is (C).** Five percent of sales between $200 and $600 is $0.05(600) =$ $30. 8% of sales over $600 is $0.08(200) =$ $16. Total commission $= $30 + $16 = 46.

12. **The correct answer is (B).** Increase is 9000. Percent of increase is figured on original.

$$\frac{9000}{3000} = 3 = 300\%$$

13. **The correct answer is (E).**

$$16\frac{2}{3}\% = \frac{1}{6}$$
$$6 = \frac{1}{6}x$$
$$36 = x$$

36 students in class: 6 failed, 30 passed

14. **The correct answer is (D).**

$$40\% = \frac{2}{5}$$
$$\frac{2}{5} \text{ of } 95\% = 38\%$$

15. **The correct answer is (B).**

Let s = sales

$$\$100 + 0.05s = 360$$
$$0.05s = 260$$
$$5s = 26,000$$
$$s = \$5200$$

ARITHMETIC AND GEOMETRIC SEQUENCES

A *sequence* is a list of numbers in which there is a first number, a second number, a third number, and so on. For example, the "sequence of multiples of 3" is the sequence containing the numbers 3, 6, 9, 12, 15, 18, 21, 24, ... It is standard to denote the first term of a sequence as a_1, the second term as a_2, and a general term as a_n.

Arithmetic Sequences

An *arithmetic sequence* is a sequence in which the difference between any two consecutive numbers is constant. For example, the sequence given above is an arithmetic sequence because the difference between each term is 3.

In an arithmetic sequence, the difference between each term is called the *common difference* and is symbolized by the letter d. Therefore, if a_1 is the first term of an arithmetic sequence, and d is the common difference, the second term, a_2, is equal to $a_1 + d$. The third term, a_3, would be $a_1 + d + d = a_1 + 2d$, the fourth term, a_4, would be $a_1 + 3d$, and so on. The nth term, a_n, of an arithmetic sequence would be equal to $a_1 + (n - 1)d$.

> Write the first six terms of the arithmetic sequence whose first term is 5 and whose common difference is 4.

The first term is 5. To find the following terms, continually add the common difference 4 to each preceding term. Thus, the first six terms are:

5
$5 + 4 = 9$
$9 + 4 = 13$
$13 + 4 = 17$
$17 + 4 = 21$
$21 + 4 = 25$

Therefore, the first six terms are 5, 9, 13, 17, 21, and 25.

> What is the 10th term of the arithmetic sequence whose first term is 2 and whose common difference is 7?

Using the formula $a_1 + (n - 1)d$, with $a_1 = 2$, $d = 7$, and $n = 10$, compute $a_1 + (n - 1)d = 2 + (10 - 1)7 = 2 + (9)7 = 2 + 63 = 65$.

Geometric Sequences

A *geometric sequence* is a sequence in which each successive term is obtained by multiplying the previous term by the same number. For example, the sequence 3, 9, 27, 81, 243, 729, ... is a geometric sequence because each term is obtained by multiplying the previous term by 3.

In a geometric sequence, the number that a term is multiplied by in order to obtain the next term is called the *common ratio* and is symbolized by the letter r. Therefore, if a_1 is the first term of a geometric sequence, and r is the common ratio, the second term, a_2, is equal to $a_1 \times r$. The third term, a_3, would be $a_1 \times r \times r = a_1 \times r^2$, the fourth term, a_4, would be $a_1 \times r^3$, and so on. The nth term, a_n, of a geometric sequence would be equal to $a_1 \times r^{n-1}$.

> Write the first four terms of the geometric sequence whose first term is 2 and whose common ratio is 3.

The first term is 2. To find the following terms, continually multiply the common ratio 3 by the preceding term. Thus, the first four terms are:

2

$2 \times 3 = 6$

$6 \times 3 = 18$

$18 \times 3 = 54$

Therefore, the first four terms are 2, 6, 18, and 54.

> What is the fifth term of the geometric sequence whose first term is 1 and whose common ratio is 4?

Using the formula $a_1 \times r^{n-1}$, with $a_1 = 1$, $r = 4$, and $n = 5$, compute $a_1 \times r^{n-1} = 1 \times 4^{5-1} = 4^4 = 256$. Sequences have real-life applications, and you might be asked on the SAT to solve problems like the one below.

> Suppose that a car that cost $20,000 loses 20% of its value each year. What is the value of the car after 6 years?

Since the car loses 20% of its value each year, then each year the car is worth $100\% - 20\% = 80\%$ of its value the year before. The values of the car each year form a geometric progression with first term 20,000 and common ratio $80\% = 0.80$. To find the value of the car after 6 years, use the formula $a_1 \times r^{n-1}$, with $a_1 = 20,000$, $r = 0.80$, and $n = 7$ (the first term is at time zero), we compute $a_1 \times r^{n-1} = 20,000 \times (0.80)^6 = \$5242.88$.

EXERCISES: ARITHMETIC AND GEOMETRIC SEQUENCES

Directions: Work out each problem. Circle the letter of your choice.

1. What is the sixth term of an arithmetic sequence whose first term is 8 and whose common difference is 5?
   (A) 18
   (B) 23
   (C) 28
   (D) 33
   (E) 38

2. What is the eighth term of an arithmetic sequence whose third term is 12 and whose common difference is 5?
   (A) 32
   (B) 37
   (C) 42
   (D) 47
   (E) 52

3. What is the third term of a geometric progression whose first term is 4 and whose common ratio is 2?
   (A) 8
   (B) 16
   (C) 32
   (D) 48
   (E) 64

4. What is the sixth term of a geometric sequence whose fourth term is 12 and whose common ratio is 3?
   (A) 36
   (B) 108
   (C) 324
   (D) 972
   (E) 2916

5. The population of a particular city begins at 2500, and doubles every year. What is the population in the city after 9 years?
   (A) 40,000
   (B) 80,000
   (C) 160,000
   (D) 320,000
   (E) 1,280,000

6. Janet saved $3500 in 2006. If each year after this she saves $750 more than the year before, how much will she save in 2011?
   (A) $5750
   (B) $6500
   (C) $7250
   (D) $8000
   (E) $8750

7. In a contest, the first name drawn wins a prize of $320. Each following name drawn wins half as much as the previous winner. How much money will be won by the person whose name is drawn fifth?
   (A) $10
   (B) $20
   (C) $40
   (D) $60
   (E) $80

8. Peter buys a house that costs $100,000. If the house loses 5% of its value each year, to the nearest dollar, what will be the value of the house after 6 years?
   (A) $63,025
   (B) $66,342
   (C) $69,834
   (D) $73,509
   (E) $77,378

9. The population of a small town is 250. If the population of the town doubles every year, what will the population of the town be after 7 years?

(A) 4000
(B) 8000
(C) 16,000
(D) 32,000
(E) 64,000

10. The number of bacteria in a colony starts at 50 and doubles every 4 hours. The formula for the number of bacteria in the colony is $50 \times 2^{t/4}$, where t is the number of hours that have elapsed. How many bacteria will there be in the colony after 24 hours?

(A) 400
(B) 800
(C) 1600
(D) 3200
(E) 6400

ANSWER KEY AND EXPLANATIONS

1. D	3. B	5. E	7. B	9. D
2. B	4. B	6. C	8. D	10. D

1. **The correct answer is (D).** Using the formula $a_1 + (n-1)d$, with $a_1 = 8$, $d = 5$, and $n = 6$, then $a_1 + (n-1)d = 8 + (6-1)5 = 8 + (5)5 = 8 + 25 = 33$.

2. **The correct answer is (B).** The trick to solving this problem is to realize that being given the third term of a sequence and being asked for the eighth term is the same as being given the first term and being asked for the sixth term. Using the formula $a_1 + (n-1)d$, with $a_1 = 12$, $d = 5$, and $n = 6$, then $a_1 + (n-1)d = 12 + (6-1)5 = 12 + (5)5 = 12 + 25 = 37$.

3. **The correct answer is (B).** Using the formula $a_1 \times r^{n-1}$, with $a_1 = 4$, $r = 2$, and $n = 3$, then $a_1 \times r^{n-1} = 4 \times 2^2 = 4 \times 4 = 16$.

4. **The correct answer is (B).** Being given the fourth term of a geometric sequence and being asked for the sixth term is the same as being given the first term and being asked for the third term. Using the formula $a_1 \times r^{n-1}$, with $a_1 = 12$, $r = 3$, and $n = 3$, then $a_1 \times r^{n-1} = 12 \times 3^2 = 12 \times 9 = 108$.

5. **The correct answer is (E).** The problem asks for the tenth term of a geometric sequence with the first term of 2500 and common ratio of 2 (first term is at time zero). Using the formula $a_1 \times r^{n-1}$, with $a_1 = 2500$, $r = 2$, and $n = 10$, then $a_1 \times r^{n-1} = 2500 \times 2^9 = 2500 \times 512 = 1,280,000$.

6. **The correct answer is (C).** The problem asks for the sixth term of an arithmetic progression with the first term of 3500, and common difference of 750. Using the formula $a_1 + (n-1)d$, with $a_1 = 3500$, $d = 750$, and $n = 6$, then $a_1 + (n-1)d = 3500 + (6-1)750 = 3500 + (5)750 = 3500 + 3750 = 7250$.

7. **The correct answer is (B).** The problem is looking for the fifth term of a geometric sequence with first term of 320 and common ratio of $\frac{1}{2}$. Using the formula $a_1 \times r^{n-1}$, with $a_1 = 320$, $r = 0.5$, and $n = 5$, then $a_1 \times r^{n-1} = 320 \times (0.5)^4 = 320 \times 0.0625 = 20$.

8. **The correct answer is (D).** The problem asks for the seventh term of a geometric sequence with first term of 100,000 and common ratio of $100\% - 5\% = 95\% = 0.95$. Using the formula $a_1 \times r^{n-1}$, with $a_1 = 100,000$, $r = 0.95$, and $n = 7$, then $a_1 \times r^{n-1} = 100,000 \times (0.95)^6 = 100,000 \times 0.73509 = 73,509$.

9. **The correct answer is (D).** The problem is looking for the eighth term of a geometric sequence with first term of 250 and common ratio of 2. Using the formula $a_1 \times r^{n-1}$, with $a_1 = 250$, $r = 2$, and $n = 8$, then $a_1 \times r^{n-1} = 250 \times 2^7 = 250 \times 128 = 32,000$.

10. **The correct answer is (D).** While this may look complex, this is actually an easy question. Simply evaluate the expression $50 \times 2^{t/4}$, with $t = 24$. The value is $50 \times 2^{t/4} = 50 \times 2^{24/4} = 50 \times 2^6 = 50 \times 64 = 3200$.

SUMMING IT UP

- If the arithmetic looks complex, try to simplify it first.

- If there's no graphic or picture for a problem, draw one.

- If a problem is presented in different units, remember to convert and work the problem in the same unit.

Basic Algebra Review

OVERVIEW

- Signed numbers
- Linear equations
- Exponents
- Quadratic equations
- Literal expressions
- Roots and radicals
- Monomials and polynomials
- Problem solving in algebra
- Inequalities
- Defined operation problems
- Summing it up

SIGNED NUMBERS

To solve algebra problems, you must be able to compute accurately with signed numbers.

Addition: To add signed numbers with the same sign, add the magnitudes of the numbers and keep the same sign. To add signed numbers with different signs, subtract the magnitudes of the numbers and use the sign of the number with the greater magnitude.

Subtraction: Change the sign of the number being subtracted and follow the rules for addition.

Multiplication: If there is an odd number of negative signs, the product is negative. An even number of negative signs gives a positive product.

Division: If the signs are the same, the quotient is positive. If the signs are different, the quotient is negative.

chapter 11

EXERCISES: SIGNED NUMBERS

Directions: Work out each problem. Circle the letter next to your choice.

1. When +3 is added to −5, what is the sum?
   - (A) −8
   - (B) +8
   - (C) −2
   - (D) +2
   - (E) −15

2. When −4 and −5 are added, what is the sum?
   - (A) −9
   - (B) +9
   - (C) −1
   - (D) +1
   - (E) +20

3. Subtract −6 from +3.
   - (A) −3
   - (B) +3
   - (C) +18
   - (D) −9
   - (E) +9

4. When −5 is subtracted from +10, what is the result?
   - (A) +5
   - (B) +15
   - (C) −5
   - (D) −15
   - (E) −50

5. (−6)(−3) equals
   - (A) −18
   - (B) +18
   - (C) +2
   - (D) −9
   - (E) +9

6. What is the product of $(-6)\left(+\dfrac{1}{2}\right)(-10)$?
   - (A) $-15\dfrac{1}{2}$
   - (B) $+15\dfrac{1}{2}$
   - (C) −30
   - (D) +30
   - (E) +120

7. When the product of (−4) and (+3) is divided by (−2), the quotient is
   - (A) $+\dfrac{1}{2}$
   - (B) $+3\dfrac{1}{2}$
   - (C) +6
   - (D) $-\dfrac{1}{2}$
   - (E) −6

ANSWER KEY AND EXPLANATIONS

1. C	3. E	5. B	7. C
2. A	4. B	6. D	

1. **The correct answer is (C).** In adding numbers with opposite signs, subtract their magnitudes ($5 - 3 = 2$) and use the sign of the number with the greater magnitude (negative).

2. **The correct answer is (A).** In adding numbers with the same sign, add their magnitudes ($4 + 5 = 9$) and keep the same sign.

3. **The correct answer is (E).** Change the sign of the second number and follow the rules for addition.

$$
\begin{array}{r}
+\ \ \ 3 \\
+\ +\ 6 \\
\hline
+\ \ \ 9
\end{array}
$$

4. **The correct answer is (B).** Change the sign of the second number and follow the rules for addition.

$$
\begin{array}{r}
+\ \ 10 \\
+\ \ \ 5 \\
\hline
+\ \ 15
\end{array}
$$

5. **The correct answer is (B).** The product of two negative numbers is a positive number.

6. **The correct answer is (D).** The product of an even number of negative numbers is positive.

$$
\overset{3}{\cancel{6}}\left(\dfrac{1}{\cancel{2}}\right)(10) = 30
$$

7. **The correct answer is (C).**

$$(-4)(+3) = -12$$

Dividing a negative number by a negative number gives a positive quotient.

$$\dfrac{-12}{-2} = +6$$

TIP

If you have a string of multiplications and divisions to do and the number of negative factors is even, the result will be positive; if the number of negative factors is odd, the result will be negative.

LINEAR EQUATIONS

The next step in solving algebra problems is mastering linear equations. Whether an equation involves numbers or only variables, the basic steps are the same.

Four-Step Strategy

1 If there are fractions or decimals, remove them by multiplication.

2 Collect all terms containing the unknown for which you are solving on the same side of the equation. Remember that whenever a term crosses the equal sign from one side of the equation to the other, it must pay a toll. That is, it must change its sign.

3 Determine the coefficient of the unknown by combining similar terms or factoring when terms cannot be combined.

4 Divide both sides of the equation by this coefficient.

Solve for x: $5x - 3 = 3x + 5$

$2x = 8$

$x = 4$

Solve for x: $ax - b = cx + d$

$ax - cx = b + d$

$x(a - c) = b + d$

$x = \dfrac{b + d}{a - c}$

Solve for x: $\dfrac{3}{4}x + 2 = \dfrac{2}{3}x + 3$

Multiply by 12: $9x + 24 = 8x + 36$

$x = 12$

Solve for x: $0.7x + 0.04 = 2.49$

Multiply by 100: $70x + 4 = 249$

$70x = 245$

$x = 3.5$

Need extra help in linear equations? Check out http://bit.ly/hippo_alg1 and http://bit.ly/hippo_alg2.

Simultaneous Equations

http://bit.ly/hippo_alg3

In solving equations with two unknowns, you must work with two equations simultaneously. The object is to eliminate one of the two unknowns and solve for the resulting single unknown.

Solve for x: $2x - 4y = 2$
$3x + 5y = 14$

Multiply the first equation by 5:

$10x - 20y = 10$

Multiply the second equation by 4:

$12x + 20y = 56$

Since the y-terms now have the same numerical coefficients, but with opposite signs, you can eliminate them by adding the two equations. If they had the same signs, you would eliminate them by subtracting the equations.

Add the equations:

$$10x - 20y = 10$$
$$12x + 20y = 56$$
$$\overline{22x = 66}$$
$$x = 3$$

Since you were only asked to solve for x, stop here. If you were asked to solve for both x and y, you would now substitute 3 for x in either equation and solve the resulting equation for y.

$$3(3) + 5y = 14$$
$$9 + 5y = 14$$
$$\overline{5y = 5}$$
$$y = 11$$

Solve for x:

$$ax + by = c$$
$$dx + ey = f$$

Multiply the first equation by e:

$$aex + bey = ce$$

Multiply the second equation by b:

$$bdx + bey = bf$$

Since the y-terms now have the same coefficient, with the same sign, eliminate these terms by subtracting the two equations.

$$
\begin{array}{r}
aex + bey = ce \\
-(bdx + bey = bf) \\
\hline
aex - bdx = ce - bf
\end{array}
$$

Factor to determine the coefficient of x:

$$x(ae - bd) = ce - bf$$

Divide by the coefficient of x:

$$x = \frac{ce - bf}{ae - bd}$$

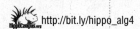 http://bit.ly/hippo_alg4

EXERCISES: LINEAR EQUATIONS

Directions: Work out each problem. Circle the letter of your choice.

1. If $5x + 6 = 10$, then x equals

   (A) $\dfrac{16}{5}$

   (B) $\dfrac{5}{16}$

   (C) $-\dfrac{5}{4}$

   (D) $\dfrac{4}{5}$

   (E) $\dfrac{5}{4}$

2. Solve for x: $ax = bx + c$

   (A) $\dfrac{b+c}{a}$

   (B) $\dfrac{c}{a-b}$

   (C) $\dfrac{c}{b-a}$

   (D) $\dfrac{a-b}{c}$

   (E) $\dfrac{c}{a+b}$

3. Solve for k: $\dfrac{k}{3} + \dfrac{k}{4} = 1$

   (A) $\dfrac{11}{8}$

   (B) $\dfrac{8}{11}$

   (C) $\dfrac{7}{12}$

   (D) $\dfrac{12}{7}$

   (E) $\dfrac{1}{7}$

4. If $x + y = 8p$ and $x - y = 6q$, then x is

   (A) $7pq$

   (B) $4p + 3q$

   (C) pq

   (D) $4p - 3q$

   (E) $8p + 6q$

5. If $7x = 3x + 12$, then $2x + 5 =$

   (A) 10

   (B) 11

   (C) 12

   (D) 13

   (E) 14

6. In the equation $y = x^2 + rx - 3$, for what value of r will $y = 11$ when $x = 2$?

   (A) 6

   (B) 5

   (C) 4

   (D) $3\dfrac{1}{2}$

   (E) 0

7. If $1 + \dfrac{1}{t} = \dfrac{t+1}{t}$, what does t equal?

   (A) $+1$ only

   (B) $+1$ or -1 only

   (C) $+1$ or $+2$ only

   (D) No values

   (E) All values except 0

8. If $0.23m = 0.069$, then $m =$

   (A) 0.003

   (B) 0.03

   (C) 0.3

   (D) 3

   (E) 30

9. If $35rt + 8 = 42rt$, then $rt =$

(A) $\dfrac{8}{7}$

(B) $\dfrac{8}{87}$

(C) $\dfrac{7}{8}$

(D) $\dfrac{87}{8}$

(E) $-\dfrac{8}{7}$

10. For what values of n is $n + 5$ equal to $n - 5$?

(A) No value

(B) 0

(C) All negative values

(D) All positive values

(E) All values

ANSWER KEY AND EXPLANATIONS

1. D	3. D	5. B	7. E	9. A
2. B	4. B	6. B	8. C	10. A

1. **The correct answer is (D).**

$$5x = 4$$
$$x = \frac{4}{5}$$

2. **The correct answer is (B).**

$$ax - bx = c \qquad x(a - b) = c \qquad x = \frac{c}{a - b}$$

3. **The correct answer is (D).** Multiply by 12:

$$4k + 3k = 12$$
$$7k = 12$$
$$k = \frac{12}{7}$$

4. **The correct answer is (B).** Add equations to eliminate y:

$$x + y = 8p$$
$$\underline{x - y = 6q}$$
$$2x \quad = 8p + 6q$$

Divide by 2: $x = 4p + 3q$

5. **The correct answer is (B).** Solve for x:

$$4x = 12$$
$$x = 3$$
$$2x + 5 = 2(3) + 5 = 1$$

6. **The correct answer is (B).** Substitute given values:

$$11 = 4 + 2r - 3$$
$$10 = 2r$$
$$r = 5$$

7. **The correct answer is (E).**

Multiply by t: $t + 1 = t + 1$

This is an identity and is therefore true for all values. However, since t was a denominator in the given equation, t may not equal 0, because you can never divide by 0.

8. **The correct answer is (C).** Multiply by 100 to make coefficient an integer.

$$23m = 6.9$$
$$m = 0.3$$

9. **The correct answer is (A).** Even though this equation has two unknowns, you are asked to solve for rt, which may be treated as a single unknown.

$$8 = 7rt$$
$$\frac{8}{7} = rt$$

10. **The correct answer is (A).** There is no number such that, when 5 is added, you get the same result as when 5 is subtracted. Do not confuse choices (A) and (B). Choice (B) would mean that the number 0 satisfies the equation, which it does not.

EXPONENTS

An exponent is a mathematical notation indicating that a number, called the base, has been multiplied one or more times by itself. For example, in the term 2^3, the 2 is the base and the ^{3} is the exponent. This term means "two times two times two" and is read "two to the third power." The word power tells how many times the base number appears in the multiplication.

$x^3 = x$ times x times x

$x^2 = x$ times x

$x^1 = x$

$x^0 = 1$

The Three Rules of Exponents

1 To multiply powers of the same base, add the exponents.

x^2 times $x^3 = x^{2+3} = x^5$

x^5 times $x^4 = x^{5+4} = x^9$

2 To divide powers of the same base, subtract the exponent of the divisor from the exponent of the dividend.

$$\frac{x^6}{x^2} = x^{6-2} = x^4$$

$$\frac{x^{10}}{x^3} = x^{10-3} = x^7$$

3 To find the power of a power, multiply the exponents.

$(x^2)^3 = x^{(2)(3)} = x^6$

$(x^3y^5)^2 = x^{(3)(2)}y^{(5)(2)} = x^6y^{10}$

A variable base with an even exponent has two values, one positive and one negative.

$x^2 = 25$; x could be positive 5 or negative 5.

A variable base can be zero (unless otherwise stated in the problem). In that case, no matter what the exponent, the value of the term is zero.

Is x^4 always greater than x^2? No; if x is zero, then x^4 and x^2 are equal.

When the base is a fraction between 0 and 1, the larger the exponent, the smaller the value of the term.

Which is greater, $\left(\frac{37}{73}\right)$ or $\left(\frac{37}{73}\right)^2$? The correct answer is $\left(\frac{37}{73}\right)$ because $\left(\frac{37}{73}\right)$ is almost $\frac{1}{2}$, while $\left(\frac{37}{73}\right)^2$ is about $\frac{1}{4}$.

Need extra help in exponents? Check out:

 http://bit.ly/hippo_alg17    http://bit.ly/hippo_alg19

 http://bit.ly/hippo_alg18    http://bit.ly/hippo_alg20

EXERCISES: EXPONENTS

Directions: Work out each problem. Circle the letter of your choice.

1. If x and y are not equal to 0, then $x^{12}y^6$ must be

   I. Positive

   II. Negative

   III. An integer

   IV. A mixed fraction

   (A) I only

   (B) II only

   (C) III only

   (D) IV only

   (E) I and III only

2. $(x^2y^3)^4 =$

   (A) x^6y^7

   (B) x^8y^{12}

   (C) $x^{12}y^8$

   (D) x^2y

   (E) x^6y^9

3. $\dfrac{x^{16}y^6}{x^4y^2} =$

   (A) $x^{20}y^8$

   (B) x^4y^3

   (C) x^5y^6

   (D) $x^{12}y^3$

   (E) $x^{12}y^4$

4. If $x^4 = 16$ and $y^2 = 36$, then the *maximum* possible value for $x - y$ is

   (A) -20

   (B) 20

   (C) -4

   (D) 6

   (E) 8

5. $p^8 \times q^4 \times p^4 \times q^8 =$

   (A) $p^{12}q^{12}$

   (B) p^4q^4

   (C) $p^{32}q^{32}$

   (D) $p^{64}q^{64}$

   (E) $p^{16}q^{16}$

ANSWER KEY AND EXPLANATIONS

| 1. A | 2. B | 3. E | 4. E | 5. A |

1. **The correct answer is (A).** If x and y are not 0, then the even exponents would force x^{12} and y^6 to be positive.

2. **The correct answer is (B).** To raise a power to a power, multiply the exponents. $x^{(2)(4)}y^{(3)(4)} = x^8y^{12}$

3. **The correct answer is (E).** All fractions are implied division. When dividing terms with a common base and different exponents, subtract the exponents. Therefore, $16 - 4 = 12$ and $6 - 2 = 4$.

4. **The correct answer is (E).** x could be positive 2 or negative 2. y could be positive 6 or negative 6. The four possible values for $x - y$ are as follows:

$$2 - 6 = -4$$
$$2 - (-6) = 8$$
$$-2 - 6 = -8$$
$$-2 - (-6) = 4$$

The maximum value would be 8.

5. **The correct answer is (A).** The multiplication signs do not change the fact that this is the multiplication of terms with a common base and different exponents. Solve this kind of problem by adding the exponents.

$$p^{8+4} \times q^{4+8} = p^{12}q^{12}$$

QUADRATIC EQUATIONS

Roots and Factoring

In solving quadratic equations, remember that there will always be two roots, even though these roots may be equal. A complete quadratic equation is of the form $ax^2 + bx + c = 0$ and, in the SAT, can always be solved by factoring.

Factor: $x^2 + 7x + 12 = 0$

$(x + 3)(x + 4) = 0$

The last term of the equation is positive; therefore, both factors must have the same sign, since the last two terms multiply to a positive product. The middle term is also positive; therefore, both factors must be positive, since they also add to a positive sum.

$(x + 4)(x + 3) = 0$

If the product of two factors is 0, each factor may be set equal to 0, yielding the values for x of -4 or -3.

Factor: $x^2 + 7x - 18 = 0$

$(x + 9)(x - 2) = 0$

Now you are looking for two numbers with a product of -18: therefore, they must have opposite signs. To yield $+7$ as a middle coefficient, the numbers must be $+9$ and -2.

$(x + 9)(x - 2) = 0$

This equation gives the roots -9 and $+2$.

Incomplete quadratic equations are those in which b or c is equal to 0.

Solve for x: $x^2 - 16 = 0$

$x^2 = 16$

$x = \pm 4$

Remember, there must be two roots.

Solve for x: $4x^2 - 9 = 0$

$4x^2 = 9$

$x^2 = \dfrac{9}{4}$

$x = \pm \dfrac{3}{2}$

ALERT!

Don't forget: In working with any equation, if you move a term from one side of the equal sign to the other, you must change its sign.

http://bit.ly/hippo_alg9

http://bit.ly/hippo-alg10

> Solve for x: $x^2 + 4x = 0$

Never divide through an equation by the unknown, as this would yield an equation of lower degree having fewer roots than the original equation. Always factor this type of equation.

$x(x + 4) = 0$

The roots are 0 and −4.

> Solve for x: $4x^2 - 9x = 0$

$x(4x - 9) = 0$

The roots are 0 and $\dfrac{9}{4}$.

Radicals

In solving equations containing radicals, always get the radical alone on one side of the equation; then square both sides to remove the radical and solve. Remember that all solutions to radical equations must be checked, as squaring both sides may sometimes result in extraneous roots.

> Solve for x: $\sqrt{x+5} = 7$

$x + 5 = 49$
$x = 44$

Checking, we have $\sqrt{49} = 7$, which is true.

> Solve for x: $\sqrt{x} = -6$

You may have written the answer: $x = 36$.

Checking, we have $\sqrt{36} = -6$, which is not true, as the radical sign means the positive, or principal, square root only. This equation has no solution because $\sqrt{36} = 6$, not −6.

 http://bit.ly/hippo_alg22

Solve for x: $\sqrt{x^2 + 6} - 3 = x$

$$\sqrt{x^2 + 6} - 3 = x$$

$$\sqrt{x^2 + 6} = x + 3$$

$$x^2 + 6 = x^2 + 6x + 9$$

$$6 = 6x + 9$$

$$-3 = 6x$$

$$-\frac{1}{2} = x$$

Checking, we have
$$\sqrt{6\frac{1}{4}} - 3 = -\frac{1}{2}$$

$$\sqrt{\frac{25}{4}} - 3 = -\frac{1}{2}$$

$$\frac{5}{2} - 3 = -\frac{1}{2}$$

$$2\frac{1}{2} - 3 = -\frac{1}{2}$$

$$-\frac{1}{2} = -\frac{1}{2}$$

This is a true statement. Therefore, $-\frac{1}{2}$ is a true root.

EXERCISES: QUADRATIC EQUATIONS

Directions: Work out each problem. Circle the letter of your choice.

1. Solve for x: $x^2 - 2x - 15 = 0$
   (A) $+5$ or -3
   (B) -5 or $+3$
   (C) -5 or -3
   (D) $+5$ or $+3$
   (E) None of these

2. Solve for x: $x^2 + 12 = 8x$
   (A) $+6$ or -2
   (B) -6 or $+2$
   (C) -6 or -2
   (D) $+6$ or $+2$
   (E) None of these

3. Solve for x: $4x^2 = 12$
   (A) $\sqrt{3}$
   (B) 3 or -3
   (C) $\sqrt{3}$ or $-\sqrt{3}$
   (D) $\sqrt{3}$ or $\sqrt{-3}$
   (E) 9 or -9

4. Solve for x: $3x^2 = 4x$
   (A) $\dfrac{4}{3}$
   (B) $\dfrac{4}{3}$ or 0
   (C) $-\dfrac{4}{3}$ or 0
   (D) $\dfrac{4}{3}$ or $-\dfrac{4}{3}$
   (E) None of these

5. Solve for x: $\sqrt{x^2 + 7} - 2 = x - 1$
   (A) No values
   (B) $\dfrac{1}{3}$
   (C) $-\dfrac{1}{3}$
   (D) -3
   (E) 3

ANSWER KEY AND EXPLANATIONS

1. A	2. D	3. C	4. B	5. E

1. **The correct answer is (A).**
$$(x-5)(x+3) = 0$$
$$x = 5 \text{ or } -3$$

2. **The correct answer is (D).**
$$x^2 - 8x + 12 = 0$$
$$(x-6)(x-2) = 0$$
$$x = 6 \text{ or } 2$$

3. **The correct answer is (C).**
$$x^2 = 3$$
$$x = \sqrt{3} \text{ or } -\sqrt{3}$$

4. **The correct answer is (B).**
$$3x^2 - 4x = 0$$
$$x(3x-4) = 0$$
$$x = 0 \text{ or } \frac{4}{3}$$

5. **The correct answer is (E).**
$$\sqrt{x^2 + 7} = x + 1$$
$$x^2 + 7 = x^2 + 2x + 1$$
$$6 = 2x$$
$$x = 3$$

Checking: $\sqrt{16} - 2 = 3 - 1$
$$4 - 2 = 3 - 1$$
$$2 = 2$$

LITERAL EXPRESSIONS

If you can compute with numbers, working with variables should be easy. The computational processes are exactly the same. Just think of how you would do the problem with numbers and do exactly the same thing with letters.

> Find the number of inches in 2 feet 5 inches.

Since there are 12 inches in a foot, multiply 2 feet by 12 to change it to 24 inches and then add 5 more inches, giving an answer of 29 inches.

> Find the number of inches in f feet and i inches.

Doing exactly as you did above, multiply f by 12, giving $12f$ inches, and add i more inches, giving an answer of $12f + i$ inches.

> A telephone call from New York to Chicago costs 85 cents for the first 3 minutes and 21 cents for each additional minute. Find the cost of an 8-minute call at this rate.

The first 3 minutes cost 85 cents. There are 5 additional minutes above the first 3. These five are billed at 21 cents each, for a cost of $1.05. The total cost is $1.90.

> A telephone call costs c cents for the first 3 minutes and d cents for each additional minute. Find the cost of a call that lasts m minutes if $m > 3$.

The first 3 minutes cost c cents. The number of additional minutes is $(m - 3)$. These are billed at d cents each, for a cost of $d(m - 3)$, or $dm - 3d$. Thus, the total cost is $c + dm - 3d$. Remember that the first 3 minutes have been paid for in the basic charge; therefore, you must subtract from the total number of minutes to find the additional minutes.

 http://bit.ly/hippo_alg-31

EXERCISES: LITERAL EXPRESSIONS

Directions: Work out each problem. Circle the letter of your choice.

1. David had d dollars. After a shopping trip, he returned with c cents. How many cents did he spend?
   - (A) $d - c$
   - (B) $c - d$
   - (C) $100d - c$
   - (D) $100c - d$
   - (E) $d - 100c$

2. How many ounces are there in p pounds and q ounces?
   - (A) $\dfrac{p}{16} + q$
   - (B) pq
   - (C) $p + 16q$
   - (D) $p + q$
   - (E) $16p + q$

3. How many passengers can be seated on a plane with r rows, if each row consists of d double seats and t triple seats?
   - (A) rdt
   - (B) $rd + rt$
   - (C) $2dr + 3tr$
   - (D) $3dr + 2tr$
   - (E) $rd + t$

4. How many dimes are there in $4x - 1$ cents?
   - (A) $40x - 10$
   - (B) $\dfrac{2}{5}x - \dfrac{1}{10}$
   - (C) $40x - 1$
   - (D) $4x - 1$
   - (E) $20x - 5$

5. If u represents the tens' digit of a certain number and t represents the units' digit, then the number with the digits reversed can be represented by
   - (A) $10t + u$
   - (B) $10u + t$
   - (C) tu
   - (D) ut
   - (E) $t + u$

6. Joe spent k cents of his allowance and has r cents left. What was his allowance in dollars?
   - (A) $k + r$
   - (B) $k - r$
   - (C) $100(k + r)$
   - (D) $\dfrac{k + r}{100}$
   - (E) $100kr$

7. If p pounds of potatoes cost $\$k$, find the cost (in cents) of one pound of potatoes.
   - (A) $\dfrac{k}{p}$
   - (B) $\dfrac{k}{100p}$
   - (C) $\dfrac{p}{k}$
   - (D) $\dfrac{100k}{p}$
   - (E) $\dfrac{100p}{k}$

8. Mr. Rabner rents a car for d days. He pays m dollars per day for each of the first 7 days, and half that rate for each additional day. Find the total charge if $d > 7$.

(A) $m + 2m(d - 7)$

(B) $m + \dfrac{m}{2}(d - 7)$

(C) $7m + \dfrac{m}{2}(d - 7)$

(D) $7m + \dfrac{md}{2}$

(E) $7m + 2md$

9. A salesperson earns $900 per month plus a 10% commission on all sales over $1000. One month she sells r dollars' worth of merchandise where $r > \$1000$. How many dollars does she earn that month?

(A) $800 + 0.1r$

(B) $800 - 0.1r$

(C) $900 + 1r$

(D) $900 - 0.1r$

(E) $810 + 0.1r$

10. Elliot's allowance was just raised to k dollars per week. He gets a raise of c dollars per week every 2 years. How much will his allowance be per week y years from now?

(A) $k + cy$

(B) $k + 2cy$

(C) $k + \dfrac{1}{2}cy$

(D) $k + 2c$

(E) $ky + 2c$

ANSWER KEY AND EXPLANATIONS

1. C	3. C	5. A	7. D	9. A
2. E	4. B	6. D	8. C	10. C

1. **The correct answer is (C).** Since the answer is to be in cents, change d dollars to cents by multiplying it by 100 and subtract from that the c cents he returned with.

2. **The correct answer is (E).** There are 16 ounces in a pound. Therefore, you must multiply p pounds by 16 to change it to ounces and then add q more ounces.

3. **The correct answer is (C).** Each double seat holds 2 people, so d double seats hold $2d$ people. Each triple seat holds 3 people, so t triple seats hold $3t$ people. Therefore, each row holds $2d + 3t$ people. There are r rows, so multiply the number of people in each row by r.

4. **The correct answer is (B).** To change cents to dimes, divide by 10.

$$\frac{4x-1}{10} = \frac{4}{10}x - \frac{1}{10} = \frac{2}{5}x - \frac{1}{10}$$

5. **The correct answer is (A).** The original number would be $10u + t$. The number with the digits reversed would be $10t + u$.

6. **The correct answer is (D).** Joe's allowance was $k + r$ cents. To change this to dollars, divide by 100.

7. **The correct answer is (D).** This can be solved by using a proportion. Remember to change $\$k$ to $100k$ cents.

$$\frac{p}{100k} = \frac{1}{x}$$
$$px = 100k$$
$$x = \frac{100k}{p}$$

8. **The correct answer is (C).** He pays m dollars for each of 7 days, for a total of $7m$ dollars. Then he pays $\frac{1}{2}m$ dollars for $(d-7)$ days, for a cost of $\frac{m}{2}(d-7)$.

The total charge is $7m + \frac{m}{2}(d-7)$.

9. **The correct answer is (A).** She gets a commission of 10% of $(r - 1000)$, or $0.1(r - 1000)$, which is $0.1r - 100$. Adding this to 900 yields $800 + 0.1r$.

10. **The correct answer is (C).** Since he gets a raise only every 2 years, in y years, he will get $\frac{1}{2}y$ raises. Each raise is c dollars, so with $\frac{1}{2}y$ raises, his present allowance will be increased by $c\left(\frac{1}{2}y\right)$.

ROOTS AND RADICALS

Adding and Subtracting

Rules for adding and subtracting radicals are much the same as for adding and subtracting variables. Radicals must be exactly the same if they are to be added or subtracted, and they merely serve as a label that does not change.

$4\sqrt{2} + 3\sqrt{2} = 7\sqrt{2}$

$\sqrt{2} + 2\sqrt{2}$ cannot be added

$\sqrt{2} + \sqrt{3}$ cannot be added

Sometimes, when radicals are not the same, simplification of one or more radicals will make them the same. Remember that radicals are simplified by factoring out any perfect square factors.

$\sqrt{27} + \sqrt{75}$

$\sqrt{9 \cdot 3} + \sqrt{25 \cdot 3}$

$3\sqrt{3} + 5\sqrt{3} = 8\sqrt{3}$

Multiplying and Dividing

In multiplying and dividing, treat radicals in the same way as you treat variables. They are factors and must be handled as such.

$\sqrt{2} \cdot \sqrt{3} = \sqrt{6}$

$2\sqrt{5} \cdot 3\sqrt{7} = 6\sqrt{35}$

$\left(2\sqrt{3}\right)^2 = 2\sqrt{3} \cdot 2\sqrt{3} = 4 \cdot 3 = 12$

$\dfrac{\sqrt{75}}{\sqrt{3}} = \sqrt{25} = 5$

$\dfrac{10\sqrt{3}}{5\sqrt{3}} = 2$

Simplifying

To simplify radicals that contain a sum or difference under the radical sign, add or subtract first, then take the square root.

$$\sqrt{\dfrac{x^2}{9} + \dfrac{x^2}{16}} = \sqrt{\dfrac{16x^2 + 9x^2}{144}} = \sqrt{\dfrac{25x^2}{144}} = \dfrac{5|x|}{12}$$

If you take the square root of each term before combining, you would have $\frac{x}{3} + \frac{x}{4}$, or $\frac{7x}{12}$, which is clearly not the same answer. Remember that $\sqrt{25}$ is 5. However, if you write that $\sqrt{25}$ as $\sqrt{16+9}$, you cannot say it is $4 + 3$ or 7. *Always* combine the quantities within a radical sign into a single term before taking the square root.

Finding Square Roots

To find the number of digits in the square root of a number, remember that the first step in the procedure for finding a square root is to pair off the numbers in the radical sign on either side of the decimal point. Every pair of numbers under the radical gives one number in the answer.

What is the square root of 61,504?

(A) 245

(B) 246

(C) 247

(D) 248

(E) 249

The only answer among the choices that will end in 4 when squared is 248. **The correct answer is (D).**

TIP

If a number ends in 9, its square root would have to end in a digit that, when multiplied by itself, would end in 9. This might be either 3 or 7. Only one of these would probably be among the choices; very few SAT problems call for this much computation.

EXERCISES: ROOTS AND RADICALS

Directions: Work out each problem. Circle the letter of your choice.

1. What is the sum of $\sqrt{12} + \sqrt{27}$?
   - **(A)** $\sqrt{29}$
   - **(B)** $3\sqrt{5}$
   - **(C)** $13\sqrt{3}$
   - **(D)** $5\sqrt{3}$
   - **(E)** $7\sqrt{3}$

2. What is the difference between $\sqrt{150}$ and $\sqrt{54}$?
   - **(A)** $2\sqrt{6}$
   - **(B)** $16\sqrt{6}$
   - **(C)** $\sqrt{96}$
   - **(D)** $6\sqrt{2}$
   - **(E)** $8\sqrt{6}$

3. What is the product of $\sqrt{18x}$ and $\sqrt{2x}$?
   - **(A)** $6x^2$
   - **(B)** $6x$
   - **(C)** $36x$
   - **(D)** $36x^2$
   - **(E)** $6\sqrt{x}$

4. If $\dfrac{1}{x} = \sqrt{0.25}$, what does x equal?
   - **(A)** 2
   - **(B)** 0.5
   - **(C)** 0.2
   - **(D)** 20
   - **(E)** 5

5. If $n = 3.14$, find n^3 to the nearest hundredth.
   - **(A)** 3.10
   - **(B)** 30.96
   - **(C)** 309.59
   - **(D)** 3095.91
   - **(E)** 30,959.14

6. The square root of 24,336 is exactly
   - **(A)** 152
   - **(B)** 153
   - **(C)** 155
   - **(D)** 156
   - **(E)** 158

7. The square root of 306.25 is exactly
   - **(A)** 0.175
   - **(B)** 1.75
   - **(C)** 17.5
   - **(D)** 175
   - **(E)** 1750

8. Divide $6\sqrt{45}$ by $3\sqrt{5}$.
   - **(A)** 9
   - **(B)** 4
   - **(C)** 54
   - **(D)** 15
   - **(E)** 6

9. $\sqrt{\dfrac{y^2}{25} + \dfrac{y^2}{16}} =$
   - **(A)** $\dfrac{2y}{9}$
   - **(B)** $\dfrac{9y}{20}$
   - **(C)** $\dfrac{y}{9}$
   - **(D)** $\dfrac{|y|\sqrt{41}}{20}$
   - **(E)** $\dfrac{41y}{20}$

10. $\sqrt{a^2 + b^2}$ is equal to
    - **(A)** $a + b$
    - **(B)** $a - b$
    - **(C)** $(a + b)(a - b)$
    - **(D)** $\sqrt{a^2} + \sqrt{b^2}$
    - **(E)** None of these

ANSWER KEY AND EXPLANATIONS

1. D	3. B	5. B	7. C	9. D
2. A	4. A	6. D	8. E	10. E

1. **The correct answer is (D).**
$$\sqrt{12} = \sqrt{4}\sqrt{3} = 2\sqrt{3}$$
$$\sqrt{27} = \sqrt{9}\sqrt{3} = 3\sqrt{3}$$
$$2\sqrt{3} + 3\sqrt{3} = 5\sqrt{3}$$

2. **The correct answer is (A).**
$$\sqrt{150} = \sqrt{25}\sqrt{6} = 5\sqrt{6}$$
$$\sqrt{54} = \sqrt{9}\sqrt{6} = 3\sqrt{6}$$
$$5\sqrt{6} - 3\sqrt{6} = 2\sqrt{6}$$

3. **The correct answer is (B).**
$$\sqrt{18x} \bullet \sqrt{2x} = \sqrt{36x^2} = 6x$$

4. **The correct answer is (A).**
$$\sqrt{0.25} = 0.5$$
$$\frac{1}{x} = 0.5$$
$$1 = 0.5x$$
$$10 = 5x$$
$$2 = x$$

5. **The correct answer is (B).** $(3)^3$ would be 27, so the answer should be a little larger than 27.

6. **The correct answer is (D).** The only answer that will end in 6 when squared is choice (D).

7. **The correct answer is (C).** The square root of this number must have two digits before the decimal point.

8. **The correct answer is (E).**
$$\frac{6\sqrt{45}}{3\sqrt{5}} = 2\sqrt{9} = 2 \bullet 3 = 6$$

9. **The correct answer is (D).**
$$\sqrt{\frac{y^2}{25} + \frac{y^2}{16}} = \sqrt{\frac{16y^2 + 25y^2}{400}}$$
$$= \sqrt{\frac{41y^2}{400}} = \frac{|y|\sqrt{41}}{20}$$

10. **The correct answer is (E).** Never take the square root of a sum separately. There is no way to simplify $\sqrt{a^2 + b^2}$.

MONOMIALS AND POLYNOMIALS

When we add a collection of expressions together, each expression is called a *term*. *Monomial* means one term. For example, we might say that $2x + 3y^2 + 7$ is the sum of three terms or three monomials. When we talk about a monomial, we generally mean a term that is just the product of constants and variables, possibly raised to various powers. Examples might be 7, $2x$, $-3y^2$, and $4x^2z^5$. The constant factor is called the *coefficient* of the variable factor. Thus, in $-3y^2$, -3 is the coefficient of y^2.

If we restrict our attention to monomials of the form Axn, the sums of such terms are called *polynomials* (in one variable). Expressions like $3x + 5$, $2x^2 - 5x + 8$, and $x^4 - 7x^5 - 11$ are all examples of polynomials. The highest power of the variable that appears is called the *degree* of the polynomial. The three examples just given are of degree 1, 2, and 5, respectively.

In evaluating monomials and polynomials for negative values of the variable, the greatest pitfall is keeping track of the minus signs. Always remember that in an expression like $-x^2$, the power 2 is applied to the x, and the minus sign in front should be thought of as (-1) times the expression. If you want to have the power apply to $-x$, you must write $(-x)^2$.

> Find the value of $3x - x^3 - x^2$, when $x = -2$.

Substitute -2 every place you see an x, thus:

$3(-2) - (-2)^3 - (-2)^2 = -6 - (-8) - (+4) = -6 + 8 - 4 = -2$

 http://bit.ly/hippo_alg11

Combining Monomials

Monomials with identical variable factors can be added together by adding their coefficients. So $3x^2 + 4x^2 = 7x^2$. Of course, subtraction is handled the same way, thus:

$3x^4 - 9x^4 = -6x^4$

Monomials are multiplied by taking the product of their coefficients and taking the product of the variable part by adding exponents of factors with like bases. So, $(3xy^2)(2xy^3) = 6x^2y^5$.

Monomial fractions can be simplified to simplest form by dividing out common factors of the coefficients and then using the usual rules for subtraction of exponents in division. An example might be:

$$\frac{6x^3y^5}{2x^4y^3} = \frac{3y^2}{x}$$

Combine into a single monomial: $\dfrac{8x^3}{4x^2} - 6x$

The fraction simplifies to $2x$, and $2x - 6x = -4x$.

Combining Polynomials and Monomials

http://bit.ly/hippo_alg12

Polynomials are added or subtracted by just combining like monomial terms in the appropriate manner. Thus,

$(3x^2 - 3x - 4) + (2x^2 + 5x - 11)$

is summed by removing the parentheses and combining like terms, to yield

$5x^2 + 2x - 15$

In subtraction, when you remove the parentheses with a minus sign in front, be careful to change the signs of *all* the terms within the parentheses. So:

http://bit.ly/hippo_alg16

$$\left(3x^2 - 3x - 4\right) - \left(2x^2 + 5x - 11\right)$$
$$= 3x^2 - 3x - 4 - 2x^2 - 5x + 11$$
$$= x^2 - 8x + 7$$

(Did you notice that $3x^2 - 2x^2 = 1x^2$ but the "1" is not shown?)

http://bit.ly/hippo-alg15

To multiply a polynomial by a monomial, use the distributive law to multiply each term in the polynomial by the monomial factor. For example, $2x(2x^2 + 5x - 11) = 4x^3 + 10x^2 - 22x$.

When multiplying a polynomial by a polynomial, you are actually repeatedly applying the distributive law to form all possible products of the terms in the first polynomial with the terms in the second polynomial. The most common use of this is in multiplying two *binomials* (polynomials with two terms), such as $(x + 3)(x - 5)$. In this case, there are four terms in the result, $x \times x = x^2$; $x(-5) = -5x$; $3 \times x = 3x$; and, $3 \times (-5) = -15$; but the two middle terms are added together to give $-2x$. Thus, the product is $x^2 - 2x - 15$.

This process is usually remembered as the FOIL method. That is, form the products of First, Outer, Inner, Last, as shown in the figure below.

$(x + 3)(x - 5) = x^2 + (-5x + 3x) - 15$

If d is an integer, and $(x + 2)(x + d) = x^2 - kx - 10$, what is the value of $k + d$?

The product of the two last terms, $2d$, must be -10. Therefore, $d = -5$. If $d = -5$, then the sum of the outer and inner products becomes $-5x + 2x = -3x$, which equals $-kx$. Hence, $k = 3$, and $k + d = 3 + (-5) = -2$.

Factoring Monomials

Factoring a monomial simply involves reversing the distributive law. For example, if you are looking at $4x^2 + 12xy$, you should see that $4x$ is a factor of both terms. Hence, you could just as well write this as $4x(x + 3y)$. Multiplication using the distributive law will restore the original formulation.

If $3x - 4y = -2$, what is the value of $9x - 12y$?

Although you seem to have one equation in two unknowns, you can still solve the problem, because you do not need to know the values of the individual variables. Just rewrite: $9x - 12y = 3(3x - 4y)$. Since $3x - 4y = -2$, $9x - 12y$ is 3 times -2, or -6.

http://bit.ly/hippo_alg13

EXERCISES: MONOMIALS AND POLYNOMIALS

Directions: Work out each problem. Circle the letter of your choice.

1. $6x^3(x^2)^3 =$
   (A) $6x^7$
   (B) $6x^8$
   (C) $6x^9$
   (D) $6x^{10}$
   (E) $6x^{12}$

2. $(3w^2y^3)^4 =$
   (A) $18w^8y^{12}$
   (B) $18w^6y^7$
   (C) $81w^6y^7$
   (D) $81w^8y^{12}$
   (E) $81w^8y^7$

3. $5x^3(-3x^8) =$
   (A) $15x^{11}$
   (B) $-15x^{11}$
   (C) $-15x^{24}$
   (D) $15x^{24}$
   (E) $15x^5$

4. $\left(\dfrac{2}{3}\right)^3 =$
   (A) $\dfrac{8}{27}$

   (B) $\dfrac{6}{9}$

   (C) $\dfrac{4}{9}$

   (D) $\dfrac{16}{27}$

   (E) $\dfrac{16}{9}$

ANSWER KEY AND EXPLANATIONS

1. C	2. D	3. B	4. A

1. The correct answer is (C).

$$6x^3\left(x^2\right)^3 = 6 \times x^3 \times \left(x^2\right)^3$$
$$= 6 \times x^3 \times x^{(2 \times 3)}$$
$$= 6 \times x^3 \times x^6$$
$$= 6 \times x^9$$
$$= 6x^9$$

2. The correct answer is (D).

$$\left(3w^2 y^3\right)^4 = \left(3\right)^4 \times w^{(2 \times 4)} \times y^{(3 \times 4)}$$
$$= 81 \times w^8 \times y^{12}$$
$$= 81 w^8 y^{12}$$

3. The correct answer is (B).

$$5x^3\left(-3x^8\right) = 5 \times x^3 \times (-3) \times x^8$$
$$= 5 \times (-3) \times x^3 \times x^8$$
$$= -15 \times x^{3+8}$$
$$= -15x^{11}$$

4. The correct answer is (A).

$$\left(\frac{2}{3}\right)^3 = \frac{2^3}{3^3}$$
$$= \frac{8}{27}$$

PROBLEM SOLVING IN ALGEBRA

When you are working with algebraic word problems, remember that before you begin working you should be absolutely certain that you understand precisely what you are to answer. Once this is done, represent what you are looking for algebraically. Write an equation that translates the words of the problem to the symbols of mathematics. Then solve that equation by the techniques reviewed previously.

This section reviews the types of algebra problems most frequently encountered on the SAT. Thoroughly familiarizing yourself with the problems that follow will help you to translate and solve all kinds of verbal problems.

Solving Two Linear Equations in Two Unknowns

Many word problems lead to equations in two unknowns. Usually, one needs two equations to solve for both unknowns, although there are exceptions. There are two generally used methods to solve two equations in two unknowns. They are the method of *substitution* and the method of *elimination by addition and subtraction*.

http://bit.ly/hippo_alg5

We'll illustrate both methods via example. Here is one that uses the method of substitution.

> Mr. Green took his four children to the local craft fair. The total cost of their admission tickets was $14. Mr. and Mrs. Molina and their six children had to pay $23. What was the cost of an adult ticket to the craft fair, and what was the cost of a child's ticket?

Expressing all amounts in dollars, let x = cost of an adult ticket and let y = cost of a child's ticket.

For the Greens: $x + 4y = 14$

For the Molinas: $2x + 6y = 23$

The idea of the method of substitution is to solve one equation for one variable in terms of the other and then substitute that solution into the second equation. So we solve the first equation for x, because that is the simplest one to isolate:

$x = 14 - 4y$

and substitute into the second equation:

$2(14 - 4y) + 6y = 23$

This gives us one equation in one unknown that we can solve:

$28 - 8y + 6y = 23$

$-2y = -5; y = 2.5$

Now that we know $y = 2.5$, we substitute this into $x = 14 - 4y$ to get:

$x = 14 - 4(2.5) = 4$

Thus, the adult tickets were $4.00 each, and the children's tickets were $2.50 each.

Here is an example using the method of elimination.

> Paul and Denise both have after-school jobs. Two weeks ago, Paul worked 6 hours, Denise worked 3 hours, and they earned a total of $39. Last week, Paul worked 12 hours, Denise worked 5 hours, and they earned a total of $75. What is each one's hourly wage?

Again, let us express all amounts in dollars. Let x = Paul's hourly wage, and let y = Denise's hourly wage.

For the first week: $6x + 3y = 39$

For the second week: $12x + 5y = 75$

The idea of the method of elimination is that adding equal quantities to equal quantities gives a true result. So we want to add some multiple of one equation to the other one so that if we add the two equations together, one variable will be eliminated. In this case, it is not hard to see that if we multiply the first equation by -2, the coefficient of x will become -12. Now when we add the two equations, x will be eliminated. Hence,

$$
\begin{aligned}
-12x - 6y &= -78 \\
\underline{12x + 5y} &= \underline{75} \\
-y &= -3
\end{aligned}
$$

Thus, $y = 3$. We now substitute this into either of the two equations. Let's use the first:

$6x + (3)(3) = 39; x = 5.$

Thus, Denise makes only $3 per hour, while Paul gets $5.

http://bit.ly/hippo_alg6

http://bit.ly/hippo-alg7

Word Problems in One or Two Unknowns

Word problems can be broken down into a number of categories. To do *consecutive integer* problems, you need to remember that consecutive integers differ by 1, so a string of such numbers can be represented as $n, n + 1, n + 2, \ldots$

Consecutive even integers differ by 2, so a string of such numbers can be represented as $n, n + 2, n + 4, \ldots$ Consecutive odd integers also differ by 2! So a string of such numbers can also be represented as $n, n + 2, n + 4, \ldots$

Rate-time-distance problems require you to know the formula $d = rt$. That is, distance equals rate times time.

Here are some examples of several types of word problems.

> Sibyl is 5 years older than Moira. Three years ago, Sibyl was twice as old as Moira. How old is Sibyl?

If you have trouble setting up the equations, try using numbers. Suppose that Moira is 11. If Sibyl is 5 years older than Moira, how old is Sibyl? She is 16. You got from 11 to 16 by adding 5. So, if S is Sibyl's age and M is Moira's age, $S = M + 5$. Three years ago, Sibyl was $S - 3$, and Moira was $M - 3$. So, from the second sentence, $S - 3 = 2(M - 3)$ or $S - 3 = 2M - 6$; or, adding 3 to both sides,

$S = 2M - 3$

Now, substituting $S = M + 5$,

$M + 5\ 2M - 3$

$M = 8$

This means Sybil is $8 + 5 = 13$.

> Three consecutive integers are written in increasing order. If the sum of the first and second and twice the third is 93, what is the second number?

Calling the smallest number x, the second is $x + 1$, and the third is $x + 2$. Therefore,

$$x + (x + 1) + 2(x + 2) = 93$$
$$x + x + 1 + 2x + 4 = 93$$
$$4x + 5 = 93$$
$$4x = 88$$
$$x = 22$$

Hence the middle number is $22 + 1 = 23$.

> It took Andrew 15 minutes to drive downtown at 28 miles per hour to get a pizza. How fast did he have to drive back in order to be home in 10 minutes?

15 minutes is $\frac{1}{4}$ of an hour. Hence, going 28 miles per hour, the distance to the pizza parlor can be computed using the formula $d = rt$; $d = (28)\left(\frac{1}{4}\right) = 7$ miles. Since 10 minutes is $\frac{1}{6}$ of an hour, we have the equation $7 = r\left(\frac{1}{6}\right)$. Multiplying by 6, $r = 42$ mph.

Fraction Problems

A fraction is a ratio between two numbers. If the value of a fraction is $\frac{2}{3}$, it does not mean the numerator must be 2 and the denominator 3. The numerator and denominator could be 4 and 6, respectively, or 1 and 1.5, or 30 and 45, or any of infinitely many other combinations. All you know is that the ratio of numerator to denominator will be 2:3. Therefore, the numerator may be represented by $2x$, the denominator by $3x$, and the fraction by $\frac{2x}{3x}$.

The value of a fraction is $\frac{3}{4}$. If 3 is subtracted from the numerator and added to the denominator, the value of the fraction is $\frac{2}{5}$. Find the original fraction.

Let the original fraction be represented by $\frac{3x}{4x}$. If 3 is subtracted from the numerator and added to the denominator, the new fraction becomes $\frac{3x-3}{4x+3}$.

The value of the new fraction is $\frac{2}{5}$.

$$\frac{3x-3}{4x+3}=\frac{2}{5}$$

Cross-multiply to eliminate fractions.

$$15x-15=8x+6$$
$$7x=21$$
$$x=3$$

Therefore, the original fraction is

$$\frac{3x}{4x}=\frac{9}{12}$$

EXERCISES: PROBLEM SOLVING IN ALGEBRA

Directions: Work out each problem. Circle the letter of your choice.

1. A box contains five blocks numbered 1, 2, 3, 4, and 5. Johnnie picks a block and replaces it. Lisa then picks a block. What is the probability that the sum of the numbers they picked is even?

   (A) $\dfrac{9}{25}$

   (B) $\dfrac{2}{5}$

   (C) $\dfrac{1}{2}$

   (D) $\dfrac{13}{25}$

   (E) $\dfrac{3}{5}$

2. If a fleet of m buses uses g gallons of gasoline every two days, how many gallons of gasoline will be used by 4 buses every five days?

   (A) $\dfrac{10g}{m}$

   (B) $10gm$

   (C) $\dfrac{10m}{g}$

   (D) $\dfrac{20g}{m}$

   (E) $\dfrac{5g}{4m}$

3. A faucet is dripping at a constant rate. If, at noon on Sunday, 3 ounces of water have dripped from the faucet into a holding tank and, at 5 p.m. on Sunday, a total of 7 ounces have dripped into the tank, how many ounces will have dripped into the tank by 2:00 a.m. on Monday?

   (A) 10

   (B) $\dfrac{51}{5}$

   (C) 12

   (D) $\dfrac{71}{5}$

   (E) $\dfrac{81}{5}$

4. If A and B are positive integers and $24AB$ is a perfect square, then which of the following CANNOT be possible?

   I. Both A and B are odd.

   II. AB is a perfect square.

   III. Both A and B are divisible by 6.

   (A) I only

   (B) II only

   (C) III only

   (D) I and II only

   (E) I, II, and III

ANSWER KEY AND EXPLANATIONS

| 1. D | 2. A | 3. D | 4. D |

1. **The correct answer is (D).** Since each person had 5 choices, there are 25 possible pairs of numbers. The only way the sum could be odd is if one person picked an odd number and the other picked an even number. Suppose that Johnnie chose the odd number and Lisa the even one. Johnnie had 3 possible even numbers to select from, and for each of these, Lisa had 2 possible choices, for a total of $(3)(2) = 6$ possibilities. However, you could have had Johnnie pick an even number and Lisa pick an odd one, and there are also 6 ways to do that. Hence, out of 25 possibilities, 12 have an odd total, and 13 have an even total. The probability of an even total, then, is choice (D), $\frac{13}{25}$.

2. **The correct answer is (A).** Running m buses for two days is the same as running one bus for $2m$ days. If we use g gallons of gasoline, each bus uses $\frac{g}{2m}$ gallons each day. So if you multiply the number of gallons per day used by each bus by the number of buses and the number of days, you should get total gasoline usage. That is, $\frac{g}{2m} \times (4)(5) = \frac{10g}{m}$.

3. **The correct answer is (D).** In 5 hours, 4 ounces $(7 - 3)$ have dripped. Therefore, the "drip rate" is $\frac{4}{5}$ of an ounce per hour. From 5:00 p.m. on Sunday until 2:00 a.m. on Monday is 9 hours, causing the total to be:

$$7 + \frac{4}{5} \times 9 = 7\frac{36}{5} = \frac{71}{5}$$

4. **The correct answer is (D).** The prime factorization of 24 is $2^3 \times 3$; hence, if $24AB$ is a perfect square, then AB must have a factor of 2 and a factor of 3. This means, first of all, that both A and B cannot be odd. So statement I cannot be possible. Statement II also cannot be possible, because if AB were a perfect square and $24AB$ were also a perfect square, then 24 would be a perfect square, which it is not. Of course, if, for example, A were 6 and B were 36, $24AB$ would be a perfect square with both A and B divisible by 6, so statement III is possible. Hence, the correct choice is (D).

INEQUALITIES

Algebraic inequality statements are solved just as equations are solved. However, you must remember that whenever you multiply or divide by a negative number, the order of the inequality, that is, the inequality symbol, must be reversed.

Solve for x: $3 - 5x > 18$

http://bit.ly/hippo_alg8

Add -3 to both sides:

$-5x > 15$

Divide by -5, remembering to reverse the inequality:

$x < -3$

Solve for x: $5x - 4 > 6x - 6$

Collect all x-terms on the left and numerical terms on the right. As with equations, remember that if a term crosses the inequality symbol, the term changes sign.

$-x > -2$

Divide (or multiply) by -1:

$x < 2$

Postulates and Theorems

In working with geometric inequalities, certain postulates and theorems should be reviewed. The list follows:

- If unequal quantities are added to unequal quantities of the same order, the result is unequal quantities in the same order.

- If equal quantities are added to, or subtracted from, unequal quantities, the results are unequal in the same order.

- If unequal quantities are subtracted from equal quantities, the results are unequal in the opposite order.

- Doubles or halves of unequals are unequal in the same order.

- If the first of three quantities is greater than the second, and the second is greater than the third, then the first is greater than the third.

- The sum of two sides of a triangle must be greater than the third side.

- If two sides of a triangle are unequal, the angles opposite these sides are unequal, with the greater angle opposite the greater side.

- If two angles of a triangle are unequal, the sides opposite these angles are unequal, with the greater side opposite the greater angle.

- An exterior angle of a triangle is greater than either remote interior angle.

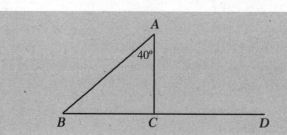

If *BCD* is a straight line and $m \angle A = 40°$, then angle *ACD* contains

(A) 40°

(B) 140°

(C) less than 40°

(D) more than 40°

(E) 100°

An exterior angle of a triangle is always greater than either of the remote interior angles. **The correct answer is (D).**

Which of the following statements is true regarding the triangle?

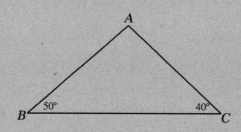

(A) $AB > AC$

(B) $AC > BC$

(C) $AB > BC$

(D) $AC > AB$

(E) $BC > AB + AC$

Since a comparison between two sides of a triangle depends upon the angles opposite these sides. The greater side is always opposite the greater angle. Since angle *A* contains 90°, the greatest side of this triangle is $\overline{BC}$, followed by $\overline{AC}$ and then $\overline{AB}$. **The correct answer is (D).**

EXERCISES: INEQUALITIES

Directions: Work out each problem. Circle the letter of your choice.

1. If $x < y$, $2x = A$, and $2y = B$, then
   - **(A)** $A = B$.
   - **(B)** $A < B$.
   - **(C)** $A > B$.
   - **(D)** $A < x$.
   - **(E)** $B < y$.

2. If $a > b$ and $c > d$, then
   - **(A)** $a = c$.
   - **(B)** $a < d$.
   - **(C)** $a + d = b + c$.
   - **(D)** $a + c < b + d$.
   - **(E)** $a + c > b + d$.

3. If $ab > 0$ and $a < 0$, which of the following is negative?
   - **(A)** b
   - **(B)** $-b$
   - **(C)** $-a$
   - **(D)** $(a - b)$
   - **(E)** $-(a + b)$

4. If $4 - x > 5$, then
   - **(A)** $x > 1$.
   - **(B)** $x > -1$.
   - **(C)** $x < 1$.
   - **(D)** $x < -1$.
   - **(E)** $x = -1$.

5. Point X is located on line segment $\overline{AB}$ and point Y is located on line segment $\overline{CD}$. If $AB = CD$ and $AX > CY$, then
   - **(A)** $XB > YD$
   - **(B)** $XB < YD$
   - **(C)** $AX > XB$
   - **(D)** $AX < XB$
   - **(E)** $AX > AB$

6. If $w > x$, $y < z$, and $x > z$, then which of the following must be true?
   - **(A)** $w > x > y > z$
   - **(B)** $w > x > z > y$
   - **(C)** $x > z > y > w$
   - **(D)** $z < y < x < w$
   - **(E)** $z < x < y < w$

7. If x and y are positive integers such that $0 < (x + y) < 10$, then which of the following must be true?
   - **(A)** $x < 8$
   - **(B)** $x > 3$
   - **(C)** $x > y$
   - **(D)** $x + y = 5$
   - **(E)** $x - y \leq 7$

8. In the diagram below, which of the following is always true?

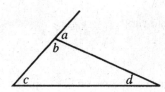

  I. $a > b$

  II. $c > a$

  III. $d > a$

(A) I only

(B) II and III only

(C) I, II, and III

(D) II only

(E) None of these

9. If point X is on line segment $\overline{AB}$, all of the following may be true EXCEPT

(A) $AX = XB$

(B) $AX > XB$

(C) $AX < XB$

(D) $AB > XB$

(E) $AX + XB < AB$

10. If $x > 0$, $y > 0$, and $x - y < 0$, then

(A) $x > y$

(B) $x < y$

(C) $x + y < 0$

(D) $y - x < 0$

(E) $x = -y$

ANSWER KEY AND EXPLANATIONS

1. B	3. A	5. B	7. E	9. E
2. E	4. D	6. B	8. E	10. B

1. **The correct answer is (B).** Doubles of unequals are unequal in the same order.

2. **The correct answer is (E).** If unequal quantities are added to unequal quantities of the same order, the results are unequal in the same order.

3. **The correct answer is (A).** If the product of two numbers is > 0 (positive), then either both numbers are positive or both are negative. Since $a < 0$ (negative), b must also be negative.

4. **The correct answer is (D).**

   $4 - x > 5$
   $-x > 1$

   Divide by -1 and change the inequality sign.

   $x < -1$

5. **The correct answer is (B).**

   If unequal quantities are subtracted from equal quantities, the results are unequal in the same order.

6. **The correct answer is (B).** The first and third statements assert:

   $w > x$ and $x > z$, therefore $w > x > z$

   The second statement says that y is less than z, therefore:

   $w > x > z > y$

7. **The correct answer is (E).** Perhaps using numbers is the easiest way to explain this item:

   (A) x could be 8 and y could be 1:
     $0 < (8 + 1) < 10$
   (B) x could be 3 and y could be 6:
     $0 < (3 + 6) < 10$
   (C) This is wrong as just shown above.
   (D) This too is wrong as shown above.
   (E) The largest possible value for x is 8, and the smallest possible value for y is 1. So the greatest possible value for $x - y$ is 7.

8. **The correct answer is (E).** An exterior angle of a triangle must be greater than either remote interior angle. There is no fixed relationship between an exterior angle and its adjacent interior angle.

9. **The correct answer is (E).** Point X could be so located to make each of the other choices true, but the whole segment $\overline{AB}$ will always be equal to the sum of its parts $\overline{AX}$ and $\overline{XB}$.

10. **The correct answer is (B).** If x and y are both positive, but $x - y$ is negative, then y must be a greater number than x.

DEFINED OPERATION PROBLEMS

"Defined operation" is another name for "function." A function problem might look like this: The function of x is obtained by squaring x and then multiplying the result by 3. If you wanted to know $f(4)$, you would square 4 and multiply that product by 3; the answer would be 48. On the SAT, the $f(x)$ symbol is not normally used. Instead the test-makers use arbitrary symbols and define what function they represent. You approach these symbols as you would a function: talk to yourself about what the function does. In math you usually change words into mathematical notation, but with functions you change mathematical notation into words:

$!x = 2x + 4$

What does the "!" do in this problem? It takes x and doubles it and then adds four.

What is the value of $!6$?

$!6 = 2(6) + 4 = 16$

EXERCISES: DEFINED OPERATION PROBLEMS

Directions: Work out each problem. Circle the letter of your choice.

1. $\&x$ is such that $\&x = \dfrac{x^3}{2}$. What is the value of $\&4$?

   (A) 8
   (B) 16
   (C) 32
   (D) 40
   (E) 64

2. $\$x$ is such that $\$x$ is equal to the largest integer less than x. What is the value of $\$6.99$ times $\$-2.01$?

   (A) 18
   (B) 12
   (C) −12
   (D) −18
   (E) −21

3. The operation # is defined in the following way for any two numbers:

   $p \# q = (p - q)$ times $(q - p)$.

   If $p \# q = -1$, then which of the following are true:

   I. p could equal 5 and q could equal 4
   II. p could equal 4 and q could equal 5
   III. p could equal 1 and q could equal −1
   IV. p could equal −1 and q could equal 1

   (A) I and II only
   (B) I and III only
   (C) II and IV only
   (D) III and IV only
   (E) I, II, III, IV

4. Every letter in the alphabet has a number value that is equal to its place in the alphabet; the letter A has a value of 1 and C a value of 3. The number value of a word is obtained by adding up the value of the letters in the word and then multiplying that sum by the length of the word. The word "DFGH" would have a number value of

   (A) 22
   (B) 44
   (C) 66
   (D) 100
   (E) 108

5. Let $^\wedge x^\wedge$ be defined such that $^\wedge x^\wedge = x + \dfrac{1}{x}$. The value of $^\wedge 6^\wedge + {}^\wedge 4^\wedge + {}^\wedge 2^\wedge$ is

   (A) 12
   (B) $12\dfrac{7}{12}$
   (C) $12\dfrac{11}{12}$
   (D) $13\dfrac{1}{2}$
   (E) $13\dfrac{5}{12}$

ANSWER KEY AND EXPLANATIONS

| 1. C | 2. D | 3. A | 4. D | 5. C |

1. **The correct answer is (C).**

$$4^3 = 64$$
$$64 \div 2 = 32$$

2. **The correct answer is (D).** The key phrase in the problem is "the largest integer." The largest integer less than 6.99 is 6 (not 7, this problem does not say to round the numbers) and the largest integer less than −2.01 is −3 (not −2, as −2 is greater than −2.01).

3. **The correct answer is (A).** The best way to solve this is to plug the values into the equation:

$(5 - 4) \bullet (4 - 5) = -1$

$(4 - 5) \bullet (5 - 4) = -1$

$(1 - -1) \bullet (-1 - 1) = -4$

$(-1 - 1) \bullet (1 - -1) = -4$

Statements I and II give the stated value, −1.

4. **The correct answer is (D).**

D = 4, F = 6, G = 7, H = 8

So the sum of the letters would be 25. 25 multiplied by 4 (the length of the word) is 100.

5. **The correct answer is (C).** The work of this problem is adding up the reciprocals of the numbers.

$6 + 4 + 2 = 12$

$$\frac{1}{6} + \frac{1}{4} + \frac{1}{2} = \frac{2}{12} + \frac{3}{12} + \frac{6}{12} = \frac{11}{12}$$

SUMMING IT UP

- In complex questions, don't look for easy solutions.

- Always keep in mind what is being asked.

- Keep the negatives and positives straight when you're doing polynomial math.

- Don't be distracted by strange symbols.

Geometry Review

OVERVIEW

- Geometric notation
- Angle measurement
- Intersecting lines
- Perimeter
- Area
- Circles
- Volume
- Triangles
- Parallel lines
- Polygons
- Coordinate geometry
- Summing it up

GEOMETRIC NOTATION

1 A point is represented by a dot, and denoted by a capital letter.

$\bullet\, P$

Point P

2 A *line* can be denoted in two different ways. First, a small letter can be placed next to the line. For example, the diagram below depicts line *l*. The arrowheads on both ends of the line indicate that lines extend infinitely in both directions.

$\longleftrightarrow l$

3 A *line* can also be denoted by placing a small double-headed arrow over two of its points. The diagram below depicts line $\overleftrightarrow{AB}$.

$\overset{\longleftrightarrow}{\underset{A \qquad\qquad B}{\bullet \qquad\qquad \bullet}}$

4 A *line segment* is the part of a line between two of its points, which are called the endpoints of the line segment. A line segment is denoted by placing a small line segment over the two endpoints. Thus, the diagram below depicts the line segment $\overline{AB}$.

$\underset{A \qquad\qquad B}{\bullet\!\!-\!\!-\!\!-\!\!-\!\!-\!\!-\!\!-\!\!\bullet}$

5 The length of a line segment is denoted by placing its two endpoints next to each other. In the diagram below, $CD = 7$.

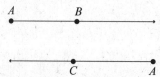

6 Two line segments that have the same length are said to be *congruent*. The symbol for congruence is ≅. Thus, if $AB = 12$ and $EF = 12$, then $\overline{AB}$ is congruent to $\overline{EF}$, or $\overline{AB} \cong \overline{EF}$.

7 A *ray* is the part of a line beginning at one point, called the *endpoint,* and extending infinitely in one direction. A ray is denoted by placing a small one-headed arrow over its endpoint and another point on the ray. The first diagram below depicts the ray $\overrightarrow{AB}$, and the second diagram depicts the ray $\overrightarrow{AC}$.

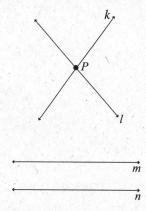

8 Two lines that cross each other are said to *intersect*. Two lines that do not intersect are said to be *parallel*. The symbol | | is used to represent parallel lines. In the diagrams below, line k intersects line l at point P, while lines m and n are parallel, that is, $m \,||\, n$.

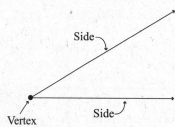

ANGLE MEASUREMENT

1 When two rays share a common endpoint, they form *angles*. The point at which the rays intersect is called the *vertex* of the angle, and the rays themselves are called the *sides* of the angle.

2 The symbol for angle is ∠. Angles can be denoted in several different ways, as shown in the diagram below. The most common way to denote an angle is to name a point on one side, then the vertex, and then a point on the other side as shown in the diagram.

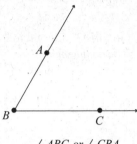

∠ABC or ∠CBA

Angles can also be denoted by writing a letter or a number within the angle, as shown below. If there is no ambiguity, an angle can be named by simply naming the vertex.

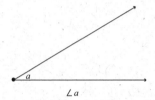   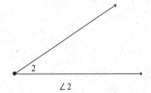   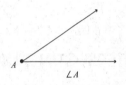

3 The size of an angle is measured in *degrees*. The symbol for degree is °. A full circle contains 360°, and all other angles can be measured as a fractional part of a full circle. Typically, the measure of an angle is written in the interior of the angle, near the vertex.

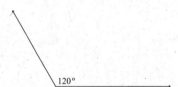   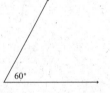

4 A *straight angle* is an angle that measures 180°.

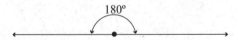

5 A *right angle* is an angle that measures 90°. Note, as shown in the diagram below, the symbol ∟ is used to represent a right angle.

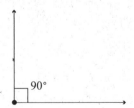

6 The measure of an angle is denoted by writing the letter m followed by the name of the angle. For example, m∠*ABC* = 45° tells that angle *ABC* has a measure of 45°.

7 Two angles that have the same number of degrees are said to be *congruent*. Thus, if m∠*P* = m∠*Q*, then ∠*P* ≅ ∠*Q*.

8 Two angles whose measures add up to 180° are said to be *supplementary*. Two angles whose measures add up to 90° are said to be *complementary*.

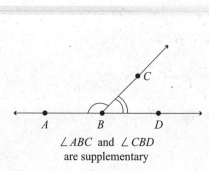

∠*ABC* and ∠*CBD*
are supplementary

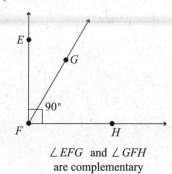

∠*EFG* and ∠*GFH*
are complementary

INTERSECTING LINES

1 When two lines intersect, four angles are formed. The angles opposite each other are congruent.

∠1 ≅ ∠3 and

∠2 ≅ ∠4

2 When two lines intersect, the angles adjacent to each other are supplementary.

m∠5 + m∠6 = 180°

m∠6 + m∠7 = 180°

m∠7 + m∠8 = 180°

m∠8 + m∠5 = 180°

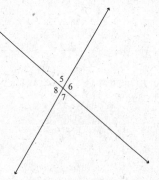

If you know the measure of any one of the four angles formed when two lines intersect, you can determine the measures of the other three. For example, if m∠1 = 45°, then m∠3 = 45°, and m∠2 = m∠4 = 180° − 45° = 135°.

③ Two lines that intersect at right angles are said to be *perpendicular*. In the figure below, $\overline{AB}$ is perpendicular to $\overline{CD}$. This can be denoted as $\overline{AB} \perp \overline{CD}$.

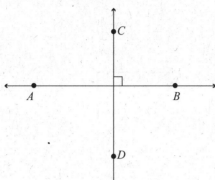

Note that all four of the angles in the diagram above are right angles.

PERIMETER

❶ Any polygon = sum of all sides

$P = 5 + 8 + 11 = 24$

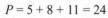

❷ Circle = π*d*

(called circumference)

Circle = π*d* = 2π*r*

Circle = π(12) = 12π

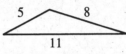

③ The distance covered by a wheel in one revolution is equal to the circumference of the wheel.

In one revolution, this wheel covers $\pi \bullet \dfrac{14}{\pi}$, or 14 feet.

AREA

❶ Rectangle = *bh*

Area = 6 • 3 = 18

❷ Parallelogram = *bh*

Area = 8 • 4 = 32

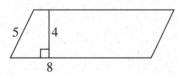

3 Square = s^2 or $\frac{1}{2}d^2$

Area = $6^2 = 36$

Area = $\frac{1}{2}(10)(10) = 50$

4 Triangle = $\frac{1}{2}bh$

Area = $\frac{1}{2}(12)(4) = 24$

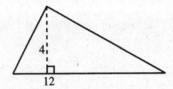

5 Equilateral triangle = $\frac{s^2}{4}\sqrt{3}$

Area = $\frac{36}{4}\sqrt{3} = 9\sqrt{3}$

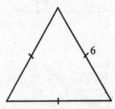

6 Trapezoid = $\frac{1}{2}h(b_1 + b_2)$

Area = $\frac{1}{2}(5)(16) = 40$

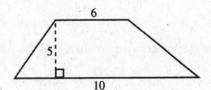

7 Circle = πr^2

Area = $\pi(6)^2 = 36\pi$

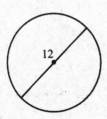

CIRCLES

❶ A *circle* is a closed flat figure formed by a set of points all of which are the same distance from a point called the *center*. The boundary of the circle is called the *circumference*, and the distance from the center to any point on the circumference is called the *radius*. A circle is denoted by naming the point at its center, that is, the circle whose center is at point *P* is called circle *P*.

❷ A *diameter* of a circle is a line segment that passes through the center of the circle, and whose endpoints lie on the circle. The diameter of a circle is twice as long as its radius. Typically, the letter *r* is used to represent the radius of a circle, and the letter *d* is used to represent the diameter.

 $2r = d$

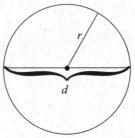

❸ A *chord* of a circle is a line segment both of whose endpoints lie on the circumference of the circle. The chords of a circle have different lengths, and the length of the longest chord is equal to the diameter.

$\overline{AB}$, $\overline{CD}$, and $\overline{EF}$ are chords of circle *O*. $\overline{EF}$ is also a diameter.

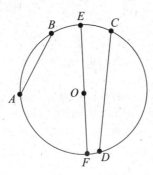

TIP

When an SAT problem asks you to find the area of a shaded region, you probably won't be able to calculate it directly. That's OK—instead, think of the shaded region as being whatever is left over when one region is subtracted or removed from a larger region. Use the formulas you know to find those two regions, and perform the necessary subtraction.

4 A *tangent* is a line that intersects the circle at exactly one point. A radius drawn to the point of intersection is perpendicular to the tangent line.

$$\overline{OQ} \perp \overline{CD}$$

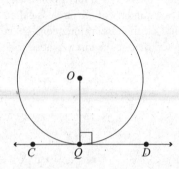

5 An *arc* is a piece of the circumference of a circle. The symbol ∩ placed on top of the two end-points is used to denote an arc. For example, $\overset{\frown}{MN}$ is indicated in the figure below.

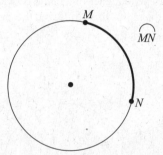

6 A *central angle* is an angle that is formed by two radii of a circle. As the diagram below shows, the vertex of a central angle is the center of the circle.

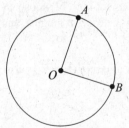

Central Angle ∠ AOB

7 A central angle is equal in degrees to the measure of the arc that it intercepts. That is, a 40° central angle intercepts a 40° arc, and a 90° central angle intercepts a 90° arc.

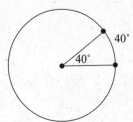
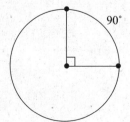

VOLUME

1 The volume of a rectangular solid is equal to the product of its length, width, and height.

$V = lwh$

$V = (6)(2)(4) = 48$

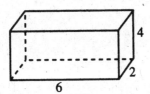

2 The volume of a cube is equal to the cube of an edge.

$V = e^3$

$V = (5)^3 = 125$

3 The volume of a cylinder is equal to π times the square of the radius of the base times the height.

$V = \pi r^2 h$

$V = \pi(5)^2(3) = 75\pi$

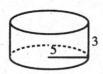

TRIANGLES

1 A *polygon* is a flat closed figure that consists of straight line segments called *sides*. A *triangle* is a polygon with three sides. A *vertex* of a triangle is a point at which two of its sides meet. The symbol for a triangle is $\triangle$, and a triangle can be named by writing its three vertices in any order.

$\triangle ABC$ contains sides $\overline{AB}$, $\overline{BC}$, and $\overline{AC}$, and angles $\angle A$, $\angle B$, and $\angle C$.

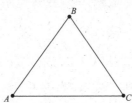

2 The sum of the measures of the angles in a triangle is 180°. Therefore, if the measures of any two of the angles in a triangle are known, the measure of the third angle can be determined.

3 In any triangle, the longest side is opposite the largest angle and the shortest side is opposite the smallest angle. In the triangle below, if $a° > b° > c°$, then $\overline{BC} > \overline{AC} > \overline{AB}$.

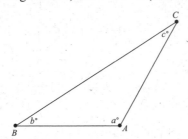

4 If two sides of a triangle are congruent, the angles opposite these sides are also congruent.

If $\overline{AB} = \overline{AC}$, then $\angle B \cong \angle C$.

5 If two angles of a triangle are congruent, the sides opposite these angles are also congruent.

If $\angle B \cong \angle C$ then $\overline{AB} = \overline{AC}$.

6 A triangle with all three sides the same length is called an *equilateral* triangle. In an equilateral triangle, all three angles are congruent and measure 60°.

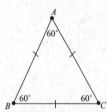

7 In the diagram below, $\angle 1$ is called an *exterior* angle. The measure of an exterior angle of a triangle is equal to the sum of the measures of the two *remote interior* angles, that is, the two interior angles that are the farthest away from the exterior angle.

$m\angle 1 = 115°$

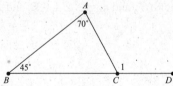

8 If two angles of one triangle are congruent to two angles of a second triangle, the third angles are also congruent.

$\angle D \cong \angle A$

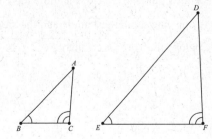

Right Triangles

1 Pythagorean theorem

$$(\text{leg})^2 + (\text{leg})^2 = (\text{hypotenuse})^2$$
$$4^2 + 5^2 = x^2$$
$$16 + 25 = x^2$$
$$41 = x^2$$
$$\sqrt{41} = x$$

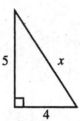

2 Pythagorean triples: These are sets of numbers that satisfy the Pythagorean theorem. When a given set of numbers such as 3-4-5 forms a Pythagorean triple ($3^2 + 4^2 = 5^2$), any multiples of this set, such as 6-8-10 or 15-20-25 also form a Pythagorean triple. The most common Pythagorean triples that should be memorized are:

3-4-5
5-12-13
8-15-17
7-24-25

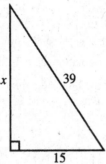

Squaring the numbers 15 and 39 in order to apply the Pythagorean theorem would take too much time. Instead, recognize the hypotenuse as 3(13). Suspect a 5-12-13 triangle. Since the given leg is 3(5), the missing leg must be 3(12), or 36, with no computation and a great saving of time.

3 The 30°-60°-90° triangle

a) The leg opposite the 30° angle is $\frac{1}{2} \times \text{hypotenuse}$.

b) The leg opposite the 60° angle is $\frac{1}{2} \times \text{hypotenuse} \times \sqrt{3}$.

c) An altitude in an equilateral triangle forms a 30°-60°-90° triangle and is therefore equal to $\frac{1}{2}\text{hypotenuse} \times \sqrt{3}$.

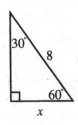 $x = 4$

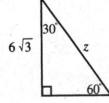 $y = 5\sqrt{3}$

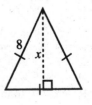 $z = 12$

$x = 4\sqrt{3}$

4 The 45°-45°-90° triangle (isosceles right triangle)

a) Each leg is $\frac{1}{2} \times \text{hypotenuse} \times \sqrt{2}$.

b) Hypotenuse is $\text{leg} \times \sqrt{2}$.

c) The diagonal in a square forms a 45°-45°-90° triangle and is therefore equal to the length of one side $\times \sqrt{2}$.

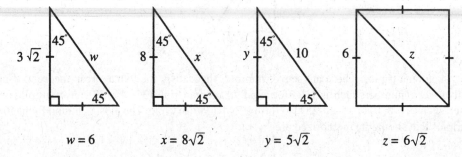

$w = 6$ $x = 8\sqrt{2}$ $y = 5\sqrt{2}$ $z = 6\sqrt{2}$

5 One way to solve SAT questions that involve 30°-60°-90° triangles and 45°-45°-90° triangles is to use right triangle trigonometric relationships. In the triangle below, side $\overline{AB}$ is called the side *adjacent* to $\angle A$, side $\overline{BC}$ is called the side *opposite* $\angle A$, and side $\overline{AC}$ is the *hypotenuse*. Relative to $\angle A$, the trigonometric ratios *sine, cosine,* and *tangent* are defined as shown.

$$\text{sine } a° = \sin a° = \frac{\text{opposite}}{\text{hypotenuse}}$$

$$\text{cosine } a° = \cos a° = \frac{\text{adjacent}}{\text{hypotenuse}}$$

$$\text{tangent } a° = \tan a° = \frac{\text{opposite}}{\text{adjacent}}$$

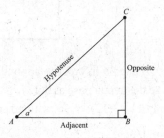

The table below shows the values of the sine, cosine, and tangent for 30°, 45°, and 60°.

Angle a	$\sin a°$	$\cos a°$	$\tan a°$
30°	$\frac{1}{2}$	$\frac{\sqrt{3}}{2}$	$\frac{\sqrt{3}}{3}$
45°	$\frac{\sqrt{2}}{2}$	$\frac{\sqrt{2}}{2}$	1
60°	$\frac{\sqrt{3}}{3}$	$\frac{1}{2}$	$\sqrt{3}$

By using the values of sine, cosine, and tangent above, problems involving 30°-60°-90° triangles and 45°-45°-90° triangles can also be solved. For example, consider the 30°-60°-90° triangle with hypotenuse of length 8. The computations that follow show how to determine the lengths of the other two sides.

sine $60° = \dfrac{\text{opposite}}{\text{hypotenuse}} = \dfrac{y}{8}$. Also, since sine $60° = \dfrac{\sqrt{3}}{2}$, then $\dfrac{y}{8} = \dfrac{\sqrt{3}}{2}$. Cross-multiply to

get $2y = 8\sqrt{3}$, or $y = \dfrac{8\sqrt{3}}{2} = 4\sqrt{3}$. Note that this is the same answer that would be obtained

using the properties of 30°-60°-90° triangles.

cos $60° = \dfrac{\text{adjacent}}{\text{hypotenuse}} = \dfrac{x}{8}$. Also, since cos $60° = \dfrac{1}{2}$, then $\dfrac{x}{8} = \dfrac{1}{2}$. Cross-multiply to get

2$x = 8$, or $x = 4$. This, again, is the same answer that would be obtained using the properties of 30°-60°-90° triangles above.

PARALLEL LINES

1 If two parallel lines are cut by a transversal, the alternate interior angles are congruent.

If $\overleftrightarrow{AB} \parallel \overleftrightarrow{CD}$, then
$\angle 1 \cong \angle 3$ and
$\angle 2 \cong \angle 4$.

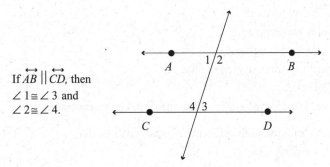

2 If two parallel lines are cut by a transversal, the corresponding angles are congruent.

If $\overleftrightarrow{AB} \parallel \overleftrightarrow{CD}$, then
$\angle 1 \cong \angle 5$,
$\angle 2 \cong \angle 6$,
$\angle 3 \cong \angle 7$, and
$\angle 4 \cong \angle 8$.

③ If two parallel lines are cut by a transversal, interior angles on the same side of the transversal are supplementary.

If $\overleftrightarrow{AB} \parallel \overleftrightarrow{CD}$, then
∠ 1 is supplementary to ∠ 4 and
∠ 2 is supplementary to ∠ 3.

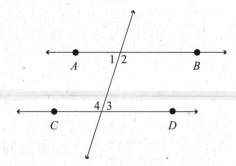

POLYGONS

① The sum of the measures of the angles of a polygon of n sides is $(n - 2)180°$. Since *ABCDE* has 5 sides, m∠A + m∠B + m∠C + m∠D + m∠E = $(5 - 2)180° = 3(180°) = 540°$.

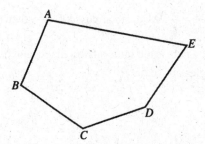

② In a parallelogram
a) Opposite sides are parallel.
b) Opposite sides are congruent.
c) Opposite angles are congruent.
d) Consecutive angles are supplementary.
e) Diagonals bisect each other.
f) Each diagonal bisects the parallelogram into two congruent triangles.

③ In a rectangle, in addition to the properties listed in (2), above,
a) All angles are right angles.
b) Diagonals are congruent.

④ In a rhombus, in addition to the properties listed in (2), above,
a) All sides are congruent.
b) Diagonals are perpendicular.
c) Diagonals bisect the angles.

⑤ A square has all of the properties listed in (2), (3), and (4), above.

Similar Polygons

1 Corresponding angles of similar polygons are congruent.

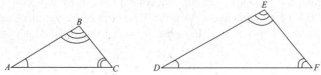

2 Corresponding sides of similar polygons are in proportion.

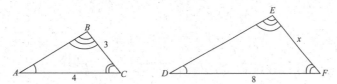

If triangle *ABC* is similar to triangle *DEF*, and the sides are given as marked, then $\overline{EF}$ must be equal to 6, as the ratio between corresponding sides is 4:8, or 1:2.

3 When figures are similar, all corresponding linear ratios are equal. The ratio of one side to its corresponding side is the same as perimeter to perimeter, altitude to altitude, etc.

4 When figures are similar, the ratio of their areas is equal to the square of the ratio between two corresponding linear quantities.

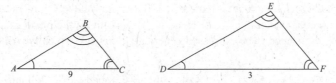

Note: Triangles are not drawn to scale.

If triangle *ABC* is similar to triangle *DEF*, the area of triangle *ABC* will be 9 times that of triangle *DEF*. The ratio of sides is 9:3, or 3:1. The ratio of areas will be the square of 3:1, or 9:1.

5 When figures are similar, the ratio of their volumes is equal to the cube of the ratio between two corresponding linear quantities.

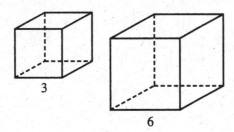

The volume of the larger cube is 8 times the volume of the smaller cube. If the ratio of sides is 3:6, or 1:2, the ratio of volumes is the cube of this, or 1:8.

COORDINATE GEOMETRY

1 Lines and other geometric figures can be positioned on a plane by means of the *rectangular coordinate system*. The rectangular coordinate system consists of two number lines that are perpendicular and cross each other at their *origins* (0 on each of the number lines). The horizontal number line is called the *x*-axis, and the vertical number line is called the *y*-axis.

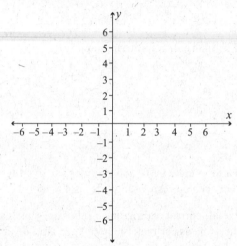

2 Any point on the plane can be designated by a pair of numbers. The first number is called the *x-coordinate*, and indicates how far to move to the left (negative) or to the right (positive) on the *x-axis*, and the second number is called the *y-coordinate* and tells how far to move up (positive) or down (negative) on the *y-axis*. Generically, a point on the plane can be written as (x, y). When two points need to be expressed generically, they are typically written as (x_1, y_1) and (x_2, y_2).

The points $(2,3)$, $(-4,1)$, $(-5,-2)$, $(2,-4)$, and $(5,0)$ are graphed on a coordinate system as shown.

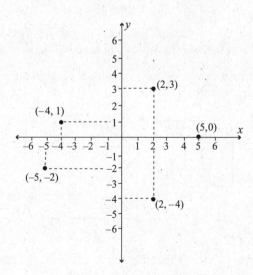

❸ Distance between two points:

$$\sqrt{(x_2-x_1)^2+(y_2-y_1)^2}$$

The distance from $(-2,3)$ to $(4,-1)$ is:

$$\sqrt{[4-(-2)]^2+[-1-(3)]^2}$$
$$\sqrt{(6)^2+(-4)^2}=\sqrt{36+16}=\sqrt{52}$$

❹ The midpoint of a line segment:

$$\left(\frac{x_1+x_2}{2},\frac{y_1+y_2}{2}\right)$$

The midpoint of the segment joining $(-2,3)$ to $(4,-1)$ is:

$$\left(\frac{-2+4}{2},\frac{3+(-1)}{2}\right)=\left(\frac{2}{2},\frac{2}{2}\right)=(1,1)$$

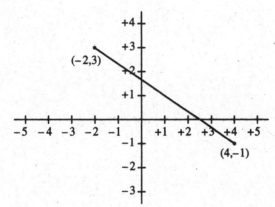

❺ The *slope* of a straight line is a number that measures how steep the line is. Traditionally, the variable m is used to stand for the slope of a line. By convention, a line that increases from left to right has a positive slope, and a line that decreases from left to right has a negative slope. A horizontal line has a slope of 0 since it is "flat," and a vertical line has no slope.

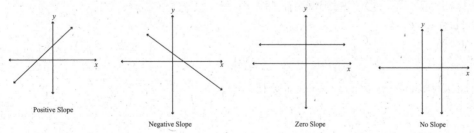

Positive Slope   Negative Slope   Zero Slope   No Slope

❻ If (x_1,y_1) and (x_2,y_2) are any two points on a line, the slope is given by the formula $m=\dfrac{(y_2-y_1)}{(x_2-x_1)}$ Therefore, for example, if a line contains the points $(5,7)$ and $(3,4)$, the slope would be $m=\dfrac{7-4}{5-3}=\dfrac{3}{2}$. A slope of $\dfrac{3}{2}$ represents the fact that, for every 2 units moved horizontally along the x-axis, the line rises vertically 3 units.

An equation of degree one that contains the variables x and/or y raised to the first power, but no higher, will always have a straight line as its graph. A very convenient way to write the equation of a line is in the *slope-intercept* form, $y = mx + b$. In this form, m represents the slope of the line, and b is the *y-intercept,* that is, the point where the graph crosses the *y-axis*.

As an example, consider the line represented by the equation $2x + 5y = 12$. Begin by writing this equation in slope-intercept form.

$2x + 5y = 12$ Subtract $2x$ from both sides

$5y = -2x + 12$ Divide both sides by 5

$$y = -\frac{2}{5}x + \frac{12}{5}$$

Therefore, the slope of the line is $-\dfrac{2}{5}$, and the y-intercept is $\dfrac{12}{5}$. The graph of this line is shown below.

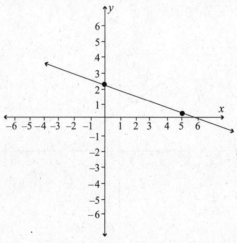

Suppose you were asked to write the equation of the line containing the point $(2,1)$ and having slope 5. Begin by taking the slope-intercept form $y = mx + b$, and substituting $m = 5$, to obtain $y = 5x + b$. To determine the value of the y-intercept b, substitute the coordinates of the point $(2,1)$ into the equation.

$y = 5x + b$ Substitute $(2,1)$

$1 = 5(2) + b$ Solve for b

$1 = 10 + b$

$b = -9$

Therefore, the equation of the line is $y = 5x - 9$.

8 Parallel lines have the same slope. Therefore, one way to tell whether two lines are parallel or not is to write them in slope-intercept form and compare the slopes. To write the equation of the line that is parallel to the line $y = 3x + 7$ and contains the point (5,2), begin by noting that the equation of the line we are looking for must have a slope of 3, just like the line $y = 3x + 7$. Thus, it must be of the form $y = 3x + b$.

$y = 3x + b$	Substitute (5,2)
$2 = 3(5) + b$	Solve for b
$2 = 15 + b$	
$b = -13$	

Therefore, the equation of the line is $y = 3x - 13$.

9 The slopes of perpendicular lines are *negative reciprocals* of each other. That is, if a line has a slope of $\frac{a}{b}$, then the slope of the perpendicular line would be $-\frac{b}{a}$. Thus, the line perpendicular to the line with slope $\frac{2}{5}$ would have a slope of $-\frac{5}{2}$.

To write the equation of the line that is perpendicular to the line $y = \frac{1}{2}x - 7$ and contains the point (4,−3), begin by noting that the equation of the line to be determined has a slope of −2. Thus, the equation must be of the form $y = -2x + b$.

$y = -2x + b$	Substitute $(4, -3)$
$-3 = -2(4) + b$	Solve for b
$-3 = -8 + b$	
$b = 5$	

Therefore, the equation of the line is $y = -2x + 5$.

EXERCISES: GEOMETRY

Directions: Work out each problem. Circle the letter next to your choice.

1. If the angles of a triangle are in the ratio 2:3:7, the triangle is
   (A) acute.
   (B) isosceles.
   (C) obtuse.
   (D) right.
   (E) equilateral.

2. If the area of a square of side x is 5, what is the area of a square of side $3x$?
   (A) 15
   (B) 45
   (C) 95
   (D) 75
   (E) 225

3. If the radius of a circle is decreased by 10%, by what percent is its area decreased?
   (A) 10
   (B) 19
   (C) 21
   (D) 79
   (E) 81

4. A spotlight is mounted on the ceiling 5 feet from one wall of a room and 10 feet from the adjacent wall. How many feet is it from the intersection of the two walls?
   (A) 15
   (B) $5\sqrt{2}$
   (C) $5\sqrt{5}$
   (D) $10\sqrt{2}$
   (E) $10\sqrt{5}$

5. A dam has the dimensions indicated in the figure. Find the area of this isosceles trapezoid.

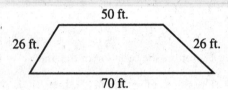

   (A) 1300
   (B) 1560
   (C) 1400
   (D) 1440
   (E) It cannot be determined from the information given.

6. In parallelogram $PQRS$, angle P is 4 times angle Q. What is the measure in degrees of angle P?
   (A) 36
   (B) 72
   (C) 125
   (D) 144
   (E) 150

7. If $\overline{PQ} \cong \overline{QS}$, $\overline{QR} \cong \overline{RS}$ and the measure of angle $PRS = 100°$, what is the measure, in degrees, of angle QPS?

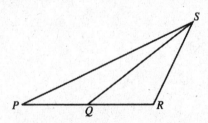

   Note: Figure not drawn to scale
   (A) 10
   (B) 15
   (C) 20
   (D) 25
   (E) 30

8. A line segment is drawn from point (3,5) to point (9,13). What are the coordinates of the midpoint of this line segment?

   (A) (3,4)

   (B) (12,18)

   (C) (6,8)

   (D) (9,6)

   (E) (6,9)

9. A rectangular box with a square base contains 6 cubic feet. If the height of the box is 18 inches, how many feet are there in each side of the base?

   (A) 1

   (B) 2

   (C) $\sqrt{3}$

   (D) $\dfrac{\sqrt{3}}{3}$

   (E) 4

10. The surface area of a cube is 150 square feet. How many cubic feet are there in the volume of the cube?

    (A) 30

    (B) 50

    (C) 100

    (D) 125

    (E) 150

11. Peter lives 12 miles west of his school and Bill lives north of the school. Peter finds that the direct distance from his house to Bill's is 6 miles shorter than the distance by way of school. How many miles north of the school does Bill live?

    (A) 6

    (B) 9

    (C) 10

    (D) $6\sqrt{2}$

    (E) None of the above

12. A square is inscribed in a circle of area 18π. Find a side of the square.

    (A) 3

    (B) 6

    (C) $3\sqrt{2}$

    (D) $6\sqrt{2}$

    (E) It cannot be determined from the information given.

13. A carpet is y yards long and f feet wide. How many dollars will it cost if the carpet sells for x cents per square foot?

    (A) xyf

    (B) $3xyf$

    (C) $\dfrac{xyf}{3}$

    (D) $\dfrac{0.03\,yf}{x}$

    (E) $0.03xyf$

14. If a triangle of base 6 has the same area as a circle of radius 6, what is the altitude of the triangle?

    (A) 6π

    (B) 8π

    (C) 10π

    (D) 12π

    (E) 14π

15. The vertex angle of an isosceles triangle is p degrees. How many degrees are there in one of the base angles?

    (A) $180 - p$

    (B) $90 - p$

    (C) $180 - 2p$

    (D) $180 - \dfrac{p}{2}$

    (E) $90 - \dfrac{p}{2}$

16. In a circle with center O, the measure of arc $RS = 132$ degrees. How many degrees are there in angle RSO?

    (A) 66°

    (B) 48°

    (C) 24°

    (D) 22°

    (E) 20°

17. The ice compartment of a refrigerator is 8 inches long, 4 inches wide, and 5 inches high. How many ice cubes will it hold if each cube is 2 inches on an edge?

(A) 8
(B) 10
(C) 12
(D) 16
(E) 20

18. In the figure, PSQ is a straight line and $\overline{RS}$ is perpendicular to $\overline{ST}$. If the measure of angle $RSQ = 48°$, how many degrees are there in angle PST?

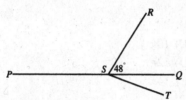

(A) 48°
(B) 90°
(C) 132°
(D) 136°
(E) 138°

19. A cylindrical pail has a radius of 7 inches and a height of 9 inches. If there are 231 cubic inches to a gallon, approximately how many gallons will this pail hold?

(A) $\dfrac{12}{7}$
(B) 6
(C) 7.5
(D) 8.2
(E) 9

20. In triangle PQR, $\overline{QS}$ and $\overline{SR}$ are angle bisectors and the measure of angle $P = 80°$. How many degrees are there in angle QSR?

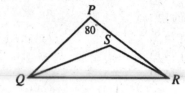

(A) 115°
(B) 120°
(C) 125°
(D) 130°
(E) 135°

21. In the figure below, the circle has center O. If $b = 40$, what is the value of a?

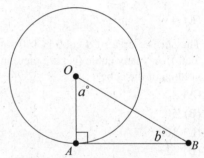

(A) 30
(B) 40
(C) 45
(D) 50
(E) 60

22. One end of a wire is attached to the top of a 70-foot high pole, and the other end is attached to a stake in the ground. If the wire makes a 30° angle with the ground, how long is the wire?

(A) 70 feet
(B) $70\sqrt{3}$ feet
(C) 140 feet
(D) $140\sqrt{2}$ feet
(E) $140\sqrt{3}$ feet

23. What is the slope of the line containing the points (4,6) and (3,8)?

(A) −2

(B) $-\dfrac{1}{2}$

(C) 0

(D) $\dfrac{1}{2}$

(E) 2

24. Which of the following represents the equation of a line with a slope of −7 and a y-intercept of 12?

(A) $y = 7x - 12$

(B) $y = -7x + 12$

(C) $y = 7x + 12$

(D) $y = 12x - 7$

(E) $y = -12x + 7$

25. Which of the following represents the equation of a line parallel to the line $y = 7x - 6$, and containing the point (1,7)?

(A) $y = 7x + 7$

(B) $y = 7x - 7$

(C) $y = -7x + 7$

(D) $y = -7x$

(E) $y = 7x$

exercises

ANSWER KEY AND EXPLANATIONS

1. C	6. D	11. B	16. C	21. D
2. B	7. C	12. B	17. D	22. C
3. B	8. E	13. E	18. E	23. A
4. C	9. B	14. D	19. B	24. B
5. D	10. D	15. E	20. D	25. E

1. **The correct answer is (C).** Represent the angles as $2x$, $3x$, and $7x$.

$$2x + 3x + 7x = 180°$$
$$12x = 180°$$
$$x = 15°$$

The angles are $30°, 45°,$ and $105°$. Since one angle is between $90°$ and $180°$, the triangle is called an obtuse triangle.

2. **The correct answer is (B).** If the sides have a ratio 1:3, the areas have a ratio 1:9. Therefore, the area of the large square is 9(5), or 45.

3. **The correct answer is (B).** If the radii of the two circles have a ratio of 10:9, the areas have a ratio of 100:81. Therefore, the decrease is 19 out of 100, or 19%.

4. **The correct answer is (C).**

$$5^2 + 10^2 = x^2$$
$$25 + 100 = x^2$$
$$x^2 = 125$$
$$x = \sqrt{125} = \sqrt{25}\sqrt{5} = 5\sqrt{5}$$

5. **The correct answer is (D).**

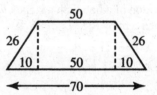

When altitudes are drawn from both ends of the upper base in an isosceles trapezoid, the figure is divided into a rectangle and two congruent right triangles. The center section of the lower base is equal to the upper base, and the remainder of the lower base is divided equally between both ends. The altitude can then be found using the Pythagorean theorem. In this case, we have a 5-12-13 triangle with all measures doubled, so the altitude is 24.

The area is $\frac{1}{2}(24)(120)$, or 1440.

6. **The correct answer is (D).** The consecutive angles of a parallelogram are supplementary, so

$$x + 4x = 180°$$
$$5x = 180°$$
$$x = 36°$$

Angle P is 4(36), or $144°$.

7. The correct answer is (C).

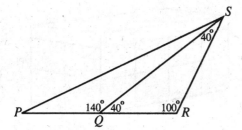

Since $\overline{QR} \cong \overline{RS}$, $\angle RQS \cong \angle RSQ$. There are 80° left in the triangle, so each of these angles is 40°. $\angle SQP$ is supplementary to $\angle SQR$, making it 140°. Since $\overline{QP} \cong \overline{QS}$, $\angle QPS \cong \angle QSP$. There are 40° left in the triangle, so each of these angles is 20°.

8. The correct answer is (E). Add the x-values and divide by 2. Add the y-values and divide by 2.

9. The correct answer is (B). Change 18 inches to 1.5 feet. Letting each side of the base be x, the volume is $1.5x^2$.

$$1.5x^2 = 6$$
$$15x^2 = 60$$
$$x^2 = 4$$
$$x = 2$$

10. The correct answer is (D). The surface area of a cube is made up of 6 equal squares. If each edge of the cube is x, then

$$6x^2 = 150$$
$$x^2 = 25$$
$$x = 5$$
$$\text{Volume} = (\text{edge})^3 = 5^3 = 125$$

11. The correct answer is (B).

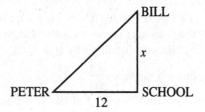

The direct distance from Peter's house to Bill's can be represented by means of the Pythagorean theorem as $\sqrt{144 + x^2}$.

Then

$$\sqrt{144 + x^2} = (12x + x) - 6$$
$$\sqrt{144 + x^2} = x + 6$$

Square both sides.

$$144 + x^2 = x^2 + 12x + 36$$
$$14 = 12x + 36$$
$$108 = 12x$$
$$9 = x$$

12. The correct answer is (B).

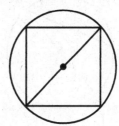

The diagonal of the square will be a diameter of the circle.

$$\pi r^2 = 18\pi$$
$$r^2 = 18$$
$$r = \sqrt{18} = \sqrt{9}\sqrt{2} = 3\sqrt{2}$$

The diameter is $6\sqrt{2}$ and, since the triangles are 45°-45°-90°, a side of the square is 6.

13. **The correct answer is (E).** To find the area in square feet, change y yards to $3y$ feet. The area is then $(3y)(f)$, or $3yf$ square feet. If each square foot costs x cents, change this to dollars by dividing x by 100. Thus, each square foot costs $\dfrac{x}{100}$ dollars. The cost of $3yf$ square feet will then be $\dfrac{3xyf}{100}$. Since $\dfrac{3}{100} = 0.03$, the correct answer is (E).

14. **The correct answer is (D).** The area of the circle is $(6)^2\pi$, or 36π. In the triangle

$$\frac{1}{2}(6)(h) = 36\pi$$
$$3h = 36\pi$$
$$h = 12\pi$$

15. **The correct answer is (E).** There are $(180 - p)$ degrees left, which must be divided between 2 congruent angles. Each angle will contain $\dfrac{(180 - p)}{2}$, or $90 - \dfrac{p}{2}$ degrees.

16. **The correct answer is (C).**

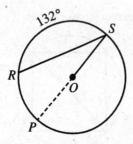

By extending SO until it hits the circle at P, arc PRS is a semicircle. Therefore, the measure of arc $PR = 48°$, and the measure of the inscribed angle $RSO = 24°$.

17. **The correct answer is (D).**

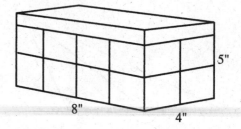

The compartment will hold 2 layers, each of which contains 2 rows of 4 cubes each. This leaves a height of 1 inch on top empty. Therefore, the compartment can hold 16 cubes.

18. **The correct answer is (E).**

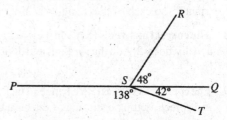

Since $\angle RST$ is a right angle, $42°$ are left for $\angle QST$. Since $\angle PSQ$ is a straight angle of $180°$, $\angle PST$ contains $138°$.

19. **The correct answer is (B).** The volume of the pail is found using the formula $V = \pi r^2 h$. Since the answers are not in terms of π, it is best to use $\dfrac{22}{7}$ as a value for π because the 7 will divide out r^2:

$$V = \frac{22}{\cancel{7}} \cdot \overset{7}{\cancel{49}} \cdot 9$$

Rather than multiply this out, which will take unnecessary time, divide by 231 and cancel wherever possible.

$$\frac{\overset{2}{\cancel{22}} \cdot \cancel{7} \cdot \overset{3}{\cancel{9}}}{\underset{\underset{3}{\cancel{33}}}{\cancel{231}}} = 6$$

20. **The correct answer is (D).** If m∠P = 80°, there are 100° left between ∠PQR and ∠PRQ. If they are both bisected, there will be 50° between ∠SQR and ∠SRQ, leaving 130° in triangle SRQ for ∠QSR.

21. **The correct answer is (D).** The line segment $\overline{AB}$ is tangent to the circle, and therefore is perpendicular to radius $\overline{OA}$.

    This means that ∠OAB is a right angle. Therefore, one of the angles in the triangle measures 90°, and another angle measures 40°. Since the sum of the three angles in a triangle is 180°, the measure of the missing angle must be 50°.

22. **The correct answer is (C).** Begin by making a diagram of the situation described in the problem.

    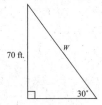

    There are two ways to solve this problem. The first is to notice that the triangle is a 30°-60°-90° triangle, and in such a triangle, the length of the side opposite the 30° angle is half of the length of the hypotenuse. Thus, the length of the wire, which is represented by the hypotenuse in the triangle, would be 2 × 70 feet = 140 feet.

    The problem can also be solved by using trigonometry. Let w stand for the length of the wire, then write $\sin 30° = \dfrac{70}{w}$. Since $\sin 30° = \dfrac{1}{2}$, the equation is $\dfrac{70}{w} = \dfrac{1}{2}$.

    Cross-multiply. $w = 140$ feet

23. **The correct answer is (A).** The formula for the slope of a line is $\dfrac{(y_2 - y_1)}{(x_2 - x_1)}$ where (x_1, y_1) and (x_2, y_2) are any two points on the line. In this problem, the two points are (4,6) and (3,8), so $m = \dfrac{(y_2 - y_1)}{(x_2 - x_1)} = \dfrac{8 - 6}{3 - 4} = \dfrac{2}{-1} = -2$.

24. **The correct answer is (B).** In the formula $y = mx + b$, m represents the slope of the line, and b represents the y-intercept. Thus, the equation $y = -7x + 12$ represents the equation of a line with slope of −7 and y-intercept of 12.

25. **The correct answer is (E).** Since parallel lines have the same slope, the slope of the line to be determined is the same as the slope of $y = 7x - 6$, which is 7. Therefore, the equation of the unknown line can be written as $y = 7x + b$, where b represents the y-intercept. In order to find the value of b, substitute the point (1,7) into $y = 7x + b$.

    $y = 7x + b$ Substitute (1,7).
    $7 = 7(1) + b$
    $7 = 7 + b$
    $b = 0$

    Therefore, the equation of the line is $y = 7x$.

    Note that a faster way to solve this problem is the trial-and-error method. Of the five answer choices, (A), (B), and (E) represent lines with slopes of 7, but only (E) contains the point (1,7).

SUMMING IT UP

- Lines and line segments are the basic building blocks for most geometry problems.

- If a geometry problem provides a figure, mine it for clues. If a geometry problem doesn't provide a figure, sketch one.

- If a geometry problem deals with a quadrilateral or circle, look to form triangles by drawing lines through the figure.

- Most geometry diagrams on the SAT are drawn to scale. If the diagram is not drawn to scale, you should redraw it.

Functions and Intermediate Algebra Review

OVERVIEW

- **Functions**
- **Integer and rational exponents**
- **Solving complex equations**
- **Linear and quadratic functions**
- **Summing it up**

FUNCTIONS

Definitions and Notation

Let D and R be any two sets of numbers. A *function* is a rule that assigns to each element of D one and only one element of R. The set D is called the *domain* of the function, and the set R is called the *range*. A function can be specified by listing all of the elements in the first set next to the corresponding elements in the second set, or by giving a rule or a formula by which elements from the first set can be associated with elements from the second set.

As an example, let the set $D = \{1, 2, 3, 4\}$ and set $R = \{5, 6, 7, 8\}$. The diagram below indicates a particular function, f, by showing how each element of D is associated with an element of R.

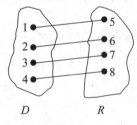

This diagram shows that the domain value of 1 is associated with the range value of 5. Similarly, 2 is associated with 6, 3 is associated with 7, and 4 is associated with 8. The function f can also be described in words by saying that f is the function that assigns to each domain value x the range value $x + 4$.

Typically, the letter x is used to represent the elements of the domain and the letter y is used to represent the elements of the range. This enables us to write the equation $y = x + 4$ to express the rule of association for the function above.

Note that as soon as a domain value x is selected, a range value y is determined by this rule. For this reason, x is referred to as the *independent variable*, and y is called the *dependent variable*.

Often, the rule of association for a function is written in *function notation*. In this notation, the symbol $f(x)$, which is read "f of x," is used instead of y to represent the range value. Therefore, the rule for our function can be written $f(x) = x + 4$. If you were asked to determine which range value was associated with the domain value of, say, 3, you would compute $f(x) = f(3) = 3 + 4 = 7$. Note that, in this notation, the letter f is typically used to stand for "function," although any other letter could also be used. Therefore, this rule could also be written as $g(x) = x + 4$.

> Using function notation, write the rule for a function that associates, to each number in the domain, a range value that is 7 less than 5 times the domain value.

$f(x) = 5x - 7$

> Use the function from the problem above to determine the range value that is associated with a domain value of -12.

$f(-12) = 5(-12) - 7 = -60 - 7 = -67$

> If $f(x) = 8x + 9$, determine the value of $f(5)$, $f(q)$, $f(p^2)$, and $f(r + 3)$.

$f(5) = 8(5) + 9 = 40 + 9 = 49$

In the same way, to determine the value of $f(q)$, simply substitute q for the value of x in the rule for $f(x)$. Therefore, $f(q) = 8q + 9$.

Similarly, $f(p^2) = 8(p^2) + 9 = 8p^2 + 9$.

Similarly, $f(r + 3) = 8(r + 3) + 9 = 8r + 24 + 9 = 8r + 33$.

Determining the Domain and Range

In the first function discussed above, you were told what numbers were in the domain and what numbers were in the range. Sometimes, however, you may be given the rule for a function without any specific information about the domain and range values. When D and R are not specified, there are some generally accepted guidelines to enable you to determine the numbers they contain.

If not otherwise specified, the domain of a function is considered to be all real numbers, except those for which the rule is undefined. A rule is undefined for any values that lead to division by 0 or to the square root of a negative number.

Determine the domain of each of the following functions:

a. $f(x) = 5x^2 - 7x + 3$

b. $g(x) = \dfrac{1}{(x-4)^2}$

c. $h(x) = \sqrt{4x - 7}$

a. The domain is the set of all real numbers, since the rule is defined for all real values of x.

b. The domain is all real numbers except $x = 4$, since the rule is undefined at 4.

c. The domain must exclude all values of x for which $4x - 7 < 0$, since square roots of negative numbers are undefined. In order to determine which values to exclude, solve the inequality

$4x - 7 < 0$, to obtain $x < \dfrac{7}{4}$. Therefore, the domain is all real numbers greater than or

equal to $\dfrac{7}{4}$.

Determining the range of a function is a little more difficult. The range of a function f is the set of all numbers that can be obtained by substituting all possible domain values in the rule for a function.

Determine the range of each of the following functions:

a. $f(x) = 12x + 3$

b. $g(x) = \dfrac{1}{x^2}$

c. $h(x) = \sqrt{5x - 7} + 4$

a. The range is the set of all real numbers, since, by selecting the appropriate value of x, any value for $f(x)$ can be obtained.

b. The range is the set of all *positive* real numbers since $\dfrac{1}{x^2} > 0$ for all real values of x (except 0).

c. Begin by noting that the $\sqrt{5x - 7} \geq 0$. Therefore, the values of $\sqrt{5x - 7} + 4$ are all real numbers greater than or equal to 4. In other words, the range is the set of all real numbers that are greater than or equal to 4.

EXERCISES: FUNCTIONS

Directions: Work out each problem. Circle the letter of your choice.

1. If $f(x) = 7 - 2x$, what is the value of $f(-14)$?
   (A) -70
   (B) -21
   (C) -9
   (D) 35
   (E) 70

2. If $g(x) = 2x^2 + 5x + 3$, what is the value of $g(x + 3)$?
   (A) $2x^2 + 17x + 36$
   (B) $2x^2 + 17x + 21$
   (C) $2x^2 + 5x + 36$
   (D) $2x^2 + 17x + 21$
   (E) $2x^2 + 11x + 27$

3. If $h(x) = 3x^2 + 5$, and $j(x) = \dfrac{3}{(x-4)^2}$, what is the value of $h(5) - j(5)$?
   (A) 0
   (B) 77
   (C) 83
   (D) 87
   (E) 93

4. What is the domain of the function $k(x) = (x - 5)^2 - (x + 4)^2$?
   (A) All real numbers
   (B) All positive real numbers
   (C) All real numbers except 5 and -4
   (D) All positive real numbers except 5
   (E) All real numbers except -4

5. What is the domain of the function $m(x) = \dfrac{6x + 7}{x^2 - x - 2}$?
   (A) All real numbers
   (B) All real numbers except $-\dfrac{7}{6}$
   (C) All real numbers except 2 and -1
   (D) All real numbers except -2 and 1
   (E) All real numbers except $-\dfrac{7}{6}$, 2, and -1

6. What is the domain of the function $p(x) = \dfrac{5x}{x^2 - 1}$?
   (A) All real numbers
   (B) All real numbers except 0
   (C) All real numbers except 1
   (D) All real numbers except 0 and 1
   (E) All real numbers except 1 and -1

7. What is the domain of the function $q(x) = \dfrac{3x^2 + 7}{\sqrt{6x - 3}}$?
   (A) All real numbers
   (B) All real numbers except $\dfrac{1}{2}$
   (C) All real numbers except $-\dfrac{1}{2}$
   (D) All real numbers greater than $\dfrac{1}{2}$
   (E) All real numbers less than or equal to $\dfrac{1}{2}$

8. What is the range of the function $r(x) = \dfrac{1}{x}$?
   (A) All real numbers
   (B) All positive real numbers
   (C) All negative real numbers
   (D) All real numbers except 0
   (E) All non-negative numbers

9. What is the range of the function $t(x) = \sqrt{5x+7}$?

   (A) All real numbers
   (B) All non-negative real numbers
   (C) All positive real numbers
   (D) All real numbers greater than $-\dfrac{7}{5}$
   (E) All real numbers greater than or equal to $-\dfrac{7}{5}$

10. Which of the following functions does NOT have a domain of all real numbers?

   (A) $f(x) = \sqrt{x^2+5}$
   (B) $g(x) = \dfrac{1}{5x^4+2}$
   (C) $h(x) = \dfrac{1}{x^2+2}$
   (D) $j(x) = \dfrac{1}{x^2-2}$
   (E) $k(x) = \dfrac{1}{\sqrt{x^2+2}}$

exercises

ANSWER KEY AND EXPLANATIONS

1. D	3. B	5. C	7. D	9. B
2. A	4. A	6. E	8. D	10. D

1. **The correct answer is (D).**

   $f(-14) = 7 - 2(-14) = 7 + 28 = 35$

2. **The correct answer is (A).**

   $g(x+3) = 2(x+3)^2 + 5(x+3) + 3 =$
   $2(x^2 + 6x + 9) + 5x + 15 + 3 =$
   $2x^2 + 12x + 18 + 5x + 15 + 3 =$
   $2x^2 + 17x + 36$

3. **The correct answer is (B).**

   $h(5) - j(5) = 3(5^2) + 5 - \dfrac{3}{(5-4)^2} = 3(25) + 5 - 3 = 77$

4. **The correct answer is (A).** There are no values for which the function $k(x)$ is undefined.

5. **The correct answer is (C).** Begin by solving the quadratic equation $x^2 - x - 2 = 0$ to determine any values for which the denominator of the function would be equal to 0.

$x^2 - x - 2 = 0$	Factor the left side
$(x - 2)(x + 1) = 0$	Set each factor equal to 0

   $x = 2, x = -1$

   Therefore, the denominator is equal to 0 when x is 2 or -1, and these two values must be excluded from the domain.

6. **The correct answer is (E).** The expression $x^2 - 1$ is equal to 0 when $x = 1$ or $x = -1$, so these two values must be excluded from the denominator.

7. **The correct answer is (D).** Exclude any values of x that lead to a denominator of 0 or to the square root of a negative number. To determine these values, solve the inequality $6x - 3 \leq 0$, and obtain $x \leq \dfrac{1}{2}$, so $x > \dfrac{1}{2}$.

8. **The correct answer is (D).** The only value that $\dfrac{1}{x}$ can never be equal to is 0. Any other range value can be obtained by letting x equal the reciprocal of the desired value.

9. **The correct answer is (B).** This function can never have a negative value; however, it can be equal to 0 or any positive number.

10. **The correct answer is (D).** The function $j(x) = \dfrac{1}{x^2 - 2}$ is undefined for $x = \pm\sqrt{2}$. For the other four choices, there are no values of x that lead to division by 0 or square roots of negative numbers.

INTEGER AND RATIONAL EXPONENTS

Chapter 11 (Basic Algebra Review) contains the definitions and the rules for positive integer exponents. The following section extends these definitions to integer and rational exponents.

Integer Exponents

Negative exponents are defined in the following way:

For any positive integer n, $x^{-n} = \dfrac{1}{x^n}$.

Therefore, for example, $4^{-2} = \dfrac{1}{4^2} = \dfrac{1}{16}$.

Similarly, $\left(\dfrac{2}{3}\right)^{-4} = \left(\dfrac{3}{2}\right)^4 = \dfrac{3^4}{2^4} = \dfrac{81}{16}$.

All of the properties of exponents discussed in Chapter 11 apply to expressions with negative exponents as well. Thus, the expression $x^{-7} \times x^4$ is equal to $x^{-3} = \dfrac{1}{x^3}$, and $\dfrac{y^{-5}}{y^{-11}} = y^{-5-(-11)} = y^{-5+11} = y^6$.

Determine the value of the following expressions:

a. 8^{-2}

b. $\left(\dfrac{1}{5}\right)^{-3}$

c. $\dfrac{3^4}{3^7}$

d. $(2^{-3})^{-2}$

---

a. $8^{-2} = \dfrac{1}{8^2} = \dfrac{1}{64}$

b. $\left(\dfrac{1}{5}\right)^{-3} = 5^3 = 125$

c. $\dfrac{3^4}{3^7} = 3^{4-7} = 3^{-3} = \dfrac{1}{3^3} = \dfrac{1}{27}$

d. $(2^{-3})^{-2} = 2^6 = 64$

If $f(x) = 5^{-x}$, what is the value of $f(-2)$?

If $f(x) = 5^{-x}$, what is the value of $f(2)$?

$f(-2) = 5^{-(-2)} = 5^2 = 25$

$f(2) = 5^{-2} = \dfrac{1}{5^2} = \dfrac{1}{25}$

Rational Exponents

The definition of exponents can also be extended to include rational numbers:

For a rational number, x to the power of $\dfrac{1}{n}$ is defined as the nth root of x. In other words, $x^{\frac{1}{n}}$ is equal to $\sqrt[n]{x}$.

Therefore, for example, $\sqrt{5}$ can be written as $5^{\frac{1}{2}}$.

Similarly, $8^{\frac{1}{3}}$ represents $\sqrt[3]{8}$ and is thus equal to 2.

Next, $x^{\frac{m}{n}}$ is defined to mean $\left(x^{\frac{1}{n}}\right)^{m}$, for $x > 0$, and $n > 0$. Therefore, when you are given a number with a rational exponent, the numerator represents the power to which the number is to be raised, and the denominator represents the root to be taken. The expression $16^{\frac{5}{4}}$ tells you to take the fourth root of 16 and then raise the result to the fifth power. This expression can be evaluated in the following way:

$$16^{\frac{5}{4}} = \left(\sqrt[4]{16}\right)^{5} = (2)^{5} = 32$$

In summary, all of the properties of exponents apply to expressions with rational exponents.

Determine the value of the following expressions:

a. $27^{\frac{1}{3}}$

b. $49^{\frac{3}{2}}$

c. $64^{-\frac{2}{3}}$

d. $\left(\dfrac{25}{36}\right)^{-\frac{3}{2}}$

a. $27^{\frac{1}{3}} = \sqrt[3]{27} = 3$

b. $49^{\frac{3}{2}} = \left(\sqrt{49}\right)^{3} = 7^{3} = 343$

c. $64^{-\frac{2}{3}} = \left(\dfrac{1}{64}\right)^{\frac{2}{3}} = \left(\sqrt[3]{\dfrac{1}{64}}\right)^{2} = \left(\dfrac{1}{4}\right)^{2} = \dfrac{1}{16}$

d. $\left(\dfrac{25}{36}\right)^{-\frac{3}{2}} = \left(\dfrac{36}{25}\right)^{\frac{3}{2}} = \left(\sqrt{\dfrac{36}{25}}\right)^{3} = \left(\dfrac{6}{5}\right)^{3} = \dfrac{6^{3}}{5^{3}} = \dfrac{216}{125}$

Simplify the following expressions:

a. $\left(25a^6\right)^{\frac{1}{2}}$

b. $\dfrac{b^{\frac{1}{3}}}{b^{-\frac{2}{3}}}$

c. $\left(c^{-\frac{1}{8}}d^{\frac{3}{4}}\right)^{16}$

a. $\left(25a^6\right)^{\frac{1}{2}} = 25^{\frac{1}{2}}\left(a^6\right)^{\frac{1}{2}} = \sqrt{25}a^3 = 5a^3$

b. $\dfrac{b^{\frac{1}{3}}}{b^{-\frac{2}{3}}} = b^{\frac{1}{3}}b^{\frac{2}{3}} = b^{\frac{1}{3}+\frac{2}{3}} = b^1 = b$

c. $\left(c^{-\frac{1}{8}}d^{\frac{3}{4}}\right)^{16} = \left(c^{-\frac{1}{8}}\right)^{16}\left(d^{\frac{3}{4}}\right)^{16} = c^{-2}d^{12} = \dfrac{d^{12}}{c^2}$

If $f(x) = 6x^{-\frac{2}{3}}$, what is the value of $f(8)$?

$f(8) = 6\left(8^{-\frac{2}{3}}\right) = 6\left(\dfrac{1}{8}\right)^{\frac{2}{3}} = 6\left(\sqrt[3]{\dfrac{1}{8}}\right)^2 = 6\left(\dfrac{1}{2}\right)^2 = 6\left(\dfrac{1}{4}\right) = \dfrac{6}{4} = \dfrac{3}{2}$

EXERCISES: INTEGER AND RATIONAL EXPONENTS

Directions: Work out each problem. Circle the letter of your choice.

1. Which of the following is equal to $(64)^{-\frac{1}{2}}$?
   (A) -32
   (B) -8
   (C) $-\dfrac{1}{8}$
   (D) $\dfrac{1}{8}$
   (E) 8

2. What is the value of $(-32)^{-\frac{1}{5}}$?
   (A) -2
   (B) $-\dfrac{1}{2}$
   (C) $-\dfrac{1}{4}$
   (D) $\dfrac{1}{2}$
   (E) 2

3. Which of the following is equal to $(xy^{-3})^2$?
   (A) $\dfrac{x}{y}$
   (B) $\dfrac{x}{y^6}$
   (C) $\dfrac{x^2}{y^6}$
   (D) $\dfrac{x^2}{y}$
   (E) $x^2 y$

4. $\dfrac{a^5 b^{-2} c^{-3}}{a^{-2} b^4 c^{-2}} =$
   (A) $\dfrac{a^7}{b^2 c}$
   (B) $\dfrac{a^7 c}{b^2}$
   (C) $\dfrac{a3}{b^2 c}$
   (D) $\dfrac{a3 c^5}{b^2}$
   (E) $\dfrac{a^7}{b^6 c}$

5. $(a^{-2} b^7 c^{-3})^{-4} =$
   (A) $\dfrac{b^3}{a^6 c}$
   (B) $\dfrac{b^3}{a^6 c^7}$
   (C) $\dfrac{a^8 c^{12}}{b^{28}}$
   (D) $\dfrac{b^{28}}{a^8 c^{12}}$
   (E) $\dfrac{a^6 c^7}{b^3}$

6. Which of the following is equal to $\left(\dfrac{8}{27}\right)^{\frac{2}{3}}$?
   (A) $-\dfrac{9}{4}$
   (B) $-\dfrac{4}{9}$
   (C) $\dfrac{4}{9}$
   (D) $\dfrac{9}{4}$
   (E) $\dfrac{81}{16}$

7. If $(5^3)^{-5} = 5^n$, what is the value of n?
   (A) -15
   (B) -8
   (C) -2
   (D) 2
   (E) 15

8. If $(7^5)^{-2} = \left(\dfrac{1}{7}\right)^p$, what is the value of p?
   (A) -10
   (B) -8
   (C) -3
   (D) 3
   (E) 10

ANSWER KEY AND EXPLANATIONS

1. D	3. C	5. C	7. A
2. B	4. E	6. D	8. E

1. **The correct answer is (D).**

$$(64)^{-\frac{1}{2}} = \left(\frac{1}{64}\right)^{\frac{1}{2}} = \sqrt{\frac{1}{64}} = \frac{1}{8}$$

2. **The correct answer is (B).**

$$(-32)^{-\frac{1}{5}} = \left(-\frac{1}{32}\right)^{\frac{1}{5}} = -\frac{1}{2}$$

3. **The correct answer is (C).**

$$\left(xy^{-3}\right)^2 = x^2 y^{-6} = \frac{x^2}{y^6}$$

4. **The correct answer is (E).**

$$\frac{a^5 b^{-2} c^{-3}}{a^{-2} b^4 c^{-2}} = a^{5-(-2)} b^{-2-4} c^{-3-(-2)} = a^7 b^{-6} c^{-1} = \frac{a^7}{b^6 c}$$

5. **The correct answer is (C).**

$$\left(a^{-2} b^7 c^{-3}\right)^{-4} = a^8 b^{-28} c^{12} = \frac{a^8 c^{12}}{b^{28}}$$

6. **The correct answer is (D).**

$$\left(\frac{8}{27}\right)^{-\frac{2}{3}} = \left(\frac{27}{8}\right)^{\frac{2}{3}} = \left(\frac{3}{2}\right)^2 = \frac{9}{4}$$

7. **The correct answer is (A).**

Since $(5^3)^{-5} = 5^{-15}$, it follows that $n = -15$.

8. **The correct answer is (E).**

$$\left(7^5\right)^{-2} = 7^{-10} = \left(\frac{1}{7}\right)^{10}.$$ Therefore, $p = 10$.

SOLVING COMPLEX EQUATIONS

Chapter 11 (Basic Algebra Review) describes how to solve linear and quadratic equations. The following section discusses how to solve some of the more complex equations and inequalities that appear on the SAT.

Equations Involving Rational Expressions

A *rational expression* is a fraction that contains variables in the numerator and/or the denominator. The quickest way to solve equations containing rational expressions is to determine the least common denominator (LCD) of all of the fractions in the equation and then to eliminate the fractions by multiplying each term in the equation by this LCD. The four steps in solving such an equation are:

1 Find the LCD of all of the rational expressions in the equation.

2 Multiply *every* term on both sides of the equation by this LCD.

3 Solve the resulting equation using the methods previously explained.

4 Check the solution to make certain that it actually solves the equation.

Note that step 4, checking the solution, is crucial because sometimes the process produces a solution that does not actually solve the equation. Such solutions are called *extraneous* solutions and need to be eliminated.

Solve for x: $\dfrac{7x}{5} + \dfrac{3}{8} = 10$

The LCD of the two fractions in the equation is 40, so every term must be multiplied by 40.

$$40\left(\frac{7x}{5}\right) + 40\left(\frac{3}{8}\right) = 40(10) \qquad \text{Perform the multiplications.}$$

$$8(7x) + 5(3) = 400$$

$$56x + 15 = 400 \qquad \text{Subtract 15 from both sides.}$$

$$56x = 385 \qquad \text{Divide both sides by 56.}$$

$$x = \frac{385}{56} = \frac{55}{8} = 6\frac{7}{8}$$

Check that the answer is correct by substituting $\dfrac{55}{8}$ into the original equation.

Solve for x: $\dfrac{5}{x-4} - \dfrac{3}{x+4} = \dfrac{36}{x^{12}-16}$

Begin by finding the LCD of the three fractions. Note that since $x^2 - 16 = (x - 4)(x + 4)$, the LCD is $(x - 4)(x + 4)$. Each term must be multiplied by this.

$$(x-4)(x+4)\left(\frac{5}{x-4}\right) - (x-4)(x+4)\left(\frac{3}{x+4}\right) = \left(\frac{36}{x^2-16}\right)(x-4)(x+4)$$

$(x+4)(5) - (x-4)(3) = 36$	Distribute.
$5x + 20 - 3x + 12 = 36$	Combine like terms.
$2x + 32 = 36$	Subtract 32 from both sides.
$2x = 4$	Divide by 2.
$x = 2$	

To check the solution, substitute 2 into the equation:

$$\frac{5}{x-4} - \frac{3}{x+4} = \frac{36}{x^2-16}$$

$$\frac{5}{2-4} - \frac{3}{2+4} = \frac{36}{2^2-16}$$

$$-\frac{5}{2} - \frac{3}{6} = -\frac{36}{12}$$

$$-3 = -3$$

Therefore, the solution is $x = 2$.

Solve for x: $\dfrac{1}{5} - \dfrac{1}{6} = \dfrac{1}{x}$

The LCD is $30x$. Multiply all terms by the LCD.

$$(30x)\left(\frac{1}{5}\right) - (30x)\left(\frac{1}{6}\right) = \left(\frac{1}{x}\right)(30x)$$

$$6x - 5x = 30$$

$$x = 30$$

If you check the value $x = 30$ in the original equation, you will find that it works.

Absolute Value Equations

The *absolute value* of a number represents the distance that the number is from the number 0 on a number line. For example, the absolute value of the number 6 is 6, since the number 6 is 6 units away from the number 0 on the number line. By the same logic, the absolute value of the number −6 is also 6, since −6 is also 6 units away from 0 on the number line.

 http://bit.ly/hippo_alg24

The absolute value of a number n is represented by the symbol $|n|$. Therefore, $|6| = 6$, and $|-6| = 6$. Intuitively, the absolute value of a number can be thought of as the value of the number without regard to its sign. The absolute value of 0 is equal to 0.

Find the value of each expression.
a. $|-6-7|$
b. $-|-9|$
c. $-|-12+(-4)|$

a. $|-6-7| = |-13| = 13$

b. $-|-9| = -(9) = -9$

c. $-|-12+(-4)| = -|-16| = -(16) = -16$

Calculate the value of $|-5| - |12| + |-4||-3|$.

$|-5| - |12| + |-4||-3| = 5 - 12 + (4)(3) = 5 - 12 + 12 = 5$

Equations involving absolute values typically have more than one solution. For example, the solutions to the equation $|x| = 12$ will be any numbers that are a distance of 12 from the origin. There are two such numbers, 12 and -12, so this equation has two answers, 12 and -12.

Solve the equation $|y| + 4 = 9$.

Begin by subtracting 4 from both sides in order to get the absolute value by itself on one side. The result is the equation $|y| = 5$, so $y = 5$ or -5.

Solve the equation $|2x+3| = 11$.

In order to solve the equation $|2x+3| = 11$, recognize that the equation is true for any value of x for which $2x + 3 = 11$ or $2x + 3 = 11$. Solving these two equations separately will give you the two solutions to $|2x+3| = 11$.

$2x + 3 = 11$ or $2x + 3 = -11$

$2x = 8$ or $2x = -14$

$x = 4$ or $x = -7$

Therefore, the two solutions are $x = 4$ and $x = -7$.

Solve for y: $3|2y| + 2 = 17$

Begin by isolating the absolute value.

$3|2y| + 2 = 7$	Subtract 2 from both sides.
$3|2y| = 15$	Divide both sides by 3.
$|2y| = 5$	Therefore,

$$2y = 5 \quad \text{or} \quad 2y = -5$$
$$y = \frac{5}{2} \quad \text{or} \quad -\frac{5}{2}$$

If $f(x) = 2|x|^3$, what is the value of $f(-3)$?

$$f(x) = 2|-3|^3 = 2(3)^3 = 2(27) = 54$$

EXERCISES: SOLVING COMPLEX EQUATIONS

Directions: Work out each problem. Circle the letter of your choice.

1. Solve for x: $\dfrac{2}{x-2} - \dfrac{5}{x+2} = \dfrac{2}{x^2-4}$

   (A) $x = -4$
   (B) $x = -2$
   (C) $x = 0$
   (D) $x = 2$
   (E) $x = 4$

2. Solve for y: $\dfrac{4}{y-2} - \dfrac{3}{y+2} = \dfrac{12}{y^2-4}$

   (A) $y = -4$
   (B) $y = -2$
   (C) $y = 2$
   (D) $y = -2$ and 2
   (E) There are no solutions.

3. Solve for a: $\dfrac{3}{a-7} + \dfrac{5}{a^2-13a+42} = \dfrac{7}{a-6}$

   (A) $a = -18$
   (B) $a = -9$
   (C) $a = 9$
   (D) $a = 18$
   (E) $a = -9$ and 9

4. Solve for b: $\dfrac{b}{8} + \dfrac{b}{12} + \dfrac{b}{24} > 2$

   (A) $b > 4$
   (B) $b > 8$
   (C) $b > 12$
   (D) $b > 18$
   (E) $b > 24$

5. What is the value of
   $-\left|-4+(-7)\right| + \left|(-13)(5)\right|$?

   (A) 54
   (B) 62
   (C) 68
   (D) 76
   (E) 93

6. Solve for p: $\left|p-2\right| = 12$

   (A) $p = 10, -14$
   (B) $p = 14, -14$
   (C) $p = 10, -10$
   (D) $p = 14, -10$
   (E) $p = 14, 10$

7. Solve for q: $4 = \left|1-3q\right|$

   (A) $q = -1, \dfrac{5}{3}$
   (B) $q = 1, -\dfrac{5}{3}$
   (C) $q = 1, \dfrac{5}{3}$
   (D) $q = -1, -\dfrac{5}{3}$
   (E) $q = -1$

8. Solve for r: $\left|5-3(2-r)\right| = 0$

   (A) $r = -\dfrac{1}{3}$
   (B) $r = \dfrac{1}{3}$
   (C) $r = \dfrac{1}{3}, -\dfrac{1}{3}$
   (D) $r = 3, -3$
   (E) There are no solutions.

9. Solve for t: $\dfrac{t}{4} + \dfrac{2t}{9} \geq \dfrac{3t-14}{6}$

   (A) $t \leq 84$
   (B) $t \leq 42$
   (C) $t \geq 42$
   (D) $t \geq 84$
   (E) $t \geq 168$

10. If $f(x) = 5\left|9-x\right| + 2\left|x\right|$, what is the value of $f(16)$?

    (A) -3
    (B) 3
    (C) 53
    (D) 67
    (E) 157

ANSWER KEY AND EXPLANATIONS

1. E	3. C	5. A	7. A	9. A
2. E	4. B	6. D	8. B	10. D

1. **The correct answer is (E).** The LCD of the fractions in the equation $\dfrac{2}{x-2} - \dfrac{5}{x+2} = \dfrac{2}{x^2-4}$ is $(x-2)(x+2)$. Multiply all terms by the LCD.

$$(x-2)(x+2)\frac{2}{x-2} - (x-2)(x+2)\frac{5}{x+2}$$
$$= \frac{2}{x^2-4}(x-2)(x+2)$$
$$2(x+2) - 5(x-2) = 2$$
$$2x + 4 - 5x + 10 = 2$$
$$3x = 12$$
$$x = 4$$

Remember that you should check the answer to make certain that is solves the equation.

2. **The correct answer is (E).** The LCD of the fractions in the equation $\dfrac{4}{y-2} - \dfrac{3}{y+2} = \dfrac{12}{y^2-4}$ is $y^2 - 4$.

$$(y-2)(y+2)\frac{4}{y-2} - (y-2)(y+2)\frac{3}{y+2}$$
$$= (y-2)(y+2)\frac{12}{y^2-4}$$
$$4(y+2) - 3(y-2) = 12$$
$$4y + 8 - 3y + 6 = 12$$
$$y + 14 = 12$$
$$y = -2$$

Note that when you substitute $y = -2$ into the equation, two of the denominators become 0 and are, therefore, undefined. This means that $y = -2$ is an extraneous solution, and the equation actually has no solutions.

3. **The correct answer is (C).** Note that $a^2 - 13a + 42 = (a-7)(a-6)$, so the LCD of the fractions in the equation is $(a-7)(a-6)$. Now, multiply by the LCD.

$$(a-7)(a-6)\frac{3}{a-7} +$$
$$(a-7)(a-6)\frac{5}{(a-7)(a-6)} =$$
$$\frac{7}{a-6}(a-7)(a-6)$$
$$3a - 18 + 5 = 7(a-7)$$
$$3a - 13 = 7a - 49$$
$$4a = 36$$
$$a = 9$$

This solution checks.

4. **The correct answer is (B).** In the inequality $\dfrac{b}{8} + \dfrac{b}{12} + \dfrac{b}{24} > 2$, multiply by the LCD of 24.

$$(24)\frac{b}{8} + (24)\frac{b}{12} + (24)\frac{b}{24} > 2(24)$$
$$3b + 2b + b > 48$$
$$6b > 48$$
$$b > 8$$

5. **The correct answer is (A).**

$$-\left|-4 + (-7)\right| + \left|(-13)(5)\right| =$$
$$-\left|-11\right| + \left|-65\right| = -(11) + 65 = 54$$

6. **The correct answer is (D).** To solve $\left|p - 2\right| = 12$, you need to solve two equations:

$$p - 2 = 12 \quad \text{or} \quad p - 2 = -12$$
$$p = 14 \quad \text{or} \quad p = -10$$

7. **The correct answer is (A).** To solve
$4 = |1 - 3q|$, you need to solve two equations:

$4 = 1 - 3q$ or $4 = -(1 - 3q)$

$3 = -3q$ or $4 = -1 + 3q$

$q = -1$ or $5 = 3q$

$q = -1$ or $q = \dfrac{5}{3}$

8. **The correct answer is (B).**

$|5 - 3(2 - r)| = 0$

Simplify the expression inside the absolute value signs:

$|5 - 6 + 3r| = 0$

$|-1 + 3r| = 0$

The only way this equation can be true is if $-1 + 3r = 0$, or $3r = 1$, so $r = \dfrac{1}{3}$.

9. **The correct answer is (A).** To solve
$\dfrac{t}{4} + \dfrac{2t}{9} \geq \dfrac{3t - 14}{6}$, multiply by the LCD of 36.

$(36)\dfrac{t}{4} + (36)\dfrac{2t}{9} \geq (36)\dfrac{3t - 14}{6}$

$9t + 8t \geq 6(3t - 14)$

$17t \geq 18t - 84$

$-t \geq -84$

$t \leq 84$

10. **The correct answer is (D).**

$f(\cdots) = |\ - \ | + |\ \ |$

$= 5|-7| + 32$

$= 5(7) + 32$

$= 35 + 32 = 67$

LINEAR AND QUADRATIC FUNCTIONS

A *linear function* is a function of the form $f(x) = mx + b$, where m and b are real numbers. A *quadratic function* is a function of the form $g(x) = ax^2 + bx + c$, where $a \neq 0$, and a, b, and c are real numbers. These functions are important because they can be used to model many real-world occurrences.

Applications of Linear Functions

In order to manufacture a new car model, a carmaker must initially spend \$750,000 to purchase the equipment needed to start the production process. After this, it costs \$7500 to manufacture each car. In this case, the *cost function* that associates the cost of manufacturing cars to the number of cars manufactured is $C(x) = 7500x + 750,000$, where x represents the number of cars manufactured, and $C(x)$ represents the cost of x cars. For example, the cost of making 7 cars is $C(7) = 7500(7) + 750,000 = 52,500 + 750,000 = \$802,500$.

The above cost function is a linear function with $b = 750,000$ and $m = 7500$. What is the domain of this function? Note that even though nothing has been specifically said about the domain, the only values that make sense as domain values are the non-negative integers, 0, 1, 2, 3, 4, 5,... In such a situation, assume that the domain only contains the values that make sense.

Using the cost function for the carmaker discussed in the example above, how much would it cost to make 24 cars?

To solve this, you need to determine the value of $C(24)$.

$C(24) = 7500(24) + 750,000 = 180,000 + 750,000 = \$930,000$

Using the same cost function, determine how many cars could be made for \$990,000.

In this problem, you are told that the value of $C(x)$ is \$990,000, and you need to find the value of x. To do this, solve the equation

$990,000 = 75000(x) + 750,000$	Subtract 750,000 from both sides.
$240,000 = 7500x$	Divide by 7500.
$32 = x$	Therefore, for \$990,000, 32 cars can be manufactured.

In the town of Kenmore, a taxi ride costs \$2.50 plus an extra \$0.50 per mile. Write a function that represents the cost of taking a taxi ride, using x to represent the number of miles traveled.

$C(x) = \$2.50 + 0.50x$

If a ride costs \$0.50 a mile, then the cost for x miles will be $0.50x$. Add to this the initial fee of \$2.50 a ride.

The Graph of a Linear Function

Typically, when a function is graphed, the independent variable is graphed along the x-axis, and the dependent variable is graphed along the y-axis.

The taxi ride function from the previous problem is a linear function. In order to graph this function, you must first determine the domain. Note that the domain, once again, must consist of non-negative numbers. Next, determine a few values that satisfy the rule for the function. For example, when $x = 0$, $C(0) = \$2.50 + 0.50(0) = \$2.50$. A few additional simple computations will lead to the following table of values.

x	C(x)
0	$2.50
1	$3.00
2	$3.50
3	$4.00

If these points are plotted on a graph, you will see that they all lie on the same line. The entire graph of the taxi ride cost function is shown below.

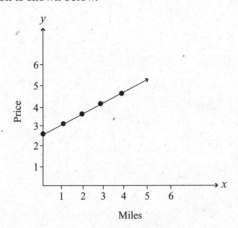

In general, the graph of any linear function is either a straight line or (depending on the domain) a portion of a straight line. The value of m represents the slope of the line, and the value of b is the y-intercept.

Applications of Quadratic Functions

Quadratic functions can also be used to model certain real-world happenings. To understand these functions better, suppose a coffee manufacturer has a revenue function given by $R(x) = 40,000x - 2000x^2$, where x represents the amount of coffee produced in tons per week. Let's consider some of the values for this function.

If $x = 0$, $R(x) = 40,000(0) - 2000(0)^2 = 0$ represents the obvious fact that if no coffee is produced there is no revenue.

That $R(1) = 40,000 - 2000 = 38,000$ tells that the revenue from 1 ton of coffee is $38,000.

Similar computations show that $R(10) = \$200,000$ and $R(11) = \$198,000$.

Note that the revenue is smaller if 11 tons of coffee are produced than if 10 tons are produced. There are a number of possible reasons for this. Perhaps, for example, at the 11-ton level, more is produced than can be sold, and the coffee company must pay to store the overage.

The Graph of a Quadratic Function

As you just saw, the graph of a linear function is always a straight line. To determine what the graph of a quadratic function looks like, consider the graph of the quadratic function $R(x) = 40,000x - 2000x^2$. Negative numbers must be excluded from the domain. A few computations lead to the table below.

x	R(x)
0	0
3	102,000
5	150,000
9	198,000
10	200,000
11	198,000
15	150,000
17	102,000
20	0

The graph of $R(x)$ is shown below.

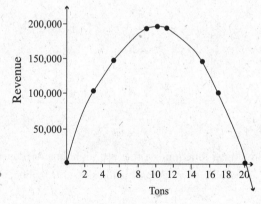

The graph shown above is called a *parabola*. This parabola is said to "open down." The highest point on the parabola, (10, 200,000), is called the *extreme point*.

Recall that the general form of a quadratic function is $g(x) = ax^2 + bx + c$. In general, the graph of any quadratic function will be a parabola. If $a > 0$, the parabola will "open up," and if $a < 0$, the parabola will "open down." If the parabola opens up, its extreme point is the minimum value of the function, and if the parabola opens down, its extreme point is the maximum value of the function.

The coordinates of the extreme point of a parabola are $\left[\dfrac{-b}{2a}, f\left(\dfrac{-b}{2a} \right) \right]$.

Sketch the graph of the function $f(x) = x^2 - x - 2$.

Since the function is quadratic, the graph will be a parabola. Note that the value of a, the number in front of the x^2-term is 1, so the parabola opens up. The x-coordinate of the minimum point is $x = \dfrac{-b}{2a} = \dfrac{-(-1)}{2(1)} = \dfrac{1}{2}$ of this point is $f\left(\dfrac{1}{2}\right) = \left(\dfrac{1}{2}\right)^2 - \dfrac{1}{2} - 2 = \dfrac{1}{4} - \dfrac{1}{2} - 2 = -2\dfrac{1}{4}$.

In order to sketch a parabola, it is helpful to determine a few points on either side of the extreme point.

x	f(x)
−2	4
−1	0
0	−2
1	−2
2	0
3	4

The graph is shown below.

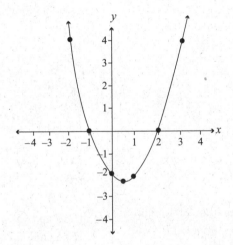

What is the relationship between the graph of the function $h(x) = ax^2 + bx$ and the graph of the function $j(x) = ax^2 + bx + 7$?

If (x, y) is a point on the graph of $h(x)$, then $(x, y + 7)$ will be a point on the graph of $j(x)$. Therefore, the two graphs have exactly the same size and shape. The graph of $j(x)$ can be obtained by taking the graph of $h(x)$ and "lifting" each point 7 units, that is, increasing the y-coordinate of each point by 7.

EXERCISES: LINEAR AND QUADRATIC FUNCTIONS

Directions: Work out each problem. Circle the letter of your choice.

1. A taxi company charges \$2.25 for the first mile, and \$0.45 for each mile thereafter. If x stands for the number of miles a passenger travels, which of the following functions relates the length of the trip to its cost?

   (A) $f(x) = 2.25 + 0.45(x + 1)$
   (B) $f(x) = 2.25 + 0.45(1 - x)$
   (C) $f(x) = 2.25 + 0.45(x - 1)$
   (D) $f(x) = 2.25x + 0.45(x - 1)$
   (E) $f(x) = 2.25 + 0.45x$

2. The Amp Corporation manufactures home video systems. The cost function for the Amp45 system is $C(x) = 3x^2 - 2x + 7$, where x represents the number of systems manufactured, and the cost is in dollars. How much does it cost to manufacture 18 of these systems?

   (A) \$943
   (B) \$972
   (C) \$974
   (D) \$2903
   (E) \$2917

3. Which of the following best describes the graph of the function $f(x) = 5x - 7$?

   (A) A horizontal line
   (B) A line that increases from left to right
   (C) A line that decreases from left to right
   (D) A parabola that opens up
   (E) A parabola that opens down

4. Which of the following best describes the graph of the function $g(x) = -5x^2 + 7x - 23$?

   (A) A horizontal line
   (B) A line that increases from left to right
   (C) A line that decreases from left to right
   (D) A parabola that opens up
   (E) A parabola that opens down

5. At the Four Seasons bowling alley, it costs \$1.50 to rent shoes and \$2.50 for each game played. Which of the following functions relates the number of games played, x, to the cost in dollars?

   (A) $f(x) = 4.00x$
   (B) $f(x) = 2.50 + 1.50x$
   (C) $f(x) = 1.50x - 2.50$
   (D) $f(x) = 2.50x + 1.50$
   (E) $f(x) = 2.50x - 1.50x$

6. In order to raise money for a charity, Deb makes cakes to sell at a school bake sale. Her profit function is $P(x) = \$4.50x - \$15$. How many cakes must she sell in order to earn \$66 for the charity?

   (A) 15
   (B) 16
   (C) 18
   (D) 20
   (E) 22

7. For which domain values of the function $f(x) = x^2 + 3x - 10$ does $f(x) = 0$?

   (A) 2
   (B) −2
   (C) −5
   (D) 2 and −5
   (E) 5 and −2

8. At which point does the graph of the function $g(x) = -12x + 6$ cross the y-axis?

   (A) $(0,6)$
   (B) $(6,0)$
   (C) $(0,2)$
   (D) $(2,0)$
   (E) $(0, \frac{1}{2})$

9. The functions $f(x) = 16x - 7$ and $g(x) = 16x + 5$ are graphed on the same coordinate axis. Which of the following best describes the appearance of the graph?

(A) Two intersecting lines, one with y-intercept of -7, the other with y-intercept of 5

(B) Two parallel lines, one with y-intercept of -7, and the other with y-intercept of 5

(C) Two parallel lines, one with y-intercept of 7, and the other with y-intercept of -5

(D) Two intersecting lines, one with y-intercept of 7, the other with y-intercept of -5

(E) Two parabolas that intersect in two points

10. What is the x-coordinate of the extreme point of the function $f(x) = 7x^2 - 28x + 16$?

(A) $x = \dfrac{1}{2}$

(B) $x = -\dfrac{1}{2}$

(C) $x = 2$

(D) $x = -2$

(E) $x = 4$

ANSWER KEY AND EXPLANATIONS

1. C	3. B	5. D	7. D	9. B
2. A	4. E	6. C	8. A	10. C

1. **The correct answer is (C).** The cost for the first mile on a trip of x miles is $2.25. After this, there are still $x - 1$ miles to go, and the cost for each of these miles is $0.45. Therefore, the total cost of the trip, in dollars, is $2.25 + 0.45(x - 1)$.

2. **The correct answer is (A).** You need to determine the value of $C(18)$.

   $C(18) = 3(18)^2 - 2(18) + 7 =$
   $3(324) - 36 + 7 = 972 - 36 + 7 = 943$

3. **The correct answer is (B).** The function $f(x) = 5x - 7$ is a linear function, which means that its graph is a straight line. The slope of the line is the coefficient of x, that is, 5. A line with a positive slope increases from left to right.

4. **The correct answer is (E).** The function $g(x) = -5x^2 + 7x - 23$ is a quadratic function, so its graph will be a parabola. Because the coefficient of the x^2-term is negative, the parabola opens down.

5. **The correct answer is (D).** The cost of x games, at $2.50 a game, is $2.50x$. Adding the $1.50 cost of shoe rental to this leads to the function $f(x) = 2.50x + 1.50$.

6. **The correct answer is (C).** You are asked to find the value of x for which $4.50x - 15 = 66$.

   $4.50x - 15 = 66$
   $4.50x - 15 = 66$ Add 15 to both sides
   $\quad 4.50x = 81$ Divide by 450
   $\qquad\quad x = 18$

   Therefore, Deb must sell 18 cakes to make $66.

7. **The correct answer is (D).** In order to answer this question, you need to solve the quadratic equation $x^2 + 3x - 10 = 0$.

   $x^2 + 3x - 10 = 0$ Factor the left-hand side.
   $(x + 5)(x - 2) = 0$ Set each factor equal to 0
   $x + 5 = 0 \qquad x - 2 = 0$
   $\quad x = -5 \qquad\quad x = 0$

   Thus, $f(x) = x^2 + 3x - 10 = 0$ at $x = -5$ and $x = 2$.

8. **The correct answer is (A).** For a linear function, the y-intercept is equal to the value of the constant. Therefore, $g(x) = -12x + 6$ crosses the y-axis at $(0,6)$

9. **The correct answer is (B).** The two functions are both linear, so their graphs are straight lines. Note that the coefficient of the x-term in each case is 16. Since this coefficient represents the slope of the function, both functions are lines with slopes of 16. Lines with the same slopes are parallel. The constant term of a linear function is the y-intercept, so one line has a y-intercept of -7, and the other has a y-intercept of 5.

10. **The correct answer is (C).** The extreme point of a quadratic function is given by the formula $x = \dfrac{-b}{2a}$, where a is the coefficient of the x^2-term and b is the coefficient of the x-term. In this case, then, the extreme point is $x = \dfrac{-b}{2a} = \dfrac{-(-28)}{2(7)} = \dfrac{28}{14} = 2$.

SUMMING IT UP

- A function is an expression or rate that takes one or more values and generates a new value.

- The four steps in solving an equation involving rational expressions are:

  1 Find the LCD of all of the rational expressions in the equation.

  2 Multiply *every* term on both sides of the equation by this LCD.

  3 Solve the resulting equation using the methods previously explained.

  4 Check the solution to make certain that it actually solves the equation.

Data Analysis, Statistics, and Probability Review

chapter 14

OVERVIEW

- Averages
- Weighted Average
- Counting and permutations
- Probability
- Data interpretation
- Summing it up

AVERAGES

Arithmetic Mean, Median, and Mode

Typically, when asked to find the *average* of a group of n numbers, students add up all the numbers in the group and then divide by n. This type of average, which is more precisely called the *arithmetic mean,* is just one of a number of different types of averages, each of which is computed in a different way and conveys a different type of information. Two other types of averages, known as the *median* and the *mode*, also occasionally appear on the SAT.

In order to avoid ambiguity, when an SAT question involves the computation of the arithmetic mean, it will use the word *average* followed by the words *arithmetic mean* in parentheses. When an SAT average question involves the median or the mode, the words *median* and *mode* will be specifically used. The arithmetic mean is by far the most common type of average used on the SAT.

The Arithmetic Mean

To find the average (arithmetic mean) of a group of n numbers, simply add the numbers and divide by n.

> Find the average (arithmetic mean) of 32, 50, and 47.

$$
\begin{array}{r}
32 \\
50 \\
+47 \\
\hline
129
\end{array}
\qquad
\begin{array}{r}
43 \\
3\overline{)129}
\end{array}
$$

Another type of arithmetic mean problem gives you the arithmetic mean and asks for the missing term.

> The average (arithmetic mean) of three numbers is 43. If two of the numbers are 32 and 50, find the third number.

Using the definition of arithmetic mean, write the equation:

$$\frac{32+50+x}{3} = 43$$
$$32 + 50 + x = 129$$
$$82 + x = 129$$
$$x = 47$$

Median and Mode

In order to find the *median* of a group of numbers, list the numbers in numerical order from smallest to largest. The median is the number in the middle. For example, the median of the numbers 3, 3, 5, 9, and 10 is 5. Note that, typically, the median and the arithmetic mean are not the same. In this problem, for example, the arithmetic mean is $30 \div 5 = 6$.

If there is an even number of numbers, the median is equal to the arithmetic mean of the two numbers in the middle. For example, to find the median of 3, 3, 5, 7, 9, and 10, note that the two middle numbers are 5 and 7. The median, then, is $\frac{5+7}{2} = 6$.

The *mode* of a group of numbers is simply the number that occurs most frequently. Therefore, the mode of the group of numbers 3, 3, 5, 7, 9, and 10 is 3. If all of the numbers in a group only appear once, then there is no mode.

> What is the product of the arithmetic mean, the median, and the mode of the following group of eight numbers?
>
> 2, 7, 8, 9, 9, 9, 10, and 10

The sum of the eight numbers is 64, so the arithmetic mean is $64 \div 8 = 8$.

The median is the arithmetic mean of the two numbers in the middle. Since these numbers are both 9, the median is $\frac{9+9}{2} = 9$.

The mode is the number that occurs most often, which is also 9. The product of these three "averages" is $8 \times 9 \times 9 = 648$.

WEIGHTED AVERAGE

If asked to find the arithmetic mean of a group of numbers in which some of the numbers appear more than once, simplify the computation by using the *weighted average* formula. For example, suppose the question asks for the average (arithmetic mean) age of a group of 10 friends. If four of the friends are 17, and six of the friends are 19, determine the average in the usual way:

$$\text{Average age} = \frac{17+17+17+17+19+19+19+19+19+19}{10} = \frac{182}{10} = 18.2$$

However, the computation can be done more quickly by taking the *weights* of the ages into account. The age 17 is weighted four times, and the age 19 is weighted six times. The average can then be computed as follows:

$$\text{Average age} = \frac{4(17)+6(19)}{10} = \frac{182}{10} = 18.2$$

> Andrea has four grades of 90 and two grades of 80 during the spring semester of calculus. What is her average (arithmetic mean) in the course for this semester?

```
90   or      90 • 4 = 360
90
90
90          +80 • 2 = 160
80
+80
6)520    6)520
  2        2
86        86
  3        3
```

Be sure not to average 90 and 80, since there are four grades of 90 and only two grades of 80.

Average Rate

The *average rate* for a trip is the total distance covered, divided by the total time spent. Recall that distance can be determined by multiplying the rate by the time, that is, $d = rt$.

> In driving from New York to Boston, Mr. Portney drove for 3 hours at 40 miles per hour and 1 hour at 48 miles per hour. What was his average rate for this portion of the trip?

$$\text{Average rate} = \frac{\text{Total distance}}{\text{Total time}}$$

$$\text{Average rate} = \frac{3(40)+1(48)}{3+1}$$

$$\text{Average rate} = \frac{168}{4} = 42 \text{ miles per hour}$$

Since more of the trip was driven at 40 mph than at 48 mph, the average should be closer to 40 than to 48, which it is. This will help you to check your answer, or to pick out the correct choice in a multiple-choice question.

EXERCISES: AVERAGES

Directions: Work out each problem. Circle the letter next to your choice.

1. Dan had an average (arithmetic mean) of 72 on his first four math tests. After taking the next test, his average (arithmetic mean) dropped to 70. Which of the following is his most recent test grade?

   (A) 60
   (B) 62
   (C) 64
   (D) 66
   (E) 68

2. What is the average (arithmetic mean) of $\sqrt{0.64}$, 0.85, and $\frac{9}{10}$?

   (A) $\frac{21}{25}$
   (B) 3.25
   (C) 2.55
   (D) 85%
   (E) $\frac{4}{5}$

3. The average (arithmetic mean) of two numbers is XY. If the first number is Y, what is the other number?

   (A) $2XY-Y$
   (B) $XY-2Y$
   (C) $2XY-X$
   (D) X
   (E) $XY-Y$

4. 30 students had an average (arithmetic mean) of X, while 20 students had an average (arithmetic mean) of 80. What is the average (arithmetic mean) for the entire group?

   (A) $\frac{X+80}{50}$
   (B) $\frac{X+80}{2}$
   (C) $\frac{50}{X+80}$
   (D) $\frac{3}{5}X+32$
   (E) $\frac{30X+80}{50}$

5. What is the average (arithmetic mean) of the first 15 positive integers?

   (A) 7
   (B) 7.5
   (C) 8
   (D) 8.5
   (E) 9

6. A man travels a distance of 20 miles at 60 miles per hour and then returns over the same route at 40 miles per hour. What is his average rate for the round trip in miles per hour?

   (A) 50
   (B) 48
   (C) 47
   (D) 46
   (E) 45

7. A number p equals $\frac{3}{2}$ the average (arithmetic mean) of 10, 12, and q. What is q in terms of p?

   (A) $\frac{2}{3}p - 22$

   (B) $\frac{4}{3}p - 22$

   (C) $2p - 22$

   (D) $\frac{1}{2}p + 11$

   (E) $\frac{9}{2}p - 22$

8. Susan has an average (arithmetic mean) of 86 in three examinations. What grade must she receive on her next test to raise her average (arithmetic mean) to 88?

   (A) 90
   (B) 92
   (C) 94
   (D) 96
   (E) 100

9. The heights of the 5 starters on Redwood High's basketball team are 5'11", 6'3", 6', 6'6", and 6'2". The average (arithmetic mean) height of these players is

   (A) 6'1".
   (B) 6'2".
   (C) 6'3".
   (D) 6'4".
   (E) 6'5".

10. What is the average (arithmetic mean) of all numbers from 1 to 100 that end in 2?

    (A) 46
    (B) 47
    (C) 48
    (D) 50
    (E) None of the above

11. For the numbers a, b, and c, the average (arithmetic mean) is three times the median. If $a < b < c$, what is the value of b in terms of a and c?

    (A) $\dfrac{3}{(x-4)^2}$

    (B) $\dfrac{a+c}{8}$

    (C) $\dfrac{a+c}{4}$

    (D) $\dfrac{a+c}{2}$

    (E) $a + c$

12. For which of the following sets of numbers is the arithmetic mean less than the mode?

    (A) $\{3, 3, 5, 6, 7\}$
    (B) $\{3, 4, 4, 4, 5\}$
    (C) $\{3, 4, 5, 5, 12\}$
    (D) $\{3, 4, 5, 5, 8\}$
    (E) $\{2, 3, 4, 4, 5\}$

ANSWER KEY AND EXPLANATIONS

1. B	4. D	7. C	10. B
2. D	5. C	8. C	11. B
3. A	6. B	9. B	12. E

1. **The correct answer is (B).**

$$\frac{4(72)+x}{5}=70$$
$$288+x=350$$
$$x=62$$

2. **The correct answer is (D).** In order to find the average (arithmetic mean) of these three numbers, they should all be expressed as decimals.

$$\sqrt{0.64}=0.8$$
$$0.85=0.85$$
$$\frac{9}{10}=0.9$$

$$\text{Average}=\frac{0.8+0.85+0.9}{3}=\frac{2.55}{3}=0.85$$

(arithmetic mean)

This is equal to 85%.

3. **The correct answer is (A).**

$$\frac{Y+x}{2}=XY$$
$$Y+x=2XY$$
$$x=2XY-Y$$

4. **The correct answer is (D).**

$$\frac{30(X)+20(80)}{50}=\text{Average}$$

(arithmetic mean)

$$\frac{30(X)+1600}{50}=\frac{3X+160}{5}=\frac{3}{5}X+32$$

5. **The correct answer is (C).** Positive integers begin with 1.

$$\frac{1+2+3+4+5+6+7+8+9+10+11+12+13+14+15}{15}$$

Since these numbers are evenly spaced, the average (arithmetic mean) will be the middle number, 8.

6. The correct answer is (B).

$$\text{Average rate} = \frac{\text{Total distance}}{\text{Total time}}$$

Total distance = $20 + 20 = 40$

Since time = $\dfrac{\text{distance}}{\text{rate}}$, time for first part of trip is $\dfrac{20}{60}$, or $\dfrac{1}{3}$ hour, while time for the

second part of trip is $\dfrac{20}{40}$, or $\dfrac{1}{2}$ hour.

Total time = $\dfrac{1}{3} + \dfrac{1}{2}$, or $\dfrac{5}{6}$ hour

Average rate = $\dfrac{40}{\dfrac{5}{6}} = 40 \bullet \dfrac{6}{5} = 48$ mph

7. The correct answer is (C).

$$p = \frac{3}{2}\left(\frac{10+12+q}{3}\right)$$

$$p = \frac{10+12+q}{2}$$

$$2p = 22 + q$$

$$2p - 22 = q$$

8. The correct answer is (C).

$$\frac{3(86)+x}{4} = 88$$

$$258 + x = 352$$

$$x = 94$$

9. The correct answer is (B).

```
      5'11"
      6'3"
      6'0"
      6'6"
      6'2"
29'22" = 5)30'10"
          6'2"
```

10. The correct answer is (B).

$$\frac{2+12+22+32+42+52+62+72+82+92}{10}$$

Since these numbers are equally spaced, the average (arithmetic mean) is the middle number. However, since there is an even number of addends, the average (arithmetic mean) will be halfway between the middle two. Halfway between 42 and 52 is 47.

11. **The correct answer is (B).** Since a is the smallest number, c is the largest, and b is the number in the middle, b is the median. The fact that the arithmetic mean is three times the median tells that

$$\frac{a+b+c}{3}=3b \qquad \text{Multiply by 3.}$$
$$a+b+c=9b \qquad \text{Subtract } b \text{ from both sides.}$$
$$a+c=8b \qquad \text{Divide both sides by 8.}$$
$$b=\frac{a+c}{8}$$

12. **The correct answer is (E).** The mode of the set in choice (E) is 4, while the arithmetic mean is $\frac{2+3+4+4+5}{5}=\frac{18}{5}$. This is the only set with the property that the arithmetic mean is less than the mode.

COUNTING AND PERMUTATIONS

The Fundamental Counting Principle

Consider the two sets $A = \{2, 3\}$ and $B = \{5, 7, 11\}$. Suppose you wanted to determine how many sets could be formed containing one element from set A and one element from set B. Note that, for each of the two possible choices from set A, there are three possible choices from set B. Thus, there are $2 \times 3 = 6$ sets that can be formed. They are $\{2, 5\}$, $\{2, 7\}$, $\{2, 11\}$, $\{3, 5\}$, $\{3, 7\}$, and $\{3, 11\}$.

In general, if one selection can be made in m possible ways, and a second selection can be made in n possible ways, then there are mn possible ways to make both selections. This principle can be extended to any number of selections, as shown below.

Jaime has 5 different ties and 7 different shirts. How many different shirt-and-tie outfits can he make?

Jaime can make $5 \times 7 = 35$ different shirt-and-tie combinations.

How many different 3-digit numbers can be formed using the digits 1, 3, 5, 7, and 9, if each digit can be used more than once?

There are 5 choices for the first digit, 5 choices for the second digit, and 5 choices for the third digit. Therefore, there are $5 \times 5 \times 5 = 125$ different 3-digit numbers.

Permutations

A *permutation* is any arrangement of the members of a set in a specific order. Consider, for example, the set $C = \{x, y, z\}$. There are six different ways in which the members of this set can be ordered: *xyz, xzy, yxz, yzx, zxy,* and *zyx.* In other words, there are 6 permutations of the set C.

To determine the number of permutations of set C without writing all of them down, note that there are three possible choices for the first element of the permutation, after which there are two possible choices for the second element of the permutation, and then only one remaining choice for the final element. Using the fundamental counting principle, there are $3 \times 2 \times 1$ permutations of the set C.

There are 5 students who plan to perform at a talent show. How many different possible performance orders are there?

There are 5 different possible choices for the student who will perform first. After this, there are 4 choices for the second performer, 3 choices for the third performer, 2 choices for the fourth performer, and 1 choice for the final performer. Therefore, there are $5 \times 4 \times 3 \times 2 \times 1 = 120$ orders.

At the Wardlaw School, 6 students are running for student council. If the student council has one president, one vice president, and one secretary, how many possible election results are there?

There are 6 possible choices for president. After the president has been selected, there are 5 remaining choices for vice president, and then 4 remaining choices for secretary. Overall, there are 6 × 5 × 4 = 120 possible election outcomes.

EXERCISES: COUNTING AND PERMUTATIONS

Directions: Work out each problem. Circle the letter of your choice.

1. If $A = \{3, 6, 9\}$, $B = \{4, 8\}$, and $C = \{5, 10, 15, 20\}$, how many different sets can be formed containing one member of A, one member of B, and one member of C?

   (A) 9
   (B) 12
   (C) 18
   (D) 24
   (E) 36

2. Sharon is ordering a sandwich. She has 3 different choices of bread, 5 different choices of meat, and 2 different choices of cheese. How many different possible sandwiches are there?

   (A) 10
   (B) 15
   (C) 18
   (D) 25
   (E) 30

3. A traveler can travel from Buffalo to Grand Island by plane, boat, or car. She can then go from Grand Island to Niagara Falls by car or by train. In how many ways can the traveler go from Buffalo to Grand Island and then to Niagara Falls?

   (A) 2
   (B) 3
   (C) 4
   (D) 5
   (E) 6

4. ActionAthletics, a sporting goods store, has 5 entrance doors. In how many different ways can a customer enter and leave the store if the same entrance is NOT used both ways?

   (A) 5
   (B) 10
   (C) 15
   (D) 20
   (E) 25

5. How many four-digit numbers can be formed from the digits 4, 5, 6, and 7, if each digit can be used more than once?

   (A) 16
   (B) 24
   (C) 64
   (D) 256
   (E) 1024

6. How many four-digit *even* numbers can be formed from the digits 4, 5, 6, and 7, if each digit can be used more than once?

   (A) 14
   (B) 64
   (C) 128
   (D) 192
   (E) 256

7. How many *even* four-digit numbers that are larger than 6999 can be formed from the digits 4, 5, 6, and 7, if each digit can be used more than once?

   (A) 11
   (B) 16
   (C) 32
   (D) 64
   (E) 128

8. How many four-digit numbers can be formed from the digits 4, 5, 6, and 7, if each digit can only be used once?

(A) 10
(B) 24
(C) 48
(D) 128
(E) 256

10. In how many different ways can a judge award first and second place in a contest with 9 participants?

(A) 17
(B) 48
(C) 64
(D) 72
(E) 81

9. How many three-digit positive even integers are there?

(A) 360
(B) 405
(C) 450
(D) 500
(E) 1000

ANSWER KEY AND EXPLANATIONS

1. D	3. E	5. D	7. C	9. C
2. E	4. D	6. C	8. B	10. D

1. **The correct answer is (D).** There are 3 choices for the member from A, 2 choices for the member from B, and 4 choices for the member from C. Overall, there are $3 \times 2 \times 4 = 24$ different sets that can be formed.

2. **The correct answer is (E).** With 3 choices of bread, 5 choices of meat, and 2 choices of cheese, there are $3 \times 5 \times 2 = 30$ different sandwiches possible.

3. **The correct answer is (E).** There are 3 choices for travel from Buffalo to Grand Island, and then 2 choices for travel from Grand Island to Niagara Falls. Overall, there are $3 \times 2 = 6$ ways to go from Buffalo to Grand Island and then to Niagara Falls.

4. **The correct answer is (D).** There are 5 choices of doorway on the way in, but only 4 choices on the way out. Overall, there are $5 \times 4 = 20$ different ways to enter and then leave the store.

5. **The correct answer is (D).** There are 4 choices for each digit in the number, and, therefore, $4 \times 4 \times 4 \times 4 = 256$ different four-digit numbers.

6. **The correct answer is (C).** For the number to be even, there are only 2 different choices for the last digit, 4 or 6. There still are, however, 4 different choices for each of the first three digits. Thus, there are $4 \times 4 \times 4 \times 2 = 128$ different numbers possible.

7. **The correct answer is (C).** For the number to be larger than 6999, the first digit must be 7. For the number to be even, the last digit must be 4 or 6. There are, however, four possibilities for each of the two middle digits. Thus, there are $1 \times 4 \times 4 \times 2 = 32$ different numbers.

8. **The correct answer is (B).** There are 4 choices for the first digit, 3 choices for the second digit, 2 choices for the third digit, and 1 choice for the last digit. Overall, there are $4 \times 3 \times 2 \times 1 = 24$ different numbers possible.

9. **The correct answer is (C).** For the number to be even, the last digit must be 0, 2, 4, 6, or 8, so there are 5 choices for the last digit. The first digit can be anything other than 0, so there are 9 choices for first digit. The middle digit can be anything, so there are 10 choices for middle digit. In total, there are $9 \times 10 \times 5 = 450$ three-digit positive even integers.

10. **The correct answer is (D).** There are 9 ways to choose the winner, and then 8 ways to choose second place. Overall, there are $9 \times 8 = 72$ different possibilities.

PROBABILITY

In the study of probability, an *experiment* is a process that yields one of a certain number of possible outcomes. For example, tossing a coin is an experiment with two possible outcomes: Heads or tails. Throwing a die is an experiment with six possible outcomes because there are six sides: 1, 2, 3, 4, 5, or 6.

Probability is a numerical way of measuring the likelihood that a specific outcome will happen. The probability of a specific outcome is always a number between 0 and 1. An outcome with a probability of 0 cannot possibly happen, and an event with probability of 1 will definitely happen. Therefore, the nearer the probability of an event is to 0, the less likely the event is to happen, and the nearer the probability of an event is to 1, the more likely the event is to happen.

If an experiment has n possible equally likely outcomes, the probability of each specific outcome is defined to be $\dfrac{1}{n}$. In the coin-tossing experiment, the probability of heads is $\dfrac{1}{2}$, since heads is one of the two equally likely outcomes. When a die is thrown, the probability of tossing a 5 is $\dfrac{1}{6}$, since tossing a 5 is one of six equally likely outcomes.

> Minh selects a card at random from a deck of 52 cards. What is the probability that he selects the three of clubs?

When a card is selected at random from a full deck, there are 52 equally likely outcomes. Therefore, the probability that he selects the three of clubs is $\dfrac{1}{52}$.

If a die is thrown, what would be the probability that the result is an odd number? There are three possible odd number results, 1, 3, and 5, and the probability of each of these outcomes is $\dfrac{1}{6}$. To determine the probability of getting an odd number, simply add up the probabilities of the three favorable outcomes: $\dfrac{1}{6}+\dfrac{1}{6}+\dfrac{1}{6}=\dfrac{3}{6}=\dfrac{1}{2}$. Therefore, the probability of getting an odd number is $\dfrac{1}{2}$. This example suggests a general formula for computing probabilities:

$$\text{The probability of an event occurring} = \frac{\text{The number of favorable outcomes}}{\text{The number of possible outcomes}}$$

> Tiffany selects a card at random from a deck of 52 cards. What is the probability that she selects a jack?

There are 4 jacks in the deck, so there are 4 favorable outcomes out of 52. Thus, the probability that she selects a jack is $\dfrac{4}{52}=\dfrac{1}{13}$.

In the diagram below, *ABCD* is a square, and point *E* is on $\overline{AB}$. If a point on the interior of the square is selected at random, what is the probability that it will be in the shaded region?

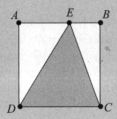

The first thing to realize is that the area of triangle *CED* is half of the area of the square. This is true since the length of the base of the triangle is the same as the length of the base of the square, and the height of the triangle is also the same as the height of the square. If we called the length of the base *b*, and the height *h*, then we can say that the area of the square is *bh*, and the area of the triangle is $\frac{1}{2}bh$. Therefore, the question is asking for the probability that a point will be selected from among half of the points in the interior of the square. Since half of the outcomes are favorable, the probability would be $\frac{1}{2}$.

EXERCISES: PROBABILITY

Directions: Work out each problem. Circle the letter next to your choice.

1. Keshawn has 5 coins in his pocket: a penny, a nickel, a dime, a quarter, and a half-dollar. If he removes one coin from his pocket at random, what is the probability that the coin is worth *at least* 10 cents?
   - (A) $\frac{1}{5}$
   - (B) $\frac{1}{3}$
   - (C) $\frac{2}{5}$
   - (D) $\frac{3}{5}$
   - (E) $\frac{2}{3}$

2. Kimberly places 5 red marbles, 3 green marbles, and 8 yellow marbles in a bag. If a marble is selected at random from the bag, what is the probability that it will NOT be green?
   - (A) $\frac{3}{16}$
   - (B) $\frac{3}{13}$
   - (C) $\frac{1}{3}$
   - (D) $\frac{11}{16}$
   - (E) $\frac{13}{16}$

3. Kimberly places 5 red marbles, 3 green marbles, and 8 yellow marbles in a bag. If a marble is selected at random from the bag, what is the probability that it will be green or yellow?
   - (A) $\frac{3}{16}$
   - (B) $\frac{5}{16}$
   - (C) $\frac{3}{8}$
   - (D) $\frac{1}{2}$
   - (E) $\frac{11}{16}$

4. Becca selects a card at random from a deck of 52 cards. What is the probability that she selects a club?
   - (A) $\frac{1}{52}$
   - (B) $\frac{1}{26}$
   - (C) $\frac{1}{13}$
   - (D) $\frac{1}{8}$
   - (E) $\frac{1}{4}$

5. A spinner is in the shape of a circle with 10 sectors of the same size numbered 1 through 10. On a particular spin, what are the odds that the pointer will end up on a number that is divisible by 4?
   - (A) $\frac{1}{10}$
   - (B) $\frac{1}{5}$
   - (C) $\frac{3}{10}$
   - (D) $\frac{2}{5}$
   - (E) $\frac{1}{2}$

6. In the diagram below, *ABCD* is a square, and points *E*, *F*, *G*, and *H* are the midpoints of its sides. If a point is selected at random from the interior of square *ABCD*, what is the probability that the point will be in the shaded area?

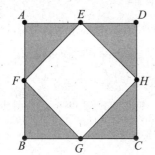

(A) $\dfrac{1}{4}$

(B) $\dfrac{1}{3}$

(C) $\dfrac{1}{2}$

(D) $\dfrac{2}{3}$

(E) $\dfrac{3}{4}$

7. The diagram below shows a circle of radius 1 contained inside a circle of radius 3. If a point is selected at random from the interior of the circle of radius 3, what is the probability that the point will also be in the interior of the circle of radius 1?

(Big circle has radius 3, small circle has radius 1)

(A) $\dfrac{1}{12}$

(B) $\dfrac{1}{9}$

(C) $\dfrac{1}{6}$

(D) $\dfrac{1}{3}$

(E) $\dfrac{1}{2}$

8. In the diagram below, *WXYZ* is a rectangle with a semicircle inscribed inside it. If a point is selected at random from the interior of the rectangle, what is the probability that the point lies within the shaded region?

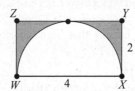

(A) $\dfrac{4-\pi}{4}$

(B) $\dfrac{\pi}{8}$

(C) $\dfrac{4-\pi}{2}$

(D) $\dfrac{2}{\pi}$

(E) $\dfrac{\pi}{4}$

ANSWER KEY AND EXPLANATIONS

1. D	3. E	5. B	7. B
2. E	4. E	6. C	8. A

1. **The correct answer is (D).** Three of the five coins are worth at least 10 cents. Therefore, the probability that a selected coin will be worth at least 10 cents is $\frac{3}{5}$. Be careful. The question does not ask if a dime will be selected.

2. **The correct answer is (E).** There are a total of $5 + 3 + 8 = 16$ marbles in the bag. Since 3 of the marbles are green, it follows that $16 - 3 = 13$ are not green. Thus, the probability that a selected marble is not green is $\frac{13}{16}$.

3. **The correct answer is (E).** This problem uses the same set up as problem 2. There are 16 marbles in the bag, and $3 + 8 = 11$ are green or yellow. Therefore, the probability that a green or yellow marble is selected is $\frac{11}{16}$.

4. **The correct answer is (E).** There are 13 clubs in a deck of 52 cards. Therefore, the probability that Becca selects a club is $\frac{13}{52} = \frac{1}{4}$.

5. **The correct answer is (B).** The only numbers between 1 and 10 that are divisible by 4 are 4 and 8. Therefore, in two of the ten possible outcomes the pointer will end up on a number divisible by 4. Thus, the probability is $\frac{2}{10} = \frac{1}{5}$.

6. **The correct answer is (C).** It is easier to solve this problem if you have numbers to work with. Say that each side of the square is of length 2. Then, the area of the square is 4. Now, focus on triangle GHC. Since H and G are midpoints of the sides of the square, $CG = 1$, and $CH = 1$. Using these as the base and height of right triangle CGH, the area of the triangle is $\frac{1}{2}bh = \frac{1}{2}(1)(1) = \frac{1}{2}$. The

shaded area of the figure consists of four congruent triangles, each of area $\frac{1}{2}$, so the total shaded area is $\frac{1}{2} \times 4 = 2$. Therefore, the overall area of the square is 4, and the shaded area is 2. The probability that a point selected at random will be in the shaded area is $\frac{2}{4} = \frac{1}{2}$.

7. **The correct answer is (B).** The area of the larger circle is $A = \pi r^2 = \pi(3^2) = 9\pi$. The area of the smaller circle is $A = \pi r^2 = \pi(1^2) = \pi$. Therefore, the probability that a point selected at random from the interior of the larger circle would also be within the small circle is $\frac{\pi}{9\pi} = \frac{1}{9}$.

8. **The correct answer is (A).** The area of the rectangle is $2 \times 4 = 8$. The semicircle has a radius of 2, so its area is $A = \frac{1}{2}\pi r^2 = \frac{1}{2}\pi(2^2) = \frac{1}{2}\pi(4) = 2\pi$. This means that the shaded region has an area of $8 - 2\pi$. Therefore, the probability that a point selected at random from the interior of the rectangle would also be in the shaded region is $\frac{8 - 2\pi}{8} = \frac{4 - \pi}{4}$.

DATA INTERPRETATION

Working with Data in Tables

Some SAT questions ask you to solve mathematical problems based on data contained in tables. All such problems are based on problem-solving techniques that have already been reviewed. The trick when working with tables is to make certain that you select the correct data needed to solve the problem. Take your time reading each table so that you understand exactly what information the table contains. Carefully select data from the correct row and column. As you will see, things are even trickier when a problem involves more than one table.

In order to illustrate problem solving with tables, consider the two tables below. The three following questions are based on the data within these tables.

Paul, Mark, and Bob are computer salespeople. In addition to their regular salaries, they each receive a commission for each computer they sell. The number of computers that each salesperson sold during a particular week, as well as their commission amounts, is shown in the tables below.

NUMBER OF COMPUTERS SOLD

	Monday	Tuesday	Wednesday	Thursday	Friday
Paul	9	3	12	6	4
Mark	6	3	9	1	5
Bob	8	4	5	7	8

COMMISSION PER SALE

Paul	$15
Mark	$20
Bob	$25

> What is the total amount of the commissions that Bob earned over the entire week?

This problem only concerns Bob, so ignore the information for Mark and Paul. Over the course of the week, Bob sold $8 + 4 + 5 + 7 + 8 = 32$ computers. The second table tells us that Bob earns $25 per sale, so the total amount of his commission would be $25 \times 32 = \$800$.

> What is the total amount of commission money earned by Paul, Mark, and Bob on Thursday?

To solve this problem, focus only on what happened on Thursday. Ignore the data for the other four days. Be careful not to add the number of computers sold by the three people, since they each earn a different commission per sale.

- On Thursday, Paul sold 6 computers and earned a $15 commission for each computer sold, so Paul earned $15 × 6 = $90.

- Mark sold 1 computer, so, based on his $20 commission, he earned $20.

- Bob sold 7 computers, and earned a $25 commission per machine, so he made $25 × 7 = $175.

- Overall, the amount of commission on Thursday is $90 + $20 + $175 = $285.

> On what day did Paul and Mark earn the same amount in commission?

You can save yourself a lot of time if you look at the tables before you start to compute. Note that Mark's commission is larger than Paul's, and so, the only way they could have earned the same amount is if Paul sold more computers than Mark. The only days that Paul sold more computers than Mark were Monday, Wednesday, and Thursday, so those are the only days that need to be considered.

- By observation, you can see that on Thursday Paul made much more in commission than Mark, so eliminate Thursday.

- On Monday, Paul earned $15 × 9 = $135 and Mark earned $20 × 6 = $120. This means that the answer must be Wednesday.

- To be certain, note that on Wednesday Paul earned $15 × 12 = $180, and Mark earned $20 × 9 = $180 also.

Correlation and Scatterplots

If two variables have a relationship such that when one variable changes, the other changes in a predictable way, the two variables are *correlated*. For example, there is a correlation between the number of hours an employee works each week and the amount of money the employee earns—the more hours the employee works, the more money the employee earns. Note that in this case, as the first variable increases, the second variable increases as well. These two variables are *positively correlated*.

Sometimes, when one variable increases, a second variable decreases. For example, the more that a store charges for a particular item, the fewer of that item will be sold. In this case, these two variables are *negatively correlated*.

Sometimes two variables are not correlated, that is, a change in one variable does not affect the other variable in any way. For example, the number of cans of soda that a person drinks each day is not correlated with the amount of money the person earns.

One way to determine whether two variables are correlated or not is to sketch a *scatterplot*. A scatterplot is a graph on which the *x*-axis represents the value of one variable and the *y*-axis represents the value of the other variable. Several values of one variable and the corresponding values of the other variable are measured and plotted on the graph:

- If the points appear to form a straight line, or are close to forming a straight line, then it is likely that the variables are correlated.

- If the line has a positive slope (rises up left to right), the variables are positively correlated.

- If the line has a negative slope (goes down left to right), the variables are negatively correlated.

- If the points on the scatterplot seem to be located more or less at random, then it is likely that the variables are not correlated.

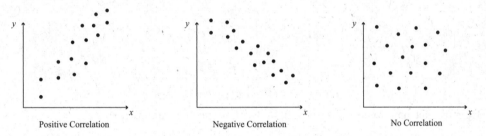

Positive Correlation   Negative Correlation   No Correlation

It is rare that the points on a scatterplot will all lie exactly on the same line. However, if there is a strong correlation, it is likely that there will be a line that could be drawn on the scatterplot that comes close to all of the points. Statisticians call the line that comes the closest to all of the points on a scatterplot the "line of best fit." Without performing any computations, it is possible to visualize the location of the line of best fit, as the diagrams below show:

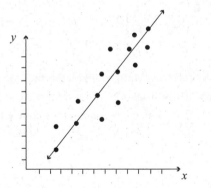
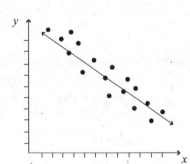

Which of the following slopes is the closest to the slope of the line of best fit for the scatterplot below?

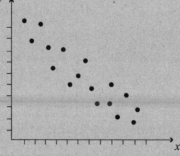

(A) 3

(B) 1

(C) 0

(D) −1

(E) −3

Begin by sketching in the line of best fit in its approximate location.

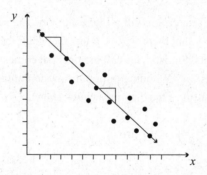

This line has a negative slope, since it decreases from left to right. In addition, the slope appears to be about −1, because if you move one unit horizontally from a point on the line, you need to move one unit vertically downward to return to the line. **The correct answer is choice (D).**

EXERCISES: DATA INTERPRETATION

Directions: Work out each problem. Circle the letter of your choice.

QUESTIONS 1–3 REFER TO THE FOLLOWING INFORMATION.

The tables below show the discount percentages for various categories of items at Wilson's Department Store, and the regular prices for three specific items.

WILSON'S DEPARTMENT STORE

Discount Amounts During Sale

Furniture	20% Discount
Clothing	15% Discount
Electronics	10% Discount

Regular Prices

Desk	$350
Shirt	$20
Television	$180

1. What is the price of the television during the sale?
   - **(A)** $18
   - **(B)** $144
   - **(C)** $153
   - **(D)** $162
   - **(E)** $280

2. If Tony buys a shirt and a desk during the sale, how much money does he save?
   - **(A)** $37
   - **(B)** $55.50
   - **(C)** $73
   - **(D)** $74
   - **(E)** $297

3. During the sale, how much greater is the savings on a television set than on a shirt?
   - **(A)** $3
   - **(B)** $12
   - **(C)** $15
   - **(D)** $18
   - **(E)** $145

QUESTIONS 4–6 REFER TO THE FOLLOWING INFORMATION.

HOURS WORKED: WEEK 1

	Mon	Tues	Wed	Thurs	Fri	Sat	Sun
Ms. Chin	8	8	7	$6\frac{1}{2}$	8	4	3
Ms. Montoya	$6\frac{1}{2}$	6	$5\frac{1}{2}$	6	7	8	3

SALARY SCALE—DOLLARS PER HOUR

Ms. Chin	$8
Ms. Montoya	$11

4. During Week 1, Ms. Chin worked how many more weekday (Monday through Friday) hours than Ms. Montoya worked?
   - **(A)** 2
   - **(B)** $2\frac{1}{2}$
   - **(C)** 6
   - **(D)** $6\frac{1}{2}$
   - **(E)** 7

5. If Ms. Chin is a manager, and managers earn an extra $1.50 per hour for weekend (Saturday and Sunday) work, how much money did Ms. Chin earn on Saturday and Sunday?
   - **(A)** $49
   - **(B)** $52
   - **(C)** $56
   - **(D)** $66.50
   - **(E)** $99

6. How much more money did Ms. Montoya earn on Thursday than did Ms. Chin?
   - **(A)** $5.50
   - **(B)** $14
   - **(C)** $15.50
   - **(D)** $17
   - **(E)** $66

In this election, Haynes and Cogswell were the
only ones who received votes.

	District A	District B	District C	District D
Cogswell	150	350	300	200
Haynes	100	200	450	150

7. What percent of the votes cast in District C
   did Haynes receive?
   (A) 40%
   (B) 45%
   (C) 60%
   (D) 65%
   (E) 70%

8. What is the ratio of the total number of votes
   received by Cogswell to the total number
   of votes received by Haynes?
   (A) 3:2
   (B) 10:9
   (C) 5:4
   (D) 4:5
   (E) 9:10

9. The scatterplot below depicts the relationship between two variables, x and y. Which
   of the following best describes the line that
   best fits the data in the scatterplot?

   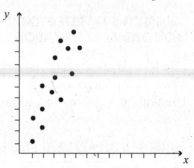

   (A) The slope of the line of best fit is −3.
   (B) The slope of the line of best fit is −1.
   (C) The slope of the line of best fit is 0.
   (D) The slope of the line of best fit is 1.
   (E) The slope of the line of best fit is 3.

10. Below is a scatterplot depicting the relation-
    ship between the variable a and the variable
    b. Which of the following best describes the
    relationship depicted in the graph?

    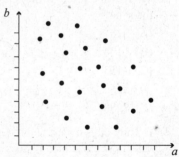

    (A) There is a strong positive correlation
    between the two variables.
    (B) There is a strong negative correlation
    between the two variables.
    (C) The two variables are not correlated.
    (D) As the value of a increases, the value
    of b increases.
    (E) As the value of a increases, the value
    of b decreases.

ANSWER KEY AND EXPLANATIONS

| 1. D | 3. C | 5. D | 7. C | 9. E |
| 2. C | 4. D | 6. B | 8. B | 10. C |

1. **The correct answer is (D).** The regular price of a television is $180. There is a 10% discount on electronic items, so the television is discounted $180 × 10% = $18. Therefore, its selling price is $180 − $18 = $162.

2. **The correct answer is (C).** Note that this question asks for the amount of money that Tony saves, and not the cost of the items. The shirt costs $20, and he saves 15% on clothing, so $20 × 15% = $3 savings on the shirt. The desk costs $350, and he saves 20% on furniture, so $350 × 20% = $70 savings on the desk. Overall, Tony saves $70 + $3 = $73.

3. **The correct answer is (C).** The savings on the television is $180 × 10% = $18. In the above problem, the savings on a shirt is $3. Therefore, the savings on the television is $18 − $3 = $15 greater than the savings on the shirt.

4. **The correct answer is (D).** Be careful to count only weekdays in this problem. Ms. Chin worked $8+8+7+6\frac{1}{2}+8=37\frac{1}{2}$ hours. During the same time period, Ms. Montoya worked $6\frac{1}{2}+6+5\frac{1}{2}+6+7=31$ hours. Therefore, Ms. Chin worked $37\frac{1}{2}-31=6\frac{1}{2}$ hours more.

5. **The correct answer is (D).** Ms. Chin's hourly salary on weekends is $8 + $1.50 = $9.50. On the weekend, she worked 4 + 3 = 7 hours, so she earned $9.50 × 7 = $66.50.

6. **The correct answer is (B).** Ms. Montoya earns $11 an hour, so on Thursday she earned $11 × 6 = $66. On Thursday, Ms. Chin earned $8\times6\frac{1}{2}=\$52$. Therefore, Ms. Montoya earned $66 − $52 = $14 more.

7. **The correct answer is (C).** Haynes received 450 out of a total of 450 + 300 = 750 votes. Therefore, he received $\frac{450}{750}=60\%$ of the vote.

8. **The correct answer is (B).** Cogswell received 1000 votes in total, and Haynes received 900. The ratio of Cogswell to Haynes, therefore, is 1000 to 900, or 10:9.

9. **The correct answer is (E).** The figure below shows the scatterplot with the approximate line of best fit sketched in.

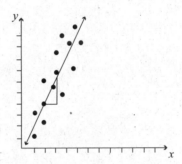

Since the line increases from left to right, the line has a positive slope. Also note that, if you move one unit horizontally away from a point on the line, you need to move approximately 3 units vertically to return to the line. Therefore, the slope of the line of best fit is approximately 3.

10. **The correct answer is (C).** The points on the scatterplot appear to be randomly arranged on the graph. This is an indication that the values of a and b are not correlated.

SUMMING IT UP

- Not all problems that deal with averages will ask you to solve for the average of a set of quantities.

- The trick when working with tables is to make sure you select the correct data needed to solve the problem.

- Take your time reading each table.

PART VI

FIVE PRACTICE TESTS

Preface to the Practice Tests

OVERVIEW

- **Simulate test-taking conditions**
- **Timing drills can help when you are short on time**
- **Summing it up**

The practice tests in this book make up one of the most important parts of your SAT preparation. Use them as benchmarks as you work through the other chapters in this book. Each test gives you a great opportunity to gauge your progress and focus your ongoing study. Together, the tests map the growth of your skills and demonstrate your SAT readiness. And, when you take the practice exams under simulated test-taking conditions, they give you a wonderful opportunity to adjust to the test-taking environment. When you enter the testing room, you'll know what to expect—and you'll be ready to score high on the exam.

SIMULATE TEST-TAKING CONDITIONS

Above and beyond everything else, the five practice exams in this part of the book help you prepare for the experience of taking a timed, standardized test. Taking these tests will improve your familiarity with the SAT, reduce your number of careless errors, and increase your overall level of confidence. To make sure that you get the most out of this practice, you should do everything in your power to simulate actual test-taking conditions. The following sections outline the best methods for simulating testing conditions when you work through the practice exams.

Find a Block of Time

Because the SAT is administered in one long block of time, the best way to simulate test-taking conditions is to take an entire practice exam in one sitting. This means that you should set aside $3\frac{1}{2}$ hours of consecutive time to take the practice tests.

If you find it difficult to find $3\frac{1}{2}$ quiet hours at home, maybe take the test in the library. If you decide to take a test at home, take precautions. Turn off the ringer on all nearby telephones, ask your parents to hold your calls, and convince siblings to stay out of your room. Easier said than done, right? Although infrequent interruptions won't completely invalidate your testing experience, you should try to avoid them.

Work at a Desk and Wear a Watch

Don't take a practice test while you are lounging on your bed. After all, the SAT people won't let you take the test lying down! Clear off sufficient space on a desk or table to work comfortably. Wear a watch to properly administer the sections under timed conditions. Or use a timer. Most sections of the SAT are 25 minutes. The time for each section is marked on the section, so check the beginning of each section and set your timer or your watch for that amount of time.

You are not allowed to explore other sections on the test while you are supposed to be working on a particular one. So when you take your practice tests, don't look ahead or back. Take the full time to complete each section.

Practice on a Weekend Morning

Since the SAT is typically administered at 8:30 a.m. on Saturday (or Sunday for religious observers), why not take the exam at the exact same time on a weekend morning? You should be most energetic in the morning anyway. If you are not a morning person, now is a good time to become one since that's when you'll have to take the actual SAT! When you take the practice test, allow yourself two breaks. Give yourself a 5-minute break after Section 3 to run to the bathroom, eat a snack, and resharpen your pencils. After Section 6, give yourself a 1-minute stretch break. During this time on SAT day, you are not allowed to leave the room or speak with anyone. To simulate this, stand up after Section 6, take a minute to collect your thoughts, and then proceed to Section 7.

TIMING DRILLS CAN HELP WHEN YOU ARE SHORT ON TIME

We know that it will be extremely difficult for you to find $3\frac{1}{2}$ hours of consecutive time during which to take full practice examinations. You have a life, after all—homework, social commitments, family responsibilities, etc. Maybe you'll only be able to take one or two complete examinations under simulated testing conditions. But you can do *timing drills* to get valuable practice in shorter periods of time. Timing drills are short groups of questions that allow you to work on your weaknesses under timed conditions.

If you feel that you need work on a particular type of math question, the first thing you should do is revisit earlier portions of the book for review. For example, if multiple-choice math gives you difficulty, read Chapter 8 and do the exercises. If the grid-ins are a problem for you, check Chapter 9. Once you have studied the strategies, do specific timing drills to get extra review and practice. To use the tests as timing drills follow these six steps:

1 Find a 20-question multiple-choice section or a 10-question grid-in subsection in a test.

2 Answer the questions.

3 Check your answers.

4 Review your results and look for patterns among your answers.

5 Try to determine whether you need to review arithmetic, basic or intermediate algebra, geometry, data analysis, statistics, or probability.

6 Review the appropriate chapters.

Follow the same procedure for the critical reading section and for the writing section. Choose particular areas to work on like sentence completions and identifying sentence errors and find specific sections of tests to answer.

Timing drills are exercises for the mind. You often read or hear people say that if you exercise just 20 minutes a day, three times a week, you can stay in shape. Well, if you do timing drills regularly, they work the same way. In just 15 to 30 minutes a sitting, you can keep mentally fit for the SAT. Try the drills. They're fast and very effective.

Critical Reading Timing Drills

You should also revisit earlier chapters to combat your critical reading weaknesses. Once you have, you can do the same kind of timing drills. If you feel that you need work on every type of critical reading question and you don't have time to take an entire practice test, take a full 30-minute section. This will give you a chance to practice sentence completions and reading questions in a timed format. If you find sentence completions particularly troubling, allow 7 minutes to answer a drill of 9 or 10 questions. And if critical reading is your stumbling block, allow 15 minutes to answer either a lengthy passage (10 or more questions) or a double passage.

A Table of Timing Drills

We know that doing all of this might appear to be excessive. But remember that your goal is to take these practice tests in as true an environment as possible so that you're prepared to take the real SAT. You will be accustomed to sitting for a long period of time, but you will get two breaks. This knowledge will make you considerably less anxious on test day.

The following table puts all of the timing drill information in a one-stop format, so you can refer to it often when planning your SAT study time.

Type of Question	Number of Questions	Time to Allot
Multiple-choice math (full section)	20	25 minutes
Multiple-choice math (part of a section)	10	12 minutes
Multiple-choice math (part of a section)	15	20 minutes
Grid-ins	10	13 minutes
Sentence completions	9	5 minutes
Sentence completions	8	5 minutes
Reading comprehension (full section)	16	20 minutes
Reading comprehension (part of a section)	8	10 minutes
Reading comprehension (part of a section)	12	15 minutes
Writing the essay	1	25 minutes
Identifying sentence errors	19	13 minutes
Improving sentences	25	17 minutes
Improving paragraphs	6	5 minutes

SUMMING IT UP

If you are going to take a full practice examination, try to simulate test-taking conditions by doing the following:

- To take a full-length practice test, you'll need approximately $3\frac{1}{2}$ quiet hours.

- Work at a desk and wear a watch when you take the practice exams.

- If temptation may lead you to sneak a peak at the answers during the practice exam, cover them up before you start the test.

- Whenever possible, take the full practice tests on weekend mornings.

- If you don't have the time to take a full test, or you need to work on a specific type of question, take the appropriate timing drills.

ANSWER SHEET PRACTICE TEST 2

SECTION 1: ESSAY

_____

_____

_____

_____

_____

_____

_____

_____

_____

_____

_____

_____

_____

_____

_____

_____

_____

_____

_____

_____

_____

_____

_____

_____

_____

_____

_____

If a section has fewer questions than answer ovals, leave the extra ovals blank.

SECTION 2

1 (A) (B) (C) (D) (E)	11 (A) (B) (C) (D) (E)	21 (A) (B) (C) (D) (E)	31 (A) (B) (C) (D) (E)
2 (A) (B) (C) (D) (E)	12 (A) (B) (C) (D) (E)	22 (A) (B) (C) (D) (E)	32 (A) (B) (C) (D) (E)
3 (A) (B) (C) (D) (E)	13 (A) (B) (C) (D) (E)	23 (A) (B) (C) (D) (E)	33 (A) (B) (C) (D) (E)
4 (A) (B) (C) (D) (E)	14 (A) (B) (C) (D) (E)	24 (A) (B) (C) (D) (E)	34 (A) (B) (C) (D) (E)
5 (A) (B) (C) (D) (E)	15 (A) (B) (C) (D) (E)	25 (A) (B) (C) (D) (E)	35 (A) (B) (C) (D) (E)
6 (A) (B) (C) (D) (E)	16 (A) (B) (C) (D) (E)	26 (A) (B) (C) (D) (E)	36 (A) (B) (C) (D) (E)
7 (A) (B) (C) (D) (E)	17 (A) (B) (C) (D) (E)	27 (A) (B) (C) (D) (E)	37 (A) (B) (C) (D) (E)
8 (A) (B) (C) (D) (E)	18 (A) (B) (C) (D) (E)	28 (A) (B) (C) (D) (E)	38 (A) (B) (C) (D) (E)
9 (A) (B) (C) (D) (E)	19 (A) (B) (C) (D) (E)	29 (A) (B) (C) (D) (E)	39 (A) (B) (C) (D) (E)
10 (A) (B) (C) (D) (E)	20 (A) (B) (C) (D) (E)	30 (A) (B) (C) (D) (E)	40 (A) (B) (C) (D) (E)

SECTION 3

1 (A) (B) (C) (D) (E)	11 (A) (B) (C) (D) (E)	21 (A) (B) (C) (D) (E)	31 (A) (B) (C) (D) (E)
2 (A) (B) (C) (D) (E)	12 (A) (B) (C) (D) (E)	22 (A) (B) (C) (D) (E)	32 (A) (B) (C) (D) (E)
3 (A) (B) (C) (D) (E)	13 (A) (B) (C) (D) (E)	23 (A) (B) (C) (D) (E)	33 (A) (B) (C) (D) (E)
4 (A) (B) (C) (D) (E)	14 (A) (B) (C) (D) (E)	24 (A) (B) (C) (D) (E)	34 (A) (B) (C) (D) (E)
5 (A) (B) (C) (D) (E)	15 (A) (B) (C) (D) (E)	25 (A) (B) (C) (D) (E)	35 (A) (B) (C) (D) (E)
6 (A) (B) (C) (D) (E)	16 (A) (B) (C) (D) (E)	26 (A) (B) (C) (D) (E)	36 (A) (B) (C) (D) (E)
7 (A) (B) (C) (D) (E)	17 (A) (B) (C) (D) (E)	27 (A) (B) (C) (D) (E)	37 (A) (B) (C) (D) (E)
8 (A) (B) (C) (D) (E)	18 (A) (B) (C) (D) (E)	28 (A) (B) (C) (D) (E)	38 (A) (B) (C) (D) (E)
9 (A) (B) (C) (D) (E)	19 (A) (B) (C) (D) (E)	29 (A) (B) (C) (D) (E)	39 (A) (B) (C) (D) (E)
10 (A) (B) (C) (D) (E)	20 (A) (B) (C) (D) (E)	30 (A) (B) (C) (D) (E)	40 (A) (B) (C) (D) (E)

SECTION 4

1 (A) (B) (C) (D) (E)	11 (A) (B) (C) (D) (E)	21 (A) (B) (C) (D) (E)	31 (A) (B) (C) (D) (E)
2 (A) (B) (C) (D) (E)	12 (A) (B) (C) (D) (E)	22 (A) (B) (C) (D) (E)	32 (A) (B) (C) (D) (E)
3 (A) (B) (C) (D) (E)	13 (A) (B) (C) (D) (E)	23 (A) (B) (C) (D) (E)	33 (A) (B) (C) (D) (E)
4 (A) (B) (C) (D) (E)	14 (A) (B) (C) (D) (E)	24 (A) (B) (C) (D) (E)	34 (A) (B) (C) (D) (E)
5 (A) (B) (C) (D) (E)	15 (A) (B) (C) (D) (E)	25 (A) (B) (C) (D) (E)	35 (A) (B) (C) (D) (E)
6 (A) (B) (C) (D) (E)	16 (A) (B) (C) (D) (E)	26 (A) (B) (C) (D) (E)	
7 (A) (B) (C) (D) (E)	17 (A) (B) (C) (D) (E)	27 (A) (B) (C) (D) (E)	
8 (A) (B) (C) (D) (E)	18 (A) (B) (C) (D) (E)	28 (A) (B) (C) (D) (E)	
9 (A) (B) (C) (D) (E)	19 (A) (B) (C) (D) (E)	29 (A) (B) (C) (D) (E)	
10 (A) (B) (C) (D) (E)	20 (A) (B) (C) (D) (E)	30 (A) (B) (C) (D) (E)	

SECTION 5

Note: ONLY the answers entered on the grid are scored. Handwritten answers at the top of the column are NOT scored.

1 Ⓐ Ⓑ Ⓒ Ⓓ Ⓔ   6 Ⓐ Ⓑ Ⓒ Ⓓ Ⓔ
2 Ⓐ Ⓑ Ⓒ Ⓓ Ⓔ   7 Ⓐ Ⓑ Ⓒ Ⓓ Ⓔ
3 Ⓐ Ⓑ Ⓒ Ⓓ Ⓔ   8 Ⓐ Ⓑ Ⓒ Ⓓ Ⓔ
4 Ⓐ Ⓑ Ⓒ Ⓓ Ⓔ   9 Ⓐ Ⓑ Ⓒ Ⓓ Ⓔ
5 Ⓐ Ⓑ Ⓒ Ⓓ Ⓔ   10 Ⓐ Ⓑ Ⓒ Ⓓ Ⓔ

11. 12. 13. 14. 15.

16. 17. 18. 19. 20.

SECTION 6

1	Ⓐ Ⓑ Ⓒ Ⓓ Ⓔ	11 Ⓐ Ⓑ Ⓒ Ⓓ Ⓔ	21 Ⓐ Ⓑ Ⓒ Ⓓ Ⓔ	31 Ⓐ Ⓑ Ⓒ Ⓓ Ⓔ
2	Ⓐ Ⓑ Ⓒ Ⓓ Ⓔ	12 Ⓐ Ⓑ Ⓒ Ⓓ Ⓔ	22 Ⓐ Ⓑ Ⓒ Ⓓ Ⓔ	32 Ⓐ Ⓑ Ⓒ Ⓓ Ⓔ
3	Ⓐ Ⓑ Ⓒ Ⓓ Ⓔ	13 Ⓐ Ⓑ Ⓒ Ⓓ Ⓔ	23 Ⓐ Ⓑ Ⓒ Ⓓ Ⓔ	33 Ⓐ Ⓑ Ⓒ Ⓓ Ⓔ
4	Ⓐ Ⓑ Ⓒ Ⓓ Ⓔ	14 Ⓐ Ⓑ Ⓒ Ⓓ Ⓔ	24 Ⓐ Ⓑ Ⓒ Ⓓ Ⓔ	34 Ⓐ Ⓑ Ⓒ Ⓓ Ⓔ
5	Ⓐ Ⓑ Ⓒ Ⓓ Ⓔ	15 Ⓐ Ⓑ Ⓒ Ⓓ Ⓔ	25 Ⓐ Ⓑ Ⓒ Ⓓ Ⓔ	35 Ⓐ Ⓑ Ⓒ Ⓓ Ⓔ
6	Ⓐ Ⓑ Ⓒ Ⓓ Ⓔ	16 Ⓐ Ⓑ Ⓒ Ⓓ Ⓔ	26 Ⓐ Ⓑ Ⓒ Ⓓ Ⓔ	36 Ⓐ Ⓑ Ⓒ Ⓓ Ⓔ
7	Ⓐ Ⓑ Ⓒ Ⓓ Ⓔ	17 Ⓐ Ⓑ Ⓒ Ⓓ Ⓔ	27 Ⓐ Ⓑ Ⓒ Ⓓ Ⓔ	37 Ⓐ Ⓑ Ⓒ Ⓓ Ⓔ
8	Ⓐ Ⓑ Ⓒ Ⓓ Ⓔ	18 Ⓐ Ⓑ Ⓒ Ⓓ Ⓔ	28 Ⓐ Ⓑ Ⓒ Ⓓ Ⓔ	38 Ⓐ Ⓑ Ⓒ Ⓓ Ⓔ
9	Ⓐ Ⓑ Ⓒ Ⓓ Ⓔ	19 Ⓐ Ⓑ Ⓒ Ⓓ Ⓔ	29 Ⓐ Ⓑ Ⓒ Ⓓ Ⓔ	39 Ⓐ Ⓑ Ⓒ Ⓓ Ⓔ
10	Ⓐ Ⓑ Ⓒ Ⓓ Ⓔ	20 Ⓐ Ⓑ Ⓒ Ⓓ Ⓔ	30 Ⓐ Ⓑ Ⓒ Ⓓ Ⓔ	40 Ⓐ Ⓑ Ⓒ Ⓓ Ⓔ

SECTION 7

1	Ⓐ Ⓑ Ⓒ Ⓓ Ⓔ	6 Ⓐ Ⓑ Ⓒ Ⓓ Ⓔ	11 Ⓐ Ⓑ Ⓒ Ⓓ Ⓔ
2	Ⓐ Ⓑ Ⓒ Ⓓ Ⓔ	7 Ⓐ Ⓑ Ⓒ Ⓓ Ⓔ	12 Ⓐ Ⓑ Ⓒ Ⓓ Ⓔ
3	Ⓐ Ⓑ Ⓒ Ⓓ Ⓔ	8 Ⓐ Ⓑ Ⓒ Ⓓ Ⓔ	13 Ⓐ Ⓑ Ⓒ Ⓓ Ⓔ
4	Ⓐ Ⓑ Ⓒ Ⓓ Ⓔ	9 Ⓐ Ⓑ Ⓒ Ⓓ Ⓔ	14 Ⓐ Ⓑ Ⓒ Ⓓ Ⓔ
5	Ⓐ Ⓑ Ⓒ Ⓓ Ⓔ	10 Ⓐ Ⓑ Ⓒ Ⓓ Ⓔ	15 Ⓐ Ⓑ Ⓒ Ⓓ Ⓔ

SECTION 8

1	Ⓐ Ⓑ Ⓒ Ⓓ Ⓔ	6 Ⓐ Ⓑ Ⓒ Ⓓ Ⓔ	11 Ⓐ Ⓑ Ⓒ Ⓓ Ⓔ	16 Ⓐ Ⓑ Ⓒ Ⓓ Ⓔ
2	Ⓐ Ⓑ Ⓒ Ⓓ Ⓔ	7 Ⓐ Ⓑ Ⓒ Ⓓ Ⓔ	12 Ⓐ Ⓑ Ⓒ Ⓓ Ⓔ	17 Ⓐ Ⓑ Ⓒ Ⓓ Ⓔ
3	Ⓐ Ⓑ Ⓒ Ⓓ Ⓔ	8 Ⓐ Ⓑ Ⓒ Ⓓ Ⓔ	13 Ⓐ Ⓑ Ⓒ Ⓓ Ⓔ	18 Ⓐ Ⓑ Ⓒ Ⓓ Ⓔ
4	Ⓐ Ⓑ Ⓒ Ⓓ Ⓔ	9 Ⓐ Ⓑ Ⓒ Ⓓ Ⓔ	14 Ⓐ Ⓑ Ⓒ Ⓓ Ⓔ	19 Ⓐ Ⓑ Ⓒ Ⓓ Ⓔ
5	Ⓐ Ⓑ Ⓒ Ⓓ Ⓔ	10 Ⓐ Ⓑ Ⓒ Ⓓ Ⓔ	15 Ⓐ Ⓑ Ⓒ Ⓓ Ⓔ	20 Ⓐ Ⓑ Ⓒ Ⓓ Ⓔ

SECTION 9

1	Ⓐ Ⓑ Ⓒ Ⓓ Ⓔ	6 Ⓐ Ⓑ Ⓒ Ⓓ Ⓔ	11 Ⓐ Ⓑ Ⓒ Ⓓ Ⓔ
2	Ⓐ Ⓑ Ⓒ Ⓓ Ⓔ	7 Ⓐ Ⓑ Ⓒ Ⓓ Ⓔ	12 Ⓐ Ⓑ Ⓒ Ⓓ Ⓔ
3	Ⓐ Ⓑ Ⓒ Ⓓ Ⓔ	8 Ⓐ Ⓑ Ⓒ Ⓓ Ⓔ	13 Ⓐ Ⓑ Ⓒ Ⓓ Ⓔ
4	Ⓐ Ⓑ Ⓒ Ⓓ Ⓔ	9 Ⓐ Ⓑ Ⓒ Ⓓ Ⓔ	14 Ⓐ Ⓑ Ⓒ Ⓓ Ⓔ
5	Ⓐ Ⓑ Ⓒ Ⓓ Ⓔ	10 Ⓐ Ⓑ Ⓒ Ⓓ Ⓔ	15 Ⓐ Ⓑ Ⓒ Ⓓ Ⓔ

PRACTICE TEST 2

Section 1

Essay • 25 Minutes

Directions: Think carefully about the statement below and the assignment that follows it.

There is an old saying, "The squeaky hinge gets the grease." If you do not make your needs known and heard in our society, you will not succeed in having them satisfied.

Assignment: What is your opinion of the idea that assertiveness is necessary in order to have issues acted upon? Plan and write an essay that develops your ideas logically. Support your opinion with specific evidence taken from your personal experience, your observations of others, or your reading.

STOP

END OF SECTION 1. IF YOU HAVE ANY TIME LEFT, GO OVER
YOUR WORK IN THIS SECTION ONLY. DO NOT WORK IN
ANY OTHER SECTION OF THE TEST.

Section 2
26 Questions • 25 Minutes

Directions: Each of the following questions consists of an incomplete sentence followed by five words or pairs of words. Choose that word or pair of words that, when substituted for the blank space or spaces, best completes the meaning of the sentence and mark the letter of your choice on your answer sheet.

In view of the extenuating circumstances and the defendant's youth, the judge recommended ____.

(A) conviction

(B) a defense

(C) a mistrial

(D) leniency

(E) life imprisonment

The correct answer is (D).

1. Because the elder Johnson was regarded with much ____ by an appreciative public, the younger quite naturally received ____.
   (A) disdain .. kudos
   (B) awe .. respect
   (C) curiosity .. familiarity
   (D) contemplation .. abandonment
   (E) pleasantry .. laughs

2. Her temperament was exceedingly ____, angry one minute but serene the next.
   (A) mercurial
   (B) steadfast
   (C) distraught
   (D) archetypal
   (E) circumspect

3. Traveling by automobile was ____ to him, but he thought nothing of bobsledding, which had been his ____ for many years.
   (A) tiresome .. profession
   (B) tiring .. outlet
   (C) harrowing .. hobby
   (D) a threat .. relief
   (E) exciting .. fun

4. Perennial flowers, such as irises, remain ____ every winter, but they ____ in the spring.
   (A) fertile .. wither
   (B) arable .. congeal
   (C) dormant .. burgeon
   (D) distended .. contract
   (E) attenuated .. rebound

5. The ____ customer was ____ by the manager's prompt action and apology.
   (A) pecuniary .. appalled
   (B) weary .. enervated
   (C) sedulous .. consoled
   (D) intrepid .. mortified
   (E) irate .. mollified

6. His ____ manner served to hide the fact that he secretly indulged in the very vices he publicly ____.
   (A) sedulous .. dispelled
   (B) sanctimonious .. condemned
   (C) dogmatic .. espoused
   (D) stentorian .. prescribed
   (E) candid .. promulgated

7. Because of the _____ caused by the flood, living conditions in the area have _____; many people have lost all their belongings.

(A) trepidation .. augmented

(B) morass .. careened

(C) censure .. abated

(D) devastation .. deteriorated

(E) vertigo .. ameliorated

8. Propaganda is a(n) _____ of truth, a mixture of half-truths and half-lies calculated to deceive.

(A) revision

(B) perversion

(C) dissension

(D) perception

(E) invasion

9. Though brilliantly presented, the report was _____ since the information on which it was based was erroneous.

(A) informative

(B) erudite

(C) laudable

(D) worthless

(E) verbose

Directions: Each passage below is followed by a set of questions. Read each passage, then answer the accompanying questions, basing your answers on what is stated or implied in the passage and in any introductory material provided. Mark the letter of your choice on your answer sheet.

QUESTIONS 10 AND 11 ARE BASED ON THE FOLLOWING PASSAGE.

Online file swapping of music became a severe problem for the music industry in the early 1990s. With the advent of DVDs, the movie industry found itself with a similar
5 problem. Studio presidents estimated that 600,000 movies a day were being illegally downloaded from the Internet. According to industry figures, film studios lost $3 billion a year to online pirates. The music industry
10 began to win its fight against online file sharers by pursuing lawsuits against them. Some of those sued were young teenagers. The music industry also began to work with technology companies to license music
15 downloading. Some film industry analysts believed that similar actions would stop film piracy.

10. The word *pirates* (line 9) refers to

(A) young teenagers.

(B) technology companies.

(C) anyone who downloads files.

(D) studio presidents.

(E) those who share files without paying.

11. The purpose of the passage is to

(A) scare people into not sharing files.

(B) discuss the similarities between the issues facing the film and music industries and how the music industry solved it.

(C) discuss the problems facing the music and film industries.

(D) discuss the way the music industry handled the problem of piracy.

(E) suggest ways that the film industry could solve its problem.

QUESTIONS 12 AND 13 ARE BASED ON THE FOLLOWING PASSAGE.

In the last movie you saw, did you notice the soda the hero was drinking? How about the car the female star was driving? Actors in TV shows and in movies have always
5 drunk sodas and driven cars, but now the name on the soda can and the emblem on the car are more prominent. Advertisers have figured out that they can get exposure for their products by having them featured
10 prominently on TV and in movies. Movie studios have figured out that they can be paid for these so-called "embeds." So what? The next time you order soda X over Y, think about whether the last movie you saw
15 featured X or Y. Have you been manipulated by an advertiser and a movie producer?

12. The author's purpose in writing this piece is to

(A) inform his or her audience of a new advertising practice.

(B) persuade the reader of the dangers of a new advertising practice.

(C) explain an advertising practice.

(D) chastise advertisers about their practices.

(E) chastise both advertisers and movie studios over their practices.

13. The best definition of *embeds* (line 12) is

(A) the placing of advertisers' products within the context of a movie or TV show for a fee.

(B) paying for advertising.

(C) accepting payment for promoting products within a movie or TV show.

(D) products placed within the context of a movie or TV show in exchange for a fee.

(E) promotional fees.

QUESTIONS 14–20 ARE BASED ON THE FOLLOWING PASSAGE.

This passage is taken from the first book of short stories published by Willa Cather (1873–1947), better known for her novels of the western past such as O Pioneers! *For obvious reasons, "Paul's Case" is subtitled "A Study in Temperament."*

It was Paul's afternoon to appear before the faculty of the Pittsburgh High School to account for his various misdemeanors. He had been suspended a week ago, and his
5 father had called at the Principal's office and confessed his perplexity about his son. Paul entered the faculty room suave and smiling. His clothes were a trifle outgrown, and the tan velvet on the collar of his open overcoat
10 was frayed and worn; but for all that there was something of the dandy in him, and he wore an opal pin in his neatly knotted black four-in-hand, and a red carnation in his buttonhole. This latter adornment the faculty
15 somehow felt was not properly significant of the contrite spirit befitting a boy under the ban of suspension.

Paul was tall for his age and very thin, with high, cramped shoulders and a narrow chest.
20 His eyes were remarkable for a certain hysterical brilliancy, and he continually used them in a conscious, theatrical sort of way, peculiarly offensive in a boy. The pupils were abnormally large, as though he
25 was addicted to belladonna, but there was a glassy glitter about them which that drug does not produce.

When questioned by the Principal as to why he was there Paul stated, politely enough,
30 that he wanted to come back to school. This was a lie, but Paul was quite accustomed to lying; found it, indeed, indispensable for overcoming friction. His teachers were asked to state their respective charges against
35 him, which they did with such a rancor and aggrievedness as evinced that this was not a usual case. Disorder and impertinence were among the offenses named, yet each of his instructors felt that it was scarcely possible
40 to put into words the cause of the trouble, which lay in a sort of hysterically defiant manner of the boy's; in the contempt which

they all knew he felt for them, and which he seemingly made not the least effort to
45 conceal. Once, when he had been making a synopsis of a paragraph at the blackboard, his English teacher had stepped to his side and attempted to guide his hand. Paul had started back with a shudder and thrust his
50 hands violently behind him. The astonished woman could scarcely have been more hurt and embarrassed had he struck at her. The insult was so involuntary and definitely personal as to be unforgettable. In one way
55 and another he had made all of his teachers, men and women alike, conscious of the same feeling of physical aversion. In one class he habitually sat with his hand shading his eyes; in another he always looked out the
60 window during the recitation; in another he made a running commentary on the lecture, with humorous intention.

His teachers felt this afternoon that his whole attitude was symbolized by his shrug and
65 his flippantly red carnation flower, and they fell upon him without mercy, his English teacher leading the pack. He stood through it smiling, his pale lips parted over his white teeth. (His lips were constantly twitching,
70 and he had a habit of raising his eyebrows that was contemptuous and irritating to the last degree.) Older boys than Paul had broken down and shed tears under that baptism of fire, but his set smile did not once desert
75 him, and his only sign of discomfort was the nervous trembling of the fingers that toyed with the buttons of his overcoat, and an occasional jerking of the other hand that held his hat. Paul was always smiling,
80 always glancing about him, seeming to feel that people might be watching him and trying to detect something. This conscious expression, since it was as far as possible from boyish mirthfulness, was usually
85 attributed to insolence or "smartness."

14. The subtitle "A Study in Temperament" suggests that Cather wants to examine
   (A) a certain type of character.
   (B) reactions under pressure.
   (C) how people change over time.
   (D) people and their settings.
   (E) inner rage.

15. Cather makes it clear in the first paragraph that the faculty of the high school
   (A) are perplexed by Paul's actions.
   (B) find Paul's demeanor inappropriate.
   (C) cannot understand Paul's words.
   (D) want only the best for Paul.
   (E) are annoyed at Paul's disruption of their day.

16. As it is used in lines 21 and 41, *hysterical* seems to imply
   (A) hilarious.
   (B) raving.
   (C) uncontrolled.
   (D) frothing.
   (E) delirious.

17. To keep the reader from sympathizing with the faculty, Cather compares them metaphorically to
   (A) rabbits.
   (B) wolves.
   (C) dictators.
   (D) comedians.
   (E) warships.

18. The word *smartness* (line 85) is used to mean
   (A) wit.
   (B) intelligence.
   (C) impudence.
   (D) reasonableness.
   (E) resoucefulness.

19. Which adjective does NOT describe Paul as Cather presents him here?

(A) paranoid

(B) defiant

(C) proud

(D) flippant

(E) candid

20. By the end of the selection, we find that the faculty

(A) resents and loathes Paul.

(B) admires and trusts Paul.

(C) struggles to understand Paul.

(D) are physically revolted by Paul.

(E) may learn to get along with Paul.

QUESTIONS 21–26 ARE BASED ON THE FOLLOWING PASSAGE.

Thomas Jefferson wrote in 1787 to his nephew, Peter Carr, a student at the College of William and Mary. Here, Jefferson gives advice about Peter's proposed course of study.

Paris, August 10, 1787

Dear Peter, ____ I have received your two letters of Decemb. 30 and April 18 and am very happy to find by them, as well as by letters from Mr. Wythe, that you have been

5   so fortunate as to attract his notice and good will: I am sure you will find this to have been one of the more fortunate events of your life, as I have ever been sensible it was of mine. I inclose you a sketch of the sciences

10 to which I would wish you to apply in such order as Mr. Wythe shall advise: I mention also the books in them worth your reading, which submit to his correction. Many of these are among your father's books, which

15 you should have brought to you. As I do not recollect those of them not in his library, you must write to me for them, making out a catalogue of such as you think you shall have occasion for in 18 months from the date

20 of your letter, and consulting Mr. Wythe on the subject. To this sketch I will add a few particular observations.

1. Italian. I fear the learning of this language will confound your French and

25 Spanish. Being all of them degenerated dialects of the Latin, they are apt to mix in conversation. I have never seen a person speaking the three languages who did not mix them. It is a delightful language, but

30 late events having rendered the Spanish more useful, lay it aside to prosecute that.

2. Spanish. Bestow great attention on this, and endeavor to acquire an accurate knowledge of it. Our future connections

35 with Spain and Spanish America will render that language a valuable acquisition. The ancient history of a great part of America too is written in that language. I send you a dictionary.

40   3. Moral philosophy. I think it lost time to attend lectures in this branch. He who made us would have been a pitiful bungler if he had made the rules of our moral conduct a matter of science. For one man of science,

45 there are thousands who are not. What would have become of them? Man was destined for society. His morality therefore was to be formed to this object. He was endowed with a sense of right and wrong merely

50 relative to this. This sense is as much a part of his nature as the sense of hearing, seeing, feeling; it is the true foundation of morality. . . . The moral sense, or conscience, is as much a part of man as his leg or arm. It is

55 given to all human beings in a stronger or weaker degree, as force of members is given them in a greater or less degree. . . . State a moral case to a ploughman and a professor. The former will decide it as well, and often

60 better than the latter, because he has not been led astray by artificial rules. . . .

21. As he refers to Mr. Wythe, Jefferson seems to
    (A) affect an air of condescension.
    (B) reject many of that man's opinions.
    (C) warn his nephew not to repeat his mistakes.
    (D) relive pleasant memories from his youth.
    (E) dispute his nephew's preconceived notions.

22. Jefferson encourages his nephew to study Spanish because
    (A) it is related to Latin.
    (B) it will prove useful in international relations.
    (C) there are many good dictionaries available.
    (D) it will prove helpful in learning Italian.
    (E) it is the language of history.

23. By "lost time" (line 40), Jefferson means
    (A) wasted time.
    (B) the past.
    (C) missing time.
    (D) youth.
    (E) about time.

24. Jefferson's main objection to attending lectures in moral philosophy is that
    (A) it could be taught as well by farmers.
    (B) it is innate and cannot be taught.
    (C) it is better practiced outside school.
    (D) very few people understand what it means.
    (E) parents, not professors, should be the instructors.

25. The example of the ploughman and the professor is used to
    (A) illustrate the uselessness of education.
    (B) demonstrate the path to true knowledge.
    (C) explain the universality of morality.
    (D) define the nature of conscience.
    (E) disprove Mr. Wythe's theory of moral conduct.

26. Jefferson compares conscience to a physical limb of the body to show
    (A) that it is natural and present in all human beings.
    (B) how easily we take it for granted.
    (C) that without it, men are powerless.
    (D) how mental and physical states are integrated.
    (E) what is meant by "the arm of the law."

STOP

END OF SECTION 2. IF YOU HAVE ANY TIME LEFT, GO OVER YOUR WORK IN THIS SECTION ONLY. DO NOT WORK IN ANY OTHER SECTION OF THE TEST.

Section 3

20 Questions • 25 Minutes

Directions: Solve the following problems using any available space on the page for scratch-work. On your answer sheet fill in the choice that best corresponds to the correct answer.

Notes: The figures accompanying the problems are drawn as accurately as possible unless otherwise stated in specific problems. Again, unless otherwise stated, all figures lie in the same plane. All numbers used in these problems are real numbers. Calculators are permitted for this test.

Reference Information

Circle:
$C = 2\pi r$
$A = \pi r^2$

Rectangle:
$A = lw$

Rectangular Solid:
$V = lwh$

Cylinder:
$V = \pi r^2 h$

Triangle:
$A = \frac{1}{2} bh$
$a^2 + b^2 = c^2$

The number of degrees of arc in a circle is 360.
The measure in degrees of a straight angle is 180.
The sum of the measures in degrees of the angles of a triangle is 180.

1. $0.2 \times 0.02 \times 0.002 =$
   (A) 0.08
   (B) 0.008
   (C) 0.0008
   (D) 0.00008
   (E) 0.000008

2. If it costs $1.30 a square foot to lay linoleum, what will be the cost of laying 20 square yards of linoleum? (3 ft. = 1 yd.)
   (A) $47.50
   (B) $49.80
   (C) $150.95
   (D) $249.00
   (E) $234.00

3. In a family of five, the heights of the members are 5 feet 1 inch, 5 feet 7 inches, 5 feet 2 inches, 5 feet, and 4 feet 7 inches. The average height is
   (A) 4 feet $4\frac{1}{5}$ inches.
   (B) 5 feet.
   (C) 5 feet 1 inch.
   (D) 5 feet 2 inches.
   (E) 5 feet 3 inches.

4. Three times the first of three consecutive odd integers is 3 more than twice the third. Find the third integer.
   (A) 7
   (B) 9
   (C) 11
   (D) 13
   (E) 15

5. In the figure below, the largest possible circle is cut out of a square piece of tin. The area, in square inches, of the remaining piece of tin is approximately

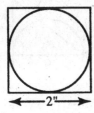

←— 2" —→

(A) 0.14
(B) 0.75
(C) 0.86
(D) 1.0
(E) 3.14

6. The figure shows one square inside another and a rectangle of diagonal T. The best approximation of the value of T, in inches, is given by which of the following inequalities?

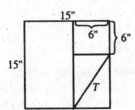

(A) $8 < T < 9$
(B) $9 < T < 10$
(C) $10 < T < 11$
(D) $11 < T < 12$
(E) $12 < T < 13$

7. If nails are bought at 35 cents per dozen and sold at 3 for 10 cents, the total profit on $5\frac{1}{2}$ dozen is

(A) 25 cents.

(B) $27\frac{1}{2}$ cents.

(C) $28\frac{1}{2}$ cents.

(D) $31\frac{1}{2}$ cents.

(E) 35 cents.

8. The total number of eighths in $2\frac{3}{4}$ is
(A) 11
(B) 14
(C) 19
(D) 22
(E) 24

9. What is the difference when $-x - y$ is subtracted from $-x^2 + 2y$?
(A) $x^2 - x - 3y$
(B) $-3x + y$
(C) $x^2 + 3y$
(D) $-x^2 + x - 3y$
(E) $-x^2 + x + 3y$

10. If $2^m = 4x$ and $2^w = 8x$, what is m in terms of w?
(A) $w - 1$
(B) $w + 1$
(C) $2w - 1$
(D) $2w + 1$
(E) w^2

11. $1\frac{1}{4}$ subtracted from its reciprocal is

(A) $\dfrac{9}{20}$

(B) $\dfrac{1}{5}$

(C) $-\dfrac{1}{20}$

(D) $-\dfrac{1}{5}$

(E) $-\dfrac{9}{20}$

12. The total number of feet in x yards, y feet, and z inches is

(A) $3x + y + \dfrac{z}{12}$

(B) $12(x + y + z)$

(C) $x + y + z$

(D) $\dfrac{x}{36} + \dfrac{y}{12} + z$

(E) $x + 3y + 36z$

13. If five triangles are constructed having sides of the lengths indicated below, which triangle will NOT be a right triangle?

(A) 5-12-13

(B) 3-4-5

(C) 8-15-17

(D) 9-40-41

(E) 12-15-18

14. Of the following, which one may be used correctly to compute $26 \times 3\dfrac{1}{2}$?

(A) $(26 \times 30) + \left(26 \times \dfrac{1}{2}\right)$

(B) $(20 \times 3) + \left(6 \times \dfrac{1}{2}\right)$

(C) $\left(20 \times \dfrac{1}{2}\right) + (6 \times 3)$

(D) $(20 \times 3) + \left(26 \times \dfrac{1}{2}\right) + \left(6 \times \dfrac{1}{2}\right)$

(E) $\left(26 \times \dfrac{1}{2}\right) + (20 \times 3) + (6 \times 3)$

15. In the figure, ST is tangent to the circle at T. RT is a diameter. If $RS = 12$, and $ST = 8$, what is the area of the circle?

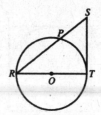

(A) 5π

(B) 8π

(C) 9π

(D) 20π

(E) 40π

16. What would be the marked price of an article if the cost is \$12.60 and the gain is 10% of the selling price?

(A) \$11.34

(B) \$12.48

(C) \$13.66

(D) \$13.86

(E) \$14.00

17. If the average weight of boys who are John's age and height is 105 lbs., and if John weighs 110% of the average, then how many pounds does John weigh?

(A) 110

(B) 110.5

(C) 112

(D) 114.5

(E) 115.5

18. Sonya has 4 twenty-dollar bills, 3 ten-dollar bills, 7 five-dollar bills, and 6 one-dollar bills in her wallet. If she removes one bill from her wallet at random, what is the probability that this particular bill will be enough for her to purchase an $8.50 item?

(A) $\dfrac{1}{5}$

(B) $\dfrac{7}{20}$

(C) $\dfrac{2}{5}$

(D) $\dfrac{13}{20}$

(E) $\dfrac{7}{10}$

19. The Cyber Corporation buys a new machine for $80,000. If the machine loses 15% of its value each year, what is its value after 4 years?

(A) $41,760.50
(B) $42,750
(C) $43,350
(D) $49,130
(E) $57,800

20. For which of the following sets of numbers is the median greater than the mode?

    I. {7, 7, 9, 10, 11}
   II. {−2, −1, 0, 1, 1}
  III. {12, 13, 13, 14, 15}

(A) I only
(B) II only
(C) III only
(D) I and III only
(E) I, II, or III

STOP

END OF SECTION 3. IF YOU HAVE ANY TIME LEFT, GO OVER YOUR WORK IN THIS SECTION ONLY. DO NOT WORK IN ANY OTHER SECTION OF THE TEST.

Section 4
35 Questions • 25 Minutes

> **Directions:** Some of the sentences below contain an error in grammar, usage, word choice, or idiom. Other sentences are correct. Parts of each sentence are underlined and lettered. The error, if there is one, is contained in one of the underlined parts of the sentence. Assume that all other parts of the sentence are correct and cannot be changed. For each sentence, select the one underlined part that must be changed to make the sentence correct and mark its letter on your answer sheet. If there is no error in a sentence, mark answer space E. No sentence contains more than one error.

> Being that it's such a lovely day, we
>   A   B
> are having a difficult time concentrating
>   C   D
> on our assignment. No error
>   E
>
> **The correct answer is (A).**

1. My brother's mother-in-law always flouts
         A   B   C
    her newly acquired possessions in a
    most boastful manner. No error
      D   E

2. If the letter was placed on the table an
             A
    hour ago, it is certain to be there now.
      B   C   D
    No error
     E

3. If you exceed to their unreasonable
          A   B
    demands this time, they will not hesitate
                       C
    to impose on you again. No error
      D   E

4. In the four years since the course
    was instituted, no more than ten students
      A   B
    has signed up for it in any one semester.
        C   D
    No error
     E

5. It is to be hoped that the reward will be
         A
    commensurate to all the effort that
      B   C
    we expended. No error
      D   E

6. Although Dolores is in this country since
      A   B
    she was a little girl, she still thinks of
                    C
    Colombia as home. No error
      D   E

7. There were at least three new innovations
         A   B
    that the chairman suggested at the first
           C
    meeting over which he presided. No error
           D   E

8. The singer <u>was oblivious of</u> the
                          A
<u>orchestra leader's</u> agitation
                          B
<u>immediately before</u> the <u>last aria.</u>
                          C   D
<u>No error</u>
      E

9. <u>There</u> <u>chartered flight</u> to Amsterdam was
      A   B
delayed for several hours <u>because of</u> a
                                              C
strike by <u>airline employees.</u> <u>No error</u>
                          D   E

10. <u>To impress</u> a prospective employer, <u>one</u>
        A   B
should dress neatly, <u>be prompt,</u> and
                                  C
<u>displaying</u> interest in the job. <u>No error</u>
        D   E

11. Each <u>successive</u> appeal <u>for donations</u>
                    A   B
<u>have</u> elicited a wider and <u>more</u>
      C   D
enthusiastic response. <u>No error</u>
                                  E

12. <u>Neither her parents</u> <u>nor</u> her grandmother
                    A   B
<u>is going</u> to be available <u>on Friday night.</u>
        C   D
<u>No error</u>
      E

13. <u>My older brother</u> <u>and myself</u> will both
                    A   B
<u>play percussion instruments,</u> but my sister
                          C
will <u>sing a solo.</u> <u>No error</u>
            D   E

14. If the costume is not <u>your's,</u> then please
                                      A
<u>ascertain if</u> it is <u>Mary's</u> or <u>Jane's.</u> <u>No error</u>
        B   C   D   E

15. <u>The consensus of opinion</u> was that the
                    A
time was not ripe <u>for the election</u> of such
                              B
a liberal <u>candidate: therefore,</u> we decided
                    C
to wait until next year to
<u>nominate Mr. Jones.</u> <u>No error</u>
            D   E

16. Fewer <u>then</u> a hundred people were
        A   B
<u>in attendance</u> and the performers
            C
<u>were quite</u> disappointed. <u>No error</u>
        D   E

17. <u>I will award</u> the prize <u>to whoever</u>
            A   B
completes <u>his work with</u> the greatest
                    C
<u>amount of accuracy.</u> <u>No error</u>
            D   E

18. Andrew, my <u>father's younger</u> brother,
            A   B
<u>will not be at</u> the picnic, much to the
            C
<u>families disappointment.</u> <u>No error</u>
            D   E

19. His <u>parents'</u> graduation gift cannot be
            A
<u>compared with</u> <u>any present</u> that
            B   C
<u>was given</u> to him at the time. <u>No error</u>
        D   E

Directions: The sentences below may contain problems in grammar, usage, word choice, sentence construction, or punctuation. Part or all of each sentence is underlined. Following each sentence you will find five ways of expressing the underlined part. Answer choice (A) always repeats the original underlined section. The other four answer choices are all different. You are to select the lettered answer that produces the most effective sentence. If you think the original sentence is best, choose (A) as your answer. If one of the other choices makes a better sentence, mark your answer sheet for the letter of that choice. Do not choose an answer that changes the meaning of the original sentence.

I have always enjoyed singing as well as to dance.

(A) singing as well as to dance
(B) singing as well as dancing
(C) to sing as well as dancing
(D) singing in addition to dance
(E) to sing in addition to dancing

The correct answer is (B).

20. Having been financially independent for the past three years, his parents no longer pay for his tuition.
(A) his parents no longer pay for his tuition
(B) his tuition is no longer paid by his parents
(C) he no longer relies on his parents to pay his tuition
(D) he does not need his parents any longer
(E) his parents do not pay his tuition any more

21. The silent movie star was unable to make the transition to "talkies" because she spoke in a stilted manner and affectedly.
(A) because she spoke in a stilted manner and affectedly
(B) because she spoke in a stilted and affected manner
(C) because of speaking in a stilted manner and affectedly
(D) since she speaks in a stilted and affected manner
(E) since her speech is stilted and affected

22. When the department was expanded it was clearly a wise move.
(A) When the department was expanded it was clearly a wise move.
(B) Expanding the department it was clearly a wise move.
(C) Expanding the department was clearly a wise move.
(D) Clearly, it was a wise move for the department to be expanded.
(E) When the department was expanded, clearly, the move was wise.

23. Except for the fact that you are missing three pages of work, your portfolio appears to be of extremely high caliber.
(A) Except for the fact that
(B) Besides that
(C) Due to the fact that
(D) Excepting that
(E) Excepting

24. The ribbon on this machine is like my typewriter.
(A) like my typewriter
(B) like my typewriter's
(C) similar to my typewriter
(D) like to my typewriter
(E) likely my typewriter's

25. Everyone in the family except I and Tracy had gone to the drive-in.
(A) except I and Tracy
(B) except Tracy and me
(C) but Tracy and I
(D) accept me and Tracy
(E) with the exception of I and Tracy

26. At first it seemed an impossible <u>feat, and with careful planning</u> and great expense it became a reality.

   (A) feat, and with careful planning

   (B) feat; and with careful planning

   (C) feat, but with careful planning

   (D) fete, but by planning carefully

   (E) feet, and by planning carefully

27. Beginning in World War II, objective tests were <u>put into use widely</u> by the Army to measure intelligence and ability.

   (A) put into use widely

   (B) use widely

   (C) used widely

   (D) used far and wide

   (E) being put into use widely

28. The applicant expressed an avid interest in astronomy, photography, and <u>he's an opera fan</u>.

   (A) he's an opera fan

   (B) he's a fan of opera

   (C) he loves opera

   (D) in opera

   (E) opera

29. A heap of broken glass and twisted metal, <u>the wreck, he thought, was</u> an eyesore.

   (A) the wreck, he thought, was

   (B) the wreckage, he thought, was

   (C) the wreck to his thought was

   (D) he considered the wreck to be

   (E) he thought the wreck was

Directions: Questions 30–35 are based on a passage that might be an early draft of a student's essay. Some sentences in this draft need to be revised or rewritten to make them both clear and correct. Read the passage carefully; then answer the questions that follow it. Some questions require decisions about diction, usage, tone, or sentence structure in particular sentences or parts of the sentences. Other questions require decisions about organization, development, or appropriateness of language in the essay as a whole. For each question, choose the answer that makes the intended meaning clearer and more precise and that follows the conventions of Standard Written English.

(1) Jazz is still my favorite! (2) I spent my vacation studying rock and roll, folk, classical, rhythm and blues, and reggae, even a few minutes of punk and heavy metal, and I enjoyed nearly everything I heard, but when all was said and done, the winner was jazz, which I have listened to for many years now, ever since I was a youngster. (3) Rolling Stones, Beatles, Dylan, Baez, Bach, Brahms, B.B. King, Bob Marley, Jimmy Cliff. (4) I love them all! (5) But in the final analysis, truth be told, I'd choose Miles, Brubeck, Coltrane, and Monk over them all. (6) Or maybe Bird and Diz, Wynton, Branford, Modern Jazz Quartet.

(7) Especially late at night, I enjoy turning on the radio to catch a show or two. (8) I also enjoy going downtown to a club to hear live music. (9) Recently I spent a lovely Sunday eating lunch while being entertained by a group of excellent young artists. (10) They were just beginning to make a name for themselves. (11) Their playing was very exciting. (12) College radio stations often program an hour or two of jazz daily, and so does several of the local public radio networks.

(13) I have a number of hobbies—playing sports, traveling, and exercising, for example—but my favorite and most relaxing is listening to music. (14) As I suggested earlier, my taste is eclectic; therefore, I sometimes find it hard to choose between jazz and rock and roll, folk, classical, rhythm and blues, and reggae. (15) But when it comes right down to it, jazz is still my favorite type of music.

30. Which of the following is the best way to improve the structure of sentence (2)?

(A) I spent my vacation studying rock and roll, folk, classical, rhythm and blues, and reggae; even a few minutes of punk and heavy metal; and I enjoyed nearly everything I heard; but when all was said and done, the winner was jazz; which I have listened to for many years now, ever since I was a youngster.

(B) I spent my vacation studying rock and roll, folk, classical, rhythm and blues, and reggae, even a few minutes of punk and heavy metal and I enjoyed nearly everything I heard, but when all was said and done, the winner was jazz, which I have listened to for many years now ever since I was a youngster.

(C) I spent my vacation studying rock and roll, folk, classical, rhythm and blues, and reggae I even listened to a few minutes of punk and heavy metal; and I enjoyed nearly everything I heard; but when all was said and done the winner was jazz; I have listened to it for many years now ever since I was a youngster.

(D) I spent my vacation studying rock and roll, folk, classical, rhythm and blues and reggae, punk and heavy metal, and I enjoyed nearly everything I heard, but when all was said and done, the winner was jazz, which I have listened to for many years now, since I was a youngster.

(E) I spent my vacation studying rock and roll, folk, classical, rhythm and blues, reggae, and even a few minutes of punk and heavy metal. I enjoyed nearly everything I heard, but when all was said and done, the winner was jazz, which I have listened to for many years now, ever since I was a youngster.

31. Which of the following would be the best way to improve the first paragraph?

(A) Add and develop one or two examples.

(B) Eliminate one or two examples.

(C) Revise to eliminate clichés and be more concise.

(D) Correct spelling errors.

(E) Add a thesis statement.

32. The second paragraph should be revised in order to

(A) eliminate the inappropriate analogy.

(B) improve the organization.

(C) make the tone more consistent.

(D) make the vocabulary more sophisticated.

(E) discuss the tunes played by the young artists.

33. Which of the following is the best way to combine sentences (9) and (10)?

(A) While being entertained at lunch by a group of young artists who were just beginning to make a name for themselves.

(B) Recently I spent a lovely Sunday eating lunch while being entertained by a group of excellent young artists who were just beginning to make a name for themselves.

(C) Recently at Sunday lunch, a group of young artists entertained me, beginning to make a name for themselves.

(D) A group of young artists entertained me recently at lunch beginning to make a name for themselves.

(E) While at lunch recently, a group of young artists making a name for themselves entertained me.

34. Which of the following is the best way to revise the underlined portion of sentence (12) below?

College radio stations often program an hour or two of jazz daily, and so does several of the local public radio networks.

(A) daily; and so does several of the local public radio networks.

(B) daily; as well as several of the local public radio networks.

(C) daily, as well as several of the local public radio networks.

(D) daily, and so do several of the local public radio networks.

(E) on a daily basis, and so does several of the local public radio networks.

35. Which of the following is the best revision of the underlined portion of sentence (14) below?

As I suggested earlier, my taste is eclectic; therefore, I sometimes find it hard to choose between jazz, rock and roll, folk, classical, rhythm and blues, and reggae.

(A) my taste is eclectic; therefore, I sometimes find it hard to choose among

(B) my tastes are eclectic; therefore I sometimes find it hard to choose between

(C) my taste is eclectic, therefore, I sometimes find it hard to choose among

(D) my taste is eclectic, so I sometimes find it hard to choose between

(E) since my taste is eclectic, therefore I sometimes find it hard to choose between

STOP

END OF SECTION 4. IF YOU HAVE ANY TIME LEFT, GO OVER YOUR WORK IN THIS SECTION ONLY. DO NOT WORK IN ANY OTHER SECTION OF THE TEST.

Section 5

20 Questions • 25 Minutes

Directions: Solve the following problems using any available space on the page for scratchwork. On your answer sheet fill in the choice that best corresponds to the correct answer.

Notes: The figures accompanying the problems are drawn as accurately as possible unless otherwise stated in specific problems. Again, unless otherwise stated, all figures lie in the same plane. All numbers used in these problems are real numbers. Calculators are permitted for this test.

Reference Information

Circle: $C = 2\pi r$, $A = \pi r^2$
Rectangle: $A = lw$
Rectangular Solid: $V = lwh$
Cylinder: $V = \pi r^2 h$
Triangle: $A = \frac{1}{2}bh$, $a^2 + b^2 = c^2$

The number of degrees of arc in a circle is 360.
The measure in degrees of a straight angle is 180.
The sum of the measures in degrees of the angles of a triangle is 180.

1. The average temperatures for five days were 82°, 86°, 91°, 79°, and 91°. What is the mode for these temperatures?
   (A) 79°
   (B) 82°
   (C) 85.8°
   (D) 86°
   (E) 91°

2. If $-2x + 5 = 2 - (5 - 2x)$, what is the value of x?
   (A) -2
   (B) $\frac{1}{2}$
   (C) 2
   (D) 3
   (E) 5

3. What is the value of $3\left(\frac{81}{16}\right)^{-\frac{3}{4}}$?
   (A) $\frac{8}{27}$
   (B) $\frac{3}{4}$
   (C) $\frac{8}{9}$
   (D) $\frac{9}{8}$
   (E) $\frac{4}{3}$

4. What is the sum of the solutions of the equation $|2x - 7| = 11$?
   (A) -9
   (B) -7
   (C) 5
   (D) 7
   (E) 9

5. What is the slope of the line that contains the points $(-6,-5)$ and $(-2,7)$?
   (A) -3
   (B) $-\dfrac{1}{3}$
   (C) 0
   (D) $\dfrac{1}{3}$
   (E) 3

6. Nine playing cards from the same deck are placed as shown in the figure below to form a large rectangle of area 180 sq. in. How many inches are there in the perimeter of this large rectangle?

   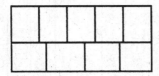

   (A) 29
   (B) 58
   (C) 64
   (D) 116
   (E) 210

7. If each of the dimensions of a rectangle is increased 100%, the area is increased
   (A) 100%.
   (B) 200%.
   (C) 300%.
   (D) 400%.
   (E) 500%.

8. A recipe for a cake calls for $2\dfrac{1}{2}$ cups of milk and 3 cups of flour. With this recipe, a cake was baked using 14 cups of flour. How many cups of milk were required?
   (A) $10\dfrac{1}{3}$
   (B) $10\dfrac{3}{4}$
   (C) 11
   (D) $11\dfrac{3}{5}$
   (E) $11\dfrac{2}{3}$

9. In the figure below, M and N are midpoints of the sides PR and PQ, respectively, of $\triangle PQR$. What is the ratio of the area of $\triangle MNS$ to that of $\triangle PQR$?

   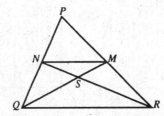

   (A) 2:5
   (B) 2:9
   (C) 1:4
   (D) 1:8
   (E) 1:12

10. What is 10% of $\dfrac{1}{3}x$, if $\dfrac{2}{3}x$ is 10% of 60?
    (A) 0.1
    (B) 0.2
    (C) 0.3
    (D) 0.4
    (E) 0.5

Student-Produced Response Questions

Directions: Solve each of these problems. Write the answer in the corresponding grid on the answer sheet and fill in the ovals beneath each answer you write. Here are some examples.

Answer: $\frac{3}{4} = .75$; show answer either way   **Answer: 325**

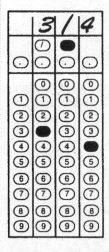 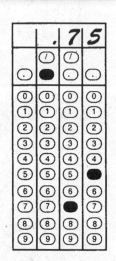 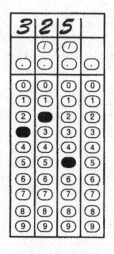 

Note: A mixed number such as $3\frac{1}{2}$ must be gridded as 7/2 or as 3.5. If gridded as "3 1/2," it will be read as "thirty-one halves."

Note: Either position is correct.

11. In the figure below, $BA \perp AD$ and $CD \perp AD$. Using the values indicated in the figure, what is the area of polygon $ABCD$?

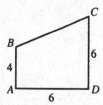

12. In the figure below, $AC = BC$. If m$\angle B =$ 50°, what is the measure of $\angle ECD$? (Do not grid the degree symbol.)

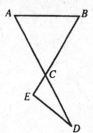

13. What is the value of $-m^2 n^3$, when $m = -2$ and $n = -1$?

14. Given a square, a rectangle, a trapezoid, and a circle, if one of these figures is selected at random, what is the probability that the figure has four right angles?

15. Given the concentric circles below, if radius JN is 3 times JU, then the ratio of the shaded area to the area of sector NJL is 1:b. What is the value of b?

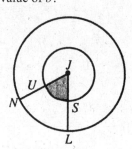

16. In a 3-hour examination of 350 questions, there are 50 mathematical problems. If twice as much time should be allowed for each mathematical problem as for each of the other questions, how many minutes should be spent on the mathematical problems?

17. In a pantry there are 28 cans of vegetables. Eight of these have labels with white lettering, 18 have labels with green lettering, and 8 have labels with neither white nor green lettering. How many cans have both white and green lettering?

18. B, C, and D divide $\overline{AE}$ into 4 equal parts. $\overline{AB}$, $\overline{BC}$, and $\overline{CD}$ are divided into 4 equal parts as shown. $\overline{DE}$ is divided into 3 equal parts as shown.

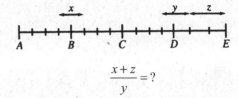

$$\frac{x+z}{y} = ?$$

19. How many 5-digit odd numbers can be formed from the digits 1, 2, 4, 6, and 8, if each digit can only be used once?

20. If $f(x) = 5x + 12$, what is the value of $f(p + 3) - f(p)$?

STOP

END OF SECTION 5. IF YOU HAVE ANY TIME LEFT, GO OVER YOUR WORK IN THIS SECTION ONLY. DO NOT WORK IN ANY OTHER SECTION OF THE TEST.

Section 6

26 Questions • 25 Minutes

Directions: Each of the following questions consists of an incomplete sentence followed by five words or pairs of words. Choose that word or pair of words that, when substituted for the blank space or spaces, best completes the meaning of the sentence and mark the letter of your choice on your answer sheet.

In view of the extenuating circumstances and the defendant's youth, the judge recommended ____.

(A) conviction

(B) a defense

(C) a mistrial

(D) leniency

(E) life imprisonment

The correct answer is (D).

1. He dashed into the house, ran for the phone, and answered ____, tripping over the cord.
   (A) hesitantly
   (B) nobly
   (C) soothingly
   (D) distantly
   (E) breathlessly

2. The criminal record of the witness caused the jury to ____ his testimony.
   (A) affirm
   (B) belie
   (C) retract
   (D) acquit
   (E) discredit

3. Although the storm left the family ____, it could not ____ their spirits.
   (A) discordant .. raise
   (B) moribund .. drench
   (C) destitute .. dampen
   (D) sodden .. excite
   (E) indolent .. inhibit

4. By a stroke of luck the troops ____, avoiding a crushing ____.
   (A) converged .. blow
   (B) prevailed .. defeat
   (C) diverged .. siege
   (D) retrenched .. retreat
   (E) interceded .. assault

5. You must act with ____ if you want to buy your airline ticket before tomorrow's price increase.
   (A) celerity
   (B) clemency
   (C) facility
   (D) lassitude
   (E) laxity

6. The ____ background music hinted of the dangers threatening the movie's heroine.
   (A) trenchant
   (B) ebullient
   (C) sardonic
   (D) portentous
   (E) precocious

7. Nineteenth-century advances in women's rights were gradual and ____; years might separate one advance from the next.

   (A) reticent
   (B) onerous
   (C) incumbent
   (D) docile
   (E) sporadic

8. Since several offices have been ____ across the street, the old directory is now ____.

   (A) refurbished .. adequate
   (B) relocated .. obsolete
   (C) deployed .. reserved
   (D) transmuted .. oblivious
   (E) removed .. upgraded

Directions: The reading passage below is followed by a set of questions. Read the passage and answer the accompanying questions, basing your answers on what is stated or implied in the passage. Mark the letter of your choice on your answer sheet.

QUESTIONS 9 AND 10 ARE BASED ON THE FOLLOWING PASSAGE.

Samuel Gompers (1850–1924) is credited with building the American Federation of Labor (AFL) into the influential organization it became. Gompers was the son of poor
5 Jewish immigrants. A cigar maker by trade, he was elected to the presidency of the Cigar Makers Union Local 144 in 1885. The following year he was elected to the legislative committee of the Federation of Organized
10 Trades and Labor Councils. Gompers spearheaded the reconstitution and renaming of the organization as the American Federation of Labor. With the exception of 1895, Gompers served as president until his death.
15 He focused the AFL on collective bargaining and the passage of legislation affecting jobs and working conditions.

9. The last line of the passage

   (A) explains why Gompers is considered so important.
   (B) describes the work of the AFL.
   (C) describes the goals of the AFL.
   (D) is the author's opinion.
   (E) describes Gompers's influence on the AFL.

10. The word *reconstitution* (line 11) means

    (A) made healthy again.
    (B) a new legal document.
    (C) rewrite a legal document.
    (D) a rebuilding.
    (E) a restoring.

QUESTIONS 11 AND 12 ARE BASED ON THE FOLLOWING PASSAGE.

Berthe Morisot was one of the early Impressionist painters. She showed her work in the Paris exhibition in 1874 that gained the movement its name. Her work hung
5 alongside that of Monet, Degas, Renoir, and Pissaro. Most critics, however, were kind neither to the group as a whole nor to individual artists. One critic wrote of Morisot's work, "That young lady is not
10 interested in reproducing trifling details. When she has a hand to paint, she makes exactly as many brushstrokes lengthwise as there are fingers, and the business is done. Stupid people who are finicky about the
15 drawing of a hand don't understand a thing about Impressionism. . . ."

11. The tone of the art critic is

    (A) sarcastic.
    (B) condescending.
    (C) appreciative.
    (D) humorous.
    (E) detached.

12. The word *finicky* (line 14) most probably means

(A) unknowing.

(B) fastidious.

(C) uncomprehending.

(D) ignorant.

(E) unaware.

QUESTIONS 13 AND 14 ARE BASED ON THE FOLLOWING PASSAGE.

[W]hen I became President . . . the idea that our natural resources were inexhaustible still obtained, and there was yet no real knowledge of their extent and condition.
5 The relation of the conservation of natural resource to the problems of National welfare and National efficiency had not yet dawned on the public mind. The reclamation of arid public lands in the West was still a matter for
10 private enterprise alone; and our magnificent river system, with its superb possibilities for public usefulness, was dealt with by the National Government not as a unit, but as a disconnected series of pork-barrel
15 problems . . .

—President Theodore Roosevelt

13. What does the author mean when he writes "the idea that our natural resources were inexhaustible still obtained" (lines 1–3)?

(A) Natural resources were easily gotten.

(B) People thought that natural resources could be easily gotten.

(C) People liked the idea that natural resources were easily gotten

(D) People still believed that natural resources were limitless.

(E) Natural resources were limitless.

14. The author is making a connection between

(A) national welfare and national efficiency.

(B) conservation and reclamation.

(C) conservation and the national good.

(D) natural resources and reclamation.

(E) public usefulness and pork-barrel projects.

QUESTIONS 15–26 ARE BASED ON THE FOLLOWING PASSAGE.

A major step forward in the history of the novel, Don Quixote *was penned by Miguel de Cervantes and first published in Spain in 1605. Driven mad by his constant perusal of tales of chivalry, Alonso Quijano changes his name to Don Quixote and rides off to seek adventure. This passage describes his first expedition.*

Once these preparations were completed, he was anxious to wait no longer before putting his ideas into effect, impelled to this by the thought of the loss the world suffered by
5 his delay, seeing the grievances there were to redress, the wrongs to right, the injuries to amend, and the debts to discharge. So, telling nobody of his intentions, and quite unobserved, one morning before dawn—it
10 was on one of those sweltering July days—he armed himself completely, mounted Rocinante, put on his badly-mended headpiece, slung on his shield, seized his lance and went out into the plain through the back gate of
15 his yard, pleased and delighted to see with what ease he had started on his fair design. But scarcely was he in open country when he was assailed by a thought so terrible that it almost made him abandon the enterprise
20 he had just begun. For he suddenly remembered that he had never received the honor of knighthood, and so, according to the laws of chivalry, he neither could nor should take arms against any knight, and even if he had
25 been knighted he was bound, as a novice, to wear plain armor without a device on his shield until he should gain one by his prowess. These reflections made him waver in his resolve, but as his madness outweighed
30 any other argument, he made up his mind to have himself knighted by the first man he met, in imitation of many who had done the same, as he had read in the books which had so influenced him. As to plain armor,
35 he decided to clean his own, when he had time, till it was whiter than ermine. With this he quieted his mind and went on his way, taking whatever road his horse chose, in the belief that in this lay the essence of
40 adventure.

As our brand-new adventurer journeyed
along, he talked to himself, saying: "Who
can doubt that in ages to come, when the
authentic story of my famous deeds comes to
45 light, the sage who writes of them will say,
when he comes to tell of my first expedition
so early in the morning: 'Scarce had the
ruddy Apollo spread the golden threads of
his lovely hair over the broad and spacious
50 face of the earth, and scarcely had the forked
tongues of the little painted birds greeted
with mellifluous harmony the coming of
the rosy Aurora who, leaving the soft bed
of her jealous husband, showed herself at
55 the doors and balconies of the Manchegan
horizon, when the famous knight, Don
Quixote de la Mancha, quitting the slothful
down, mounted his famous steed Rocinante
and began to journey across the ancient and
60 celebrated plain of Montiel'?" That was, in
fact, the road that our knight actually took, as
he went on: "Fortunate the age and fortunate
the times in which my famous deeds will
come to light, deeds worthy to be engraved
65 in bronze, carved in marble and painted on
wood, as a memorial for posterity. And you,
sage enchanter, whoever you may be, to
whose lot it falls to be the chronicler of this
strange history, I beg you not to forget my
70 good Rocinante, my constant companion on
all my rides and journeys!" And presently
he cried again, as if he had really been in
love: "O Princess Dulcinea, mistress of
this captive heart! You did me great injury
75 in dismissing me and inflicting on me the
cruel rigour of your command not to appear
in your beauteous presence. Deign, lady,
to be mindful of your captive heart, which
suffers such griefs for love of you."

80 He went on stringing other nonsense on to
this, all after the fashion he had learnt in his
reading, and imitating the language of his
books as best he could. And all the while he
rode so slowly and the sun's heat increased
85 so fast that it would have been enough to
turn his brain, if he had had any.

15. The word *redress* in line 6 most nearly
means to
(A) locate a residence.
(B) put on clothes.
(C) downplay.
(D) correct.
(E) confuse.

16. As described in lines 20–28, Don Quixote
was hesitant to fight because he
(A) was afraid for his life.
(B) didn't believe in violence.
(C) would break the established code of
chivalry.
(D) would lose his wife if he fought for
what he truly believed.
(E) was indifferent to the cause.

17. The word *device* in line 26 probably means
(A) emblem.
(B) tool.
(C) gadget.
(D) trick.
(E) metal.

18. The words that best describe the first speech
Cervantes has Don Quixote make (lines
42–60) are
(A) informative and deliberate.
(B) profound and resolute.
(C) dull and ill-conceived.
(D) shocking and defamatory.
(E) flowery and overwrought.

19. What does Don Quixote mean when he says
"quitting the slothful down" (lines 57–58)?
(A) Leaving the farm
(B) Climbing into the saddle
(C) Feeling happier and more energetic
(D) Recovering from illness
(E) Getting out of bed

20. The phrase "as if he had really been in love" (lines 72–73) is used to illuminate Don Quixote's

    (A) need for attention.
    (B) starved spirit.
    (C) dementia.
    (D) unhappy childhood.
    (E) inability to emote.

21. Cervantes has his hero address his remarks to

    (A) God.
    (B) the reader.
    (C) his horse.
    (D) a mythical historian and a princess.
    (E) an unknown knight.

22. The last line of the selection reminds us that

    (A) the story takes place in Spain.
    (B) Don Quixote is mad.
    (C) Rocinante has no destination in mind.
    (D) other knights have taken this same route.
    (E) the long day is about to end.

23. We first suspect that Don Quixote is not quite the hero he seems when he recalls that

    (A) he left his armor at home.
    (B) his horse is named Rocinante.
    (C) he is not a real knight.
    (D) Dulcinea holds him captive.
    (E) he started his journey with ease.

24. According to the author, Don Quixote's speech is affected by

    (A) romantic books he has read.
    (B) the language of seventeenth-century Spain.
    (C) letters received from Dulcinea.
    (D) the speeches of Alfonso X.
    (E) his night visions.

25. Cervantes's opinion of the literature of his day seems to be that it is

    (A) written by madmen.
    (B) argumentative and controversial.
    (C) not up to the standards of the previous century.
    (D) sentimental drivel.
    (E) derivative.

26. The best word to describe Cervantes's feeling toward his hero might be

    (A) disdainful.
    (B) revolted.
    (C) indifferent.
    (D) mocking.
    (E) appreciative.

STOP

END OF SECTION 6. IF YOU HAVE ANY TIME LEFT, GO OVER YOUR WORK IN THIS SECTION ONLY. DO NOT WORK IN ANY OTHER SECTION OF THE TEST.

Section 7

15 Questions • 20 Minutes

Directions: Solve the following problems using any available space on the page for scratchwork. On your answer sheet fill in the choice that best corresponds to the correct answer.

Notes: The figures accompanying the problems are drawn as accurately as possible unless otherwise stated in specific problems. Again, unless otherwise stated, all figures lie in the same plane. All numbers used in these problems are real numbers. Calculators are permitted for this test.

Reference Information

Circle:
$C = 2\pi r$
$A = \pi r^2$

Rectangle:
$A = lw$

Rectangular Solid:
$V = lwh$

Cylinder:
$V = \pi r^2 h$

Triangle:
$A = \frac{1}{2}bh$

$a^2 + b^2 = c^2$

The number of degrees of arc in a circle is 360.
The measure in degrees of a straight angle is 180.
The sum of the measures in degrees of the angles of a triangle is 180.

1. What is the total savings in purchasing thirty 13-cent lollipops for a class party at a reduced rate of $1.38 per dozen?

   (A) $0.35
   (B) $0.38
   (C) $0.40
   (D) $0.45
   (E) $0.50

2. A gallon of water is equal to 231 cubic inches. How many gallons of water are needed to fill a fish tank that measures 11" high, 14" long, and 9" wide?

   (A) 6
   (B) 8
   (C) 9
   (D) 14
   (E) 16

3. The area of a right triangle is 12 square inches. The ratio of its legs is 2:3. Find the number of inches in the hypotenuse of this triangle.

   (A) $\sqrt{13}$
   (B) $\sqrt{26}$
   (C) $3\sqrt{13}$
   (D) $2\sqrt{13}$
   (E) $4\sqrt{13}$

4. A rectangular solid block of metal weighs 3 ounces. How many pounds will a similar block of the same metal weigh if the edges are twice as long?

(A) $\dfrac{3}{8}$

(B) $\dfrac{3}{4}$

(C) $1\dfrac{1}{2}$

(D) 3

(E) 24

5. A college graduate goes to work for x dollars per week. After several months, the company gives all the employees a 10% pay cut. A few months later, the company gives all the employees a 10% raise. What is the college graduate's new salary?

(A) $0.90x$
(B) $0.99x$
(C) x
(D) $1.01x$
(E) $1.11x$

6. What is the net amount of a bill of $428 after a discount of 6% has been allowed?

(A) $432.62
(B) $430.88
(C) $414.85
(D) $412.19
(E) $402.32

7. A certain type of board is sold only in lengths of multiples of 2 feet, from 6 feet to 24 feet. A builder needs a larger quantity of this type of board in $5\dfrac{1}{2}$-foot lengths. For minimum waste, the lengths in feet to be ordered should be

(A) 6
(B) 12
(C) 18
(D) 22
(E) 24

8. A cube has an edge that is 4 inches long. If the edge is increased by 25%, then the volume is increased by approximately

(A) 25%.
(B) 48%.
(C) 73%.
(D) 95%.
(E) 122%.

9. The ratio of $\dfrac{1}{4}$ to $\dfrac{3}{5}$ is

(A) 1 to 3.
(B) 3 to 20.
(C) 5 to 12.
(D) 3 to 4.
(E) 5 to 4.

10. Which of the following numbers is the smallest?

(A) $\sqrt{3}$

(B) $\dfrac{1}{\sqrt{3}}$

(C) $\dfrac{\sqrt{3}}{3}$

(D) $\dfrac{1}{3}$

(E) $\dfrac{1}{3\sqrt{3}}$

11. The radius of a circle that has a circumference equal to the perimeter of a hexagon whose sides are each 22 inches long is closest in length to which of the following?

(A) 7
(B) 14
(C) 21
(D) 24
(E) 28

12. In the first year of the U.S. Stickball League, the Bayonne Bombers won 50% of their games. During the second season of the league, the Bombers won 65% of their games. If there were twice as many games played in the second season as in the first, what percentage of the games did the Bombers win in the first two years of the league?

(A) 115%

(B) 60%

(C) 57.5%

(D) 55%

(E) It cannot be determined from the information given.

13. If the total weight of an apple is $\frac{4}{5}$ of its weight plus $\frac{4}{5}$ of an ounce, what is its weight in ounces?

(A) $1\frac{3}{5}$

(B) $3\frac{1}{2}$

(C) 4

(D) $4\frac{4}{5}$

(E) 5

14. At which point does the graph of the function $J(x) = 6x - 18$ cross the x-axis?

(A) $(3,0)$

(B) $(0,3)$

(C) $(\frac{1}{3},0)$

(D) $(0,\frac{1}{3})$

(E) $(-18,0)$

15. What is the domain of the function $h(x) = \frac{5x+15}{x^2+1}$?

(A) All real numbers except -3

(B) All real numbers except -1

(C) All real numbers except -1 and 1

(D) All real numbers except -3 and -1

(E) All real numbers

STOP

END OF SECTION 7. IF YOU HAVE ANY TIME LEFT, GO OVER YOUR WORK IN THIS SECTION ONLY. DO NOT WORK IN ANY OTHER SECTION OF THE TEST.

Section 8

16 Questions • 20 Minutes

Directions: The two passages given below deal with a related topic. Following the passages are questions about the content of each passage or about the relationship between the two passages. Answer the questions based upon what is stated or implied in the passages and in any introductory material provided. Mark the letter of your choice on your answer sheet.

Questions 1–4 Are Based On The Following Passages.

The following two passages represent two views of global warming.

Passage 1

It is very likely that the U.S. will get substantially warmer. Temperatures are projected to rise more rapidly in the next 100 years than in the last 10,000 years. It is also likely
5   that there will be more precipitation overall, with more of it coming in heavy downpours. In spite of this, some areas are likely to get drier as increased evaporation due to higher temperatures outpaces increased precipi-
10 tation. Droughts and flash floods are likely to become more frequent and intense. . . . It is likely that rising temperatures will cause further permafrost thawing, damaging roads, buildings, and forests in Alaska.

—Report of the National Assessment Synthesis Team

Passage 2

[The global-warming] hypothesis predicts that global temperatures will rise significantly, indeed catastrophically, if atmospheric carbon dioxide rises. Most of
5   the increase in atmospheric carbon dioxide has occurred during the past 50 years, and the increase has continued during the past 20 years. Yet there has been no significant increase in atmospheric temperature during
10 those 50 years and during the 20 years with the highest carbon dioxide levels, temperatures have decreased. . . . So we needn't worry about human use of hydrocarbons warming the earth. We also needn't worry
15 about environmental calamities, even if the current, natural warming trend continues:

After all the earth has been much warmer during the past 3,000 years. . . .

—Arthur B. Robinson and Zachary W. Robinson, "Global Warming Is a Myth"

1. The most appropriate title for Passage 1 would be
   (A) "Global Warming: An Important Issue"
   (B) "What Global Warming?"
   (C) "Attempts at Understanding Global Warming"
   (D) "Effects of Global Warming on the Environment"
   (E) "Global Warming and Temperatures"

2. The tone of Passage 1 is
   (A) evocative.
   (B) lyrical.
   (C) sentimental.
   (D) direct.
   (E) factual.

3. The purpose of Passage 2 appears to be to
   (A) set the record straight about the global warming crisis.
   (B) ridicule those who believe in global warming.
   (C) refute the idea that car emissions contribute to global warming.
   (D) argue each point about the impact of global warming.
   (E) attack conservationists.

4. In comparison with Passage 1, the authors of Passage 2

(A) use few facts to bolster their argument.

(B) use broad generalizations.

(C) use hypotheses rather than proven evidence.

(D) base their argument on faulty evidence.

(E) base their argument on what has happened rather than on what may happen.

QUESTIONS 5–16 ARE BASED ON THE FOLLOWING PASSAGES.

The struggle of African Americans to make economic and political progress within the socioeconomic structure of the United States has been long and filled with setbacks. These two passages document some of the events in that long struggle and seek to explain why the struggle was so difficult.

Passage 1—The Economic Scene

Because of slavery, which lasted until 1865, and undereducation, African Americans have been at a disadvantage in terms of socioeconomic progress until well into the
5 twentieth century. Segregated schools were often not on a par with the schools in which whites were educated; consequently, when African Americans competed for jobs with whites, they often found they could not.

10 Increased opportunities for African Americans followed in the wake of the civil rights movement, and as a result, African Americans were able to gain higher levels of education and achieve more managerial
15 positions within the various professions. In the 1980s, African Americans moved into the upper middle class in large numbers.

Consistently in the last five decades, African Americans have moved into higher-status
20 jobs, have opened their own businesses, and have increased their levels of education. Because of such progress, it is safe to assume that those African Americans who

have become upwardly mobile would not
25 be able to tolerate racial discrimination as it existed prior to the civil rights movement.

While progress has been made in some segments of the African American population, less progress has occurred among
30 low-income African Americans. Many low-income African Americans do not have a place in the class structure because of racial segregation and poverty, particularly in urban areas. When segregation and poverty
35 prevail, urban neighborhoods become places of high crime, poor schools, and poorly maintained homes.

Thus, what has emerged in the 1990s is a widening socioeconomic gap between low-
40 income African Americans and the African Americans who have been able to improve their socioeconomic status.

Passage 2—The Political Scene

Only with the enforcement of the Reconstruction Act of 1867 and the ratification of the Fifteenth Amendment to the Constitution did African Americans first win
5 seats in Congress. Hiram Revels of Mississippi became the first African American to serve in Congress when he took his seat in the Senate on February 25, 1870. Joseph Rainey of South Carolina became the first
10 African American member of the House of Representatives later in 1870.

African Americans throughout the South became politically active soon after emancipation and the close of the Civil
15 War. A generation of African American leaders emerged who nearly unanimously adhered to the Republican Party because it had championed the rights of African Americans. African Americans elected to
20 Congress during Reconstruction found the national legislature an effective forum for the advocacy of political equality. Following the end of federal Reconstruction in 1877, African Americans continued to win election
25 to Congress, and carried on the struggle for civil rights and economic opportunity.

During the 1890s and early 1900s, no African American won election to Congress, in part because of restrictive state election codes

30 in some southern states. During World War
I and in the following decade, however,
African American migration to northern
cities established the foundations for
political organization in urban centers. Over
35 the next three decades African Americans
won congressional seats in New York City,
Detroit, and Philadelphia. In the wake of the
civil rights movement and the enforcement
of the Voting Rights Act of 1965, African
40 Americans regained seats in the South. Since
the 1930s, nearly all African American representatives have been Democrats.

Since the nineteenth century, African-
American members of Congress have served
45 as advocates for all African Americans
as well as representatives for their constituencies. During Reconstruction and the
late nineteenth century, African American
representatives called on their colleagues
50 to protect the voting rights of African
Americans. They also called for expanded
educational opportunities and land grants
for freed African Americans. In the mid-
twentieth century, African American rep-
55 resentatives turned to the needs of urban
communities and urged federal programs for
improved housing and job training. These
representatives served as defenders of the
civil rights movement and proponents of
60 legislation to end segregation. The Congressional Black Caucus demonstrated a special
concern for the protection of civil rights; the
guarantee of equal opportunity in education,
employment, and housing; and a broad array
65 of foreign and domestic policy issues.

Since the victories of the civil rights
movement in the 1960s, African American
men and women have won election to Congress from increasingly diverse regions of
70 the country. Whether from largely urban
districts, suburban areas, or more recently
from rural Mississippi, these members of
Congress have maintained their common
concern with economic issues that affect
75 African Americans with the protection of
civil rights.

The collected biographies of African
Americans who served in the House and
Senate provide an important perspective

80 on the history of the Congress and the role
of African Americans in American politics.
Their stories offer eloquent testimony to
the long struggle to extend the ideals of
the founders to encompass all citizens of
85 the United States.

5. The author's attitude in Passage 1 is primarily one of

(A) complete detachment.

(B) unbridled outrage.

(C) indifference.

(D) disinterest.

(E) objectivity.

6. Passage 1 indicates that socioeconomic
progress for African Americans has been
slow because of

(A) prejudice.

(B) insurmountable poverty.

(C) slavery and undereducation.

(D) generally slow economic progress in
the United States.

(E) immigrants from Central America.

7. The phrase "on a par" (Passage 1, line 6)
means

(A) in the same location.

(B) at odds with.

(C) in competition with.

(D) on the same level.

(E) on a different level.

8. According to Passage 1, African Americans
have done all of the following in the last five
decades EXCEPT

(A) move into higher-status jobs.

(B) open their own businesses.

(C) tolerate more racial discrimination.

(D) achieve more managerial positions.

(E) increase their level of education.

Section 9

15 Questions • 10 Minutes

Directions: The sentences below may contain problems in grammar, usage, word choice, sentence construction, or punctuation. Part or all of each sentence is underlined. Following each sentence you will find five ways of expressing the underlined part. Answer choice (A) always repeats the original underlined section. The other four answer choices are all different. You are to select the lettered answer that produces the most effective sentence. If you think the original sentence is best, choose (A) as your answer. If one of the other choices makes a better sentence, mark your answer sheet for the letter of that choice. Do not choose an answer that changes the meaning of the original sentence.

I have always enjoyed singing as well as to dance.

(A) singing as well as to dance

(B) singing as well as dancing

(C) to sing as well as dancing

(D) singing in addition to dance

(E) to sing in addition to dancing

The correct answer is (B).

1. Although her parents, naturally, were worried, they did not try and dissuade her.
   (A) did not try and dissuade
   (B) didn't try and dissuade
   (C) tried not dissuading
   (D) did not try to dissuade
   (E) do not try and dissuade

2. Critics agree that Keats poetry is among the most beautiful in the English language.
   (A) Critics agree that Keats poetry
   (B) Critic's agree that Keats poetry
   (C) Critics agree that Keat's poetry
   (D) Critics agree that Keats' poetry
   (E) Critics' agree that Keats' poetry

3. She was the singer, I was told, whom won the grand prize at the talent show.
   (A) whom won the grand prize
   (B) which won the grand prize
   (C) of whom won the grand prize
   (D) whosoever won the grand prize
   (E) who won the grand prize

4. The data are not sufficient to require an investigation.
   (A) The data are not sufficient to require
   (B) The data is not sufficient to require
   (C) The data is not sufficient for requiring
   (D) The data are not, sufficient for the requiring of
   (E) The data is not enough to require

5. The material was highly inflammable, we were advised to use extreme caution.
   (A) highly inflammable, we were advised
   (B) not highly inflammable and so we were advised
   (C) highly flammable, advising us
   (D) greatly flammable, we were advised
   (E) highly inflammable, and so we were advised

6. The instructor entered the auditorium, glanced angrily about the room, and then strides up to the podium.

   (A) and then strides up to
   (B) striding up to
   (C) and then strode up to
   (D) afterward he strode on
   (E) in which he strode up to

7. If a person wants to be well educated, they must be prepared to devote many hours to reading and studying.

   (A) If a person wants to be well educated, they
   (B) If a person wants to be well educated, one
   (C) When a person wants an education, they
   (D) A person who wants to be well educated
   (E) A person who wants to be well educated, he

8. The meeting degenerated into a heated argument about economical conditions throughout the world.

   (A) economical conditions throughout the world
   (B) worldwide economic conditions
   (C) economics conditions of the world
   (D) economy condition throughout the world
   (E) economical conditions worldwide

9. The door had barely slammed behind me when I began to regret that we quarreled.

   (A) when I began to regret that we quarreled.
   (B) before I began to regret that we quarreled.
   (C) before I begun to regret that we quarreled.
   (D) when I had began to regret that we quarreled.
   (E) when I began to regret that we had quarreled.

10. They had not been informed of the length of the program or of how much it would cost.

   (A) of how much it would cost.
   (B) of what it would cost.
   (C) of the cost.
   (D) of how much it cost.
   (E) that it would cost to attend.

11. Please check her background to see whether she is capable to do whatever is necessary to assure the success of the project.

   (A) whether she is capable to do whatever
   (B) whether she is capable of doing whatever
   (C) if she is capable to do whatever
   (D) whether or not she is capable to do whatever
   (E) whether it is possible for her to be capable to do

12. Both Mr. Blake and his son had been invited to the opening, but he was unable to attend on such short notice.

   (A) he was unable to attend
   (B) he was not able to attend
   (C) attendance was out of the question
   (D) Mr. Blake was unable to attend
   (E) he found it impossible to attend

13. When the stores were having a half-price sale. it was nearly impossible to get a parking space in the shopping center.

   (A) When the stores were having a half-price sale,

   (B) When the stores have a half-price sale,

   (C) Although the stores were having a half-price sale,

   (D) If the stores were having a half-price sale,

   (E) If the stores have a half-price sale,

14. "Loan them your car, so they can go to the game with us," Dad said.

   (A) "Loan them your car, so they can go

   (B) "Loan them your car; so they can go

   (C) "Loan them your car. So they can go

   (D) "Lend them your car, so they can go

   (E) "Lend them your car: they can go

15. They would prefer to go to the stadium regardless of the weather than watching the game on television.

   (A) regardless of the weather than watching the game

   (B) irregardless of the weather than watching the game

   (C) irregardless of the weather than to watch the game

   (D) regardless of the weather then to watch the game

   (E) regardless of the weather than to watch the game

STOP

END OF SECTION 9. IF YOU HAVE ANY TIME LEFT, GO OVER YOUR WORK IN THIS SECTION ONLY. DO NOT WORK IN ANY OTHER SECTION OF THE TEST.

ANSWER KEY AND EXPLANATIONS

Section 1: Writing
Sample Essay 1

If you want something, you've got to ask for it, the old saying goes. It's not enough to wait quietly for someone to read your mind and satisfy your desires. Rather it is necessary to speak out and take action, to be the "squeaky hinge" that will get "the grease."

This concept is proven by the actions of a number of groups in our country. For instance, if the civil rights activists of the 1950s and 1960s had not made plenty of noise and demanded satisfaction of their legal rights, who knows how much progress would have been made in the area of human rights by now. Similarly, organizations that feed the homeless or that take care of the poor also must make enough political noise so that they will have access to government funds to continue their good work.

However, making too much noise can have a reverse effect. If the public's perception is that a person or group is complaining too much, or asking for too much, then that group may be acting in a counterproductive manner. So it is important to strike the proper balance.

With all the budgetary cuts on local, state, and federal levels, it is crucial for public interest groups to "squeak" for the "grease." Without attention from media and without money from private individuals or government sources, it is extremely difficult for organizations or agencies to exist and succeed.

Analysis of Essay 1

This is an excellent essay. It focuses clearly upon the topic and does not stray. The organization into four well-defined paragraphs is well handled. Both the first and last paragraphs cleverly make reference to words in the quotation (*squeaky hinge, squeak, grease*) so that the reader is always aware of the citation that is at the heart of the essay.

The punctuation is accurate. The vocabulary is mature. The content is well developed. The writer makes use of appropriate transitional phrases and words (*For instance, however*). The essay takes into account both the positive and negative aspects of the issue and then comes to a strong and valid conclusion. This is a well-written paper.

Sample Essay 2

It just doesn't pay to suffer in silence any more. If you keep still, no one will know you're around or if they do they will not care. If you have a complaint you have to yell or make noise. Then people will hear you and take action.

For example, I remember that my father once told me that he worked in a factory under very poor conditions and everyone felt that their had to be improvement so they went to the boss and gave him a list of there demands. They waited many weeks maybe even months and there was no results. Finally all the men got together and had a sit-in at the plant and they made a lot of noise and then the boss arrange for a meeting and even improved the problems.

Many of us were brought up and told to be polite and not to make trouble. We were told to listen to our parents and obey our teachers. But now we know that there are times when the people in authority can be wrong. Police make mistakes. Innocent people are sent to jail. And parents aren't always right either.

I think that the conclusion we have to come to is that if we want to get any action and make changes in the world or in our living conditions then we have to make a fuss and raise our voices. We see from our study of history and current events that it was only when people went out and took action that they were able to change their society and improve their living conditions because then people had to listen and hear what was said and they were force to take action and make changes.

Analysis of Essay 2

Although the essay shows a sense of organization (there are four paragraphs with a clear introduction and conclusion), there appears to be a lack of specific examples to substantiate arguments. Thus, in the final paragraph, the conclusion reached is that "it was only when people went out and took action that they were able to change their society . . . ." This statement is not followed by a specific example or even a historical allusion. Certainly the illustration of the factory workers in the second paragraph is valid and indicates that the writer is aware of the need for specifics.

There is a problem in tone. The second person "you" is used in the first paragraph and then abandoned. It would be preferable to use a third-person construction throughout the essay. Errors in technical English also detract. Omission of the final "d" in the past tense of verbs (*arrange, force*), errors of agreement (*everyone . . . they*), and spelling errors (*their* for *there*) also hurt the writing.

Section 2

1. B	7. D	12. B	17. B	22. B
2. A	8. B	13. D	18. C	23. A
3. C	9. D	14. A	19. E	24. B
4. C	10. E	15. B	20. A	25. C
5. E	11. B	16. C	21. D	26. A
6. B				

1. **The correct answer is (B).** An "appreciative public" is likely to give the elder Johnson's son *respect*.

2. **The correct answer is (A).** A person who is angry one minute but serene the next is said to be *mercurial* (changeable).

3. **The correct answer is (C).** Irony or paradox is indicated by the phrase "but he thought nothing of." It is ironic that automobile travel should be *harrowing*, or frightening, to someone whose *hobby* was bobsledding, a dangerous sport.

4. **The correct answer is (C).** A perennial flower is one that blooms every year. In the winter it lies *dormant* (inactive), but the following spring it *burgeons* (sprouts) anew.

5. **The correct answer is (E).** A manager who apologizes must be dealing with an *irate* (angry) customer. As a result of the apology, the customer was *mollified* (soothed and pacified).

6. **The correct answer is (B).** Normally, vices are publicly *condemned*. Secret indulgence in them might, however, be hidden by a *sanctimonious* (excessively righteous) manner.

7. **The correct answer is (D).** A flood that destroys people's belongings causes *devastation*. Living conditions in the area can be said to have *deteriorated* (worsened).

8. **The correct answer is (B).** A *perversion* of the truth is a deviation from the truth, or the half-truths and half-lies mentioned in the second half of the sentence.

9. **The correct answer is (D).** As indicated by the word *though*, the sentence requires a contrast. Since the presentation was positive, the blank should be filled by a negative; *worthless* is the best choice to describe a report full of errors.

10. **The correct answer is (E).** Choice (A) is a good distracter if you read the passage too quickly. The qualifier "some" says that not all illegal file sharers are young teens. You need to read the passage quickly but also concentrate on what you are reading.

11. **The correct answer is (B).** Only choice (B) contains both parts of the purpose.

12. **The correct answer is (B).** The tone of the passage tells you the answer: to persuade.

13. **The correct answer is (D).** The word *embeds* is used as a noun. Although choice (A) is close, it does not define a noun but the process.

14. **The correct answer is (A).** Only the first choice explains the subtitle. The other choices may be included under the idea "A Study in Temperament," but they are not the main idea.

15. **The correct answer is (B).** The faculty may be perplexed, choice (A), but the first paragraph focuses on their feeling that Paul's dress and behavior are not properly contrite.

16. **The correct answer is (C).** Paul seems to be unable to control his odd mannerisms, but he is not actually frenzied, as choices (B), (D), or (E) would suggest.

17. **The correct answer is (B).** The faculty "fell upon him without mercy, his English teacher leading the pack" (lines 66–67). The comparison is to a pack of wolves.

18. **The correct answer is (C).** All of these choices could mean "smartness," but only *impudence* makes sense in context.

19. **The correct answer is (E).** There is evidence for every other choice in the descriptions of Paul's actions. The point is made in lines 31–33 that Paul often lies; he cannot be called "candid."

20. **The correct answer is (A).** Paul is physically revolted by the faculty, not vice versa, choice (D). The faculty's attack on Paul indicates their hatred for him.

21. **The correct answer is (D).** Jefferson is "ever sensible" that meeting and attracting the good will of Mr. Wythe was "one of the more fortunate events" of his life (line 7).

22. **The correct answer is (B).** Jefferson says "Our future connections with Spain and Spanish America will render that language a valuable acquisition." (lines 34–36)

23. **The correct answer is (A).** Point 3 is all about the fact that no one needs to study moral philosophy. In other words, to study it is a waste of time.

24. **The correct answer is (B).** Lines 40–44 explain this reasoning.

25. **The correct answer is (C).** Jefferson's point is that either one is as likely to decide a moral argument fairly; morality is bred into everyone and does not require an advanced degree.

26. **The correct answer is (A).** Choices (B), (C), and (D) may be true, but Jefferson only covers the first point, that morality is as natural as an arm or leg, and is given to all "in a stronger or weaker degree" (lines 55–56).

Section 3

1. E	5. C	9. E	13. E	17. E
2. E	6. C	10. A	14. E	18. B
3. C	7. B	11. E	15. D	19. A
4. E	8. D	12. A	16. E	20. A

Note: A 🔲 following a math answer explanation indicates that a calculator could be helpful in solving that particular problem.

1. **The correct answer is (E).** Count the number of decimal places in the terms to be multiplied; this adds up to 6. It should be clear that the last number must be 8.

   There must be six decimal places accounted for and thus there must be five zeros in front of the 8. 🔲

2. **The correct answer is (E).** 20 square yards = 180 square feet. At \$1.30 per square foot, it will cost \$234.00. 🔲

3. **The correct answer is (C).**

   5 ft. 1 in.
   5 ft. 7 in.
   5 ft. 2 in.
   5 ft.
   <u>4 ft. 7 in.</u>
   24 ft. in. , or 25 ft. 5 in.

   Average = 25 ft. 5 in. ÷ 5 = 5 ft. 1 in. 🔲

4. **The correct answer is (E).**
   Let x = first integer
   $x + 2$ = second integer
   $x + 4$ = third integer

   $3(x) = 3 + 2(x + 4)$
   $3x = 3 + 2x + 8$
   $x = +11$

   The third integer is 15.

5. **The correct answer is (C).**
   Area of square = $2^2 = 4$
   Area of circle = $\pi \cdot 1^2 = \pi$
   Difference = $4 - \pi = 4 - 3.14 = 0.86$
   🔲

6. **The correct answer is (C).** The right triangle, of which T is the hypotenuse, has legs that are obviously 6 inches and 9 inches.
   Hence, $T^2 = 6^2 + 9^2$
   $T^2 = 36 + 81 = 117$
   $T = \sqrt{117}$
   or $10 < T = < 11$. 🔲

7. **The correct answer is (B).** $5\frac{1}{2}$ dozen nails are bought for $5\frac{1}{2}$ dozen × 35 cents per dozen = 192.5 cents. There are 66 nails in $5\frac{1}{2}$ dozen and $66 \div 3 = 22$ sets sold at 10 cents per set, so 22 sets × 10 cents per set = 220 cents. The profit is $220 - 192.5 = 27\frac{1}{2}$ cents. 🔲

8. **The correct answer is (D).**
   $2\frac{3}{4} \div \frac{1}{8} = \frac{11}{4} \div \frac{1}{8} = \frac{11}{4} \times 8 = 22$ 🔲

9. **The correct answer is (E).**
   $-x^2 + 2y - (-x - y)$
   $= -x^2 + 2y + x + y$
   $= -x^2 + x + 3y$

10. **The correct answer is (A).**
    Multiply the equation $2^m = 4x$ by 2
    $2(2^m) = 2(4x)$
    $2^{m+1} = 8x = 2^w$
    $\therefore w = m + 1$ and $m = w - 1$

11. **The correct answer is (E).** The reciprocal of $1\frac{1}{4}$ is $\frac{4}{5}$. $\frac{4}{5} - \frac{5}{4} = \frac{16}{20} - \frac{25}{20} = -\frac{9}{20}$. 🔲

12. The correct answer is (A). x yards =

$3x$ feet; y feet = y feet; z inches = $\dfrac{z}{12}$ feet. Therefore,

x yards + y feet + z inches =

$3x$ feet + y feet + $\dfrac{z}{12}$ feet,

or $3x + y + \dfrac{z}{12}$ feet .

13. The correct answer is (E). If a triangle is a right triangle, then the squares of two sides will add up to the square of the hypotenuse. $12^2 = 144$. $15^2 = 225$. $18^2 = 324$. $144 + 225 \neq 324$. ▧

14. The correct answer is (E). By the distributive law, $26 \times 3\dfrac{1}{2} = (26 \times 3) + \left(26 \times \dfrac{1}{2}\right)$. By the distributive law, $26 \times 3 = (20 \times 3) + (6 \times 3)$. Therefore,

$26 \times 3\dfrac{1}{2} = \left(26 \times \dfrac{1}{2}\right) + (20 \times 3) + (6 \times 3)$. ▧

15. The correct answer is (D). Angle T is a right angle. By the Pythagorean theorem, $RT^2 + ST^2 = RS^2$. Since $RS = 12$ and $ST = 8$, RT must

equal $\sqrt{80}$, so, $OT = \dfrac{1}{2}\sqrt{80}$. By the formula for the area of a circle ($A = \pi r^2$), area equals $(\pi)\left(\dfrac{1}{2}\right)^2\left(\sqrt{80}\right)^2$, or $(\pi)\left(\dfrac{1}{4}\right)(80)$, which equals 20π. ▧

16. The correct answer is (E). If the gain is 10% of the selling price, then $12.60 is 90%. Therefore, 100% is equal to $14.00. ▧

17. The correct answer is (E). If John weighs 110% of the average, he weighs 10% more than the average weight of 105 lbs., or $0.10 \times 105 = 10.5$ lbs. John weighs $105 + 10.5 = 115.5$ lbs. ▧

18. The correct answer is (B). Sonya has a total of $4 + 3 + 7 + 6 = 20$ bills in her wallet. Of these, the 4 twenty-dollar bills and the 3 ten-dollar bills would enable her to buy an $8.50 item, so 7 of the 20 bills would be enough for her to make the purchase.

Therefore, the probability is $\dfrac{7}{20}$.

19. The correct answer is (A). If the machine loses 15% of its value each year, then each year its value is 85% of what it was the year before. Therefore, we are looking for the fifth term of a geometric sequence with first term $80,000 at time zero, and common ratio 0.85. Using the formula $a_n = a_1 \times r^{n-1}$, we can compute $a_5 = \$80{,}000 \times (0.85)^4 = \$41{,}760.50$.

20. The correct answer is (A). In Set I, the median (the number in the middle when the numbers are arranged in order) is 9, and the mode (the most frequently occurring number) is 7. Thus, in Set I, the median is greater than the mode. In Set II, the median is 0 and the mode is 1, so the median is *not* greater than the mode. In Set III, the median is 13 and the mode is 13, so again the median is not greater than the mode. Thus, the required property only holds for Set I.

Section 4

1. C	8. E	15. A	22. C	29. A
2. E	9. A	16. B	23. A	30. E
3. A	10. D	17. E	24. B	31. C
4. C	11. C	18. D	25. B	32. B
5. B	12. E	19. C	26. C	33. B
6. B	13. B	20. C	27. C	34. D
7. B	14. A	21. B	28. E	35. A

1. **The correct answer is (C).** *Flouts*, meaning "scorns," is incorrect. The correct word is *flaunts*, meaning "makes a display of."

2. **The correct answer is (E).** The sentence is correct.

3. **The correct answer is (A).** The writer has confused *exceed*, meaning "surpass," with *accede*, meaning "yield."

4. **The correct answer is (C).** *Students* is plural and takes a plural verb; hence, ". . . ten students *have signed up*."

5. **The correct answer is (B).** The correct idiom is *commensurate with*, not *to*.

6. **The correct answer is (B).** The context requires the present perfect for action (or state of being) that began at a point in the past and has continued to the present: "Dolores *has been* in this country since. . . ."

7. **The correct answer is (B).** *New innovations* is redundant since *innovations* means "new concepts"; therefore, omit *new*.

8. **The correct answer is (E).** The sentence is correct.

9. **The correct answer is (A).** *There*, meaning "in that place," should be *their*, meaning "belonging to them."

10. **The correct answer is (D).** *Displaying* should be *display* to parallel *dress* and *be*.

11. **The correct answer is (C).** The subject is singular: *appeal*. Therefore the verb should be singular: *has elicited*.

12. **The correct answer is (E).** The sentence is correct.

13. **The correct answer is (B).** *Myself* is incorrect since neither an intensive nor a reflexive is required. The correct word is *I*.

14. **The correct answer is (A).** The possessive pronoun is *yours*, without the apostrophe.

15. **The correct answer is (A).** *Consensus of opinion* is redundant; *of opinion* should be deleted.

16. **The correct answer is (B).** *Than*, not *then*, is used in a comparison.

17. **The correct answer is (E).** The sentence is correct.

18. **The correct answer is (D).** The plural *families* is incorrect; the possessive *family's* is required.

19. **The correct answer is (C).** The correct expression is "any *other* present."

20. **The correct answer is (C).** The subject of the introductory phrase and the main clause is *he*, not *his parents* or *his tuition*. Both choices (C) and (D) provide the required subject, but choice (D) changes the meaning of the original sentence.

21. **The correct answer is (B).** The original is incorrect because the two modifiers of *spoke* are not parallel. Choices (B), (D), and (E) correct the error in parallelism, but choices (D) and (E) introduce a new error by changing the tense of the dependent clause from the past to the present tense.

22. **The correct answer is (C).** The pronoun *it* is ambiguous and unnecessary in choices (A) and (B). Choice (C) omits the unnecessary *it* and uses the active rather than the passive voice, thus making a more effective statement than either choice (D) or (E).

23. **The correct answer is (A).** The sentence is correct.

24. **The correct answer is (B).** Choices (A), (C), and (D) all liken a part to a whole, a ribbon to a typewriter. What is intended is to liken the *ribbon on this machine* to the *ribbon on the writer's machine,* as in choice (B).

25. **The correct answer is (B).** The object of the preposition *except* must be in the objective case: not *I* but *me.* That rules out choices (A), (C), and (E). Choice (D) confuses *except* with *accept.*

26. **The correct answer is (C).** *But* is the conjunction needed to show contrast between the clauses. Choice (D) confuses *feat* with *fete.*

27. **The correct answer is (C).** *Put into use* takes three words to say what *used* says by itself.

28. **The correct answer is (E).** The original is incorrect because it is not a parallel construction. Choices (B) and (C) have the same problem. Choice (D) contains an incorrect *in.*

29. **The correct answer is (A).** The sentence is correct. The introductory phrase modifies *the wreck,* and so that term must immediately follow *metal.*

30. **The correct answer is (E).** The best way to improve sentence (2) is to break it up into two shorter and more manageable sentences as in choice (E). Choice (A) uses semicolons incorrectly. Choices (B), (C), and (D) are all unnecessarily long and complicated. Also, choices (B) and (C) need a comma between *now* and *ever since I was a youngster.*

31. **The correct answer is (C).** Such phrases as "all was said and done," "in the final analysis," and "truth be told" are clichés and should be eliminated.

32. **The correct answer is (B).** The organization of the second paragraph is weak. Sentence (12) does not necessarily follow the preceding sentences. The entire paragraph should be strengthened and more tightly organized.

33. **The correct answer is (B).** Choice (A) is a fragment. Choice (C) is awkward because of the placement of the final phrase. Choices (D) and (E) are also clumsily phrased and garbled.

34. **The correct answer is (D).** There is a problem of subject-verb agreement here. The subject *networks* is plural and requires a plural verb, *do.* Choices (A) and (E) do not correct this error. Choices (B) and (C) are awkward and ungrammatical.

35. **The correct answer is (A).** The transitional adverb *therefore* should be followed by a comma; therefore, choices (B) and (E) are incorrect. Choices (B), (D), and (E) use the preposition *between* rather than *among.* When three or more objects follow, the preposition should be *among.* Choice (C) is a run-on sentence.

Section 5

1. E	5. E	9. E	13. 4	17. 6
2. C	6. B	10. C	14. 0.5	18. 2
3. C	7. C	11. 30	15. 9	19. 24
4. D	8. E	12. 80	16. 45	20. 15

Note: A ▤ following a math answer explanation indicates that a calculator could be helpful in solving that particular problem.

1. **The correct answer is (E).** The *mode* is the data element that occurs the most often. In this case, the mode is 91°.

2. **The correct answer is (C).**

$-2x + 5 = 2 - (5 - 2x)$

$-2x + 5 = 2 - 5 + 2x$

$-2x + 5 = -3 + 2x$ Add $2x$ to both sides

$5 = -3 + 4x$ Add $+3$ to both sides

$8 = 4x$ Divide by 4

$2 = x$

3. **The correct answer is (C).**

$$3\left(\frac{81}{16}\right)^{-\frac{3}{4}} = 3\left(\frac{16}{81}\right)^{\frac{3}{4}} = 3\left(\frac{2}{3}\right)^3 = 3\left(\frac{8}{27}\right) = \frac{8}{9}$$

4. **The correct answer is (D).** The equation $|2x - 7| = 11$ is true when $2x - 7 = 11$ and when $2x - 7 = -11$.

$2x - 7 = 11$ $2x - 7 = -11$

$2x = 18$ $2x = -4$

$x = 9$ $x = -2$

Therefore, the two solutions are 9 and −2, and their sum is 7.

5. **The correct answer is (E).** The slope of a line is given by the formula $m = \dfrac{y_2 - y_1}{x_2 - x_1}$. In this case, we can compute

$$m = \frac{7 - (-5)}{-2 - (-6)} = \frac{7 + 5}{-2 + 6} = \frac{12}{4} = 3$$

6. **The correct answer is (B).** Let L = length of each card and W = width of each card. Then $5W$ = length of large rectangle and $L + W$ = width of large rectangle. So, area of large rectangle =

$5W(L + W) = 180$, also

$9LW = 180$ or $LW = 20$

$5LW + 5W^2 = 180$

$LW + W^2 = 36$

$20 + W^2 = 36$

$W^2 = 16$

$W = 4$ and $L = 5$

Thus, perimeter $= 2[5W + (L + W)]$

$= 2(20 + 9) = 58$ ▤

7. **The correct answer is (C).** If each of the dimensions is doubled, the area of the new rectangle is four times the size of the original one. The increase is three times, or 300%.   ▤

8. **The correct answer is (E).** This is a proportion of $\dfrac{2\frac{1}{2}}{3} = \dfrac{x}{14}$, or $x = \dfrac{35}{3}$, or $11\frac{2}{3}$.   ▤

9. **The correct answer is (E).** $MN = \frac{1}{2}QR$ and $\overline{MN}$ is parallel to $\overline{QR}$. This makes $\triangle MNS$ similar to $\triangle QSR$ in a ratio of 1:2, so the altitude from S to $\overline{MN}$ must be half of the altitude from S to $\overline{QR}$. It follows that the altitude from S to $\overline{MN}$ is $\frac{1}{3}$ of the distance from $\overline{MN}$ to $\overline{QR}$, and because the distance from $\overline{MN}$ to $\overline{QR}$ is half the overall altitude from P to $\overline{QR}$, the altitude of $\triangle MNS$ is $\frac{1}{3} \times \frac{1}{2} = \frac{1}{6}$ of the altitude of $\triangle PQR$.

The area of
$$\triangle PQR = \frac{1}{2}(QR)\left(\text{altitude from } P \text{ to } \overline{QR}\right).$$
The area of
$$\triangle MNS = \frac{1}{2}(MN)\left(\text{altitude from } S \text{ to } \overline{MN}\right)$$
$$= \frac{1}{2}\left[\frac{1}{2}(QR)\right]\left[\frac{1}{6}\left(\text{altitude from } P \text{ to } \overline{QR}\right)\right]$$
$$= \frac{1}{12} \times \text{the area of } \triangle PQR.$$

Therefore, the ratio of the two areas is 1:12.

10. **The correct answer is (C).**
Given $\frac{2}{3}x = \frac{1}{10}(60) = 6$.
$\therefore x = 9$
Find $\frac{1}{10}\left(\frac{1}{3}x\right) = \frac{1}{30}(9) = \frac{3}{10} = 0.3$

11. **The correct answer is 30.**

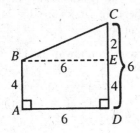

Area of rectangle $ABED = bh = 6(4) = 24$
Area of $\triangle BEC = \frac{1}{2}bh = \frac{1}{2}(6)(2) = 6$
Area of polygon $= 24 + 6 = 30$

12. **The correct answer is 80.** If $AC = BC$, then $m\angle A = m\angle B = 50°$.

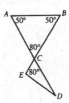

In $\triangle ABC$:
$m\angle ACB = 180° - (m\angle A + m\angle B)$
$m\angle ACB = 80°$
$m\angle ACB = m\angle ECD$ (vertical angles)
$m\angle ECD = 80°$

13. **The correct answer is 4.**
$-m^2 n^3 = -(-2)^2(-1)^3 = -(4)(-1) = 4$

14. **The correct answer is 0.5.** The *square* has four right angles.

The *rectangle* has four right angles.

The *trapezoid* does not have four right angles.

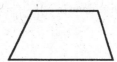

The *circle* does not have four right angles.

Probability of four right angles
$$= \frac{\text{number of successes}}{\text{number of possibilities}} = \frac{2}{4} = \frac{1}{2} = 0.5$$

15. The correct answer is 9.

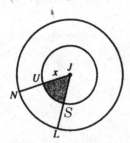

If $JU = x$, then $JN = 3x$. The area of the smaller circle $= \pi(x)^2 = \pi x^2$. The area of the larger circle $= \pi(3x)^2 = 9x^2(\pi) = 9\pi x^2$ $\therefore b = 9$

$$\frac{\text{Area } JUS}{\text{Area } NJL} = \frac{\text{Area of smaller circle}}{\text{Area of larger circle}}$$

$$= \frac{\pi x^2}{9\pi x^2} = \frac{1}{9} = 1:b$$

16. The correct answer is 45. Letting m be the time per regular question, $2m$ is the time per math problem. The total time for all the regular questions is $300m$ and $50(2m)$ is the total time for all the math problems. Since the exam is 3 hours, or 180 minutes, $300m + 100m = 180$ minutes, $400m = 180$, and $m = \frac{180}{400} = \frac{9}{20}$. The time to do a math problem is $2\left(\frac{9}{20}\right) = \frac{9}{10}$. All 50 math problems can be done in $50\left(\frac{9}{10}\right) = 45$ minutes.

17. The correct answer is 6.

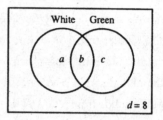

$a + b = 8, \; b + c = 18, \; d = 8$

$$\underset{28}{\underline{\text{Total}}} = \underset{8}{\underline{a + b}} + c + \underset{8}{\underline{d}}$$

$$28 = 8 + c + 8$$

$$\therefore c = 12$$

Since $b + c = 18$ and $c = 12$
$\therefore b = 6$

18. The correct answer is 2.

$$x = \frac{2}{4}, \; y = \frac{1}{4} + \frac{1}{3}, \; z = \frac{2}{3}$$

$$\frac{x + z}{y} = \frac{\left(\frac{2}{4}\right) + \left(\frac{2}{3}\right)}{\frac{1}{4} + \frac{1}{3}} = \frac{2\left(\frac{1}{4} + \frac{1}{3}\right)}{\left(\frac{1}{4} + \frac{1}{3}\right)} = 2$$

19. The correct answer is 24. The only possible units digit is 1, since any other unit's digit would create an even number. After the digit 1 is selected as the unit's digit, there are 4 possible remaining choices for the ten's digit, then 3 choices for the hundred's digit, 2 choices for the thousand's digit, and 1 choice for the ten thousand's digit. Overall, then, there are $4 \times 3 \times 2 \times 1 = 24$ five-digit odd numbers.

20. The correct answer is 15. To begin, $f(p + 3) = 5(p + 3) + 12 = 5p + 15 + 12 = 5p + 27$. Similarly, $f(p) = 5p + 12$. Thus, $f(p + 3) - f(p) = 5p + 27 - (5p + 12) = 5p + 27 - 5p - 12 = 15$.

Section 6

1. E	7. E	12. B	17. A	22. B
2. E	8. B	13. D	18. E	23. C
3. C	9. E	14. C	19. E	24. A
4. B	10. D	15. D	20. C	25. D
5. A	11. A	16. C	21. D	26. D
6. D				

1. **The correct answer is (E).** If he "dashed into the house," then he was in a hurry and probably out of breath.

2. **The correct answer is (E).** A criminal record may indeed cause a jury to *discredit* (disbelieve) a witness's testimony.

3. **The correct answer is (C).** A catastrophic storm might leave a family *destitute* (living in poverty). For the second blank, the word *although* indicates a shift in mood from negative to positive; poverty could not *dampen* (depress) the family's spirits.

4. **The correct answer is (B).** "By a stroke of luck" implies good fortune; the troops likely *prevailed* (were victorious), thereby avoiding a crushing *defeat*.

5. **The correct answer is (A).** If the price is going up tomorrow, you must do your buying with *celerity* (swiftness).

6. **The correct answer is (D).** If danger threatens, the music would likely be *portentous* (ominous).

7. **The correct answer is (E).** If years separated one advance from the next, progress in women's rights was *sporadic* (occasional or scattered over time).

8. **The correct answer is (B).** Offices that are now across the street have been *relocated* (moved). As a result, the directory is *obsolete* (out of date).

9. **The correct answer is (E).** While one could infer that the final sentence deals with Gompers's importance, a better answer based on the passage as written is that the line describes his influence on the AFL.

10. **The correct answer is (D).** Choices (A), (B), and (C) are distracters meant to confuse you with meanings close to that of the root word.

11. **The correct answer is (A).** The tone has more of a biting edge than condescending and certainly more than humorous, which is a good distracter if you read so quickly that you miss the biting edge.

12. **The correct answer is (B).** Knowing that the art critic was being sarcastic will help you eliminate the choices that relate to a literal interpretation of the passage and a mistaken belief that *finicky* means either choices (A), (C), or (D).

13. **The correct answer is (D).** The word *obtained* might throw you off, but it means "held true" in this context, not "gotten."

14. **The correct answer is (C).** The answer choices pick out phrases from the passage, but only choice (C) correctly connects Roosevelt's idea of conservation and the national good.

15. **The correct answer is (D).** In the text, the author discusses Quixote's desire to change wrongs to right and redress grievances. In this context, *redress* means to fix, change, or correct for the better.

16. **The correct answer is (C).** Because Don Quixote is not a knight, to take up arms against another knight would be a breach in the code of chivalry.

17. **The correct answer is (A).** Don Quixote is worried that he cannot wear armor with a *device* on his shield that denotes his knighthood. The only appropriate choice is (A).

18. **The correct answer is (E).** With such malapropisms as "forked tongues" of birds, Cervantes imbues his hero with language that mimics the flowery language of the romances he reads.

19. **The correct answer is (E).** In his florid, overblown language, Don Quixote tells of getting out of bed to ride off on his adventure. "The slothful down" seems to refer to the down mattress on which he sleeps.

20. **The correct answer is (C).** Don Quixote is talking to himself and calling on a woman who may or may not exist. His speech cries out for his love for Dulcinea, but Cervantes pulls the reader back with this line to show that Quixote is mad.

21. **The correct answer is (D).** Don Quixote speaks first to the "sage enchanter" who might chronicle his tale (line 67) and then to Dulcinea, "mistress of this captive heart" (lines 73–74).

22. **The correct answer is (B).** The sun's heat "would have been enough to turn his brain, if he had had any." Cervantes is again reminding the reader that Don Quixote is out of his mind.

23. **The correct answer is (C).** The story up to this point might be the tale of any knight somewhat down on his luck, but in lines 29–33, Cervantes jolts the reader into realizing that Don Quixote is out of his mind—he is not even a real knight.

24. **The correct answer is (A).** Cervantes refers to the romantic books that fill Don Quixote's head in lines 33–34 and 81–83.

25. **The correct answer is (D).** Although he never comes right out and says so, Cervantes's mocking reproduction of the language of romantic books makes it clear that he does not think much of the writing styles he imitates. The fact that the hero who speaks the way such writers write is completely mad is another ironic twist that reveals Cervantes's opinion.

26. **The correct answer is (D).** Throughout, Cervantes uses a gently mocking tone to show Don Quixote's ridiculousness.

Section 7

1. D	4. C	7. D	10. E	13. C
2. A	5. B	8. D	11. C	14. A
3. D	6. E	9. C	12. B	15. E

Note: A ▤ following a math answer explanation indicates that a calculator could be helpful in solving that particular problem.

1. **The correct answer is (D).** Buying the lollipops singly would cost: 30 pops × \$0.13 per pop = \$3.90. The reduced rate is \$1.38 per dozen. Thirty pops is $2\frac{1}{2}$ dozen, so the cost for 30 pops is \$1.38 × 2.5 = \$3.45. The savings with this reduced rate is \$3.90 − \$3.45 = \$0.45. ▤

2. **The correct answer is (A).** The volume of the fish tank is 11" × 14" × 9" = 1386 cu. in. The amount needed to fill the tank is 1386 cu. in. ÷ 231 cu. in./gal. = 6 gallons. ▤

3. **The correct answer is (D).** Let legs be $2x$ and $3x$. Then, $(2x)^2 + (3x)^2 = $ (hypotenuse)^2, and

$$\frac{1}{2} \cdot 2x \cdot 3x = 12$$
$$3x^2 = 12$$
$$x^2 = 4$$
$$x = 2$$

Thus, $4^2 + 6^2 = $ (hypotenuse)^2

$16 + 36 = 52$

hypotenuse $= \sqrt{52} = 2\sqrt{13}$ ▤

4. **The correct answer is (C).** The weights are proportional to the volumes, and the volumes vary as the cubes of their dimensions. If the edges are doubled, the volume becomes $2^3 = 8$ times as large. Hence, the weight $= 8 \times 3 = 24$ ounces $= 1\frac{1}{2}$ lbs. ▤

5. **The correct answer is (B).** The graduate starts at x dollars per week. After the pay cut, the graduate receives 90% of the original salary. The 10% raise adds 9% to the salary (10% of 90%), so the new salary is $0.99x$.

6. **The correct answer is (E).**

$\$428.00 - (0.06) \times \$428.00 = \$402.32.$ ▤

7. **The correct answer is (D).** There will be no waste if the lengths are multiples of $5\frac{1}{2}$ feet. This occurs between 6 and 24 feet only for 22 feet. ▤

8. **The correct answer is (D).** A cube with an edge of 4 has a volume of 64 cubic inches. A cube with an edge of 5 has a volume of 125 cubic inches. The percentage increase is $\frac{61}{64}$, or approximately 95%. ▤

9. **The correct answer is (C).**

$$\frac{1}{4} : \frac{3}{5} = \frac{1}{4} \div \frac{3}{5}$$
$$= \frac{1}{4} \times \frac{5}{3}$$
$$= \frac{5}{12}$$
$$= 5 : 12$$ ▤

10. **The correct answer is (E).**

$\sqrt{3} = 1.73$ (approx.)

$$\frac{1}{\sqrt{3}} = \frac{\sqrt{3}}{3} = \frac{1.73}{3} = 0.57$$

$$\frac{\sqrt{3}}{3} = \frac{1.73}{3} = 0.57$$

$$\frac{1}{3} = 0.333.....$$

$$\frac{1}{3\sqrt{3}} = \frac{\sqrt{3}}{3 \times 3} = \frac{\sqrt{3}}{9} = \frac{1.73}{9} = 0.19$$

Thus, the smallest is $\frac{1}{3\sqrt{3}}$. ▤

11. **The correct answer is (C).** A hexagon with 22-inch sides has a perimeter of 6×22, or 132 inches.

$$C = 2\pi r$$
$$132 = 2\pi r$$
$$132 = 2(3.14)r$$
$$132 = 6.28r$$
$$21.02 = r$$

12. **The correct answer is (B).** We are not told how many games the Bombers played, but we know that the ratio of the number of games played in the second year to that in the first is 2:1. Problems like this can be solved by plugging in real numbers. Let's say that there were 50 games in the first year, so they won 25. In the second year there were 100 games, so they won 65 games. Altogether they won 90 out of 150 games, and this fraction can be simplified to 3 out of 5, or 60%.

13. **The correct answer is (C).** Let $x =$ weight in ounces of the apple. Then,

$$x = \frac{4}{5}x + \frac{4}{5}$$
$$5x = 4x + 4$$
$$x = 4$$

14. **The correct answer is (A).** The graph will cross the x-axis at the point where the function (that is, the y-coordinate) has a value of 0. As result, the following equation needs to be solved: $6x - 18 = 0$

$$6x - 18 = 0 \qquad \text{Add 18 to both sides}$$
$$6x = 18 \qquad \text{Divide both sides by 6}$$
$$x = 3$$

Therefore, the point is $(3,0)$.

15. **The correct answer is (E).** The function will be undefined for any values of x that yield a denominator of 0. Note that the smallest value that x^2 can have is 0, so $x^2 + 1$ is always positive. Thus, the denominator is never 0, and the domain is all real numbers.

Section 8

1. D	5. E	9. E	13. D
2. D	6. C	10. E	14. A
3. A	7. D	11. D	15. B
4. E	8. C	12. B	16. D

1. **The correct answer is (D).** While the passage does discuss the importance of global warming, most of the content relates to the actual impacts that are likely.

2. **The correct answer is (D).** Just mentioning downpours doesn't make the passage lyrical. You probably didn't fall for that, but you might have chosen choice (E). The passage doesn't state these outcomes as absolute but qualifies them with the word *likely*, so factual is not the correct answer.

3. **The correct answer is (A).** Like Passage 1, the tone is direct. Car emissions aren't mentioned, and there is no mention of the impact of rising temperatures, which is the point of Passage 1, so you know choice (D) can't be right.

4. **The correct answer is (E).** The biggest contrast between Passage 1 and Passage 2 in terms of content or style is the use of past data rather than future possibilities.

5. **The correct answer is (E).** Most of the choices are extremes, either extreme outrage or extreme lack of interest. The author takes more of an objective middle ground in outlining the history of African-American economics.

6. **The correct answer is (C).** In the first sentence of the passage, the author indicates that slavery and undereducation hindered economic progress for African Americans until well into the twentieth century.

7. **The correct answer is (D).** The context of the sentence indicates that the best answer is "on the same level."

8. **The correct answer is (C).** On the contrary, in the last five decades African Americans have become much less tolerant of racial discrimination.

9. **The correct answer is (E).** The passage generally implies that the civil rights movement did help African Americans in their quest for economic and political equality.

10. **The correct answer is (E).** The passage acknowledges that progress has been made in some segments of the African-American population, but that the gap is widening between lower-income and higher-income African Americans.

11. **The correct answer is (D).** See lines 5–8. Hiram Revels was the first African American in Congress, but he was elected to the Senate. Choice (A) may be true, but it is not mentioned in the passage.

12. **The correct answer is (B).** Compare lines 15–19 and 40–42.

13. **The correct answer is (D).** The context makes it clear that "turned to" means "concentrated on" or "devoted themselves to."

14. **The correct answer is (A).** Political organizations in southern states in the nineteenth century are mentioned in lines 19–22; political organizations in northern states in the twentieth century are cited in lines 32–34.

15. **The correct answer is (B).** In Passage 2, the author expresses admiration in the last paragraph, where the representatives' "long struggle to extend the ideals of the founders to encompass all citizens of the United States" is cited.

16. **The correct answer is (D).** Although the author of Passage 2 points out that political gain occurred immediately following the Civil War, he also indicates that African Americans suffered political powerlessness from 1890–1900. Therefore, there were bumps in the road.

Section 9

1. D	5. E	9. E	13. A
2. D	6. C	10. C	14. D
3. E	7. D	11. B	15. E
4. A	8. B	12. D	

1. **The correct answer is (D).** The verb *try* takes the preposition *to*, not the conjunction *and*.

2. **The correct answer is (D).** *Keats* must be possessive: *Keats'. Critics* is simply plural. Only choice (D) solves both problems.

3. **The correct answer is (E).** *Who* is correct as the subject of the verb *won*.

4. **The correct answer is (A).** The sentence is correct, since *data* is a plural subject and requires a plural verb, *are*.

5. **The correct answer is (E).** Choice (A) and (D) are run-ons. Choice (B) reverses the intended meaning and choice (C) does not make sense. Note that *flammable* and *inflammable* are synonyms; the prefix *in* is an intensive.

6. **The correct answer is (C).** The third verb must be in the same tense as the first two verbs: *entered, glanced,* and *strode*. Choices (D) and (E) fail to maintain the parallel structure of choice (C).

7. **The correct answer is (D).** *A person* takes the singular pronoun *he* or *she*; therefore, choices (A), (B), and (C) are incorrect. Choice (E) contains a superfluous *he*.

8. **The correct answer is (B).** *Economics* is a noun meaning the study of the production, distribution, and consumption of wealth. *Economical* is an adjective meaning *thrifty*. The adjective that refers to the science of economics is *economic*.

9. **The correct answer is (E).** The quarrel began before the speakers began to regret it; therefore, the past perfect *had quarreled* is needed.

10. **The correct answer is (C).** For parallel structure, the sentence should be "of the cost."

11. **The correct answer is (B).** The correct idiom is "capable of doing."

12. **The correct answer is (D).** As written it is unclear, to whom the "he" refers. Choice (D) clarifies the antecedent.

13. **The correct answer is (A).** The sentence is correct.

14. **The correct answer is (D).** *Lend* is the verb; *loan* is the noun.

15. **The correct answer is (E).** For parallel structure, *watching* should be *to watch*.

COMPUTING YOUR SCORES

To get a sense of your progress in preparing for the SAT, you need to compute individual multiple-choice critical reading, math, and writing raw scores for this practice test. Keep in mind that these formulas have been simplified to give you a "quick and dirty" sense of where you are scoring, not a perfectly precise score.

To Compute Your Raw Scores

1 Enter the number of correct answers for each critical reading, math, and multiple-choice writing section under Number of Questions Correct.

2 Enter the number of incorrect answers (not blanks) for each critical reading, math, and multiple-choice writing section under Number of Questions Incorrect.

3 Total the number correct and number incorrect.

4 Follow this formula: Take the total correct and subtract one quarter of the total incorrect. Round up in your favor to compute your raw score.

Critical Reading Section	Total Number of Questions	Number of Questions Correct	Number of Questions Incorrect
2	26		
6	26		
8	16		
Totals	68	Total Correct:	Total Incorrect:

Critical Reading Raw Score = Total Correct − ($\frac{1}{4}$ × Total Incorrect) = ____

Math Section	Total Number of Questions	Number of Questions Correct	Number of Questions Incorrect
3	20		
5	20		
7	15		
Totals	55	Total Correct:	Total Incorrect:

Math Raw Score = Total Correct − ($\frac{1}{4}$ × Total Incorrect) = ____

Multiple-Choice Writing Section	Total Number of Questions	Number of Questions Correct	Number of Questions Incorrect
4	35		
9	15		
Total	50	Total Correct:	Total Incorrect:

Multiple-Choice Writing Raw Score = Total Correct − ($\frac{1}{4}$ × Total Incorrect) = ____

CONVERSION SCALES

CRITICAL READING

Raw Score	Scaled Score	Raw Score	Scaled Score
68	800	30	480
65	760	25	440
60	710	20	410
55	670	15	370
50	620	10	340
45	590	5	290
40	550	0	230
35	520		

MATH

Raw Score	Scaled Score	Raw Score	Scaled Score
55	800	20	510
50	760	15	480
45	690	10	440
40	650	5	340
35	610	0	200
30	580		
25	550		

MULTIPLE-CHOICE WRITING

Raw Score	Scaled Score	Raw Score	Scaled Score
50	800	20	470
45	760	15	420
40	680	10	370
35	620	5	320
30	580	0	270
25	520		

SELF-EVALUATION CHARTS

Critical Reading: Raw Score

Excellent	60–68
Good	50–59
Average	30–49
Fair	20–29
Poor	0–19

Math: Raw Score

Excellent	50–55
Good	40–49
Average	20–39
Fair	10–19
Poor	0–9

answers practice test 2

ANSWER SHEET PRACTICE TEST 3

SECTION 1: ESSAY

_____
_____
_____
_____
_____
_____
_____
_____
_____
_____
_____
_____
_____
_____
_____
_____
_____
_____
_____
_____
_____
_____
_____
_____
_____
_____
_____
_____

answer sheet

If a section has fewer questions than answer ovals, leave the extra ovals blank.

SECTION 2

1 Ⓐ Ⓑ Ⓒ Ⓓ Ⓔ   11 Ⓐ Ⓑ Ⓒ Ⓓ Ⓔ   21 Ⓐ Ⓑ Ⓒ Ⓓ Ⓔ   31 Ⓐ Ⓑ Ⓒ Ⓓ Ⓔ
2 Ⓐ Ⓑ Ⓒ Ⓓ Ⓔ   12 Ⓐ Ⓑ Ⓒ Ⓓ Ⓔ   22 Ⓐ Ⓑ Ⓒ Ⓓ Ⓔ   32 Ⓐ Ⓑ Ⓒ Ⓓ Ⓔ
3 Ⓐ Ⓑ Ⓒ Ⓓ Ⓔ   13 Ⓐ Ⓑ Ⓒ Ⓓ Ⓔ   23 Ⓐ Ⓑ Ⓒ Ⓓ Ⓔ   33 Ⓐ Ⓑ Ⓒ Ⓓ Ⓔ
4 Ⓐ Ⓑ Ⓒ Ⓓ Ⓔ   14 Ⓐ Ⓑ Ⓒ Ⓓ Ⓔ   24 Ⓐ Ⓑ Ⓒ Ⓓ Ⓔ   34 Ⓐ Ⓑ Ⓒ Ⓓ Ⓔ
5 Ⓐ Ⓑ Ⓒ Ⓓ Ⓔ   15 Ⓐ Ⓑ Ⓒ Ⓓ Ⓔ   25 Ⓐ Ⓑ Ⓒ Ⓓ Ⓔ   35 Ⓐ Ⓑ Ⓒ Ⓓ Ⓔ
6 Ⓐ Ⓑ Ⓒ Ⓓ Ⓔ   16 Ⓐ Ⓑ Ⓒ Ⓓ Ⓔ   26 Ⓐ Ⓑ Ⓒ Ⓓ Ⓔ   36 Ⓐ Ⓑ Ⓒ Ⓓ Ⓔ
7 Ⓐ Ⓑ Ⓒ Ⓓ Ⓔ   17 Ⓐ Ⓑ Ⓒ Ⓓ Ⓔ   27 Ⓐ Ⓑ Ⓒ Ⓓ Ⓔ   37 Ⓐ Ⓑ Ⓒ Ⓓ Ⓔ
8 Ⓐ Ⓑ Ⓒ Ⓓ Ⓔ   18 Ⓐ Ⓑ Ⓒ Ⓓ Ⓔ   28 Ⓐ Ⓑ Ⓒ Ⓓ Ⓔ   38 Ⓐ Ⓑ Ⓒ Ⓓ Ⓔ
9 Ⓐ Ⓑ Ⓒ Ⓓ Ⓔ   19 Ⓐ Ⓑ Ⓒ Ⓓ Ⓔ   29 Ⓐ Ⓑ Ⓒ Ⓓ Ⓔ   39 Ⓐ Ⓑ Ⓒ Ⓓ Ⓔ
10 Ⓐ Ⓑ Ⓒ Ⓓ Ⓔ   20 Ⓐ Ⓑ Ⓒ Ⓓ Ⓔ   30 Ⓐ Ⓑ Ⓒ Ⓓ Ⓔ   40 Ⓐ Ⓑ Ⓒ Ⓓ Ⓔ

SECTION 3

1 Ⓐ Ⓑ Ⓒ Ⓓ Ⓔ   11 Ⓐ Ⓑ Ⓒ Ⓓ Ⓔ   21 Ⓐ Ⓑ Ⓒ Ⓓ Ⓔ   31 Ⓐ Ⓑ Ⓒ Ⓓ Ⓔ
2 Ⓐ Ⓑ Ⓒ Ⓓ Ⓔ   12 Ⓐ Ⓑ Ⓒ Ⓓ Ⓔ   22 Ⓐ Ⓑ Ⓒ Ⓓ Ⓔ   32 Ⓐ Ⓑ Ⓒ Ⓓ Ⓔ
3 Ⓐ Ⓑ Ⓒ Ⓓ Ⓔ   13 Ⓐ Ⓑ Ⓒ Ⓓ Ⓔ   23 Ⓐ Ⓑ Ⓒ Ⓓ Ⓔ   33 Ⓐ Ⓑ Ⓒ Ⓓ Ⓔ
4 Ⓐ Ⓑ Ⓒ Ⓓ Ⓔ   14 Ⓐ Ⓑ Ⓒ Ⓓ Ⓔ   24 Ⓐ Ⓑ Ⓒ Ⓓ Ⓔ   34 Ⓐ Ⓑ Ⓒ Ⓓ Ⓔ
5 Ⓐ Ⓑ Ⓒ Ⓓ Ⓔ   15 Ⓐ Ⓑ Ⓒ Ⓓ Ⓔ   25 Ⓐ Ⓑ Ⓒ Ⓓ Ⓔ   35 Ⓐ Ⓑ Ⓒ Ⓓ Ⓔ
6 Ⓐ Ⓑ Ⓒ Ⓓ Ⓔ   16 Ⓐ Ⓑ Ⓒ Ⓓ Ⓔ   26 Ⓐ Ⓑ Ⓒ Ⓓ Ⓔ   36 Ⓐ Ⓑ Ⓒ Ⓓ Ⓔ
7 Ⓐ Ⓑ Ⓒ Ⓓ Ⓔ   17 Ⓐ Ⓑ Ⓒ Ⓓ Ⓔ   27 Ⓐ Ⓑ Ⓒ Ⓓ Ⓔ   37 Ⓐ Ⓑ Ⓒ Ⓓ Ⓔ
8 Ⓐ Ⓑ Ⓒ Ⓓ Ⓔ   18 Ⓐ Ⓑ Ⓒ Ⓓ Ⓔ   28 Ⓐ Ⓑ Ⓒ Ⓓ Ⓔ   38 Ⓐ Ⓑ Ⓒ Ⓓ Ⓔ
9 Ⓐ Ⓑ Ⓒ Ⓓ Ⓔ   19 Ⓐ Ⓑ Ⓒ Ⓓ Ⓔ   29 Ⓐ Ⓑ Ⓒ Ⓓ Ⓔ   39 Ⓐ Ⓑ Ⓒ Ⓓ Ⓔ
10 Ⓐ Ⓑ Ⓒ Ⓓ Ⓔ   20 Ⓐ Ⓑ Ⓒ Ⓓ Ⓔ   30 Ⓐ Ⓑ Ⓒ Ⓓ Ⓔ   40 Ⓐ Ⓑ Ⓒ Ⓓ Ⓔ

SECTION 4

1 Ⓐ Ⓑ Ⓒ Ⓓ Ⓔ   11 Ⓐ Ⓑ Ⓒ Ⓓ Ⓔ   21 Ⓐ Ⓑ Ⓒ Ⓓ Ⓔ   31 Ⓐ Ⓑ Ⓒ Ⓓ Ⓔ
2 Ⓐ Ⓑ Ⓒ Ⓓ Ⓔ   12 Ⓐ Ⓑ Ⓒ Ⓓ Ⓔ   22 Ⓐ Ⓑ Ⓒ Ⓓ Ⓔ   32 Ⓐ Ⓑ Ⓒ Ⓓ Ⓔ
3 Ⓐ Ⓑ Ⓒ Ⓓ Ⓔ   13 Ⓐ Ⓑ Ⓒ Ⓓ Ⓔ   23 Ⓐ Ⓑ Ⓒ Ⓓ Ⓔ   33 Ⓐ Ⓑ Ⓒ Ⓓ Ⓔ
4 Ⓐ Ⓑ Ⓒ Ⓓ Ⓔ   14 Ⓐ Ⓑ Ⓒ Ⓓ Ⓔ   24 Ⓐ Ⓑ Ⓒ Ⓓ Ⓔ   34 Ⓐ Ⓑ Ⓒ Ⓓ Ⓔ
5 Ⓐ Ⓑ Ⓒ Ⓓ Ⓔ   15 Ⓐ Ⓑ Ⓒ Ⓓ Ⓔ   25 Ⓐ Ⓑ Ⓒ Ⓓ Ⓔ   35 Ⓐ Ⓑ Ⓒ Ⓓ Ⓔ
6 Ⓐ Ⓑ Ⓒ Ⓓ Ⓔ   16 Ⓐ Ⓑ Ⓒ Ⓓ Ⓔ   26 Ⓐ Ⓑ Ⓒ Ⓓ Ⓔ
7 Ⓐ Ⓑ Ⓒ Ⓓ Ⓔ   17 Ⓐ Ⓑ Ⓒ Ⓓ Ⓔ   27 Ⓐ Ⓑ Ⓒ Ⓓ Ⓔ
8 Ⓐ Ⓑ Ⓒ Ⓓ Ⓔ   18 Ⓐ Ⓑ Ⓒ Ⓓ Ⓔ   28 Ⓐ Ⓑ Ⓒ Ⓓ Ⓔ
9 Ⓐ Ⓑ Ⓒ Ⓓ Ⓔ   19 Ⓐ Ⓑ Ⓒ Ⓓ Ⓔ   29 Ⓐ Ⓑ Ⓒ Ⓓ Ⓔ
10 Ⓐ Ⓑ Ⓒ Ⓓ Ⓔ   20 Ⓐ Ⓑ Ⓒ Ⓓ Ⓔ   30 Ⓐ Ⓑ Ⓒ Ⓓ Ⓔ

SECTION 5

Note: ONLY the answers entered on the grid are scored.

Handwritten answers at the top of the column are NOT scored.

1. (A) (B) (C) (D) (E)   6. (A) (B) (C) (D) (E)
2. (A) (B) (C) (D) (E)   7. (A) (B) (C) (D) (E)
3. (A) (B) (C) (D) (E)   8. (A) (B) (C) (D) (E)
4. (A) (B) (C) (D) (E)   9. (A) (B) (C) (D) (E)
5. (A) (B) (C) (D) (E)   10. (A) (B) (C) (D) (E)

11.   12.   13.   14.   15.

16.   17.   18.   19.   20.

SECTION 6

1 (A) (B) (C) (D) (E)	11 (A) (B) (C) (D) (E)	21 (A) (B) (C) (D) (E)	31 (A) (B) (C) (D) (E)
2 (A) (B) (C) (D) (E)	12 (A) (B) (C) (D) (E)	22 (A) (B) (C) (D) (E)	32 (A) (B) (C) (D) (E)
3 (A) (B) (C) (D) (E)	13 (A) (B) (C) (D) (E)	23 (A) (B) (C) (D) (E)	33 (A) (B) (C) (D) (E)
4 (A) (B) (C) (D) (E)	14 (A) (B) (C) (D) (E)	24 (A) (B) (C) (D) (E)	34 (A) (B) (C) (D) (E)
5 (A) (B) (C) (D) (E)	15 (A) (B) (C) (D) (E)	25 (A) (B) (C) (D) (E)	35 (A) (B) (C) (D) (E)
6 (A) (B) (C) (D) (E)	16 (A) (B) (C) (D) (E)	26 (A) (B) (C) (D) (E)	36 (A) (B) (C) (D) (E)
7 (A) (B) (C) (D) (E)	17 (A) (B) (C) (D) (E)	27 (A) (B) (C) (D) (E)	37 (A) (B) (C) (D) (E)
8 (A) (B) (C) (D) (E)	18 (A) (B) (C) (D) (E)	28 (A) (B) (C) (D) (E)	38 (A) (B) (C) (D) (E)
9 (A) (B) (C) (D) (E)	19 (A) (B) (C) (D) (E)	29 (A) (B) (C) (D) (E)	39 (A) (B) (C) (D) (E)
10 (A) (B) (C) (D) (E)	20 (A) (B) (C) (D) (E)	30 (A) (B) (C) (D) (E)	40 (A) (B) (C) (D) (E)

SECTION 7

1 (A) (B) (C) (D) (E)	6 (A) (B) (C) (D) (E)	11 (A) (B) (C) (D) (E)
2 (A) (B) (C) (D) (E)	7 (A) (B) (C) (D) (E)	12 (A) (B) (C) (D) (E)
3 (A) (B) (C) (D) (E)	8 (A) (B) (C) (D) (E)	13 (A) (B) (C) (D) (E)
4 (A) (B) (C) (D) (E)	9 (A) (B) (C) (D) (E)	14 (A) (B) (C) (D) (E)
5 (A) (B) (C) (D) (E)	10 (A) (B) (C) (D) (E)	15 (A) (B) (C) (D) (E)

SECTION 8

1 (A) (B) (C) (D) (E)	6 (A) (B) (C) (D) (E)	11 (A) (B) (C) (D) (E)	16 (A) (B) (C) (D) (E)
2 (A) (B) (C) (D) (E)	7 (A) (B) (C) (D) (E)	12 (A) (B) (C) (D) (E)	17 (A) (B) (C) (D) (E)
3 (A) (B) (C) (D) (E)	8 (A) (B) (C) (D) (E)	13 (A) (B) (C) (D) (E)	18 (A) (B) (C) (D) (E)
4 (A) (B) (C) (D) (E)	9 (A) (B) (C) (D) (E)	14 (A) (B) (C) (D) (E)	19 (A) (B) (C) (D) (E)
5 (A) (B) (C) (D) (E)	10 (A) (B) (C) (D) (E)	15 (A) (B) (C) (D) (E)	20 (A) (B) (C) (D) (E)

SECTION 9

1 (A) (B) (C) (D) (E)	6 (A) (B) (C) (D) (E)	11 (A) (B) (C) (D) (E)
2 (A) (B) (C) (D) (E)	7 (A) (B) (C) (D) (E)	12 (A) (B) (C) (D) (E)
3 (A) (B) (C) (D) (E)	8 (A) (B) (C) (D) (E)	13 (A) (B) (C) (D) (E)
4 (A) (B) (C) (D) (E)	9 (A) (B) (C) (D) (E)	14 (A) (B) (C) (D) (E)
5 (A) (B) (C) (D) (E)	10 (A) (B) (C) (D) (E)	15 (A) (B) (C) (D) (E)

Section 1

Essay • 25 Minutes

Directions: Think carefully about the statement below and the assignment that follows it.

There is an old saying, "There is nothing new under the sun."

Assignment: What is your opinion of the idea that everything today is a repetition of something that occurred earlier? Plan and write an essay that develops your ideas logically. Support your opinion with specific evidence taken from your personal experience, your observations of others, or your reading.

STOP

END OF SECTION 1. IF YOU HAVE ANY TIME LEFT, GO OVER YOUR WORK IN THIS SECTION ONLY. DO NOT WORK IN ANY OTHER SECTION OF THE TEST.

practice test 3

Section 2

26 Questions • 25 Minutes

Directions: Each of the following questions consists of an incomplete sentence followed by five words or pairs of words. Choose that word or pair of words that when substituted for the blank space or spaces, best completes the meaning of the sentence and mark the letter of your choice on your answer sheet.

In view of the extenuating circumstances and the defendant's youth, the judge recommended ____.

(A) conviction

(B) a defense

(C) a mistrial

(D) leniency

(E) life imprisonment

The correct answer is (D).

---

1. An audience that laughs in all the wrong places can ____ even the most experienced actor.
   (A) disparage
   (B) allay
   (C) disconcert
   (D) upbraid
   (E) satiate

2. Their assurances of good faith were hollow; they ____ on the agreement almost at once.
   (A) conferred
   (B) expiated
   (C) recapitulated
   (D) obtruded
   (E) reneged

3. If we ____ our different factions, then together we can gain the majority in the legislature.
   (A) amalgamate
   (B) manifest
   (C) preclude
   (D) alienate
   (E) deviate

4. The Eighteenth Amendment, often called the Prohibition Act, ____ the sale of alcoholic beverages.
   (A) prolonged
   (B) preempted
   (C) sanctioned
   (D) proscribed
   (E) encouraged

5. The police received a(n) ____ call giving them valuable information, but the caller would not give his name out of fear of ____.
   (A) private .. impunity
   (B) anonymous .. reprisals
   (C) professional .. dissension
   (D) enigmatic .. refusal
   (E) adamant .. transgression

6. A person who is ____ is slow to adapt to a new way of life.
   (A) nonchalant
   (B) intractable
   (C) rabid
   (D) insolent
   (E) doughty

7. Though they came from _____ social backgrounds, the newly married couple shared numerous interests and feelings.
   (A) desultory
   (B) obsolete
   (C) malleable
   (D) disparate
   (E) deleterious

8. The _____ was a _____ of gastronomic delights.
   (A) internist .. progeny
   (B) gourmet .. connoisseur
   (C) scientist .. facilitator
   (D) xenophobe .. promoter
   (E) tyro .. master

9. Mrs. Jenkins, upon hearing that her arm was broken, looked _____ at the doctor.
   (A) jovially
   (B) plaintively
   (C) fortuitously
   (D) serendipitously
   (E) opportunely

Directions: Each passage below is followed by a set of questions. Read each passage, then answer the accompanying questions, basing your answers on what is stated or implied in the passage and in any introductory material provided. Mark the letter of your choice on your answer sheet.

QUESTIONS 10 AND 11 ARE BASED ON THE FOLLOWING PASSAGE.

Edouard Manet was one of the foremost painters of the mid and late nineteenth century. Although he was a friend of the Impressionists, he never became one of
5 them. He chose not to exhibit with them in an effort to remain fixed in the public's mind as the finest painter of the era. While experimental in his style and techniques, he did not go as far as Impressionists such
10 as Degas and Pissaro or his sister-in-law Berthe Morisot. Manet's paintings, however, served as a model for younger painters looking for different ways to capture light, movement, detail, and color. Manet himself
15 had studied earlier painters and owed much to the Spanish, Italian, and Dutch masters.

10. The purpose of the passage is to
    (A) describe the difference between Manet's work and that of the Impressionists.
    (B) discuss Manet's ego.
    (C) discuss Manet's legacy to later painters.
    (D) discuss Manet's relation to Impressionism.
    (E) explain why Manet chose not to exhibit with the Impressionists.

11. The phrase "he did not go as far as Impressionists" (line 9) means that
    (A) Manet was less creative.
    (B) Manet did not travel as much as the Impressionists in looking for subjects.
    (C) Manet's works were more traditional than those of the Impressionists.
    (D) the Impressionists exhibited more than Manet did.
    (E) Manet was less interested in public opinion.

QUESTIONS 12 AND 13 ARE BASED ON THE FOLLOWING PASSAGE.

This, then, is . . . the duty of the man of wealth: first, to set an example of modest, unostentatious living, shunning display or extravagance; to provide moderately
5 for legitimate wants of those dependent upon him; and after doing so to consider all surplus revenues which come to him simply as trust funds, which he is called upon to administer, and strictly bound as
10 matter of duty to administer in the manner which, in his judgment, is best calculated to produce the most beneficial results for the community—the man of wealth thus becoming the mere agent and trustee for his
15 poorer brethren, bringing to their service his superior wisdom, experience, and ability to administer, ...

—Andrew Carnegie,
"The Gospel of Wealth"

12. The word *unostentatious* (line 3) means
    (A) not pretending.
    (B) stable.
    (C) not showy.
    (D) real.
    (E) lacking in luster.

13. The passage implies that the author believes that
    (A) wisdom comes with wealth.
    (B) wealthy men are wise.
    (C) the wealthy and the poor are locked in a battle for the resources of wealth.
    (D) the poor are not able to take care of themselves.
    (E) the wealthy need to step in to help the poor.

QUESTIONS 14–21 ARE BASED ON THE FOLLOWING PASSAGE.

The Great Famine, which occurred in Ireland between 1845–1848, affected the country so profoundly that today, more than 100 years later, it is still discussed both in Irish-American communities in the United States and in Ireland. The passage presents a timeline of the famine and some of the events leading up to it.

During the mid-1840s, from 1845–1848, the potato crop in Ireland failed, creating a famine that ravaged the population. This event, the Great Famine, was one of the most
5 significant events in the 8000-year history of this island nation, and the effects of it continue to haunt the Irish, both those who still live in Ireland and those who live in the United States. The most immediate effect of
10 the famine was the dramatic decline in the Irish population—either through death from starvation and disease or through emigration to other countries.

In Ireland, the potato had historically been
15 the mainstay of the diet of a large proportion of the rural population. Highly nutritional, the potato was easy to plant and easy to harvest. If a family of six had one acre of land, it could grow a potato crop that would
20 feed them for almost a year. However, dependence on one crop had its downside as well. Potatoes could not be stored for long, and farmers who had grown so accustomed to dealing with this one crop neglected to
25 plant other crops as a hedge against possible failures.

Rapid population increases in the years preceding the Great Famine had created a country whose expanding population was
30 often poverty-stricken. Expanding population, coupled with landowners' lack of responsibility toward tenant-farmers, led to a system where tenant-farmers frequently subdivided their land so that they could gain
35 a bit of rent themselves. Consequently, the rural areas were dotted with small plots of land, most of which were used for potato farming. Prior to the famine, urban areas in Ireland were also experiencing economic
40 distress because of a decline in Irish industry

that resulted in unemployment and poverty in cities such as Dublin.

In 1845, the year the famine began, a good potato crop was expected, so it came as a
45 great surprise when nearly half of the crop of the country failed because of a blight that had come from North America. This particular blight was unusual inasmuch as when the potato was dug from the ground,
50 it appeared to be healthy; it was only after a day or two that the potato began to rot.

Despite the fact that only half the crop failed in 1845, starvation and disease plagued the entire country because many starving people,
55 some of whom were infected with contagious diseases, roamed the countryside looking for food and spreading disease. Then, in 1846, the crop failed completely. In 1847, there was another partial failure, but because people
60 had eaten their seed potatoes in 1846, the crop was much smaller in 1847. Then again in 1848, the crop failed completely.

As if the crop failures were not enough, other factors affected the seriousness of the
65 situation. Various contagious diseases such as typhus, dysentery, and several different types of fever spread rapidly. Landlords evicted tenant-farmers, and the government did very little to provide relief. Nor did it
70 help that the winter of 1846–1847 was one of the coldest on record.

When the famine was over in 1849, a cholera epidemic struck Ireland, so that by 1850 the country found its population reduced
75 from 8.5 million to 6.5 million. One million people had died from disease and starvation, and one million had left Ireland for Britain, Europe, or North America.

The results of the Great Famine were pro-
80 found. Farming in Ireland changed from a one-crop economy to an agricultural economy that included livestock and other crops, such as grains. The seeds of animosity toward Great Britain, which had not helped
85 the Irish in their time of need, were sown. And a pattern of emigration was established that lasts until today.

14. The word *ravaged* (line 3) means
   (A) pillaged.
   (B) devastated.
   (C) wasted.
   (D) sacked.
   (E) assisted.

15. According to the passage, the potato became a staple of the Irish diet for all of the following reasons EXCEPT
   (A) it was filled with nutrients.
   (B) it was easy to plant.
   (C) it was easy to harvest.
   (D) the soil was good for potatoes.
   (E) one acre could support a whole family.

16. The passage implies that
   (A) dependence on one crop was sensible.
   (B) the potato was not the only crop in Ireland.
   (C) the dependence on one crop had no downside.
   (D) the Irish were a happy people.
   (E) dependence on one crop was dangerous.

17. According to the passage, rural life in the years before the Great Famine can best be described as
   (A) prosperous.
   (B) declining in population.
   (C) harsh.
   (D) decreasing in tenant-farmers.
   (E) expanding in farm size.

18. Irish farmers tended to subdivide their farms repeatedly because
   (A) the farms were getting too large.
   (B) they had big families.
   (C) it was easier to farm a smaller plot.
   (D) they needed rent payments.
   (E) they wanted to diversify their crops.

19. The word *blight* (line 48) means
   (A) curse.
   (B) disease.
   (C) injury.
   (D) omen.
   (E) impairment.

20. Disease plagued the Irish during the famine because

(A) the potato was diseased.

(B) immigrants brought disease.

(C) starving Irish carried disease from place to place.

(D) living conditions were not sanitary.

(E) they were not prepared.

21. All of the following were results of the famine EXCEPT that the Irish

(A) emigrated to new lands.

(B) began to raise livestock.

(C) were no longer dependent on one crop.

(D) became independent from Great Britain.

(E) became angered at the British.

QUESTIONS 22–26 ARE BASED ON THE FOLLOWING PASSAGE.

Thomas Bulfinch (1796–1867) was a teacher and writer known for his popularization of myths and legends. In this excerpt from Bulfinch's Mythology, *he tells the story behind the Trojan War.*

Minerva was the goddess of wisdom, but on one occasion she did a very foolish thing; she entered into competition with Juno and Venus for the prize of beauty. It happened
5 thus: At the nuptials of Peleus and Thetis all the gods were invited with the exception of Eris, or Discord. Enraged at her exclusion, the goddess threw a golden apple among the guests, with the inscription, "For the fairest."
10 Thereupon Juno, Venus, and Minerva each claimed the apple. Jupiter, not willing to decide in so delicate a matter, sent the goddesses to Mount Ida, where the beautiful shepherd Paris was tending his flocks, and
15 to him was committed the decision. The goddesses accordingly appeared before him. Juno promised him power and riches, Minerva glory and renown in war, and Venus the fairest of women for his wife, each
20 attempting to bias his decision in her own favor. Paris decided in favour of Venus and gave her the golden apple, thus making the two other goddesses his enemies. Under the protection of Venus, Paris sailed to Greece,
25 and was hospitably received by Menelaus, king of Sparta. Now Helen, the wife of Menelaus, was the very woman whom Venus had destined for Paris, the fairest of her sex. She had been sought as a bride by
30 numerous suitors, and before her decision was made known, they all, at the suggestion of Ulysses, one of their number, took an oath that they would defend her from all injury and avenge her cause if necessary.
35 She chose Menelaus, and was living with him happily when Paris became their guest. Paris, aided by Venus, persuaded her to elope with him, and carried her to Troy, whence arose the famous Trojan war, the theme of
40 the greatest poems of antiquity, those of Homer and Virgil.

Menelaus called upon his brother chieftains of Greece to fulfill their pledge, and join him in his efforts to recover his wife. They
45 generally came forward, but Ulysses, who had married Penelope, and was very happy in his wife and child, had no disposition to embark in such a troublesome affair. He therefore hung back and Palamedes was
50 sent to urge him. When Palamedes arrived at Ithaca, Ulysses pretended to be mad. He yoked an ass and an ox together to the plough and began to sow salt. Palamedes, to try him, placed the infant Telemachus before
55 the plough, whereupon the father turned the plough aside, showing plainly that he was no madman, and after that could no longer refuse to fulfill his promise. Being now himself gained for the undertaking,
60 he lent his aid to bring in other reluctant chiefs, especially Achilles. This hero was the son of that Thetis at whose marriage the apple of Discord had been thrown among the goddesses. Thetis was herself one of the
65 immortals, a sea-nymph, and knowing that her son was fated to perish before Troy if he went on the expedition, she endeavoured to prevent his going. She sent him away to the court of King Lycomedes, and induced him
70 to conceal himself in the disguise of a maiden among the daughters of the king. Ulysses, hearing he was there, went disguised as a merchant to the palace and offered for sale female ornaments, among which he

75 had placed some arms. While the king's daughters were engrossed with the other contents of the merchant's pack, Achilles handled the weapons and thereby betrayed himself to the keen eye of Ulysses, who

80 found no great difficulty in persuading him to disregard his mother's prudent counsels and join his countrymen in the war.

22. Bulfinch describes Jupiter as unwilling to "decide in so delicate a matter" (lines 11–12), implying that

(A) Jupiter is usually heavy-handed.

(B) any decision is bound to offend someone.

(C) Jupiter is overly sensitive.

(D) the problems are so obscure that no one can judge them.

(E) all three goddesses are fragile and dainty.

23. The word *disposition* (line 47) is used to mean

(A) inclination.

(B) nature.

(C) integrity.

(D) value.

(E) habit.

24. The sowing of salt is used by Bulfinch to show

(A) Ulysses's attempt to be found insane.

(B) the difficulty of cultivating in rocky soil.

(C) how the tears of the gods created the sea.

(D) the gods' punishment of those who disobey them.

(E) Ulysses's talent as a soldier rather than a farmer.

25. Why does Ulysses display arms among the ornaments?

(A) To test Achilles into revealing himself

(B) As a declaration of war

(C) To mislead the daughters of the king

(D) To complete his disguise as a merchant

(E) Because he wants to start an altercation

26. A reasonable title for this narrative might be

(A) "Disputes and Deceit."

(B) "Achilles and Ulysses."

(C) "Beauty and the Beast."

(D) "The Pettiness of the Gods."

(E) "The Apple of Discord Leads to War."

STOP

END OF SECTION 2. IF YOU HAVE ANY TIME LEFT, GO OVER YOUR WORK IN THIS SECTION ONLY. DO NOT WORK IN ANY OTHER SECTION OF THE TEST.

Section 3

20 Questions • 25 Minutes

Directions: Solve the following problems using any available space on the page for scratchwork. On your answer sheet fill in the choice that best corresponds to the correct answer.

Notes: The figures accompanying the problems are drawn as accurately as possible unless otherwise stated in specific problems. Again, unless otherwise stated, all figures lie in the same plane. All numbers used in these problems are real numbers. Calculators are permitted for this test.

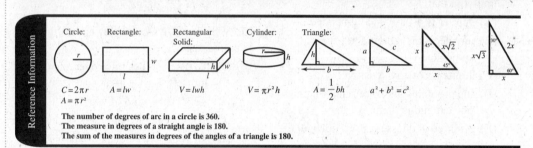

Reference Information

$C = 2\pi r$ $A = lw$ $V = lwh$ $V = \pi r^2 h$ $A = \frac{1}{2}bh$ $a^2 + b^2 = c^2$
$A = \pi r^2$

The number of degrees of arc in a circle is 360.
The measure in degrees of a straight angle is 180.
The sum of the measures in degrees of the angles of a triangle is 180.

1. One angle of a triangle is 82°. The other two angles are in the ratio 2:5. Find the number of degrees in the smallest angle of the triangle.
   - **(A)** 14
   - **(B)** 25
   - **(C)** 28
   - **(D)** 38
   - **(E)** 82

2. Village A has a population of 6800, which is decreasing at a rate of 120 per year. Village B has a population of 4200, which is increasing at a rate of 80 per year. In how many years will the populations of the two villages be equal?
   - **(A)** 9
   - **(B)** 11
   - **(C)** 13
   - **(D)** 14
   - **(E)** 16

3. If $*x$ is defined such that $*x = x^2 - 2x$, the value of $*2 - *1$ is:
   - **(A)** −1
   - **(B)** 0
   - **(C)** 1
   - **(D)** 2
   - **(E)** 4

4. In a right triangle, the ratio of the legs is 1:2. If the area of the triangle is 25 square units, what is the length of the hypotenuse?
   - **(A)** $\sqrt{5}$
   - **(B)** $5\sqrt{5}$
   - **(C)** $5\sqrt{3}$
   - **(D)** $10\sqrt{3}$
   - **(E)** $25\sqrt{5}$

5. In the graph below, the axes and the origin are not shown. If point P has coordinates $(3,7)$, what are the coordinates of point Q, assuming each box is one unit?

   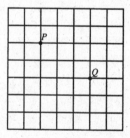

   - **(A)** (5,6)
   - **(B)** (1,10)
   - **(C)** (6,9)
   - **(D)** (6,5)
   - **(E)** (5,10)

6. If $r = 5x$, how many tenths of r does $\frac{1}{2}$ of x equal?

(A) 1
(B) 2
(C) 3
(D) 4
(E) 5

7. *ABCD* is a parallelogram, and *DE = EC*.

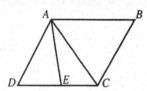

What is the ratio of the area of triangle *ADE* to the area of the parallelogram?

(A) 2:5
(B) 1:2
(C) 1:3
(D) 1:4
(E) It cannot be determined from the information given.

8. In any square, the length of one side is

(A) one half the diagonal of the square.
(B) the square root of the perimeter of the square.
(C) about 0.7 the length of the diagonal of the square.
(D) the square root of the diagonal.
(E) one fourth the area.

9. A pulley having a 9-inch diameter is belted to a pulley having a 6-inch diameter, as shown in the figure. If the large pulley runs at 120 rpm, how fast does the small pulley run, in revolutions per minute?

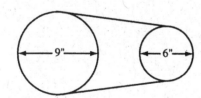

(A) 80
(B) 100
(C) 160
(D) 180
(E) 240

10. The number of degrees through which the hour hand of a clock moves in 2 hours and 12 minutes is:

(A) 66
(B) 72
(C) 126
(D) 732
(E) 792

11. The average of 8 numbers is 6; the average of 6 other numbers is 8. What is the average of all 14 numbers?

(A) 6
(B) $6\frac{6}{7}$
(C) 7
(D) $7\frac{2}{7}$
(E) $8\frac{1}{7}$

12. If x is between 0 and 1, which of the following increases as x increases?

I. $1 - x^2$
II. $x - 1$
III. $\dfrac{1}{x^2}$

(A) I and II only
(B) II and III only
(C) I and III only
(D) II only
(E) I only

13. In the series 3, 7, 12, 18, 25, . . . the 9th term is

(A) 50.
(B) 63.
(C) 75.
(D) 86.
(E) 88.

14. Simplify: $\dfrac{x^2 - y^2}{x - y}$

(A) $\dfrac{xy}{x + y}$
(B) $\dfrac{x + y}{xy}$
(C) $x + y$
(D) xy
(E) $x^2 + y^2 - 1$

15. The front wheels of a wagon are 7 feet in circumference and the back wheels are 9 feet in circumference. When the front wheels have made 10 more revolutions than the back wheels, what distance, in feet, has the wagon gone?

(A) 126
(B) 180
(C) 189
(D) 315
(E) 630

16. A rectangular flower bed, dimensions 16 yards by 12 yards, is surrounded by a walk 3 yards wide. What is the area of the walk in square yards?

(A) 78 square yards
(B) 93 square yards
(C) 132 square yards
(D) 204 square yards
(E) 396 square yards

17. Doreen can wash her car in 15 minutes, while her younger brother Dave takes twice as long to do the same job. If they work together, how many minutes will the job take them?

(A) 5
(B) $7\frac{1}{2}$
(C) 10
(D) $22\frac{1}{2}$
(E) 30

18. What is the equation of the line that is parallel to $y = 5x + 7$ and contains the point $(1,3)$?

(A) $y = -5x + 8$
(B) $y = 5x - 2$
(C) $y = 5x + 3$
(D) $y = 5x + 2$
(E) $y = -\frac{1}{5}x + \frac{16}{15}$

19. Which of the following is equal to $\left(f^{\frac{2}{5}} g^{-\frac{1}{10}} \right)^{20}$?

(A) $\dfrac{f^2}{g^4}$

(B) $\dfrac{g^2}{f^8}$

(C) $\dfrac{1}{f^8 g^2}$

(D) $\dfrac{f^8}{g^2}$

(E) $f^8 g^2$

20. Which values of x must be excluded from the domain of $q(x) = \sqrt{4x - 9}$?

(A) All values of x that are less than $\dfrac{9}{4}$

(B) All values of x that are less than or equal to $\dfrac{9}{4}$

(C) All values of x that are greater than $\dfrac{9}{4}$

(D) All values of x that are greater than or equal to $\dfrac{9}{4}$

(E) All values of x that are between $-\dfrac{9}{4}$ and $\dfrac{9}{4}$

STOP

END OF SECTION 3. IF YOU HAVE ANY TIME LEFT, GO OVER YOUR WORK IN THIS SECTION ONLY. DO NOT WORK IN ANY OTHER SECTION OF THE TEST.

Section 4

35 Questions • 25 Minutes

Directions: Some of the sentences below contain an error in grammar, usage, word choice, or idiom. Other sentences are correct. Parts of each sentence are underlined and lettered. The error, if there is one, is contained in one of the underlined parts of the sentence. Assume that all other parts of the sentence are correct and cannot be changed. For each sentence, select the one underlined part that must be changed to make the sentence correct and mark its letter on your answer sheet. If there is no error in a sentence, mark answer space E. No sentence contains more than one error.

Being that it's such a lovely day, we
   A   B
are having a difficult time concentrating
   C   D
on our assignment. No error
              E

The correct answer is (A).

1. The paper attempted to magnify the
                 A
importance of Defoe's novel's by
                  B
belittling the achievements of his
  C
predecessors. No error
    D   E

2. If the game went into extra innings, the
          A B
relief pitcher would have won it for the
    C   D
visiting team. No error
        E

3. It is all together too early to
      A
forecast accurately what the rate of
    B   C
inflation will be by year's end.
             D
No error
  E

4. My girlfriend and myself plan
  A   B
to get married next year, if we are able to
  C   D
finish our education by that time. No error
                 E

5. Even after Richard Cory killed himself
in the famous poem , many of the
 A
townspeople who had envied him
  B   C
probably still wished they could have
           D
lived in his situation. No error
         E

6. When my mother first learned to knit, she
made a beautiful sweater for my father;
                  A
it only didn't fit him too well. No error
 B   C   D   E

7. Hardly no one is able to compete in
  A   B
professional sports after the age of forty.
  C   D
No error
  E

8. The census statistics was a complex
          A
source of information, in that the
           B
demographers knew that certain groups of
people were more likely to respond
    C
than others. No error
   D   E

9. <u>Admirers</u> of American ballet have made
   A

   the claim that <u>its</u> stars can dance <u>as well</u>
   B   C

   or <u>better than</u> the best of the Russian
   D

   artists. <u>No error</u>
   E

10. <u>During the winter recess,</u> I <u>plan to study</u>
    A   B

    for final examinations in the library
    <u>since it is</u> very quiet <u>there</u>. <u>No error</u>
    C   D   E

11. If he <u>had had</u> the <u>foresight</u> to <u>call first for</u>
    A   B   C

    an appointment, his reception
    <u>would of been</u> more friendly. <u>No error</u>
    D   E

12. Bill, not to mention his friends, <u>are</u>
    A

    <u>to be held</u> <u>accountable</u> for the damage
    B   C

    <u>done</u> to the student lounge. <u>No error</u>
    D   E

13. Everyone was asked, <u>in fact ordered,</u>
    A

    <u>to take</u> <u>their</u> coat to the locker room
    B   C

    <u>prior to</u> the game. <u>No error</u>
    D   E

14. She <u>could hardly</u> <u>accept</u> the invitation
    A   B

    <u>since</u> it was extended in <u>so half-hearted</u>
    C   D

    a manner. <u>No error</u>
    E

15. <u>In regards to</u> the problem <u>presented</u>, I
    A   B

    feel that all <u>aspects</u> must be considered
    C

    carefully. <u>No error</u>
    D   E

16. I hope you do not feel <u>too</u> <u>badly</u>, but I
    A   B

    must <u>inform</u> you that it is quite <u>likely</u>
    C   D

    your application will be rejected. <u>No error</u>
    E

17. <u>There is</u> certainly sufficient reasons <u>for</u>
    A   B

    <u>his being rejected</u> by the
    C

    <u>group's membership.</u> <u>No error</u>
    D   E

18. <u>All the members</u> of the group
    A

    <u>were required</u> to swear that they would
    B

    tell <u>the honest truth</u> even though they
    C

    disliked <u>the concept</u> of an investigation.
    D

    <u>No error</u>
    E

19. A person may study <u>diligently</u>,
    A

    <u>but without</u> adequate sleep <u>you</u> cannot
    B   C

    expect to do <u>well</u>. <u>No error</u>
    D   E

Directions: The sentences below may contain problems in grammar, usage, word choice, sentence construction, or punctuation. Part or all of each sentence is underlined. Following each sentence you will find five ways of expressing the underlined part. Answer choice (A) always repeats the original underlined section. The other four answer choices are all different. You are to select the lettered answer that produces the most effective sentence. If you think the original sentence is best, choose (A) as your answer. If one of the other choices makes a better sentence, mark your answer sheet for the letter of that choice. Do not choose an answer that changes the meaning of the original sentence.

I have always enjoyed singing as well as to dance.

(A) singing as well as to dance

(B) singing as well as dancing

(C) to sing as well as dancing

(D) singing in addition to dance

(E) to sing in addition to dancing

The correct answer is (B).

20. It is perfectly satisfactory to give the sample test to whomever you think needs it.
    (A) whomever you think needs it
    (B) whomsoever has a need for it
    (C) whosoever you think has a need of it
    (D) whoever you think needs it
    (E) who you think has need of it

21. The painting titled "Solitude" is certainly one of the most remarkable studies that was done by Gauguin.
    (A) that was done by Gauguin
    (B) that has been done
    (C) that were done by Gauguin
    (D) which Gauguin done
    (E) that Gauguin done

22. Due to the pressure being placed on the workers to meet the deadline, all leaves had to be cancelled.
    (A) Due to the pressure being placed
    (B) Due to the pressure placed
    (C) Due to the pressure having been placed
    (D) Notwithstanding the pressure being placed
    (E) Because of the pressure being placed

23. He plays the violin with ease and with skill: hardly taking time to glance at the score.
    (A) skill; hardly taking time
    (B) skill, hardly taking time
    (C) skill; scarcely taking time
    (D) skill. Hardly taking time
    (E) skill, he hardly takes time

24. When I was riding on the bus to school, my best friend comes and sits besides me.
    (A) comes and sits beside me
    (B) comes and sits besides me
    (C) came and sat beside me
    (D) came and sat besides me
    (E) comes to sit beside me

25. If the highway is widened, the maple trees <u>that give such beauty to the summer and the fall</u> will have to be cut down.

(A) that give such beauty to the summer and the fall

(B) that had given such beauty to the summer and the fall

(C) that makes the summer and fall so beautiful

(D) which makes it so beautiful in the summer and the fall

(E) that makes it so beautiful all summer and fall

26. Lou, a tenor in the men's chorus, sings better <u>than any tenor</u> in the chorus.

(A) than any tenor

(B) than any other tenor

(C) then any tenor

(D) of all the tenors

(E) then the tenors

27. When the first quarter ended, the home team <u>were leading by ten points.</u>

(A) were leading by ten points

(B) leads by ten points

(C) is leading by ten points

(D) was leading by ten points

(E) has a ten-point lead

28. Avoiding fatty foods, exercising regularly, <u>and visits to the doctor for annual blood tests were recommended</u> as an important regimen.

(A) and visits to the doctor for annual blood tests were recommended

(B) and visits to the doctor for annual blood testing was recommended

(C) and visiting the doctor for annual blood tests were recommended

(D) and annual visits to the doctor for blood tests were recommended

(E) and visiting the doctor for annual blood tests was recommended

29. In the second act, <u>it shows very clearly that</u> her motivation is greed.

(A) it shows very clearly that

(B) it very clearly shows that

(C) the author shows very clearly that

(D) it is showed very clearly how

(E) the author showed how

Directions: Questions 30–35 are based on a passage that might be an early draft of a student's essay. Some sentences in this draft need to be revised or rewritten to make them both clear and correct. Read the passage carefully; then answer the questions that follow it. Some questions require decisions about diction, usage, tone, or sentence structure in particular sentences or parts of sentences. Other questions require decisions about organization, development, or appropriateness of language in the essay as a whole. For each question, choose the answer that makes the intended meaning clearer and more precise and that follows the conventions of Standard Written English.

(1) Voting is not only a privilege, it is also a responsibility. (2) There are people who say that it doesn't really make any difference whether or not you vote. (3) They say it is almost predetermined who will win an election. (4) They claim that only those with a good deal of money are chosen to run for office. (5) They further state that poor people are never selected to run for office.

(6) In many countries, a free and open election is unheard of. (7) There is a one party system. (8) As a result, the average citizen's right to vote is nonexistent. (9) To vote in an unchallenged way, to exercise free speech, and enjoy open political debate are all forbidden by the state. (10) How they must envy us when they see what we enjoy in our country. (11) Even if our choice is limited, at least we can vote for whomever we feel has the best qualifications.

(12) And yet, there are those who ignore this situation. (13) They don't realize how fortunate we are, they are like pessimists who see only the half-empty glass, not the half-full one. (14) For years, women and minorities have struggled for the right to vote. (15) Now that we have it, you shouldn't waste it.

30. Which of the following best describes the writer's intention in sentence (1)?

(A) To present two points of view

(B) To suggest that a solution is needed

(C) To present a "straw man"

(D) To change a reader's opinion

(E) To present the main thesis of the essay

31. Which of the following is the best way to combine sentences (3), (4), and (5)?

(A) Claiming that only the wealthy are chosen to run for office, they say that winning an election is almost predetermined.

(B) They claim that only the rich can afford to run and poor people are never chosen.

(C) Since it requires a good deal of money to run for public office, the choice of candidates is determined in advance.

(D) Election results are predetermined since only the rich are chosen to run and the poor are disenfranchised.

(E) Since it is predetermined who will win an election, they claim only the wealthy, and never the poor, are selected.

32. Which of the following best characterizes sentence (5)?

(A) It provides an alternate viewpoint.

(B) It restates sentence (4), without adding anything new.

(C) It provides a summary to the introductory paragraph.

(D) It provides a bridge between paragraph one and paragraph two.

(E) It adds further proof that the system is not working.

33. Which of the following is the best revision of the underlined portion of sentence (11) below?

Even if our choice is limited, at least we can vote <u>for whomever we feel has the best qualifications.</u>

(A) for whomever we feel is the best qualified.

(B) for the candidate whom we feel has the best qualifications.

(C) for whoever we feel has the best qualifications.

(D) for whomever we feel have the best qualifications.

(E) for the candidates whom we feel have the best qualifications.

34. Which of the following is the best revision of the underlined portion of sentence (13) below?

They don't realize how fortunate <u>we are, they are like</u> the pessimists who see only the half-empty glass, not the half-full one.

(A) they are, they are like

(B) they are, they act like

(C) we are, they behave like

(D) we are, like

(E) we are; acting like

35. In light of the sentence that precedes it, which is the best way to revise sentence (15) below?

<u>Now that we have it, you shouldn't waste it.</u>

(A) Now that the right to vote has been achieved, it shouldn't be wasted.

(B) You shouldn't waste the vote, if you have it.

(C) Now that this important right has been gained, work for it.

(D) Since other nations are not so lucky, we shouldn't waste our right to vote.

(E) You shouldn't waste the right, once you have the vote.

STOP

END OF SECTION 4. IF YOU HAVE ANY TIME LEFT, GO OVER YOUR WORK IN THIS SECTION ONLY. DO NOT WORK IN ANY OTHER SECTION OF THE TEST.

Section 5

20 Questions • 25 Minutes

Directions: Solve the following problems using any available space on the page for scratchwork. On your answer sheet fill in the choice that best corresponds to the correct answer.

Notes: The figures accompanying the problems are drawn as accurately as possible unless otherwise stated in specific problems. Again, unless otherwise stated, all figures lie in the same plane. All numbers used in these problems are real numbers. Calculators are permitted for this test.

Reference Information

Circle: $C = 2\pi r$ $A = \pi r^2$

Rectangle: $A = lw$

Rectangular Solid: $V = lwh$

Cylinder: $V = \pi r^2 h$

Triangle: $A = \frac{1}{2}bh$ $a^2 + b^2 = c^2$

The number of degrees of arc in a circle is 360.
The measure in degrees of a straight angle is 180.
The sum of the measures in degrees of the angles of a triangle is 180.

1. If $X = \{6, 12\}$, $Y = \{5, 10, 15, 20\}$, and $Z = \{4, 8, 16\}$, how many different sets can be formed that contain exactly one element from X, one element from Y, and one element from Z?

   (A) 3
   (B) 6
   (C) 12
   (D) 24
   (E) 36

2. What is the eighth term of the arithmetic sequence when the first term is 5 and the common difference is 4?

   (A) 25
   (B) 29
   (C) 33
   (D) 37
   (E) 41

3. In order to raise money for a class trip, Claudia sells ice cream bars at a high school basketball game. Her profit function is $P(x) = \$1.25x - \$12$, where x represents the number of ice cream bars sold. How many ice cream bars would she need to sell in order to raise $78 for the trip?

   (A) 62
   (B) 66
   (C) 68
   (D) 70
   (E) 72

4. $\left(\sqrt{18} - \sqrt{8}\right)^2 =$

   (A) 1
   (B) $\sqrt{2}$
   (C) 2
   (D) 10
   (E) 260

5. The distance from the center of a circle to a chord is 5. If the length of the chord is 24, what is the length of the radius of the circle?

   (A) 5
   (B) 10
   (C) 12
   (D) 13
   (E) 26

6. If the base of a rectangle is increased by 30% and the altitude is decreased by 20%, the area is increased by

(A) 4%.

(B) 5%.

(C) 10%.

(D) 25%.

(E) 104%.

7. Using a 9 × 12-inch sheet of paper lengthwise, a typist leaves a 1-inch margin on each side and a $1\frac{1}{2}$-inch margin on top and bottom. What fractional part of the page is used for typing?

(A) $\frac{5}{12}$

(B) $\frac{7}{12}$

(C) $\frac{5}{9}$

(D) $\frac{3}{4}$

(E) $\frac{21}{22}$

8. In the figure, $PQRS$ is a parallelogram, and $ST = TV = VR$. What is the ratio of the area of triangle SPT to the area of the parallelogram?

Note: Figure is not drawn to scale.

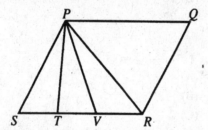

(A) $\frac{1}{6}$

(B) $\frac{1}{5}$

(C) $\frac{2}{7}$

(D) $\frac{1}{3}$

(E) It cannot be determined from the information given.

9. Given formula $A = P\,(1 + rt)$, then $t =$

(A) $A - P - Pr$

(B) $\dfrac{A + P}{Pr}$

(C) $\dfrac{A}{P} - r$

(D) $\dfrac{A - P}{Pr}$

(E) $\dfrac{A - r}{Pr}$

10. If $p > q$ and $r < 0$, which of the following is (are) true?

  I. $pr < qr$

  II. $p + r > q + r$

  III. $p - r < q - r$

(A) I only

(B) II only

(C) I and III only

(D) I and II only

(E) I, II, and III

Student-Produced Response Questions

Directions: Solve each of these problems. Write the answer in the corresponding grid on the answer sheet and fill in the ovals beneath each answer you write. Here are some examples.

Answer: $\frac{3}{4} = .75$; show answer either way

Answer: 325

Note: A mixed number such as $3\frac{1}{2}$ must be gridded as 7/2 or as 3.5. If gridded as "3 1/2," it will be read as "thirty-one halves."

Note: Either position is correct.

11. If the cost of a party is to be split equally among 11 friends, each would pay $15.00. If 20 persons equally split the same cost, how much would each person pay?

12. In the figure below, $\angle N = (9x - 40)°$, $\angle J = (4x + 30)°$, and $\angle JLR = (8x + 40)°$. What is the measure of $\angle J$? (Do not grid the degree symbol.)

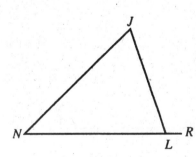

13. $\dfrac{2^2 + 3^2}{5^2} + \dfrac{1}{10} =$

14. In the figure below, two circles are tangent to each other and each is tangent to three sides of the rectangle. If the radius of each circle is 3, then the area of the shaded portion is $a - b\pi$. What is the value of a?

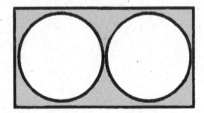

15. The measures of the angles of a triangle are in the ratio of 3:5:7. What is the measure, in degrees, of the smallest angle? (Do not grid the degree symbol.)

16. The length of the line segment whose end points are $(3,-2)$ and $(-4,5)$ is $b\sqrt{2}$. What is the value of b?

17. Jessica caught five fish with an average weight of 10 pounds. If the first fish weighs 9 pounds, the second weighs 9 pounds, and the third fish weighs 10 pounds, what is the average (arithmetic mean) weight of the other two fish?

18. In the figure below, what is the area of △*NKL*?

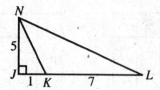

19. How many 5-digit *odd* numbers that are less than 50,000 can be formed from the digits 8, 6, 4, 3, and 1 if each digit can be used more than once?

20. What is the average (arithmetic mean) of the median and the mode of the following group of ten numbers: −5, −3, 0, 1, 1, 2, 3, 3, 3, 5?

STOP

END OF SECTION 5. IF YOU HAVE ANY TIME LEFT, GO OVER YOUR WORK IN THIS SECTION ONLY. DO NOT WORK IN ANY OTHER SECTION OF THE TEST.

Section 6

26 Questions • 25 Minutes

Directions: Each of the following questions consists of an incomplete sentence followed by five words or pairs of words. Choose the word or pair of words that, when substituted for the blank space or spaces, best completes the meaning of the sentence and mark the letter of your choice on your answer sheet.

In view of the extenuating circumstances and the defendant's youth, the judge recommended ____.

(A) conviction

(B) a defense

(C) a mistrial

(D) leniency

(E) life imprisonment

The correct answer is (D).

---

1. The ____ was greatest when the pitcher paused before delivering the last strike.
   (A) game
   (B) crowd
   (C) cheering
   (D) sportsmanship
   (E) tension

2. Her ____ instincts led her to fund the construction of a hospital for the poor.
   (A) far-ranging
   (B) humanitarian
   (C) humble
   (D) popular
   (E) eclectic

3. After years of ____ war, the Great Wall was constructed to ____ the Chinese people.
   (A) internecine .. instigate
   (B) destructive .. resurrect
   (C) unceasing .. protect
   (D) amicable .. unite
   (E) pitiable .. win

4. His remarks were so ____ that we could not decide which of the possible meanings was correct.
   (A) facetious
   (B) ambiguous
   (C) cogent
   (D) impalpable
   (E) congruent

5. In an attempt to ____ a strike, the two sides agreed to negotiate through the night.
   (A) arbitrate
   (B) herald
   (C) trigger
   (D) transmute
   (E) avert

6. Elder statesmen used to be ____ for their wisdom when respect for age was part of every person's upbringing.
   (A) deplored
   (B) exonerated
   (C) rebuked
   (D) venerated
   (E) exiled

7. Being less than perfectly prepared, she approached the exam with ____.
   (A) aplomb
   (B) trepidation
   (C) indifference
   (D) confidence
   (E) duplicity

8. As citizens, we would be ____ if we did not make these facts public.
   (A) derelict
   (B) pejorative
   (C) impersonal
   (D) private
   (E) derogatory

Directions: Each passage below is followed by a set of questions. Read each passage, then answer the accompanying questions, basing your answers on what is stated or implied in the passage. Mark the letter of your choice on your answer sheet.

QUESTIONS 9 AND 10 ARE BASED ON THE FOLLOWING PASSAGE.

In 1903, the Wright brothers proved that airplanes were viable, but it was not until 1941 that Frank Whittle proved that planes could fly without a propeller. On May 15,
5 1941, Whittle's Gloster E.28/39 had its first sustained flight. The problem that Whittle overcame was engine size. Jet planes require a steady stream of air to push them forward. The first attempts at jet engine
10 design resulted in engines that were too heavy. Whittle figured out how to build a light-weight, more efficient engine. His invention was the first in a series of innovations that resulted in the huge jets that fly
15 400 passengers at a time across the country in less than 6 hours.

9. The word *viable* (line 2) means
   (A) healthy.
   (B) capable of life.
   (C) worthwhile.
   (D) possible.
   (E) routine.

10. The passage implies that the Wright brothers' plane
    (A) had a propeller.
    (B) had an inefficient engine.
    (C) was lightweight.
    (D) had a more efficient engine than Whittle's.
    (E) was not related to the development of jet planes.

QUESTIONS 11 AND 12 ARE BASED ON THE FOLLOWING PASSAGE.

Pesticides were supposed to save the world's crops from insects, but were found over time to be harmful to the environment and to humans. DDT is a case in point. Now
5 scientists are creating insects to save us from insects—and it is not just insects that are being created. Scientists are also engineering microbes whose mission is to kill destructive insects found in nature. The problem is
10 that no one knows for sure whether these "designer" insects and microbes can harm the environment and humans. No long-term studies have as yet been conducted on them, and government agencies such
15 as the Department of Agriculture and the Environmental Protection Agency have not approved many of them.

11. The word *designer* (line 11) refers to the fact that
    (A) the insects and microbes are not found in nature.
    (B) the insects and microbes have been developed for specific purposes.
    (C) the insects and microbes have certain specific features that are unnatural.
    (D) the insects and microbes are not natural, but have been created by scientists for specific purposes.
    (E) genetic engineers can pick and choose characteristics like fashion designers choose fabrics, colors, and details.

12. The author uses the reference to DDT to

(A) note that the new insects and microbes are also harmful.

(B) imply that the new insects and microbes may be harmful.

(C) state that the new insects and microbes are as harmful as the pesticides turned out to be.

(D) make a case for long-term study of the genetically engineered insects and microbes.

(E) reinforce the fact that pesticides were used before long-term studies showed their harm just as advocates want the new insects and microbes to be used without study.

QUESTIONS 13 AND 14 ARE BASED ON THE FOLLOWING PASSAGE.

The place of secondhand smoke in causing disease has been under study for years. A mid-sized city in a western state unexpectedly added to the data. Smoking in
5 public and in workplaces was banned and six months later the ban was lifted. During the time that smoking was prohibited in public places, the rate of hospital admissions for heart attacks was 24. During the
10 typical six-month period, the rate is 40 admissions. The researchers believed that this drop was evidence of the negative effects of secondhand smoke. Secondhand smoke contributes to heart attacks by elevating
15 heart rate and decreasing the ability of blood vessels to dilate.

13. The tone of the passage is

(A) informational.

(B) strident.

(C) challenging.

(D) informal.

(E) accusatory.

14. The phrase *typical six-month period* (line 10) refers to

(A) the time of the study.

(B) any time other than the six months during the ban.

(C) the six months before the study.

(D) the six months after the study.

(E) an unspecified time period.

QUESTIONS 15–26 ARE BASED ON THE FOLLOWING PASSAGE.

Louisa May Alcott (1832–1888) was a beloved author of books for children, but she also wrote gothic tales and short stories for adults. This excerpt is from "Mrs. Gay's Prescription."

The poor little woman looked as if she needed rest but was not likely to get it; for the room was in a chaotic state, the breakfast
5 table presented the appearance of having been devastated by a swarm of locusts, the baby began to fret, little Polly set up her usual whine of "I want sumpin to do," and a pile of work loomed in the corner waiting
10 to be done.

"I don't see how I ever shall get through it all," sighed the despondent matron as she hastily drank a last cup of tea, while two great tears rolled down her cheeks, as she
15 looked from one puny child to the other, and felt the weariness of her own tired soul and body more oppressive than ever.

A good cry was impending, when there came a brisk ring at the door, a step in the hall, and
20 a large, rosy woman came bustling in, saying in a cheery voice as she set a flower pot down upon the table, "Good morning! Nice day, isn't it? Came in early on business and brought you one of my Lady Washingtons,
25 you are so fond of flowers."

"Oh, it's lovely! How kind you are. Do sit down if you can find a chair; we are all behind hand today, for I was up half the night with poor baby, and haven't energy
30 enough to go to work yet," answered Mrs. Bennet, with a sudden smile that changed her whole face, while baby stopped fretting to stare at the rosy clusters, and Polly found

employment in exploring the pocket of the newcomer, as if she knew her way there.

35 "Let me put the pot on your stand first, girls are so careless, and I'm proud of this. It will be an ornament to your parlor for a week," and opening a door Mrs. Gay carried the plant to a sunny bay window where many
40 others were blooming beautifully.

Mrs. Bennet and the children followed to talk and admire, while the servant leisurely cleared the table.

"Now give me that baby, put yourself in
45 the easy chair, and tell me all about your worries," said Mrs. Gay, in the brisk, commanding way which few people could resist.

"I'm sure I don't know where to begin," sighed Mrs. Bennet, dropping into the com-
50 fortable seat while baby changed bearers with great composure.

"I met your husband and he said the doctor had ordered you and these chicks off to Florida for the winter. John said he didn't
55 know how he should manage it, but he meant to try."

"Isn't it dreadful? He can't leave his business to go with me, and we shall have to get Aunt Miranda to come and see to him and
60 the boys while I'm gone, and the boys can't bear her strict, old-fashioned ways, and I've got to go that long journey all alone and stay among strangers, and these heaps of fall work to do first, and it will cost an
65 immense sum to send us, and I don't know what is to become of me."

Here Mrs. Bennet stopped for breath, and Mrs. Gay asked briskly, "What is the matter with you and the children?"

70 "Well, baby is having a hard time with his teeth and is croupy, Polly doesn't get over scarlet fever well, and I'm used up; no strength or appetite, pain in my side and low spirits. Entire change of scene, milder
75 climate, and less work for me, is what we want, the doctor says. John is very anxious about us, and I feel regularly discouraged."

"I'll spend the day and cheer you up a bit. You just rest and get ready for a new start
80 tomorrow; it is a saving of time to stop short now and then and see where to begin next. Bring me the most pressing job of work. I can sew and see to this little rascal at the same time."

15. The "little woman" referred to in line 1 is
   (A) Lady Washington.
   (B) Alcott's mother.
   (C) a servant.
   (D) Mrs. Bennet.
   (E) Mrs. Gay.

16. When Alcott compares the breakfast table to something "devastated by a swarm of locusts" (line 6), she means
   (A) that it is a mess left by an uncaring mob.
   (B) that children are no more meaningful than insects to Mrs. Bennet.
   (C) to indicate Mrs. Bennet's flightiness.
   (D) to illustrate the horror of Mrs. Bennet's life.
   (E) that the Bennets are pests.

17. All of the following contribute to the Bennets' "chaotic state" of affairs EXCEPT
   (A) the overall appearance of the breakfast table.
   (B) the fretting of the baby.
   (C) the contribution of Polly.
   (D) the uncompleted pile of work.
   (E) the optimism of Mrs. Gay.

18. The word *despondent* in line 12 most nearly means
   (A) different.
   (B) daring.
   (C) excited.
   (D) exasperated.
   (E) dilapidated.

19. Had Mrs. Gay not arrived when she did, Alcott leads us to suspect that
    (A) Mrs. Bennet would have gone back to bed.
    (B) the children would have continued to cry.
    (C) Mrs. Bennet would have accomplished little all day.
    (D) sickness would have overtaken the entire family.
    (E) the servant would have left the dishes untended.

20. The "rosy clusters" in line 33 are
    (A) Mrs. Gay's cheeks.
    (B) Mrs. Bennet's cheeks.
    (C) flowers.
    (D) candies from Mrs. Gay's pockets.
    (E) embroidered pockets.

21. In lines 38–40 Alcott
    (A) reveals Mrs. Bennet's only talent.
    (B) uses the sunny parlor as a symbol of hope.
    (C) contrasts Mrs. Gay's sunniness with Mrs. Bennet's dullness.
    (D) contrasts Mrs. Bennet's plants with her children.
    (E) opens the door to Mrs. Bennet's despair.

22. When Mrs. Bennet says that she's "used up" (line 72), she means that she
    (A) has no energy.
    (B) is abused.
    (C) is exploited.
    (D) has spent all her money.
    (E) has given up.

23. The word *pressing* (line 82) means
    (A) heavy.
    (B) ardent.
    (C) forceful.
    (D) important.
    (E) concentrated.

24. Mrs. Bennet's friend's disposition is indicated by
    (A) her name.
    (B) her speech.
    (C) her clothing.
    (D) both (A) and (B).
    (E) both (B) and (C).

25. Alcott implies that Mrs. Bennet's real problem is
    (A) her inability to cope.
    (B) a touch of fever.
    (C) the cold winter weather.
    (D) unsympathetic children.
    (E) a lack of common sense.

26. Mrs. Gay's primary quality seems to be her
    (A) lethargy.
    (B) obliviousness.
    (C) anxiety.
    (D) dignity.
    (E) practical nature.

STOP

END OF SECTION 6. IF YOU HAVE ANY TIME LEFT, GO OVER YOUR WORK IN THIS SECTION ONLY. DO NOT WORK IN ANY OTHER SECTION OF THE TEST.

Section 7

15 Questions • 20 Minutes

Directions: Solve the following problems using any available space on the page for scratchwork. On your answer sheet fill in the choice that best corresponds to the correct answer.

Notes: The figures accompanying the problems are drawn as accurately as possible unless otherwise stated in specific problems. Again, unless otherwise stated, all figures lie in the same plane. All numbers used in these problems are real numbers. Calculators are permitted for this test.

Reference Information

Circle:
$C = 2\pi r$
$A = \pi r^2$

Rectangle:
$A = lw$

Rectangular Solid:
$V = lwh$

Cylinder:
$V = \pi r^2 h$

Triangle:
$A = \frac{1}{2}bh$

$a^2 + b^2 = c^2$

The number of degrees of arc in a circle is 360.
The measure in degrees of a straight angle is 180.
The sum of the measures in degrees of the angles of a triangle is 180.

---

1. Which one of the following quantities has the least value?

(A) $\dfrac{4}{5}$

(B) $\dfrac{7}{9}$

(C) 0.76

(D) $\dfrac{5}{7}$

(E) $\dfrac{9}{11}$

2. A salesperson earns twice as much in December as in each of the other months of a year. What part of this salesperson's entire year's earnings is earned in December?

(A) $\dfrac{1}{7}$

(B) $\dfrac{2}{13}$

(C) $\dfrac{1}{6}$

(D) $\dfrac{2}{11}$

(E) $\dfrac{3}{14}$

3. If $x = -1$, then $3x^3 + 2x^2 + x + 1 =$

(A) -5

(B) -1

(C) 1

(D) 2

(E) 5

4. $0.03\% \times 0.21 =$

(A) 0.63

(B) 0.063

(C) 0.0063

(D) 0.00063

(E) 0.000063

5. An equilateral triangle 3 inches on a side is cut up into smaller equilateral triangles 1 inch on a side. What is the greatest number of such triangles that can be formed?

(A) 3

(B) 6

(C) 9

(D) 12

(E) 15

6. A square 5 units on a side has one vertex at the point (1,1) and has sides that are parallel to the x– and y-axes. Which one of the following points *cannot* be diagonally opposite that vertex?

   (A) (6,6)

   (B) (−4,6)

   (C) (−4,−4)

   (D) (6,−4)

   (E) (4,−6)

7. Five equal squares are placed side by side to make a single rectangle whose perimeter is 372 inches. Find the number of square inches in the area of one of these squares.

   (A) 72

   (B) 324

   (C) 900

   (D) 961

   (E) 984

8. The water level of a swimming pool, 75 feet by 42 feet, is to be raised 4 inches. How many gallons of water must be added to accomplish this? (7.48 gal. = 1 cubic ft.)

   (A) 140

   (B) 7854

   (C) 31,500

   (D) 94,500

   (E) 727,650

9. What part of the total quantity is represented by a 24-degree sector of a circle graph?

   (A) $6\frac{2}{3}\%$

   (B) 12%

   (C) $13\frac{1}{3}\%$

   (D) 15%

   (E) 24%

10. The square of a fraction between 0 and 1 is

    (A) less than the original fraction.

    (B) greater than the original fraction.

    (C) twice the original fraction.

    (D) less than the cube of the fraction.

    (E) not necessarily any of the preceding.

11. A circle is inscribed in a given square and another circle is circumscribed about the same square. What is the ratio of the area of the inscribed circle to the area of the circumscribed circle?

    (A) 1:4

    (B) 4:9

    (C) 1:2

    (D) 2:3

    (E) 3:4

12. If $\frac{3}{7}$ of a bucket can be filled in 1 minute, how many minutes will it take to fill the rest of the bucket?

    (A) $\frac{7}{3}$

    (B) $\frac{4}{3}$

    (C) 1

    (D) $\frac{3}{4}$

    (E) $\frac{4}{7}$

13. In the figure below, the side of the large square is 14. The four smaller squares are formed by joining the midpoints of opposite sides. Find the value of Y.

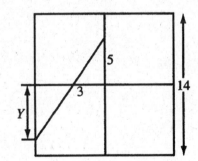

    (A) 5

    (B) 6

    (C) $6\frac{5}{8}$

    (D) $6\frac{2}{3}$

    (E) 6.8

14. In how many different ways can 6 books be arranged on a shelf if one of the books, book X, has to be first?

(A) 120
(B) 640
(C) 720
(D) 3125
(E) 7776

15. If $P = \{2, 3, 5\}$, $Q = \{5, 10, 15\}$, and $R = \{2, 5, 15, 25\}$, which of the following sets represents $P \cap Q \cap R$?

(A) $\{5\}$
(B) $\{2, 5\}$
(C) $\{2, 5, 10\}$
(D) $\{2, 5, 15\}$
(E) $\{2, 3, 5, 10, 15, 25\}$

STOP

END OF SECTION 7. IF YOU HAVE ANY TIME LEFT, GO OVER YOUR WORK IN THIS SECTION ONLY. DO NOT WORK IN ANY OTHER SECTION OF THE TEST.

Section 8

16 Questions • 20 Minutes

Directions: The two passages given below deal with a related topic. Following the passages are questions about the content of each passage or about the relationship between the two passages. Answer the questions based upon what is stated or implied in the passages and in any introductory material provided. Mark the letter of your choice on your answer sheet.

QUESTIONS 1–4 ARE BASED ON THE FOLLOWING PASSAGES.

The following two passages represent two views of the Constitution.

Passage 1

If you make the citizens of this country agree to become the subjects of one great consolidated empire of America, your government will not have sufficient energy to keep them
5 together. Such a government is incompatible with the genius of republicanism. There will be no checks, no real balances, in this government. What can avail your specious, imaginary balances, your rope-dancing,
10 chain-rattling ridiculous ideal checks and contrivances?

—Patrick Henry

Passage 2

In order to lay a due foundation for that separate and distinct exercise of the different powers of government, which to a certain extent is admitted on all hands to
5 be essential to the preservation of liberty; it is evident that each department should have a will of its own; and consequently should be so constituted that the members of each should have as little agency as pos-
10 sible in the appointment of the members of the others. . . . It is equally evident that the members of each department should be as little dependent as possible on those of the others for the emoluments annexed to
15 their offices.

—James Madison

1. The word *genius* (line 6) in Passage 1 means
   (A) great intellect.
   (B) great ability.
   (C) intellectual rigor.
   (D) strong influence.
   (E) essential quality.

2. The tone of Passage 1 is
   (A) humorous.
   (B) rational.
   (C) ironic.
   (D) angry.
   (E) exaggerated.

3. When Passage 2 refers to *as little agency as possible in the appointment of the members* (lines 9–10) it means
   (A) as little inter-office rivalry as possible.
   (B) having small departments.
   (C) as little influence as possible in staffing other departments.
   (D) having little discretion in staffing a department—one's own or others.
   (E) paying as little attention as possible to other departments.

4. All of the following are major differences between Passages 1 and 2 EXCEPT
   (A) tone.
   (B) the use of specific examples to support the author's argument.
   (C) word choice.
   (D) subject matter.
   (E) sentence structure.

QUESTIONS 5–16 ARE BASED ON THE FOLLOWING PASSAGES.

The two American women described in the following passages, Mary Harris (Mother Jones) and Rachel Carson, lived almost a century apart, yet in the face of great obstacles both fought for a vision of life that they believed in.

Passage 1—Mother Jones, the Miners' Angel

Mary Harris (Mother Jones) was born in County Cork, Ireland, in the late 1830s, and came to be known in the United States as the "miners' angel" for the work that she
5 did on behalf of coal miners from West Virginia to Colorado. Working at a time when very few women were active in the public arena, Harris worked tirelessly on behalf of workers, who were often mistreated during
10 that part of the nineteenth century. She helped to organize unions among the textile workers, steel workers, brewery workers, and coal miners.

And who was this woman? Born in Ireland
15 during a time of Irish rebellion against the British, Mary Harris was quite familiar with unrest and violence. The Irish at that point in their troubled history could not vote, hold office, or buy land, and Mary's family was
20 known in County Cork as dissident rebels who fought the British oppressors. Forced to leave Ireland for political reasons, the Harris family fled to the United States with waves of other Irish immigrants. In the United States
25 Mary Harris married George Jones, an iron worker, who was a member of a trade union in Chicago. It was in Chicago that Mary Jones, after the untimely loss of her husband and young family to yellow fever, began her
30 early union work. Finding herself homeless after the Chicago fire in 1871, Mary began to spend time at the hall where the Knights of Labor held their meetings. It was through what she learned at these meetings that
35 she became a radical union organizer. Remaining loyal to the Knights of Labor through its growing pains of the 1870s and 1880s, she continued to fight for the rights of working people who suffered greatly due
40 to the capriciousness of employers, who could reduce their wages at the first sign of economic difficulty. Railroad workers were particularly oppressed, and it was to their cause that Mary Jones first gave her
45 support, working with Eugene V. Debs, who had organized the American Railway Union. But it was in the coal fields of Pennsylvania during the 1890s that Mary made her most significant contributions. It was here that she
50 received the name "Mother Jones" from the miners because she called them "her boys." She convinced the miners she was willing to risk her life for them, and earned their undying love and gratitude. Although she
55 organized textile workers, fought for child labor laws, and spent time with Colorado miners, her heart was always with the miners of West Virginia; she returned time after time to help them organize, often placing
60 her own life in danger.

Mother Jones lived to be 100 years old, and during her lifetime, she crossed the country time and again to fight battles for fair labor laws. A woman of vision with a
65 clear understanding of the rights of workers, she was buried in Mt. Olive, Illinois, in a union cemetery next to miners who were killed in an 1898 labor dispute.

Passage 2—Rachel Carson, Protector of the Environment

Today we can hardly imagine a world without newspapers and magazines that express deep concern about the environment; without Earth Day speeches and marches,
5 and without elected officials assuring their constituencies that they will do everything in their power to assure that the ecological balance is preserved in their areas. But in 1962, when Rachel Carson's *Silent Spring*
10 was first published, this was not the case. Carson, a former marine biologist for the Fish and Game Service, disturbed many who had a vested interest in maintaining the status quo as far as the environment
15 was concerned. Her credibility as a scientist and her deep and abiding personal courage enabled Carson to withstand the steady onslaught of criticism heaped on her during her lifetime. This criticism seemed
20 to be directed at her on several levels—as a woman whose emotional response to the

situation was getting in the way of scientific
accuracy and as a scientist who believed that
man should accommodate to nature rather
25 than try to control it.

And what exactly was it that Rachel Carson
did that was so disturbing? She pointed out
the dangers of pesticides, DDT in particular,
to the environment. Designed to contain
30 insect pests in gardens and on farmland,
the pesticides were permeating the soil,
the rivers, and adhering to tree leaves and
branches that were the home for various
birds and unharmful insects.

35 Carson contended that the levels of chemical
pesticides in major rivers, ground water,
wildlife, soil, fish, earth-worms, and
humans, for example, were at levels that
were alarming. The synthetic insecticides,
40 according to Carson, were so potent that
they were able to penetrate systems and
remain there for years, perhaps leading to
a breakdown in tissue and immune systems,
and possibly causing malignancies. Arsenic,
45 the chief ingredient in insecticides and
pesticides at the time of Carson's writing,
is extremely toxic, causing reactions in
livestock near areas dusted with arsenic
sprays. Arsenic absorbed in the soil has even
50 been found in plant tissues, thereby causing
unsprayed plants to take up toxicity from the
soil. As residue from the pesticides continues
to build up in the soil over the years, more
and more plant life is contaminated.

55 The furor caused by Carson's writing was
mostly felt by the chemical companies
that produced pesticides. Not willing to
acknowledge the potential hazards of their
products, they resisted by seeking to dis-
60 credit Carson. And despite her credentials,
Carson was discredited for a period of time.
However, in 1970 with the establishment of
the Environmental Protection Agency, the
nation became more concerned with issues
65 that Carson had raised. Even though not as
much progress has been made as Carson
might have wished, DDT has been banned
in the United States.

Rachel Carson, a scientist of vision and
70 determination, was able to change the course
of history and bring environmental issues
to the attention of the world.

5. According to Passage 1, the work of Mary
Harris was particularly noteworthy because
(A) she was an Irish immigrant.
(B) she fought for workers' rights.
(C) everyone was sure that she would
fail.
(D) no one was supporting workers at
that time.
(E) very few women worked in the
public sector.

6. The author implies that Mother Jones became
a champion of workers' rights because
(A) she experienced injustices in her
native Ireland.
(B) no other work was open to her.
(C) the workers prevailed upon her to
take up their cause.
(D) she knew how hard life in the textile
mills was.
(E) workers were so mistreated in the
midnineteenth century.

7. Mother Jones's family responded to the
oppression of the British by
(A) joining the rebels.
(B) emigrating to Australia.
(C) becoming involved in local
government.
(D) joining the Labor Party.
(E) establishing large land holdings.

8. Mother Jones learned to become a radical
union organizer through her association with
(A) Irish rebels.
(B) the Knights of Labor.
(C) West Virginia coal miners.
(D) textile workers.
(E) County Cork Association.

9. When Passage 1 refers to the *capriciousness
of employers* (line 40), it means employers
(A) were subject to no rules.
(B) were generous.
(C) were interested in profits.
(D) hired only nonunion workers.
(E) were not interested in workers'
problems.

10. According to Passage 1, Eugene V. Debs organized the

(A) Knights of Labor.

(B) Textile Workers' Union.

(C) American Railway Union.

(D) Coal Miners' Union.

(E) Steel Workers' Union.

11. In Passage 2, the word *constituencies* (line 6) means

(A) an advisory committee.

(B) financial contributors.

(C) campaign workers.

(D) legislative body.

(E) a group of citizens.

12. According to Passage 2, the reaction to Carson's findings and recommendations during her lifetime was

(A) completely indifferent.

(B) highly supportive.

(C) somewhat critical.

(D) negative and hostile.

(E) positive and accepting.

13. Rachel Carson pointed out the hazards to the environment associated with

(A) pesticides.

(B) acid rain.

(C) smog.

(D) destruction of the rain forest.

(E) noise pollution.

14. According to Passage 2, Carson maintained that the use of insecticides was responsible for all of the following EXCEPT

(A) human tissue breakdown.

(B) breakdown of the immune system.

(C) breathing difficulties.

(D) malignancies.

(E) plant tissue contamination.

15. One of the most toxic ingredients in insecticides, according to the passage, is

(A) synthetic toxins.

(B) DDT.

(C) arsenic.

(D) Agent Orange.

(E) poisonous herbs.

16. The authors of the two passages would agree that a quality shared by Mother Jones and Rachel Carson was

(A) need for power.

(B) desire for the limelight.

(C) belief in a cause.

(D) understanding of the media.

(E) interest in monetary reward.

STOP

END OF SECTION 8. IF YOU HAVE ANY TIME LEFT, GO OVER YOUR WORK IN THIS SECTION ONLY. DO NOT WORK IN ANY OTHER SECTION OF THE TEST.

Section 9

15 Questions • 10 Minutes

Directions: The sentences below may contain problems in grammar, usage, word choice, sentence construction, or punctuation. Part or all of each sentence is underlined. Following each sentence you will find five ways of expressing the underlined part. Answer choice (A) always repeats the original underlined section. The other four answer choices are all different. You are to select the lettered answer that produces the most effective sentence. If you think the original sentence is best, choose (A) as your answer. If one of the other choices makes a better sentence, mark your answer sheet for the letter of that choice. Do not choose an answer that changes the meaning of the original sentence.

I have always enjoyed singing as well as to dance.

(A) singing as well as to dance

(B) singing as well as dancing

(C) to sing as well as dancing

(D) singing in addition to dance

(E) to sing in addition to dancing

The correct answer is (B).

1. Between you and me, it is no longer as important as it once was for you to pay cash for your supplies.
   (A) Between you and me, it is no longer as important as it once was
   (B) Between you and me, it is no longer so important as it once was
   (C) Between you and I, it is no longer so important as it once was
   (D) Between you and I, it is no longer as important as it once was
   (E) Between us, it is not as important as it once was

2. In the final act, the climactic scene is when the mother and father are reunited.
   (A) is when the mother and father
   (B) is where the mother and father
   (C) occurs at the point when they
   (D) occurs where the mother and father
   (E) occurs when the mother and father

3. There is really no valid excuse for him refusing to accept the invitation.
   (A) for him refusing to accept
   (B) for his refusing to accept
   (C) for his refusal of accepting
   (D) of his refusal to accept
   (E) for his refusing to except

4. I ordered the sort of a dessert that no one except her could finish.
   (A) the sort of a dessert that no one except her could
   (B) the sort of a dessert that no one except she could
   (C) the type of dessert she only could
   (D) a dessert no one could
   (E) the sort of dessert that no one except her could

5. The examiner told us that the instructions were to be read by us carefully.
   (A) that the instructions were to be read by us carefully
   (B) that the instructions were read by us carefully
   (C) that careful reading of the instructions was required of us
   (D) to read the instructions carefully
   (E) carefully to read the instructions

6. <u>After failing the first examination,</u> the teacher recommended that Tony come in after school for extra help.
   - (A) After failing the first examination,
   - (B) After he had failed the first examination,
   - (C) Having failed the first examination,
   - (D) Failing the first examination,
   - (E) He failed the first examination,

7. After years of walk-ons and bit parts, I finally awoke to the realization that <u>I never have and never will be the actor I had dreamed of becoming.</u>
   - (A) I never have and never will be the actor I had dreamed of becoming
   - (B) never have I and never will I be the actor of my dreams
   - (C) I never have been and never will be the actor I had dreamed of becoming
   - (D) I never had and never will be the actor I dreamed of becoming
   - (E) never had I been and never would I be an actor like I dreamed of

8. Although some of the writers honored the picket line, many others went to work at the <u>studios, which ended the strike</u> almost as soon as it had begun.
   - (A) studios, which ended the strike
   - (B) studios, thus ended the strike
   - (C) studios, which had ended the strike
   - (D) studios, ending the strike
   - (E) studios; ending the strike

9. The manufacturers are obliged to contact all those workers <u>whom they think may have been</u> contaminated.
   - (A) whom they think may have been
   - (B) who they think may have been
   - (C) whom they think might have been
   - (D) who they think were
   - (E) that they think may have been

10. <u>Evaluating other's performances makes</u> one more critical of one's own effort.
    - (A) Evaluating other's performances makes
    - (B) Evaluating other's performances make
    - (C) Evaluating others' performances makes
    - (D) Evaluating others' performances make
    - (E) Evaluation of other performances make

11. To visit the recently reconstructed Globe Theatre is to stand <u>where Shakespeare once stood.</u>
    - (A) where Shakespeare once stood
    - (B) where Shakespeare has once stood
    - (C) where Shakespeare had once stood
    - (D) where Shakespeare once was standing
    - (E) in the place where Shakespeare once was

12. The student had interesting hobbies; she liked <u>photography and going to plays and baseball games.</u>
    - (A) photography and going to plays and baseball games.
    - (B) photography, going to plays and baseball games.
    - (C) photography, going to plays and attending baseball games.
    - (D) taking pictures and going to plays and baseball games.
    - (E) taking pictures, going to plays and going to baseball games.

13. Although the coach wanted Chris to play, he <u>did not try and stretch</u> the eligibility rules.
    - (A) did not try and stretch
    - (B) didn't try and stretch
    - (C) tried not stretching
    - (D) did not try to stretch
    - (E) do not try and stretch

14. We believe that the United Nations has an important <u>goal, to raise</u> peoples and nations above their parochial concerns for the purpose of world peace.
    - (A) goal, to raise
    - (B) goal, raising
    - (C) goal; to raise
    - (D) goals. To raise
    - (E) goal: raising

15. The opponents of the garage plan use the council meetings as a forum to vent their anger and to ridicule the council, <u>taking their time and showing disrespect</u>.
    - (A) taking their time and showing disrespect
    - (B) by taking their time as well as showing disrespect
    - (C) taking their time and showing their disrespect
    - (D) having taken their time and then showing disrespect
    - (E) taking its time and showing disrespect

STOP

END OF SECTION 9. IF YOU HAVE ANY TIME LEFT, GO OVER YOUR WORK IN THIS SECTION ONLY. DO NOT WORK IN ANY OTHER SECTION OF THE TEST.

ANSWER KEY AND EXPLANATIONS

Section 1: Writing

Sample Essay 1

What the old saying, "There is nothing new under the sun," means is that no matter how hard we try to achieve something new, it has been done before, and maybe even better. This is a very pessimistic attitude but I think it's true.

For example, poverty. There have always been poor people. We try to help them but it doesn't really matter since no matter how hard we try there will always be poor people. Sometimes I feel that the government isn't doing enough to help the poor but yet I know that it's like throwing money into a bottomless pit. Still I suppose we can't give up, we must keep trying.

There is also the problem of communication. Parents and children and children and parents have a really hard time getting to communicate with each other. We call it the generation gap but no matter what name we give it the problem has always been with us. I remember that my mother was once complaining to my aunt about her children and my aunt said, "So, what else is new?" Meaning that this is nothing that is different and has always been with us.

Human nature doesn't change. People are prejudice today and have always been. Only before they use to hide it away and not call someone prejudice but today we say that there is prejudice against women, ethnic groups, and old people and we pass laws trying to make it illegal to discriminate. We can make it illegal but we can't change peoples emotion and feeling and what's going inside of them.

So I guess the saying is right that there is really nothing new. People are people and have always had the same problems and same feelings. Only maybe today we can pass laws and also develop better ways of education so that we can learn to control our feelings so that we will not hurt other people so much as we once did. Then even though will be "nothing new under the sun" at least what is old will not do too much harm. As the saying goes, "There is nothing new under the sun."

Analysis of Essay 1

The writer uses five paragraphs to develop the essay. The introduction cites the maxim and then the writer returns to it in the concluding paragraph, citing it twice. The repetition of the quotation to tie the first and last paragraphs together is a good device. However, it would have been better to eliminate one of the quotations in the last paragraph, or, at least, to paraphrase it.

The writer makes good use of specific examples (poverty and the generation gap) in the developmental paragraphs to compare the past with the present to support the thesis.

Unfortunately, the weaknesses in technical English detract from the ideas presented. There are several serious errors in sentence structure; there is a fragment at the beginning of the second paragraph and a fragment concluding the third paragraph. The writer should review the use of the comma after introductory subordinate clauses (sentence three, paragraph two, following try) and in long compound sentences. The final "d" is omitted in "prejudiced" and "used" (as in the fourth paragraph) and the final "s" in "emotions" and in "feelings" (in the same paragraph). Also, in the same paragraph, the apostrophe is omitted in the possessive "people's." Avoiding repetitious phrases would tighten the essay and strengthen the response.

Sample Essay 2

In many ways it is true that "there is nothing new under the sun"; but in many ways it's not true. For although people continue to exist and act in much the same way as they have for thousands of years, there have been numerous changes and developments in the twentieth century that the ancient people could never have imagined.

Certainly there is still the terrible problem of war. Humankind has not yet learned the futility of continuing to wage war, of destroying people and natural wonders. This is the perhaps saddest example one can provide to illustrate the statement. Unfortunately, other unpleasant examples abound. Disease and prejudice remain with us, for instance, and there is little likelihood of their eradication in our lifetime.

On a happier note, there are things that continue to please people as they have since the beginning of time. People still sing and dance and have families. There is still work to give people satisfaction and feed themselves.

However, there are many new things under the sun—people exploring outer space, creating new machines to make life easier or better, developing the computer chip, decoding the human genome. These would surely surprise earlier generations.

Thus, it is a matter of perspective whether or not the statement, "There is nothing new under the sun," is accurate. It might depend on the century in which a person is living or on the point of view of the observer.

Analysis of Essay 2

The writer shows a sense of organization. The essay is developed in five paragraphs with a clear introduction, three-paragraph development, and conclusion. Paragraphs two and three, in addition, show that the writer organized material first with negative details and then with positive ones.

Technical English is exemplary. The writer appears to be well aware of rules governing punctuation and sentence structure. The use of transitional words *however* and *thus* to begin paragraphs four and five is very good.

The composition is excellent and shows that the writer can develop an essay with ease.

Section 2

1. C	7. D	12. C	17. C	22. B
2. E	8. B	13. B	18. D	23. A
3. A	9. B	14. B	19. B	24. A
4. D	10. D	15. D	20. C	25. A
5. B	11. C	16. E	21. D	26. E
6. B				

1. **The correct answer is (C).** Audience laughter at the wrong moment can easily *disconcert* (upset or confuse) an actor.

2. **The correct answer is (E).** Since the assurances of good faith were "hollow," it is not surprising that those who made them *reneged* on (went back on) their agreement.

3. **The correct answer is (A).** To win the majority, we must unite, or *amalgamate,* the different factions.

4. **The correct answer is (D).** A law known as the Prohibition Act would naturally be expected to *proscribe* (outlaw) something.

5. **The correct answer is (B).** A caller who will not give his name is by definition *anonymous.* Since he is giving information to the police, he may well fear *reprisals* (retaliation) by a criminal.

6. **The correct answer is (B).** An *intractable,* or stubborn, individual is likely to have trouble adapting to a new way of life. Choice (A), *nonchalant,* means unconcerned. Choice (C), *rabid,* means furious. Choice (D), *insolent,* means rude. And choice (E), *doughty,* means valiant.

7. **The correct answer is (D).** The key word *though* indicates that the word in the blank should be opposite in meaning from *shared.* The only choice that satisfies this condition is *disparate* (very different; having nothing in common).

8. **The correct answer is (B).** If you understand that *gastronomic* is an adjective having to do with eating, the only possible choice is (B). A *gourmet* (person who appreciates good food) is a *connoisseur,* or expert, in food.

9. **The correct answer is (B).** The phrase "her arm was broken" points to a negative word choice for this sentence. The only negative word is *plaintively,* which means *sadly.* All other choices are positive.

10. **The correct answer is (D).** Although the other answer choices are pieces of information stated or implied in the passage, the overriding purpose is to discuss the connection between Manet and the Impressionists.

11. **The correct answer is (C).** There is no reason to believe that the author means either choices (A) or (D), and the passage disproves choice (E). Choice (B) is too literal a reading of the word *far.*

12. **The correct answer is (C).** The prefix *un-* is a hint that the word means not or a lack of. Choice (A) is a distracter. A synonym for unostentatious is unpretentious, which is not the same as "not pretending."

13. **The correct answer is (B).** Choice (A) is the opposite of Carnegie's belief. Men are wealthy because they are wise, or wealth comes to the wise. Choice (E) may have confused you. This is not implied in the passage, but stated.

14. **The correct answer is (B).** While answers (A), (C), and (D) are all synonyms for *ravaged*, the context of the sentence supports the choice of *devastated*.

15. **The correct answer is (D).** Nowhere in the passage is the quality of the soil mentioned as a reason for the dependence on the potato as a staple.

16. **The correct answer is (E).** While not directly stated in the passage, the author certainly implies that the dependence on one crop was dangerous.

17. **The correct answer is (C).** The passage certainly describes Irish life as characterized by poverty and oppression from landlords, so *harsh* is the correct answer.

18. **The correct answer is (D).** The passage states that farmers were compelled to subdivide in order to make rent payments to their landlords.

19. **The correct answer is (B).** The best answer according to the context of the sentence is *disease*, particularly since in the sentence the word applies to the crop.

20. **The correct answer is (C).** While some of the other responses may be true, they are not stated in the passage.

21. **The correct answer is (D).** The Irish did not gain their independence during this period; no reference to Irish independence is made in the passage.

22. **The correct answer is (B).** Jupiter is being asked to decide which of three goddesses is the fairest—it is a no-win decision, since it is bound to anger two of the three.

23. **The correct answer is (A).** Ulysses has no inclination to embark on the adventure, since he is happy at home with his family.

24. **The correct answer is (A).** "Ulysses pretended to be mad" (line 51), and one of the methods he chose was to hitch up a mismatched team and sow something that could not grow.

25. **The correct answer is (A).** Again Bulfinch expects his readers to understand Ulysses' clever ploy without its being spelled out. Achilles is disguised as a woman, but he is inappropriately interested in manly objects.

26. **The correct answer is (E).** This is an accurate summary of the main themes in the passage.

answers practice test 3

Section 3: Math

1. C	5. D	9. D	13. B	17. C
2. C	6. A	10. A	14. C	18. B
3. C	7. D	11. B	15. D	19. D
4. B	8. C	12. D	16. D	20. A

Note: A ▦ following a math answer explanation indicates that a calculator could be helpful in solving that particular problem.

1. **The correct answer is (C).** Let the other two angles be $2x$ and $5x$. Thus,

   $$2x + 5x + 82 = 180$$
   $$7x = 98$$
   $$x = 14$$
   $$2x = 28$$
   $$5x = 70$$

   Smallest angle = 28°   ▦

2. **The correct answer is (C).** Let x = number of years for two populations to be equal. Then,

   $$6800 - 120x = 4200 + 80x$$
   $$2600 = 200x$$
   $$x = 13$$

3. **The correct answer is (C).** Simply plug the two values into the formula.

   $2^2 - 2(2) = 0$ and $1^2 - 2(1) = -1$
   *2 - *1 = 0 - (-1) = 1.   ▦

4. **The correct answer is (B).**

   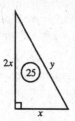

   $$\frac{1}{2} \cdot x \cdot 2x = 25$$
   $$x^2 = 25$$
   $$x = 5$$
   $$2x = 10$$
   $$y^2 = 5^2 + 10^2$$
   $$y^2 = 25 + 100$$
   $$y^2 = 125$$
   $$y = \sqrt{125} = \sqrt{25 \times 5}$$
   $$y = 5\sqrt{5}$$ ▦

5. **The correct answer is (D).** The abscissa of Q is 3 more than that of P. The ordinate of Q is 2 less than that of P. Hence, coordinates of Q are $(3 + 3, 7 - 2) = (6,5)$.

6. **The correct answer is (A).** $r = 5x$ Divide both sides by 10.

   $$\frac{r}{10} = \frac{5}{10}x$$

   or $\frac{1}{10}r = \frac{1}{2}x$

   Hence, 1 is the answer.

7. **The correct answer is (D).** The area of triangle *ADE* equals the area of triangle *AEC*, since they have the same base and altitude. The area of triangle *ABC* equals that of triangle *ADC*, since the diagonal of a parallelogram divides it equally.

8. **The correct answer is (C).** If the side of a square is *s*, its diagonal is the hypotenuse of a right triangle with two sides as its legs. The length of the diagonal is:

$$\sqrt{s^2 + s^2} = \sqrt{2s^2}$$
$$= \sqrt{s^2}\sqrt{2}$$
$$= s\sqrt{2}$$
$$\approx 1.41s$$

So $s = \dfrac{\text{diagonal}}{1.41} \approx 0.7(\text{diagonal})$.

9. **The correct answer is (D).** This is an inverse proportion; that is:

$$\frac{9}{6} = \frac{x}{120}$$
$$6x = 1080$$
$$x = 180$$

10. **The correct answer is (A).** Thinking of a clock in terms of degrees, there are 360 degrees from 12 noon to 12 midnight. In 1 hour, there are 360 degrees ÷ 12 hours = 30 degrees per hour. In 2 hours, the hour hand moves 2 hours × 30 degrees per hour = 60 degrees. Therefore, in 2 hours and 12 minutes, the hour hand moves 66 degrees.

11. **The correct answer is (B).**

$$8 \times 6 = 48$$
$$6 \times 8 = 48$$
$$48 + 48 = 96 \text{ (sum of all 14 numbers)}$$

$$\text{Average} = \frac{96}{14} = 6\frac{6}{7}$$

12. **The correct answer is (D).**

I. As *x* increases, $(1 - x^2)$ decreases.

II. As *x* increases, $(x - 1)$ increases.

III. As *x* increases, $\dfrac{1}{x^2}$ decreases.

Hence, only II increases.

13. **The correct answer is (B).** In the 3, 7, 12, 18, 25,... series, the differences are 4, 5, 6, 7, 8,....

Thus, the series progresses as follows: 3, 7, 12, 18, 25, 33, 42, 52, 63.

14. **The correct answer is (C).** The numerator is the difference between perfect squares; $x^2 - y^2$ is equal to the product of $(x+y)$ and $(x-y)$. Therefore, $\dfrac{x^2 + y^2}{x - y} = \dfrac{(x+y)(x-y)}{x-y} = x + y$

15. **The correct answer is (D).** The distance traveled is the circumference of the wheel times the number of revolutions. If *r* is the number of revolutions of the back wheel, $r + 10$ will be the number of revolutions of the front wheel. They will have traveled the same distance, so 7 ft. × $(r + 10) = 9$ ft. × *r*, and $r = 35$. The wagon has gone 9 ft. × 35 revolutions = 315 ft.

16. **The correct answer is (D).** The dimensions of the flower bed including the walk are $(12 + 6)$ and $(16 + 6)$. Thus, the area is 18 yds × 22 yds = 396 square yds. The area of the flower bed alone is $12 \times 16 = 192$ square yds. Therefore, the area of the walk is 396 square yds − 192 square yds = 204 square yds.

17. **The correct answer is (C).** Dave takes 30 minutes to wash the car alone.

$$\frac{x}{15} + \frac{x}{30} = 1$$
$$2x + x = 30$$
$$3x = 30$$
$$x = 10$$

18. The correct answer is (B). The slope of the line $y = 5x + 7$ is 5, and a line parallel to this line would have the same slope. Therefore, the desired line is of the form $y = 5x + b$. Substitute $(1,3)$ into this equation to compute the value of b.

$y = 5x + b$

$3 = 5(1) + b$

$3 = 5 + b$

$b = -2$

Therefore, the equation is $y = 5x - 2$.

19. The correct answer is (D).

$$\left(f^{\frac{2}{5}} g^{-\frac{1}{10}}\right)^{20} \left(f^{-\frac{2}{5}}\right)^{20} \left(g^{-\frac{1}{10}}\right)^{20} = f^{\frac{40}{5}} g^{-\frac{20}{10}} =$$

$$f^8 g^{-2} = \frac{f^8}{g^2}$$

20. The correct answer is (A). Since square roots of negative numbers are not defined, exclude all values of x for which $4x - 9 < 0$.

$4x - 9 < 0$ Add 9 to both sides.

$\quad 4x < 9$

$\quad\quad x < \dfrac{9}{4}$

Section 4: Writing

1. B	8. A	15. A	22. E	29. C
2. A	9. C	16. B	23. B	30. E
3. A	10. E	17. A	24. C	31. A
4. B	11. D	18. C	25. A	32. B
5. E	12. A	19. C	26. B	33. C
6. B	13. C	20. D	27. D	34. D
7. A	14. E	21. C	28. C	35. A

1. **The correct answer is (B).** The sentence requires the word *novels* (plural), not *novel's* (possessive).

2. **The correct answer is (A).** The past subjunctive *had gone* is needed in the first clause to coordinate with the past conditional in the second clause (*would have won*).

3. **The correct answer is (A).** *All together*, which means "everybody or everything together," should be *altogether*, which means "entirely or completely."

4. **The correct answer is (B).** As part of the compound subject, the correct pronoun is *I*, not *myself*.

5. **The correct answer is (E).** The sentence is correct.

6. **The correct answer is (B).** *Only* should precede *it*.

7. **The correct answer is (A).** *Hardly no one* is a double negative and is incorrect. The correct phrase is *Hardly any one*.

8. **The correct answer is (A).** What is the subject, *census* (singular) or *statistics* (plural)? *Statistics*. *Census* is used as an adjective. The plural subject means you would need a plural verb, *were*. The answer is (A).

9. **The correct answer is (C).** The phrase *as well as* is needed for a complete comparison: *its stars can dance as well as the best*.

10. **The correct answer is (E).** The sentence is correct.

11. **The correct answer is (D).** The correct form is *would have been*.

12. **The correct answer is (A).** The singular subject *Bill* requires the singular verb *is*.

13. **The correct answer is (C).** The singular pronoun *his* (or *her*) is required to agree with the singular antecedent *everyone*.

14. **The correct answer is (E).** The sentence is correct.

15. **The correct answer is (A).** The correct phrase is *In regard to*.

16. **The correct answer is (B).** The adjective *bad* is required after the verb *feel*.

17. **The correct answer is (A).** The verb *is*, a singular form, is incorrect; the correct form is *are* to agree with the plural subject *reasons*.

18. **The correct answer is (C).** *Honest truth* is redundant, since by its very definition *truth* is honest.

19. **The correct answer is (C).** Do not switch from the third person (*person*) to the second person (*you*) in the middle of a sentence.

20. **The correct answer is (D).** The nominative *whoever* is required as the subject of the verb *need*. Nothing is gained by changing the simple *need* to the more cumbersome *has need of*.

21. **The correct answer is (C).** The antecedent of *that* is the plural *studies*; therefore, the verb must also be plural (*were done*). Choices (A) and (B) use singular verbs. Choices (D) and (E) are ungrammatical.

22. **The correct answer is (E).** The subordinate clause should be introduced by a subordinating conjunction, such as *Because*, and not by the phrase *Due to*.

23. **The correct answer is (B).** The semicolon is incorrect since a comma is required to separate the independent clause from the dependent clause. Choice (E) is incorrect since a comma cannot be employed to separate two independent clauses.

24. **The correct answer is (C).** The first verb (*was riding*) sets the time for the verbs to follow (*came and sat*); choices (A), (B), and (E) shift from past to present tense. Choice (D) incorrectly uses *besides*, which means "in addition to," in place of *beside,* which means close to.

25. **The correct answer is (A).** The sentence is correct. The antecedent of *that* is *trees*, so the verb must be plural.

26. **The correct answer is (B).** In the comparison, the correct phrase is "than any *other* ...."

27. **The correct answer is (D).** The collective noun *team* when thought of as a unit takes a singular verb. Since the first verb (*ended*) is past tense, the second must also reflect past time (*was leading*). Choice (A) is a plural verb form. Choices (B), (C), and (E) are all present tense.

28. **The correct answer is (C).** Correct parallel structure requires all of the phrases to begin with *ing* verb forms as in choices (C) and (E). However, the compound subject requires a plural verb (*were recommended*), which is found only in choice (C).

29. **The correct answer is (C).** The pronoun *it* is unclear; the verb *shows* requires a more definite subject. Both choices (C) and (E) provide a suitable subject. However, the author showed *that*, not *how*, her motivation is greed,

30. **The correct answer is (E).** Since the entire essay concerns the concept that in a free and open society like ours, the citizenry has both the right and the obligation to participate in the election process, sentence (1) presents the main thesis of the essay.

31. **The correct answer is (A).** Choices (C), (D), and (E) omit the concept that these ideas are only claims, not statements of fact. Choice (B) omits the claim that the winner is almost predetermined. Therefore, choice (A) is best.

32. **The correct answer is (B).** Sentence (4) offers the claim that only those with money are selected; sentence (5) claims that poor people are never selected. Thus, sentence (5) is merely a negative restatement of sentence (4) and offers no new information.

33. **The correct answer is (C).** *Whomever* is incorrect usage. The sentence requires a subject pronoun, the subject of the verb *has*. *Whom* and *whomever* are object pronouns. Choice (C) is best since it provides the subject pronoun *whoever*.

34. **The correct answer is (D).** Choices (A), (B), and (C) are incorrect since none corrects the original comma splice error. Choice (E) is wrong because the semicolon is used incorrectly. Choice (D) is best.

35. **The correct answer is (A).** Choice (A) is best since it is both clear and consistent with the tone of the passage.

Section 5: Math

1. D	5. D	9. D	13. 0.62	17. 11
2. C	6. A	10. D	14. 72	18. $\dfrac{35}{2}$
3. E	7. B	11. 8.25	15. 36	19. 750
4. C	8. A	12. 70	16. 7	20. 2.25

Note: A ▤ following a math answer explanation indicates that a calculator could be helpful in solving that particular problem.

1. **The correct answer is (D).** There are 2 choices for the element from set X, 4 choices for the element from set Y, and 3 choices for the element from set Z. Overall, there are $2 \times 4 \times 3 = 24$ different sets that can be formed.

2. **The correct answer is (C).** Using the formula $a_n = a_1 + (n-1)d$, with $a_1 = 5$, $d = 4$, and $n = 8$, we compute $a_8 = a_1 + (n-1)d = 5 + (8-1)4 = 5 + 7(4) = 5 + 28 = 33$.

3. **The correct answer is (E).** You need to determine the value of x for which

   $1.25x - \$12 = \$78$.
   $1.25x - \$12 = \$78$ Add \$12 to both sides.
   $\quad \$1.25x = \$90$ Divide both sides by \$1.25.
   $\qquad x = 72$

4. **The correct answer is (C).**
   $(\sqrt{18} - \sqrt{8})^2 = (3\sqrt{2} - 2\sqrt{2})^2 = (\sqrt{2})^2 = 2$

5. **The correct answer is (D).**

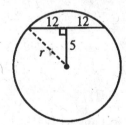

   A radius drawn perpendicular to a chord bisects the chord. Construct the radius as shown above.

   $5^2 + 12^2 = r^2$
   $25 + 144 = r^2$
   $\quad 169 = r^2$
   $\qquad 13 = r$

6. **The correct answer is (A).** An increase of 30% in the base b means that the new base will be $b + 0.30b$. A 20% decrease in the new altitude a means that the new altitude will be $a - 0.20a$. The new area is $(b + 0.30b)(a - 0.20a) = 1.04ba$. The new area is 104% of the old, an increase of 104% − 100% = 4%. ▤

7. **The correct answer is (B).** Typing space is $12 - 3 = 9$ inches long and $9 - 2 = 7$ inches wide.

   Part used $= \dfrac{9 \times 7}{9 \times 12} = \dfrac{7}{12}$

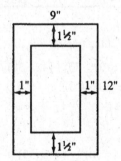

8. **The correct answer is (A).**

   Triangle $SPT = \dfrac{1}{3}\triangle PSR$ since they have common altitude and the base $ST = \dfrac{1}{3}SR$.
   But, $\triangle PSR = \dfrac{1}{2} \times PQRS$.
   Hence, $\triangle SPT = \dfrac{1}{3} \times \dfrac{1}{2} \times PQRS = \dfrac{1}{6} \times PQRS$.

9. **The correct answer is (D).**
   $A = P(1 + rt)$
   $A = P + Prt$
   $A - P = Prt$

   Divide both sides by Pr.

   $t = \dfrac{A - P}{Pr}$

10. The correct answer is (D).

I. Since $r < 0$, multiplying both sides of $p > q$ by r reverses the inequality to $pr < qr$.

II. Also, $p + r > q + r$.

III. However, subtracting r from both sides leaves the inequality in same order.

Hence, I and II only.

11. The correct answer is 8.25.

$$\frac{x}{11} = 15$$
$$x = 165$$
$$\frac{165}{20} = 8.25$$

12. The correct answer is 70.

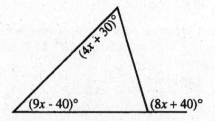

An exterior angle of a triangle is equal to the sum of the two remote interior angles.

$$8x + 40 = (9x - 40) + (4x + 30)$$
$$8x + 40 = 13x - 10$$
$$5x = 50$$
$$x = 10$$
$$\angle J = (4x + 30)° = (40 + 30)° = 70°$$

13. The correct answer is 0.62.

$$\frac{2^2 + 3^2}{5^2} + \frac{1}{10} = \frac{4 + 9}{25} + \frac{1}{10}$$
$$= \frac{13}{25} + \frac{1}{10}$$

The least common denominator is 50.

$$= \frac{26}{50} + \frac{5}{50} = \frac{31}{50} = 0.62$$

14. The correct answer is 72. The shaded area is the area of the rectangle minus the area of the two circles.

Area of the rectangle $= 6(12) = 72$

Area of circle $= \pi r^2 = 9\pi$

Shaded area $= 72 - 2(9\pi)$
$$= 72 - 18\pi$$
$$= a - b\pi$$

$\therefore a = 72$ and $b = 18$

15. The correct answer is 36.

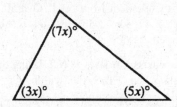

Let $3x =$ the measure of one of the angles
$5x =$ the measure of the 2nd angle
$7x =$ the measure of the 3rd angle
$$3x + 5x + 7x = 180$$
$$15x = 180$$
$$x = 12$$

The smallest angle $= 3x = 36°$.

16. The correct answer is 7.

$$b = \sqrt{(x_2 - x_1)^2 + (y_2 - y_1)^2}$$
$$= \sqrt{(3 - (-4))^2 + (-2 - 5)^2}$$
$$= \sqrt{7^2 + (-7)^2}$$
$$= \sqrt{49 + 49} = \sqrt{98} = \sqrt{49}\sqrt{2}$$
$$= 7\sqrt{2} = b\sqrt{2}$$

$\therefore b = 7$

17. The correct answer is 11.

$$\frac{9 + 9 + 10 + x + y}{5} = 10$$
$$28 + x + y = 50$$
$$x + y = 22$$

The average of x and y is
$$\frac{x + y}{2} = \frac{22}{2} = 11$$

18. **The correct answer is** $\dfrac{35}{2}$.

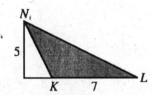

$$\text{Area } \triangle NKL = \frac{1}{2}(b)(h)$$
$$= \frac{1}{2}(7)(5) = 17.5 = \frac{35}{2}$$ 🖩

19. **The correct answer is 750.** In order for the number to be less than 50,000, the ten-thousand's digit must be 4, 3, or 1. Thus, there are 3 choices for the ten-thousand's digit. In order for the number to be odd, the unit's digit must be 3 or 1, so there are 2 choices for unit's digit. There are five possible choices for the other three digits, so overall, there are $3 \times 5 \times 5 \times 5 \times 2 = 750$ numbers.

20. **The correct answer is 2.25.** The mode of a group of numbers is the number that occurs most frequently. In this case, the mode is 3. In a group with an even number of members, the median is the arithmetic mean of the two numbers in the middle. In this case, the median would be the average of 1 and 2, which is 1.5. Thus, you need to find the average of 1.5 and 3. Compute that $\dfrac{1.5+3}{2} = \dfrac{4.5}{2} = 2.25$.

answers practice test 3

Section 6

1. E	7. B	12. E	17. E	22. A
2. B	8. A	13. A	18. D	23. D
3. C	9. D	14. B	19. C	24. D
4. B	10. A	15. D	20. C	25. A
5. E	11. E	16. A	21. B	26. E
6. D				

1. **The correct answer is (E).** *Tension* is likely to mount before a pitcher delivers the last strike of a game—especially during a pause.

2. **The correct answer is (B).** Funding a hospital for the poor may properly be called a *humanitarian* act. It may or may not be popular.

3. **The correct answer is (C).** This is the only answer in which both words are correct in relation to each other as well as to the sense of the sentence.

4. **The correct answer is (B).** The word that means "having more than one meaning" is *ambiguous*.

5. **The correct answer is (E).** The two sides might negotiate, or bargain, through the night in an attempt to *avert*, or prevent, a strike.

6. **The correct answer is (D).** The missing word must mean the same as "respect for age." The correct choice is *venerated*.

7. **The correct answer is (B).** It is likely that someone who is unprepared would approach an exam with *trepidation,* or apprehension, not with *aplomb* (self-assurance), *indifference* (lack of concern), *confidence,* or *duplicity* (hypocrisy).

8. **The correct answer is (A).** The only word that makes sense in this context is *derelict,* meaning neglectful of duty, or remiss.

9. **The correct answer is (D).** Remember that you are looking for the best answer. Choices

(B) and (D) are both meanings of *viable,* but only choice (D) makes sense.

10. **The correct answer is (A).** The only reference to the Wright brothers' plane is in the opening sentence. The discussion of efficient engines and weight is about Whittle's plane.

11. **The correct answer is (E).** Choice (D) says something similar to choice (E) but without using the simile *fashion designer,* a clear connection to the word in the question and in the passage.

12. **The correct answer is (E).** Choice (A) has not been proven because of the lack of study. Choice (B) is close to the answer, but choice (E) is a fuller statement, and, therefore, a better choice.

13. **The correct answer is (A).** The passage is straightforward and direct.

14. **The correct answer is (B).** The ban was atypical, so choice (A) can't be the right answer. Choice (E) can't be correct, because the time is specified as *the typical six-month period.*

15. **The correct answer is (D).** Introduced as the "little woman" and "despondent matron," Mrs. Bennet is named in paragraph 4. Alcott's epithets for Mrs. Bennet emphasize her weakness.

16. **The correct answer is (A).** Mrs. Bennet's family has left her this mess with as little concern as a swarm of insects might have. Locusts are not particularly horrible; had Alcott used a more potent simile, choice (D) might be correct.

17. **The correct answer is (E).** Mrs. Gay's presence has a beneficial effect on the chaotic Bennets. All of the other items either directly contribute to the chaos or are by-products of it.

18. **The correct answer is (D).** In this context, *despondent* most nearly means sad, frustrated, or exasperated. This is explained in the context of lines 12–14 during which the reader learns that Mrs. Bennet is crying.

19. **The correct answer is (C).** Before Mrs. Gay's arrival, Mrs. Bennet was about to have "a good cry" (line 18). There is no indication that she would have been able to cope with her household duties.

20. **The correct answer is (C).** The flowers Mrs. Gay brings echo the rosiness of Mrs. Gay herself—she is earlier described as "a large, rosy woman" (line 20).

21. **The correct answer is (B).** In contrast to Mrs. Bennet's disorderly breakfast room, her front parlor is sunny and filled with blooming flowers. This gives hope that things may change. Even though the blooming flowers are a contrast to the sickly children, this is not the main purpose of the sentence.

22. **The correct answer is (A).** Mrs. Bennet's lack of energy is her primary quality.

23. **The correct answer is (D).** Mrs. Gay, in her practical way, requests the job that is most vital, knowing that to get that job out of the way will improve Mrs. Bennet's spirits.

24. **The correct answer is (D).** Mrs. Gay has a name that suits her, and every speech she makes reveals her good humor and energy.

25. **The correct answer is (A).** Mrs. Bennet seems paralyzed by her situation. The "weariness of her own tired soul and body" oppresses her (line 16), and she surveys her household with despair.

26. **The correct answer is (E).** The last paragraph of the passage best expresses this quality. Mrs. Gay's get-things-done attitude is contrasted with Mrs. Bennet's ineffectiveness.

answers practice test 3

Section 7

1. D	4. E	7. D	10. A	13. D
2. B	5. C	8. B	11. C	14. A
3. B	6. E	9. A	12. B	15. A

Note: A 🖩 following a math answer explanation indicates that a calculator could be helpful in solving that particular problem.

1. The correct answer is (D).

$$\frac{4}{5} = 0.8$$

$$\frac{7}{9} = 9\overline{)7.00}^{\,0.78}$$

$$\frac{5}{7} = 7\overline{)5.00}^{\,0.71}$$

$$\frac{9}{11} = 11\overline{)9.00}^{\,0.82}$$

Thus, $\frac{5}{7}$ is the smallest quantity. 🖩

2. The correct answer is (B). Let x = amount earned each month. $2x$ = amount earned in December. Then, $11x + 2x = 13x$ (entire earnings).

$$\frac{2x}{13x} = \frac{2}{13}$$

3. The correct answer is (B).

$$3x^3 + 2x^2 + x + 1$$
$$= 3(-1)^3 + 2(-1)^2 + (-1) + 1$$
$$= 3(-1) + 2(1) - 1 + 1$$
$$= -3 + 2 + 0$$
$$= -1$$ 🖩

4. The correct answer is (E). Convert the percent to decimal form before multiplying.

$$0.03\% = 0.0003$$

$$0.0003 \times 0.21 = 0.000063$$

The number of decimal places in the product must be equal to the sum of the number of decimal places in the terms to be multiplied. 🖩

5. The correct answer is (C). Since the ratio of the sides is 3:1, the ratio of the areas is 9:1.

The subdivision into 9 triangles is shown.

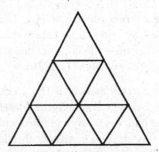

6. The correct answer is (E). The opposite vertices may be any of the number pairs $(1\pm5, 1\pm5)$, or $(6,6)$, $(-4,-4)$, $(-4,6)$, and $(6,-4)$.

Thus, $(4,-6)$ is not possible.

7. The correct answer is (D).

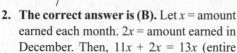

Perimeter of rectangle $= x + 5x + x + 5x$

$$\text{Thus, } 12x = 372$$
$$x = 31$$

Area of square $= 31^2 = 961$

8. The correct answer is (B). Four inches is $\frac{1}{3}$ ft. The volume of the added level is

$$75 \times 42 \times \frac{1}{3} = 1050 \text{ cubic ft.}$$ There are 7.48 gallons in 1 cubic ft., so 1050 cubic ft. $\times$ 7.48 gal./cubic ft. = 7854 gallons. 🖩

9. **The correct answer is (A).** There are 360 degrees in a circle. A 24-degree sector is

$$\frac{24}{360} = 0.067, \text{ or about } 6\frac{2}{3}\% \text{ of a circle.}$$

10. **The correct answer is (A).** In these fractions the numerator n is always less than the denominator d. After squaring the fraction $\left(\frac{n}{d}\right)^2 = \frac{n^2}{d^2}$, the new fraction is less than the original since the denominator is getting larger faster than the numerator.

11. **The correct answer is (C).** Let r = radius of inscribed circle and s = radius of circumscribed circle. Then, in right triangle OPQ,

$$PQ = OQ = r \text{ and } s = OP = r\sqrt{2}.$$

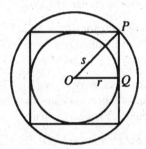

Area of inscribed circle = πr^2

Area of circumscribed circle = πs^2

$= \pi(r\sqrt{2})^2 = 2\pi r^2$

Ratio = $\dfrac{\pi r^2}{2\pi r^2} = 1:2$

12. **The correct answer is (B).** Let x = number of minutes to fill $\frac{4}{7}$ of bucket. Then,

$$\frac{\frac{3}{7}}{1} = \frac{\frac{4}{7}}{x}, \text{ or } \frac{3}{1} = \frac{4}{x}$$

$$3x = 4 \quad x = \frac{4}{3}$$

13. **The correct answer is (D).** The similar triangles in the configuration produce the proportion:

$$\frac{3}{5} = \frac{4}{Y}$$

$$3Y = 20$$

$$Y = 6\frac{2}{3}$$

14. **The correct answer is (A).** Begin by placing book X in the first position. After this is done, there are 5 remaining books that could possibly be placed in the second position, then 4 books that could go in the third position, 3 books for the fourth position, 2 books for the fifth position, and 1 book for the final position. Overall, there are $5 \times 4 \times 3 \times 2 \times 1 = 120$ possible orders.

15. **The correct answer is (A).** The set $P \cap Q \cap R$ contains only the elements that are in all three sets. The element 5 is the only element in all three sets.

Section 8

1. E	5. E	9. A	13. A
2. D	6. A	10. C	14. C
3. A	7. A	11. E	15. C
4. D	8. B	12. D	16. C

1. **The correct answer is (E).** Choices (A), (B), and (C) are good distracters. Don't look for the most familiar answer. SAT vocabulary questions test unusual meanings of words.

2. **The correct answer is (D).** While some of the phrasing may seem humorous today, ratifying the Constitution was deadly serious. This is one instance when paying attention to the author of the passage would have helped. From your history classes, you should remember Patrick Henry of "Give me liberty or give me death" fame.

3. **The correct answer is (A).** Did you remember to restate the author's words before reading the answer choices?

4. **The correct answer is (D).** Whereas Madison sets out his points and uses details to support them, Henry paints a set of broad generalizations backed up with no facts or examples. Madison's tone is direct, whereas Henry's is angry, perhaps even inflammatory. Madison's diction and sentence structure is erudite and complex, whereas Henry sticks to mostly simple sentences and easily understood words. Both are discussing the system of checks and balances.

5. **The correct answer is (E).** The author makes the point that Mary's work was most unusual because women did not work in the public arena during the mid-nineteenth century.

6. **The correct answer is (A).** The passage, with its emphasis on Mary's history of standing up for human rights, certainly implies that previous injustices influenced her later work with workers.

7. **The correct answer is (A).** The passage clearly states that Mary's family joined the Irish rebels.

8. **The correct answer is (B).** When Mary found herself homeless (lines 30–31), she lived at the union hall and became involved with the Knights of Labor.

9. **The correct answer is (A).** The context of the sentence that mentions that employers could reduce wages whenever they wished supports the choice of (A).

10. **The correct answer is (C).** The passage clearly states that Debs founded the American Railway Union (lines 45–46).

11. **The correct answer is (E).** The context of the sentence indicates that "a group of citizens" is the best choice.

12. **The correct answer is (D).** During Carson's lifetime, the response to her work was negative and hostile; it was only later that her work was appreciated for its vision.

13. **The correct answer is (A).** Carson's work concerned the effect of pesticides on the environment (lines 29–31).

14. **The correct answer is (C).** Nowhere in the passage are breathing difficulties mentioned as a side effect of using insecticides.

15. **The correct answer is (C).** The passage mentions arsenic (lines 44–46) as the most toxic ingredient.

16. **The correct answer is (C).** The choice must be "belief in a cause," as the other choices are contrary to the picture painted of each woman in the passages.

Section 9

1. A	5. D	9. B	13. D
2. E	6. B	10. C	14. A
3. B	7. C	11. A	15. E
4. E	8. D	12. D	

1. **The correct answer is (A).** The sentence is correct.

2. **The correct answer is (E).** The construction *is when* is unidiomatic. Choice (C) is wrong since it is unclear. Choice (E) adds precision and clarity and is the best choice.

3. **The correct answer is (B).** Before the gerund (*refusing*), the possessive *his* is required. Choice (E) confuses *accept,* meaning "to take when offered," with *except,* meaning "to leave out."

4. **The correct answer is (E).** The correct idiom is *sort of*, not *sort of a*. The preposition *except* takes *her* as its object. Choice (D) is grammatically correct, but changes the meaning of the original sentence.

5. **The correct answer is (D).** Choices (A), (B), and (C) all shift from the active to the passive voice. Choice (E) misplaces *carefully.*

6. **The correct answer is (B).** Adding a subject *(he)* to the dependent clause corrects the original dangling modifier. Although choice (E) provides the necessary subject, it also creates a comma splice.

7. **The correct answer is (C).** Because *have* and *will* are completed by different forms of the verb *to be* (*have been* and *will be*), both forms must appear in the sentence. Choice

(E) provides the missing verb form but uses *like* incorrectly.

8. **The correct answer is (D).** The use of *which* creates confusion as to whether the *studios* or the *working writers* ended the strike. Choice (B) creates a comma splice, and choice (E) uses a semicolon incorrectly.

9. **The correct answer is (B).** The insertion of *they think* does not alter the fact that *who* is needed as the subject of the verb *may have been contaminated.*

10. **The correct answer is (C).** *Evaluating* is the subject of the verb and, therefore, *makes* is correct. *Others'* is the correct plural possessive form.

11. **The correct answer is (A).** The sentence is correct.

12. **The correct answer is (D).** A parallel construction is required here; however, the second *going* in choice (E) is unnecessary.

13. **The correct answer is (D).** The verb *try* takes the preposition *to,* not the conjunction *and.*

14. **The correct answer is (A).** The sentence is correct.

15. **The correct answer is (E).** The antecedent for *their* is *council* used as a collective noun. To correct the error and clarify meaning, the singular *its* is correct.

COMPUTING YOUR SCORES

To get a sense of your progress in preparing for the SAT, you need to compute individual multiple-choice critical reading, math, and writing raw scores for this Practice Test. Keep in mind that these formulas have been simplified to give you a "quick and dirty" sense of where you are scoring, not a perfectly precise score.

To Compute Your Raw Scores

1 Enter the number of correct answers for each critical reading, math, and multiple-choice writing section under Number of Questions Correct.

2 Enter the number of incorrect answers (not blanks) for each critical reading, math, and multiple-choice writing section under Number of Questions Incorrect.

3 Total the number correct and number incorrect.

4 Follow this formula: Take the total correct and minus one quarter of the total incorrect. Round up in your favor to compute your raw score.

Critical Reading Section	Total Number of Questions	Number of Questions Correct	Number of Questions Incorrect
2	26		
6	26		
8	16		
Totals	68	Total Correct:	Total Incorrect:

Critical Reading Raw Score = Total Correct − ($\frac{1}{4}$ × Total Incorrect) = ____

Math Section	Total Number of Questions	Number of Questions Correct	Number of Questions Incorrect
3	20		
5	20		
7	15		
Totals	55	Total Correct:	Total Incorrect:

Math Raw Score = Total Correct − ($\frac{1}{4}$ × Total Incorrect) = ____

Multiple-Choice Writing Section	Total Number of Questions	Number of Questions Correct	Number of Questions Incorrect
4	35		
9	15		
Total	50	Total Correct:	Total Incorrect:

Multiple-Choice Writing Raw Score = Total Correct − ($\frac{1}{4}$ × Total Incorrect) = ____

CONVERSION SCALES

CRITICAL READING

Raw Score	Scaled Score	Raw Score	Scaled Score
68	800	30	480
65	760	25	440
60	710	20	410
55	670	15	370
50	620	10	340
45	590	5	290
40	550	0	230
35	520		

MATH

Raw Score	Scaled Score	Raw Score	Scaled Score
55	800	20	510
50	760	15	480
45	690	10	440
40	650	5	340
35	610	0	200
30	580		
25	550		

MULTIPLE-CHOICE WRITING

Raw Score	Scaled Score	Raw Score	Scaled Score
50	800	20	470
45	760	15	420
40	680	10	370
35	620	5	320
30	580	0	270
25	520		

SELF-EVALUATION CHARTS

Critical Reading: Raw Score

Excellent	60–68
Good	50–59
Average	30–49
Fair	20–29
Poor	0–19

Math: Raw Score

Excellent	50–55
Good	40–49
Average	20–39
Fair	10–19
Poor	0–99

ANSWER SHEET PRACTICE TEST 4

SECTION 1: ESSAY

answer sheet

If a section has fewer questions than answer ovals, leave the extra ovals blank.

SECTION 2

1 (A) (B) (C) (D) (E)   11 (A) (B) (C) (D) (E)   21 (A) (B) (C) (D) (E)   31 (A) (B) (C) (D) (E)
2 (A) (B) (C) (D) (E)   12 (A) (B) (C) (D) (E)   22 (A) (B) (C) (D) (E)   32 (A) (B) (C) (D) (E)
3 (A) (B) (C) (D) (E)   13 (A) (B) (C) (D) (E)   23 (A) (B) (C) (D) (E)   33 (A) (B) (C) (D) (E)
4 (A) (B) (C) (D) (E)   14 (A) (B) (C) (D) (E)   24 (A) (B) (C) (D) (E)   34 (A) (B) (C) (D) (E)
5 (A) (B) (C) (D) (E)   15 (A) (B) (C) (D) (E)   25 (A) (B) (C) (D) (E)   35 (A) (B) (C) (D) (E)
6 (A) (B) (C) (D) (E)   16 (A) (B) (C) (D) (E)   26 (A) (B) (C) (D) (E)   36 (A) (B) (C) (D) (E)
7 (A) (B) (C) (D) (E)   17 (A) (B) (C) (D) (E)   27 (A) (B) (C) (D) (E)   37 (A) (B) (C) (D) (E)
8 (A) (B) (C) (D) (E)   18 (A) (B) (C) (D) (E)   28 (A) (B) (C) (D) (E)   38 (A) (B) (C) (D) (E)
9 (A) (B) (C) (D) (E)   19 (A) (B) (C) (D) (E)   29 (A) (B) (C) (D) (E)   39 (A) (B) (C) (D) (E)
10 (A) (B) (C) (D) (E)   20 (A) (B) (C) (D) (E)   30 (A) (B) (C) (D) (E)   40 (A) (B) (C) (D) (E)

SECTION 3

1 (A) (B) (C) (D) (E)   11 (A) (B) (C) (D) (E)   21 (A) (B) (C) (D) (E)   31 (A) (B) (C) (D) (E)
2 (A) (B) (C) (D) (E)   12 (A) (B) (C) (D) (E)   22 (A) (B) (C) (D) (E)   32 (A) (B) (C) (D) (E)
3 (A) (B) (C) (D) (E)   13 (A) (B) (C) (D) (E)   23 (A) (B) (C) (D) (E)   33 (A) (B) (C) (D) (E)
4 (A) (B) (C) (D) (E)   14 (A) (B) (C) (D) (E)   24 (A) (B) (C) (D) (E)   34 (A) (B) (C) (D) (E)
5 (A) (B) (C) (D) (E)   15 (A) (B) (C) (D) (E)   25 (A) (B) (C) (D) (E)   35 (A) (B) (C) (D) (E)
6 (A) (B) (C) (D) (E)   16 (A) (B) (C) (D) (E)   26 (A) (B) (C) (D) (E)   36 (A) (B) (C) (D) (E)
7 (A) (B) (C) (D) (E)   17 (A) (B) (C) (D) (E)   27 (A) (B) (C) (D) (E)   37 (A) (B) (C) (D) (E)
8 (A) (B) (C) (D) (E)   18 (A) (B) (C) (D) (E)   28 (A) (B) (C) (D) (E)   38 (A) (B) (C) (D) (E)
9 (A) (B) (C) (D) (E)   19 (A) (B) (C) (D) (E)   29 (A) (B) (C) (D) (E)   39 (A) (B) (C) (D) (E)
10 (A) (B) (C) (D) (E)   20 (A) (B) (C) (D) (E)   30 (A) (B) (C) (D) (E)   40 (A) (B) (C) (D) (E)

SECTION 4

1 (A) (B) (C) (D) (E)   11 (A) (B) (C) (D) (E)   21 (A) (B) (C) (D) (E)   31 (A) (B) (C) (D) (E)
2 (A) (B) (C) (D) (E)   12 (A) (B) (C) (D) (E)   22 (A) (B) (C) (D) (E)   32 (A) (B) (C) (D) (E)
3 (A) (B) (C) (D) (E)   13 (A) (B) (C) (D) (E)   23 (A) (B) (C) (D) (E)   33 (A) (B) (C) (D) (E)
4 (A) (B) (C) (D) (E)   14 (A) (B) (C) (D) (E)   24 (A) (B) (C) (D) (E)   34 (A) (B) (C) (D) (E)
5 (A) (B) (C) (D) (E)   15 (A) (B) (C) (D) (E)   25 (A) (B) (C) (D) (E)   35 (A) (B) (C) (D) (E)
6 (A) (B) (C) (D) (E)   16 (A) (B) (C) (D) (E)   26 (A) (B) (C) (D) (E)
7 (A) (B) (C) (D) (E)   17 (A) (B) (C) (D) (E)   27 (A) (B) (C) (D) (E)
8 (A) (B) (C) (D) (E)   18 (A) (B) (C) (D) (E)   28 (A) (B) (C) (D) (E)
9 (A) (B) (C) (D) (E)   19 (A) (B) (C) (D) (E)   29 (A) (B) (C) (D) (E)
10 (A) (B) (C) (D) (E)   20 (A) (B) (C) (D) (E)   30 (A) (B) (C) (D) (E)

SECTION 5

Note: ONLY the answers entered on the grid are scored. Handwritten answers at the top of the column are NOT scored.

1 (A) (B) (C) (D) (E)   6 (A) (B) (C) (D) (E)
2 (A) (B) (C) (D) (E)   7 (A) (B) (C) (D) (E)
3 (A) (B) (C) (D) (E)   8 (A) (B) (C) (D) (E)
4 (A) (B) (C) (D) (E)   9 (A) (B) (C) (D) (E)
5 (A) (B) (C) (D) (E)   10 (A) (B) (C) (D) (E)

11. 12. 13. 14. 15.

16. 17. 18. 19. 20.

SECTION 6

1 Ⓐ Ⓑ Ⓒ Ⓓ Ⓔ	11 Ⓐ Ⓑ Ⓒ Ⓓ Ⓔ	21 Ⓐ Ⓑ Ⓒ Ⓓ Ⓔ	31 Ⓐ Ⓑ Ⓒ Ⓓ Ⓔ
2 Ⓐ Ⓑ Ⓒ Ⓓ Ⓔ	12 Ⓐ Ⓑ Ⓒ Ⓓ Ⓔ	22 Ⓐ Ⓑ Ⓒ Ⓓ Ⓔ	32 Ⓐ Ⓑ Ⓒ Ⓓ Ⓔ
3 Ⓐ Ⓑ Ⓒ Ⓓ Ⓔ	13 Ⓐ Ⓑ Ⓒ Ⓓ Ⓔ	23 Ⓐ Ⓑ Ⓒ Ⓓ Ⓔ	33 Ⓐ Ⓑ Ⓒ Ⓓ Ⓔ
4 Ⓐ Ⓑ Ⓒ Ⓓ Ⓔ	14 Ⓐ Ⓑ Ⓒ Ⓓ Ⓔ	24 Ⓐ Ⓑ Ⓒ Ⓓ Ⓔ	34 Ⓐ Ⓑ Ⓒ Ⓓ Ⓔ
5 Ⓐ Ⓑ Ⓒ Ⓓ Ⓔ	15 Ⓐ Ⓑ Ⓒ Ⓓ Ⓔ	25 Ⓐ Ⓑ Ⓒ Ⓓ Ⓔ	35 Ⓐ Ⓑ Ⓒ Ⓓ Ⓔ
6 Ⓐ Ⓑ Ⓒ Ⓓ Ⓔ	16 Ⓐ Ⓑ Ⓒ Ⓓ Ⓔ	26 Ⓐ Ⓑ Ⓒ Ⓓ Ⓔ	36 Ⓐ Ⓑ Ⓒ Ⓓ Ⓔ
7 Ⓐ Ⓑ Ⓒ Ⓓ Ⓔ	17 Ⓐ Ⓑ Ⓒ Ⓓ Ⓔ	27 Ⓐ Ⓑ Ⓒ Ⓓ Ⓔ	37 Ⓐ Ⓑ Ⓒ Ⓓ Ⓔ
8 Ⓐ Ⓑ Ⓒ Ⓓ Ⓔ	18 Ⓐ Ⓑ Ⓒ Ⓓ Ⓔ	28 Ⓐ Ⓑ Ⓒ Ⓓ Ⓔ	38 Ⓐ Ⓑ Ⓒ Ⓓ Ⓔ
9 Ⓐ Ⓑ Ⓒ Ⓓ Ⓔ	19 Ⓐ Ⓑ Ⓒ Ⓓ Ⓔ	29 Ⓐ Ⓑ Ⓒ Ⓓ Ⓔ	39 Ⓐ Ⓑ Ⓒ Ⓓ Ⓔ
10 Ⓐ Ⓑ Ⓒ Ⓓ Ⓔ	20 Ⓐ Ⓑ Ⓒ Ⓓ Ⓔ	30 Ⓐ Ⓑ Ⓒ Ⓓ Ⓔ	40 Ⓐ Ⓑ Ⓒ Ⓓ Ⓔ

SECTION 7

1 Ⓐ Ⓑ Ⓒ Ⓓ Ⓔ	6 Ⓐ Ⓑ Ⓒ Ⓓ Ⓔ	11 Ⓐ Ⓑ Ⓒ Ⓓ Ⓔ
2 Ⓐ Ⓑ Ⓒ Ⓓ Ⓔ	7 Ⓐ Ⓑ Ⓒ Ⓓ Ⓔ	12 Ⓐ Ⓑ Ⓒ Ⓓ Ⓔ
3 Ⓐ Ⓑ Ⓒ Ⓓ Ⓔ	8 Ⓐ Ⓑ Ⓒ Ⓓ Ⓔ	13 Ⓐ Ⓑ Ⓒ Ⓓ Ⓔ
4 Ⓐ Ⓑ Ⓒ Ⓓ Ⓔ	9 Ⓐ Ⓑ Ⓒ Ⓓ Ⓔ	14 Ⓐ Ⓑ Ⓒ Ⓓ Ⓔ
5 Ⓐ Ⓑ Ⓒ Ⓓ Ⓔ	10 Ⓐ Ⓑ Ⓒ Ⓓ Ⓔ	15 Ⓐ Ⓑ Ⓒ Ⓓ Ⓔ

SECTION 8

1 Ⓐ Ⓑ Ⓒ Ⓓ Ⓔ	6 Ⓐ Ⓑ Ⓒ Ⓓ Ⓔ	11 Ⓐ Ⓑ Ⓒ Ⓓ Ⓔ	16 Ⓐ Ⓑ Ⓒ Ⓓ Ⓔ
2 Ⓐ Ⓑ Ⓒ Ⓓ Ⓔ	7 Ⓐ Ⓑ Ⓒ Ⓓ Ⓔ	12 Ⓐ Ⓑ Ⓒ Ⓓ Ⓔ	17 Ⓐ Ⓑ Ⓒ Ⓓ Ⓔ
3 Ⓐ Ⓑ Ⓒ Ⓓ Ⓔ	8 Ⓐ Ⓑ Ⓒ Ⓓ Ⓔ	13 Ⓐ Ⓑ Ⓒ Ⓓ Ⓔ	18 Ⓐ Ⓑ Ⓒ Ⓓ Ⓔ
4 Ⓐ Ⓑ Ⓒ Ⓓ Ⓔ	9 Ⓐ Ⓑ Ⓒ Ⓓ Ⓔ	14 Ⓐ Ⓑ Ⓒ Ⓓ Ⓔ	19 Ⓐ Ⓑ Ⓒ Ⓓ Ⓔ
5 Ⓐ Ⓑ Ⓒ Ⓓ Ⓔ	10 Ⓐ Ⓑ Ⓒ Ⓓ Ⓔ	15 Ⓐ Ⓑ Ⓒ Ⓓ Ⓔ	20 Ⓐ Ⓑ Ⓒ Ⓓ Ⓔ

SECTION 9

1 Ⓐ Ⓑ Ⓒ Ⓓ Ⓔ	6 Ⓐ Ⓑ Ⓒ Ⓓ Ⓔ	11 Ⓐ Ⓑ Ⓒ Ⓓ Ⓔ
2 Ⓐ Ⓑ Ⓒ Ⓓ Ⓔ	7 Ⓐ Ⓑ Ⓒ Ⓓ Ⓔ	12 Ⓐ Ⓑ Ⓒ Ⓓ Ⓔ
3 Ⓐ Ⓑ Ⓒ Ⓓ Ⓔ	8 Ⓐ Ⓑ Ⓒ Ⓓ Ⓔ	13 Ⓐ Ⓑ Ⓒ Ⓓ Ⓔ
4 Ⓐ Ⓑ Ⓒ Ⓓ Ⓔ	9 Ⓐ Ⓑ Ⓒ Ⓓ Ⓔ	14 Ⓐ Ⓑ Ⓒ Ⓓ Ⓔ
5 Ⓐ Ⓑ Ⓒ Ⓓ Ⓔ	10 Ⓐ Ⓑ Ⓒ Ⓓ Ⓔ	15 Ⓐ Ⓑ Ⓒ Ⓓ Ⓔ

PRACTICE TEST 4

Section 1
Essay • 25 Minutes

Directions: Think carefully about the statement below and the assignment that follows it.

It has been said that "old age is not a defeat, but a victory." And yet it is extremely difficult for many people to meet the expenses brought on by long-term illnesses. The elderly, especially, are often at a loss when it comes to providing for health care for themselves or for family members. For this reason, the federal government should provide additional insurance to assist people during periods of long-term catastrophic illness.

Assignment: What is your opinion of the idea that the federal government should provide insurance for long-term catastrophic illness for the elderly? Plan and write an essay that develops your ideas logically. Support your opinion with specific evidence taken from your personal experience, your observations of others, or your reading.

STOP

END OF SECTION 1. IF YOU HAVE ANY TIME LEFT, GO OVER YOUR WORK IN THIS SECTION ONLY. DO NOT WORK IN ANY OTHER SECTION OF THE TEST.

Section 2

26 Questions • 25 Minutes

Directions: Each of the following questions consists of an incomplete sentence followed by five words or pairs of words. Choose that word or pair of words that, when substituted for the blank space or spaces, best completes the meaning of the sentence and mark the letter of your choice on your answer sheet.

> In view of the extenuating circumstances and the defendant's youth, the judge recommended ____.
>
> (A) conviction
> (B) a defense
> (C) a mistrial
> (D) leniency
> (E) life imprisonment
>
> **The correct answer is (D).**

1. Unsure of her skills in English, the young girl was ____ when called on to speak in class.
   (A) remunerative
   (B) transient
   (C) reticent
   (D) sartorial
   (E) resilient

2. Anyone familiar with the facts could ____ his arguments, which seemed logical but were actually ____.
   (A) refute .. specious
   (B) support .. protracted
   (C) repeat .. recumbent
   (D) review .. cogent
   (E) elicit .. prodigious

3. Each spring the ____ tree put out fewer and fewer leaves.
   (A) ambient
   (B) malignant
   (C) desultory
   (D) moribund
   (E) reclusive

4. The building had been ____; she could not even be sure exactly where it had stood.
   (A) jettisoned
   (B) debilitated
   (C) mitigated
   (D) berated
   (E) obliterated

5. The bully's menacing, ____ manner was actually just for show; in reality it was entirely ____.
   (A) imperturbable .. vapid
   (B) truculent .. affected
   (C) stringent .. credulous
   (D) supercilious .. blatant
   (E) parsimonious .. contentious

6. The municipality attracted the country's scientific elite and ____ them, insulating them entirely from the problems of ordinary civilian life.
   (A) cajoled
   (B) muted
   (C) mused
   (D) cosseted
   (E) impeded

7. Although the bank executive gave the appearance of a(n) ____ businessman, he was really a ____.
   - (A) dedicated .. capitalist
   - (B) respectable .. reprobate
   - (C) depraved .. profligate
   - (D) empathetic .. philanthropist
   - (E) churlish .. miscreant

8. During a campaign, politicians often engage in ____ debate, attacking each other's proposals in a torrent of ____ words.
   - (A) acerbic .. amiable
   - (B) acrimonious .. angry
   - (C) intensive .. nebulous
   - (D) garrulous .. inarticulate
   - (E) impassioned .. vapid

9. He was uneven in his approach to the problem, at once ____ and ____.
   - (A) surly .. unwilling
   - (B) sincere .. well-meaning
   - (C) harmonious .. foolhardy
   - (D) conscientious .. frivolous
   - (E) careless .. insouciant

Directions: Each passage below is followed by a set of questions. Read each passage, then answer the accompanying questions, basing your answers on what is stated or implied in the passage and any introductory material provided. Mark the letter of your choice on your answer sheet.

QUESTIONS 10 AND 11 ARE BASED ON THE FOLLOWING PASSAGE.

In recent years the outsourcing of work to companies in India has grown exponentially. U.S. corporations interested in cutting costs in areas such as call centers and data analysis
5 have found a ready source of workers among India's huge and well-educated population. Some experts estimate that there are more technology engineers in Bangalore than in all of Silicon Valley, the hub of technology
10 development in the United States. One reason that outsourcing is possible is the dramatic decrease in telecommunications costs. New types of interactive software also encourage a long-distance workforce.
15 Third, salaries for starting engineers in India are as much as 87 percent lower than those in the United States.

10. The word *exponentially* (line 2) means
    - (A) an unknown variable.
    - (B) the quality of a number.
    - (C) relating to an exponent.
    - (D) increasing in an extraordinarily large way.
    - (E) symbolically.

11. The purpose of the passage is to
    - (A) express indignation at the movement of jobs overseas.
    - (B) explain why outsourcing is occurring.
    - (C) suggest ways to combat outsourcing.
    - (D) alert readers to the issue.
    - (E) explain why there is no alternative to outsourcing overseas.

QUESTIONS 12 AND 13 ARE BASED ON THE FOLLOWING PASSAGE.

President after president has appointed commission after commission to inquire into and report upon Indian affairs, and to make suggestions as to the best methods of managing
5   them. The reports are filled with eloquent statements of wrongs done to the Indians, of perfidies on the part of the Government; they counsel, as earnestly as words can, a trial of the simple and unperplexing expedients
10   of telling truth, keeping promises, making fair bargains, dealing justly in all ways and all things. . . . [A]ny one of [these reports], . . . read by the right-thinking, right-feeling men and women , . . would initiate a revo-
15   lution, which would not subside until the Indians' wrongs were, so far as is now left possible, righted.

—Helen Hunt Jackson,
A Century of Dishonor

12. What does Jackson mean by the phrase "a trial of the simple and unperplexing expedients" (lines 8–9)?

   (A) The introduction of a lawsuit as quickly as possible

   (B) A simple plea for justice

   (C) A test of the court system as quickly as possible

   (D) A quick test of the government's actions

   (E) A test of the use of straightforward action

13. The phrase "so far as is now left possible" (lines 16–17) implies that

   (A) any interest in righting injustices to Indians is small.

   (B) there are not enough "right-thinking, right-feeling men and women" to fight for the Indians' rights.

   (C) there are some injustices that will no longer be able to be reversed.

   (D) a revolution for Indian rights is unlikely.

   (E) it is too late for a revolution for Indian rights.

QUESTIONS 14–21 ARE BASED ON THE FOLLOWING PASSAGE.

The following speech was delivered at the height of the 1960s civil rights movement by Dr. Martin Luther King, head of the Southern Christian Leadership Conference and the movement's most eloquent spokesperson.

We have come to this hallowed spot to remind America of the fierce urgency of Now. This is no time to engage in the luxury of cooling off or to take the tranquilizing drug
5   of gradualism. Now is the time to make real the promises of democracy. Now is the time to rise from the dark and desolate valley of segregation to the sunlit path of racial justice. Now is the time to lift our nation from the
10   quicksands of racial injustice to the solid rock of brotherhood. Now is the time to make justice a reality for all of God's children.

It would be fatal for the nation to overlook the urgency of the moment. This sweltering
15   summer of the Negro's legitimate discontent will not pass until there is an invigorating autumn of freedom and equality. . .Those who hope that the Negro needed to blow off steam and will now be content will have
20   a rude awakening if the nation returns to business as usual. And there will be neither rest nor tranquility in America until the Negro is granted his citizenship rights. The whirlwinds of revolt will continue to shake
25   the foundations of our nation until the bright day of justice emerges.

But there is something that I must say to my people, who stand on the warm threshold which leads into the palace of justice: In the
30   process of gaining our rightful place, we must not be guilty of wrongful deeds. Let us not seek to satisfy our thirst for freedom by drinking from the cup of bitterness and hatred. We must forever conduct our struggle
35   on the high plane of dignity and discipline. We must not allow our creative protest to degenerate into physical violence. Again and again, we must rise to the majestic heights of meeting physical force with soul force.
40   The marvelous new militancy which has engulfed the Negro community must not lead us to a distrust of all white people, for

many of our white brothers, as evidenced
by their presence here today, have come to
45 realize that their destiny is tied up with our
destiny. And they have come to realize that
their freedom is inextricably bound to our
freedom. We cannot walk alone.

And as we walk, we must make the pledge
50 that we shall always march ahead. We cannot
turn back. There are those who are asking
the devotees of civil rights, "When will you
be satisfied?" We can never be satisfied
as long as the Negro is the victim of the
55 unspeakable horrors of police brutality...We
cannot be satisfied as long as the Negro's
basic mobility is from a smaller ghetto to a
larger one. We can never be satisfied as long
as our children are stripped of their selfhood
60 and robbed of their dignity by signs stating
"For Whites Only." We cannot be satisfied
as long as a Negro in Mississippi cannot
vote and a Negro in New York believes he
has nothing for which to vote. No, no, we
65 are not satisfied, and we will not be satisfied
until "justice rolls down like waters and
righteousness like a mighty stream."

I am not unmindful that some of you have
come out of great trials and tribulations.
70 Some of you have come fresh from narrow
jail cells. And some of you have come
from areas where your quest—quest for
freedom—left you battered by the storms
of persecution and staggered by the winds
75 of police brutality. You have been the
veterans of creative suffering. Continue to
work with the faith that unearned suffering
is redemptive. Go back to Mississippi, go
back to Alabama, go back to South Carolina,
80 go back to Louisiana, go back to the slums
and ghettos of our northern cities, knowing
that somehow this situation can and will be
changed. Let us not wallow in the valley
of despair, I say to you today, my friends.

14. When King says in lines 77–78 that "un-
earned suffering is redemptive," he means
that it
   (A) provokes police brutality.
   (B) confers sanctity, or holiness, upon the
       sufferer.
   (C) is bound to continue forever.
   (D) strips children of their dignity or
       self-worth.
   (E) will never be repaid.

15. In the passage, King's attitude is generally
   (A) prejudiced.
   (B) cynical.
   (C) fearful.
   (D) optimistic.
   (E) neutral.

16. Which quotation best suggests the main idea
of the speech?
   (A) "... we must not be guilty of wrongful
       deeds."
   (B) "We cannot walk alone."
   (C) "We cannot be satisfied as long as
       the Negro's basic mobility is from a
       smaller ghetto to a larger one."
   (D) "... to remind America of the fierce
       urgency of Now."
   (E) ". . . this situation can and will be
       changed."

17. The tone of this speech can best be
described as
   (A) inspirational.
   (B) boastful.
   (C) defiant.
   (D) sad.
   (E) buoyant.

18. King's attitude toward white Americans
appears to be based on
   (A) noncommitment.
   (B) contempt for authority.
   (C) mutual distrust.
   (D) mutual respect.
   (E) negativism.

19. King's remarks indicate that he considers the racial problem a national problem because

(A) all white Americans are prejudiced.

(B) African Americans are moving to the suburbs.

(C) all areas of American life are affected.

(D) the United States Constitution supports segregation.

(E) laws will be broken if the problem is left unattended.

20. In the passage, King implies that the struggle for racial justice can be best won through

(A) marching on Washington.

(B) civil disorder.

(C) creative protest.

(D) challenging unjust laws.

(E) doing nothing.

21. In this speech, King specifically recommends

(A) nonviolent resistance.

(B) faith in God.

(C) Communist ideas.

(D) social turmoil.

(E) turbulent revolt.

QUESTIONS 22–26 ARE BASED ON THE FOLLOWING PASSAGE.

Agustín Yáñez was the author of many short stories, most of them based in or around Guadalajara, Mexico, his hometown. "Alda," from which this passage is excerpted, is from a collection entitled Archipiélago de Mujeres.

I never met my first love. She must have been a sweet and sad child. Her photographs inspire my imagination to reconstruct the outlines of her soul, simple and austere as

5 a primitive church, extensive as a castle, stately as a tower, deep as a well. Purity of brow, which, like the throat, the hands, the entire body, must have been carved in crystal or marble; the very soft lines of the face; the

10 deep-set eyes with a look of surprise, sweet and sad, beneath the veil of the eyelashes; a brief mouth with fine lips, immune to sensuality; docile hair, harmonious and still; simply dressed in harmony with the obvious

15 distinction and nobility of her bearing; all of her, aglow with innocence and a certain gravity in which are mixed the delights of childhood and the reverie of first youth. Her photographs invite one to try to imagine the

20 timbre and rhythm of her voice, the ring of her laughter, the depth of her silences, the cadence of her movements, the direction and intensity of her glances. Her arms must have moved like the wings of a musical and

25 tranquil bird; her figure must have yielded with the gentleness of a lily in an April garden. How many times her translucent hands must have trimmed the lamps of the vigilant virgins who know not the day or the

30 hour; in what moments of rapture did her mouth and eyes accentuate their sadness? When did they emphasize her sweet smile?

No, I never met her. And yet, even her pictures were with me for a long time after

35 she died. Long before then, my life was filled with her presence, fashioned of unreal images, devoid of all sensation; perhaps more faithful, certainly more vivid, than these almost faded photographs. Hers was

40 a presence without volume, line or color; an elusive phantom, which epitomized the beauty of all faces without limiting itself to any one, and embodied the delicacy of the best and loftiest spirits, indefinitely.

45 I now believe that an obscure feeling, a fear of reality, was the cause of my refusal to exchange the formless images for a direct knowledge of her who inspired them. How many times, just when the senses might have

50 put a limit to fancy did I avoid meeting her; and how many others did Fate intervene! On one of the many occasions that I watched the house in which my phantom lived, I decided to knock; but the family was out.

22. What does Yáñez mean when he says "I never met my first love" (line 1)?

(A) He loved unconditionally.

(B) His first love died young.

(C) He never fell in love.

(D) He fell in love with someone he never really knew.

(E) His first love was not a human being.

23. The description in the first paragraph moves from

(A) sound to sight.

(B) smell to sight to sound.

(C) sight to touch.

(D) sight to sound to movement.

(E) touch to sound to sight.

24. The word *docile* (line 13) is used to imply

(A) wildness.

(B) conformity.

(C) manageability.

(D) indifference.

(E) willingness.

25. Unlike the previous paragraphs, the third paragraph

(A) suggests an explanation for the author's behavior.

(B) describes the author's photographs of Alda.

(C) mentions the elusive qualities of Alda.

(D) compares Alda to someone else the author loved later.

(E) expresses regret for losing Alda's love.

26. How might you reword the phrase "the senses might have put a limit to fancy" (lines 49–50)?

(A) If I were sensible, I would not have fantasized.

(B) My good taste enabled me to dream without limits.

(C) Good sense would have made things plainer.

(D) I could sense that she wanted to end my dreams.

(E) Seeing her might have stopped my fantasies.

STOP

END OF SECTION 2. IF YOU HAVE ANY TIME LEFT, GO OVER YOUR WORK IN THIS SECTION ONLY. DO NOT WORK IN ANY OTHER SECTION OF THE TEST.

Section 3

20 QUESTIONS • 25 MINUTES

Directions: Solve the following problems using any available space on the page for scratchwork. On your answer sheet, fill in the choice that best corresponds to the correct answer.

Notes: The figures accompanying the problems are drawn as accurately as possible unless otherwise stated in specific problems. Again, unless otherwise stated, all figures lie in the same plane. All numbers used in these problems are real numbers. Calculators are permitted for this test.

Reference Information

Circle:
$C = 2\pi r$
$A = \pi r^2$

Rectangle:
$A = lw$

Rectangular Solid:
$V = lwh$

Cylinder:
$V = \pi r^2 h$

Triangle:
$A = \frac{1}{2}bh$

$a^2 + b^2 = c^2$

45°–45° triangle: x, x, $x\sqrt{2}$

30°–60° triangle: x, $x\sqrt{3}$, $2x$

The number of degrees of arc in a circle is 360.
The measure in degrees of a straight angle is 180.
The sum of the measures in degrees of the angles of a triangle is 180.

---

1. If $9x + 5 = 23$, what is the numerical value of $18x + 5$?

(A) 46
(B) 41
(C) 36
(D) 32
(E) It cannot be determined from the information given.

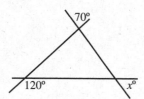

2. In the figure above, $x =$

(A) 35°
(B) 50°
(C) 70°
(D) 90°
(E) 110°

3. If $2y = \frac{1}{3}$, then $\frac{1}{4y} =$

(A) $\frac{3}{2}$
(B) $\frac{3}{4}$
(C) $\frac{2}{5}$
(D) $\frac{1}{5}$
(E) $\frac{4}{3}$

4. Pieces of wire are soldered together so as to form the edges of a cube, whose volume is 64 cubic inches. The number of inches of wire used is

(A) 24.
(B) 48.
(C) 64.
(D) 96.
(E) 120.

5. If a box of notepaper costs $4.20 after a 40% discount, what was its original price?

   (A) $2.52
   (B) $4.60
   (C) $5.33
   (D) $7.00
   (E) $10.50

6. *A* is 15 years old. *B* is one third older. How many years ago was *B* twice as old as *A*?

   (A) 3
   (B) 5
   (C) 7.5
   (D) 8
   (E) 10

7. The distance, *s*, in feet that an object falls in *t* seconds when dropped from a height is obtained by use of the formula $s = 16t^2$. How many feet will an object fall in 8 seconds?

   (A) 256
   (B) 1024
   (C) 2048
   (D) 15,384
   (E) 16,000

8. Three circles are tangent externally to one another and have radii of 2 inches, 3 inches, and 4 inches, respectively. How many inches are in the perimeter of the triangle formed by joining the centers of the three circles?

   (A) 9
   (B) 12
   (C) 15
   (D) 18
   (E) 21

9. One tenth is what part of three fourths?

   (A) $\dfrac{3}{40}$
   (B) $\dfrac{1}{8}$
   (C) $\dfrac{2}{15}$
   (D) $\dfrac{15}{2}$
   (E) $\dfrac{40}{3}$

10. The area of square *PQRS*, which is centered at the origin, is 49. What are the coordinates of *Q*?

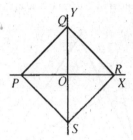

   (A) $(\dfrac{7}{2}\sqrt{2},0)$
   (B) $(0,\dfrac{7}{2}\sqrt{2})$
   (C) $(0,7)$
   (D) $(7,0)$
   (E) $(0,7\sqrt{2})$

11. If one half of the female students in a certain college eat in the cafeteria and one third of the male students eat there, what fractional part of the student body eats in the cafeteria?

   (A) $\dfrac{5}{12}$
   (B) $\dfrac{2}{5}$
   (C) $\dfrac{3}{4}$
   (D) $\dfrac{5}{6}$
   (E) It cannot be determined from the information given.

12. A recent report states that if you were to eat each meal in a different restaurant in New York City, it would take you more than 19 years to cover all of New York City's eating places, assuming that you eat three meals a day. On the basis of this information, the number of restaurants in New York City

   (A) exceeds 20,500.
   (B) is closer to 20,000 than 21,000.
   (C) exceeds 21,000.
   (D) exceeds 21,000 but does not exceed 21,500.
   (E) is fewer than 20,500.

13. In the figure below, $AB = BC$ and angle BEA is a right angle. If the length of DE is four times the length of BE, then what is the ratio of the area of $\triangle ACD$ to the area of $\triangle ABC$?

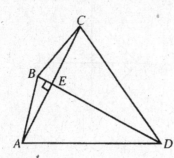

(A) 1:4

(B) 1:2

(C) 2:1

(D) 4:1

(E) It cannot be determined from the information given.

14. A pound of water has evaporated from 6 pounds of seawater containing 4% salt. What is the percentage of salt in the remaining solution?

(A) 3.6%

(B) 4%

(C) 4.8%

(D) 5.2%

(E) 6%

15. What is the product of 75^3 and 75^7?

(A) $(75)^5$

(B) $(75)^{10}$

(C) $(150)^{10}$

(D) $(5625)^{10}$

(E) $(75)^{21}$

16. The distance from City A to City B is 150 miles, and the distance from City A to City C is 90 miles. Therefore, it is necessarily true that

(A) the distance from B to C is 60 miles.

(B) six times the distance from A to B equals 10 times the distance from A to C.

(C) the distance from B to C is 240 miles.

(D) the distance from A to B exceeds by 30 miles twice the distance from A to C.

(E) three times the distance from A to C exceeds by 30 miles twice the distance from A to B.

17. If $a + b = 3$ and $ab = 4$, then $\dfrac{1}{a} + \dfrac{1}{b} =$

(A) $\dfrac{3}{4}$

(B) $\dfrac{3}{7}$

(C) $\dfrac{4}{7}$

(D) $\dfrac{1}{7}$

(E) $\dfrac{1}{12}$

18. If $f(x) = x^2 - 2x - 8$, for which value(s) of x does $f(x) = 0$?

(A) $x = 4$

(B) $x = -4, 2$

(C) $x = 2, 4$

(D) $x = -4, -2$

(E) $x = -2, 4$

19. If $(x) = \dfrac{x+5}{x-1}$ and $g(x) = \dfrac{x+2}{x+3}$, for which values of x is $h(x) - g(x)$ undefined?

    (A) $x = -3$ and 1

    (B) $x = -5$ and -3

    (C) $x = -2$ and 1

    (D) $x = -1$ and 3

    (E) $x = -3$

20. Which of the following is equal to $\left(-\dfrac{27}{8}\right)^{-\frac{1}{3}}$?

    (A) $-\dfrac{3}{2}$

    (B) $-\dfrac{2}{3}$

    (C) $\dfrac{2}{3}$

    (D) $\dfrac{3}{2}$

    (E) $\dfrac{8}{3}$

STOP

END OF SECTION 3. IF YOU HAVE ANY TIME LEFT, GO OVER YOUR WORK IN THIS SECTION ONLY. DO NOT WORK IN ANY OTHER SECTION OF THE TEST.

Section 4

35 Questions • 25 Minutes

> **Directions:** Some of the sentences below contain an error in grammar usage, word choice, or idiom. Other sentences are correct. Parts of each sentence are underlined and lettered. The error, if there is one, is contained in one of the underlined parts of the sentence. Assume that all other parts of the sentence are correct and cannot be changed. For each sentence, select the one underlined part that must be changed to make the sentence correct and mark its letter on your answer sheet. If there is no error in a sentence, mark answer space E. No sentence contains more than one error.

> <u>Being that</u> <u>it's</u> such a lovely day, we
>   A   B
> <u>are having</u> a difficult time <u>concentrating</u>
>   C   D
> on our assignment. <u>No error</u>
>   E
>
> **The correct answer is (A).**

1. She <u>poured over</u> the travel brochure <u>as if</u>
       A   B
she <u>had never seen</u> photographs of
       C
snowcapped mountains <u>before</u>. <u>No error</u>
               D   E

2. <u>At the heart of</u> the New England town
    A
was the <u>common</u>, a <u>public</u> pasture for the
       B   C
<u>citizens'</u> sheep and cattle. <u>No error</u>
  D   E

3. <u>Being</u> a <u>real estate</u> agent <u>it</u> requires
  A   B   C
<u>passing</u> a licensing examination. <u>No error</u>
  D   E

4. These oranges taste <u>more sweetly</u> <u>than</u>
              A   B
any <u>others</u> I've <u>ever</u> tried. <u>No error</u>
   C   D   E

5. <u>In applying</u> for the loan, <u>one is required</u>
  A   B
<u>to supply</u> copies of your <u>federal</u> income
  C   D
tax return. <u>No error</u>
        E

6. <u>Coming from</u> the rain forests, we
   A
<u>never dreamed</u> that the desert <u>could be</u>
  B   C
<u>so beautiful</u>. <u>No error</u>
  D   E

7. <u>On</u> the following day, the blizzard <u>grew</u>
 A   B
even <u>worst</u>, <u>surpassing</u> all previous
    C   D
records. <u>No error</u>
      E

8. All <u>but</u> seven passengers, three crewmen,
   A
and a small dog <u>was</u> lost <u>when</u> the ship
        B   C
sank. <u>No error</u>
  D   E

9. <u>Everybody</u> in the choir <u>except for</u> Meryl
  A   B
and <u>I</u> <u>had sung</u> the hymn previously.
  C D
<u>No error</u>
E

10. She wrote <u>that</u> they had visited Chartres
     A
and <u>saw</u> the <u>cathedral</u> <u>there</u>. <u>No error</u>
  B   C   D   E

11. Quickly and <u>in a brusque way</u>, the press
        A
agent <u>informed</u> the reporters that the tour
    B
<u>had had</u> <u>to be canceled</u>. <u>No error</u>
 C   D   E

12. Traditionally, the <u>street number</u> of a house
                     A

in a Japanese town reflected the relative

antiquity of the building <u>rather than</u>
                             B

<u>its location</u>; the oldest house was number
    C

one, the next oldest number two,
<u>and so forth</u>. <u>No error</u>
   D   E

13. Please ask <u>she</u> and the other applicant
            A

<u>to call</u> on Friday <u>to arrange</u> <u>interviews</u>.
  B   C   D
<u>No error</u>
  E

14. One must organize <u>their</u> time efficiently
                   A

<u>in order</u> to complete <u>all</u> the assignments
  B   C

<u>promptly</u>. <u>No error</u>
  D   E

15. Though <u>well intentioned</u>, his <u>advise</u>
          A   B
was <u>usually</u> <u>ineffectual</u>. <u>No error</u>
     C   D   E

16. <u>After the fall</u> of the leader, the country
    A

became a <u>theocracy</u>, a state <u>in which</u>
        B   C

the government is <u>not separate of</u> the
               D

church. <u>No error</u>
       E

17. The <u>noise</u> of <u>him</u> typing <u>reverberated</u>
    A   B   C

<u>through</u> the cabin. <u>No error</u>
  D   E

18. In 1901, McKinley was <u>fatally</u> shot, <u>and</u>,
                A   B

at forty-two, Teddy Roosevelt <u>was</u>
  C   D

president. <u>No error</u>
       E

19. *The Front Page*, a play by Ben Hecht and

Charles MacArthur <u>and written</u> in 1928,
                  A

<u>was</u> the <u>basis for</u> <u>Howard Hawks'</u> film
 B   C   D

His Girl Friday. <u>No error</u>
         E

Directions: The sentences below may contain problems in grammar, usage, word choice, sentence construction, and punctuation. Part or all of each sentence is underlined. Following each sentence you will find five ways of expressing the underlined part. Answer choice (A) always repeats the original underlined section. The other four answer choices are all different. You are to select the lettered answer that produces the most effective sentence. If you think the original sentence is best, choose (A) as your answer. If one of the other choices makes a better sentence, mark your answer sheet for the letter of that choice. Do not choose an answer that changes the meaning of the original sentence.

I have always enjoyed singing as well as to dance.

(A) singing as well as to dance

(B) singing as well as dancing

(C) to sing as well as dancing

(D) singing in addition to dance

(E) to sing in addition to dancing

The correct answer is (B).

20. Noticing how close the other car was to him, his hands began to shake and he broke out in a sweat.

(A) Noticing how close the other car was to him,

(B) Noticing how closely the other car was following him,

(C) When he noticed how close the other car was to him,

(D) After noticing how close the other car was to him,

(E) He noticed how close the other car was to him,

21. The money had been split equally between the four gang members.

(A) had been split equally between the four gang members

(B) was split equally between the four gang members

(C) had been split into equal shares between the four gang members

(D) had been split equally among the four gang members

(E) had been split equal by the four gang members

22. Hardcover books usually last longer than paperbacks; of course, paperbacks usually are less expensive to purchase.

(A) than paperbacks; of course,

(B) then paperbacks of course,

(C) then paperbacks. Of course,

(D) than paperbacks, of course,

(E) than paperbacks, of course

23. In the six months since the truce was declared, several minor skirmishes occurring along the border.

(A) several minor skirmishes occurring along the border

(B) several minor skirmishes breaking out along the border

(C) there have been several minor skirmishes along the border

(D) along the border there has been several minor skirmishes

(E) the several skirmishes along the border have been minor

24. I have a fever of 101°, so I have lain in bed all day.

(A) so I have lain

(B) so I laid

(C) but I lay

(D) so I have laid

(E) but I lied

25. The desire for public acclaim and recognition is universal, yet it is rarely achieved.

(A) yet it is rarely achieved

(B) yet its rarely achieved

(C) yet it is rarely satisfied

(D) however it is rarely achieved

(E) yet it is achieved rarely

26. The computer <u>has the capability for process-ing</u> all the relevant data within a half hour.
    (A) has the capability for processing
    (B) has the capacity for processing
    (C) has the capability in processing
    (D) can process
    (E) processes

27. <u>Neither one of the twins has been</u> inoculated against polio.
    (A) Neither one of the twins has been
    (B) Neither one nor the other of the twins has been
    (C) Neither one or the other twin has been
    (D) Neither one of the twins have been
    (E) Neither one of the twins been

28. <u>Not only reading in poor light but she warned that sitting</u> too close to the television can strain the eyes.
    (A) Not only reading in poor light but she warned that sitting
    (B) Not only reading in poor light she warned, but sitting
    (C) She warned that not only reading in poor light but also sitting
    (D) In addition to reading in poor light, she warned that sitting
    (E) Not only reading in poor light, but she also warned that sitting

29. <u>If I would have realized how much</u> the music disturbed her, I would have turned the volume down.
    (A) If I would have realized how much
    (B) If I realize how much
    (C) Had I realized how much
    (D) When I realized how much
    (E) If I would have realized to what extent

Directions: Questions 30–35 are based on a passage that might be an early draft of a student's essay. Some sentences in this draft need to be revised or rewritten to make them both clear and correct. Read the passage carefully; then answer the questions that follow it. Some questions require decisions about diction, usage, tone, or sentence structure in particular sentences or parts of sentences. Other questions require decisions about organization, development, or appropriateness of language in the essay as a whole. For each question, choose the answer that makes the intended meaning clearer and more precise and that follows the conventions of Standard Written English.

(1) Advocates of a student dress code maintain that proper attire and proper behavior are interrelated. (2) If a student dresses correctly, they will also behave correctly. (3) At least, that's what is claimed.

(4) I do not believe that this is a valid assumption. (5) I know many young people who come to class in a very informal fashion. (6) They wear sweat suits or cut-off jeans. (7) Sometimes they dress so sloppily that teachers or their peers make remarks to them. (8) And yet their grades are quite acceptable, or often even more than acceptable. (9) I feel that as long as a person performs well academically, the way they dress should be of no concern to others.

(10) I suppose that one day psychologists will conduct studies to test whether or not attire affects behavior. (11) If these studies prove that poor attire results in poor behavior, then school administrators will be justified in trying to establish and enforce a dress code. (12) But until that day comes, dress the way you feel most comfortable.

30. Which of the following is the best way to combine sentences (2) and (3)?

(A) If you dress well, you will behave well, at least so they say.

(B) They claim that if a student dresses correctly, they will also behave correctly.

(C) They claim that students who dress well also behave well.

(D) As claimed by them, correct dress and correct behavior go hand-in-hand.

(E) At least they claim that to dress correctly means you will behave correctly.

31. Which of the following best describes the chief purpose of sentence (4)?

(A) To change the opinion of the reader

(B) To prepare the reader for a second point of view

(C) To offer an illustration or example

(D) To provide a partial summary

(E) To help the reader evaluate paragraph one

32. Which of the following is the best way to combine sentences (5) and (6)?
   (A) I know many people who come to class dressed very informally in sweats or cut-off jeans.
   (B) I know many students who dress informally, they even wear sweat suits or cut-off jeans.
   (C) Many students I know come to class in sweats or jeans, this is informal dress.
   (D) Students come to class dressed in sweats or other ways.
   (E) If there are students who come to class dressed informally, wearing sweat suits or cut-off jeans.

33. Which of the following best describes the purpose of paragraph two?
   (A) To provide a transition
   (B) To continue the philosophy of the first paragraph
   (C) To summarize the material previously offered
   (D) To present material opposing that already presented
   (E) To offer two diametrically opposing opinions

34. Which of the following is the best revision of the underlined portion of sentence (9) below?

   I feel that as long as a person performs well academically, the way they dress should be of no concern to others.
   (A) how they dress should be of no concern to others.
   (B) the way they dress should not concern others.
   (C) their dress should be of no concern to others.
   (D) what they wear or how they dress should be their own concern.
   (E) the way he or she dresses should be of no concern to others.

35. Considering the sentences preceding it, which of the following is the best revision of sentence (12)?
   (A) But until that day comes, students should dress the way that is most comfortable for them.
   (B) But until that day, stop deciding on a dress code for students.
   (C) But until that day comes, don't tell students how to dress.
   (D) Wait until that day to tell students how to dress.
   (E) Until that day, don't attempt to enforce a dress code or regulate school attire.

STOP

END OF SECTION 4. IF YOU HAVE ANY TIME LEFT, GO OVER YOUR WORK IN THIS SECTION ONLY. DO NOT WORK IN ANY OTHER SECTION OF THE TEST.

Section 5

20 Questions • 25 Minutes

Directions: Solve the following problems using any available space on the page for scratchwork. On your answer sheet, fill in the choice that best corresponds to the correct answer.

Notes: The figures accompanying the problems are drawn as accurately as possible unless otherwise stated in specific problems. Again, unless otherwise stated, all figures lie in the same plane. All numbers used in these problems are real numbers. Calculators are permitted for this test.

Reference Information

Circle: Rectangle: Rectangular Solid: Cylinder: Triangle:

$C = 2\pi r$
$A = \pi r^2$ $A = lw$ $V = lwh$ $V = \pi r^2 h$ $A = \frac{1}{2} bh$ $a^2 + b^2 = c^2$

The number of degrees of arc in a circle is 360.
The measure in degrees of a straight angle is 180.
The sum of the measures in degrees of the angles of a triangle is 180.

---

1. Jamal bought two dozen apples for $3. At this rate, how much will 18 apples cost?
   - **(A)** $1.20
   - **(B)** $2.25
   - **(C)** $2.50
   - **(D)** $2.75
   - **(E)** $4.50

2. What is $\frac{1}{10}\%$ of $\frac{1}{10}$ of 10?
   - **(A)** 0.000001
   - **(B)** 0.00001
   - **(C)** 0.0001
   - **(D)** 0.001
   - **(E)** 0.01

3. If T is the set of all integers between 10 and 99 that are perfect squares, and S is the set of all integers between 10 and 99 that are perfect cubes, how many elements are there in the set $S \cap T$?
   - **(A)** 0
   - **(B)** 1
   - **(C)** 2
   - **(D)** 7
   - **(E)** 8

4. What is the fifth term of the geometric sequence whose first term is 3 and whose common ratio is 2?
   - **(A)** 16
   - **(B)** 24
   - **(C)** 32
   - **(D)** 48
   - **(E)** 96

5. The numbers v, w, x, y, and z are five consecutive integers. If $v < w < x < y < z$, and none of the integers is equal to 0, what is the value of the average (arithmetic mean) of the five numbers divided by the median of the five numbers?
   - **(A)** 0
   - **(B)** 1
   - **(C)** 2.5
   - **(D)** 5
   - **(E)** It cannot be determined from the information given.

6. If a cubic inch of metal weighs 2 pounds, a cubic foot of the same metal weighs how many pounds?

   (A) 8
   (B) 24
   (C) 96
   (D) 288
   (E) 3456

7. If the number of square inches in the area of a circle is equal to the number of inches in its circumference, what is the diameter of the circle in inches?

   (A) 4
   (B) π
   (C) 2
   (D) $\dfrac{\pi}{2}$
   (E) 1

8. John is now three times Pat's age. Four years from now John will be x years old. In terms of x, how old is Pat now?

   (A) $\dfrac{x+4}{3}$
   (B) $3x$
   (C) $x+4$
   (D) $x-4$
   (E) $\dfrac{x-4}{3}$

9. When the fractions $\dfrac{2}{3}$, $\dfrac{5}{7}$, $\dfrac{8}{11}$, and $\dfrac{9}{13}$ are arranged in ascending order of size, what is the result?

   (A) $\dfrac{8}{11}, \dfrac{5}{7}, \dfrac{9}{13}, \dfrac{2}{3}$
   (B) $\dfrac{5}{7}, \dfrac{8}{11}, \dfrac{2}{3}, \dfrac{9}{13}$
   (C) $\dfrac{2}{3}, \dfrac{8}{11}, \dfrac{5}{7}, \dfrac{9}{13}$
   (D) $\dfrac{2}{3}, \dfrac{9}{13}, \dfrac{5}{7}, \dfrac{8}{11}$
   (E) $\dfrac{9}{13}, \dfrac{2}{3}, \dfrac{8}{11}, \dfrac{5}{7}$

10. In a certain course, a student takes eight tests, all of which count equally. When figuring out the final grade, the instructor drops the best and the worst grades and averages the other six. The student calculates that his average for all eight tests is 84%. After dropping the best and the worst grades the student averages 86%. What was the average of the best and the worst test?

    (A) 68
    (B) 72
    (C) 78
    (D) 88
    (E) It cannot be determined from the information given.

Student-Produced Response Questions

Directions: Solve each of these problems. Write the answer in the corresponding grid on the answer sheet and fill in the ovals beneath each answer you write. Here are some examples.

Answer: $\frac{3}{4} = .75$; show answer either way

Answer: 325

Note: A mixed number such as $3\frac{1}{2}$ must be gridded as 7/2 or as 3.5. If gridded as "3 1/2," it will be read as "thirty-one halves."

Note: Either position is correct.

11. $\dfrac{\dfrac{-1}{3}}{3} - \dfrac{3}{\dfrac{-1}{3}} =$

12. Dawn's average for four math tests is 80. What score must she receive on her next exam to increase her average by three points?

13. In the figure below, square *WXYZ* is formed by connecting the midpoints of the sides of square *ABCD*. If the length of *AB* = 6, what is the area of the shaded region?

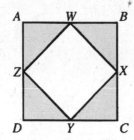

14. Thirty-thousand two hundred forty minutes is equivalent to how many weeks?

15. In the figure below, line l_1 is parallel to l_2. Transversals t_1 and t_2 are drawn. What is the value of $a + b + c + d$? (Do not grid the degree symbol.)

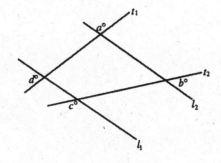

16. A car travels from town A to town B, a distance of 360 miles, in 9 hours. How many hours would the same trip have taken had the car traveled 5 mph faster?

17. In the figure below, *KJ* bisects ∠*J*. The measure of ∠*K* is 40° and the measure of ∠*L* is 20°. What is the measure of ∠*N*? (Do not grid the degree symbol.)

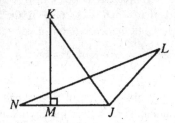

18. The area of a circle that is inscribed in a square with a diagonal of 8 is *a*π. What is the value of *a*?

19. Bobby can travel from Woodbridge to Kenmore by either bus or taxi. He can then travel to Amherst by train, plane, or bus. From Amherst, he can travel to Batavia by boat, taxi, or bus. In how many different ways can Bobby travel from Woodbridge to Kenmore to Amherst and then to Batavia?

20. If *D* is the set containing all of the numbers between 11 and 29 that are not prime, and *E* is the set containing all multiples of 3, how many elements are there in the set *D* ∩ *E*?

STOP

END OF SECTION 5. IF YOU HAVE ANY TIME LEFT, GO OVER YOUR WORK IN THIS SECTION ONLY. DO NOT WORK IN ANY OTHER SECTION OF THE TEST.

Section 6

26 Questions • 25 Minutes

Directions: Each of the following questions consists of an incomplete sentence followed by five words or pairs of words. Choose the word or pair of words that, when substituted for the blank space or spaces, *best* completes the meaning of the sentence and mark the letter of your choice on your answer sheet.

In view of the extenuating circumstances and the defendant's youth, the judge recommended ____.

(A) conviction

(B) a defense

(C) a mistrial

(D) leniency

(E) life imprisonment

The correct answer is (D).

1. Her clear ____ of the situation kept the meeting from breaking up into ____.
   (A) grasp .. chaos
   (B) vision .. anarchy
   (C) knowledge .. uproar
   (D) control .. harmony
   (E) idea .. laughter

2. The mayor remained ____ in her commitment to ____ the rise of unemployment among her constituents.
   (A) firm .. uphold
   (B) wavering .. identify
   (C) steadfast .. stem
   (D) uncertain .. staunch
   (E) alone .. approach

3. A ____ old stone farmhouse, it had been a landmark since before the Civil War.
   (A) corrupt
   (B) sturdy
   (C) rickety
   (D) ramshackle
   (E) vital

4. Because she thought her hateful cousin's behavior was ____, it ____ her to hear the adults praise him.
   (A) intangible .. thrilled
   (B) putative .. baffled
   (C) laconic .. encouraged
   (D) insipid .. demeaned
   (E) obnoxious .. galled

5. A public official must be ____ in all his or her actions to avoid even the appearance of impropriety.
   (A) redolent
   (B) unctuous
   (C) baleful
   (D) circumspect
   (E) propitious

6. So many people turned out for the meeting that there were not enough seats to ____ them all.
   (A) count
   (B) ascertain
   (C) accommodate
   (D) delineate
   (E) delegate

7. The editorial accused the mayor of _____ for making promises he knew he could not _____.

  (A) hypocrisy .. fulfill
  (B) revulsion .. condone
  (C) impunity .. reprise
  (D) liability .. improve
  (E) petulance .. verify

8. She was _____ as a child, accepting without question everything she was told.

  (A) obstreperous
  (B) recalcitrant
  (C) credulous
  (D) truculent
  (E) tearful

Directions: The reading passage below is followed by a set of questions. Read the passage and answer the accompanying questions, basing your answers on what is stated or implied in the passage. Mark the letter of your choice on your answer sheet.

QUESTIONS 9 AND 10 ARE BASED ON THE FOLLOWING PASSAGE.

I'm sure that Shakespeare would have wanted us to compare his plays with our own lives, and weigh their true value in the scale of that relationship. There are so many
5   brilliant theories and studies that demand that we compare the plays to ideas, favourite productions, and right answers; often one can feel quite stupid (or clever) in the face of it all, but either way we may miss the
10 chance to compare the plays with our own lives. . . . We are not synthetic Elizabethans harking back to an imagined time. . . . Like Shakespeare and his fellows we have reconstructed an urban amphitheatre to resonate
15 with words and stories for our time.

—Mark Rylance, Artistic Director, the Globe Theatre, London

9. The phrase "synthetic Elizabethans" (line 11) probably means

  (A) the artifice of acting.
  (B) artificial people.
  (C) manufactured nostalgia.
  (D) pretending to be from an earlier era.
  (E) imaginary people.

10. The writer implies that

  (A) academic critiques of Shakespeare's plays are silly.
  (B) academic critiques of Shakespeare's plays miss the essential meaning of the plays.
  (C) people should ignore academic critiques of Shakespeare's plays.
  (D) the reconstructed Globe Theatre is the proper place to view Shakespeare's plays.
  (E) one can enjoy the plays without being Elizabethan.

QUESTIONS 11 AND 12 ARE BASED ON THE FOLLOWING PASSAGE.

One reason that fashions soon become out-of-date is that our society values novelty; new things are considered desirable rather than a threat to established traditions. Another
5 reason is that designers and apparel makers, who profit by producing popular new styles, encourage change. Finally, new fashions are a means of showing social status, as well as appearing attractive. The latest styles are
10 adopted first by the wealthy who can afford them. Afterward inexpensive copies are made available to people of lower status. Sometimes, however, a reverse process takes place. Blue jeans were for many years
15 the traditional clothes of the working class. Today they have become very popular with . . . the middle and upper classes.

—*Sociology: The Search for Social Patterns*

11. All of the following are reasons why fashions in the United States change rapidly EXCEPT

(A) upper-class people tire of their clothes more quickly than other social classes.

(B) wearing new fashions confers attractiveness on the wearer.

(C) wearing new fashions demonstrates social status.

(D) newness is valued.

(E) clothing designers and manufacturers change styles often in order to make more money.

12. While not directly stated, the passage implies that

(A) newness is a valued quality in U.S. society.

(B) tradition is less valued than newness in U.S. society.

(C) tradition and novelty are equally important in U.S. society.

(D) newness is not valued in some societies.

(E) maintaining the balance between tradition and novelty is a universal issue.

QUESTIONS 13 AND 14 ARE BASED ON THE FOLLOWING PASSAGE.

"Ice is the beginning of Antarctica and ice is its end. . . . Ice creates more ice, and ice defines ice. . . . This is a world derived from a single substance—water, water, in a single
5 crystalline state, snow, transformed into a lithosphere composed of a single mineral, ice. This is earthscape transfigured into icescape." A reader could infer from this quotation by environmental historian Steven
10 Pyne that the world's coldest continent is nothing but ice. Antarctica is actually land—mountains and rocks. Deposits of coal have been found under the ice and scientists think that oil, gold, and iron among other minerals
15 are under the ice's surface.

13. The tone of the quotation is

(A) formal.

(B) dense with jargon.

(C) lyrical.

(D) informal.

(E) direct.

14. The phrase "earthscape transfigured into icescape" (lines 7–8) probably means that

(A) where we would expect land there is ice.

(B) our perception of land has been changed to include ice.

(C) land was transformed into ice.

(D) the terrain is ice.

(E) the land was turned miraculously into ice.

QUESTIONS 15–26 ARE BASED ON THE FOLLOWING PASSAGE.

Alexander Wilson was a poet and a naturalist. Born in Scotland in 1766, he emigrated to Pennsylvania in 1794 and soon became a full-time naturalist. This excerpt on hummingbird nests is from a 9-volume work titled American Ornithology, *published from 1808–1814.*

About the twenty-fifth of April the Hummingbird usually arrives in Pennsylvania; and about the tenth of May begins to build its nest. This is generally fixed on the upper
5 side of a horizontal branch, not among the twigs, but on the body of the branch itself.

Yet I have known instances where it was
attached by the side to an old moss-grown
trunk; and others where it was fastened on
10 a strong rank stalk, or weed, in the garden;
but these cases are rare. In the woods it very
often chooses a white oak sapling to build
on; and in the orchard, or garden, selects
a pear tree for that purpose. The branch is
15 seldom more than ten feet from the ground.
The nest is about an inch in diameter, and
as much in depth. A very complete one is
now lying before me, and the materials of
which it is composed are as follows: —The
20 outward coat is formed of small pieces of
bluish grey lichen that vegetates on old
trees and fences, thickly glued on with
the saliva of the bird, giving firmness and
consistency to the whole, as well as keeping
25 out moisture. Within this are thick matted
layers of the fine wings of certain flying
seeds, closely laid together; and lastly, the
downy substance from the great mullein,
and from the stalks of the common fern,
30 lines the whole. The base of the nest is
continued round the stem of the branch, to
which it closely adheres; and, when viewed
from below, appears a mere mossy knot or
accidental protuberance. The eggs are two,
35 pure white, and of equal thickness at both
ends. . . . On a person's approaching their
nest, the little proprietors dart around with a
humming sound, passing frequently within
a few inches of one's head; and should the
40 young be newly hatched, the female will
resume her place on the nest even while you
stand within a yard or two of the spot. The
precise period of incubation I am unable to
give; but the young are in the habit, a short
45 time before they leave the nest, of thrusting
their bills into the mouths of their parents,
and sucking what they have brought them. I
never could perceive that they carried them
any animal food; tho, from circumstances
50 that will presently be mentioned, I think it
highly probable they do. As I have found
their nest with eggs so late as the twelfth of
July, I do not doubt but that they frequently,
and perhaps usually, raise two broods in the
55 same season.

15. In line 4, the word "fixed" most nearly means
(A) changed.
(B) improved.
(C) found.
(D) understood.
(E) undermined.

16. According to the author, all of the following are places where one could find a humming-bird EXCEPT
(A) on the upper side of a branch.
(B) on a moss-grown trunk.
(C) on a white oak sapling.
(D) on a pear tree.
(E) in the meadow.

17. Why does Wilson mention the "old moss-grown trunk" and "strong rank stalk" (lines 8–10)?
(A) To compare relative sizes of birds
(B) To establish the birds' eating patterns
(C) To illustrate nontypical nesting behaviors
(D) To delineate plant life in Pennsylvania
(E) To complete a list of related flora

18. When Wilson remarks that the birds' nests resemble an "accidental protuberance" (line 34), he implies that
(A) the nests are messily constructed.
(B) nests may be destroyed accidently.
(C) the nests are usually invisible.
(D) the nests are designed to blend into their surroundings.
(E) most nests resemble the beak of the bird itself.

19. The phrase "little proprietors" (line 37) refers to
(A) children in the orchard.
(B) eggs.
(C) naturalists.
(D) shop owners.
(E) nesting pairs of hummingbirds.

20. When Wilson remarks that he "never could perceive" hummingbirds feeding their nestlings animal food (lines 47–49), he is suggesting

(A) that his eyesight is failing.

(B) his limitations as an observer.

(C) that animal food may, in fact, be eaten.

(D) that no animal food is eaten.

(E) that hummingbirds eat only at night.

21. The fact that Wilson has found nests with eggs "so late as the twelfth of July" (lines 52–53) indicates that

(A) birds do not lay eggs before June.

(B) most eggs are found earlier than July 12.

(C) the eggs are not likely to hatch.

(D) the birds began nesting late in the season.

(E) some birds abandon their nests.

22. The hummingbirds' nest is composed of all of the following EXCEPT

(A) moss.

(B) lichen.

(C) the wings of flying seeds.

(D) a downy substance from fern stalks.

(E) hummingbird saliva.

23. How does Wilson reconstruct the makeup of the nest?

(A) By taking apart a nest that hangs in the orchard

(B) By watching a hummingbird build a nest in the stable

(C) By reading a report by John Audubon

(D) By inspecting a nest that lies on his desk

(E) By making a copy of a nest he has observed

24. Which of the following can be inferred about the hummingbirds' habits?

(A) They flourish only in Pennsylvania.

(B) Their broods each consist of a single egg.

(C) They migrate in the spring.

(D) They always raise two broods in a season.

(E) They spend the winter in Pennsylvania.

25. The main purpose of this passage is to describe

(A) the nesting behavior of the hummingbird.

(B) the mating behavior of the hummingbird.

(C) the relative size of the hummingbird.

(D) hummingbirds in Pennsylvania.

(E) young hummingbird fledglings.

26. If Wilson were to study crows, he would be likely to

(A) stuff and mount them.

(B) observe them in the wild.

(C) read all about them.

(D) mate them in a laboratory.

(E) dissect them.

STOP

 END OF SECTION 6. IF YOU HAVE ANY TIME LEFT, GO OVER YOUR WORK IN THIS SECTION ONLY. DO NOT WORK IN ANY OTHER SECTION OF THE TEST.

Section 7

15 Questions • 20 Minutes

Directions: Solve the following problems using any available space on the page for scratchwork. On your answer sheet fill in the choice that best corresponds to the correct answer.

Notes: The figures accompanying the problems are drawn as accurately as possible unless otherwise stated in specific problems. Again, unless otherwise stated, all figures lie in the same plane. All numbers used in these problems are real numbers. Calculators are permitted for this test.

Reference Information

Circle: $C = 2\pi r$ $A = \pi r^2$

Rectangle: $A = lw$

Rectangular Solid: $V = lwh$

Cylinder: $V = \pi r^2 h$

Triangle: $A = \frac{1}{2}bh$ $a^2 + b^2 = c^2$

The number of degrees of arc in a circle is 360.
The measure in degrees of a straight angle is 180.
The sum of the measures in degrees of the angles of a triangle is 180.

---

1. In the figure, what percent of the area of rectangle *PQRS* is shaded?

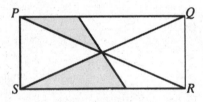

(A) 20
(B) 25
(C) 30
(D) $33\frac{1}{3}$
(E) 35

2. One wheel has a diameter of 30 inches and a second wheel has a diameter of 20 inches. The first wheel traveled a certain distance in 240 revolutions. In how many revolutions did the second wheel travel the same distance?

(A) 120
(B) 160
(C) 360
(D) 420
(E) 480

3. 1.86×10^5 is equivalent to

(A) 18,600
(B) 186,000
(C) 18,600,000
(D) $186 \times 500,000$
(E) 1,860,000

4. How many of the numbers between 100 and 300 begin or end with 2?

(A) 20
(B) 40
(C) 100
(D) 110
(E) 180

5. The area of a square is $49x^2$. What is the length of a diagonal of the square?

(A) $7x$
(B) $7x\sqrt{2}$
(C) $14x$
(D) $7x^2$
(E) $\frac{7x}{\sqrt{2}}$

6. If shipping charges to a certain point are 62 cents for the first 5 ounces and 8 cents for each additional ounce, the weight of a package, in pounds, for which the charges are $1.66 is

(A) $\dfrac{7}{8}$

(B) 1

(C) $1\dfrac{1}{8}$

(D) $1\dfrac{1}{4}$

(E) $1\dfrac{1}{2}$

7. If 15 cans of food are needed for 7 adults for two days, the number of cans needed to feed 4 adults for seven days is

(A) 15.

(B) 20.

(C) 25.

(D) 30.

(E) 35.

8. A rectangular sign is cut down by 10% of its height and 30% of its width. What percent of the original area remains?

(A) 30%

(B) 37%

(C) 57%

(D) 63%

(E) 70%

9. If the average (arithmetic mean) of a series of numbers is 20 and their sum is 160, how many numbers are in the series?

(A) 8

(B) 16

(C) 32

(D) 48

(E) 80

10. If the result of squaring a number is less than the number, the number is

(A) negative and greater than −1.

(B) negative and less than −1.

(C) a positive fraction greater than 1.

(D) positive and less than 1.

(E) 1 and only 1.

11. $(x)^6 + (2x^2)^3 + (3x^3)^2 =$

(A) $5x^5 + x^6$

(B) $17x^5 + x^6$

(C) $6x^6$

(D) $18x^6$

(E) $6x^{18}$

12. The scale of a map is $\dfrac{3}{4}$ inch $= 10$ miles . If the distance on the map between two towns is 6 inches, the actual distance in miles is

(A) 45.

(B) 60.

(C) 75.

(D) 80.

(E) 90.

13. If $d = m - \dfrac{50}{m}$, and m is a positive number, then as m increases in value, d

(A) increases in value.

(B) decreases in value.

(C) remains unchanged.

(D) increases, then decreases.

(E) decreases, then increases.

14. If $\dfrac{x}{12}+\dfrac{x}{18}=1$, what is the value of x?

(A) $\dfrac{1}{5}$

(B) $3\dfrac{2}{5}$

(C) $6\dfrac{4}{5}$

(D) $7\dfrac{1}{5}$

(E) 20

15. One end of a piece of rope is tied to the top of a flagpole, and the other end is attached to a stake in the ground. If the rope makes a 45° angle with the ground, and the distance from the base of the flagpole to the stake is 20 feet, how long is the piece of rope?

(A) $10\sqrt{2}$ feet

(B) 20 feet

(C) $20\sqrt{2}$ feet

(D) $20\sqrt{3}$ feet

(E) 40 feet

STOP

END OF SECTION 7. IF YOU HAVE ANY TIME LEFT, GO OVER YOUR WORK IN THIS SECTION ONLY. DO NOT WORK IN ANY OTHER SECTION OF THE TEST.

practice test

Section 8

16 Questions • 20 Minutes

> **Directions:** The two passages below deal with a related topic. Following the passages are questions about the content of each passage or about the relationship between the two passages. Answer the questions based upon what is stated or implied in the passages and in any introductory material provided. Mark the letter of your choice on your answer sheet.

QUESTIONS 1–4 ARE BASED ON THE FOLLOWING PASSAGES.

The following passages represent two views of the value of hybrid cars, cars that are powered by gasoline and by electricity depending on whether they are in traffic or on the open road.

Passage 1

Advocates of hybrids believe that they offer the best short-term solution to some long-term problems. By combining a regular gasoline-powered engine with an
5　electric engine, hybrids cut down on gas consumption and decrease the pollution caused by gasoline engines. These cars help auto makers meet government regulations for fuel efficiency and emissions controls.
10　Auto makers do not think that hybrids are the answer for the future, but these small cars provide a way for conservation-conscious consumers to do something for the environment. Auto makers see another benefit
15　to the development process for hybrids. The technology that has gone into creating and refining the dual-powered hybrid will help with the longer-term development of cars powered by hydrogen fuel cells.

Passage 2

Opponents of hybrids believe that auto makers should be focusing on a longer-term solution. They believe that either hydrogen fuel cells or diesel fuel or both are better
5　alternatives than hybrids. The cost of hybrids is higher than comparably sized gasoline-powered cars, forcing consumers who want "green" cars to pay anywhere from $2,500 to $4,000 more. Opponents say that the higher
10　sticker price means lower demand and less likelihood of automobile companies making

their development dollars back. Naysayers point to Europe as an example of lack of demand. Gasoline prices are much higher
15　there than in the United States, but no mass movement from gasoline-powered cars to hybrids has occurred.

1. According to Passage 1, hybrids are beneficial for all of the following reasons EXCEPT they
   - **(A)** decrease gas consumption.
   - **(B)** provide information for the development of hydrogen fuel cells.
   - **(C)** decrease pollution.
   - **(D)** provide an alternative for car buyers who want to protect the environment.
   - **(E)** add to the profit margin for auto makers.

2. The lack of demand discussed in Passage 2 is said to result from
   - **(A)** the lack of fuel efficiency of the hybrids.
   - **(B)** the higher price of hybrids.
   - **(C)** buyers' waiting for the alternatives to hybrids to come on the market.
   - **(D)** the high price of gas.
   - **(E)** a general lack of interest in conserving gasoline.

3. In Passage 2, *"green" cars* (line 8) probably refers to the fact that the
   - **(A)** technology is new and relatively untested over a long period of time.
   - **(B)** technology is experimental.
   - **(C)** cars are environmentally friendly.
   - **(D)** opponents are jealous because they did not come up with the technology first.
   - **(E)** cars are expensive.

4. In contrast to Passage 1, the writer of Passage 2 uses

(A) jargon.

(B) a dismissive attitude toward the arguments of the other side.

(C) a straightforward, direct style.

(D) examples to support the argument.

(E) complex sentence structures.

QUESTIONS 5–16 ARE BASED ON THE FOLLOWING PASSAGES.

Achilles, the Greek hero, and Cuchulain, the Champion of Ireland, achieved mythical status because of their acts of courage. The following passages compare the two heroes and their heroic feats.

Passage 1—Achilles, Defender of Honor

When Achilles heard that his friend Patroclus had been killed in battle, he became so despondent that his friends feared he might end his own life. When word of his complete
5 and agonizing distress reached his mother, Thetis, in the depths of the ocean where she resided, she raced to his side. She found him in a highly distraught state, feeling guilty that he, in some way, might have been
10 responsible for his friend's demise. His only consolation were thoughts of revenge for which he needed the help of Hector. However, his mother reminded him that he was without armor, having lost his recently
15 in battle. His mother, however, promised him that she would procure for him a suit of armor from Vulcan far superior to the one he had lost. Achilles agreed and Thetis immediately repaired to Vulcan's palace.
20 Thetis found Vulcan busy at his forge making magical tripods that moved forward when they were wanted, and retreated when dismissed. Vulcan immediately honored Thetis's request for a set of armor for her son,
25 and ceasing his own work, hastened to meet her demands. Vulcan created a magnificent suit of armor for Achilles. The shield was adorned with elaborate ornaments. The helmet had a gold crest, and the body of
30 the armor was perfectly suited to his body and of the very finest workmanship. The armor was completed in one night. When

Thetis received it, she descended to earth, and laid it down at Achilles' feet at the first
35 dawn of day.

Seeing the armor brought the first signs of life to Achilles that he had felt since the death of his friend Patroclus. The armor was so splendid that Achilles was stunned at the
40 sight of it. Achilles went into battle with his new armor, consumed with rage and thirst for vengeance that made him an unbeatable foe. The bravest warriors fled from him or were killed by his lance.

Passage 2—Cuchulain, Champion of Ireland

In days of yore, the men of Ulster sought to choose a champion. They enlisted the help of Curoi of Kerry, a wise man, to help them reach their decision. Three brave men,
5 Laegire, Connall Cearnach, and Cuchulain indicated that they wished to be considered. Each was told that he would have to meet the challenge of a terrible stranger. When the stranger arrived, all were in awe of him.
10 "Behold my axe," the stranger said. "My challenge is this. Whoever will take the axe today may cut my head off with it, provided that I may, in like manner, cut off his head tomorrow. If you have no champions who
15 dare face me, I will say that the men of Ulster have lost their courage and should be ashamed."

Laegire was the first to accept the challenge. The giant laid his head on a block.
20 With one blow the hero severed it from the body. Thereupon the giant arose, took the head and the axe, and headless, walked slowly from the hall. The following night the giant returned, sound as ever, to claim the
25 fulfillment of Laegire's promise. However, Laegire did not come forward. The stranger scoffed at the men of Ulster because their great champion showed no courage. He could not face the blow he should receive
30 in return for the one he gave.

The men from Ulster were sorely ashamed, but Connall Cearnach, the second aspiring champion, made another pact with the stranger. He, too, gave a blow which
35 beheaded the giant. But again, when the giant

returned whole and sound on the following evening, the champion was not there.

Now it was the turn of Cuchulain, who as the others had done, cut off the giant's
40 head at one stroke. The next day everyone watched Cuchulain to see what he would do. They would not have been surprised if he had not appeared. This champion, however, was there. He was not going to disgrace
45 Ulster. Instead, he sat with great sadness in his place. "Do not leave this place till all is over," he said to his king. "Death is coming to me soon, but I must honor my promise, for I would rather die than break my word."

50 At the end of the day the giant appeared.

"Where is Cuchulain?' he cried.

"Here I am," answered Cuchulain.

"Cuchulain, your speech is morose, and the fear of death is obviously foremost in your
55 thoughts, but at least you have honored your promise."

Cuchulain went towards the giant, as he stood with his great axe ready, and knelt to receive the blow.

60 The would-be champion of Ulster laid his head on the block.

When the giant did not immediately use his axe, Cuchulain said, "Slay me now with haste, for I did not keep you waiting
65 last night."

The stranger raised his axe so high that it crashed upwards through the rafters of the hall, like the crash of trees falling in a storm. When the axe came down with a sound that
70 shook the room, all men looked fearfully at Cuchulain. But to the surprise of all, the descending axe had not even touched him; it had come down with the blunt side on the ground, and Cuchulain knelt there
75 unharmed. Smiling at him and leaning on his axe, stood no terrible and hideous stranger, but Curoi of Kerry, who had taken on the form of the giant to test the champions. He was now there to give his decision.

80 "Rise up, Cuchulain," said Curoi. "There is none among all the heroes of Ulster to equal you in courage and loyalty and truth. The Championship is yours." Thereupon Curoi vanished. The assembled warriors gathered
85 around Cuchulain, and all with one voice acclaimed him the champion.

5. The word *despondent* in Passage 1 (line 3) means
   (A) very depressed.
   (B) in need of food.
   (C) angry.
   (D) embarrassed.
   (E) belligerent.

6. Achilles' feelings of guilt were related to
   (A) the loss of his armor.
   (B) the loss of his last battle.
   (C) his estrangement from his mother.
   (D) the death of his friend.
   (E) his relationship with Vulcan.

7. In Passage 1, line 19, the word *repaired* means
   (A) glazed.
   (B) retired.
   (C) replenished.
   (D) returned.
   (E) untouched.

8. Although not stated directly in the passage, it is obvious that Vulcan
   (A) blames Achilles for his friend's death.
   (B) is a lower-level god.
   (C) is extremely powerful.
   (D) loves Thetis.
   (E) does not wish to help Achilles.

9. Achilles' feeling as he went into battle can best be described as
   (A) guilty.
   (B) nervous.
   (C) confident.
   (D) depressed.
   (E) arrogant.

10. According to Passage 2, when the men of Ulster wished to select a champion, they enlisted the help of
    (A) Curoi.
    (B) the king.
    (C) Laegire.
    (D) Connall.
    (E) Cearnach.

11. The challenge that the would-be champion had to meet involved
    (A) fighting a giant with an axe.
    (B) beheading a giant.
    (C) competing against other men of Ulster.
    (D) winning a match with the king.
    (E) fighting Curoi of Kerry.

12. According to the passage, the giant was unusual because he
    (A) was so tall.
    (B) was so huge.
    (C) defeated all his opponents.
    (D) remained alive while headless.
    (E) had three eyes.

13. In Passage 2, the word *sorely* (line 31) means
    (A) feverishly.
    (B) utterly.
    (C) angrily.
    (D) bitterly.
    (E) pitifully.

14. Cuchulain appeared as promised to meet the giant because he
    (A) was afraid.
    (B) knew the giant would not kill him.
    (C) knew the giant was Curoi.
    (D) did not wish to fail his king.
    (E) gave his word.

15. In Passage 2, line 53, the word *morose* most nearly means
    (A) serious and somber.
    (B) riotous and humorous.
    (C) indifferent and detached.
    (D) informed and knowledgeable.
    (E) satisfied.

16. Cuchulain is sometimes called the "Irish Achilles," probably because of his
    (A) honesty.
    (B) bravery.
    (C) strength.
    (D) wisdom.
    (E) intelligence.

STOP

END OF SECTION 8. IF YOU HAVE ANY TIME LEFT, GO OVER YOUR WORK IN THIS SECTION ONLY. DO NOT WORK IN ANY OTHER SECTION OF THE TEST.

Section 9
15 Questions • 10 Minutes

Directions: The sentences below may contain problems in grammar, usage, word choice, sentence construction, or punctuation. Part or all of each sentence is underlined. Following each sentence you will find five ways of expressing the underlined part. Answer choice (A) always repeats the original underlined section. The other four answer choices are all different. You are to select the lettered answer that produces the most effective sentence. If you think the original sentence is best, choose (A) as your answer. If one of the other choices makes a better sentence, mark your answer sheet for the letter of that choice. Do not choose an answer that changes the meaning of the original sentence.

I have always enjoyed singing as well as to dance.

- **(A)** singing as well as to dance
- **(B)** singing as well as dancing
- **(C)** to sing as well as dancing
- **(D)** singing in addition to dance
- **(E)** to sing in addition to dancing

The correct answer is (B).

1. I prefer him singing his own material to his performances of other people's songs.
   - **(A)** him singing his own material
   - **(B)** him when he is singing his own material
   - **(C)** him to sing his own material
   - **(D)** him singing his own material himself
   - **(E)** his singing his own material

2. The geometrical design of the quilt was traditional, but using strikingly modern fabrics.
   - **(A)** using strikingly modern fabrics
   - **(B)** strikingly modern fabrics were used
   - **(C)** using striking modern fabrics
   - **(D)** making use of strikingly modern fabrics
   - **(E)** the fabrics used were strikingly modern

3. He handwrote his application sloppily and filled with spelling errors.
   - **(A)** He handwrote his application sloppily and filled with spelling errors.
   - **(B)** He sloppily wrote his application by hand and it was filled with spelling errors.
   - **(C)** His application was sloppily hand-written and filled with spelling errors.
   - **(D)** He handwrote his application, it was sloppy and filled with spelling errors.
   - **(E)** His application was handwritten sloppy and filled with spelling errors.

4. Only Congress can declare war officially however the Commander-in-Chief of the armed forces has the power to order a military action without consulting Congress.
   - **(A)** war officially however
   - **(B)** war, officially; however,
   - **(C)** war, officially, however,
   - **(D)** war. Officially, however,
   - **(E)** war officially. However

5. <u>For one to accept constructive criticism without getting resentful is a sign that one is mature.</u>

(A) For one to accept constructive criticism without getting resentful is a sign that one is mature.

(B) It is a sign that one is mature when one accepts constructive criticism without getting resentful.

(C) Accepting constructive criticism without one getting resentful is a sign of maturity.

(D) A mature sign is to accept constructive criticism without resentment.

(E) Accepting constructive criticism without resentment is a sign of maturity.

6. The day was <u>windy and cold and snowed continuously</u>.

(A) windy and cold and snowed continuously

(B) windy and cold, and it snowed continuously

(C) wind, cold, and snowed continuously

(D) windy and therefore cold and snowy

(E) windy and cold because it snowed continuously

7. <u>To keep the raccoon was cruel,</u> and letting it go was dangerous.

(A) To keep the raccoon was cruel,

(B) To keep the raccoon being cruel,

(C) Keeping the raccoon being cruel,

(D) Keeping the raccoon was cruel,

(E) Keeping the raccoon it was cruel

8. My sister asked me <u>if I knew Jim and will he be at the dance.</u>

(A) if I knew Jim and will he be at the dance.

(B) whether I know Jim and would he be at the dance.

(C) whether I knew Jim and whether he would be at the dance.

(D) did I know Jim and will he be at the dance?

(E) if I knew Jim and would he be at the dance?

9. The reviewer declared <u>how there was a dearth of serious books</u> being published on issues of social importance.

(A) how there was a dearth of serious books

(B) as how there was a dearth of serious books

(C) a dearth of serious books

(D) why there was a dearth of serious books

(E) that there was a dearth of serious books

10. I think that each applicant should be interviewed in person <u>before they are granted admission to the program</u>.

(A) before they are granted admission to the program

(B) prior to their being granted admission to the program

(C) before being granted admission to the program

(D) before admission is granted to them

(E) before they can be granted admission

11. Perhaps in this way <u>we will lessen the amount of traffic accidents that occur</u> among 16- to 24-year olds and thus decrease car insurance costs to this group.

(A) we will lessen the amount of traffic accidents that occur

(B) we will lessen the number of traffic accidents that occur

(C) we will shorten the number of traffic accidents that occur

(D) we will decrease the amount of traffic accidents that occur

(E) we will alleviate the amount of traffic accidents that occur

12. The acquisition of a new building, along with several less expensive issues, <u>are going to be voted on at the next executive session</u>.

    (A) are going to be voted on at the next executive session

    (B) are up for a vote at the next executive session

    (C) are expected to be voted on at the next executive session

    (D) is going to be voted on at the next executive session

    (E) is going to be put for a vote, at the next executive session

13. No one among the students was more disgruntled <u>than she when the assignment was handed out</u>.

    (A) than she when the assignment was handed out

    (B) than her when the assignment was handed out

    (C) when the assignment was handed out than her

    (D) when the assignment was handed out to her

    (E) when she was handed the assignment

14. Jake is <u>the smallest of any boy</u> in his kindergarten class.

    (A) the smallest of any boy

    (B) smaller than any boy

    (C) the smaller of any of the boys

    (D) the smallest of any of the boys

    (E) the smallest boy

15. <u>Although spring is well advanced,</u> patches of old snow could be seen among the evergreens.

    (A) Although spring is well advanced,

    (B) Although spring was well advanced,

    (C) Although spring had well advanced,

    (D) Spring was well advanced;

    (E) Spring, having advanced,

STOP

END OF SECTION 9. IF YOU HAVE ANY TIME LEFT, GO OVER YOUR WORK IN THIS SECTION ONLY. DO NOT WORK IN ANY OTHER SECTION OF THE TEST.

ANSWER KEY AND EXPLANATIONS

Section 1

Sample Essay 1

We are all living longer thanks to medical knowledge, and perhaps we should be grateful for this. But I am not at all sure this is true. Sometimes I feel that living longer presents many problems.

For example, I know that my friends grandmother is now in a nursing home where she is suffering a slow death. Each week the family pays huge amounts of money to keep her in the home. Soon all of her savings will be gone and her husband will be reduced to living on welfare if he survives. This is only one case but there are many others.

The goverment should step in and assist. People who have worked all of their lives and have paid taxes should expect some help in their final years of live. Help in the way of additional money would be of great emotional and economic value. We provide social security it is true, but this is not enough to cover unusual medical expenses. We cannot desert these victims of old age when they are ill. We must help.

I urge the government to help provide funds to cover home care and to relieve our ill seniors of the worry and dispair that comes from catastrophic illness. We know that the physical pain they bear is great. Lets at least take away some of the economic hurt.

Analysis of Sample Essay 1

This is a well-organized four-paragraph response. The writer provides a good introduction, which presents the topic and a strong conclusion to summarize the position taken. In addition, in the second paragraph an example is offered to illustrate the problem. The vocabulary and sentence structure are good, as is the somewhat emotional tone.

The few spelling errors (*government, live, despair*) and the omissions of apostrophes (*friends grandmother, lets*) could be corrected through careful revision. The closing sentence, although effective, would be better phrased by avoiding the address to the reader and maintaining a third-person approach. A possible revision could be: "The federal government should at least take away some of the economic hurt."

Sample Essay 2

The federal government should definitely provide enough insurance coverage so that families or individuals face with the problem of long-term catastrophic illness will be able to meet the rising cost of healthcare. Without government assistance, many people today are unable to provide proper care for seriously sick relatives, and as the population of older people increases, the problem will only get worse.

Right now my cousins are faced with a problem that is a good illustration of the need for a better health care program. Their mother has been ill for nearly a year, suffering from heart disease and diabetes. First she was in the hospital, then in a nursing home. Medicare covered a lot of her expenses at first, but not all. Later, the family had to pay from their own savings, and when their funds got low, they took her out of the hospital. Besides, she was not really so happy there, and they missed her too.

At home my cousins have a nurse, which is very expensive. They both work so they need someone to look after mother. But again they are hurting for money and are getting worry about what to do. If they had government coverage, they could keep her at home and take good care of her for as long as it takes.

In conclusion, my observation of this very sad situation proves that the federal government should help people who have long-term illnesses.

Analysis of Sample Essay 2

This is an interesting and well-written essay. It begins with a strong statement of the author's thesis and employs a two-paragraph personal example to support its view. The writer demonstrates an understanding of the question and an ability to organize a coherent and logical response.

Although the essay is developed in some depth, it would appear that the conclusion is somewhat skimpy. Perhaps the writer might have budgeted the allotted time more effectively to provide for an additional sentence in the final paragraph. In addition, the concluding sentence of paragraph two might have been deleted and more careful proofreading might have eliminated the two ending errors (*face—faced* in paragraph one; *worry—worried* in paragraph three).

Section 2

1. C	7. B	12. E	17. A	22. D
2. A	8. B	13. C	18. D	23. D
3. D	9. D	14. B	19. C	24. C
4. E	10. D	15. D	20. C	25. A
5. B	11. B	16. E	21. A	26. E
6. D				

1. **The correct answer is (C).** If the young girl was unsure of her English skills, she was likely to be *reticent* (shy and restrained) when asked to speak.

2. **The correct answer is (A).** Arguments that only seemed logical were likely to be *specious* (false), and anyone familiar with the facts could *refute* (disprove) them.

3. **The correct answer is (D).** A tree that puts out fewer and fewer leaves is probably *moribund* (dying).

4. **The correct answer is (E).** If no trace of the building remained, it had been *obliterated* (destroyed completely).

5. **The correct answer is (B).** A manner that is menacing or threatening is said to be *truculent.* If, however, it is put on only for show, it is merely *affected.*

6. **The correct answer is (D).** Those who are protected from the harsh world around them are pampered, or *cosseted.* The other choices make no sense.

7. **The correct answer is (B).** The transitional word *although* sets up a contrast suggesting that one choice will be positive and one choice will be negative. The only possible choice is (B). Someone only appearing to be a *respectable* businessman may in reality be a *reprobate,* or a scoundrel.

8. **The correct answer is (B).** The word *attacking* indicates the need for two strong negative words. Only choice (B) satisfies this requirement with *acrimonious,* meaning harsh or bitter, and *angry.*

9. **The correct answer is (D).** *Conscientious* (extremely careful) and *frivolous* (silly) are opposing characteristics.

10. **The correct answer is (D).** *Exponentially* is related to the word *exponent,* but isn't used here in a math sense.

11. **The correct answer is (B).** The tone of the passage should have told you that choices (A), *indignation,* and (E), *resignation,* are incorrect. The content will tell you that choices (C) and (D) aren't correct. This is a straightforward explanation of why outsourcing is occurring.

12. **The correct answer is (E).** If you read the question quickly and didn't go back to the passage, you might have chosen choices (A), (B), or (C) because each seems to work with the word *trial.* Always go back to the passage.

13. **The correct answer is (C).** This is another example of why it's important to go back to the passage to check your answer. On a quick read of the question and the answers, you might have been distracted by the use of words from the passage and chosen any of one of the wrong answers.

14. **The correct answer is (B).** King urges his listeners to "continue to work with the faith that unearned suffering is redemptive." Even if you did not know the meaning of *redemptive,* you could infer that it promised something positive. Of the choices, only (B) satisfies this condition.

15. **The correct answer is (D).** The last paragraph gives King's belief that"...this situation can and will be changed."

16. **The correct answer is (E).** This is stated in the last paragraph and sums up the point of the entire speech.

17. **The correct answer is (A).** King is attempting to inspire his listeners.

18. **The correct answer is (D).** Lines 41–46 state that this new attitude "...must not lead us to a distrust of all white people, for many of our white brothers . . . have come to realize that their destiny is tied up with our destiny."

19. **The correct answer is (C).** King states in lines 21–23: "And there will be neither rest nor tranquility in America until the Negro is granted his citizenship rights."

20. **The correct answer is (C).** Paragraph three specifically mentions creative protest.

21. **The correct answer is (A).** The second paragraph discusses "the whirlwinds of revolt" that will continue until justice prevails; the third paragraph urges listeners to obey the law, as ". . . we must not be guilty of wrongful deeds." Thus, "nonviolent resistance" is the best response.

22. **The correct answer is (D).** This is a completely literal statement. As the rest of the passage makes clear, the narrator never really knew Alda.

23. **The correct answer is (D).** To answer this synthesis/analysis question will require looking back at the paragraph and tracing its structure. The narrator describes what Alda looked like, speculates on what she sounded like, and guesses what she moved like, in that order.

24. **The correct answer is (C).** *Docile* has several connotations, but a look back at the citation in question will tell you that only two of the choices could easily be applied to hair, and choice (A) is exactly opposite to the meaning the narrator intends.

25. **The correct answer is (A).** In the first sentence of paragraph three, the author suggests that his fear of reality was the reason he failed to meet Alda. This is the first time he has made such a suggestion. Paragraph three might also be said to support choice (C), but so do paragraphs one and two. Choices (D) and (E) are not supported anywhere in the passages.

26. **The correct answer is (E).** Here is an example of an oddly worded phrase that cannot be easily deciphered. By testing the choices in place of the phrase in context, however, the reasonable translation is clear.

Section 3

1. B	5. D	9. C	13. D	17. A
2. B	6. E	10. B	14. C	18. E
3. A	7. B	11. E	15. B	19. A
4. B	8. D	12. A	16. B	20. B

Note: A  following a math answer explanation indicates that a calculator could be helpful in solving that particular problem.

1. **The correct answer is (B).**

   If $9x + 5 = 23$, $9x = 18$, and $x = 2$.
   Thus, $18x + 5 = 36 + 5 = 41$.

2. **The correct answer is (B).**

   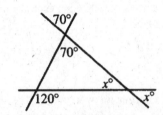

   $120 = 70 + x$
   $x = 50$

3. **The correct answer is (A).**

   $$2y = \frac{1}{3}$$
   $$6y = 1$$
   $$y = \frac{1}{6}$$
   $$\frac{1}{4y} = \frac{1}{4\left(\frac{1}{6}\right)} = \frac{1}{\frac{2}{3}} = \frac{3}{2}$$

4. **The correct answer is (B).** The volume of

   a cube is $V = s_3$. A side of this cube is $\sqrt[3]{64}$ in. Since there are 12 edges to a cube, the amount of wire needed is 12×4 in., or 48 inches.

5. **The correct answer is (D).**

   Let x = original price
   Then $0.60x = \$4.20$
   or $6x = \$42.00$
   $x = \$7.00$

6. **The correct answer is (E).**

   $$A = \quad 15$$
   $$B = \quad 15 + \frac{1}{3}(15) = 20$$

   $15 - n$ is A's age n years ago

   $20 - n$ is B's age n years ago

   $$(20 - n) = \quad 2(15 - n)$$
   $$20 - n = \quad 30 - 2n$$
   $$n = \quad 10$$

7. **The correct answer is (B).** By simple substitutions, $s = 16 \times 8 \times 8$, or 1024.

8. **The correct answer is (D).** The line of center of two tangent circles passes through the point of tangency. Hence, perimeter of $\triangle = (2 + 3) + (3 + 4) + (4 + 2) = 5 + 7 + 6 = 18$.

   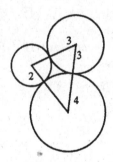

9. **The correct answer is (C).**

   $$\frac{1}{10} = x \bullet \frac{3}{4} = \frac{3x}{4}$$
   $$30x = 4$$
   $$x = \frac{2}{15}$$

10. **The correct answer is (B).** Since $QR = 7$, and triangle QOR is a right isosceles triangle, $OQ = \dfrac{7}{\sqrt{2}} = \dfrac{7\sqrt{2}}{2}$. Hence, coordinates of Q are $(0, \dfrac{7}{2}\sqrt{2})$.

11. **The correct answer is (E).** There is no indication as to the exact percentage of students who eat in the cafeteria, since we do not know how many boys or girls there are.

12. **The correct answer is (A).** Three meals a day times 365 days per year means there are $3 \times 365 = 1095$ meals in one year. Over 19 years, there are $1095 \times 19 = 20,805$ meals. Therefore, the number of restaurants in New York City exceeds 20,500.

13. **The correct answer is (D).** Both of the triangles share a common base, AC. The difference in their area is accounted for by the difference in their altitudes. Since we are given a right angle we know that DE is the altitude of the larger triangle and BE is the altitude of the smaller triangle. Since the ratio of those two segments is 4:1, then the areas must be in the ratio of 4:1.

14. **The correct answer is (C).** The original 6 pounds contained 0.24 pounds of salt. Now, the same 0.24 pounds are in 5 pounds of solution, so the percentage is $\dfrac{0.24}{5}(100) = 4.8\%$. 🖩

15. **The correct answer is (B).** By the Law of Exponents:

$(75)^3 \bullet (75)^7 = (75)^{3+7} = (75)^{10}$ 🖩

16. **The correct answer is (B).** Cities A, B, and C need not be on a straight line; therefore, one cannot add or subtract miles. Six times the distance between A and B is $150 \times 6 = 900$, which is 10 times the distance between A and C, or $10 \times 90 = 900$.

17. **The correct answer is (A).**

$\dfrac{1}{a} + \dfrac{1}{b} = \dfrac{b+a}{ab} = \dfrac{3}{4}$

18. **The correct answer is (E).** In order to determine when $f(x) = 0$, solve the equation $x^2 - 2x - 8 = 0$.

$x^2 - 2x - 8 = 0$	Factor the left-hand side.
$(x-4)(x+2) = 0$	Set each factor equal to 0.
$x - 4 = 0, \ x + 2 = 0$	Solve each equation.
$x = 4, -2$	

19. **The correct answer is (A).** The function $h(x)$ is defined for all real numbers except $x = 1$, since this would create a denominator of 0. Similarly, $g(x)$ is undefined at $x = -3$. Overall, then, $h(x) - g(x)$ is undefined at -3 and 1.

20. **The correct answer is (B).**

$\left(-\dfrac{27}{8}\right)^{-\frac{1}{3}} = \left(-\dfrac{8}{27}\right)^{\frac{1}{3}} = -\dfrac{2}{3}$

Section 4

1. A	8. B	15. B	22. A	29. C
2. E	9. C	16. D	23. C	30. C
3. C	10. B	17. B	24. A	31. B
4. A	11. A	18. E	25. C	32. A
5. B	12. E	19. A	26. D	33. D
6. E	13. A	20. C	27. A	34. E
7. C	14. A	21. D	28. C	35. A

1. **The correct answer is (A).** The correct verb is *to pore over*, meaning "to study carefully."

2. **The correct answer is (E).** The sentence is correct.

3. **The correct answer is (C).** The subject is *being a real estate agent*. The pronoun *it* is superfluous.

4. **The correct answer is (A).** Since *taste* is a verb referring to one of the senses, it should be modified by an adjective (*sweeter*), not an adverb (*more sweetly*).

5. **The correct answer is (B).** *You are required* is needed to agree with *your tax return*.

6. **The correct answer is (E).** The sentence is correct.

7. **The correct answer is (C).** To compare weather conditions for two days, use the comparative *worse*.

8. **The correct answer is (B).** When *all* refers to the total number of persons or things in a group, it takes a plural verb: *All . . . were lost.*

9. **The correct answer is (C).** The preposition *except for* takes an objective pronoun: *except for Meryl and me.*

10. **The correct answer is (B).** Since *wrote* is past tense, the events that preceded the writing must be described in the past perfect: *had visited* and *had seen.*

11. **The correct answer is (A).** Use the adverb *brusquely* to parallel the adverb *quickly.*

12. **The correct answer is (E).** The sentence is correct.

13. **The correct answer is (A).** The object of the verb *ask* must be in the objective case; *she*, the nominative case, must be replaced by *her.*

14. **The correct answer is (A).** A singular possessive pronoun (*one's*, *his*, or *her*) is required to agree with the singular subject *one*.

15. **The correct answer is (B).** The sentence requires the noun *advice*, not the verb *advise.*

16. **The correct answer is (D).** As an adjective and as a verb, *separate* uses *from*: The government is not separate *from* the church.

17. **The correct answer is (B).** The noise was not of *him* but of *his typing.*

18. **The correct answer is (E).** The sentence is correct.

19. **The correct answer is (A).** The phrase *and written* should simply be *written.*

20. **The correct answer is (C).** The sentence should be rephrased so that it does not seem as if *his hands* were *noticing*. Although choice (E) corrects the misplaced modifier, it creates a run-on sentence.

21. **The correct answer is (D).** The correct word is *among* (not *between*) the four gang members.

22. **The correct answer is (A).** The sentence is correct.

23. The correct answer is (C). The original sentence lacks a complete verb in the main clause. Both choices (C) and (E) provide a verb that agrees with the subject, but choice (E) changes the meaning of the original sentence.

24. The correct answer is (A). The sentence is correct. *So* establishes the cause-effect relationship; *have lain* is the present perfect form of *to lie*.

25. The correct answer is (C). The *it* does not refer to acclaim and recognition, which could be *achieved*. It refers to *desire*, which is either *satisfied* or *not satisfied*.

26. The correct answer is (D). The original uses five words where two will do.

27. The correct answer is (A). The sentence is correct. *Neither one* is singular and takes the singular verb form *has been*.

28. The correct answer is (C). The original idea poses two problems in parallel structure: (1) The two warnings must branch off grammatically from the subject that *warns*. (2) If the *not only* correlative form is used, it should be balanced by a phrase like *but also*. Only choice (C) meets both requirements.

29. The correct answer is (C). The sentence deals with a condition that is not a fact but a possibility. The verb used to express the condition contrary to fact should be in the subjunctive mood; the verb used to explain the possible conclusion should be in the conditional mood. The first clause should read: *Had I realized* or *If I had realized*.

30. The correct answer is (C). Choice (A) switches unnecessarily to the second person (*you*). Choice (B) has an agreement problem, using the plural pronoun *they* to refer to the singular noun *student*. Choices (D) and (E) are awkward. Choice (C) is best.

31. The correct answer is (B). Sentence (4) states that the material presented in the first paragraph, that a dress code is important, may not be valid. This paves the way for the presentation of another point of view.

32. The correct answer is (A). Choices (B) and (C) contain comma-splice errors. Choice (E) is a fragment. Choice (D) is awkward and omits details. Choice (A) is best.

33. The correct answer is (D). Paragraph one presents the opinion of those who favor a dress code. Paragraph two presents arguments against a dress code. Since paragraph two offers material opposing that already presented, choice (D) is best.

34. The correct answer is (E). The antecedent of *they* appears to be *a person*, but *they* is a plural pronoun and *person* is a singular noun. Choices (A), (B), (C), and (D) do not address this problem. Choice (E) does and is correct.

35. The correct answer is (A). Choice (A) is best because it is the only choice that phrases the sentence in the third person and not in the imperative (command) form.

Section 5

1. B	5. B	9. D	13. 18	17. 60
2. D	6. E	10. C	14. 3	18. 8
3. B	7. A	11. 8.89	15. 360	19. 18
4. D	8. E	12. 95	16. 8	20. 6

Note: A 🔲 following a math answer explanation indicates that a calculator could be helpful in solving that particular problem.

1. **The correct answer is (B).** Set up a proportion comparing apples to dollars.

$$\frac{\text{apples}}{\text{dollars}} \to \frac{24}{3} = \frac{18}{x}$$

$$8 = \frac{18}{x}$$

$$8x = 18$$

$$x = \frac{18}{8} = 2.25$$

2. **The correct answer is (D).** Rewrite $\frac{1}{10}$ as 0.1. Note that $\frac{1}{10}\% = 0.1\% = 0.001$. Therefore, $\frac{1}{10}\%$ of $\frac{1}{10}$ of 10 = 0.001 × 0.1 × 10 = 0.001.

3. **The correct answer is (B).** Set $T = \{16, 25, 36, 49, 64, 81\}$ and set $S = \{27, 64\}$. The only element that these sets have in common is 64. Thus, $S \cap T = \{64\}$.

4. **The correct answer is (D).** Using the formula $a_n = a_1 \times r^{n-1}$, with $a_1 = 3$, $r = 2$, and $n = 5$, determine that $a_5 = 3 \times 2^{5-1} = 3 \times 2^4 = 3 \times 16 = 48$.

5. **The correct answer is (B).** The average (arithmetic mean) of five consecutive integers is the number in the middle; therefore, the average is x. To find the median of five integers, arrange them in numerical order. The median will also be the number in the middle, x. Finally, note that x divided by x is equal to 1.

6. **The correct answer is (E).** One cubic foot equals 12^3 cubic inches, or 1728. Thus, one cubic foot of the metal would weigh 3456 pounds. 🔲

7. **The correct answer is (A).** The area of the circle is πr^2 and the circumference is $2\pi r$. If the area equals the circumference, solve the equation $\pi r^2 = 2\pi r$, or $r = 2$. The diameter is $2r$, or 4 inches.

8. **The correct answer is (E).** Let's substitute J for John and P for Pat.

(J is 3 times P) $J = 3P$

(J in four years) $x = J + 4$

(substitute $3P$ for J) $x = 3P + 4$

$$x - 4 = 3P$$

$$\frac{x - 4}{3} = P$$

You can also reason this way: If John will be x years old in 4 years, then he is $x - 4$ years old now. Since Pat's age is now one third of John's, Pat is now $\frac{x-4}{3}$ years old.

9. **The correct answer is (D).** Renaming the fractions as decimals, $\frac{2}{3} = 0.666\ldots$, $\frac{5}{7} = 0.7142\ldots$, $\frac{8}{11} = .7272\ldots$, and $\frac{9}{13} = 0.6923$. So the order is $\frac{2}{3}, \frac{9}{13}, \frac{5}{7}, \frac{8}{11}$.

10. **The correct answer is (C).** If the average for the eight tests is 84%, then the sum of the eight tests must be 8 times 84, or 672. For the six tests, the sum must be 6 times 86, or 516. The two dropped tests must have accounted for 156 points. 156 divided by 2 is 78.

11. The correct answer is 8.89.

$$\frac{\frac{-1}{3}}{3} - \frac{3}{\frac{-1}{3}} = \frac{-\frac{1}{3}}{\frac{3}{1}} - \frac{\frac{3}{1}}{-\frac{1}{3}}$$

$$= -\frac{1}{3}\left(\frac{1}{3}\right) - \frac{3}{1}\left(-\frac{3}{1}\right)$$

$$= -\frac{1}{9} + 9$$

$$= 8\frac{8}{9} = \frac{80}{9} = 8.89$$

12. The correct answer is 95. The sum of Dawn's scores for the first four tests is 80(4) = 320.

$$\frac{320 + x}{5} = 83$$

$$320 + x = 415$$

$$x = 95$$

13. The correct answer is 18.

Area of a square = (side)² or $\dfrac{(\text{diagonal})^2}{2}$

Area of $ABCD$ = (side)² = 6² = 36

Area of $WXYZ$ = $\dfrac{(\text{diagonal})^2}{2} = \dfrac{6^2}{2}$

Shaded area = 36 − 18 = 18

14. The correct answer is 3.

1 week = 7 days

1 day = 24 hours

1 hour = 60 minutes

$$\frac{30,240}{7(24)(60)} = 3$$

15. The correct answer is 360. The sum of the interior angles of a quadrilateral is 360°.

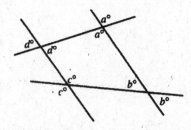

$\therefore a + b + c + d = 360$

16. The correct answer is 8.

Distance = rate × time

$$360 = r(9)$$

$$40 = r$$

If r were 40 + 5 = 45

$$d = rt$$

$$360 = 45t$$

$$t = 8$$

17. The correct answer is 60.

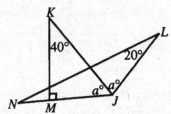

$$40 + 90 + a = 180$$

$$a = 50$$

$$\angle J = 2(50) = 100°$$

$$\angle N + \angle J + \angle L = 180°$$

$$\angle N + 100° + 20° = 180°$$

$$\angle N = 60°$$

18. **The correct answer is 8.**

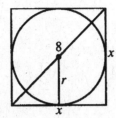

$$x^2 + x^2 = 8^2$$
$$2x^2 = 64$$
$$x = 4\sqrt{2}$$

The side of the square $= 4\sqrt{2}$.

The radius of the circle $= \dfrac{1}{2}\left(4\sqrt{2}\right) = 2\sqrt{2}$.

$$A = \pi r^2$$
$$= \pi\left(2\sqrt{2}\right)^2 = 8\pi = a\pi \therefore a = 8$$

19. **The correct answer is 18.** There are 2 ways to complete the first leg of the trip. After this, there are 3 ways to complete the second leg of the trip, and then 3 ways to complete the third leg of the trip. Overall, there are $2 \times 3 \times 3 = 18$ ways to make the entire trip.

20. **The correct answer is 6.** The set D contains the numbers between 11 and 29 that are not prime. Specifically, $D = \{12, 14, 15, 16, 18, 20, 21, 22, 24, 25, 26, 27, 28\}$. Of the members of D, the numbers 12, 15, 18, 21, 24, and 27 are also multiples of 3. Therefore, $D \cap E = \{12, 15, 18, 21, 24, 27\}$.

Section 6

1. A	7. A	12. D	17. C	22. A
2. C	8. C	13. C	18. D	23. D
3. B	9. D	14. D	19. E	24. C
4. E	10. C	15. C	20. C	25. A
5. D	11. A	16. E	21. B	26. B
6. C				

1. **The correct answer is (A).** Keeping a meeting from breaking up requires more than a clear *idea* or *vision*; it requires control, or a *grasp* of the situation.

2. **The correct answer is (C).** The word *commitment* signals the appropriate actions of the mayor; to be *steadfast* in her commitment, she must *stem*, or check, the increase of economic problems for the people who voted her into office.

3. **The correct answer is (B).** For the farmhouse to have been a landmark since before the Civil War, it must have been well built, or *sturdy*.

4. **The correct answer is (E).** If she thought her cousin was hateful, it is most likely that she found his behavior *obnoxious* (offensive) and that she was *galled*, or irritated, to hear him praised.

5. **The correct answer is (D).** *Circumspect*, meaning "watchful or wary," is the only choice that makes sense.

6. **The correct answer is (C).** *Accommodate*, meaning "to provide space for," is the only answer that makes sense.

7. **The correct answer is (A).** To make promises you know you cannot *fulfill* is *hypocrisy*. No other choice correctly fills both blanks.

8. **The correct answer is (C).** One who accepts without question is *credulous* (tending to believe readily).

9. **The correct answer is (D).** Choice (A) is a good distracter because it sounds important and authoritative, but it's wrong. Choice (E) is almost right, but choice (D) includes the idea of a previous time and is, therefore, the better choice of the two and the best choice of all five answers.

10. **The correct answer is (C).** The author may be slightly dismissive of academic critiques, but he doesn't ridicule them, so choice (A) isn't correct. The author doesn't introduce the subject of meaning as such, so choice (B) doesn't work. Choices (D) and (E) are distracters using words from the passage but distorting the passage's meaning.

11. **The correct answer is (A).** Choice (A) can't even be inferred from the content of the passage. Note that choices (B) and (C) are not listed separately in the passage, but the use of the coordinating conjunction *as well as* gives them equal status.

12. **The correct answer is (D).** The second clause in the first sentence can be interpreted to mean that in some societies novelty is not valued because it threatens traditions. Sentence 1 proves that choice (A) is incorrect. No information is given that could be the basis of inferring choices (B), (C), or (E).

13. **The correct answer is (C).** Pyne paints a "sing-song" image of Antarctica through his choice of words and sentence structure.

14. **The correct answer is (D).** There is no mention of people in the quotation, so choices (A) and (B) are probably not the best. Choice (C) is impossible, as is choice (E). That leaves choice (D) as the most logical and best choice.

15. **The correct answer is (C).** In this context, the word *fixed* means situated or found.

16. **The correct answer is (E).** All of the other choices are explicitly mentioned by the author as the nesting places of the hummingbird.

17. **The correct answer is (C).** Wilson states that nests are sometimes attached to such objects, but "these cases are rare" (line 11).

18. **The correct answer is (D).** The nest is not easily seen, but it is not invisible, as choice (C) suggests. Wilson describes seeing it from below (lines 32–33).

19. **The correct answer is (E).** Wilson refers to the proprietors darting around to protect the nest (lines 36–37).

20. **The correct answer is (C).** Wilson believes that hummingbirds *do* feed their young such food, saying, "I think it highly probable they do" (lines 50–51). However, he has not seen it.

21. **The correct answer is (B).** Since Wilson takes this to mean that hummingbirds may raise two broods (lines 54–55), the only possible answer here is (B).

22. **The correct answer is (A).** According to the passage (lines 19–30), the nest is composed of bluish-grey lichen glued on with hummingbird saliva, the wings of flying seeds, and downy substances from fern stalks and from the great mullein (another kind of plant).

23. **The correct answer is (D).** Lines 17–18 show that Wilson is looking at something that "is now lying before me."

24. **The correct answer is (C).** It can be inferred from the sentence that the hummingbirds migrate into Pennsylvania (presumably from the South) "about the twenty-fifth of April." None of the other choices is supported by the passage.

25. **The correct answer is (A).** Although other details about the hummingbird are included, the passage focuses on hummingbirds' nesting.

26. **The correct answer is (B).** Most of Wilson's observations in this piece happen in the wild; it is safe to assume that he would study crows the same way.

Section 7

1. B	4. D	7. D	10. D	13. A
2. C	5. B	8. D	11. D	14. D
3. B	6. C	9. A	12. D	15. C

Note: A 🖩 following a math answer explanation indicates that a calculator could be helpful in solving that particular problem.

1. **The correct answer is (B).**

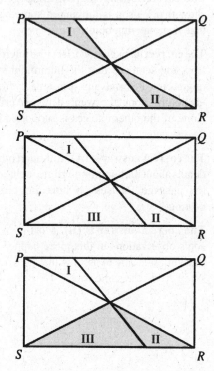

PR and *SQ* are diagonals of rectangle *PQRS*.

The diagonals of a rectangle divide the rectangle into four triangles of equal area. $\triangle$I and $\triangle$II are equal.

Since $\triangle$III + $\triangle$II = 25% of rectangle *PQRS*, $\triangle$III and $\triangle$I = 25% of rectangle *PQRS* as well.

2. **The correct answer is (C).** The number of revolutions is inversely proportional to the size of the wheel. Thus, $\frac{30}{20} = \frac{n}{240}$. Where $n =$ number of revolutions for second wheel,

$$20n = 7200$$
$$n = 360 \quad 🖩$$

3. **The correct answer is (B).** $1.86 \times 10^5 = 1.86 \times 100,000 = 186,000$ 🖩

4. **The correct answer is (D).** All the numbers from 200 to 299 begin with 2. There are 100 of these. Then all numbers like 102, 112, . . ., 192 end with 2. There are 10 of these.

Hence, there are 110 such numbers.

5. **The correct answer is (B).** If the area is $49x^2$, the side of the square is $7x$. Therefore, the diagonal of the square must be the hypotenuse of a right isosceles triangle of leg $7x$.

Hence, diagonal $= 7x\sqrt{2}$.

6. **The correct answer is (C).** The amount paid for weight over 5 ounces is $1.66 - 0.62 = 1.04$. At $0.08 for each additional ounce,

$$\frac{\$1.04}{\$0.08} = 13 \text{ ounces of additional weight.}$$

The total weight is 13 ounces + 5 ounces = 18 ounces.

$$18 \text{ ounces} \times \left(\frac{1 \text{ lb.}}{16 \text{ oz.}}\right) = 1\frac{1}{8} \text{ lbs}.$$

7. **The correct answer is (D).** Each adult needs 15 cans/7 adults $= \frac{15}{7}$ cans in two days, or $\left(\frac{1}{2}\right)\left(\frac{15}{7}\right) = \frac{15}{14}$ cans per adult per day. Multiply this by the number of adults and by the number of days:

$$\frac{15}{14} (4 \text{ adults})(7 \text{ days}) = 30 \text{ cans of food} \quad 🖩$$

8. The correct answer is (D). Let the original sign be 10 by 10.

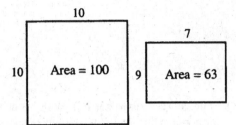

Then, the new sign is 9 by 7.

$$\frac{63}{100} = 63\%$$

9. The correct answer is (A). The average is found by taking the sum of a list of numbers and dividing the sum by the number in the list. If n is the number of numbers in the series, $160 \div n = 20$, so $n = 8$ numbers.

10. The correct answer is (D). Squaring a negative number will make it positive, so choices (A) and (B) are not true. $1^2 = 1$, so choice (E) is not true. Squaring any number greater than 1 will always be larger than the number itself, but squaring a fraction less than 1, where the denominator is larger than the numerator, will make the denominator much larger than the numerator, thus making the whole fraction smaller.

11. The correct answer is (D).

$$x^6 + (2x^2)^3 + (3x^3)^2 = x^6 + 8x^6 + 9x^6 = 18x^6$$

12. The correct answer is (D). Set up a proportion and solve for x:

$$\frac{\frac{3}{4}\text{ in.}}{6\text{ in.}} = \frac{10\text{ mi.}}{x\text{ mi}}$$

$$\frac{3}{4}x = 60$$

$$x = 80$$

13. The correct answer is (A). If h is any positive quantity, then letting $d_h = (m+h) - \frac{50}{m+h}$, we can see that d_h is greater than d, since h is greater than zero, and $\frac{50}{m}$ is greater than $\frac{50}{m+h}$. Therefore, d increases as m does.

14. The correct answer is (D). Begin by multiplying all terms of the equation by the LCD of 36.

$$36\left(\frac{x}{12}\right) + 36\left(\frac{x}{18}\right) = 1(36)$$

$$3x + 2x = 36$$

$$5x = 36$$

$$x = \frac{36}{5} = 7\frac{1}{5}$$

15. The correct answer is (C). Begin by making a sketch of the flagpole and rope.

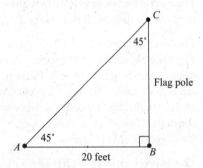

Note that $\angle B$ is a right angle, and the other two angles measure 45°. The easiest way to solve this problem is to recognize that the triangle is a 45-45-90 triangle, that the length of one of the legs is 20, and that the hypotenuse needs to be found. Using the properties of a 45-45-90 triangle, the hypotenuse is equal to the length of the leg times $\sqrt{2}$. Thus, the hypotenuse is $20\sqrt{2}$ feet.

This problem can also be solved by using trigonometric ratios. Let h represent the length of the hypotenuse, so

$$\cos 45° = \frac{\text{Adjacent}}{\text{Hypotenuse}} = \frac{20}{h}$$

Now, since $\cos 45° = \frac{\sqrt{2}}{2}$, we have

$$\frac{\sqrt{2}}{2} = \frac{20}{h} \quad \text{Cross-multiply.}$$

$$h\sqrt{2} = 40 \quad \text{Divide both sides by } \sqrt{2}.$$

$$h = \frac{40}{\sqrt{2}} = \frac{40}{\sqrt{2}} \times \frac{\sqrt{2}}{\sqrt{2}} = \frac{40\sqrt{2}}{2} = 20\sqrt{2}$$

Note that, while you obtain the same answer either way, it is much faster to use the properties of a 45-45-90 triangle than it is to use trigonometry to solve the problem.

answers practice test 4

Section 8

1. E	5. A	9. C	13. B
2. B	6. D	10. A	14. E
3. C	7. D	11. B	15. A
4. D	8. C	12. D	16. B

1. **The correct answer is (E).** Passage 1 doesn't even mention money. Remember with EXCEPT questions that you are looking for the wrong answer.

2. **The correct answer is (B).** This answer is very clearly discussed in Passage 2.

3. **The correct answer is (C).** If you didn't know the use of the word *green,* you could figure it out by going back to Passage 1 to see if it says who the likely buyer of a hybrid is. It says that "conservation-conscious consumers" buy them. Conservation equals environment equals green.

4. **The correct answer is (D).** The author of Passage 2 gives the difference in dollars between hybrid and gasoline-powered cars and also cites Europe as an example of why opponents think hybrids won't sell well.

5. **The correct answer is (A).** The context of the sentence, with its reference to taking his own life, supports this choice.

6. **The correct answer is (D).** Sentence three specifically cites the cause of Achilles' feelings of guilt.

7. **The correct answer is (D).** In this context, Thetis is traveling or returning to Vulcan.

8. **The correct answer is (C).** The passage refers to Vulcan's palace and his ability to create magical tripods, indicating that he is quite powerful.

9. **The correct answer is (C).** With his new armor and his feelings of righteousness, Achilles is confident as he goes into battle.

10. **The correct answer is (A).** Sentence two in Passage 2 states that they enlisted the help of Curoi of Kerry.

11. **The correct answer is (B).** The champion did not have to fight the giant; the champion had to behead the giant.

12. **The correct answer is (D).** Although choices (A) and (B) might be appealing, the fact that the giant remained alive while headless was what made him so unusual.

13. **The correct answer is (B).** The context of the sentence supports definition (B), as the men of Ulster were completely, or *utterly,* ashamed.

14. **The correct answer is (E).** Cuchulain is a man to whom his word is his bond; he had to meet the giant because he gave his word.

15. **The correct answer is (A).** His speech is serious and sad because he is afraid of imminent death.

16. **The correct answer is (B).** The quality that Achilles and Cuchulain share is courage.

Section 9

1. E	5. E	9. E	13. A
2. E	6. B	10. C	14. E
3. C	7. D	11. B	15. B
4. D	8. C	12. D	

1. **The correct answer is (E).** If the *material* and the *performances* are his, so is the singing.

2. **The correct answer is (E).** The design and the fabrics are being compared. The verb form should be parallel, as in choice (E).

3. **The correct answer is (C).** Parallel ideas should be expressed in parallel form. If the application had two faults, they should be expressed in parallel form. Choice (B) contains a faulty antecedent for *it*. Choice (D) contains a comma splice. Choice (E) fails to use commas.

4. **The correct answer is (D).** The original choice (A) is a run-on sentence. Choice (B) correctly separates the clauses but incorrectly adds a comma before *officially*. Choice (C) creates a run-on sentence. Choice (E) omits the comma required after *however*. Choice (D) resolves all problems. It assigns *officially* to the President's powers, it puts *however* in the right place, and it uses the punctuation required when such an adverb is tucked inside the sentence.

5. **The correct answer is (E).** The original sentence takes 16 words to say what choice (E) says in 10 words.

6. **The correct answer is (B).** *Windy* and *cold* can modify *day*, but *snowed continuously* cannot; therefore, choices (A) and (C) are incorrect. Choices (D) and (E) are illogical. Choice (B) is both correct and logical.

7. **The correct answer is (D).** The most effective means of phrasing this sentence is to use two parallel clauses. Since the subject of the second clause is *letting it go*, the best subject for the first clause is *keeping the raccoon*. The addition of the pronoun *it* in choice (E) makes this version incorrect.

8. **The correct answer is (C).** An indirect question ends with a period, not a question mark, so eliminate choices (D) and (E). Of the remaining choices, only choice (C) is consistent in the tense of the verbs used (*asked, knew, would be*).

9. **The correct answer is (E).** *That* is needed to introduce the subordinate clause; *how*, meaning for what purpose or for what reason, does not make sense in the sentence.

10. **The correct answer is (C).** The pronoun agreeing with *each applicant* must be singular. Since active voice is preferable to passive voice, choice (D), choice (C) is the best answer.

11. **The correct answer is (B).** Traffic accidents can be counted, so the correct phrasing is *number of traffic accidents*, not *amount*. Choice (C) uses *shorten* incorrectly.

12. **The correct answer is (D).** The subject of the sentence is *acquisition*, which is singular, so the verb must be singular.

13. **The correct answer is (A).** The sentence is correct.

14. **The correct answer is (E).** Jake can't be the smallest of any boy, only the smallest boy.

15. **The correct answer is (B).** The verb *could be seen* is past tense, so the correct tense sequence puts spring in the past tense also. (Present tense would be *can be seen*.)

COMPUTING YOUR SCORES

To get a sense of your progress in preparing for the SAT, you need to compute individual multiple-choice critical reading, math, and writing raw scores for this Practice Test. Keep in mind that these formulas have been simplified to give you a "quick and dirty" sense of where you are scoring, not a perfectly precise score.

To Compute Your Raw Scores

1. Enter the number of correct answers for each critical reading, math, and multiple-choice writing section under Number of Questions Correct.

2. Enter the number of incorrect answers (not blanks) for each critical reading, math, and multiple-choice writing section under Number of Questions Incorrect.

3. Total the number correct and number incorrect.

4. Follow this formula: Take the total correct and subtract one quarter of the total incorrect. Round up in your favor to compute your raw score.

Critical Reading Section	Total Number of Questions	Number of Questions Correct	Number of Questions Incorrect
2	26		
6	26		
8	16		
Totals	68	Total Correct:	Total Incorrect:

Critical Reading Raw Score = Total Correct − ($\frac{1}{4}$ × Total Incorrect) = ____

Math Section	Total Number of Questions	Number of Questions Correct	Number of Questions Incorrect
3	20		
5	20		
7	15		
Totals	55	Total Correct:	Total Incorrect:

Math Raw Score = Total Correct − ($\frac{1}{4}$ × Total Incorrect) = ____

Multiple-Choice Writing Section	Total Number of Questions	Number of Questions Correct	Number of Questions Incorrect
4	35		
9	15		
Total	50	Total Correct:	Total Incorrect:

Multiple-Choice Writing Raw Score = Total Correct − ($\frac{1}{4}$ × Total Incorrect) = ____

CONVERSION SCALES

CRITICAL READING

Raw Score	Scaled Score	Raw Score	Scaled Score
68	800	30	480
65	760	25	440
60	710	20	410
55	670	15	370
50	620	10	340
45	590	5	290
40	550	0	230
35	520		

MATH

Raw Score	Scaled Score	Raw Score	Scaled Score
55	800	20	510
50	760	15	480
45	690	10	440
40	650	5	340
35	610	0	200
30	580		
25	550		

MULTIPLE-CHOICE WRITING

Raw Score	Scaled Score	Raw Score	Scaled Score
50	800	20	470
45	760	15	420
40	680	10	370
35	620	5	320
30	580	0	270
25	520		

SELF-EVALUATION CHARTS

Critical Reading: Raw Score

Excellent	60–68
Good	50–59
Average	30–49
Fair	20–29
Poor	0–19

Math: Raw Score

Excellent	50–55
Good	40–49
Average	20–39
Fair	10–19
Poor	0–9

ANSWER SHEET PRACTICE TEST 5

SECTION 1: ESSAY

_____
_____
_____
_____
_____
_____
_____
_____
_____
_____
_____
_____
_____
_____
_____
_____
_____
_____
_____
_____
_____
_____
_____
_____
_____
_____
_____
_____

answer sheet

If a section has fewer questions than answer ovals, leave the extra ovals blank.

SECTION 2

1 Ⓐ Ⓑ Ⓒ Ⓓ Ⓔ	11 Ⓐ Ⓑ Ⓒ Ⓓ Ⓔ	21 Ⓐ Ⓑ Ⓒ Ⓓ Ⓔ	31 Ⓐ Ⓑ Ⓒ Ⓓ Ⓔ
2 Ⓐ Ⓑ Ⓒ Ⓓ Ⓔ	12 Ⓐ Ⓑ Ⓒ Ⓓ Ⓔ	22 Ⓐ Ⓑ Ⓒ Ⓓ Ⓔ	32 Ⓐ Ⓑ Ⓒ Ⓓ Ⓔ
3 Ⓐ Ⓑ Ⓒ Ⓓ Ⓔ	13 Ⓐ Ⓑ Ⓒ Ⓓ Ⓔ	23 Ⓐ Ⓑ Ⓒ Ⓓ Ⓔ	33 Ⓐ Ⓑ Ⓒ Ⓓ Ⓔ
4 Ⓐ Ⓑ Ⓒ Ⓓ Ⓔ	14 Ⓐ Ⓑ Ⓒ Ⓓ Ⓔ	24 Ⓐ Ⓑ Ⓒ Ⓓ Ⓔ	34 Ⓐ Ⓑ Ⓒ Ⓓ Ⓔ
5 Ⓐ Ⓑ Ⓒ Ⓓ Ⓔ	15 Ⓐ Ⓑ Ⓒ Ⓓ Ⓔ	25 Ⓐ Ⓑ Ⓒ Ⓓ Ⓔ	35 Ⓐ Ⓑ Ⓒ Ⓓ Ⓔ
6 Ⓐ Ⓑ Ⓒ Ⓓ Ⓔ	16 Ⓐ Ⓑ Ⓒ Ⓓ Ⓔ	26 Ⓐ Ⓑ Ⓒ Ⓓ Ⓔ	36 Ⓐ Ⓑ Ⓒ Ⓓ Ⓔ
7 Ⓐ Ⓑ Ⓒ Ⓓ Ⓔ	17 Ⓐ Ⓑ Ⓒ Ⓓ Ⓔ	27 Ⓐ Ⓑ Ⓒ Ⓓ Ⓔ	37 Ⓐ Ⓑ Ⓒ Ⓓ Ⓔ
8 Ⓐ Ⓑ Ⓒ Ⓓ Ⓔ	18 Ⓐ Ⓑ Ⓒ Ⓓ Ⓔ	28 Ⓐ Ⓑ Ⓒ Ⓓ Ⓔ	38 Ⓐ Ⓑ Ⓒ Ⓓ Ⓔ
9 Ⓐ Ⓑ Ⓒ Ⓓ Ⓔ	19 Ⓐ Ⓑ Ⓒ Ⓓ Ⓔ	29 Ⓐ Ⓑ Ⓒ Ⓓ Ⓔ	39 Ⓐ Ⓑ Ⓒ Ⓓ Ⓔ
10 Ⓐ Ⓑ Ⓒ Ⓓ Ⓔ	20 Ⓐ Ⓑ Ⓒ Ⓓ Ⓔ	30 Ⓐ Ⓑ Ⓒ Ⓓ Ⓔ	40 Ⓐ Ⓑ Ⓒ Ⓓ Ⓔ

SECTION 3

1 Ⓐ Ⓑ Ⓒ Ⓓ Ⓔ	11 Ⓐ Ⓑ Ⓒ Ⓓ Ⓔ	21 Ⓐ Ⓑ Ⓒ Ⓓ Ⓔ	31 Ⓐ Ⓑ Ⓒ Ⓓ Ⓔ
2 Ⓐ Ⓑ Ⓒ Ⓓ Ⓔ	12 Ⓐ Ⓑ Ⓒ Ⓓ Ⓔ	22 Ⓐ Ⓑ Ⓒ Ⓓ Ⓔ	32 Ⓐ Ⓑ Ⓒ Ⓓ Ⓔ
3 Ⓐ Ⓑ Ⓒ Ⓓ Ⓔ	13 Ⓐ Ⓑ Ⓒ Ⓓ Ⓔ	23 Ⓐ Ⓑ Ⓒ Ⓓ Ⓔ	33 Ⓐ Ⓑ Ⓒ Ⓓ Ⓔ
4 Ⓐ Ⓑ Ⓒ Ⓓ Ⓔ	14 Ⓐ Ⓑ Ⓒ Ⓓ Ⓔ	24 Ⓐ Ⓑ Ⓒ Ⓓ Ⓔ	34 Ⓐ Ⓑ Ⓒ Ⓓ Ⓔ
5 Ⓐ Ⓑ Ⓒ Ⓓ Ⓔ	15 Ⓐ Ⓑ Ⓒ Ⓓ Ⓔ	25 Ⓐ Ⓑ Ⓒ Ⓓ Ⓔ	35 Ⓐ Ⓑ Ⓒ Ⓓ Ⓔ
6 Ⓐ Ⓑ Ⓒ Ⓓ Ⓔ	16 Ⓐ Ⓑ Ⓒ Ⓓ Ⓔ	26 Ⓐ Ⓑ Ⓒ Ⓓ Ⓔ	36 Ⓐ Ⓑ Ⓒ Ⓓ Ⓔ
7 Ⓐ Ⓑ Ⓒ Ⓓ Ⓔ	17 Ⓐ Ⓑ Ⓒ Ⓓ Ⓔ	27 Ⓐ Ⓑ Ⓒ Ⓓ Ⓔ	37 Ⓐ Ⓑ Ⓒ Ⓓ Ⓔ
8 Ⓐ Ⓑ Ⓒ Ⓓ Ⓔ	18 Ⓐ Ⓑ Ⓒ Ⓓ Ⓔ	28 Ⓐ Ⓑ Ⓒ Ⓓ Ⓔ	38 Ⓐ Ⓑ Ⓒ Ⓓ Ⓔ
9 Ⓐ Ⓑ Ⓒ Ⓓ Ⓔ	19 Ⓐ Ⓑ Ⓒ Ⓓ Ⓔ	29 Ⓐ Ⓑ Ⓒ Ⓓ Ⓔ	39 Ⓐ Ⓑ Ⓒ Ⓓ Ⓔ
10 Ⓐ Ⓑ Ⓒ Ⓓ Ⓔ	20 Ⓐ Ⓑ Ⓒ Ⓓ Ⓔ	30 Ⓐ Ⓑ Ⓒ Ⓓ Ⓔ	40 Ⓐ Ⓑ Ⓒ Ⓓ Ⓔ

SECTION 4

1 Ⓐ Ⓑ Ⓒ Ⓓ Ⓔ	11 Ⓐ Ⓑ Ⓒ Ⓓ Ⓔ	21 Ⓐ Ⓑ Ⓒ Ⓓ Ⓔ	31 Ⓐ Ⓑ Ⓒ Ⓓ Ⓔ
2 Ⓐ Ⓑ Ⓒ Ⓓ Ⓔ	12 Ⓐ Ⓑ Ⓒ Ⓓ Ⓔ	22 Ⓐ Ⓑ Ⓒ Ⓓ Ⓔ	32 Ⓐ Ⓑ Ⓒ Ⓓ Ⓔ
3 Ⓐ Ⓑ Ⓒ Ⓓ Ⓔ	13 Ⓐ Ⓑ Ⓒ Ⓓ Ⓔ	23 Ⓐ Ⓑ Ⓒ Ⓓ Ⓔ	33 Ⓐ Ⓑ Ⓒ Ⓓ Ⓔ
4 Ⓐ Ⓑ Ⓒ Ⓓ Ⓔ	14 Ⓐ Ⓑ Ⓒ Ⓓ Ⓔ	24 Ⓐ Ⓑ Ⓒ Ⓓ Ⓔ	34 Ⓐ Ⓑ Ⓒ Ⓓ Ⓔ
5 Ⓐ Ⓑ Ⓒ Ⓓ Ⓔ	15 Ⓐ Ⓑ Ⓒ Ⓓ Ⓔ	25 Ⓐ Ⓑ Ⓒ Ⓓ Ⓔ	35 Ⓐ Ⓑ Ⓒ Ⓓ Ⓔ
6 Ⓐ Ⓑ Ⓒ Ⓓ Ⓔ	16 Ⓐ Ⓑ Ⓒ Ⓓ Ⓔ	26 Ⓐ Ⓑ Ⓒ Ⓓ Ⓔ	
7 Ⓐ Ⓑ Ⓒ Ⓓ Ⓔ	17 Ⓐ Ⓑ Ⓒ Ⓓ Ⓔ	27 Ⓐ Ⓑ Ⓒ Ⓓ Ⓔ	
8 Ⓐ Ⓑ Ⓒ Ⓓ Ⓔ	18 Ⓐ Ⓑ Ⓒ Ⓓ Ⓔ	28 Ⓐ Ⓑ Ⓒ Ⓓ Ⓔ	
9 Ⓐ Ⓑ Ⓒ Ⓓ Ⓔ	19 Ⓐ Ⓑ Ⓒ Ⓓ Ⓔ	29 Ⓐ Ⓑ Ⓒ Ⓓ Ⓔ	
10 Ⓐ Ⓑ Ⓒ Ⓓ Ⓔ	20 Ⓐ Ⓑ Ⓒ Ⓓ Ⓔ	30 Ⓐ Ⓑ Ⓒ Ⓓ Ⓔ	

SECTION 5

Note: ONLY the answers entered on the grid are scored. Handwritten answers at the top of the column are NOT scored.

1 Ⓐ Ⓑ Ⓒ Ⓓ Ⓔ   6 Ⓐ Ⓑ Ⓒ Ⓓ Ⓔ
2 Ⓐ Ⓑ Ⓒ Ⓓ Ⓔ   7 Ⓐ Ⓑ Ⓒ Ⓓ Ⓔ
3 Ⓐ Ⓑ Ⓒ Ⓓ Ⓔ   8 Ⓐ Ⓑ Ⓒ Ⓓ Ⓔ
4 Ⓐ Ⓑ Ⓒ Ⓓ Ⓔ   9 Ⓐ Ⓑ Ⓒ Ⓓ Ⓔ
5 Ⓐ Ⓑ Ⓒ Ⓓ Ⓔ 10 Ⓐ Ⓑ Ⓒ Ⓓ Ⓔ

11. 12. 13. 14. 15.

16. 17. 18. 19. 20.

SECTION 6

1 Ⓐ Ⓑ Ⓒ Ⓓ Ⓔ	11 Ⓐ Ⓑ Ⓒ Ⓓ Ⓔ	21 Ⓐ Ⓑ Ⓒ Ⓓ Ⓔ	31 Ⓐ Ⓑ Ⓒ Ⓓ Ⓔ
2 Ⓐ Ⓑ Ⓒ Ⓓ Ⓔ	12 Ⓐ Ⓑ Ⓒ Ⓓ Ⓔ	22 Ⓐ Ⓑ Ⓒ Ⓓ Ⓔ	32 Ⓐ Ⓑ Ⓒ Ⓓ Ⓔ
3 Ⓐ Ⓑ Ⓒ Ⓓ Ⓔ	13 Ⓐ Ⓑ Ⓒ Ⓓ Ⓔ	23 Ⓐ Ⓑ Ⓒ Ⓓ Ⓔ	33 Ⓐ Ⓑ Ⓒ Ⓓ Ⓔ
4 Ⓐ Ⓑ Ⓒ Ⓓ Ⓔ	14 Ⓐ Ⓑ Ⓒ Ⓓ Ⓔ	24 Ⓐ Ⓑ Ⓒ Ⓓ Ⓔ	34 Ⓐ Ⓑ Ⓒ Ⓓ Ⓔ
5 Ⓐ Ⓑ Ⓒ Ⓓ Ⓔ	15 Ⓐ Ⓑ Ⓒ Ⓓ Ⓔ	25 Ⓐ Ⓑ Ⓒ Ⓓ Ⓔ	35 Ⓐ Ⓑ Ⓒ Ⓓ Ⓔ
6 Ⓐ Ⓑ Ⓒ Ⓓ Ⓔ	16 Ⓐ Ⓑ Ⓒ Ⓓ Ⓔ	26 Ⓐ Ⓑ Ⓒ Ⓓ Ⓔ	36 Ⓐ Ⓑ Ⓒ Ⓓ Ⓔ
7 Ⓐ Ⓑ Ⓒ Ⓓ Ⓔ	17 Ⓐ Ⓑ Ⓒ Ⓓ Ⓔ	27 Ⓐ Ⓑ Ⓒ Ⓓ Ⓔ	37 Ⓐ Ⓑ Ⓒ Ⓓ Ⓔ
8 Ⓐ Ⓑ Ⓒ Ⓓ Ⓔ	18 Ⓐ Ⓑ Ⓒ Ⓓ Ⓔ	28 Ⓐ Ⓑ Ⓒ Ⓓ Ⓔ	38 Ⓐ Ⓑ Ⓒ Ⓓ Ⓔ
9 Ⓐ Ⓑ Ⓒ Ⓓ Ⓔ	19 Ⓐ Ⓑ Ⓒ Ⓓ Ⓔ	29 Ⓐ Ⓑ Ⓒ Ⓓ Ⓔ	39 Ⓐ Ⓑ Ⓒ Ⓓ Ⓔ
10 Ⓐ Ⓑ Ⓒ Ⓓ Ⓔ	20 Ⓐ Ⓑ Ⓒ Ⓓ Ⓔ	30 Ⓐ Ⓑ Ⓒ Ⓓ Ⓔ	40 Ⓐ Ⓑ Ⓒ Ⓓ Ⓔ

SECTION 7

1 Ⓐ Ⓑ Ⓒ Ⓓ Ⓔ	6 Ⓐ Ⓑ Ⓒ Ⓓ Ⓔ	11 Ⓐ Ⓑ Ⓒ Ⓓ Ⓔ
2 Ⓐ Ⓑ Ⓒ Ⓓ Ⓔ	7 Ⓐ Ⓑ Ⓒ Ⓓ Ⓔ	12 Ⓐ Ⓑ Ⓒ Ⓓ Ⓔ
3 Ⓐ Ⓑ Ⓒ Ⓓ Ⓔ	8 Ⓐ Ⓑ Ⓒ Ⓓ Ⓔ	13 Ⓐ Ⓑ Ⓒ Ⓓ Ⓔ
4 Ⓐ Ⓑ Ⓒ Ⓓ Ⓔ	9 Ⓐ Ⓑ Ⓒ Ⓓ Ⓔ	14 Ⓐ Ⓑ Ⓒ Ⓓ Ⓔ
5 Ⓐ Ⓑ Ⓒ Ⓓ Ⓔ	10 Ⓐ Ⓑ Ⓒ Ⓓ Ⓔ	15 Ⓐ Ⓑ Ⓒ Ⓓ Ⓔ

SECTION 8

1 Ⓐ Ⓑ Ⓒ Ⓓ Ⓔ	6 Ⓐ Ⓑ Ⓒ Ⓓ Ⓔ	11 Ⓐ Ⓑ Ⓒ Ⓓ Ⓔ	16 Ⓐ Ⓑ Ⓒ Ⓓ Ⓔ
2 Ⓐ Ⓑ Ⓒ Ⓓ Ⓔ	7 Ⓐ Ⓑ Ⓒ Ⓓ Ⓔ	12 Ⓐ Ⓑ Ⓒ Ⓓ Ⓔ	17 Ⓐ Ⓑ Ⓒ Ⓓ Ⓔ
3 Ⓐ Ⓑ Ⓒ Ⓓ Ⓔ	8 Ⓐ Ⓑ Ⓒ Ⓓ Ⓔ	13 Ⓐ Ⓑ Ⓒ Ⓓ Ⓔ	18 Ⓐ Ⓑ Ⓒ Ⓓ Ⓔ
4 Ⓐ Ⓑ Ⓒ Ⓓ Ⓔ	9 Ⓐ Ⓑ Ⓒ Ⓓ Ⓔ	14 Ⓐ Ⓑ Ⓒ Ⓓ Ⓔ	19 Ⓐ Ⓑ Ⓒ Ⓓ Ⓔ
5 Ⓐ Ⓑ Ⓒ Ⓓ Ⓔ	10 Ⓐ Ⓑ Ⓒ Ⓓ Ⓔ	15 Ⓐ Ⓑ Ⓒ Ⓓ Ⓔ	20 Ⓐ Ⓑ Ⓒ Ⓓ Ⓔ

SECTION 9

1 Ⓐ Ⓑ Ⓒ Ⓓ Ⓔ	6 Ⓐ Ⓑ Ⓒ Ⓓ Ⓔ	11 Ⓐ Ⓑ Ⓒ Ⓓ Ⓔ
2 Ⓐ Ⓑ Ⓒ Ⓓ Ⓔ	7 Ⓐ Ⓑ Ⓒ Ⓓ Ⓔ	12 Ⓐ Ⓑ Ⓒ Ⓓ Ⓔ
3 Ⓐ Ⓑ Ⓒ Ⓓ Ⓔ	8 Ⓐ Ⓑ Ⓒ Ⓓ Ⓔ	13 Ⓐ Ⓑ Ⓒ Ⓓ Ⓔ
4 Ⓐ Ⓑ Ⓒ Ⓓ Ⓔ	9 Ⓐ Ⓑ Ⓒ Ⓓ Ⓔ	14 Ⓐ Ⓑ Ⓒ Ⓓ Ⓔ
5 Ⓐ Ⓑ Ⓒ Ⓓ Ⓔ	10 Ⓐ Ⓑ Ⓒ Ⓓ Ⓔ	15 Ⓐ Ⓑ Ⓒ Ⓓ Ⓔ

Section 1

Essay • 25 Minutes

Directions: Think carefully about the statement below and the assignment that follows it.

At a recent conference on global issues, several panels debated possible solutions to problems facing the world today. There was no consensus on the solutions or even on the nature of the problems. Some considered nuclear proliferation to be the most serious issue. Others concentrated on global warming, whereas some put forth world poverty as the most serious issue.

Assignment: What in your opinion is the most serious problem facing the world today? Plan and write an essay that develops your ideas logically. Support your opinion with specific evidence taken from your personal experience, your observations of others, or your reading.

STOP

END OF SECTION 1. IF YOU HAVE ANY TIME LEFT, GO OVER YOUR WORK IN THIS SECTION ONLY. DO NOT WORK IN ANY OTHER SECTION OF THE TEST.

practice test 5

Section 2
26 Questions • 25 Minutes

Directions: Each of the following questions consists of an incomplete sentence followed by five words or pairs of words. Choose that word or pair of words that, when substituted for the blank space or spaces, best completes the meaning of the sentence and mark the letter of your choice on your answer sheet.

In view of the extenuating circumstances and the defendant's youth, the judge recommended ____ .

(A) conviction

(B) a defense

(C) a mistrial

(D) leniency

(E) life imprisonment

The correct answer is (D).

1. ____ by her family, the woman finally agreed to sell the farm.
   (A) Decimated
   (B) Importuned
   (C) Encumbered
   (D) Interpolated
   (E) Designated

2. The ghost of his royal father ____ the young Hamlet to avenge his murder.
   (A) enervates
   (B) parlays
   (C) marauds
   (D) exhorts
   (E) inculcates

3. Concerned for his children's safety, the father tried to ____ in them a(n) ____ attitude toward strangers.
   (A) obviate .. hospitable
   (B) ingratiate .. assiduous
   (C) insinuate .. salubrious
   (D) assimilate .. benevolent
   (E) inculcate .. wary

4. A life of hardship and poverty has ____ them to petty physical discomforts.
   (A) ascribed
   (B) inured
   (C) remonstrated
   (D) deferred
   (E) impugned

5. Displeased with the ____ of his novel, the author withdrew from the television project.
   (A) adaptation
   (B) compilation
   (C) transliteration
   (D) transfusion
   (E) resurgence

6. Because he changed his mind nearly every day, the governor had a reputation for ____ .
   (A) impudence
   (B) impartiality
   (C) perspicuity
   (D) prevarication
   (E) vacillation

7. Her ____ smile ____ all those who saw it.
   (A) devastating .. replenished
   (B) penultimate .. inured
   (C) radiant .. obliged
   (D) sunny .. tanned
   (E) bright .. dazzled

8. Although he was known as a ____ old miser, his anonymous gifts to charity were always ____ .
   (A) grasping .. tasteless
   (B) spendthrift .. gracious
   (C) gregarious .. selfish
   (D) penurious .. generous
   (E) stingy .. mangy

9. With one _____ motion, Brian disarmed his assailant and gained his freedom.
   (A) maladroit
   (B) deft
   (C) ponderous
   (D) superfluous
   (E) brusque

10. The platypus is a biological _____; although it's classed as a mammal, it has a duck-like bill and lays eggs.
   (A) euphemism
   (B) exemplar
   (C) antidote
   (D) periphery
   (E) anomaly

Directions: The reading passage below is followed by a set of questions. Read the passage and answer the accompanying questions, basing your answers on what is stated or implied in the passage. Mark the letter of your choice on your answer sheet.

QUESTIONS 11 AND 12 ARE BASED ON THE FOLLOWING PASSAGE.

Amy Cheney Beach (1867–1944) was the first formally acknowledged woman composer of classical music in the United States. When she expressed a desire to study music
5 in Europe, the head of the Boston Symphony told her mother that a lady should stay home. At 18, she married Henry H.A. Beach, a doctor and amateur musician. He encouraged his wife to spend her time composing music
10 rather than performing as a pianist. Beach taught herself musical composition and composed over 150 works during her life, including an opera. The Boston Symphony premiered her *Gaelic Symphony* and also
15 her *Piano Concerto*. After her husband's death, Beach lived in Europe for three years.

11. By using the phrase "first formally acknowledged woman composer," (lines 2–3), the writer implies that
   (A) Beach was the first woman to have her music played by an orchestra.
   (B) Beach was the first woman to compose classical music.
   (C) Beach was recognized during her lifetime as a pianist first.
   (D) there may have been other women composers, but they preferred to remain unknown.
   (E) there were other women who composed classical music, but they remain unknown.

12. The writer probably included the final sentence
   (A) to present more information about Beach.
   (B) to provide a connection with information presented earlier in the paragraph.
   (C) to complete the biographical sketch about Beach.
   (D) to underline the unfairness of women's role.
   (E) as a strong conclusion.

QUESTIONS 13 AND 14 ARE BASED ON THE FOLLOWING PASSAGE.

During one hundred and fifty years we have built up a form of self-government and a social system which is peculiarly our own. It differs essentially from all others in the
5 world. . . . It is founded upon a particular conception of self-government in which decentralized local responsibility is the very base. Further than this, it is founded upon the conception that only through ordered
10 liberty, freedom, and equal opportunity to the individual will his initiative and enterprise spur on the march of progress. And in our insistence upon equality of opportunity has our system advanced beyond all the world.

—Herbert Hoover

13. The word *peculiarly* (line 3) means

(A) oddly.
(B) bizarrely.
(C) singularly.
(D) curiously.
(E) strangely.

14. The "march of progress" (line 12) can be achieved only through

(A) decentralized local responsibility.
(B) ordered liberty and freedom.
(C) individual initiative and enterprise.
(D) equal opportunity.
(E) the American view of self-government.

QUESTIONS 15–26 ARE BASED ON THE FOLLOWING PASSAGE

The history of a place is preserved in various ways, including through its landmarks, historic buildings, and public areas. The following passage discusses Los Angeles and what is being done there to preserve its place in history.

An outsider approaches the subject gingerly, lest civic feelings be bruised. Los Angeles gives the impression of having erased much of its history by allowing the city's
5 development to run unchecked. Insiders like Dolores Hayden . . . pull no punches: "It is . . . common," she wrote, "for fond residents to quote Gertrude Stein's sentence about Oakland when summing up urban design
10 in Los Angeles: 'There's no there, there.'" Hayden has also acknowledged that Los Angeles is generally "the first (American city) singled out as having a problem about sense of place." Both statements come from
15 a handsome brochure-cum-itinerary, drawn up by Hayden, Gail Dubrow, and Carolyn Flynn to introduce The Power of Place, a local nonprofit group with a mission to retrieve some of the city's misplaced "there."

20 Founded by Hayden in 1982, The Power of Place lays special emphasis on redressing an imbalance in memory—and memorials. As Hayden has pointed out, in 1987 less than half the population of Los Angeles was
25 Anglo-American; yet almost 98 percent of the city's cultural historic landmarks were devoted to the history and accomplishments of Anglo-Americans. Even these personages come from a narrow spectrum
30 of achievers—in Hayden's phrase, "a small minority of landholders, bankers, business leaders, and their architects"—almost all of whom were male. . . .

The likeliest explanation for this under-
35 representation may be an urban variation on the great-man theory of history: History is what public figures do, and by their civic monuments shall ye know them—especially the structures they designed or built.
40 In Hayden's view, however, "The task of choosing a past for Los Angeles is a political as well as an historic and cultural one," and the unexamined preference for architecture

as the focus of historic preservation efforts
45 can slight less conscious but perhaps equally
powerful human forces. Hayden's goal has
been to supplement the city's ample supply
of monocultural landmarks and memorials
with others representing its ethnic and
50 gender-based diversity. Accordingly, some
sites need new status as official landmarks,
others need reinterpretation. Other sites
no longer contain structures emblematic
of their histories or are located in blighted
55 neighborhoods; these do not readily lend
themselves to resuscitation through reno-
vation and commercial development, as
preservationists have managed elsewhere.

The Power of Place has identified nine
60 places on which to concentrate in the first
phase of its work: development of a walking
tour of little-known Los Angeles sites, for
which The Power of Place brochure serves
as a guide.

65 The most ethnically evocative of these sites
is probably Vignes Vineyard/Wolf-skill
Grove, neighboring plots that once supported a share of the vineyards and citrus
groves abounding in early 19th-century Los
70 Angeles. The first cultivators of the wine
grapes and citrus were Franciscan mission-
aries and their Native American converts.
The padres gave way to white entrepreneurs;
the Native Americans to various waves
75 of immigrants, including Chinese, then
Japanese, and finally, Mexicans. . . .

The Power of Place brochure concludes its
summary of what is known about each stop
on the walking tour with a postscript called
80 Placemaking, which describes the site's
current status and suggests ways to make it
more redolent of its past. For the vineyard/
grove complex, the current situation is not
atypical: "Present uses . . . are commercial
85 and industrial." Then comes word of what
seems to be a minor miracle: "One tall
slender grapefruit tree . . . has been preserved and relocated in the courtyard of the
Japanese American Cultural and Community
90 Center. . . ." Suggestions for recapturing
more of the past proposed by The Power
of Place include returning orange trees to
the Wolfskill site and installing historical
markers on the Vignes site.

15. Which of the following most accurately
summarizes the main idea of the passage?
(A) Multicultural landmarks are better
than monocultural ones.
(B) The Power of Place is attempting to
correct an imbalance in Los Angeles
historical landmarks.
(C) Los Angeles has a limited sense of
place because it has not adequately
preserved its history.
(D) Dolores Hayden has an iconoclastic
viewpoint on the state of historical
preservation in Los Angeles.
(E) Los Angelenos do not care about
their surroundings.

16. The author uses the phrase "civic feelings"
(line 2) to mean the
(A) allegiance of a city's residents to their
city.
(B) emotions that breed courtesy and
good behavior.
(C) respect for each other shown by
people who think of themselves as
civilized.
(D) defensiveness that city residents
sometimes show toward outsiders.
(E) regularity with which citizens vote.

17. What is the danger of allowing the development of Los Angeles to "run unchecked"
(line 5)?
(A) The roadways will become overrun
with traffic.
(B) Developers will use up all arable
land.
(C) Smog will become an even bigger
environmental concern.
(D) Much of the city's cultural history
will be lost to modernization.
(E) People will emigrate from Los
Angeles in search of more suitable
living conditions.

18. In quoting Gertrude Stein's saying, "There's no there, there" (line 10), Dolores Hayden most likely means to say that

(A) the same lack of urban design that characterizes Oakland is also typical of Los Angeles.

(B) a sprawling city like Los Angeles often has no particular center where residents congregate.

(C) Los Angeles's historic monuments focus too exclusively on a particular segment of the population.

(D) Los Angeles is not an old city historically.

(E) Los Angeles seems to have no outstanding characteristics that define it as a place.

19. According to Dolores Hayden, most of the historical landmarks of Los Angeles

(A) do not enhance a sense of place among the people of Los Angeles.

(B) have been chosen according to political rather than aesthetic criteria.

(C) are not representative of the history of all of the people of Los Angeles.

(D) should be replaced by landmarks that celebrate the accomplishments of minorities and women.

(E) are not on a par with historical landmarks elsewhere.

20. With which of the following statements about the people memorialized by most existing Los Angeles monuments would Dolores Hayden be most likely to agree?

  I. They were usually of a higher social class than were the people highlighted by The Power of Place.

 II. Their accomplishments are more conspicuous than are those of the people highlighted by The Power of Place.

III. They made greater contributions to the economic development of Los Angeles than did the people highlighted by The Power of Place.

(A) I only

(B) I, II, and III

(C) I and III only

(D) I and II only

(E) II only

21. Which of the following statements most accurately characterizes Hayden's view on historic preservation, as those views are described in the passage?

(A) Political and economic considerations should have no place in the designation of cultural and historic landmarks.

(B) Plants and other natural phenomena make better historic landmarks than do buildings and other human artifacts.

(C) Some parts of history cannot be memorialized in surviving buildings and landmarks, so new ways must be found to more fully recapture the past.

(D) The homes and workplaces of working people should be preserved whenever possible because the history of working people is more important than that of so-called "great men."

(E) The past cannot be memorialized in anything but buildings and landmarks so that every care must be taken to preserve them.

22. Which one of the following is cited in the passage as a difficulty The Power of Place faces in preserving the history of women and minorities?

  (A) Most citizens of Los Angeles are uninterested in the preservation effort.

  (B) Few written records of the history of women and minorities have been preserved.

  (C) Women and minorities are not in support of the efforts on their behalf.

  (D) Many of the historical sites have completely changed in the intervening years.

  (E) Funding for historical preservation tends to go to groups that memorialize famous public figures.

23. The author of the passage seems to value the Vignes/Wolfskill site most for

  (A) its well-preserved state.

  (B) the main uses the site has served over the years.

  (C) its evocation of one of the most important industries in nineteenth-century Los Angeles.

  (D) the variety of cultural groups whose history is represented there.

  (E) its connection to the early founders of Los Angeles.

24. For Hayden, "Placemaking" (line 80) most nearly means

  (A) finding ways to overcome urban blight.

  (B) capturing the character of the city by evoking the past of all its people.

  (C) restoring an historic site to its previous condition.

  (D) showing the city's residents how particular sites have been used in the past.

  (E) creating new landmarks.

25. The author most likely refers to the existence of a grapefruit tree at the Vignes/Wolfskill site as "a minor miracle" (line 86) because

  (A) the tree's slenderness indicates that it has survived so far only because of exceptionally good care.

  (B) grapefruit trees grow best in groves rather than singly.

  (C) citrus trees, once common at the site, have been replaced by businesses and factories.

  (D) grapefruit trees are not native to the area and often do not grow well there.

  (E) the area has been so heavily vandalized.

26. In the author's view, all of the following would most likely be *undervalued* cultural landmarks EXCEPT

  (A) indigenous trees.

  (B) endangered species of animal and plant life.

  (C) historic buildings in dilapidated areas.

  (D) city hall.

  (E) Chinatown.

STOP

END OF SECTION 2. IF YOU HAVE ANY TIME LEFT, GO OVER YOUR WORK IN THIS SECTION ONLY. DO NOT WORK IN ANY OTHER SECTION OF THE TEST.

Section 3

20 Questions • 25 Minutes

Directions: Solve the following problems using any available space on the page for scratchwork. On your answer sheet, fill in the choice that best corresponds to the correct answer.

Notes: The figures accompanying the problems are drawn as accurately as possible unless otherwise stated in specific problems. Again, unless otherwise stated, all figures lie in the same plane. All numbers used in these problems are real numbers. Calculators are permitted for this test.

Circle: $C = 2\pi r$ $A = \pi r^2$
Rectangle: $A = lw$
Rectangular Solid: $V = lwh$
Cylinder: $V = \pi r^2 h$
Triangle: $A = \frac{1}{2}bh$ $a^2 + b^2 = c^2$

The number of degrees of arc in a circle is 360.
The measure in degrees of a straight angle is 180.
The sum of the measures in degrees of the angles of a triangle is 180.

1. If for all real numbers (a.b.c. − d.e.f.) = (a − d) × (b − e) × (c − f), then (4.5.6. − 1.2.3.) =
   - (A) −27
   - (B) 0
   - (C) 27
   - (D) 54
   - (E) 108

2. The sum of an odd number and an even number is
   - (A) sometimes an even number.
   - (B) always divisible by 3 or 5 or 7.
   - (C) always an odd number.
   - (D) always a prime number.
   - (E) always divisible by 2.

3. If $6x + 12 = 9$, $x^2 =$
   - (A) $\frac{21}{6}$
   - (B) $-\frac{1}{2}$
   - (C) $\frac{9}{12}$
   - (D) $\frac{1}{4}$
   - (E) $\frac{9}{6}$

4. Under certain conditions, sound travels at about 1100 ft. per second. If 88 ft. per second is approximately equivalent to 60 miles per hour, the speed of sound in miles per hour under the above conditions is closest to
   - (A) 730.
   - (B) 740.
   - (C) 750.
   - (D) 760.
   - (E) 780.

5. If on a blueprint $\frac{1}{4}$ inch equals 12 inches, what is the actual length in feet of a steel bar that is represented on the blueprint by a line $3\frac{3}{8}$ inches long?
   - (A) $2\frac{1}{2}$
   - (B) $3\frac{3}{8}$
   - (C) $6\frac{3}{4}$
   - (D) 9
   - (E) $13\frac{1}{2}$

6. If one angle of a triangle is three times a second angle and the third angle is 20 degrees more than the second angle, the second angle, in degrees, is

(A) 64.

(B) 50.

(C) 40.

(D) 34.

(E) 32.

7. If $x = \dfrac{3}{2}$ and $y = 2$, then $x + y^2 - \dfrac{1}{2} =$

(A) 5

(B) 10

(C) $11\dfrac{1}{2}$

(D) $9\dfrac{1}{2}$

(E) $\dfrac{6}{2}$

8. A math class has 27 students in it. Of those students, 14 are also enrolled in history and 17 are enrolled in English. What is the minimum percentage of the students in the math class who are also enrolled in history *and* English?

(A) 15%

(B) 22%

(C) 49%

(D) 63%

(E) 91%

9. A cylindrical container has a diameter of 14 inches and a height of 6 inches. Since 1 gallon equals 231 cubic inches, the capacity of the tank in gallons is approximately

(A) $\dfrac{2}{3}$.

(B) $1\dfrac{1}{7}$.

(C) $2\dfrac{2}{7}$.

(D) $2\dfrac{2}{3}$.

(E) 4.

10. If $\dfrac{1}{x+y} = 6$ and $x = 2$, then $y =$

(A) $-\dfrac{11}{6}$

(B) $-\dfrac{9}{4}$

(C) -2

(D) -1

(E) 4

11. The number of grams in 1 ounce is 28.35. The number of grams in a kilogram is 1000. Therefore, the number of kilograms in 1 pound is approximately

(A) 0.045.

(B) 0.45.

(C) 1.0.

(D) 2.2.

(E) 4.5.

12. Which one of the following numbers is NOT the square of a rational number?

(A) 0.0016

(B) 0.16

(C) 1.6

(D) 16

(E) 1600

13. In the figure below, lines *l* and *m* are parallel. Which of the following must be equal to 180 degrees?

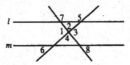

I   1 plus 3

II.   2 plus 4

III.   5 plus 6

IV.   7 plus 8

V.   8 plus 6

(A) I and II

(B) III and IV

(C) V only

(D) I, II, III, IV

(E) I, II, III, IV, V

14. If x is a fraction that ranges from $\frac{1}{4}$ to $\frac{1}{2}$ and y is a fraction that ranges from $\frac{3}{4}$ to $\frac{11}{2}$, what is the maximum value for $\frac{x}{y}$?

(A) $\frac{3}{16}$

(B) $\frac{11}{48}$

(C) $\frac{3}{8}$

(D) $\frac{11}{24}$

(E) $\frac{2}{3}$

15. These circles share a common center, point O. The smallest circle has a radius of 2; the next circle, a radius of 5; and the largest circle, a radius of 9. What fraction of the area of the largest circle is the area of the shaded region?

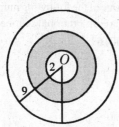

(A) $\frac{7}{27}$

(B) $\frac{25}{81}$

(C) $\frac{1}{3}$

(D) $\frac{7}{11}$

(E) $\frac{12}{17}$

16. If n and d represent positive whole numbers ($n > d$), the fractions arranged in ascending order of magnitude are represented correctly by

   I. $\dfrac{d}{n}$

   II. $\dfrac{d+1}{n+1}$

   III. $\dfrac{d-1}{n-1}$

   IV. $\dfrac{n}{d}$

   V. $\dfrac{n-1}{d-1}$

(A) III, II, I, V, IV

(B) IV, V, III, I, II

(C) II, I, IV, III, V

(D) III, V, IV, I, II

(E) III, I, II, IV, V

17. A train running between two towns arrives at its destination 10 minutes late when it goes 40 miles per hour and 16 minutes late when it goes 30 miles per hour. What is the distance in miles between the towns?

(A) $8\frac{6}{7}$

(B) 12

(C) 192

(D) 560

(E) 720

18. The diagram below depicts a circle of radius 5 with center at point O. If $AC = 8$, what is the probability that a point selected at random from the interior of the circle will also lie in the interior of triangle ABC?

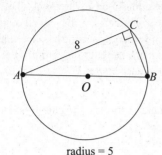

radius = 5

(A) $\dfrac{2}{5\pi}$

(B) $\dfrac{12}{25\pi}$

(C) $\dfrac{16}{25\pi}$

(D) $\dfrac{24}{25\pi}$

(E) $\dfrac{12}{5\pi}$

19. If G is the set containing all positive multiples of 3, H is the set containing all positive multiples of 5, and I is the set containing all positive multiples of 7, which of the following best describes the set $G \cap H \cap I$?

(A) The set containing all positive integers that are multiples of 3, 5, or 7

(B) The set containing all positive integers that are multiples of either 3 or 5

(C) The set containing all positive integers that are multiples of 15

(D) The set containing all positive integers that are multiples of 35

(E) The set containing all positive integers that are multiples of 105

20. For the numbers v, w, x, y, and z, the average (arithmetic mean) is 6 times the median. If $v < w < x < y < z$, which of the following is equal to x?

(A) $v + w + y + z$

(B) $\dfrac{v + w + y + z}{6}$

(C) $\dfrac{v + w + y + z}{12}$

(D) $\dfrac{v + w + y + z}{29}$

(E) $\dfrac{v + w + y + z}{58}$

STOP

END OF SECTION 3. IF YOU HAVE ANY TIME LEFT, GO OVER YOUR WORK IN THIS SECTION ONLY. DO NOT WORK IN ANY OTHER SECTION OF THE TEST.

Section 4

35 Questions • 25 Minutes

Directions: Some of the sentences below contain an error in grammar, usage, word choice, or idiom. Other sentences are correct. Parts of each sentence are underlined and lettered. The error, if there is one, is contained in one of the underlined parts of the sentence. Assume that all other parts of the sentence are correct and cannot be changed. For each sentence, select the one underlined part that must be changed to make the sentence correct and mark its letter on your answer sheet. If there is no error in a sentence, mark answer space E. No sentence contains more than one error.

Being that it's such a lovely day, we
  A   B

are having a difficult time concentrating on
  C   D

our assignment. No error
          E

The correct answer is (A).

1. The second speaker was the most amusing
               A
   of the two, though he had little
          B   C
   of substance to add. No error
     D   E

2. Anyone dissatisfied with the board's
           A
   decision should make their objections
           B   C
   known. No error
     D   E

3. All that he added as extra equipment
         A
   on the new car was two speakers, a
            B   C
   cassette deck, and a retractable antenna.
           D
   No error
     E

4. She owned a small glass pyramid
       A
   and a crystal, and she claimed that it
       B   C   D
   had a mysterious healing power. No error
                E

5. In making rounds, the chief resident in
              A
   the hospital was always
         B
   accompanied with an intern. No error
       C   D   E

6. If it is in a person's best interest, then
         A   B
   she should apply for a stipend as soon as
     C   D
   possible. No error
        E

7. When the mirror cracked yesterday,
           A
   they got very nervous about the bad luck
     B   C
   they may be in for. No error
     D   E

8. He tripped on the rock and fell, broke
     A   B C
   his ankle in the process. No error
        D   E

9. By changing the combination, the
     A
   locksmith was able to provide us with
            B
   peace of mind, convenience,
     C
   and feeling safe when we came home.
       D
   No error
     E

10. <u>Having studied</u> your report carefully,
A
<u>I am convinced</u> that <u>neither</u> of your
B   C
solutions <u>are</u> correct. <u>No error</u>
D   E

11. The <u>fabric, even though</u> it is not
A
<u>expensive, feels soft</u> <u>to the touch</u>.
B   C   D
<u>No error</u>
E

12. <u>The major affects</u> of the battle
A
<u>were made known</u> to the
B
<u>military personnel,</u> but they were not
C
revealed <u>to the media.</u> <u>No error</u>
D   E

13. <u>There was,</u> <u>contrary to</u> what you <u>believe,</u>
A   B   C
many complaints <u>about</u>
D
the poor service. <u>No error</u>
E

14. The chart <u>does appear</u> <u>to be larger</u>
A   B
<u>than any chart</u> in the room, although this
C
may well be only an <u>optical illusion.</u>
D
<u>No error</u>
E

15. <u>Even a random sampling</u> of the questions
A
<u>reveal</u> that <u>there is</u> an <u>emphasis</u> on correct
B   C   D
punctuation. <u>No error</u>
E

16. He spoke <u>softly</u> and appealed to the
A
audience, <u>using</u> such expressions <u>like</u>
B   C
"for the common <u>welfare" and "to</u>
D
help the oppressed and homeless."
<u>No error</u>
E

17. The leaders of the <u>movement</u> believed
A
<u>that</u> persuasion was a more <u>effective</u>
B   C
means than <u>to use</u> force. <u>No error</u>
D   E

18. <u>Thanks</u> <u>in large part</u> to an excellent <u>score</u>
A   B   C
and <u>imaginary</u> staging, the musical had a
D
successful run. <u>No error</u>
E

19. The influence of radio <u>on</u> American life
A
<u>during</u> the Depression years <u>were</u>
B   C
<u>profound.</u> <u>No error</u>
D   E

Directions: The sentences below may contain problems in grammar, usage, word choice, sentence construction, or punctuation. Part or all of each sentence is underlined. Following each sentence you will find five ways of expressing the underlined part. Answer choice (A) always repeats the original underlined section. The other four answer choices are all different. You are to select the lettered answer that produces the most effective sentence. If you think the original sentence is best, choose (A) as your answer. If one of the other choices makes a better sentence, mark your answer sheet for the letter of that choice. Do not choose an answer that changes the meaning of the original sentence.

I have always enjoyed singing as well as to dance.

(A) singing as well as to dance

(B) singing as well as dancing

(C) to sing as well as dancing

(D) singing in addition to dance

(E) to sing in addition to dancing

The correct answer is (B).

20. In order to achieve the highest rating in the diving competition, it is necessary to enter the water with a minimal splash.
    (A) it is necessary to enter the water
    (B) of necessity you must necessarily enter the water
    (C) the water must, as is necessary, be entered
    (D) it is entering the water with necessity
    (E) necessarily you must be entered in the water

21. The ancient Egyptians built structures that still stand after 2500 years, their accomplishments are a marvel to behold.
    (A) years, their accomplishments are a marvel to behold.
    (B) years, their accomplishing marvels that are to be beheld.
    (C) years; and they have accomplished marvelous beholdings.
    (D) years; their accomplishments are a marvel to behold.
    (E) years, beholding their accomplishments is a marvel.

22. The contract that was made between the students and the teacher stated that the students would hand in homework on the day it was scheduled to be.
    (A) on the day it was scheduled to be.
    (B) on the scheduled day.
    (C) in accordance with the planned scheduling.
    (D) on the scheduled day that it was to be.
    (E) with the schedule that was handed out.

23. The turnout for the game was very low, but those in attending enjoyed every minute of the contest.
    (A) those in attending
    (B) those in attendance
    (C) those who were in attending
    (D) the attendance of those who were there
    (E) the people being in attendance

24. People are concerned about the nearby nuclear plant because it employs new technology and that real estate prices will decrease.
    (A) that real estate prices will decrease.
    (B) that the price of real estate will decrease.
    (C) that the decrease will be in real estate.
    (D) the decrease in real estate will happen.
    (E) decreases the price of real estate.

25. <u>Several notes were sent by the principal of the school that</u> were concerned with vandalism in the gymnasium.

(A) Several notes were sent by the principal of the school that

(B) Several notes written by the principal of the school that

(C) The principal of the school sent several notes that

(D) The principal of the school in sending notes that

(E) Several of the notes sent that

26. Since no one bothered to bring a copy of the directions, <u>so they had no idea</u> how to put the tent together.

(A) so they had no idea

(B) they were having no idea

(C) they had no ideas on

(D) they had no idea

(E) their ideas were none on

27. When I mentioned that I was trying to learn a foreign language, <u>the professor recommended that I read comic books written in that language</u>.

(A) the professor recommended that I read comic books written in that language

(B) the professor made a recommendation that I be reading comic books that were written in that language

(C) the professor, who was recommended, said to read comic books

(D) the professor was recommended because he wrote comic books in that language

(E) the professor recommended to me the reading of comic books

28. The stock market fell more than sixty points in <u>one day, this is a sure sign that</u> the economic recovery is not materializing.

(A) one day, this is a sure sign that

(B) one day, this sign is sure that

(C) one day; notwithstanding the surety of the sign

(D) one day and this was a sure sign when

(E) one day, and this is a sure sign that

29. A fundamental difference between the two parties is reflected in their attitudes toward affirmative <u>action, one certainly strongly</u> endorses the concept while the other condemns it.

(A) action, one certainly strongly

(B) action, the stronger one certainly

(C) action; one strongly

(D) action which one, however strongly,

(E) action, and one certainly strongly

Directions: Questions 30–35 are based on a passage that might be an early draft of a student's essay. Some sentences in this draft need to be revised or rewritten to make them both clear and correct. Read the passage carefully; then answer the questions that follow it. Some questions require decisions about diction, usage, tone, or sentence structure in particular sentences or parts of sentences. Other questions require decisions about organization, development, or appropriateness of language in the essay as a whole. For each question, choose the answer that makes the intended meaning clearer and more precise and that follows the conventions of Standard Written English.

(1) Hopefully the government of the United States will soon make sure that all their citizens are able to have good, affordable health care. (2) If legislation is enacted and national coverage is assured, we will truly be ready to enter a new age in America. (3) It will be one in which all people—rich or poor, working or unemployed—will be provided for when they are ill.

(4) The significance of a national health care plan cannot be overstated. (5) Recently, for instance, my aunt and uncle were involved in an automobile accident. (6) Although their injuries were pretty serious, yet after some emergency treatment they didn't get a lot of medical attention. (7) Due to the fact that they didn't have much coverage. (8) So doctors and hospital staff didn't want to treat them. (9) It's hard to believe that good, hardworking people like my relatives, now they are being neglected by society.

(10) And this is only one example of a situation in which people without adequate protection are mistreated by the medical profession, there are many other stories that could be told. (11) For this reason, that's why I sincerely hope that our government will soon provide for all those needy people, like my aunt and uncle, who presently lack adequate health care coverage.

30. Which of the following is the best revision of the underlined portion of sentence (1) below?

Hopefully the government of the United States will soon make sure that all their citizens are able to have good, affordable health care.

(A) Hopefully the government of the United States will soon provide all citizens with

(B) It is hoped that the government of the United States will soon make sure that all its citizens are able to have

(C) Hopefully the government of the United States will soon make sure that all citizens would be able to have

(D) I hope that the government of the United States will soon make sure that all its citizens will be able to have

(E) I hope that the government of the United States soon makes sure that all their citizens would be able to have

31. Which of the following is the best way to combine sentences (2) and (3)?

   (A) If legislation is enacted and national coverage is assured, we will truly be ready to enter a new age in America, being one in which all people, rich or poor, will be provided for when they are ill.

   (B) If legislation is enacted and national coverage is assured, we will truly be able to enter a new age, one in which all Americans—rich or poor, working or unemployed—will be provided for when they are ill.

   (C) If legislation is enacted and national coverage is assured, we will truly be ready to enter a new age in America, it will be one in which all people, rich or poor, working or unemployed, will be provided for when they are ill.

   (D) If legislation is enacted then all people, no matter what their abilities will be provided for by their government at all times.

   (E) If we enact legislation and assure national coverage, we will be able to enter a new age in America; in which all—rich or poor, working or unemployed—will be provided for when they are ill.

32. Which of the following is the best way to revise sentences (6), (7), and (8)?

   (A) Although their injuries were serious, after some emergency treatment, they received very little medical attention. Since they did not have much coverage, doctors and hospital staff did not want to treat them.

   (B) Although their injuries were serious, yet after some emergency treatment, they didn't get a lot of medical attention. Due to the fact they didn't have much coverage, doctors and hospital staff didn't want to treat them.

   (C) Their injuries were pretty serious although after some emergency treatment they didn't get a lot medical attention, due to the fact that they didn't have much coverage. So doctors and hospital staff didn't want to treat them.

   (D) Their injuries were pretty serious, yet after some emergency treatment they did not get much medical attention. Due to the fact that they did not have much coverage, so doctor and hospitals did not want to treat them.

   (E) Although their injuries were serious, after some emergency treatment, they didn't get a lot of attention because of the fact that they didn't have much coverage so doctors and hospital staff didn't want to treat them.

33. Which of the following is the best revision of the underlined portion of sentence (9) below?

It's hard to believe that good, hard-working people like my relatives, now they are being neglected by society.

(A) relatives. Now they are being neglected by society.

(B) relatives and being neglected by society now.

(C) relatives are now being neglected by society.

(D) relatives and now they are being neglected by society.

(E) relatives have neglected society.

34. Which of the following is the reason sentence (10) should be revised?

(A) To provide another example

(B) To correct an error in usage

(C) To correct a sentence structure error

(D) To correct an error in verb agreement

(E) To correct a pronoun reference error

35. Which of the following is the best revision of the underlined portion of sentence (11) below?

For this reason, that's why I sincerely hope that our government will soon provide for all those needy people, like my aunt and uncle, who presently lack adequate health care coverage.

(A) Because this is why

(B) For this reason it is why

(C) Because of this reason is why

(D) This reason is why

(E) This is why

STOP

END OF SECTION 4. IF YOU HAVE ANY TIME LEFT, GO OVER YOUR WORK IN THIS SECTION ONLY. DO NOT WORK IN ANY OTHER SECTION OF THE TEST.

Section 5

20 Questions • 25 Minutes

Directions: Solve the following problems using any available space on the page for scratchwork. On your answer sheet, fill in the choice that best corresponds to the correct answer.

Notes: The figures accompanying the problems are drawn as accurately as possible unless otherwise stated in specific problems. Again, unless otherwise stated, all figures lie in the same plane. All numbers used in these problems are real numbers. Calculators are permitted for this test.

Reference Information

Circle: $C = 2\pi r$, $A = \pi r^2$

Rectangle: $A = lw$

Rectangular Solid: $V = lwh$

Cylinder: $V = \pi r^2 h$

Triangle: $A = \dfrac{1}{2}bh$, $a^2 + b^2 = c^2$

The number of degrees of arc in a circle is 360.
The measure in degrees of a straight angle is 180.
The sum of the measures in degrees of the angles of a triangle is 180.

---

1. What is the ratio of 6 minutes to 6 hours?
(A) 1:60
(B) 1:36
(C) 1:1
(D) 36:1
(E) 60:1

2. At Ungerville High School, the ratio of girls to boys is 2:1. If $\dfrac{3}{5}$ of the boys are on a team, and the other 40 boys are not, how many girls attend the school?
(A) 67
(B) 100
(C) 133
(D) 200
(E) 225

3. If $f(x) = x^2 + 3x + 5$ and $g(x) = 3x^2$, what is the value of $\dfrac{f(2)}{g(2)}$?
(A) $\dfrac{15}{36}$
(B) 1
(C) $\dfrac{5}{4}$
(D) $\dfrac{15}{7}$
(E) $\dfrac{11}{3}$

4. If $(11^{-3})^k = 11^{-15}$, what is the value of k?
(A) -12
(B) -5
(C) $\dfrac{1}{5}$
(D) 5
(E) 12

5. What is the positive difference between the two solutions of $3 = |1 - 2q|$?
(A) 1
(B) 2
(C) 3
(D) 4
(E) 5

6. In the figure below, *QOR* is a quadrant of a circle. *TPSO* is a rectangle, with *PS* = 6 and *PT* = 8. What is the length of arc *QR*?

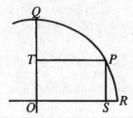

(A) 5π

(B) 10π

(C) 20π

(D) 24

(E) It cannot be determined from the information given.

7. The ice compartment in a refrigerator is 8 inches deep, 5 inches high, and 4 inches wide. How many whole ice cubes will it hold if each cube is 2 inches on each edge?

(A) 16

(B) 20

(C) 24

(D) 80

(E) 160

8. If Paul can paint a fence in 2 hours and Fred can paint the same fence in 3 hours, Paul and Fred working together can paint the fence in how many hours?

(A) $\frac{5}{6}$

(B) 1

(C) 1.2

(D) 2.5

(E) 5

9. If one third of the liquid contents of a can evaporates on the first day and three fourths of the remainder evaporates on the second day, the fractional part of the original contents remaining at the close of the second day is

(A) $\frac{1}{6}$

(B) $\frac{1}{4}$

(C) $\frac{5}{12}$

(D) $\frac{1}{2}$

(E) $\frac{7}{12}$

10. A motorist drives 60 miles to her destination at an average speed of 40 miles per hour and makes the return trip at an average rate of 30 miles per hour. What is her average speed in miles per hour for the entire trip?

(A) 17

(B) $34\frac{2}{7}$

(C) 35

(D) $43\frac{1}{3}$

(E) 70

Student-Produced Response Questions

Directions: Solve each of these problems. Write the answer in the corresponding grid on the answer sheet and fill in the ovals beneath each answer you write. Here are some examples.

Answer: $\frac{3}{4} = .75$; show answer either way   **Answer: 325**

Note: A mixed number such as $3\frac{1}{2}$ must be gridded as 7/2 or as 3.5. If gridded as "3 1/2," it will be read as "thirty-one halves."

Note: Either position is correct.

11. Jerry grew 5 inches in 2007, and 2 inches more in 2008 before reaching his final height of 5 feet 10 inches. What percentage of his final height did his 2007–2008 growth represent?

12. Seth bought $4\frac{5}{6}$ pounds of peanuts. He gave $\frac{1}{4}$ of his purchase to his sister. How many pounds of peanuts did Seth keep for himself?

13. If $p = 2r = 3s = 4t$, then $\dfrac{pr}{st} =$

14. $\sqrt{7+9+7+9+7+9+7+9} =$

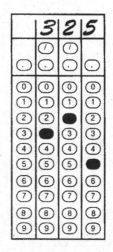

DA and *EA* trisect angle *A*.

15. In the figure above, if m∠*DMC* = 80° and m∠*ENC* = 60°, then angle *BAC* =

(Do not grid the degree symbol.)

16. $\dfrac{\dfrac{7}{8} + \dfrac{7}{8} + \dfrac{7}{8}}{\dfrac{8}{7} + \dfrac{8}{7} + \dfrac{8}{7}} =$

17. The average of 8 numbers is 6; the average of 6 other numbers is 8. What is the average of all 14 numbers?

18. If the ratio of $4a$ to $3b$ is 8 to 9, what is the ratio of $3a$ to $4b$?

19. Solve the following equation for x:
$$\frac{2x}{3} + \frac{1}{5} = 3$$

20. If $f(x) = 3|x|^3$, what is the value of $f(-2)$?

STOP

END OF SECTION 5. IF YOU HAVE ANY TIME LEFT, GO OVER YOUR WORK IN THIS SECTION ONLY. DO NOT WORK IN ANY OTHER SECTION OF THE TEST.

Section 6
26 Questions • 25 Minutes

Directions: Each of the following questions consists of an incomplete sentence followed by five words or pairs of words. Choose the word or pair of words that, when substituted for the blank space or spaces, best completes the meaning of the sentence and mark the letter of your choice on the answer sheet.

In view of the extenuating circumstances and the defendant's youth, the judge recommended ___ .

(A) conviction

(B) a defense

(C) a mistrial

(D) leniency

(E) life imprisonment

The correct answer is (D).

1. They acted in concert, each ____ for a(n) ____ of the plot.
   (A) reliable .. source
   (B) responsible .. element
   (C) unavailable .. section
   (D) appointed .. article
   (E) agreeable .. felony

2. They were unwisely ____ during their education, and ____ was the result.
   (A) neglected .. ignorance
   (B) interrupted .. consistency
   (C) befriended .. alienation
   (D) instructed .. genius
   (E) taught .. attendance

3. Most young children are highly conformist and will ____ a classmate whose appearance or manners are ____ .
   (A) welcome .. bizarre
   (B) shun .. conventional
   (C) emulate .. unusual
   (D) ostracize .. different
   (E) deride .. ordinary

4. The royal astrologers were commanded to determine the most ____ date for the king's coronation.
   (A) propitious
   (B) ostensible
   (C) aberrant
   (D) resplendent
   (E) obsequious

5. The poem by the great satirist was dripping with venom and was ____ with scorn.
   (A) contentious
   (B) discordant
   (C) redolent
   (D) sardonic
   (E) vicarious

6. The ____ rites of the fraternity were kept secret by the members and were never ____ to outsiders.
   (A) eclectic .. delegated
   (B) esoteric .. divulged
   (C) dubious .. maligned
   (D) inscrutable .. traduced
   (E) elusive .. proscribed

7. The composer was _____ enough to praise the work of a musician he detested.
   - (A) magnanimous
   - (B) loquacious
   - (C) munificent
   - (D) parsimonious
   - (E) surreptitious

8. The goodwill of its customers is a genuine but _____ asset for a company.
   - (A) insensate
   - (B) redolent
   - (C) dismissive
   - (D) intangible
   - (E) vigilant

Directions: Each passage below is followed by a set of questions. Read each passage, then answer the accompanying questions, basing your answers on what is stated or implied in the passage and in any introductory material provided. Mark the letter of your choice on your answer sheet.

QUESTIONS 9 AND 10 ARE BASED ON THE FOLLOWING PASSAGE.

The Gothic style in art and architecture developed and flourished in Europe from the mid-1100s to the end of the 1400s. Gothic architecture is characterized by the
5   rib vault and the flying buttress. The former is a combination of the barrel vault and stone rib of the earlier Romanesque style. Compared to Romanesque construction, Gothic buildings have more light and are airier.
10 Highly colorful stained glass windows, usually depicting scenes from the Bible, are also a feature of Gothic cathedrals. Among the best-known Gothic cathedrals are Notre Dame with its telltale flying but-
15 tresses; Saint-Chapelle and Chartres with their glorious stained glass windows; and the high vaults of Salisbury and Cologne.

9. The purpose of this passage is to
   - (A) compare Gothic and Romanesque cathedrals.
   - (B) compare Gothic and Romanesque styles.
   - (C) describe Gothic architecture.
   - (D) define rib vault and flying buttress.
   - (E) give examples of rib vaults and flying buttresses.

10. By singling out certain cathedrals for certain characteristics, the writer is suggesting that these cathedrals
   - (A) do not have all the characteristics described as Gothic.
   - (B) were the first to use each one of these characteristics.
   - (C) are the writer's favorites.
   - (D) are especially fine examples of the characteristics noted.
   - (E) provide the best comparison to Romanesque churches.

QUESTIONS 11 AND 12 ARE BASED ON THE FOLLOWING PASSAGE.

Your computer may be spying on you. It may be harboring spyware called adware and key loggers. Adware is used by advertising agencies to track where you go on the Web
5   and what you buy there, so they can find out what interests you. Then their clients send you ads via your computer that supposedly match your interests and possible purchasing needs. Key loggers track the information
10 you type into your computer when you send your name, address, user name, and the like. Key loggers can provide all the information a thief needs to steal your identity.

11. A good title for this passage might be

  (A) "Beware of Spyware."

  (B) "The Spy in Your Computer."

  (C) "What You Don't Know May Hurt You."

  (D) "What to Do About Spyware."

  (E) "Don't Trust the Internet."

12. Adware tracks

  (A) personal data.

  (B) a person's Internet activity.

  (C) a person's response to advertisements on Web sites.

  (D) activity on Web sites.

  (E) purchases on the Internet.

QUESTIONS 13 AND 14 ARE BASED ON THE FOLLOWING PASSAGE.

Akbar inaugurated a new era characterized by the desire to centralize everything around himself. Henceforth, he alone was entitled to make and unmake the fortunes of
5 some people, . . . [H]e decided to share the responsibility for the empire's main areas of administration (finance, army, justice and religion, and royal household) among four different ministers. From 1572 he undertook
10 an important series of reforms, ... He divided the empire into twelve provinces . . . and appointed as the head of each a governor whose duty was to administer its territory . . .

  —Valérie Berinstain, *Mughal India: Splendors of the Peacock Throne*

13. Akbar's actions indicate that he believed that

  (A) sharing power was a way to win the loyalty of subordinates.

  (B) sending possible rivals to the provinces would keep them from plotting against him.

  (C) his empire was too large for him to rule without help.

  (D) change was good for the empire.

  (E) no one person should be allowed to gain too much power.

14. Akbar could be characterized as

  (A) ruthless.

  (B) thoughtful.

  (C) shrewd.

  (D) aggressive.

  (E) sly.

QUESTIONS 15–22 ARE BASED ON THE FOLLOWING PASSAGE.

John James Audubon (1785–1851) is known primarily for his bird studies, but as this passage from Ornithological Biography *shows, he was fascinated by the behavior of other animals as well.*

The Black Bear (*Ursus americanus*), however clumsy in appearance, is active, vigilant, and persevering; possesses great strength, courage, and address; and
5 undergoes with little injury the greatest fatigues and hardships in avoiding the pursuit of the hunter. Like the Deer, it changes its haunts with the seasons, and for the same reason, namely, the desire of obtaining
10 suitable food, or of retiring to the more inaccessible parts, where it can pass the time in security, unobserved by man, the most dangerous of its enemies. During the spring months, it searches for food in the
15 low rich alluvial lands that border the rivers, or by the margins of such inland lakes as, on account of their small size, are called by us ponds. There it procures abundance of succulent roots, and of the tender juicy
20 stems of plants, on which it chiefly feeds at that season. During the summer heat, it enters the gloomy swamps, passes much of its time wallowing in the mud, like a hog, and contents itself with crayfish, roots, and
25 nettles, now and then, when hard pressed by hunger, seizing on a young pig, or perhaps a sow, or even a calf. As soon as the different kinds of berries which grow on the mountain begin to ripen, the Bears betake themselves
30 to the high grounds, followed by their cubs. In such retired parts of the country where there are no hilly grounds, it pays visits to the maize fields, which it ravages for a while. After this, the various species of nuts,
35 acorns, grapes, and other forest fruits, that form what in the western country is called

mast, attract its attention. The Bear is then seen rambling singly through the woods to gather this harvest, not forgetting to rob
40 every Bee tree it meets with, Bears being, as you well know, expert at this operation. You also know that they are good climbers, and may have been told, or at least may now be told, that the Black Bear now and then
45 houses itself in the hollow trunks of the larger trees for weeks together, when it is said to suck its paws. You are probably not aware of a habit in which it indulges, and which, being curious, must be interesting to you.

50 At one season, the Black Bear may be seen examining the lower part of the trunk of a tree for several minutes with much attention, at the same time looking around, and snuffing the air, to assure itself that no
55 enemy is near. It then raises itself on its hind legs, approaches the trunk, embraces it with its forelegs, and scratches the bark with its teeth and claws for several minutes in continuance. Its jaws clash against each
60 other, until a mass of foam runs down both sides of the mouth. After this it continues its rambles.

In various portions of our country, many of our woodsmen and hunters who have seen
65 the Bear performing the singular operation just described, imagine that it does so for the purpose of leaving behind an indication of its size and power. They measure the height at which the scratches are made, and in this
70 manner, can, in fact, form an estimate of the magnitude of the individual. My own opinion, however, is different. It seems to me that the Bear scratches on the trees, not for the purpose of showing its size or its
75 strength, but merely for that of sharpening its teeth and claws, to enable it better to encounter a rival of its own species during the amatory season. The Wild Boar of Europe clashes its tusks and scrapes the earth with
80 its feet, and the Deer rubs its antlers against the lower part of the stems of young trees or bushes, for the same purpose.

15. The bear migrates from one habitat to another in order to
   (A) teach its cubs to climb.
   (B) locate a hollow tree.
   (C) visit every bee tree.
   (D) escape from the wild boar.
   (E) find food and security.

16. The fact that Audubon calls man the bear's "most dangerous" enemy (line 13) indicates that he
   (A) is himself a hunter.
   (B) has some sympathy for hunted bears.
   (C) is an animal rights activist.
   (D) does not believe that bears are dangerous.
   (E) thinks bears are more dangerous than people.

17. The word *alluvial* (line 15) refers to
   (A) high grounds.
   (B) rocky shorelines.
   (C) river-deposited sediment.
   (D) thick underbrush.
   (E) maize fields.

18. According to the passage, black bears eat all of the following EXCEPT
   (A) bark.
   (B) maize.
   (C) mast.
   (D) honey.
   (E) crayfish.

19. Audubon believes that bears scratch trees to
   (A) show their power.
   (B) leave a mark.
   (C) sharpen their claws.
   (D) navigate.
   (E) indicate their size.

20. Audubon assumes that his reader knows about bears'
   (A) scratching behavior and threatening manner.
   (B) eating of roots and berries.
   (C) size and coloring.
   (D) fear of man.
   (E) climbing expertise and love of honey.

21. Audubon compares the bear to deer twice,

    (A) once in relation to its migratory habits, and once in comparing its rubbing behavior.

    (B) once in relation to its eating habits, and once in comparing its combative behavior.

    (C) both times having to do with its habitat.

    (D) both times having to do with hibernation.

    (E) both times having to do with size and weight.

22. From his description, it seems that Audubon's attitude toward black bears is one of

    (A) fear.

    (B) respect.

    (C) amusement.

    (D) alarm.

    (E) bewilderment.

QUESTIONS 23–26 ARE BASED ON THE FOLLOWING PASSAGE.

The study of plant life is very different from the study of animal life because of unique plant characteristics. The following passage provides an overview of those characteristics along with some plant classifications that are of interest to scientists.

Compared to animals, plants present unique problems in demographic studies. The idea of counting living individuals becomes difficult given perennials that reproduce
5 vegetatively by sending out runners or rhizomes, by splitting at the stem base, or by producing arching canes that take root where they touch the ground. In these ways some individuals, given sufficient time, can
10 extend out over a vast area.

There are five typical plant life spans, and each has a basic associated life form. *Annual plants* live for 1 year or less. Their average life span is 1–8 months, depending on the
15 species and on the environment where they are located (the same desert plant may complete its life cycle in 8 months one year and in 1 month the next, depending on the amount of rain it receives). Annuals with extremely
20 short life cycles are classified as *ephemeral* plants. An example of an ephemeral is *Boerrhavia repens* of the Sahara Desert, which can go from seed to seed in just 10 days. Annuals are herbaceous, which means that
25 they lack a secondary meristem that produces lateral, woody tissue. They complete their life cycle after seed production for several reasons: nutrient depletion, hormone changes, or inability of non-woody tissue
30 to withstand unfavorable environmental conditions following the growing season. A few species can persist for more than a year in uncommonly favorable conditions.

Biennial plants are also herbaceous, but
35 usually live for 2 years. Their first year is spent in vegetative growth, which generally takes place more below ground than above. Reproduction occurs in the second year, and this is followed by the completion of the life
40 cycle. Under poor growing conditions, or by experimental manipulation, the vegetative stage can be drawn out for more than 1 year.

Herbaceous perennials typically live for 20–30 years, although some species have
45 been known to live for 400–800 years. These plants die back to the root system and root crown at the end of each growing season. The root system becomes woody, but the above-ground system is herbaceous. They
50 have a juvenile, vegetative stage for the first 2–8 years, then bloom and reproduce yearly. Sometimes they bloom only once at the conclusion of their life cycle. Because herbaceous perennials have no growth rings,
55 it is difficult to age them. Methods that have been used to age them include counting leaf scars or estimating the rate of spread in *tussock* (clumped) forms.

Suffrutescent shrubs (hemixyles) fall some-
60 where between herbaceous perennials and true shrubs. They develop perennial, woody tissue only near the base of their stems; the rest of the shoot system is herbaceous and dies back each year. They are small and are
65 short-lived compared to true shrubs.

Woody perennials (trees and shrubs) have the longest life spans. Shrubs live on the average 30–50 years. Broadleaf trees (angiosperm) average 200–300 years, and conifer

70 (needles) trees average 500–1,000 years. Woody perennials spend approximately the first 10 percent of their life span in a juvenile, totally vegetative state before they enter a combined reproductive and vegetative state,
75 achieving a peak of reproduction several years before the conclusion of their life cycle.

Regardless of the life span, annual or perennial, one can identify about eight important age states in an individual plant
80 or population. They are: (1) viable seed, (2) seedling, (3) juvenile, (4) immature, (5) mature, (6) initial reproductive, (7) maximum vigor (reproductive and vegetative), and (8) senescent. If a population
85 shows all eight states, it is stable and is most likely a part of a *climax* community. If it shows only the last four states, it may not maintain itself and may be part of a *seral* community.

23. The author believes that plants present "unique problems in demographic studies" (lines 1–2) because

(A) they cannot be aged accurately.

(B) it is difficult to define and identify an individual.

(C) many have very short lifespans.

(D) there has been little interest in such studies.

(E) the scientific community is not capable of conducting them.

24. The best definition of *ephemeral* (line 20) might be

(A) resilient.

(B) short-lived.

(C) awkward.

(D) uncomplicated.

(E) shrub-like.

25. A plant that spends a year growing below ground and a year growing above ground before dying would be called

(A) an angiosperm.

(B) a true shrub.

(C) a meristem.

(D) ephemeral.

(E) a biennial.

26. Paragraph 5 deals mainly with

(A) suffrutescent shrubs.

(B) a form of tree shrub.

(C) a form of herbaceous perennial.

(D) a woody biennial.

(E) None of the above

STOP

END OF SECTION 6. IF YOU HAVE ANY TIME LEFT, GO OVER YOUR WORK IN THIS SECTION ONLY. DO NOT WORK IN ANY OTHER SECTION OF THE TEST.

Section 7

15 Questions • 20 Minutes

Directions: Solve the following problems using any available space on the page for scratchwork. On your answer sheet, fill in the choice that best corresponds to the correct answer.

Notes: The figures accompanying the problems are drawn as accurately as possible unless otherwise stated in specific problems. Again, unless otherwise stated, all figures lie in the same plane. All numbers used in these problems are real numbers. Calculators are permitted for this test.

Reference Information

Circle: Rectangle: Rectangular Solid: Cylinder: Triangle:

$C = 2\pi r$
$A = \pi r^2$
$A = lw$
$V = lwh$
$V = \pi r^2 h$
$A = \frac{1}{2}bh$
$a^2 + b^2 = c^2$

The number of degrees of arc in a circle is 360.
The measure in degrees of a straight angle is 180.
The sum of the measures in degrees of the angles of a triangle is 180.

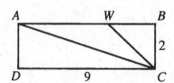

1. In the figure above, BW is one third the length of AB. What is the area of triangle ACW?

(A) 4
(B) 5
(C) 6
(D) 8
(E) 9

2. Of the following, which one is NOT equivalent to 376?

(A) $(3 \times 100) + (6 \times 10) + 16$
(B) $(2 \times 100) + (17 \times 10) + 6$
(C) $(3 \times 100) + (7 \times 10) + 6$
(D) $(2 \times 100) + (16 \times 10) + 6$
(E) $(2 \times 100) + (7 \times 10) + 106$

3. Emily can pack 6 cartons in h days. At this rate, she can pack $3h$ cartons in how many days?

(A) 18
(B) $2h$
(C) h^2
(D) $\dfrac{h^2}{2}$
(E) $2h^2$

4. What is the total length of fencing needed to enclose a rectangular area 46 feet by 34 feet (3 ft. = 1 yd.)?

(A) 26 yards 1 foot
(B) $26\dfrac{2}{3}$ yards
(C) 52 yards 2 feet
(D) $53\dfrac{1}{3}$ yards
(E) $37\dfrac{2}{3}$ yards

5. On an income of $15,000 a year, a clerk pays 15% in federal taxes and 10% of the remainder in state taxes. How much is left?

   (A) $9750
   (B) $11,475
   (C) $12,750
   (D) $13,500
   (E) $14,125

6. $(x^a)^b =$

   (A) $x \cdot a \cdot b$
   (B) x^{a+b}
   (C) x^{ab}
   (D) $(ax)^b$
   (E) b^{xa}

7. A is 300 miles from B. The path of all points equidistant from A and B can best be described as

   (A) a line $\parallel$ to AB and 150 miles north of AB.
   (B) a transverse segment cutting through AB at a 45° angle.
   (C) a circle with AB as its diameter.
   (D) the perpendicular bisector of AB.
   (E) the line AB.

8. If $y = x^2$, $z = x^3$, and $w = xy$, then $y^2 + z^2 + w^2 =$

   (A) $x^4 + x^6 + x^{10}$
   (B) $x^4 + 2x^5$
   (C) $x^4 + 2x^6$
   (D) $2x^9$
   (E) $2x^{10}$

9. The number missing in the sequence 2, 6, 12, 20, ?, 42, 56, 72 is

   (A) 24.
   (B) 30.
   (C) 36.
   (D) 38.
   (E) 40.

10. The square and the equilateral triangle in the above drawing both have a side of 6. If the triangle is placed inside the square with one side of the triangle directly on one side of the square, what is the area of the shaded region?

    (A) $36 - 18\sqrt{3}$
    (B) $36 - 9\sqrt{3}$
    (C) $36 - 6\sqrt{3}$
    (D) $36 + 6\sqrt{3}$
    (E) $36 + 9\sqrt{3}$

11. A square has a diagonal of x units. If the diagonal is increased by 2 units, what is the length of the side of the new square?

    (A) $x + 2$
    (B) $\left(x + 2\sqrt{2}\right)$
    (C) $\dfrac{(x+2)\sqrt{2}}{2}$
    (D) $(x + 2^2)$
    (E) $\dfrac{(x+2)\sqrt{2}}{4}$

12. $PQRS$ is a square and triangle PTS is an equilateral triangle. How many degrees are there in angle TRS?

    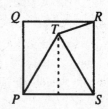

    (A) 60
    (B) 75
    (C) 80
    (D) 90
    (E) It cannot be determined from the information given.

13. In the figure, line *PQ* is parallel to line *RS,* angle *y* = 60°, and angle *z* = 130°. How many degrees are there in angle *x*?

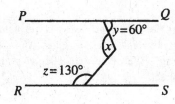

(A) 90°
(B) 100°
(C) 110°
(D) 120°
(E) 130°

QUESTIONS 14 AND 15 REFER TO THE FOLLOWING INFORMATION.

Alan rents a booth at a fair to sell pastries. Alan pays $15 for the booth. It costs Alan $0.35 to make the pastries, and he sells them for $0.75 each.

14. Which of the functions below represents Alan's profit if *x* represents the number of pastries he sells?
(A) $P(x) = \$0.40x + \$15$
(B) $P(x) = \$0.40x - \$15$
(C) $P(x) = \$1.05x + \$15$
(D) $P(x) = \$15 - \$0.40x$
(E) $P(x) = \$15 - \$1.05x$

15. How many pastries must Alan sell in order to make a profit of $45?
(A) 60
(B) 120
(C) 145
(D) 150
(E) 200

STOP

END OF SECTION 1. IF YOU HAVE ANY TIME LEFT, GO OVER YOUR WORK IN THIS SECTION ONLY. DO NOT WORK IN ANY OTHER SECTION OF THE TEST.

Section 8

16 Questions • 20 Minutes

Directions: The two passages below deal with a related topic. Following the passages are questions about the content of each passage or about the relationship between the two passages. Answer the questions based upon what is stated or implied in the passages and in any introductory material provided. Mark the letter of your choice on your answer sheet.

QUESTIONS 1–4 ARE BASED ON THE FOLLOWING PASSAGES.

The following two passages reflect different views of the causes of the American Revolution.

Passage 1

The events of 1763–1775 can have no meaning unless we understand that . . . the purpose of the general [English imperialist] program was to protect the English capitalist
5 interests which were now being jeopardized as a result of the intensification of . . . colonial capitalist competition . . . The struggle was not over high-sounding political and constitutional concepts: over the power of taxation
10 and, in the final analysis, over natural rights: but over colonial manufacturing, wild lands and furs, sugar, wine, tea and currency, all of which meant, simply, the survival or collapse of the English merchant capitalism
15 within the imperial-colonial framework of the mercantilist system.

—Louis M. Hacker,
"The First American Revolution"

Passage 2

But while [Americans] clung so persistently to the past, they were actually moving, if only half consciously and unwillingly, away from it. They were in fact on the verge of
5 a discovery that would turn the course of history in a new direction. . . . This discovery was nothing more or less than the principle of human equality. In 1774 the Americans may not have realized how close they were
10 to it, but there were others who perceived, however dimly, that the whole course of their resistance to Parliament was leading them in that direction.

—Edmund S. Morgan,
The Birth of the Republic, 1763–1789

1. The author of Passage 1 claims that the American Revolution resulted from

(A) the conflict between natural rights and taxation.

(B) the issue of taxation.

(C) colonial self-interest.

(D) constitutional issues.

(E) the clash between colonial and English self-interests.

2. The phrase "colonial capitalist competition" (lines 6–7) in Passage 1 refers to

(A) rivalry between colonial and English business interests.

(B) the imperial-colonial framework.

(C) colonial manufacturing.

(D) colonial business interests.

(E) colonial products.

3. The phrase "only half consciously and un-willingly" (line 3) in Passage 2 means that the colonists were

(A) following the logic of their argument wherever it led them.

(B) acting without serious thought to the outcome.

(C) being dragged against their will into revolution by a few men.

(D) following their instincts.

(E) not thinking about what they were doing or what the outcome would be.

4. The authors of the two passages differ over whether the American Revolution was fought

(A) as a defense of English capitalism.

(B) as a defense of colonial manufacturing.

(C) to prevent the usurpation of colonists' rights.

(D) over political or economic issues.

(E) as a result of a lack of understanding by the colonists of their place in the English capitalist system.

QUESTIONS 5-16 ARE BASED ON THE FOLLOWING PASSAGES.

In 1848, a Woman's Rights Convention was held at Seneca Falls, New York. Sponsored by Lucretia Mott, Martha Wright, Elizabeth Cady Stanton, and Mary Ann McClintock, the convention featured the creation of a "Declaration of Sentiments," a document based on America's Declaration of Independence, in which men's unfair dominion over women was described. Crusader for the rights of African Americans and women, Sojourner Truth was born a slave on a Dutch estate around 1797 and named Isabella. The first edition of her biography was written by Olive Gilbert, a white friend of hers, and published in 1850.

Passage 1—Declaration of Sentiments

The history of mankind is a history of repeated injuries and usurpations on the part of man toward woman, having in direct object the establishment of an absolute
5 tyranny over her. To prove this, let facts be submitted to a candid world.

He has never permitted her to exercise her inalienable right to the elective franchise.

He has compelled her to submit to laws, in
10 the formation of which she had no voice. He has withheld from her rights which are given to the most ignorant and degraded men—both natives and foreigners.

Having deprived her of this first right of
15 a citizen, the elective franchise, thereby leaving her without representation in the halls of legislation, he has oppressed her on all sides.

He has made her, if married, in the eye of
20 the law, civilly dead.

He has taken from her all right in property, even to the wages she earns.

He has made her, morally, an irresponsible being, as she can commit many crimes
25 with impunity, provided they be done in the presence of her husband. In the covenant of marriage, she is compelled to promise obedience to her husband, he becoming, to all intents and purposes, her master—the
30 law giving him power to deprive her of her liberty, and to administer chastisement.

He has so framed the laws of divorce, as to what shall be the proper causes, and in the case of separation, to whom the guard-
35 ianship of the children shall be given, as to be wholly regardless of the happiness of women—the law, in all cases, going upon a false supposition of the supremacy of man, and giving all power into his hands.

40 After depriving her of all rights as a married woman, if single, and the owner of property, he has taxed her to support a government which recognizes her only when her property can be made profitable to it.

45 He has endeavored, in every way that he could, to destroy her confidence in her own powers, to lessen her self-respect, and to make her willing to lead a dependent and abject life.

Passage 2—Sojourner Truth

After emancipation had been decreed by the State, some years before the time fixed for its consummation, Isabella's master told her if she would do well, and be faithful, he would
5 give her "free papers," one year before she was legally free by statute. In the year 1826, she had a badly diseased hand, which greatly diminished her usefulness; but on the arrival of July 4, 1827, the time specified for her
10 receiving her "free papers," she claimed the fulfillment of her master's promise; but he refused granting it, on account (as he alleged) of the loss he had sustained by her hand. She plead that she had worked all the time,
15 and done many things she was not wholly able to do, although she knew she had been less useful than formerly; but her master remained inflexible. Her very faithfulness probably operated against her now, and he
20 found it less easy than he thought to give up the profits of his faithful Bell, who had so long done him efficient service.

But Isabella inwardly determined that she would remain quietly with him only until
25 she had spun his wool—about one hundred pounds—and then she would leave him, taking the rest of the time to herself. "Ah!" she says, with emphasis that cannot be written, "the slaveholders are TERRIBLE
30 for promising to give you this or that, or such and such a privilege, if you will do thus and so; and when the time of fulfillment comes, and one claims the promise, they, forsooth, recollect nothing of the kind; and
35 you are, like as not, taunted with being a LIAR; or, at best, the slave is accused of not having performed *his* part or condition of the contract." "Oh!" said she, "I have felt as if I could not live through the *operation*
40 *sometimes.* Just think of us! *so* eager for our pleasures, and just foolish enough to keep feeding and feeding ourselves up with the idea that we should get what had been thus fairly promised; and when we think it is
45 almost in our hands, find ourselves flatly denied! Just think! how *could* we bear it?"

5. Both passages concern themselves with a kind of
   (A) tyranny.
   (B) liberation.
   (C) government.
   (D) security.
   (E) autonomy.

6. The word *injuries* in line 2 of the Declaration of Sentiments might be replaced with the word
   (A) bruises.
   (B) prejudice.
   (C) mistreatment.
   (D) wounds.
   (E) shocks.

7. The Declaration of Sentiments compares the status of women with those of "ignorant and degraded men" (lines 12–13) in order to
   (A) condemn people with weak bodies.
   (B) poke fun at a segment of the population.
   (C) argue that even undereducated men deserve a chance to express their opinions.
   (D) state that they are equals.
   (E) highlight the ludicrousness of women's position in society.

8. When the Declaration of Sentiments states in line 20 that a married woman is "civilly dead," this probably means that
   (A) the law ignores married women.
   (B) married women must treat their husbands courteously.
   (C) women must give up their lives to their husbands.
   (D) a man may kill his wife with impunity.
   (E) married women must not show undue emotion.

9. The word *her* as used throughout the Declaration of Sentiments refers to
   (A) an emancipated woman.
   (B) a married woman.
   (C) all women.
   (D) the author of the Declaration.
   (E) a woman who is old enough to vote.

10. According to the Declaration of Sentiments, women are only seen as useful to the government when they
    (A) promote discord.
    (B) can provide it with profit.
    (C) vote.
    (D) marry.
    (E) earn wages.

11. The word *sustained* (Passage 2, line 13), most nearly means
    (A) experienced.
    (B) maintained.
    (C) improved.
    (D) nourished.
    (E) made plentiful.

12. The narrative of Sojourner Truth implies that slaveholders' cruelty is based on
    (A) twisted emotions.
    (B) desire for profit.
    (C) fear of confrontation.
    (D) racism.
    (E) misunderstanding.

13. Truth's main objection to her slaveholder is to his
    (A) harassment.
    (B) brutality.
    (C) unfairness.
    (D) bigotry.
    (E) rudeness.

14. When Truth refers to "us" (line 40), she means
    (A) African Americans.
    (B) slaveholders.
    (C) women.
    (D) writers.
    (E) slaves.

15. The tone of both passages might be described as
    (A) resigned.
    (B) calculating.
    (C) fierce.
    (D) embittered.
    (E) hopeful.

16. Would you expect Sojourner Truth to approve of the Declaration of Sentiments?
    (A) No, because the Declaration clearly represents only white women.
    (B) No, because slavery and sexual oppression have little in common.
    (C) Yes, because she, too, is taxed to support a government that does not represent her.
    (D) Yes, because she, too, is willing to be dependent.
    (E) Yes, because she understands as well as anyone what it means to have no rights.

STOP

END OF SECTION 8. IF YOU HAVE ANY TIME LEFT, GO OVER YOUR WORK IN THIS SECTION ONLY. DO NOT WORK IN ANY OTHER SECTION OF THE TEST.

Section 9
15 Questions • 10 Minutes

Directions: The sentences below may contain problems in grammar, usage, word choice, sentence construction, or punctuation. Part or all of each sentence is underlined. Following each sentence you will find five ways of expressing the underlined part. Answer choice (A) always repeats the original underlined section. The other four answer choices are all different. You are to select the lettered answer that produces the most effective sentence. If you think the original sentence is best, choose (A) as your answer. If one of the other choices makes a better sentence, mark your answer sheet for the letter of that choice. Do not choose an answer that changes the meaning of the original sentence.

I have always enjoyed <u>singing as well as to dance</u>.

(A) singing as well as to dance

(B) singing as well as dancing

(C) to sing as well as dancing

(D) singing in addition to dance

(E) to sing in addition to dancing

The correct answer is (B).

1. Between 10 and 20 percent of the homes in the town <u>are suspected of having</u> a high level of radon contamination.
   (A) are suspected of having
   (B) are suspects in the having of
   (C) are suspicious as they have
   (D) can be suspected of having an ordinary and
   (E) seem to be suspicious in that they have

2. The students disliked the teacher and <u>demonstrating it by</u> not handing in assignments.
   (A) demonstrating it by
   (B) demonstrated it by
   (C) to demonstrate to the teacher, they were
   (D) demonstrate it by
   (E) cause a demonstration when they are

3. Everyone said that John was a natural salesman; he had a winning smile, an above-average intelligence, <u>and he was always tenaciously persistent.</u>
   (A) and he was always tenaciously persistent.
   (B) and he persisted in a tenacious manner.
   (C) and, with tenacity, he always persisted.
   (D) and a tenacious persistence.
   (E) and the ability to project his persistent tenacity.

4. Juggling, like any other skill, <u>requires many hours of practice</u> before it becomes easy.
   (A) requires many hours of practice
   (B) requires practice that can be hourless
   (C) requires, among other things, many practice hours
   (D) requires that you practice with it many hours
   (E) requires you to be practicing many hours

5. <u>As whenever the two of them were together they quarreled</u>, we decided to put each one in a different group.

   (A) As whenever the two of them were together they quarreled

   (B) As to the two of them quarreling when they were together

   (C) Since the two of them quarreled whenever they were together

   (D) Since quarreling was what happened as a result of their togetherness

   (E) Because the two of them quarreled together

6. Having tried to cover too much territory in her brief essay, <u>nothing was analyzed in any detail.</u>

   (A) nothing was analyzed in any detail.

   (B) nothing was analyzed in no detail.

   (C) the analysis was not detailed enough.

   (D) nothing that she analyzed was in detail.

   (E) she failed to analyze anything in detail.

7. If one wishes to be an individualist, <u>you must live with</u> the suspicion and resentment of those who prefer conformity.

   (A) you must live with

   (B) you have to live with

   (C) you must tolerate

   (D) one must live with

   (E) we must live with

8. Stories of huge hailstones have been <u>reported; it is claimed that</u> in Pipestone, Minnesota, in 1911, a 5.5-pound stone fell through the skylight of an office building.

   (A) reported; it is claimed that

   (B) reported, it is claimed that

   (C) reported; they claim that

   (D) reported; it is claimed how

   (E) reported; it is claim that

9. I had delayed too long by talking to Jeremy; the shop <u>was close by the time I got there.</u>

   (A) was close by the time I got there.

   (B) was close when I got there.

   (C) was closed when I got there.

   (D) had close when I got there.

   (E) had close by the time I got there.

10. She had never played tennis <u>well on any surface but grass.</u>

    (A) well on any surface but grass.

    (B) good on any surface but grass.

    (C) good on no surface but grass.

    (D) well on no surface but grass.

    (E) good on any surface except grass.

11. The principal listed the names of the students <u>whom he thought ought to be honored</u> at the assembly.

    (A) whom he thought ought to be honored

    (B) whom he thought should be honored

    (C) whom, he thought, ought to be honored

    (D) who, he thought, ought to be honored

    (E) who ought to be honored

12. <u>One of the authors points, as I interpret them,</u> is that some traditions should not be followed, or at least should be re-evaluated when they no longer make sense.

    (A) One of the authors points, as I interpret them,

    (B) One of the authors' points, as I interpret them

    (C) The author's point, as I interpret them,

    (D) One of the authors point in my interpretation,

    (E) One of the author's points, as I interpret it,

13. <u>Having packed hurriedly and left quickly,</u> he was sure he had forgotten something.

(A) Having packed hurriedly and left quickly,

(B) Having packed hurriedly and leaving quickly,

(C) Having packed hurriedly and having left quickly,

(D) Packing hurriedly and leaving quickly,

(E) Packing hurriedly and having left quickly,

14. <u>It's unfair to expect Rob and I</u> to pay for dinner when everyone else is working, too.

(A) It's unfair to expect Rob and I

(B) Its unfair to expect Rob and I

(C) It's not fair to expect Rob and I

(D) It's unfair to expect Rob and me

(E) To expect Rob and I to pay is unfair

15. While it comprises only a small percentage of the student population, <u>the club, numbering some 150 members, are very vocal.</u>

(A) the club, numbering some 150 members, are very vocal.

(B) the club numbering some 150 members are very vocal.

(C) the club with some 150 members are very vocal.

(D) the club, numbering some 150 members, is very vocal.

(E) the club of 150 members are very vocal.

STOP

END OF SECTION 9. IF YOU HAVE ANY TIME LEFT, GO OVER YOUR WORK IN THIS SECTION ONLY. DO NOT WORK IN ANY OTHER SECTION OF THE TEST.

ANSWER KEY AND EXPLANATIONS

Section 1

Sample Essay 1

There are so many problems plaguing humanity that it is hard to know where to begin to solve them. It is terribly sad to see so much hunger and poverty throughout the world—in our country and elsewhere. But perhaps the most frightening problem we face is what to do to avoid nuclear annihilation.

Destruction will not come with a "whimper" but with a "bang" I'm afraid. So many countries have nuclear weapons—large and powerful countries and smaller countries as well and then there is always the threat of terrorists getting them. The likelihood of a catastrophe, accidental or otherwise is great. Events in the United States and in Russia have proven that nuclear reactors are not all that safe. Then there are the threats made by smaller nations at war against other smaller nations. The prospect is possible and terrible.

Many people do not even bother to have children or get married nowadays. They say it's better to just enjoy the little time they have left before the world is blown up. It's a very depressing situation and not easy to explain to youngsters. Also, some people say that they can't trust politicians to do the right thing.

Therefore, this is a serious problem that must be addressed. But intelligent answers to this very difficult problem do not seem to be at hand.

Analysis of Sample Essay 1

The essay is well organized, keeping to the subject and developing its arguments in a logical progression. The introduction is well developed as it moves from the general to the specific—from "many major problems" to the problem of avoidance of nuclear annihilation.

The essay might be revised to address or elaborate on certain ideas. First, the writer should suggest how the problems noted might be addressed, since that is what the question required. Second, the discussion of the breakdown of social values and family life needs specific development and details so that it will be more germane to the central issue. Revisions are needed to make the tone more consistent. In the third paragraph, the tone becomes informal and the argument wanders.

In the second paragraph, specific examples of conflicts between nations might have provided illustration of the thesis. The second paragraph begins with an *allusion*, the technique of making indirect reference to an author or work of literature. In this case, the writer alludes to T.S. Eliot's famous line "This is how the world ends, not with a bang but a whimper"—a most appropriate way to suggest a point of view.

The concluding paragraph is signaled by a transition ("Therefore") that prepares the reader for a summation of the preceding arguments and uses some of the language of the topic that the writer has chosen to discuss. In the opening sentence the word *this* is vague and its antecedent is unclear. If the author means "the possibility of nuclear annihilation," it should be said.

Sample Essay 2

Over the past years there has been an area of concern that people have forgotten, and yet I feel that this should be our cheif concern. The area is that of pollution. Our entire world is suffering from various forms of pollution and I feel that if we do not open our eyes to this problem we will soon see the general breakdown of our universe.

Because of the increasing number of cars on our streets and the various forms of mass transportation, our air is becoming polluted. All sorts of harmful gasses are being given off into the air, and we are breathing in fumes that will surely cause us many kinds of diseases. We pollute our bodies with cigarete smoke and drugs but we also pollute our bodies with gasoline fumes and taken together we are shortening our lives.

Garbage and poisons are polluting our soil and our streams. Newspaper articles always point out that all the chemicals that we use to grow bigger and more delicious fruits and vegetables and to destroy the bugs are going to destroy us as well. The chemicals get into our foods and then we eat them, and soon we will suffer the affects. Garbage is thrown into the waters and rivers and our fish become contaminated.

Of course, poverty, nuclear war, and hunger are problems, but so is pollution, and pollution is a problem that people overlook; that is why it is so dangerous. I think that over the next few years laws should be passed to regulate air pollution, to solve the problem of garbage disposal, and to deal with the use of chemicals and agriculture. In my opinion, this should be our major concern.

Analysis of Sample Essay 2

The writer shows an intelligent handling of the topic. Choosing pollution, an area not mentioned in the question, the writer provides a thoughtful alternative approach.

The four paragraphs are well organized and well developed. The writer uses specific examples in the body of the essay. The essay is clear, generally well written, and consistent with the writer's thesis statement. The reader feels that the author strongly believes in the point of view presented.

However, the author overstates the case in writing in the introduction that "people have forgotten" pollution, and in the conclusion that "people overlook" this problem. The writer seems to be carried away by emotion rather than sticking to facts and rational tone.

More careful proofreading might result in the correction of usage and spelling errors: in paragraph one, *cheif* should be *chief;* in paragraph two, *cigarete* should be *cigarette;* in paragraph three, *affects* should be *effects*.

In paragraph three, the concluding sentence might well be eliminated, since it adds no new ideas and simply repeats what has been stated earlier in the paragraph.

Section 2

1. B	7. E	12. B	17. D	22. D
2. D	8. D	13. C	18. E	23. D
3. E	9. B	14. C	19. C	24. B
4. B	10. E	15. B	20. D	25. C
5. A	11. E	16. A	21. C	26. D
6. E				

1. **The correct answer is (B).** The word *finally* suggests that the woman agreed to sell the farm only after being *importuned*, or repeatedly urged, to do so by her family.

2. **The correct answer is (D).** The ghost urges, or *exhorts*, Hamlet to take revenge.

3. **The correct answer is (E).** Concern for the children's safety would logically lead a father to *inculcate* (teach by constant repetition) in them a *wary* attitude toward strangers.

4. **The correct answer is (B).** With a life full of hardship and poverty, they are surely *inured* (accustomed) to discomfort.

5. **The correct answer is (A).** The author probably withdrew from the project because he was displeased with the novel's *adaptation*, or change, required to turn the novel into a television program.

6. **The correct answer is (E).** *Vacillation* means fluctuation of mind or changing from one purpose to another.

7. **The correct answer is (E).** A smile could be *radiant* or *bright*, but it could logically only *dazzle* all those who saw it.

8. **The correct answer is (D).** The word *although* indicates that the blanks will be filled by opposites as in choice (D): *penurious* (stingy) and *generous*.

9. **The correct answer is (B).** To disarm someone in a single motion requires sure and swift, or *deft*, action.

10. **The correct answer is (E).** The platypus, with its curious duckbill and habit of laying eggs, is a biological *anomaly* (abnormality).

11. **The correct answer is (E).** The writer is implying that of the women who composed classical music, Beach was the first to be recognized as such.

12. **The correct answer is (B).** Choice (E) is not true, because the paragraph really has no summary conclusion, nor does it present a complete picture of Beach's life or accomplishments. For those reasons, you can rule out choice (C) also. While choices (A) and (D) are true, they aren't the best answers. Remember the difference between true and best, or correct.

13. **The correct answer is (C).** Remember to look for the unusual meanings of words in answering vocabulary questions on the SAT. The usual meanings, choices (A), (B), (D), and (E), are incorrect in the context.

14. **The correct answer is (C).** This is a convoluted passage, but the immediate cause of progress according to the passage is individual initiative and enterprise. Choices (B) and (D) combined provide the individual with the necessary environment in which to exercise initiative and enterprise.

15. **The correct answer is (B).** The Power of Place is the main subject of the passage. Dolores Hayden, choice (D), is important only because she is the founder and spokesperson of this organization; while she would probably agree with choices (A) and (C), those answers are too broad.

16. The correct answer is (A). The juxtaposition in lines 1 and 2 of "outsider" and "Los Angeles" indicates that "civic" should be taken in its original sense of "having to do with the city." That the city's feelings might be "bruised" by criticism suggests that these feelings consist of an allegiance to one's home city.

17. The correct answer is (D). According to the author, the modernization of Los Angeles threatens to rob the city of its naturally diverse cultural history.

18. The correct answer is (E). See lines 5–10. Choices (A) and (B), while they may reflect Hayden's opinions, are not what she means while quoting Stein's statement.

19. The correct answer is (C). This answer summarizes Hayden's point in saying that 98 percent of landmarks memorialize Anglo-Americans while less than half the population of Los Angeles is Anglo-American (lines 23–28).

20. The correct answer is (D). Answer I is supported by the contrast between the "land-holders, bankers, business leaders" of lines 31–32 and the workers described in the fifth paragraph. Answer II is supported in lines 36–39. Answer III is not supported in the passage; in fact, Hayden's respect for the economic contributions of working people is mentioned in lines 40–46.

21. The correct answer is (C). This is the point of the third paragraph, especially lines 42–46.

22. The correct answer is (D). See lines 52–58.

23. The correct answer is (D). The author describes the site as "ethnically evocative" (line 65) and identifies several different ethnic groups that worked there.

24. The correct answer is (B). This answer summarizes Hayden's views as they are expressed not only in lines 40–46 but throughout the passage. "Placemaking" is intended to make the site "more redolent of its past" (line 82), and the point of this redolence, as described by the first three paragraphs, is to give Los Angeles a better sense of place.

25. The correct answer is (C). The tree is a miracle only in contrast to its surroundings as described in lines 86–90.

26. The correct answer is (D). Chances are that a monument such as city hall garners significant attention from the mainstream community. After all, it is an official government landmark. The other listed attributes are more likely to get lost in the shuffle.

Section 3

1. C	5. E	9. E	13. B	17. B
2. C	6. E	10. A	14. E	18. D
3. D	7. A	11. B	15. A	19. E
4. C	8. A	12. C	16. E	20. D

Note: A 🖩 following a math answer explanation indicates that a calculator could be helpful in solving that particular problem.

1. **The correct answer is (C).** This is easily solved by plugging in the numbers:

$(4 - 1) \times (5 - 2) \times (6 - 3) = 3 \times 3 \times 3$
$= 27$ 🖩

2. **The correct answer is (C).** If $2n$ is an even number, $2n + 1$ is odd.

3. **The correct answer is (D).** Solving the equation for x gives x a value of $-\frac{1}{2}$, and

$x^2 = \left(-\frac{1}{2}\right)^2 = \frac{1}{4}$.

4. **The correct answer is (C).** Setting up a ratio,

$$\frac{88 \text{ ft. / sec.}}{60 \text{ mi. / hr.}} = \frac{100 \text{ ft. / sec.}}{x \text{ mi. / hr.}}$$
$$88x = (1100)(60)$$
$$x = 750 \text{ mi. / hr.}$$ 🖩

5. **The correct answer is (E).** Setting up a ratio,

$$\frac{\frac{1}{4} \text{ in.}}{12 \text{ in.}} = \frac{3\frac{3}{8} \text{ in.}}{x \text{ in.}}$$
$$\left(\frac{1}{4}\right)x = (12)\left(3\frac{3}{8}\right)$$
$$x = 162 \text{ in.} = 13\frac{1}{2} \text{ ft.}$$ 🖩

6. **The correct answer is (E).** Let x be the second angle. The first angle is $3x$, and the third angle is $x + 20$. The angles of a triangle must equal $180°$, so $3x + x + (x + 20) = 180$, $5x = 160$, and $x = 32$.

7. **The correct answer is (A).**

By substitution, $x + y^2 - \frac{1}{2}$ becomes

$\frac{3}{2} + (2)^2 - \frac{1}{2} = \frac{3}{2} + 4 - \frac{1}{2} = \frac{3}{2} + \frac{8}{2} - \frac{1}{2}$

$= \frac{10}{2} = 5.$ 🖩

8. **The correct answer is (A).** $14 + 17 = 31$. Therefore, there are 4 students who must be enrolled in all three courses. Four students out of $27 = \frac{4}{27} = 0.148$. Round up to 0.15, which is 15%. 🖩

9. **The correct answer is (E).** The volume of the container is the area of the circle at one end times the height. The area of the circle is $A = \pi 7^2 \approx 154$ sq. in. The volume is $154 \times 6 = 924$ cu. in. The capacity of the tank is 924 cu. in. ÷ 231 cu. in./gal. = 4 gallons. 🖩

10. **The correct answer is (A).**

$$\frac{1}{x+y} = 6$$
$$\frac{1}{2+y} = 6$$
$$6(2+y) = 1$$
$$12 + 6y = 1$$
$$6y = -11$$
$$y = -\frac{11}{6}$$

11. **The correct answer is (B).** If there are 28.35 grams per ounce, then 28.35 grams per ounce ÷ 1000 grams per kilogram = 0.02835 kilograms per ounce. Since there are 16 ounces to the pound, 0.02835 kilograms per ounce times 16 ounces per pound = 0.45 kilograms per pound. 🖩

12. **The correct answer is (C).** The square root of 0.16 is 0.4, so 0.16 is a perfect square. The square root of 16 is 4, so 16 is a perfect square. The square root of 1600 is 40, so 1600 is a perfect square. The square root of 0.0016 is 0.04, so 0.0016 is a perfect square. Only 1.6 is not a perfect square. 🖩

13. **The correct answer is (B).** Let's start by pointing out that we do not know the size of angles 1, 2, 3, or 4. We do know that the two lines are parallel and therefore 8 and 6 can be moved to their corresponding locations on the top line. Since all straight lines have 180 degrees, III and IV each equal 180 degrees.

14. **The correct answer is (E).** The maximum value is obtained by making x as large as possible and y as small as possible. Thus, we set up a fraction:

$$\frac{\frac{1}{2}}{\frac{3}{4}} = \frac{1}{2} \times \frac{4}{3} = \frac{4}{6} = \frac{2}{3}$$

15. **The correct answer is (A).** Start by finding the area of the largest circle. The radius of the largest circle is 9, so the area is 81π. The middle circle has a radius of 5, so the area is 25π. The smallest circle has a radius of 2, so the area is 4π. To find the shaded region, subtract the smaller circle from the middle and get 21π. The fraction is thus $\frac{21\pi}{81\pi}$, which can be simplified to $\frac{7}{27}$.

16. **The correct answer is (E).** The answer can quickly be obtained by using a numerical example. Let $n = 5$ and $d = 2$.

I. $\frac{2}{5}$

II. $\frac{3}{6}$

III. $\frac{1}{4}$

IV. $\frac{5}{2}$

V. $\frac{4}{1}$

$$\frac{1}{4} < \frac{2}{5} < \frac{3}{6} < \frac{5}{2} < 4$$ 🖩

17. **The correct answer is (B).** Let t be the time the train is scheduled to take. At 40 mph, the train arrives in $t + \frac{10}{60} = t + \frac{1}{6}$ hours. At 30 mph, the train takes $t + \frac{16}{60} = t + \frac{4}{15}$ hours.

The distance is the speed times the time.

$$40\left(t + \frac{1}{6}\right) = 30\left(t + \frac{4}{15}\right)$$

$$40t + \frac{40}{6} = 30t + 8$$

$$10t = 8 - \frac{40}{6}$$

$$10t = 1\frac{1}{3} \text{ hr.} = 80 \text{ min.}$$

$$t = 8 \text{ min.}$$

The distance between towns is:

$$d = (40 \text{ mph})\left(\frac{8}{60} + \frac{10}{60} \text{ hr.}\right)$$

$$= 40 \times \frac{18}{60}$$

$$= 12 \text{ miles}$$ 🖩

18. **The correct answer is (D).** Since the radius of the circle is 5, the area of the circle is $\pi r^2 = \pi(5)^2 = 25\pi$. Next, note that $\overline{AB}$ is a diameter of the circle, and is therefore of length 10. $\overline{AB}$ is also the hypotenuse of right triangle ABC, and, since $AC = 8$, it follows from the Pythagorean theorem that $BC = 6$. Using AC and BC as the base and height of the triangle, compute the area of the triangle as $A = \frac{1}{2}bh = \frac{1}{2}(8)(6) = 24$. Therefore, the probability that a point in the interior of the circle is also in the triangle is $\frac{24}{25\pi}$.

19. **The correct answer is (E).** You are looking for a description of the set that contains all positive integers that are multiples of 3 *and* 5 *and* 7. Since 3, 5, and 7 are prime numbers, the smallest number in this set is $3 \times 5 \times 7 = 105$. The other numbers in this set would be the multiples of 105, such as $2 \times 105 = 210$, $3 \times 105 = 315$, and so on.

20. **The correct answer is (D).** Begin by noting that the median of the five numbers is equal to x, the number in the middle. The average, on the other hand, is given by the expression $\frac{v+w+x+y+z}{5}$. Since the average is 6 times the median, the formula is $\frac{v+w+x+y+z}{5} = 6x$.

Multiplying both sides by 5 gives you $v + w + x + y + z = 30x$.

Subtract x from both sides to obtain $v + w + y + z = 29x$.

Divide both sides by 29, then

$$x = \frac{v+w+y+z}{29}.$$

Section 4

1. A	8. C	15. B	22. B	29. C
2. C	9. D	16. C	23. B	30. D
3. B	10. D	17. D	24. E	31. B
4. D	11. E	18. D	25. C	32. A
5. C	12. A	19. C	26. D	33. C
6. E	13. A	20. A	27. A	34. C
7. D	14. C	21. D	28. E	35. E

1. **The correct answer is (A).** When comparing only two persons or things, use the comparative forms *more* or *-er: more amusing or funnier.*

2. **The correct answer is (C).** A singular pronoun (*his* or *her*) is required to agree with the antecedent *Anyone.*

3. **The correct answer is (B).** The plural verb *were* is required to agree with the compound subject that follows.

4. **The correct answer is (D).** The plural pronoun *they* is required to agree with the plural antecedent, *a small glass pyramid and a crystal.*

5. **The correct answer is (C).** The correct idiomatic phrase is *accompanied by.*

6. **The correct answer is (E).** The sentence is correct.

7. **The correct answer is (D).** For correct sequence of tenses, the verb form *might* is required to follow *cracked* and *got.*

8. **The correct answer is (C).** The participle *breaking* is required to introduce the dependent clause.

9. **The correct answer is (D).** For parallel structure, the noun phrase *a feeling of safety* is required.

10. **The correct answer is (D).** The verb should be changed to *is* to agree with the singular subject *neither.*

11. **The correct answer is (E).** The sentence is correct.

12. **The correct answer is (A).** The correct word is *effects,* meaning *results.*

13. **The correct answer is (A).** The plural verb form *were* is required to agree with the plural subject, *complaints.*

14. **The correct answer is (C).** In this comparison, the correct phrase is "than any *other* chart."

15. **The correct answer is (B).** The singular subject, *sampling,* requires the third-person singular verb form, *reveals.*

16. **The correct answer is (C).** The correct idiomatic phrase is "such . . . *as.*"

17. **The correct answer is (D).** Use parallel forms for comparisons: *persuasion* was a more effective means than *force.*

18. **The correct answer is (D).** *Imaginary* means "existing in the imagination." The word needed here is *imaginative,* meaning "creative or original."

19. **The correct answer is (C).** The singular verb *was* is required to agree with the singular subject *influence.*

20. **The correct answer is (A).** The sentence is correct.

21. **The correct answer is (D).** The sentence contains two independent clauses. If there is not a connective, then the first clause must be followed by a semicolon.

22. **The correct answer is (B).** Choice (B) is more economical and does not end with the dangling infinitive *to be.*

23. **The correct answer is (B).** Although *in attending* might be acceptable in a different context, here the correct word is *attendance*.

24. **The correct answer is (E).** In order to keep the structure parallel, it is necessary to have a present-tense verb with an object.

25. **The correct answer is (C).** In the original sentence, it is difficult to be certain whether the school or the notes are concerned with vandalism.

26. **The correct answer is (D).** The word *so* has no function in the sentence.

27. **The correct answer is (A).** The sentence is correct.

28. **The correct answer is (E).** The original sentence would be acceptable if the comma were replaced by a semicolon. It is also acceptable to connect the clauses with *and*.

29. **The correct answer is (C).** The word *certainly* is unnecessary, and the clauses should be joined by a semicolon.

30. **The correct answer is (D).** To start the sentence with the adverb *hopefully* is poor since *hopefully* does not modify *government*. Therefore, choices (A) and (C) are weak. Choice (B) is vague, and choice (E) has a problem of reference (*their* should be *its*). Choice (D) is best because the entire essay is written from the first-person point of view, and the pronoun is correct.

31. **The correct answer is (B).** Choice (A) is weak since the phrase *being one* is poor. Choice (C) contains a comma splice error following *America*. Choice (D) does not convey the sense of the original sentence. Choice (E) is poor since the semicolon following *America* is incorrect punctuation.

32. **The correct answer is (A).** The only choice that is clear and grammatically sound, with proper punctuation and good word choice, is choice (A).

33. **The correct answer is (C).** Choice (A) makes a fragment of the first part of the sentence, and choice (B) makes a fragment of the entire sentence. Choice (D), like the original sentence, includes the extra pronoun *they*. Choice (E) changes the meaning.

34. **The correct answer is (C).** The error in sentence (10) is a comma splice error. A comma cannot separate two main clauses. A period or a semicolon should be used after *profession*. This type of error is an error in sentence structure.

35. **The correct answer is (E).** The underlined portion is redundant, as are choices (A), (B), (C), and (D).

Section 5

1. A	5. C	9. A	13. 6	17. 6.86
2. D	6. A	10. B	14. 8	18. $\frac{1}{2}$
3. C	7. A	11. 10	15. 60	19. 4.2
4. D	8. C	12. 3.63	16. .766	20. 24

Note: A 🔲 following a math answer explanation indicates that a calculator could be helpful in solving that particular problem.

1. **The correct answer is (A).**

$$\frac{6 \text{ minutes}}{6 \text{ hours}} = \frac{6 \text{ minutes}}{6(60) \text{ minutes}} = \frac{1}{60}$$

2. **The correct answer is (D).**

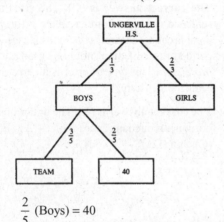

$$\frac{2}{5}(\text{Boys}) = 40$$

Therefore, the number of boys is 100. Since there are twice as many girls as boys, there are 200 girls. 🔲

3. **The correct answer is (C).** To begin, $f(2) = 2^2 + 3(2) + 5 = 4 + 6 + 5 = 15$. Similarly, $g(2) = 3(2)^2 = 3(4) = 12$. Thus, $\frac{f(2)}{g(2)} = \frac{15}{12} = \frac{5}{4}$.

4. **The correct answer is (D).** Since $(11^{-3})^k = 11^{-3k} = 11^{-15}$, it must be true that $-3k = -15$. Therefore, $k = 5$.

5. **The correct answer is (C).** The equation $3 = |1 - 2q|$ is true when $1 - 2q = 3$ and when

$$1 - 2q = -3$$

$$
\begin{array}{ll}
1 - 2q = 3 & 1 - 2q = -3 \\
-2q = 2 & -2q = -4 \\
q = -1 & q = 2
\end{array}
$$

Finally, $2 - (-1) = 2 + 1 = 3$.

6. **The correct answer is (A).** Draw OP.

Then, in right triangle OPS,

$$OP^2 = PS^2 + OS^2 = 6^2 + 8^2 = 10^2$$

$$OP = 10$$

Then, length $\overset{\frown}{QR} = \frac{1}{4} \cdot 2\pi r = \frac{1}{4} \cdot 2\pi \cdot 10 = 5\pi$

7. **The correct answer is (A).**

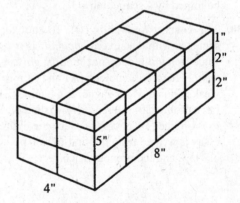

The 2-inch ice cube will fit only in the 8-inch by 4-inch by 4-inch part of the compartment. The upper inch cannot be used.

Hence, $\frac{8 \times 4 \times 4}{2 \times 2 \times 2} = 16$ cubes 🔲

8. **The correct answer is (C).** Since it takes Paul 2 hours to paint 1 fence, he paints $\frac{1}{2}$ of the fence in 1 hour. Fred paints $\frac{1}{3}$ of the fence per hour. Together their speed is $\frac{1}{2} + \frac{1}{3} = \frac{5}{6}$ fence/hr. The time to paint this fence working together is 1 fence $\div \frac{5}{6}$ fence/hr. = 1.2 hours. 🔲

9. The correct answer is (A). $\frac{3}{4}$ evaporates the second day; therefore, there is $\frac{1}{4}$ of the $\frac{2}{3}$ of liquid left after evaporation the first day. $\frac{1}{4}$ of $\frac{2}{3} = \frac{1}{6}$, so $\frac{1}{6}$ of the original contents remains after two days.

10. The correct answer is (B). The time it takes the driver to arrive at her destination is 60 miles ÷ 40 miles per hour = $1\frac{1}{2}$ hours. The time it takes to return is 60 miles ÷ 30 miles per hour = 2 hours, making the total time for this 120-mile trip $1\frac{1}{2} + 2 = 3\frac{1}{2}$ hours. The average speed for the entire trip is 120 miles ÷ $3\frac{1}{2}$ hours =

$34\frac{2}{7}$ miles per hour.   🖩

11. The correct answer is 10. First convert Jerry's final height to inches:

$5 \times 12 = 60$ $60 + 10 = 70$

Jerry's 7-inch growth is 10% of 70 inches.

12. The correct answer is 3.63. He kept $\frac{3}{4}$ of his peanuts.

$$\frac{3}{4}\left(4\frac{5}{6}\right) = \frac{3}{4}\left(\frac{29}{6}\right) = \frac{29}{8} = 3\frac{5}{8} = 3.625$$

Use 3.63.   🖩

13. The correct answer is 6.

$$\frac{pr}{st} = \frac{p\left(\dfrac{p}{2}\right)}{\left(\dfrac{p}{3}\right)\left(\dfrac{p}{4}\right)} = \frac{\dfrac{p^2}{2}}{\dfrac{p^2}{12}} = \frac{p^2}{2} \bullet \frac{12}{p^2} = 6$$

14. The correct answer is 8.

$$\sqrt{7+9+7+9+7+9+7+9} =$$
$$\sqrt{4(7+9)} = \sqrt{4(16)} = \sqrt{64} = 8 \quad 🖩$$

15. The correct answer is 60.

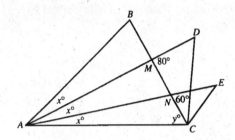

$x + y = 60$ (Exterior angle = sum of the 2 remote interior angles)

$2x + y = 80$ (Exterior angle = sum of the 2 remote interior angles)

$$\begin{array}{r} 2x + y = 80 \\ -x + y = 60 \\ \hline x \quad\quad = 20 \end{array}$$

16. The correct answer is .766.

$$\frac{\dfrac{7}{8}+\dfrac{7}{8}+\dfrac{7}{8}}{\dfrac{8}{7}+\dfrac{8}{7}+\dfrac{8}{7}} = \frac{3\left(\dfrac{7}{8}\right)}{3\left(\dfrac{8}{7}\right)} = \frac{\dfrac{7}{8}}{\dfrac{8}{7}}$$

$$= \frac{7}{8} \bullet \frac{7}{8} = \frac{49}{64} = .766 \quad 🖩$$

17. The correct answer is 6.86.

$$\text{Average} = \frac{\text{Sum}}{\text{Number of items}}$$

$\therefore$ Sum = (Avg.) (No. of items)

$$\begin{array}{r} 48 \;= (8)(6) \\ +48 \;= (6)(8) \\ \hline 96 \end{array}$$

$$\text{Average} = \frac{96}{14} = 6\frac{6}{7} = \frac{48}{7} = 6.68 \quad 🖩$$

18. The correct answer is $\dfrac{1}{2}$.

$$\frac{4a}{3b} = \frac{8}{9}$$

Multiply each side of the equation by $\dfrac{9}{16}$.

$$\frac{\overset{1}{\cancel{4}}a}{\underset{1}{\cancel{3}}b} \cdot \frac{\overset{3}{\cancel{9}}}{\underset{4}{\cancel{16}}} = \frac{\overset{1}{\cancel{8}}}{\underset{1}{\cancel{9}}} \cdot \frac{\overset{1}{\cancel{9}}}{\underset{2}{\cancel{16}}}$$

$$\frac{3a}{4b} = \frac{1}{2}$$ 🖩

19. The correct answer is 4.2. Begin by multiplying both sides of the equation by the LCD of 15.

$$15\left(\frac{2x}{3}\right) + 15\left(\frac{1}{5}\right) = 15(3)$$
$$5(2x) + 3(1) = 45$$
$$10x + 3 = 45$$
$$10x = 42$$
$$x = \frac{42}{10} = 4.2$$

20. The correct answer is 24. Compute that
$$f(-\,) = |-\,|^3 = (\ )^3 = (\ ) =$$

Section 6

1. B	7. A	12. B	17. C	22. B
2. A	8. D	13. E	18. A	23. B
3. D	9. C	14. C	19. C	24. B
4. A	10. D	15. E	20. E	25. E
5. C	11. B	16. B	21. A	26. A
6. B				

1. **The correct answer is (B).** Acting together, those involved would each be *responsible* for an *element*.

2. **The correct answer is (A).** Unwise *neglect* during someone's education could result in *ignorance*.

3. **The correct answer is (D).** A conformist is conventional, acting in accordance with the prevailing customs. Children who are conventional are likely to *ostracize* (exclude) classmates who are *different* in behavior or dress.

4. **The correct answer is (A).** The date chosen for a king's coronation would most likely be *propitious* (lucky).

5. **The correct answer is (C).** A poem dripping with venom is apt to be *redolent* with (suggestive of) scorn.

6. **The correct answer is (B).** If the rites were kept secret, the members never *divulged* (revealed) them. Furthermore, fraternity rites are very likely to be *esoteric* (known to only a select few).

7. **The correct answer is (A).** A composer who praised the work of a musician he detested would be considered *magnanimous* (extremely generous).

8. **The correct answer is (D).** *Goodwill* is a genuine asset, but it is necessarily *intangible* (incapable of being touched in the physical sense).

9. **The correct answer is (C).** This one is easy; the main idea is stated in the first sentence of the passage. The comparison to Romanesque architecture is a way to describe Gothic but is not the focus of the paragraph.

10. **The correct answer is (D).** The writer uses the phrase "among the best-known." This is your clue.

11. **The correct answer is (B).** Choices (A) and (C) are too general. Choice (B) incorporates the idea of spyware and your computer. Remember you are always looking for the best answer.

12. **The correct answer is (B).** The focus in choices (D) and (E) is on the general—any activity on a Web site and any purchasing on the Internet. Spyware focuses on individuals. Choice (B) includes the idea of an individual.

13. **The correct answer is (E).** Dividing up authority among several people points to choice (E). There is nothing in the passage to support the other choices.

14. **The correct answer is (C).** While Akbar might indeed be thoughtful, choice (C) is a more precise description. There is nothing to indicate that choice (E) applies.

15. **The correct answer is (E).** According to the first paragraph, the bear "changes its haunts with the seasons" in order to obtain "suitable food" and security.

16. **The correct answer is (B).** This is the only possible conclusion one can reach among those listed. Nothing indicates that Audubon hunts, choice (A), and he never denies that bears are dangerous, choice (D).

17. **The correct answer is (C).** Low, rich lands bordering a river are likely to be composed largely of river-deposited sediment.

18. **The correct answer is (A).** The bears scratch bark with their teeth and claws, but they do not eat it. Each of the other choices is specifically mentioned.

19. **The correct answer is (C).** Lines 75–76 put forth Audubon's theory. Others, he says, believe in theories given in choices (A), (B), and (E).

20. **The correct answer is (E).** Audubon draws back and addresses the reader directly in lines 41–44, remarking that "you well know" and "you also know" about bears' honey eating and ability to climb.

21. **The correct answer is (A).** The first comparison comes in lines 7–13 and the second comes at the end of the passage, in lines 72–82.

22. **The correct answer is (B).** Audubon makes much of the positive traits of the bear, focusing on its strength and pragmatism. He brushes over any indications that bears are fearsome, choice (A), or alarming, choice (D).

23. **The correct answer is (B).** A careful reading of paragraph 1 will tell you this. Although choices (A) and (C) are true in some cases, they have nothing to do with the opinion of the author.

24. **The correct answer is (B).** Whether or not you know this word in another context, you should be able to comprehend its meaning by reading the surrounding passage. The word is used to describe a plant with an extremely short life cycle.

25. **The correct answer is (E).** The definition of *biennial* appears in the third paragraph.

26. **The correct answer is (A).** The paragraph deals mainly with suffrutescent shrubs, which fall somewhere between herbaceous perennials and true shrubs.

Section 7

1. C	4. D	7. D	10. B	13. C
2. D	5. B	8. C	11. C	14. B
3. D	6. C	9. B	12. B	15. D

Note: A 🖩 following a math answer explanation indicates that a calculator could be helpful in solving that particular problem.

1. **The correct answer is (C).** Area $= \left(\dfrac{1}{2}\right)bh$. The base is AW, which is $\dfrac{2}{3}$ of AB, or $\dfrac{2}{3}(9) = 6$. The height is 2.

   $a = \dfrac{1}{2}(6)(2) = 6$ 🖩

2. **The correct answer is (D).** $(2 \times 100) + (16 \times 10) + 6 = 200 + 160 + 6 = 366.$ 🖩

3. **The correct answer is (D).** This is a direct proportion.

   $\dfrac{\text{cartons}}{\text{days}} \Rightarrow \dfrac{6}{h} = \dfrac{3h}{x}$

   $6x = 3h^2$

   $x = \dfrac{h^2}{2}$

4. **The correct answer is (D).** The perimeter of a 46' × 34' rectangle is 160 feet, which equals $53\dfrac{1}{3}$ yards.   🖩

5. **The correct answer is (B).** After the 15% deduction, $12,750 is left. After the 10% is deducted from $12,750, $11,475 is left. Note that you cannot simply deduct 25% from the $15,000.   🖩

6. **The correct answer is (C).** By the laws of exponents, $(x^a)^b$ is the same as $x^{a \cdot b}$.

7. **The correct answer is (D).** The path of all points equidistant from two points is the perpendicular bisector of the segment that connects the two points.

8. **The correct answer is (C).**

   $w = xy = x(x^2) = x^3$

   $y^2 + z^2 + w^2 = (x^2)^2 + (x^3)^2 + (x^3)^2$

   $= x^4 + x^6 + x^6 = x^4 + 2x^6$

9. **The correct answer is (B).** The difference between the numbers increases by 2; therefore, $? - 20 = 10$, so $? = 30$.   🖩

10. **The correct answer is (B).** The area of the square is 36. Since the triangle is equilateral, we can use the 30-60-90 rule to solve. By dropping a perpendicular, we find the altitude to be $3\sqrt{3}$. Then, the area of the triangle is $9\sqrt{3}$. Thus, the shaded area is $36 - 9\sqrt{3}$.

11. **The correct answer is (C).** When you are given the diagonal of a square, you can find the length of the side by dividing the diagonal by 2 and multiplying by $\sqrt{2}$.

12. **The correct answer is (B).**

    $m\angle TSP = 60°$

    Since $m\angle PSR = 90°$, $m\angle TSR = 90 - 60 = 30°$.

    Since $TS = PS = SR, m\angle RTS = m\angle TRS$. Thus,

    $m\angle TRS = \dfrac{1}{2}(180° - 30°) = \dfrac{1}{2}(150°) = 75°$ 🖩

13. **The correct answer is (C).**

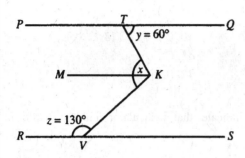

Through point K, draw KM parallel to PQ and RS. Then,

$m\angle x = m\angle MKV + m\angle MKT$

$m\angle MKV = m\angle KVS = 180 - 130 = 50°$

$m\angle MKT = m\angle QTK = 60°$

$m\angle x = 60° + 50° = 110°$

14. **The correct answer is (B).** Alan's profit for each pastry would be $\$0.75 - \$0.35 = \$0.40$, so, if he sells x pastries, he would make $\$0.40x$. After paying $\$15$ for the booth, he would have $\$0.40x - \$15$ left.

15. **The correct answer is (D).** Find the value of x that makes $P(x) = \$0.40x - \$15 = \$45$.

$\$0.40x - \$15 = \$45$ Add $\$15$ to both sides

$\$0.40x = \$60$ Divide both sides

 by $\$0.40$

$x = 150$

Section 8

1. E	5. A	9. C	13. C
2. D	6. C	10. B	14. E
3. A	7. E	11. A	15. D
4. D	8. A	12. B	16. E

1. **The correct answer is (E).** The thesis of the first passage is that both the colonists and the English were trying to protect their self-interest. The other choices are distracters; they use words and phrases that are in the passage, but they do not answer the question.

2. **The correct answer is (D).** Only choice (D) includes both choices (C) and (E), which separately are only partial answers.

3. **The correct answer is (A).** Only choice (A) includes the twin ideas of partial awareness and lack of control. The other choices focus on one or the other idea.

4. **The correct answer is (D).** Passage 1 makes the argument for an economic motive, whereas Passage 2 supports a political motive. The other choices are only partial aspects of each argument.

5. **The correct answer is (A).** The Declaration speaks of the tyranny of men over women; Truth speaks of the tyranny of the slaveholder over his slaves.

6. **The correct answer is (C).** The word *injuries* signifies general mistreatment of women by men. The forms of mistreatment that are listed are primarily legal and social; "bruises," "prejudice," "wounds," and "shocks" are never mentioned.

7. **The correct answer is (E).** The Declaration does not equate the two, as is argued in choice (D). The comparison is made to argue that if undereducated men have basic rights, so too should the average American woman.

8. **The correct answer is (A).** "In the eye of the law" is the clue here; a woman who marries is dead in the law's eyes, or ignored by the law.

9. **The correct answer is (C).** Look back at the first paragraph and you will see that the authors of the Declaration are referring to the tyranny of man over woman throughout history. *He* is all men; *her* refers to all women.

10. **The correct answer is (B).** The proof of this is in lines 42–44, wherein the woman is taxed to "support a government which recognizes her only when her property can be made profitable to it."

11. **The correct answer is (A).** In this context, *sustained* means *experienced*. The master experienced a loss in productivity because of the slave's diseased hand.

12. **The correct answer is (B).** This opinion is implied in line 13 ("the loss he had sustained by her hand") and 20–21 ("to give up the profits of his faithful Bell . . .").

13. **The correct answer is (C).** We see no signs of brutality, choice (B), but Truth's owner is clearly pictured as unfair. He breaks his promises despite Isabella's faithfulness.

14. **The correct answer is (E).** Truth is referring to those who are eager for freedom but foolish enough to believe that they will get it—slaves, in other words.

15. **The correct answer is (D).** The passages as cited cannot be considered *resigned,* choice (A), or *hopeful,* choice (E). Each is essentially a catalog of sins by an aggrieved victim.

16. **The correct answer is (E).** In fact, Sojourner Truth went on to work hard for the rights of women. Even if you did not know that, you could predict her approval based on the fact that her description of slavery parallels so thoroughly the Declaration's description of sexual oppression.

Section 9

1. A	5. C	9. C	13. C
2. B	6. E	10. A	14. D
3. D	7. D	11. D	15. D
4. A	8. A	12. E	

1. **The correct answer is (A).** The sentence is correct.

2. **The correct answer is (B).** Notice that *disliked* is in the past tense. *Demonstrating* is a gerund rather than a verb.

3. **The correct answer is (D).** It is important that the parallelism be maintained. Sometimes it is easier to hear this if you leave a few words out: ". . . he had a . . . smile . . . intelligence . . . and persistence."

4. **The correct answer is (A).** The sentence is correct.

5. **The correct answer is (C).** In addition to being least awkward, this choice places the emphasis on the two people quarreling.

6. **The correct answer is (E).** Only choice (E) meets the requirement that an introductory participle be followed by the subject of both the sentence and the participle.

7. **The correct answer is (D).** The only thing wrong with the original is that it shifts the point of view from the impersonal *one* to the personal *you*. Correct English requires that the same point of view be used throughout.

8. **The correct answer is (A).** The sentence is correct.

9. **The correct answer is (C).** There is a big difference between the shop being *close* and being *closed*.

10. **The correct answer is (A).** The sentence is correct. *Good* is an adjective and *well* is an adverb; in this case the adverb is needed to answer the question "how did she play."

11. **The correct answer is (D).** *He thought* is an interpolation that has no influence on the grammar of the sentence. As the subject of the second clause, the correct pronoun is *who*.

12. **The correct answer is (E).** The word *authors* needs an apostrophe to indicate that it is possessive, not plural. The singular possessive form is *author's,* as in choices (C) and (E). However, since choice (B) uses the plural *them* to refer to the singular subject *one,* it is incorrect.

13. **The correct answer is (C).** The tense of the main clause is simple past; therefore, the tense of the participle should be past perfect. The sense of the sentence is that the packing and leaving occurred before the idea of being sure something was forgotten. Choice (D) would make the act of being sure of forgetting and packing and leaving simultaneous. Only choice (C) has the correct form of both participles.

14. **The correct answer is (D).** *I* is the subject form of the pronoun. But the pronouns should be in the objective case, because, along with *Rob,* it is the object of the verb *expect.*

15. **The correct answer is (D).** *Club* is a collective noun in this sentence, and the verb used with it should be the singular *is,* not *are.*

COMPUTING YOUR SCORES

To get a sense of your progress in preparing for the SAT, you need to compute individual multiple-choice critical reading, math, and writing raw scores for this Practice Test. Keep in mind that these formulas have been simplified to give you a "quick and dirty" sense of where you are scoring, not a perfectly precise score.

To Compute Your Raw Scores

1 Enter the number of correct answers for each critical reading, math, and multiple-choice writing section under Number of Questions Correct.

2 Enter the number of incorrect answers (not blanks) for each critical reading, math, and multiple-choice writing section under Number of Questions Incorrect.

3 Total the number correct and number incorrect.

4 Follow this formula: Take the total correct and subtract one quarter of the total incorrect. Round up in your favor to compute your raw score.

Critical Reading Section	Total Number of Questions	Number of Questions Correct	Number of Questions Incorrect
2	26		
6	26		
8	16		
Totals	68	Total Correct:	Total Incorrect:

Critical Reading Raw Score = Total Correct $- (\frac{1}{4} \times$ Total Incorrect) = ___

Math Section	Total Number of Questions	Number of Questions Correct	Number of Questions Incorrect
3	20		
5	20		
7	15		
Totals	55	Total Correct:	Total Incorrect:

Math Raw Score = Total Correct $- (\frac{1}{4} \times$ Total Incorrect) = ___

Multiple-Choice Writing Section	Total Number of Questions	Number of Questions Correct	Number of Questions Incorrect
4	35		
9	15		
Total	50	Total Correct:	Total Incorrect:

Multiple-Choice Writing Raw Score = Total Correct $- (\frac{1}{4} \times$ Total Incorrect) = ___

CONVERSION SCALES

CRITICAL READING

Raw Score	Scaled Score	Raw Score	Scaled Score
68	800	30	480
65	760	25	440
60	710	20	410
55	670	15	370
50	620	10	340
45	590	5	290
40	550	0	230
35	520		

MATH

Raw Score	Scaled Score	Raw Score	Scaled Score
55	800	20	510
50	760	15	480
45	690	10	440
40	650	5	340
35	610	0	200
30	580		
25	550		

MULTIPLE-CHOICE WRITING

Raw Score	Scaled Score	Raw Score	Scaled Score
50	800	20	470
45	760	15	420
40	680	10	370
35	620	5	320
30	580	0	270
25	520		

SELF-EVALUATION CHARTS

Critical Reading: Raw Score

Excellent	60–68
Good	50–59
Average	30–49
Fair	20–29
Poor	0–19

Math: Raw Score

Excellent	50–55
Good	40–49
Average	20–39
Fair	10–19
Poor	0–9

ANSWER SHEET PRACTICE TEST 6

SECTION 1: ESSAY

_____

_____

_____

_____

_____

_____

_____

_____

_____

_____

_____

_____

_____

_____

_____

_____

_____

_____

_____

_____

_____

_____

_____

_____

_____

_____

answer sheet

If a section has fewer questions than answer ovals, leave the extra ovals blank.

SECTION 2

1 Ⓐ Ⓑ Ⓒ Ⓓ Ⓔ   11 Ⓐ Ⓑ Ⓒ Ⓓ Ⓔ   21 Ⓐ Ⓑ Ⓒ Ⓓ Ⓔ   31 Ⓐ Ⓑ Ⓒ Ⓓ Ⓔ
2 Ⓐ Ⓑ Ⓒ Ⓓ Ⓔ   12 Ⓐ Ⓑ Ⓒ Ⓓ Ⓔ   22 Ⓐ Ⓑ Ⓒ Ⓓ Ⓔ   32 Ⓐ Ⓑ Ⓒ Ⓓ Ⓔ
3 Ⓐ Ⓑ Ⓒ Ⓓ Ⓔ   13 Ⓐ Ⓑ Ⓒ Ⓓ Ⓔ   23 Ⓐ Ⓑ Ⓒ Ⓓ Ⓔ   33 Ⓐ Ⓑ Ⓒ Ⓓ Ⓔ
4 Ⓐ Ⓑ Ⓒ Ⓓ Ⓔ   14 Ⓐ Ⓑ Ⓒ Ⓓ Ⓔ   24 Ⓐ Ⓑ Ⓒ Ⓓ Ⓔ   34 Ⓐ Ⓑ Ⓒ Ⓓ Ⓔ
5 Ⓐ Ⓑ Ⓒ Ⓓ Ⓔ   15 Ⓐ Ⓑ Ⓒ Ⓓ Ⓔ   25 Ⓐ Ⓑ Ⓒ Ⓓ Ⓔ   35 Ⓐ Ⓑ Ⓒ Ⓓ Ⓔ
6 Ⓐ Ⓑ Ⓒ Ⓓ Ⓔ   16 Ⓐ Ⓑ Ⓒ Ⓓ Ⓔ   26 Ⓐ Ⓑ Ⓒ Ⓓ Ⓔ   36 Ⓐ Ⓑ Ⓒ Ⓓ Ⓔ
7 Ⓐ Ⓑ Ⓒ Ⓓ Ⓔ   17 Ⓐ Ⓑ Ⓒ Ⓓ Ⓔ   27 Ⓐ Ⓑ Ⓒ Ⓓ Ⓔ   37 Ⓐ Ⓑ Ⓒ Ⓓ Ⓔ
8 Ⓐ Ⓑ Ⓒ Ⓓ Ⓔ   18 Ⓐ Ⓑ Ⓒ Ⓓ Ⓔ   28 Ⓐ Ⓑ Ⓒ Ⓓ Ⓔ   38 Ⓐ Ⓑ Ⓒ Ⓓ Ⓔ
9 Ⓐ Ⓑ Ⓒ Ⓓ Ⓔ   19 Ⓐ Ⓑ Ⓒ Ⓓ Ⓔ   29 Ⓐ Ⓑ Ⓒ Ⓓ Ⓔ   39 Ⓐ Ⓑ Ⓒ Ⓓ Ⓔ
10 Ⓐ Ⓑ Ⓒ Ⓓ Ⓔ   20 Ⓐ Ⓑ Ⓒ Ⓓ Ⓔ   30 Ⓐ Ⓑ Ⓒ Ⓓ Ⓔ   40 Ⓐ Ⓑ Ⓒ Ⓓ Ⓔ

SECTION 3

1 Ⓐ Ⓑ Ⓒ Ⓓ Ⓔ   11 Ⓐ Ⓑ Ⓒ Ⓓ Ⓔ   21 Ⓐ Ⓑ Ⓒ Ⓓ Ⓔ   31 Ⓐ Ⓑ Ⓒ Ⓓ Ⓔ
2 Ⓐ Ⓑ Ⓒ Ⓓ Ⓔ   12 Ⓐ Ⓑ Ⓒ Ⓓ Ⓔ   22 Ⓐ Ⓑ Ⓒ Ⓓ Ⓔ   32 Ⓐ Ⓑ Ⓒ Ⓓ Ⓔ
3 Ⓐ Ⓑ Ⓒ Ⓓ Ⓔ   13 Ⓐ Ⓑ Ⓒ Ⓓ Ⓔ   23 Ⓐ Ⓑ Ⓒ Ⓓ Ⓔ   33 Ⓐ Ⓑ Ⓒ Ⓓ Ⓔ
4 Ⓐ Ⓑ Ⓒ Ⓓ Ⓔ   14 Ⓐ Ⓑ Ⓒ Ⓓ Ⓔ   24 Ⓐ Ⓑ Ⓒ Ⓓ Ⓔ   34 Ⓐ Ⓑ Ⓒ Ⓓ Ⓔ
5 Ⓐ Ⓑ Ⓒ Ⓓ Ⓔ   15 Ⓐ Ⓑ Ⓒ Ⓓ Ⓔ   25 Ⓐ Ⓑ Ⓒ Ⓓ Ⓔ   35 Ⓐ Ⓑ Ⓒ Ⓓ Ⓔ
6 Ⓐ Ⓑ Ⓒ Ⓓ Ⓔ   16 Ⓐ Ⓑ Ⓒ Ⓓ Ⓔ   26 Ⓐ Ⓑ Ⓒ Ⓓ Ⓔ   36 Ⓐ Ⓑ Ⓒ Ⓓ Ⓔ
7 Ⓐ Ⓑ Ⓒ Ⓓ Ⓔ   17 Ⓐ Ⓑ Ⓒ Ⓓ Ⓔ   27 Ⓐ Ⓑ Ⓒ Ⓓ Ⓔ   37 Ⓐ Ⓑ Ⓒ Ⓓ Ⓔ
8 Ⓐ Ⓑ Ⓒ Ⓓ Ⓔ   18 Ⓐ Ⓑ Ⓒ Ⓓ Ⓔ   28 Ⓐ Ⓑ Ⓒ Ⓓ Ⓔ   38 Ⓐ Ⓑ Ⓒ Ⓓ Ⓔ
9 Ⓐ Ⓑ Ⓒ Ⓓ Ⓔ   19 Ⓐ Ⓑ Ⓒ Ⓓ Ⓔ   29 Ⓐ Ⓑ Ⓒ Ⓓ Ⓔ   39 Ⓐ Ⓑ Ⓒ Ⓓ Ⓔ
10 Ⓐ Ⓑ Ⓒ Ⓓ Ⓔ   20 Ⓐ Ⓑ Ⓒ Ⓓ Ⓔ   30 Ⓐ Ⓑ Ⓒ Ⓓ Ⓔ   40 Ⓐ Ⓑ Ⓒ Ⓓ Ⓔ

SECTION 4

1 Ⓐ Ⓑ Ⓒ Ⓓ Ⓔ   11 Ⓐ Ⓑ Ⓒ Ⓓ Ⓔ   21 Ⓐ Ⓑ Ⓒ Ⓓ Ⓔ   31 Ⓐ Ⓑ Ⓒ Ⓓ Ⓔ
2 Ⓐ Ⓑ Ⓒ Ⓓ Ⓔ   12 Ⓐ Ⓑ Ⓒ Ⓓ Ⓔ   22 Ⓐ Ⓑ Ⓒ Ⓓ Ⓔ   32 Ⓐ Ⓑ Ⓒ Ⓓ Ⓔ
3 Ⓐ Ⓑ Ⓒ Ⓓ Ⓔ   13 Ⓐ Ⓑ Ⓒ Ⓓ Ⓔ   23 Ⓐ Ⓑ Ⓒ Ⓓ Ⓔ   33 Ⓐ Ⓑ Ⓒ Ⓓ Ⓔ
4 Ⓐ Ⓑ Ⓒ Ⓓ Ⓔ   14 Ⓐ Ⓑ Ⓒ Ⓓ Ⓔ   24 Ⓐ Ⓑ Ⓒ Ⓓ Ⓔ   34 Ⓐ Ⓑ Ⓒ Ⓓ Ⓔ
5 Ⓐ Ⓑ Ⓒ Ⓓ Ⓔ   15 Ⓐ Ⓑ Ⓒ Ⓓ Ⓔ   25 Ⓐ Ⓑ Ⓒ Ⓓ Ⓔ   35 Ⓐ Ⓑ Ⓒ Ⓓ Ⓔ
6 Ⓐ Ⓑ Ⓒ Ⓓ Ⓔ   16 Ⓐ Ⓑ Ⓒ Ⓓ Ⓔ   26 Ⓐ Ⓑ Ⓒ Ⓓ Ⓔ
7 Ⓐ Ⓑ Ⓒ Ⓓ Ⓔ   17 Ⓐ Ⓑ Ⓒ Ⓓ Ⓔ   27 Ⓐ Ⓑ Ⓒ Ⓓ Ⓔ
8 Ⓐ Ⓑ Ⓒ Ⓓ Ⓔ   18 Ⓐ Ⓑ Ⓒ Ⓓ Ⓔ   28 Ⓐ Ⓑ Ⓒ Ⓓ Ⓔ
9 Ⓐ Ⓑ Ⓒ Ⓓ Ⓔ   19 Ⓐ Ⓑ Ⓒ Ⓓ Ⓔ   29 Ⓐ Ⓑ Ⓒ Ⓓ Ⓔ
10 Ⓐ Ⓑ Ⓒ Ⓓ Ⓔ   20 Ⓐ Ⓑ Ⓒ Ⓓ Ⓔ   30 Ⓐ Ⓑ Ⓒ Ⓓ Ⓔ

SECTION 5

Note: ONLY the answers entered on the grid are scored. Handwritten answers at the top of the column are NOT scored.

1. Ⓐ Ⓑ Ⓒ Ⓓ Ⓔ   6. Ⓐ Ⓑ Ⓒ Ⓓ Ⓔ
2. Ⓐ Ⓑ Ⓒ Ⓓ Ⓔ   7. Ⓐ Ⓑ Ⓒ Ⓓ Ⓔ
3. Ⓐ Ⓑ Ⓒ Ⓓ Ⓔ   8. Ⓐ Ⓑ Ⓒ Ⓓ Ⓔ
4. Ⓐ Ⓑ Ⓒ Ⓓ Ⓔ   9. Ⓐ Ⓑ Ⓒ Ⓓ Ⓔ
5. Ⓐ Ⓑ Ⓒ Ⓓ Ⓔ   10. Ⓐ Ⓑ Ⓒ Ⓓ Ⓔ

11. 12. 13. 14. 15.

16. 17. 18. 19. 20.

SECTION 6

1 Ⓐ Ⓑ Ⓒ Ⓓ Ⓔ	11 Ⓐ Ⓑ Ⓒ Ⓓ Ⓔ	21 Ⓐ Ⓑ Ⓒ Ⓓ Ⓔ	31 Ⓐ Ⓑ Ⓒ Ⓓ Ⓔ
2 Ⓐ Ⓑ Ⓒ Ⓓ Ⓔ	12 Ⓐ Ⓑ Ⓒ Ⓓ Ⓔ	22 Ⓐ Ⓑ Ⓒ Ⓓ Ⓔ	32 Ⓐ Ⓑ Ⓒ Ⓓ Ⓔ
3 Ⓐ Ⓑ Ⓒ Ⓓ Ⓔ	13 Ⓐ Ⓑ Ⓒ Ⓓ Ⓔ	23 Ⓐ Ⓑ Ⓒ Ⓓ Ⓔ	33 Ⓐ Ⓑ Ⓒ Ⓓ Ⓔ
4 Ⓐ Ⓑ Ⓒ Ⓓ Ⓔ	14 Ⓐ Ⓑ Ⓒ Ⓓ Ⓔ	24 Ⓐ Ⓑ Ⓒ Ⓓ Ⓔ	34 Ⓐ Ⓑ Ⓒ Ⓓ Ⓔ
5 Ⓐ Ⓑ Ⓒ Ⓓ Ⓔ	15 Ⓐ Ⓑ Ⓒ Ⓓ Ⓔ	25 Ⓐ Ⓑ Ⓒ Ⓓ Ⓔ	35 Ⓐ Ⓑ Ⓒ Ⓓ Ⓔ
6 Ⓐ Ⓑ Ⓒ Ⓓ Ⓔ	16 Ⓐ Ⓑ Ⓒ Ⓓ Ⓔ	26 Ⓐ Ⓑ Ⓒ Ⓓ Ⓔ	36 Ⓐ Ⓑ Ⓒ Ⓓ Ⓔ
7 Ⓐ Ⓑ Ⓒ Ⓓ Ⓔ	17 Ⓐ Ⓑ Ⓒ Ⓓ Ⓔ	27 Ⓐ Ⓑ Ⓒ Ⓓ Ⓔ	37 Ⓐ Ⓑ Ⓒ Ⓓ Ⓔ
8 Ⓐ Ⓑ Ⓒ Ⓓ Ⓔ	18 Ⓐ Ⓑ Ⓒ Ⓓ Ⓔ	28 Ⓐ Ⓑ Ⓒ Ⓓ Ⓔ	38 Ⓐ Ⓑ Ⓒ Ⓓ Ⓔ
9 Ⓐ Ⓑ Ⓒ Ⓓ Ⓔ	19 Ⓐ Ⓑ Ⓒ Ⓓ Ⓔ	29 Ⓐ Ⓑ Ⓒ Ⓓ Ⓔ	39 Ⓐ Ⓑ Ⓒ Ⓓ Ⓔ
10 Ⓐ Ⓑ Ⓒ Ⓓ Ⓔ	20 Ⓐ Ⓑ Ⓒ Ⓓ Ⓔ	30 Ⓐ Ⓑ Ⓒ Ⓓ Ⓔ	40 Ⓐ Ⓑ Ⓒ Ⓓ Ⓔ

SECTION 7

1 Ⓐ Ⓑ Ⓒ Ⓓ Ⓔ	6 Ⓐ Ⓑ Ⓒ Ⓓ Ⓔ	11 Ⓐ Ⓑ Ⓒ Ⓓ Ⓔ
2 Ⓐ Ⓑ Ⓒ Ⓓ Ⓔ	7 Ⓐ Ⓑ Ⓒ Ⓓ Ⓔ	12 Ⓐ Ⓑ Ⓒ Ⓓ Ⓔ
3 Ⓐ Ⓑ Ⓒ Ⓓ Ⓔ	8 Ⓐ Ⓑ Ⓒ Ⓓ Ⓔ	13 Ⓐ Ⓑ Ⓒ Ⓓ Ⓔ
4 Ⓐ Ⓑ Ⓒ Ⓓ Ⓔ	9 Ⓐ Ⓑ Ⓒ Ⓓ Ⓔ	14 Ⓐ Ⓑ Ⓒ Ⓓ Ⓔ
5 Ⓐ Ⓑ Ⓒ Ⓓ Ⓔ	10 Ⓐ Ⓑ Ⓒ Ⓓ Ⓔ	15 Ⓐ Ⓑ Ⓒ Ⓓ Ⓔ

SECTION 8

1 Ⓐ Ⓑ Ⓒ Ⓓ Ⓔ	6 Ⓐ Ⓑ Ⓒ Ⓓ Ⓔ	11 Ⓐ Ⓑ Ⓒ Ⓓ Ⓔ	16 Ⓐ Ⓑ Ⓒ Ⓓ Ⓔ
2 Ⓐ Ⓑ Ⓒ Ⓓ Ⓔ	7 Ⓐ Ⓑ Ⓒ Ⓓ Ⓔ	12 Ⓐ Ⓑ Ⓒ Ⓓ Ⓔ	17 Ⓐ Ⓑ Ⓒ Ⓓ Ⓔ
3 Ⓐ Ⓑ Ⓒ Ⓓ Ⓔ	8 Ⓐ Ⓑ Ⓒ Ⓓ Ⓔ	13 Ⓐ Ⓑ Ⓒ Ⓓ Ⓔ	18 Ⓐ Ⓑ Ⓒ Ⓓ Ⓔ
4 Ⓐ Ⓑ Ⓒ Ⓓ Ⓔ	9 Ⓐ Ⓑ Ⓒ Ⓓ Ⓔ	14 Ⓐ Ⓑ Ⓒ Ⓓ Ⓔ	19 Ⓐ Ⓑ Ⓒ Ⓓ Ⓔ
5 Ⓐ Ⓑ Ⓒ Ⓓ Ⓔ	10 Ⓐ Ⓑ Ⓒ Ⓓ Ⓔ	15 Ⓐ Ⓑ Ⓒ Ⓓ Ⓔ	20 Ⓐ Ⓑ Ⓒ Ⓓ Ⓔ

SECTION 9

1 Ⓐ Ⓑ Ⓒ Ⓓ Ⓔ	6 Ⓐ Ⓑ Ⓒ Ⓓ Ⓔ	11 Ⓐ Ⓑ Ⓒ Ⓓ Ⓔ
2 Ⓐ Ⓑ Ⓒ Ⓓ Ⓔ	7 Ⓐ Ⓑ Ⓒ Ⓓ Ⓔ	12 Ⓐ Ⓑ Ⓒ Ⓓ Ⓔ
3 Ⓐ Ⓑ Ⓒ Ⓓ Ⓔ	8 Ⓐ Ⓑ Ⓒ Ⓓ Ⓔ	13 Ⓐ Ⓑ Ⓒ Ⓓ Ⓔ
4 Ⓐ Ⓑ Ⓒ Ⓓ Ⓔ	9 Ⓐ Ⓑ Ⓒ Ⓓ Ⓔ	14 Ⓐ Ⓑ Ⓒ Ⓓ Ⓔ
5 Ⓐ Ⓑ Ⓒ Ⓓ Ⓔ	10 Ⓐ Ⓑ Ⓒ Ⓓ Ⓔ	15 Ⓐ Ⓑ Ⓒ Ⓓ Ⓔ

Section 1

Essay • 25 Minutes

Directions: Think carefully about the statement below and the assignment that follows it.

Computers make it unnecessary for people to know how to write well in their everyday lives. No one cares if words are misspelled or if incorrect grammar is used for e-mail. The idea is to get the message out.

Assignment: What is your opinion of the idea that writing well in everyday life is no longer important? Plan and write an essay that develops your ideas logically. Support your opinion with specific evidence taken from your personal experience, your observations of others, or your reading.

STOP

END OF SECTION 1. IF YOU HAVE ANY TIME LEFT, GO OVER YOUR WORK IN THIS SECTION ONLY. DO NOT WORK IN ANY OTHER SECTION OF THE TEST.

Section 2

26 Questions • 25 Minutes

Directions: Each of the following questions consists of an incomplete sentence followed by five words or pairs of words. Choose that word or pair of words that, when substituted for the blank space or spaces, best completes the meaning of the sentence and mark the letter of your choice on your answer sheet.

In view of the extenuating circumstances and the defendant's youth, the judge recommended ____.

(A) conviction

(B) a defense

(C) a mistrial

(D) leniency

(E) life imprisonment

The correct answer is **(D)**.

1. ____ the activities of her employees, the director refused to ____ their methods.
   (A) Disarming .. condone
   (B) Applauding .. question
   (C) Repudiating .. reward
   (D) Handling .. oversee
   (E) Approving .. arrogate

2. The ____ soldier ____ at the idea that he was to go to battle.
   (A) luckless .. rejoiced
   (B) youthful .. retired
   (C) unwilling .. recoiled
   (D) frail .. relapsed
   (E) vigorous .. repined

3. The ____ treatment of the zoo animals resulted in community-wide ____.
   (A) curious .. apathy
   (B) popular .. neglect
   (C) critical .. distention
   (D) adequate .. revulsion
   (E) inhumane .. criticism

4. Unlike gold, paper money has no ____ value; it is merely a representation of wealth.
   (A) financial
   (B) inveterate
   (C) economic
   (D) intrinsic
   (E) fiscal

5. His untimely death, at first thought to be due to a ____ fever, was later ____ to poison.
   (A) degenerative .. relegated
   (B) debilitating .. ascribed
   (C) raging .. reduced
   (D) sanguine .. abdicated
   (E) pernicious .. prescribed

6. To strengthen her client's case, the lawyer sought to put the ____ of the witness in doubt.
   (A) laxity
   (B) posterity
   (C) probity
   (D) onus
   (E) sensitivity

7. During the campaign, the politicians engaged in ____ debate, accusing each other of gross misdeeds.
   (A) capricious
   (B) acrimonious
   (C) altruistic
   (D) facetious
   (E) chimerical

8. His carelessness produced a(n) ____ report
   that left everyone ____.
   (A) intelligent .. inept
   (B) ambiguous .. confused
   (C) complete .. mollified
   (D) acceptable .. angry
   (E) insipid .. inspired

9. Only a ____ person could be ____ to the
   suffering of the starving child.
   (A) churlish .. receptive
   (B) dour .. disposed
   (C) placid .. detrimental
   (D) pious .. uncivil
   (E) callous .. oblivious

Directions: Each passage below is followed by a set of questions. Read each passage, then answer the accompanying questions, basing your answers on what is stated or implied in the passage and in any introductory material provided. Mark the letter of your choice on your answer sheet.

QUESTIONS 10 AND 11 ARE BASED ON THE FOLLOWING PASSAGE.

India is part of the Asian subcontinent and is home to over 1 billion people. Only China has a larger population. A little over half of India's land is suited to agriculture, but
5 about 65 percent of Indians are farmers or farm laborers. They raise rice, wheat, cotton, cattle, sheep, and water buffalo. To increase output, the government instituted irrigation and land reclamation projects. Newer types
10 of crops and fertilizers have also been tried. India is one of the nations benefiting from the Green Revolution. Unfortunately, the initial high hopes for the Green Revolution have proved to be illusory because of the
15 high costs for the seeds and fertilizer and the environmental issues arising from the massive use of pesticides.

10. The author probably introduced the statistic about the size of India's population
    (A) in order to set up a comparison with China's population.
    (B) because it is an interesting fact.
    (C) to provide background for the discussion of the Green Revolution.
    (D) to show the seriousness of the need for food in India.
    (E) to provide context for the number of Indians who work in agriculture.

11. In adopting the Green Revolution, the Indian government evidently hoped to
    (A) increase the amount of land under cultivation.
    (B) increase the amount of food produced.
    (C) experiment with how new types of fertilizers and crops would work on Indian land.
    (D) kill off insects that were harming Indian crops.
    (E) vary the diet of Indians with new types of food.

QUESTIONS 12 AND 13 ARE BASED ON THE FOLLOWING PASSAGE.

. . . Too many of us had supposed that, built as our commonwealth was on universal suffrage, it would be proof against the complaints [slums] that harassed older states; but in fact
5   it turned out that there was extra hazard in that. Having solemnly resolved that all men are created equal and have certain inalienable rights, among them life, liberty, and the pursuit of happiness, we shut our eyes and
10   waited for the formula to work. . . . When, after a hundred years, we opened our eyes, it was upon sixty cents a day as the living wage of the working-woman in our cities.

—Jacob Riis, *The Battle with the Slums*

12. The tone that the author uses in this passage is
   (A) satiric.
   (B) resignation.
   (C) indignation.
   (D) surprise.
   (E) exasperation.

13. By "proof" (line 3) Riis means that
   (A) by being able to vote, people would ensure that everyone enjoyed life, liberty, and the pursuit of happiness.
   (B) life, liberty, and the pursuit of happiness would be automatically conferred on everyone.
   (C) evidence based on older states was incorrectly applied to the United States.
   (D) there was evidence that slums could not occur.
   (E) there was evidence that working women were earning only sixty cents a day.

QUESTIONS 14–21 ARE BASED ON THE FOLLOWING PASSAGE.

The following speech has been adapted from A Citizen is Entitled to Vote *by Susan B. Anthony, a nineteenth-century campaigner for women's rights. At the time of the speech, women were not guaranteed the right to vote.*

Friends and fellow citizens:—I stand before you tonight under indictment for the alleged crime of having voted at the last presidential election, without having a lawful right to
5   vote.

It shall be my work this evening to prove to you that in thus voting, I not only committed no crime, but instead, simply exercised my *citizen's rights*, guaranteed to me and
10   all United States citizens by the National Constitution, beyond the power of any State to deny.

The preamble of the Federal Constitution says: "We, the people of the United States, in
15   order to form a more perfect union, establish justice, insure *domestic* tranquility, provide for the common defense, promote the general welfare, and secure the blessings of liberty to ourselves and our posterity, do ordain and
20   establish this Constitution for the United States of America."

It was we, the people, not we, the white male citizens; but we, the whole people, who formed the Union. And we formed it,
25   not to give the blessings of liberty, but to secure them; not to the half of ourselves and the half of our posterity but to the whole people—women as well as men. And it is a down-right mockery to talk to women of
30   their enjoyment of the blessings of liberty while they are denied the use of the only means of securing them provided by this democratic-republican government—the ballot.

35   For any State to make sex a qualification that must ever result in the disfranchisement of one entire half of the people is a violation of the supreme law of the land. By it the blessings of liberty are forever withheld from
40   women and their female posterity. To them this government has no just powers derived from the consent of the governed. To them

this government is not a democracy. It is not a republic. It is a hateful oligarchy of sex. An
45 oligarchy of learning, where the educated govern the ignorant, might be endured; but this oligarchy of sex, which makes father, brothers, husband, sons, the oligarchs or rulers over the mother and sisters, the wife
50 and daughters of every household—which ordains all men sovereigns, all women subjects, carries dissension, discord and rebellion into every home of the nation.

Webster's Dictionary defines a citizen as a
55 person in the United States, entitled to vote and hold office.

The only question left to be settled now is, Are women persons? And I hardly believe any of our opponents will have the har-
60 dihood to say they are not. Being persons, then, women are citizens; and no State has a right to make any law, or to enforce any old law, that shall abridge their privileges or immunities. Hence, every discrimination
65 against women in the constitutions and laws of the several States is today null and void.

14. Anthony talks as if she were a
(A) defendant on trial.
(B) chairperson of a committee.
(C) legislator arguing for a new law.
(D) judge ruling at a trial.
(E) lawyer in court.

15. Anthony broadens her appeal to her audience by showing how her case could affect all
(A) existing laws.
(B) U.S. citizens.
(C) women.
(D) uneducated persons.
(E) children.

16. Anthony quotes the preamble to the Constitution in order to
(A) impress the audience with her intelligence.
(B) share common knowledge with her audience.
(C) point out which part of the preamble needs to be changed.
(D) add force to her argument.
(E) utilize a common legalistic trick.

17. According to this speech, one reason for forming the Union was to
(A) establish an aristocracy.
(B) limit the powers of the states.
(C) insure domestic harmony.
(D) draw up a Constitution.
(E) provide an international power.

18. Anthony argues that a government that denies women the right to vote is not a democracy because its powers do not come from
(A) the Constitution of the United States.
(B) the rights of the states.
(C) the consent of the governed.
(D) the vote of the majority.
(E) both houses of Congress.

19. According to this speech, an oligarchy of sex would cause
(A) women to rebel against the government.
(B) men to desert their families.
(C) poor women to lose hope.
(D) problems to develop in every home.
(E) the educated to rule the ignorant.

20. In this speech, a citizen is *defined* as a person who has the right to vote and also the right to
(A) change laws.
(B) acquire wealth.
(C) speak publicly.
(D) hold office.
(E) pay taxes.

21. Anthony argues that state laws that discriminate against women are
(A) being changed.
(B) null and void.
(C) helpful to the rich.
(D) supported only by men.
(E) supported by the Constitution.

QUESTIONS 22–26 ARE BASED ON THE FOLLOWING PASSAGE.

The Indianists were musicians who borrowed freely from Native American motifs, rhythms, and musical structures to create a style of music that was unique. The passage outlines a history of this movement.

In the late nineteenth and early twentieth centuries, Euro-American composers known as the "Indianist" school chose and adapted elements of Indian song for their own work.
5 Certain elements of Indian song styles could easily be used by these American-born but typically European-trained composers; other elements were not assimilated so easily into musical structures built on harmony and
10 into a musical aesthetic that preferred an open-throated singing style. For example, a choral setting of the "Navajo War Dance," composed by Arthur Farwell (1872–1952), does not give the illusion of being an actual
15 Navajo song. But the elements of Navajo style that caught Farwell's attention are clear: the sparse sound (few harmonies), the typical Navajo melodic skips, the pulsing beat.

Farwell got his ideas about Indian music
20 from visits to southwestern reservations and from studying transcriptions of melodies collected by Alice Fletcher, a noted scholar of Omaha ceremonial traditions. Other composers also borrowed material from
25 Fletcher's collections. The opening motif and basic melodic outline for perhaps the most famous Indianist composition, Charles Wakefield Cadman's "From the Land of the Sky Blue Waters" (published in 1901), are
30 fairly literal reproductions of an Omaha flute call and love song in Fletcher's collection. But, unlike Farwell, Cadman did not try to replicate Indian sounds. He embedded the tune in pure Euro-American harmonic
35 structures and rhythms. What seems more "Indian" is the song's narrative, describing a fearless captive maid courted by a flute player.

It is the text that marks many Indianist com-
40 positions, but the words do not usually reflect direct tribal experience. The Indianists were Romantics who seized on universal themes of love, war and death cloaked in American Indian dress. One could not know from these
45 compositions that native peoples had an everyday world of work, education, child-bearing, and food preparation. The images selected for Indianist compositions are just that: selections from a much broader array
50 of experiences.

As the Indianist composers selected sounds from or notions about Native American music for their purposes, native groups chose and adapted items from Euro-American
55 musical practice. For example, while many drum groups use a wooden drum covered with rawhide, others choose a Western-style bass drum turned on its side; in its decoration and use, it becomes a Native American
60 instrument. Similarly, many Canadian and Alaskan indigenous people have adopted the fiddle as a means of cultural self-expression. This adaptation reflects Euro-American influence, but native traditions are also
65 represented, for example, in the way songs are introduced, typically identifying the occasion for the song's composition, and in accompanying activities, such as community feasts.

70 Perhaps the most far-reaching result of European contact is the development of a pantribal style. The very concept of "American Indian" is probably a product of contact. Though there were tribal confed-
75 eracies prior to contact with Europeans, there was no need for an identity that spanned a continent to include tribal neighbors, rivals, and strangers—and no outside view to lump together people as diverse as the Kwakiutl,
80 the Hopi, the Cuna, the Pawnee, and the Natchez. However, "American Indian" and "Native American" are now recognized concepts both inside and outside the societies so identified. Though tribal affiliation
85 is a primary source of identification for most individuals, sometimes the category "American Indian" takes precedence.

One drum group that includes Arizona Pima and Kansas Potawatomi singers, for
90 example, performs songs representative of the Northern Plains rather than of the Southwest or Central Plains. Indeed, the wide-range Northern Plains-style song has come to represent "American Indian" music.
95 Its characteristic forms, sung with tense throat and pulsating voice, make it most different from Euro-American singing, and the most difficult aural pattern for a non-Indian to assimilate, let alone replicate. By
100 differentiating as much as possible from the dominant culture, by staking out that which is most markedly unique and displaying it to the outside world, native musical groups that perform in the Northern Plains style
105 confirm their cultural identity.

22. In using and adapting Native American music, the Indianist composers attempted to

(A) reflect the gamut of Native American experiences.

(B) popularize Native American music among Euro-Americans.

(C) reproduce faithfully the style and content of the music they were copying.

(D) address universal concerns using Native American motifs.

(E) indicate their appreciation of the musical form.

23. According to the passage, both Arthur Farwell and Charles Wakefield Cadman

(A) studied with Native American musicians.

(B) attempted to reproduce Native American harmonies and rhythms.

(C) used material from Alice Fletcher's collections.

(D) studied musical composition in Europe.

(E) adapted Native American melodies to European harmonies.

24. The use of a Western-style drum by some Native American drum groups is an example of how some Native Americans have

(A) put aside their own traditions in favor of Euro-American forms of cultural expression.

(B) adopted some Euro-American material goods, but not other aspects of Euro-American culture.

(C) borrowed aspects of European culture and adapted these aspects to their own use.

(D) adapted to the scarcity of traditional instruments by using instruments that are more readily available.

(E) indicated an inclination to embrace more and more Western forms.

25. The "development of a pantribal style" of music (lines 71–72) is an example of the way in which

(A) cultural groups select and adapt aspects of each other's culture when two groups meet.

(B) Native American groups formed tribal confederacies to resist the advance of the Europeans.

(C) tribal identification transcends musical style.

(D) members of the Pima and Potawatomi peoples have learned to work together.

(E) a group's culture can be modified when the group meets another cultural group.

26. According to the passage, the Northern Plains–style music has come to stand for Native American music in general because

(A) the Northern Plains style is so different from Euro-American musical styles that it sets the singers clearly apart as Native Americans.

(B) Europeans, when they first heard Northern Plains–style music, wrongly assumed that it was representative of all Native American music.

(C) Northern Plains–style music is more easily comprehended and enjoyed by Euro-Americans than most other styles of Native American music.

(D) Northern Plains tribes are predominant among Native American tribes today.

(E) Northern Plains music has been the most widely distributed music.

STOP

END OF SECTION 2. IF YOU HAVE ANY TIME LEFT, GO OVER YOUR WORK IN THIS SECTION ONLY. DO NOT WORK IN ANY OTHER SECTION OF THE TEST.

Section 3

20 Questions • 25 Minutes

Directions: Solve the following problems using any available space on the page for scratchwork. On your answer sheet, fill in the choice that best corresponds to the correct answer.

Notes: The figures accompanying the problems are drawn as accurately as possible unless otherwise stated in specific problems. Again, unless otherwise stated, all figures lie in the same plane. All numbers used in these problems are real numbers. Calculators are permitted for this test.

Circle: Rectangle: Rectangular Solid: Cylinder: Triangle:

$C = 2\pi r$
$A = \pi r^2$
$A = lw$
$V = lwh$
$V = \pi r^2 h$
$A = \frac{1}{2}bh$
$a^2 + b^2 = c^2$

The number of degrees of arc in a circle is 360.
The measure in degrees of a straight angle is 180.
The sum of the measures in degrees of the angles of a triangle is 180.

1. If $3x + 2 > 2x + 7$, then x is
   (A) 5
   (B) < 5
   (C) > 5
   (D) < 1
   (E) < -1

2. If $x \neq \frac{2}{3}$, then $\dfrac{6x^2 - 13x + 6}{3x - 2} =$
   (A) $3x - 2$
   (B) $3x - 3$
   (C) $2x - 6$
   (D) $2x - 3$
   (E) $2x2 + 3x - 3$

3. What is the length of $\overline{AC}$?

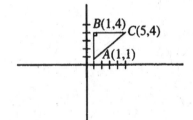

   (A) $2\frac{1}{2}$
   (B) 5
   (C) 7
   (D) 11
   (E) 25

4. If 3! means $3 \bullet 2 \bullet 1$ and 4! means $4 \bullet 3 \bullet 2 \bullet 1$, then what does $\dfrac{8!}{9!}$ equal?
   (A) 9
   (B) $\dfrac{8}{9}$
   (C) $\dfrac{1}{9}$
   (D) $\dfrac{1}{89}$
   (E) 0

5. If a distance estimated at 150 feet is really 140 feet, what is the percent of error in this estimate?
   (A) 10%
   (B) $7\frac{1}{7}\%$
   (C) $6\frac{2}{3}\%$
   (D) 1%
   (E) 0.71%

6. There are x cookies in a cookie jar. One child eats $\frac{1}{4}$ of all the cookies. A second child eats $\frac{1}{3}$ of the remaining cookies. If the remaining cookies are distributed among four other children, what fraction of the original number of cookies did each of the four children receive?
   (A) $\frac{7}{12}$
   (B) $\frac{1}{2}$
   (C) $\frac{5}{12}$
   (D) $\frac{1}{6}$
   (E) $\frac{1}{8}$

7. If $|2y-4|=6$, $y=$
   (A) $-5, 1$
   (B) -8
   (C) $-4, 3$
   (D) $5, -1$
   (E) 0

8. Given the system of equations $3x + 2y = 4$ and $6x - 3y = 6$, what does y equal?
   (A) 14
   (B) $\frac{14}{6}$
   (C) 2
   (D) $\frac{11}{7}$
   (E) $\frac{2}{7}$

9. If the radius of a circle is diminished by 20%, the area is diminished by
   (A) 20%.
   (B) 36%.
   (C) 40%.
   (D) 64%.
   (E) 400%.

10. If $x - y = 10$ and $x + y = 20$, then what is the value of $x^2 - y^2$?
    (A) 400
    (B) 200
    (C) 100
    (D) 30
    (E) It cannot be determined from the information given.

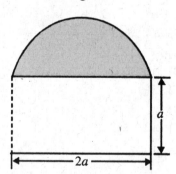

11. A semicircle surmounts a rectangle whose length is $2a$ and whose width is a, as shown in the above diagram. A formula for finding the area of the whole figure is
    (A) $2a^2 + \dfrac{\pi a^2}{2}$
    (B) $2\pi a^2$
    (C) $3\pi a^2$
    (D) $2a^2 + \pi a^2$
    (E) $2a^2 + 2\pi a^2$

12. An airplane flies 550 yards in 3 seconds. What is the speed of the airplane, expressed in miles per hour? (5,280 ft. = 1 mi.)

(A) 1125
(B) 375
(C) 300
(D) 125
(E) 90

13. Given that 1 meter = 3.28 ft., the distance run in a 100-meter race most closely approximates to

(A) 100 yards.
(B) 90 yards.
(C) 105 yards.
(D) 110 yards.
(E) 103 yards.

14. Of the following sets of fractions, which set is arranged in increasing order?

(A) $\dfrac{7}{12}, \dfrac{6}{11}, \dfrac{3}{5}, \dfrac{5}{8}$

(B) $\dfrac{6}{11}, \dfrac{7}{12}, \dfrac{5}{8}, \dfrac{3}{5}$

(C) $\dfrac{6}{11}, \dfrac{7}{12}, \dfrac{3}{5}, \dfrac{5}{8}$

(D) $\dfrac{3}{5}, \dfrac{5}{8}, \dfrac{6}{11}, \dfrac{7}{12}$

(E) $\dfrac{7}{12}, \dfrac{6}{11}, \dfrac{5}{8}, \dfrac{3}{5}$

15. If one pipe can fill a tank in $1\dfrac{1}{2}$ hours and another can fill the same tank in 45 minutes, then how many hours will it take the two pipes to fill the tank if they are working together?

(A) $\dfrac{1}{3}$

(B) $\dfrac{1}{2}$

(C) $\dfrac{5}{6}$

(D) 1

(E) $1\dfrac{1}{2}$

16. If the sum of the lengths of the edges of a cube is 48 inches, the volume of the cube in cubic inches is

(A) 64.
(B) 96.
(C) 149.
(D) 512.
(E) 1728.

17. If the length of each side of a square is $\dfrac{2x}{3} + 1$, what is the perimeter of the square?

(A) $\dfrac{8x+4}{3}$

(B) $\dfrac{8x+12}{3}$

(C) $\dfrac{2x}{3} + 4$

(D) $\dfrac{2x}{3} + 16$

(E) $\dfrac{4x}{3} + 2$

18. If $g(2) = -10$, and $g(-3) = 0$, which of the following could be the function $g(x)$?

(A) $g(x) = 3x + 9$

(B) $g(x) = 5x - 20$

(C) $g(x) = x2 - x - 12$

(D) $g(x) = x2 + x - 12$

(E) $g(x) = x2 - x + 12$

19. In the diagram below, $ABCD$ is a rectangle, and point E is on line segment $\overline{BC}$. If a point is selected at random from the interior of the rectangle $ABCD$, what is the probability that the point will also be in the shaded area?

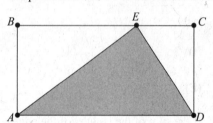

(A) $\dfrac{2}{5}$

(B) $\dfrac{1}{2}$

(C) $\dfrac{3}{5}$

(D) $\dfrac{2}{3}$

(E) It cannot be determined from the information given.

20. Which of the following describes the range of the function $p(x) = \sqrt{12x - 7} - 6$?

(A) All real numbers

(B) All real numbers less than 6 $\dfrac{7}{12}$

(C) All real numbers greater than

(D) All real numbers greater than -6

(E) All real numbers greater than or equal to -6

STOP

END OF SECTION 3. IF YOU HAVE ANY TIME LEFT, GO OVER YOUR WORK IN THIS SECTION ONLY. DO NOT WORK IN ANY OTHER SECTION OF THE TEST.

Section 4

35 Questions • 25 Minutes

Directions: Some of the sentences below contain an error in grammar, usage, word choice, or idiom. Other sentences are correct. Parts of each sentence are underlined and lettered. The error, if there is one, is contained in one of the underlined parts of the sentence. Assume that all other parts of the sentence are correct and cannot be changed. For each sentence, select the one underlined part that must be changed to make the sentence correct and mark its letter on your answer sheet. If there is no error in a sentence, mark answer space E. No sentence contains more than one error.

Being that it's such a lovely day, we
     A   B

are having a difficult time concentrating
     C   D

on our assignment. No error
                        E

The correct answer is (A).

1. When she graduates college, she will have
                 A   B
   to decide whether to continue her studies
                 C
   or seek employment. No error
        D   E

2. Farmers predicted that if the drought
               A   B
   lasted another week half the wheat crop
                        C
   was lost. No error
     D   E

3. When my grandfather comes to visit us,
                         A   B
   he takes off his shoes and sets in the easy
                               C   D
   chair all day. No error
                    E

4. It is all ready too late for us to do our
      A   B   C
   Christmas shopping in an uncrowded
                          D
   atmosphere. No error
                 E

5. Lacking the idiomatic vocabulary
   A
   necessary for true fluency, many students
                                B
   who study a foreign language in school
   are unable to converse comfortably in the
     C   D
   language. No error
              E

6. Judging from the beauty of the night, I
                    A
   believe that we are liable to have good
        B   C   D
   weather tomorrow. No error
                        E

7. Despite them being abundant, cheap,
           A   B
   and rich in protein, mussels are not
       C
   a favorite dish of most Americans.
       D
   No error
   E

8. If it is not watered today, one of the
   A
   prettiest plants on the windowsill are
     B   C   D
   going to die. No error
                  E

9. The word *atom* in Greek means "not
   divisible" because it was once belief
     A   B   C
   that the atom was the smallest possible
                                    D
   unit of matter. No error
                     E

10. Before they could <u>adjourn</u> <u>for the day</u>
                          A   B
they <u>must</u> consider the <u>group's</u> petition.
     C   D
<u>No error</u>
   E

11. The children <u>who</u> I <u>observed</u> at the
                 A   B
theater seemed <u>enchanted</u> by the <u>antics</u>
               C   D
of the puppets. <u>No error</u>
                   E

12. Most animals cannot recognize <u>their</u>
                                   A
reflection in a mirror <u>as themselves</u>; they
                       B
usually react <u>as if</u> confronted by another
              C
member of <u>their species</u>. <u>No error</u>
          D   E

13. Of the two candidates applying for the
<u>position</u> , we have <u>no doubt</u> that Jim is
A   B
<u>likely</u> to be the <u>most favored</u>. <u>No error</u>
C   D   E

14. There are <u>less</u> workers today in
              A
<u>rural areas</u> <u>than</u> there <u>were</u> a decade
B   C   D
ago. <u>No error</u>
        E

15. She is exactly the <u>kind of person</u> <u>who</u>
                       A   B
should be chosen for the position of
<u>discussion leader,</u> since she thinks clearly
C
and has a good <u>academic background</u>.
                          D
<u>No error</u>
   E

16. He <u>looked</u> <u>like</u> he <u>had seen</u> a ghost
       A   B   C
<u>when</u> his father entered the room.
D
<u>No error</u>
   E

17. I really appreciated <u>the fact</u> that you
                         A
made a special trip <u>just</u> <u>to bring</u> the
                    B   C
flowers to my mother and <u>I</u>. <u>No error</u>
                         D   E

18. The inhabitants of Pompeii in the
<u>first century A.D.</u> did not realize that the
A
high incidence of earthquakes in the area
<u>were</u> the warning sign of a <u>much greater</u>
B   C
disaster—the <u>eruption</u> of Vesuvius.
              D
<u>No error</u>
   E

19. I <u>use</u> to be a pretty good mechanic, but
     A
lately I <u>haven't</u> had the time to get my
         B
hands dirty working <u>on my car</u>—or
                    C
<u>even</u> on my toaster. <u>No error</u>
D   E

20. We were asked, indeed <u>required,</u> to tell
                                    A
the <u>honest truth</u> before the jury or else we
    B
might <u>well</u> have been accused of
      C
<u>having committed</u> perjury. <u>No error</u>
D   E

Directions: The sentences below may contain problems in grammar, usage, word choice, sentence construction, or punctuation. Part or all of each sentence is underlined. Following each sentence you will find five ways of expressing the underlined part. Answer choice (A) always repeats the original underlined section. The other four answer choices are all different. You are to select the lettered answer that produces the most effective sentence. If you think the original sentence is best, choose (A) as your answer. If one of the other choices makes a better sentence, mark your answer sheet for the letter of that choice. Do not choose an answer that changes the meaning of the original sentence.

I have always enjoyed singing as well as to dance.

(A) singing as well as to dance
(B) singing as well as dancing
(C) to sing as well as dancing
(D) singing in addition to dance
(E) to sing in addition to dancing

The correct answer is (B).

21. The committee requested that there be input from all the staff before taking a vote.
    (A) from all the staff before taking a vote
    (B) from all the staff taking a vote
    (C) before the staff took a vote on the input
    (D) from all the staff before having taken a vote
    (E) from all the staff who would take a vote

22. She could not scarcely but be affected by the plight of the homeless.
    (A) not scarcely but be affected
    (B) hardly help being effected
    (C) not help being affected
    (D) not help being effected
    (E) not scarcely be affected

23. With regards to examining the union contract, the staff spent several days discussing the various sections and then voted on it.
    (A) With regards to examining the union contract, the staff spent several days discussing the various sections and then voted on it.
    (B) As concerns the contract, the staff spent several days on a discussion that resulted in a vote.
    (C) An examination of the contract resulted in several days of voting and discussing the various sections.
    (D) After several days of discussing the various sections of the union contract, the staff voted on it.
    (E) A vote followed a discussion of the union contract by the staff which examined the sections and followed it with a vote.

24. There are, of course, three possible alternatives that we have in order to reach an equitable solution.
    (A) are, of course, three possible alternatives
    (B) is, of course three possible alternatives
    (C) are, of course, three possible choices
    (D) are of course three possible alternatives
    (E) are of course three possible choices

25. <u>In the dictionary, it indicates</u> how words should be pronounced.

    (A) In the dictionary, it indicates

    (B) In the dictionary, it has

    (C) The dictionary indicates

    (D) There in the dictionary, it indicates

    (E) In the dictionary, it has an indication

26. The actor <u>was apparently unaware or unconcerned by the small audience</u>.

    (A) was apparently unaware or unconcerned by the small audience

    (B) was apparently unaware or unconcerned, by the small audience

    (C) was not aware or unconcerned by the small audience

    (D) seemed to ignore the fact that there was a small audience

    (E) was apparently unaware of or unconcerned by the small audience

27. The main pipe broke, and they were without water for a <u>week, which created many problems for them</u>.

    (A) week, which created many problems for them

    (B) week; this situation created many problems for them

    (C) week; which situation created many problems for them

    (D) week, which is creating many problems for them

    (E) week, this created many problems for them

28. If we ever have the watch <u>inscribed: we will ask the jewelers</u> to use italic lettering for the quotation.

    (A) inscribed; we will ask the jewelers

    (B) inscribed; we'll ask the jeweler's

    (C) inscribed, we will ask the jewelers

    (D) inscribed, we will ask the jewelers'

    (E) inscribed, we will ask for the jewelers

29. <u>No one, including Walter and I. have</u> the ability to cash this check for her.

    (A) No one, including Walter and I, have

    (B) No one, including Walter and I, had

    (C) No one, including Walter and me, have

    (D) No one, including Walter and me, has

    (E) No one including Walter and me, has

Directions: Questions 30–35 are based on a passage that might be an early draft of a student's essay. Some sentences in this draft need to be revised or rewritten to make them both clear and correct. Read the passage carefully; then answer the questions that follow it. Some questions require decisions about diction, usage, tone, or sentence structure in particular sentences or parts of sentences. Other questions require decisions about organization, development, or appropriateness of language in the essay as a whole. For each question, choose the answer that makes the intended meaning clearer and more precise and that follows the conventions of Standard Written English.

(1) When my family came to the United States to live, we spoke no English. (2) My parents luckily got a job and my sister and I were very young and we did what many other immigrant children did. (3) We learned English in public school and learned our native language and culture at home with our family. (4) It was not long before we all realized that success in the United States would depend on our ability to be fluent in English.

(5) Because of my own case I think that bilingual education is not as good as English in school, native language at home. (6) But I know of other people who found a bilingual education to be just what they needed, in fact it was essential to their progress since their English was so limited. (7) However, some people I knew did drop out of school later on. (8) Some of them had been labeled learning-disabled. (9) It was really just a language problem. (10) And some of my friends' parents felt that their children's bilingual education was ineffective or harmful, while others felt it was very good for them.

(11) As a result, I cannot decide for certain whether English is being taught better to foreigners today than it was in the past. (12) But I think that I would like to see small groups of non-native speakers taught in English. (13) Then I would like them to be moved into regular classrooms as soon as possible. (14) In that way, I think they would be best served. (15) Perhaps that would be one way to solve the problem of how to help them to succeed in school and in their life in the United States.

30. Which of the following is the best way to revise sentence (2)?

(A) My parents luckily got a job. My sister and I were young. We did what many other immigrated children did.

(B) My parents luckily got a job and my sister and I were very young so we did what many other immigrants did.

(C) My parents got jobs, luckily; my very young sister and I did what many others did.

(D) Luckily, my parents got jobs. My sister and I, who were very young, did what many other immigrant children did.

(E) Luckily, my parents got jobs and my sister and I were very young. We did what many other immigrant children did.

31. Which of the following is the best way to revise sentence (5)?

    (A) Because of my own experience, I think that a bilingual education is not as good as learning English in school and the family's native language at home.

    (B) In my own case, bilingual education is not so good as English in school and native language at home.

    (C) I think than because of my own experience, English in school, native language at home is better than bilingual education.

    (D) As a result of my own case, I think that bilingual education is not as good as students who learn English in school and their native language at home.

    (E) Because of my own case, I consider bilingual education less effective than learning English in school and their native language at home.

32. Which of the following is the best revision of the underlined portion of sentence (6) below?

    But I know of other people who found a bilingual education to be just what they needed, in fact it was essential to their progress since their English was so limited.

    (A) needed; in fact it being essential

    (B) needed, being that it was essential

    (C) needed; in fact it was essential

    (D) needed; essential as it was in fact

    (E) needed. In fact essential

33. Which of the following is the best way to combine sentences (8) and (9)?

    (A) Although it was really just a language problem; some had been labeled learning-disabled.

    (B) Some of them were labeled learning-disabled, it was really just a language problem.

    (C) Some of them had been labeled learning-disabled, even though what they really had was a language problem.

    (D) Some of them were learning-disabled with a language problem.

    (E) Some of them had a language problem that made them learning-disabled.

34. Which of the following is the best revision of sentence (10)?

    (A) Some of my friends' parents felt that their children's bilingual education was ineffective or harmful, while others felt it was very good for them.

    (B) Some felt that their child's bilingual education was ineffective or harmful, but other of my friends' parents felt it was very good for them.

    (C) Though some of my friends' parents felt it was very good for them, some felt that bilingual education was ineffective or harmful.

    (D) Although some of my friends' parents felt it was very good, some felt that their children's bilingual education was ineffective or harmful.

    (E) Ineffective or harmful though it may have been to some, others of my friends' parents felt that their children's bilingual education has been very good.

35. Which of the following would be the best way to improve the last paragraph?

    (A) To incorporate transitional words or phrases

    (B) To eliminate the specious argument presented

    (C) To present a more personal point of view

    (D) To adopt a less sympathetic tone

    (E) To be more exact and concise in wording

STOP

END OF SECTION 4. IF YOU HAVE ANY TIME LEFT, GO OVER YOUR WORK IN THIS SECTION ONLY. DO NOT WORK IN ANY OTHER SECTION OF THE TEST.

Section 5

20 Questions • 25 Minutes

Directions: Solve the following problems using any available space on the page for scratchwork. On your answer sheet, fill in the choice that best corresponds to the correct answer.

Notes: The figures accompanying the problems are drawn as accurately as possible unless otherwise stated in specific problems. Again, unless otherwise stated, all figures lie in the same plane. All numbers used in these problems are real numbers. Calculators are permitted for this test.

    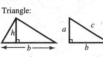

Reference Information

| Circle: | Rectangle: | Rectangular Solid: | Cylinder: | Triangle: |

$C = 2\pi r$
$A = \pi r^2$

$A = lw$

$V = lwh$

$V = \pi r^2 h$

$A = \frac{1}{2} bh$

$a^2 + b^2 = c^2$

The number of degrees of arc in a circle is 360.
The measure in degrees of a straight angle is 180.
The sum of the measures in degrees of the angles of a triangle is 180.

1. In the pentagon shown below, what is the maximum number of different diagonals that can be drawn?

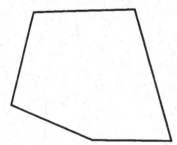

(A) 3
(B) 4
(C) 5
(D) 6
(E) 8

2. If $4x = 2(2 + x)$ and $6y = 3(2 + y)$, then $2x + 3y =$

(A) 2.
(B) 4.
(C) 8.
(D) 10.
(E) 12.

3. If J is the set of all numbers between 31 and 59 that are divisible by 3, and K is the set of all numbers between 31 and 59 that are divisible by 5, how many elements are there in the set $J \cup K$?

(A) 1
(B) 5
(C) 9
(D) 13
(E) 14

4. If $h(x) = x^2 - 8x + 7$, determine all of the values of x for which $h(x) = -8$.

(A) $x = -3$
(B) $x = 3$
(C) $x = 5$
(D) $x = -3$ and -5
(E) $x = 3$ and 5

5. If $f(x) = 5x^{-\frac{3}{2}}$, what is the value of $f(25)$?
   (A) 0.04
   (B) 0.02
   (C) 4
   (D) 25
   (E) 125

6. Line $a\|b$, while d is the distance between a and b at points C and D.

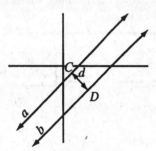

   The length of segment d
   (A) steadily increases as it is moved along lines a and b to the right.
   (B) steadily decreases as it is moved toward the left.
   (C) fluctuates in both directions.
   (D) remains constant.
   (E) None of the above

7. $(x + 9)(x + 2) =$
   (A) $x2 + 18$
   (B) $11x$
   (C) $x2 + 11$
   (D) $x2 + 11x + 18$
   (E) $9(x + 2) + 2(x + 9)$

8. The points $(3,1)$ and $(5,y)$ are $\sqrt{13}$ units apart. What does y equal?
   (A) -3
   (B) 4
   (C) $\sqrt{17}$
   (D) 10
   (E) 17

9. In a baseball game, a pitcher needs to throw nine strikes to complete an inning. If a pitcher is able to throw strikes on 85% of his pitches, how many pitches to the nearest whole number would it take for him to throw the necessary number of strikes for a nine-inning game?
   (A) 95
   (B) 97
   (C) 103
   (D) 105
   (E) 111

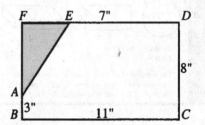

   Note: Figure not drawn to scale.

10. Triangle AFE is cut from the rectangle as shown in the figure above. The area of the remaining polygon $ABCDE$ in square inches is
    (A) 29.
    (B) 68.
    (C) 78.
    (D) 88.
    (E) 98.

Student-Produced Response Questions

Directions: Solve each of these problems. Write the answer in the corresponding grid on the answer sheet and fill in the ovals beneath each answer you write. Here are some examples.

Answer: $\frac{3}{4} = .75$; **show answer either way**   **Answer: 325**

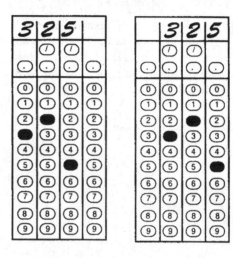

Note: A mixed number such as $3\frac{1}{2}$ must be gridded as 7/2 or as 3.5. If gridded as "3 1/2," it will be read as "thirty-one halves."

Note: Either position is correct.

11. Let the "JOSH" of a number be defined as three less than three times the number. What number is equal to its "JOSH"?

12. Machine A produces flue covers at a uniform rate of 2000 per hour. Machine B produces flue covers at a uniform rate of 5000 in $2\frac{1}{2}$ hours. After $7\frac{1}{4}$ hours, Machine A has produced how many more flue covers than Machine B?

13. 0.01 is the ratio of 0.1 to what number?

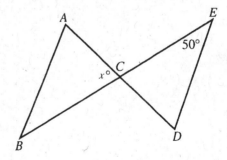

Note: Figure not drawn to scale.

14. In the figure above, *AB* is parallel to *ED* and *AC* = *BC*. If angle *E* is 50°, then what does *x* equal?

15. At NJL High School, $\frac{1}{4}$ of the school's population are seniors, $\frac{1}{5}$ are juniors, and $\frac{1}{3}$ are sophomores. If there are 390 freshmen, what is the total school population?

16. From the town of Williston Park to Albertson there are 3 different roads. From the town of Albertson to Mineola there are 5 routes. How many different paths are there to go from Williston Park to Mineola through Albertson?

17. If 12 candies cost $1.70, how many of these candies can be bought for $10.20?

18. Two roads intersect at right angles. A pole is 30 meters from one road and 40 meters from the other road. How far (in meters) is the pole from the point where the roads intersect?

19. If T is the set of all integers between 10 and 99 that are perfect squares, and S is the set of all integers between 10 and 99 that are perfect cubes, how many elements are there in the set $S \cap T$?

20. If $\dfrac{1}{t+2} + \dfrac{1}{t-2} = \dfrac{10}{t^2-4}$, what is the value of t?

STOP

END OF SECTION 5. IF YOU HAVE ANY TIME LEFT, GO OVER YOUR WORK IN THIS SECTION ONLY. DO NOT WORK IN ANY OTHER SECTION OF THE TEST.

Section 6
26 Questions • 25 Minutes

Directions: Each of the following questions consists of an incomplete sentence followed by five words or pairs of words. Choose the word or pair of words that, when substituted for the blank space or spaces, best completes the meaning of the sentence and mark the letter of your choice on your answer sheet.

In view of the extenuating circumstances and the defendant's youth, the judge recommended ___.

(A) conviction

(B) a defense

(C) a mistrial

(D) leniency

(E) life imprisonment

The correct answer is (D).

1. The society was not ____ and required much outside aid.
   (A) destitute
   (B) self-sufficient
   (C) democratic
   (D) impoverished
   (E) benevolent

2. The new regime immediately ____ laws implementing the promised reforms.
   (A) vouchsafed
   (B) ensconced
   (C) augmented
   (D) promulgated
   (E) parlayed

3. The machines were ____, and because of the below-zero temperature, it was feared they would ____.
   (A) frozen .. dehydrate
   (B) brittle .. shatter
   (C) frosty .. slide
   (D) icy .. capsize
   (E) shiny .. expand

4. A long illness can ____ even the strongest constitution.
   (A) obviate
   (B) inculcate
   (C) bolster
   (D) enervate
   (E) disparage

5. With ____ attention to detail, the careful researcher churned out his reports.
   (A) prosaic
   (B) painless
   (C) meticulous
   (D) appealing
   (E) atypical

6. A shy look from the beautiful Laura ____ him, and soon they were married.
   (A) released
   (B) controlled
   (C) enchanted
   (D) ensconced
   (E) jilted

7. The city _____ to the advancing invaders without firing a single shot.

(A) extolled

(B) regressed

(C) equivocated

(D) dissembled

(E) capitulated

8. When the two opposing sides failed to reach a _____, the long-anticipated strike became _____.

(A) consensus .. impossible

(B) transition .. general

(C) compromise .. inevitable

(D) rationale .. culpable

(E) precedent .. potential

Directions: The reading passages below are followed by sets of questions. Read the passages and answer the accompanying questions, basing your answers on what is stated or implied in the passage. Mark the letter of your choice on your answer sheet.

QUESTIONS 9 AND 10 ARE BASED ON THE FOLLOWING PASSAGE.

Born in New Orleans in 1829, Louis Moreau Gottshalk was a gifted pianist and a successful composer. Gottshalk drew on the African and Creole traditions of New
5 Orleans and was also inspired by Spanish themes. His five years in Puerto Rico produced such works as *Souvenir de Porto Rico* and *Night in the Tropics*. He once wrote, "Every evening I moved my piano out upon
10 the terrace, . . . in view of the most beautiful scenery in the world, . . . bathed by the serene and limpid atmosphere of the tropics, I played, for myself alone, everything that the scene opened up before me inspired. . .
15 it was there that I composed [*Souvenir de Porto Rico*]."

9. The phrase "everything that the scene opened up before me inspired" (lines 13–14) refers to

(A) the awareness of beauty that the scene called forth in Gottshalk.

(B) the ideas and feelings that Gottshalk became aware of as he played the piano on his terrace.

(C) an overflowing of feelings.

(D) the way the setting brought forth ideas in him for new musical compositions.

(E) the music that Gottshalk played in this setting.

10. The mood of Gottshalk's quotation is

(A) elegiac.

(B) evocative.

(C) mournful.

(D) nostalgic.

(E) informative.

QUESTIONS 11 AND 12 ARE BASED ON THE FOLLOWING PASSAGE.

A side effect of chemotherapy is that healthy tissue as well as diseased tissue can be destroyed. Cancer drugs of the future may be able to target just the diseased cells.
5 These drugs go after the epidermal growth factor receptor (EGFR) in cancer cells. This protein enables the cells to spread quickly. However, research so far on drugs specifically developed to inhibit EGFR has been
10 disappointing. The one exception has been lung cancer. Two new drugs seem to work on people with a mutation in EGFR in some cancer cells. Patients with this mutation had very aggressive cancer, but the cancer
15 reacted to the new drug. The patients were not cured, but their lives were prolonged.

11. The purpose of the new drugs is to

(A) inhibit damage to healthy tissue.

(B) kill only tumors.

(C) go after mutated EGFR.

(D) cause the mutation of EGFR.

(E) kill aggressive cancer.

12. A good title for this passage would be
    (A) "Lung Cancers React to Targeted Drugs."
    (B) "Mutations Can Be Good News."
    (C) "Future Cancer Drugs May Be More Selective."
    (D) "Disappointing Developments in Fighting Cancer."
    (E) "EGFR—the Key to Cancer Therapy."

QUESTIONS 13 AND 14 ARE BASED ON THE FOLLOWING PASSAGE.

The extremely cold weather this winter has dangerously depleted our supplies of natural gas and fuel oil . . . I congratulate the Congress for its quick action on the Emergency
5 Natural Gas Act, ... But the real problem . . . started long before this winter. . . . The amount of energy being wasted . . . is greater than the total energy that we are importing . . . . We must face the fact that
10 the energy short-age is permanent. There is no way we can solve it quickly. But if we all cooperate and make modest sacrifices, if we learn to live thriftily . . . we can find ways to adjust and to make our society more
15 efficient and our own lives more enjoyable and productive.

—President Jimmy Carter,
State of the Union Address, 1977

13. The implied purpose of this speech was to
    (A) inform the American public of certain facts.
    (B) dispel misinformation about the nature of the energy problem.
    (C) rally the public to take action.
    (D) establish the president's energy agenda.
    (E) thank Congress for its action.

14. Which of the following is a desired outcome that the president states in his speech?
    (A) A decrease in imported oil will occur.
    (B) People will learn to cooperate.
    (C) People will learn to save.
    (D) Efficiency will be increased.
    (E) The energy shortage will become permanent.

QUESTIONS 15–26 ARE BASED ON THE FOLLOWING PASSAGE.

*Anton Chekhov is the Russian playwright responsible for some of our most enduring dramas—*The Sea Gull, The Cherry Orchard, Uncle Vanya, *and others. In this letter, he writes to another important playwright, Maxim Gorky, about Gorky's latest work.*

Moscow. Oct. 22, 1901

Five days have passed since I read your play (*The Petty Bourgeois*). I have not written to you till now because I could not get hold of the fourth act; I have kept waiting for it,
5 and—I have still not got it. And so I have read only three acts, but that I think is enough to judge of the play. It is, as I expected, very good, written á la Gorky, original, very interesting; and, to begin by talking of the
10 defects, I have noticed only one, a defect incorrigible as red hair in a red-haired man—the conservatism of the form. You make new and original people sing new songs to an accompaniment that looks second-hand;
15 you have four acts, the characters deliver edifying discourses, there is a feeling of alarm before long speeches, and so on, and so on. But all that is not important, and it is all, so to speak, drowned in the good points of the
20 play. Perchikhin—how living! His daughter is enchanting, Tatyana and Piotr also, and their mother is a splendid old woman. The central figure of the play, Nil, is vigorously drawn and extremely interesting! In fact,
25 the play takes hold of one from the first act. Only, God preserve you from letting anyone act Perchikhin except Artyom, while Alekseyev-Stanislavsky must certainly play Nil. Those two figures will do just what's
30 needed; Piotr—Meierkhold. Only, Nil's part, a wonderful part, must be made two or three times as long. You ought to end the play with it, to make it the leading part. Only, do not contrast him with Piotr and
35 Tatyana, let him be by himself and them by themselves, all wonderful, splendid people independent of one another. When Nil tries to seem superior to Piotr and Tatyana, and says of himself that he is a fine fellow—the
40 element so characteristic of our decent working man, the element of modesty, is

lost. He boasts, he argues, but you know
one can see what kind of man he is without
that. Let him be merry, let him play pranks
45 through the whole four acts, let him eat a
great deal after his work—and that will be
enough for him to conquer the audience with.
Piotr, I repeat, is good. Most likely you don't
even suspect how good he is. Tatyana, too,
50 is a finished figure, only,—(a) she ought
really to be a schoolmistress, ought to be
teaching children, ought to come home
from school, ought to be taken up with her
pupils and exercise-books, and—(b) it ought
55 to be mentioned in the first or second act
that she has attempted to poison herself;
then, after that hint, the poisoning in the
third act will not seem so startling and will
be more in place. Teterev talks too much:
60 such characters ought to be shown bit by bit
among others, for in any case such people are
everywhere merely incidental—both in life
and on the stage. Make Elena dine with all
the rest in the first act, let her sit and make
65 jokes, or else there is very little of her, and
she is not clear. . . .

15. By "á la Gorky" (line 8) Chekhov seems to
mean

(A) plagiarized from another playwright.

(B) in the manner of Maxim's father.

(C) quirky.

(D) fascinating and creative.

(E) full of defects.

16. The word *incorrigible* (line 11) means

(A) offensive.

(B) irreparable.

(C) pessimistic.

(D) alarming.

(E) impossible.

17. When Chekhov compares the book to the
red-haired man in line 11, his comments are

(A) inflammatory.

(B) pessimistic.

(C) harsh.

(D) supportive.

(E) condescending.

18. When Chekhov states that the "accompaniment looks second-hand" (line 14), he means
that

(A) the music should be rewritten.

(B) the minor characters are stereotypes.

(C) the play's form is old-fashioned.

(D) the very few new characters are
introduced.

(E) the set is shabby.

19. By "all that" in line 18, Chekhov is referring
to the

(A) dramatic highlights of the play.

(B) superior development of the play's
characters.

(C) work's traditional trappings.

(D) poor acting.

(E) bizarre elements of *The Petty
Bourgeois.*

20. When Chekhov refers to Perchikhin as "living" (line 20), he means that the character

(A) dies later in the act.

(B) seems authentic.

(C) is incredibly active.

(D) lives well.

(E) seethes with rage.

21. From the passage you can infer that Nil is most likely a(n)
    (A) intellectual.
    (B) ordinary working man.
    (C) aristocrat.
    (D) murderer.
    (E) revolutionary.

22. Chekhov objects to Nil's lack of
    (A) willpower.
    (B) contrast.
    (C) superiority.
    (D) modesty.
    (E) energy.

23. Chekhov's advice about Elena (lines 63–66) is meant to
    (A) elucidate her character.
    (B) startle Gorky.
    (C) remove her from the first act.
    (D) contrast her behavior with that of Nil.
    (E) lengthen the play.

24. The word *incidental* (line 62) means
    (A) insignificant.
    (B) accidental.
    (C) coincidental.
    (D) essential.
    (E) characteristic.

25. Chekhov expresses definite opinions on each of these points EXCEPT
    (A) who should play the part of Nil.
    (B) whose part should be extended.
    (C) what Tatyana should do for a living.
    (D) how Teterev's part should be cut.
    (E) how the third act should end.

26. Chekhov suggests change in all of the following characters EXCEPT
    (A) Tatyana.
    (B) Elena.
    (C) Nil.
    (D) Teterev.
    (E) Piotr.

STOP

END OF SECTION 6. IF YOU HAVE ANY TIME LEFT, GO OVER YOUR WORK IN THIS SECTION ONLY. DO NOT WORK IN ANY OTHER SECTION OF THE TEST.

Section 7
15 Questions • 20 Minutes

Directions: Solve the following problems using any available space on the page for scratch-work. On your answer sheet, fill in the choice that best corresponds to the correct answer.

Notes: The figures accompanying the problems are drawn as accurately as possible unless otherwise stated in specific problems. Again, unless otherwise stated, all figures lie in the same plane. All numbers used in these problems are real numbers. Calculators are permitted for this test.

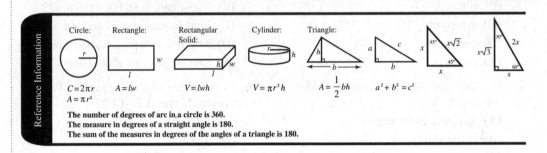

The number of degrees of arc in a circle is 360.
The measure in degrees of a straight angle is 180.
The sum of the measures in degrees of the angles of a triangle is 180.

1. If a triangle of base 7 is equal in area to a circle of radius 7, what is the altitude of the triangle?
   (A) 8π
   (B) 10π
   (C) 12π
   (D) 14π
   (E) It cannot be determined from the information given.

2. If the following numbers are arranged in order from the smallest to the largest, what will be their correct order?
   I. $\dfrac{9}{13}$
   II. $\dfrac{13}{9}$
   III. 70%
   IV. $\dfrac{1}{0.70}$

   (A) II, I, III, IV
   (B) III, II, I, IV
   (C) III, IV, I, II
   (D) II, IV, III, I
   (E) I, III, IV, II

3. The coordinates of the vertices of quadrilateral $PQRS$ are $P(0,0)$, $Q(9,0)$, $R(10,3)$, and $S(1,3)$, respectively. What is the area of $PQRS$?
   (A) $9\sqrt{10}$
   (B) $\dfrac{9}{2}\sqrt{10}$
   (C) $\dfrac{27}{2}$
   (D) 27
   (E) It cannot be determined from the information given.

4. If $8x + 4 = 64$, then $2x + 1 =$
   (A) 12
   (B) 13
   (C) 16
   (D) 24
   (E) 60

5. A circle whose radius is 7 has its center at the origin. Which of the following points are outside the circle?

    I. (4,4)

    II. (5,5)

    III. (4,5)

    IV. (4,6)

    (A) I and II only

    (B) II and III only

    (C) II, III, and IV only

    (D) II and IV only

    (E) III and IV only

6. What is the difference in area between a square with side = 9 and the surface area of a cube with edge = 3?

    (A) 516

    (B) 432

    (C) 72

    (D) 27

    (E) 18

7. A set of numbers is "quarked" if the sum of all the numbers in the set is evenly divisible by each of the numbers in the set. Which of the following sets is "quarked"?

    (A) (1, 3, 5, 7)

    (B) (4, 6, 8)

    (C) (6, 7, 8, 9)

    (D) (2, 4, 6)

    (E) (5, 10, 15, 20)

8. If $x \neq -2$, $\dfrac{3(x^2 - 4)}{x + 2} =$

    (A) $3x^2 + 4.$

    (B) $3x - 2.$

    (C) $3x - 2.$

    (D) $3x - 6.$

    (E) $3x + 6.$

9. An ice cream truck runs down a certain street 4 times a week. This truck carries 5 different flavors of ice cream bars, each of which comes in 2 different designs. Considering that the truck runs Monday through Thursday, and Monday was the first day of the month, by what day of the month could a person, buying one ice cream bar each truck run, purchase all the different varieties of ice cream bars?

    (A) 11th

    (B) 16th

    (C) 21st

    (D) 24th

    (E) 30th

10. If $N! = N(N - 1)(N - 2)\ldots[N - (N - 1)]$, what does $\dfrac{N!}{(N-2)!}$ equal?

    (A) $N2 - N$

    (B) $N^5 + N^3 - N^2 + \dfrac{N}{N^2}$

    (C) $N + 1$

    (D) 1

    (E) 6

11. Equilateral triangle ABC has a perpendicular line drawn from point A to point D. If the triangle is "folded over" on the perpendicular line so that points B and C meet, the perimeter of the new triangle is approximately what percent of the perimeter of the triangle before the fold?

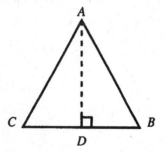

    (A) 100%

    (B) 78%

    (C) 50%

    (D) 32%

    (E) It cannot be determined from the information given.

12. To find the radius of a circle whose circumference is 60 inches,

   (A) multiply 60 by π.

   (B) divide 60 by 2π.

   (C) divide 30 by 2π.

   (D) divide 60 by π and extract the square root of the result.

   (E) multiply 60 by $\dfrac{\pi}{2}$.

13. If the outer diameter of a metal pipe is 2.84 inches and the inner diameter is 1.94 inches, what is the thickness of the metal in inches?

   (A) 0.45

   (B) 0.90

   (C) 1.42

   (D) 1.94

   (E) 2.39

14. The function $f(x) = \dfrac{8x - 24}{(3x - 7)^2}$ is defined for all real numbers EXCEPT

   (A) 3

   (B) 3 and $\dfrac{7}{3}$

   (C) $-\dfrac{7}{3}$

   (D) $\dfrac{7}{3}$

   (E) $-\dfrac{7}{3}$ and 3

15. If $P = \{2, 3, 5\}$, $Q = \{5, 10, 15\}$, and $R = \{2, 5, 15, 25\}$, which of the following sets represents $P \cap Q \cap R$?

   (A) $\{5\}$

   (B) $\{2, 5\}$

   (C) $\{2, 5, 10\}$

   (D) $\{2, 5, 15\}$

   (E) $\{2, 3, 5, 10, 15, 25\}$

STOP

END OF SECTION 7. IF YOU HAVE ANY TIME LEFT, GO OVER YOUR WORK IN THIS SECTION ONLY. DO NOT WORK IN ANY OTHER SECTION OF THE TEST.

Section 8

16 Questions • 20 Minutes

Directions: The two passages given below deal with a related topic. Following the passages are questions about the content of each passage or about the relationship between the two passages. Answer the questions based upon what is stated or implied in the passages and in any introductory material provided. Mark the letter of your choice on your answer sheet.

QUESTIONS 1–4 ARE BASED ON THE FOLLOWING PASSAGES.

The following passages provide two viewpoints on the controversy over civil service reform in the late 1800s.

Passage 1

What Civil Service reform demands, is simply that the business part of the Government shall be carried on in a sound businesslike . . . manner. . . . The spoils
5 system, which practice which turns public offices, high and low, from public trusts into objects of prey and booty for the victorious party, may without extravagance of language be called one of the greatest criminals in
10 our history. . . . It tends to divert our whole political life from its true aims. It teaches men to seek something else in politics than the public good.

—Carl Shurz

Passage 2

The Senator . . . praises the civil service system of Great Britain. . . . In England the tenure of office in the civil service is for life. They hold their offices during good
5 behavior, that is to say, during life. . . . [T]en thousand men in this city holding office for life would form a privileged class that would revolutionize the very foundations of this government. We have but one
10 life tenure under our Constitution, and if we had it to make over again we would not have that. I refer to the Supreme Court of the United States.

—Oliver P. Morton

1. According to Passage 1, the lack of a civil service system results in
   (A) the piracy of jobs.
   (B) the awarding of jobs to unqualified people.
   (C) criminals being given government jobs.
   (D) people using government office not to aid the nation but to enrich themselves.
   (E) the view that a life in politics is a way to enrich one's self.

2. The purpose of Passage 2 is to
   (A) describe the English system of civil service.
   (B) refute the English system of civil service.
   (C) compare the U.S. court system with the English system.
   (D) explain why the English civil system will not work in the United States.
   (E) praise the English civil service system.

3. Which of the following topics mentioned in Passage 2 is NOT considered in Passage 1?
   (A) Life tenure
   (B) Spoils system
   (C) Booty
   (D) The public good
   (E) Public trust

4. The tone of both Passage 1 and Passage 2 is
- **(A)** thoughtful.
- **(B)** inflammatory.
- **(C)** impassioned.
- **(D)** bombastic.
- **(E)** declamatory.

QUESTIONS 5–16 ARE BASED ON THE FOLLOWING PASSAGES.

President Lincoln referred to Harriet Beecher Stowe as "the little woman who made the great war," largely because of the furor caused by the publication of her antislavery novel Uncle Tom's Cabin. *In Passage 1, Stowe reflects on the writing of that novel. In Passage 2, Frederick Douglass, a slave who fled to freedom, speaks of his fear on the eve of his second—and successful—attempt to escape to the North from slavery.*

Passage 1—Harriet Beecher Stowe, from a letter to Mrs. Follen (1853)

I had two little curly-headed twin daughters to begin with, and my stock in this line was gradually increased, till I have been the mother of seven children, the most beautiful
5 and the most loved of whom lies buried near my Cincinnati residence. It was at his dying bed and at his grave that I learned what a poor slave mother may feel when her child is torn away from her. In those depths of
10 sorrow which seemed to me immeasurable, it was my only prayer to God that such anguish might not be suffered in vain. There were circumstances about his death of such peculiar bitterness, of what seemed almost
15 cruel suffering, that I felt that I could never be consoled for it unless this crushing of my own heart might enable me to work out some great good to others. . . .

I allude to this here because I have often
20 felt that much that is in that book ("Uncle Tom") had its root in the awful scenes and bitter sorrows of that summer. It has left now, I trust, no trace on my mind except a deep compassion for the sorrowful, especially
25 for mothers who are separated from their children. . . .

I am now writing a work which will contain, perhaps, an equal amount of matter with *Uncle Tom's Cabin*. It will contain all the
30 facts and documents upon which that story was founded, and an immense body of facts, reports of trial, legal documents, and testimony of people now living South, which will more than confirm every statement in
35 *Uncle Tom's Cabin*.

I must confess that till I began the examination of facts in order to write this book, much as I thought I knew before, I had not begun to measure the depth of the abyss.
40 The law records of courts and judicial proceedings are so incredible as to fill me with amazement whenever I think of them. It seems to me that the book cannot but be felt, and, coming upon the sensibility awaked
45 by the other, do something.

I suffer exquisitely in writing these things. It may be truly said that I suffer with my heart's blood. Many times in writing *Uncle Tom's Cabin* I thought my heart would fail utterly,
50 but I prayed earnestly that God would help me till I got through, and still I am pressed beyond measure and above strength. . . .

Passage 2—Recollection of Frederick Douglass

. . . It is impossible for me to describe my feelings as the time of my contemplated start grew near. I had a number of warm-hearted friends in Baltimore,—friends that I loved
5 almost as I did my life,—and the thought of being separated from them forever was painful beyond expression. It is my opinion that thousands would escape from slavery, who now remain, but for the strong cords
10 of affection that bind them to their friends. The thought of leaving my friends was decidedly the most painful thought with which I had to contend. The love of them was my tender point, and shook my decision
15 more than all things else. Besides the pain of separation, the dread and apprehension of a failure exceeded what I had experienced at my first attempt. The appalling defeat I then sustained returned to torment me. I felt
20 assured that, if I failed in this attempt, my case would be a hopeless one—it would seal my fate as a slave forever. I could not

hope to get off with anything less than the severest punishment, and being placed
25 beyond the means of escape. It required no very vivid imagination to depict the most frightful scenes through which I would have to pass, in case I failed. The wretchedness of slavery, and the blessedness of freedom,
30 were perpetually before me. It was life and death with me. But I remained firm and according to my resolution, on the third day of September, 1838, I left my chains, and succeeded in reaching New York without the
35 slightest interruption of any kind.

5. Harriet Beecher Stowe traces her compassion for slave mothers to her

(A) writing of *Uncle Tom's Cabin.*

(B) hatred of injustice.

(C) meeting a young woman in Cincinnati.

(D) reading of legal documents and testimony.

(E) loss of her own son.

6. According to the passage, Stowe is writing a new book that will be

(A) as long as *Uncle Tom's Cabin.*

(B) fictional, like *Uncle Tom's Cabin.*

(C) more successful than *Uncle Tom's Cabin.*

(D) both A and B.

(E) both B and C.

7. By "the depth of the abyss" (line 39), Stowe refers to the

(A) endless array of documentation.

(B) cruelty of the judicial process.

(C) suffering of young mothers.

(D) horrors of slavery.

(E) immeasurable intensity of grief.

8. In Passage 1, line 46, the word *exquisitely* most nearly means

(A) lavishly.

(B) expensively.

(C) enormously.

(D) indefinitely.

(E) superficially.

9. Stowe believes that her new book will

(A) prompt readers to read her last book.

(B) arouse empathy in readers.

(C) cause readers intense suffering.

(D) console readers of *Uncle Tom's Cabin.*

(E) infuriate readers of *Uncle Tom's Cabin.*

10. Why does Stowe want to write a follow-up to *Uncle Tom's Cabin?*

I. She believes that the book needs a sequel to complete the story.

II. She feels the need to substantiate claims that she made in the original novel.

III. She feels that a presentation of more facts will deepen the reader's understanding of the first book.

(A) I only

(B) II only

(C) I and II only

(D) III only

(E) II and III only

11. Stowe is obviously a writer who

(A) wrote with little effort.

(B) conducted little research for her writing.

(C) was deeply and emotionally involved in her work.

(D) did not understand the demands of writing.

(E) was not an enduring literary force.

12. The main idea of Passage 1 is that
    - (A) Stowe was in the right place at the right time.
    - (B) a successful writer is born, not made.
    - (C) Stowe was successful because she lived at a time when significant events were occurring in our nation.
    - (D) without Lincoln, Stowe would not have succeeded.
    - (E) a writer's life is a deeply felt one.

13. In Passage 2, Douglass acknowledges which of the following as a reason for many slaves not attempting to escape?
    - (A) Fear
    - (B) Ties to their friends
    - (C) Lack of education
    - (D) Lack of courage
    - (E) Inability to make contact with people in the North

14. According to the passage, what, in particular, tormented Douglass as he waited to make his second attempt at escape?
    - (A) Fear of reprisals
    - (B) Memories of his failed first attempt to escape
    - (C) The wretchedness of slavery
    - (D) The blessedness of freedom
    - (E) Pain of separation

15. Douglass was especially frightened at this attempt to escape because
    - (A) it was not as well-planned as his first attempt.
    - (B) his northern contact had not been established.
    - (C) he was going alone.
    - (D) failure would result in the severest punishment.
    - (E) he was leaving his friends.

16. From the picture of Douglass portrayed in Passage 2, which phrase below best describes him?
    - (A) Fearful and indecisive
    - (B) Bitter and angry
    - (C) Friendless and alone
    - (D) Confused and troubled
    - (E) Brave and persistent

STOP

END OF SECTION 8. IF YOU HAVE ANY TIME LEFT, GO OVER YOUR WORK IN THIS SECTION ONLY. DO NOT WORK IN ANY OTHER SECTION OF THE TEST.

Section 9

15 Questions • 10 Minutes

Directions: The sentences below may contain problems in grammar, usage, word choice, sentence construction, or punctuation. Part or all of each sentence is underlined. Following each sentence you will find five ways of expressing the underlined part. Answer choice (A) always repeats the original underlined section. The other four answer choices are all different. You are to select the lettered answer that produces the most effective sentence. If you think the original sentence is best, choose (A) as your answer. If one of the other choices makes a better sentence, mark your answer sheet for the letter of that choice. Do not choose an answer that changes the meaning of the original sentence.

I have always enjoyed singing as well as to dance.

(A) singing as well as to dance

(B) singing as well as dancing

(C) to sing as well as dancing

(D) singing in addition to dance

(E) to sing in addition to dancing

The correct answer is (B).

1. Recognizing the expense of the repairs, the plumbing mishap created a great deal of consternation.
   (A) Recognizing the expense of the repairs,
   (B) Recognizing the expensive repairs,
   (C) Recognizing that the repairs are expensive
   (D) Due to the repairs are going to be expensive
   (E) Recognizing the expense of the repairs, he noted that

2. Seatbelts, while unquestionably a good idea, it's sometimes a nuisance to use them.
   (A) Seatbelts, while unquestionably a good idea, it's sometimes a nuisance to use them.
   (B) Seatbelts, while unquestionably a good idea, are sometimes a nuisance.
   (C) Seatbelts are unquestionably a good idea and also they are sometimes a nuisance.
   (D) Seatbelts, while unquestionably a good idea, but sometimes a nuisance to use.
   (E) Seatbelts, while it's unquestionably a good idea to have them, it's sometimes a nuisance to use them.

3. Your application for a scholarship arriving late, however: it will still be considered by the committee.
   (A) arriving late, however; it will still be considered by the committee
   (B) arrived late, however the committee will consider it still
   (C) arrived late; however, the committee will still consider it
   (D) will be considered by the committee that arrived late
   (E) arriving late and is being considered by the committee

4. When I travel, <u>I most always enjoy seeing sights that differ from the typical tourist traps</u>.

   (A) I most always enjoy seeing sights that differ from the typical tourist traps

   (B) I almost always enjoy to see sights other than the typical tourist traps

   (C) I most always enjoy seeing sights that are different than the typical tourist traps

   (D) I almost always enjoy seeing sights that are different than the typical tourist traps

   (E) I almost always enjoy seeing sights that are different from the typical tourist traps

5. Unless treated and rewarmed, <u>hypothermia causes death</u>.

   (A) hypothermia causes death

   (B) death results from hypothermia

   (C) hypothermia kills

   (D) the victim of hypothermia will die

   (E) hypothermia will cause death

6. First choose a recipe; then <u>you should make a list of the ingredients needed</u>.

   (A) you should make a list of the ingredients needed

   (B) a list can be made of the ingredients needed

   (C) you can make a list of the ingredients needed

   (D) you should list the ingredients needed

   (E) make a list of the ingredients needed

7. Living in the city for the first time, the <u>traffic noise, she found, disrupted her sleep</u>.

   (A) the traffic noise, she found, disrupted her sleep

   (B) she found that the traffic noise disrupted her sleep

   (C) she found out how the traffic noise disrupted her sleep

   (D) her sleep, she found, was disrupted by the traffic noise

   (E) her sleep disrupted, she found, by traffic noise

8. Elgin called to find out <u>will you lend him your bicycle.</u>

   (A) will you lend him your bicycle.

   (B) will you lend him your bicycle?

   (C) did you lend him your bicycle.

   (D) will your bicycle be lent to him?

   (E) whether you will lend him your bicycle.

9. Few freshmen these days <u>are as ingenuous as him that first year</u>.

   (A) are as ingenuous as him that first year

   (B) were as ingenuous as him that first year

   (C) is as ingenuous as him that first year

   (D) are as ingenuous as he that first year

   (E) were as ingenuous as he that first year

10. Congress is expected to enact legislation soon that <u>will attempt to slow the rising trade deficit</u> that the U.S. is experiencing.

(A) will attempt to slow the rising trade deficit

(B) would attempt to slow the rising trade deficit

(C) will slow the rising trade deficit

(D) will attempt to slow the raising trade deficit

(E) would attempt to slow the raising trade deficit

11. Listening to another student's question, I frequently discover <u>that they are confused about the same points that I am.</u>

(A) that they are confused about the same points that I am

(B) that they are as confused about the same points as I am

(C) they are confused about the same points that I am

(D) that I am not the only one confused about the same points

(E) that he or she is confused about the same points that I am

12. <u>Noticing how close the other car was to him,</u> his hands began to shake and he broke out in a sweat.

(A) Noticing how close the other car was to him,

(B) Noticing how closely the other car was following him,

(C) When he noticed how close the other car was to him,

(D) After noticing how close the other car was to him,

(E) He noticed how close the other car was near to him,

13. The conditions of the contract <u>by which the strike has been settled has not yet been made public.</u>

(A) by which the strike has been settled has not yet been made public

(B) by which the strike has been settled have not yet been made public

(C) by which the strike had been settled has not yet been made public

(D) under which the strike has been settled has not yet been made public

(E) that settled the strike has not yet been made public

14. Myths are often marked by <u>anthropomorphism, the concept where animals and inanimate forces are invested</u> with human characteristics.

(A) anthropomorphism, the concept where animals and inanimate forces are invested

(B) anthropomorphism—the concept—where animals and inanimate forces are invested

(C) anthropomorphism, the concept, where animals and inanimate forces are invested

(D) anthropomorphism, the concept by which animals and inanimate forces are invested

(E) anthropomorphism, the concept that invests animals and inanimate forces

15. It is not <u>I to whom you should complain.</u>

(A) I to whom you should complain

(B) I, to whom you should complain

(C) I who you should complain to

(D) me whom you should complain to

(E) me to whom you should complain

ANSWER KEY AND EXPLANATIONS

Section 1

Sample Essay 1

Its not important to be a good writer today as it use to be. In the past people didn't have telephone and computer and telegraph and push a button and watch TV or a video or play a computer game etc. Whereas today we have all those thing, so we don't worry about writing. We can always just or make a call and say hello to a friend. So we won't have to write letters if we don't want.

Also, we won't have to write reports if we don't want. It depends on your job or occupation. Teachers and lawyers will of course have to write good essays but its not important for nurses and mechanical and computer occupations to be able to express themselves in writing.

In conclusion, students should be able to study what their interested in instead of practicing to write better in the future.

Analysis of Sample Essay 1

Essay 1 is weak. It is poorly written and developed in a sketchy manner. The writer's inclusion of TV, videos, and computer games is extraneous to the topic. Among the flaws are fragments, punctuation problems, lack of clarity or precision, and word-ending errors. Remember that although the readers don't take off points for punctuation and word-ending errors, these types of errors add to the impression that this writer is not in command of Standard Written English and, therefore, should not be given a high score.

A good deal of work is necessary if this essay is to convey its thoughts effectively. In addition to correcting the aspects noted in the first paragraph, the writer would also have to develop the content more fully while sticking to the topic and explain and support the few points made in the essay.

Sample Essay 2

Certainly modern technological advances have provided us with significant ways of improving our life style and I do not think that there are many clear thinking people who would want to get rid of the computer or word-processing software. Still there is no substitute for personal contact in the exchange of ideas and the written word provides us with exactly this sort of contact.

Letter-writing is an effective way of staying in touch with friends and cementing good professional relationships. Writing can avoid the coldness of a computer print-out and the warmth of the human voice on the telephone cannot be forgotten. There is simply no substitute for a good letter which can be re-read from time to time. Business firms often keep letters on file and refer to them when appropriate; and the sentiment of holding on to notes from a relative or friend can be a very meaningful and important part of our private life.

The well-rounded individual should seek to utilize all means to develop his power to communicate effectively and to present himself in the best possible light.

Writing clearly, coherently, and carefully will help to fulfill these objectives. Writing well should not be a lost art, part of the past, but rather a very important aspect of our daily lives.

Analysis of Sample Essay 2

Essay 2 is written in a mature style and conveys its message effectively and clearly, for the most part. It is generally well organized, progressing from an introductory statement of specific examples to a summation that reinforces the writer's views.

The comment concerning "the human voice on the telephone" (paragraph 2) might be utilized more properly in another part of the essay, or reworded to fit more coherently with the context of the paragraph. Nevertheless, the essay succeeds in conveying its point to the reader.

Section 2

1. B	7. B	12. C	17. C	22. D
2. C	8. B	13. A	18. C	23. C
3. E	9. E	14. A	19. D	24. C
4. D	10. D	15. B	20. D	25. E
5. B	11. B	16. D	21. B	26. A
6. C				

1. **The correct answer is (B).** If the director *applauds* her employees' activities, she is not likely to *question* their methods.

2. **The correct answer is (C).** An *unwilling* soldier would *recoil* at the idea of going to battle.

3. **The correct answer is (E).** The *inhumane* treatment of the zoo animals would result in *criticism*.

4. **The correct answer is (D).** Paper money is merely a representation of wealth; therefore, unlike gold, it has no *intrinsic* (inherent) value.

5. **The correct answer is (B).** The fever could be *degenerative, debilitating, raging,* or *pernicious*. However, only *ascribed* (attributed) makes sense in the second blank.

6. **The correct answer is (C).** If the lawyer can cast doubt on the *probity* (honesty or integrity) of the witness, she can probably strengthen her client's case.

7. **The correct answer is (B).** A debate in which candidates fling accusations at each other is likely to be *acrimonious* (harsh or bitter).

8. **The correct answer is (B).** Because they result from *carelessness,* both blanks should be filled by negative words. *Carelessness* is likely to produce an *ambiguous* (vague or unclear) report, which may leave everyone *confused*.

9. **The correct answer is (E).** Only a *callous* or insensitive person could be *oblivious* to, or unmindful of, the suffering of a starving child.

10. **The correct answer is (D).** You might have been torn between choices (C) and (D), but the passage discusses not just the Green Revolution but also irrigation and land reclamation projects.

11. **The correct answer is (B).** Choice (A) would be correct if the question asked about the land reclamation project or included it with the Green Revolution. Pay attention to other questions and answers as you work your way through a passage. Knowing the answer to one question may help with another.

12. **The correct answer is (C).** The use of closed and opened eyes as a device is not meant as *satire* or to feign *surprise*. The author shows no hint of *resignation* or *exasperation*.

13. **The correct answer is (A).** The answer hinges on untangling a few complex and convoluted sentences. The *proof* refers to the exercise of the vote, so choice (A) is better than choice (B). The other answers are distracters.

14. **The correct answer is (A).** The second sentence of the passage states: "I stand before you tonight under indictment for the alleged crime . . ." A defendant on trial would be under indictment for a supposed crime.

15. **The correct answer is (B).** The fourth paragraph discusses how ". . . not we, the white male citizens; but we, the whole people . . . formed the Union" to secure the blessings of liberty ". . . to the whole people—women as well as men."

16. **The correct answer is (D).** Quoting the preamble of the Constitution adds weight to her argument that all citizens, not merely white, male citizens, should have the right to vote.

17. **The correct answer is (C).** Lines 23–28 state: "...we, the whole people, who formed the Union . . . not to give the blessings of liberty, but to secure them. . . to the whole people . . . ."

18. **The correct answer is (C).** Lines 40–44 state: "To them this government has no just powers derived from the consent of the governed . . . . It is a hateful oligarchy of sex."

19. **The correct answer is (D).** Lines 51–53 describe an oligarchy of sex as a government where "all men [are] sovereigns [and] all women subjects, [inciting] dissension, discord and rebellion [in] every home . . . ."

20. **The correct answer is (D).** Lines 54–56 present the definition of a citizen ". . . as a person in the United States, entitled to vote and hold office."

21. **The correct answer is (B).** The last sentence of the passage states that ". . . every discrimination against women in the constitutions and laws of the several States is today null and void."

22. **The correct answer is (D).** As stated in lines 41–44, "The Indianists . . . seized on universal themes . . . cloaked in American Indian dress."

23. **The correct answer is (C).** Lines 19–22 say that Farwell used Fletcher's collections; lines 27–31 show that Cadman used melodies from the same collection.

24. **The correct answer is (C).** Lines 51–60 state the point of the examples in the fourth paragraph.

25. **The correct answer is (E).** The final paragraph contains the best explanation for this thesis. Choice (A), while it expresses the main idea of the passage as a whole, does not apply to the development of a pantribal style of music because in this case the Native Americans are not adapting a European cultural expression.

26. **The correct answer is (A).** See lines 100–105.

Section 3

1. C	5. B	9. B	13. D	17. B
2. D	6. E	10. B	14. C	18. C
3. B	7. D	11. A	15. B	19. B
4. C	8. E	12. B	16. A	20. E

Note: A ▣ following a math answer explanation indicates that a calculator could be helpful in solving that particular problem.

1. **The correct answer is (C).**

$$3x + 2 > 2x + 7$$
$$x + 2 > 7$$
$$x > 5$$

2. **The correct answer is (D).** By long division:

$$
\begin{array}{r}
2x - 3 \\
3x-2\overline{\smash{)}6x^2 - 13x + 6} \\
\underline{6x^2 - 4x} \\
-9x + 6 \\
\underline{-9x + 6} \\
0
\end{array}
$$

3. **The correct answer is (B).** It can easily be seen that $AB = 3$ and $BC = 4$. By the Pythagorean theorem, $(3)^2 + (4)^2 = (AC)^2$ and $AC = 5$. Also, the distance formula can be used.

$$d = \sqrt{(x - x_1)^2 + (y - y_1)^2}$$
$$= \sqrt{(5-1)^2 + (4-1)^2}$$
$$= \sqrt{(4)^2 + (3)^2} = \sqrt{25} = 5 \; ▣$$

4. **The correct answer is (C).**

$$\frac{8!}{9!} = \frac{8 \times 7 \times 6 \times 5 \times 4 \times 3 \times 2 \times 1}{9 \times 8 \times 7 \times 6 \times 5 \times 4 \times 3 \times 2 \times 1}$$

Dividing out common factors in the numerator and denominator leaves $\frac{1}{9}$.

5. **The correct answer is (B).** There was an error of 150 ft. − 140 ft. = 10 ft. The percent of error is the error divided by the actual distance, 10 ft. ÷ 140 ft. = 0.0714 × 100%, or about $7\frac{1}{7}$%. ▣

6. **The correct answer is (E).** The first child leaves $\frac{3}{4}$ of the cookies. The second child eats $\frac{1}{3}$ of $\frac{3}{4}$ and that leaves $\frac{1}{2}$. If the $\frac{1}{2}$ is divided among four children, then $\frac{1}{2}$ divided by 4 is $\frac{1}{8}$. ▣

7. **The correct answer is (D).** $|2y - 4| = 6$ means that $2y - 4 = 6$ or $2y - 4 = -6$. Solving the first equation, $y = \frac{10}{2}$, and solving the second equation gives y a value of -1. Therefore, $y =$ both 5 and -1.

8. **The correct answer is (E).** To solve this system of equations for y, the first equation must be multiplied by 2.

$$3x + 2y = 4 \rightarrow 6x + 4y = 8$$
$$6x - 3y = 6 \rightarrow 6x - 3y = 6$$

Subtracting the two equations on the right gives $7y = 2$. Therefore, $y = \frac{2}{7}$.

9. **The correct answer is (B).** If the radius r of a circle is diminished by 20%, the new radius is $r - 0.20r$. The new area is $\pi(r - 0.20r)^2 = \pi(0.64r^2)$. The new area is 64% of the old area. Thus, the area was diminished by $100\% - 64\% = 36\%$. ▣

10. **The correct answer is (B).**

$$x^2 - y^2 = (x + y)(x - y) = 10 \times 20 = 200$$

11. **The correct answer is (A).** The area of the rectangle is $(2a) \times a = 2a^2$. The area of a semicircle is $\frac{1}{2}$ the area of a circle. The radius of the semicircle is $\frac{1}{2}(2a) = a$; therefore, the area is $\frac{\pi a^2}{2}$. Add the areas of the rectangle and semicircle to get the total area, $2a^2 + \frac{\pi a^2}{2}$.

12. **The correct answer is (B).** In one second, the plane flies about 550 yds. ÷ 3 sec. = 183 yd./sec. There are 3600 seconds in one hour, so the plane flies 183 yd./sec. × 3600 sec./hr. = 658,800 yd./hr. There are 1760 yards in one mile, so the plane flies 658,800 yd./hr. ÷ 1760 yd./mi. ≈ 375 mi./hr.

13. **The correct answer is (D).** One meter equals approximately 1.10 yds. 100 meters is 100 m × 1.10 yds. per m = 110 yds.

14. **The correct answer is (C).** Use your calculator to rewrite each fraction in decimal form. The fractions become:

$$\frac{7}{12} = 7 \div 12 = 0.583$$

$$\frac{6}{11} = 6 \div 12 = 0.54$$

$$\frac{3}{5} = 3 \div 5 = 0.6$$

$$\frac{5}{8} = 5 \div 8 = 0.652$$

Arranging them in increasing order, we have, 0.54 < 0.583 < 0.6 < 0.625

So $\frac{6}{11} < \frac{7}{12} < \frac{3}{5} < \frac{5}{8}$

15. **The correct answer is (B).** The first pipe can fill the tank in $1\frac{1}{2}$, or $\frac{3}{2}$, hours, or it can do $\frac{2}{3}$ the work in 1 hour. The second pipe can fill the tank in 45 minutes, or $\frac{3}{4}$ hour, doing $\frac{4}{3}$ of the job in 1 hour. Thus, together the two pipes can do $\frac{4}{3} + \frac{2}{3} = \frac{6}{3}$ of the job in 1 hour. Therefore, the pipes working together could fill the entire tank in $\frac{1}{2}$ hour.

16. **The correct answer is (A).** There are 12 edges on a cube, so each edge is 48 in. ÷ 12 = 4 inches. The volume of the cube is $(s)^3 = (4 \text{ in.})^3 = 64$ cu. in.

17. **The correct answer is (B).** Since the perimeter of a square is four times the length of a side, it is $4\left(\frac{2x}{3} + 1\right)$, or $\frac{8x + 12}{3}$.

18. **The correct answer is (C).** Note that, if $g(x) = x^2 - x - 12$, then $g(2) = 2^2 - 2 - 12 = 4 - 2 - 12 = -10$, and $g(-3) = (-3)^2 - (-3) - 12 = 9 + 3 - 12 = 0$. Both of these properties do not hold for any of the other options.

19. **The correct answer is (B).** The key to determining the solution to this problem is to realize that both the rectangle and triangle AED have the same base and the same height. The segment $\overline{AD}$ is the base of both the rectangle and the triangle. The height of the triangle is the distance from point E to the base, and this distance is the same as the height of the rectangle. Therefore, if you write the area of the rectangle as $A = bh$, the area of the triangle is $\frac{1}{2}bh$. The probability, then, is $\frac{\frac{1}{2}bh}{bh} = \frac{1}{2}$.

20. **The correct answer is (E).** The smallest possible value of $\sqrt{12x - 7}$ is 0. Thus, the smallest possible value of $\sqrt{12x - 7}$ is −6. Therefore, −6 and any real numbers greater than −6 are possible range values.

Section 4

1. A	8. D	15. E	22. C	29. D
2. D	9. C	16. B	23. D	30. D
3. C	10. C	17. D	24. C	31. A
4. B	11. A	18. B	25. C	32. C
5. E	12. E	19. A	26. E	33. C
6. C	13. D	20. B	27. B	34. D
7. A	14. A	21. A	28. C	35. E

1. **The correct answer is (A).** The correct idiom is *graduates from college*.

2. **The correct answer is (D).** The conditional sense of the sentence requires *would be*.

3. **The correct answer is (C).** The standard form is *sits*.

4. **The correct answer is (B).** The correct word is *already*.

5. **The correct answer is (E).** The sentence is correct.

6. **The correct answer is (C).** *Liable* is used here incorrectly. The word needed here is *likely*.

7. **The correct answer is (A).** A gerund *(being)* is modified by a possessive pronoun *(their)*.

8. **The correct answer is (D).** The subject *one* requires a singular verb, *is*.

9. **The correct answer is (C).** The sentence requires the past-tense verb *believed,* not the noun *belief.*

10. **The correct answer is (C).** The verb form *could adjourn* establishes the action as past tense. Therefore, the second clause must also be in the past tense: not *must* consider but *had to* consider.

11. **The correct answer is (A).** As the object of *I observed, who* must be in the objective case: *whom.*

12. **The correct answer is (E).** The sentence is correct.

13. **The correct answer is (D).** The comparative *more* is required since *two* people are mentioned.

14. **The correct answer is (A).** The correct word is *fewer* because *workers* are countable.

15. **The correct answer is (E).** The sentence is correct.

16. **The correct answer is (B).** The correct phrase is *as if* to introduce the clause.

17. **The correct answer is (D).** The object of the preposition *to* should be *me.*

18. **The correct answer is (B).** The singular subject *incidence* requires a singular verb, *was.*

19. **The correct answer is (A).** The correct word is *used.*

20. **The correct answer is (B).** *Honest truth* is redundant.

21. **The correct answer is (A).** The sentence is correct.

22. **The correct answer is (C).** The double negative (*could not scarcely*) is incorrect. *Affected* (meaning "influenced") is correct.

23. **The correct answer is (D).** *With regards to* is unacceptable for *in regard to*. Choice (B) is awkward and wordy, choice (C) is illogical, and choice (E) is repetitious. Choice (D) offers the best expression of the thought.

24. **The correct answer is (C).** *Choices* is used for three or more items, *alternatives* for two; the commas separating *of course* are correct.

25. The correct answer is (C). There is no antecedent for the pronoun *it;* the subject of *indicates* should be *dictionary,* as in (C).

26. The correct answer is (E). *Unaware* should be followed by the preposition *of.* Choice (D) alters the sense of the sentence.

27. The correct answer is (B). The original sentence, choice (A), is awkward, since *which* seems to refer to *week,* rather than to the *situation,* which created the problem. Choices (D) and (C) have the same problem, and choice (C) uses the semicolon incorrectly. Choice (E) is a comma splice.

28. The correct answer is (C). A dependent clause introduced by a subordinating conjunction is separated from the main clause by a comma. Choice (D) is incorrect since *jewelers* is not possessive and does not require an apostrophe; choice (E) is awkward because of the preposition *for* following *ask.*

29. The correct answer is (D). The preposition *including* takes the objective case, *me.* Choice (C) is incorrect since the correct singular verb *has* (the subject is *no one*) is changed to the plural *have.* Choice (E) omits the comma after *one.*

30. The correct answer is (D). What is required is a grammatically sound and precisely worded revision. The adverb *luckily* is best placed at the beginning of the sentence.

31. The correct answer is (A). The only choice that is not awkward and does not misrepresent the material given is choice (A).

32. The correct answer is (C). A comma cannot join two independent clauses as in sentence (6). Choice (C) corrects this error by replacing the comma with a semicolon. In choices (A) and (D), the words following the semicolon do not form an independent clause. The use of *being that* in choice (B) is incorrect. Choice (E) creates a fragment.

33. The correct answer is (C). The word *it* in sentence (9) has no clear reference. Choices (A) and (B) have the same problem. In addition, choice (A) has a fragment, and choice (B) has a comma splice error. Choices (D) and (E) change the intended meaning. Choice (C) correctly eliminates the vague *it* and makes it clear that these students had a language problem, not a learning disability.

34. The correct answer is (D). Choices (A), (B), and (C) are poor since the antecedent of the pronoun *them* is not clear. Choice (E) is wrong since the sentence is awkwardly phrased.

35. The correct answer is (E). The use of the pronouns *they* and *them* in sentences (13), (14), and (15) is not always clear. One is not certain to whom the pronoun refers. Often, a precise noun would be a better choice.

Section 5

1. C	5. A	9. A	13. 10	17. 72
2. D	6. D	10. C	14. 80	18. 50
3. D	7. D	11. $\frac{3}{2}$	15. 1800	19. 1
4. E	8. B	12. 0	16. 15	20. 5

Note: A ▤ following a math answer explanation indicates that a calculator could be helpful in solving that particular problem.

1. **The correct answer is (C).**

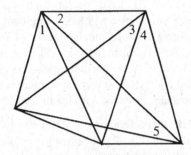

2. **The correct answer is (D).**

$$4x = 2(2+x) \qquad 6y = 3(2+y)$$
$$4x = 4+2x \qquad 6y = 6+3y$$
$$2x = 4 \qquad\qquad 3y = 6$$
$$x = 2 \qquad\qquad y = 2$$
$$2x+3y = 2(2)+3(2) = 4+6 = 10$$

3. **The correct answer is (D).** To begin, $J = \{33, 36, 39, 42, 45, 48, 51, 54, 57\}$ and $K = \{35, 40, 45, 50, 55\}$. Thus, J has 9 members, and K has 5 members. However, both sets contain the number 45, so actually there are only 13 members of the set $J \cup K$.

4. **The correct answer is (E).**

Solve the equation $x^2 - 8x + 7 = -8$.

$x^2 - 8x + 7 = -8$	Set the left-hand side equal to 0.
$x^2 - 8x + 15 = 0$	Factor the left-hand side.
$(x-5)(x-3) = 0$	Set each factor equal to 0.
$x - 5 = 0 \qquad x - 3 = 0$	
$x = 3$ and 5	

5. **The correct answer is (A).** $f(25) =$

$$5(25)^{-\frac{3}{2}} = 5\left(\frac{1}{25}\right)^{\frac{3}{2}} = 5\left(\frac{1}{5}\right)^{3} = 5\left(\frac{1}{125}\right) =$$

$$\frac{5}{125} = \frac{1}{25} = 0.04$$

6. **The correct answer is (D).** By definition, parallel lines are equidistant everywhere. Therefore, the length of segment d remains constant.

7. **The correct answer is (D).** By using the FOIL method,

$$(x + 9)(x + 2)$$

By combining like terms, this is simplified to:

$x^2 + 11x + 18$

8. **The correct answer is (B).** If the points $(3, 1)$ and $(5, y)$ are $\sqrt{13}$ units apart, then, by the distance formula,

$$\sqrt{13} = \sqrt{(5-3)^2 + (y-1)^2}$$
$$13 = (2)^2 + (y-1)^2$$
$$9 = (y-1)^2$$

Solving for y: $\quad y = 4$ or $y = -2$

Only 4 is given as an answer choice. ▤

9. **The correct answer is (A).** The total number of strikes that a pitcher must throw in a game is 9×9, or 81. Since only 85% of his pitches are strikes, he must throw 81/0.85, or 95, pitches a game. ▤

10. The correct answer is (C). The area of the rectangle is length × width = 11" × 8" = 88 sq. in. The area of the triangle is $\frac{1}{2}(\text{base})\times(\text{height})$. Its base is 8" − 3" = 5"; its height is 11" − 7" = 4". The area of the triangle is $\frac{1}{2}\times5''\times4''=10$ sq. in. The area of the polygon is 88 − 10 = 78 sq. in.

11. The correct answer is $\frac{3}{2}$.

$$\text{"JOSH"} = 3n - 3$$
$$n = 3n - 3$$
$$-2n = -3$$
$$n = \frac{3}{2} = 1.5$$

12. The correct answer is 0.

Machine A produces:

2000 flue covers/hour.

Machine B produces:

$$5000/\frac{5}{2}\text{ hr.} = 5000\left(\frac{2}{5}\right) = 2000/\text{hr.}$$

Since the rates are the same, they produce the same amount of flue covers during any period of time. So Machine A has produced 0 more than Machine B. 🔲

13. The correct answer is 10.

$$0.01 = \frac{0.1}{x}$$
$$\frac{1}{100} = \frac{\frac{1}{10}}{x} = \frac{1}{10}\bullet\frac{1}{x} = \frac{1}{10x}$$
$$\frac{1}{100} = \frac{1}{10x}$$
$$10x = 100$$
$$x = 10$$ 🔲

14. The correct answer is 80.

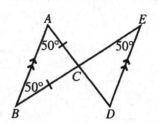

Since $ED\|AB$, angle E = angle B = 50°. (alternate interior angles)

Since $AC = BC$, angle A = angle B = 50°.

(In a triangle, opposite equal sides are equal angles.)

In $\triangle ABC$:

$$50 + 50 + x = 180$$
$$x = 80$$

15. The correct answer is 1800.

Let p = the school's population.

$$60\left(\frac{1}{4}p + \frac{1}{5}p + \frac{1}{3}p + 390 = p\right)$$
$$47p + 390(60) = 60p$$
$$13p = 390(60)$$
$$p = \frac{\overset{30}{390}(60)}{\cancel{13}} = 30(60) = 1800$$ 🔲

16. The correct answer is 15.

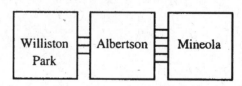

There are 3 × 5 = 15 different paths from Williston Park to Mineola through Albertson.

17. The correct answer is 72.

Establish a ratio of candies to cents.

Note: $1.70 = 170 cents and $10.20 = 1020 cents.

$$\frac{\cdots}{\text{cents}}: \frac{}{170} = \frac{x}{1020}$$
$$170x = 12(1020)$$
$$x = 72$$ 🔲

18. **The correct answer is 50.**

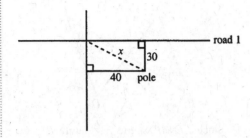

Using the Pythagorean theorem:

$$(30)^2 + (40)^2 = x^2$$
$$900 + 1600 = x^2$$
$$2500 = x^2$$
$$x = 50$$

19. **The correct answer is 1.** Set $T = \{16, 25, 36, 49, 64, 81\}$ and set $S = \{27, 64\}$. The only element that these sets have in common is 64. Thus, $S \cap T = \{64\}$.

20. **The correct answer is 5.** Begin by multiplying all terms of the equation by the LCD, which is $t^2 - 4 = (t+2)(t-2)$.

$$\left(t^2 - 4\right)\frac{1}{t+2} + \left(t^2 - 4\right)\frac{1}{t-2} = \left(t^2 - 4\right)\frac{10}{t^2 - 4}$$

$$(t-2) + (t+2) = 10$$
$$2t = 10$$
$$t = 5$$

Section 6

1. B	7. E	12. C	17. D	22. D
2. D	8. C	13. C	18. C	23. A
3. B	9. D	14. D	19. C	24. A
4. D	10. E	15. D	20. B	25. E
5. C	11. B	16. B	21. B	26. E
6. C				

1. **The correct answer is (B).** The fact that the society required outside aid indicates that it could not totally support itself. In other words, it was not *self-sufficient*.

2. **The correct answer is (D).** Since the regime is new, the laws must be newly announced and put into effect, or *promulgated*.

3. **The correct answer is (B).** *Brittle* machines might *shatter*.

4. **The correct answer is (D).** When illness strikes, even a person with a strong constitution can be *enervated* (weakened and drained of energy).

5. **The correct answer is (C).** A careful researcher would be *meticulous*.

6. **The correct answer is (C).** A shy look might *enchant* someone into matrimony, but it would not *release*, *control*, *ensconce*, or *jilt* someone to that end.

7. **The correct answer is (E).** A city that has failed to fire a single shot against an invading army has clearly *capitulated* (surrendered).

8. **The correct answer is (C).** A *compromise* (agreement) between two opposing sides might avert a strike, but without one the strike becomes *inevitable* (unavoidable).

9. **The correct answer is (D).** The scene set in motion Gottshalk's creative powers. This is borne out in the rest of the sentence, "it was there that I composed [*Souvenir de Porto Rico*]."

10. **The correct answer is (E).** There is nothing mournful, choices (A) and (C), about the quotation. While it creates the scene that Gottshalk saw each evening, choice (B), the purpose is to relate to the reader how the scene inspired his work.

11. **The correct answer is (B).** The purpose of the drugs is stated in the second sentence. In lung cancer, it appears that choice (C) is true, but that is the only type of cancer. Choice (A) is a side benefit, not the purpose of the drugs.

12. **The correct answer is (C).** The entire paragraph is about the new drugs in general. The effect on lung cancer is one example, so choices (A) and (B) are too specific. The passage indicates that except for lung cancer, these drugs that attack EGFR have not been very successful, so choice (E) overstates the effect.

13. **The correct answer is (C).** The president is calling on the public to act. While the speech provides information in part, choice (A), and thanks Congress, choice (E), neither is the overarching purpose.

14. **The correct answer is (D).** Did you note the word *states*? Choice (A) is implied, not stated. Choices (B) and (C) are incorrect, because the president uses the word *if* to introduce both cooperation and thrift. They are conditional actions, not outcomes. The energy shortage is already permanent according to the speech.

15. **The correct answer is (D).** Chekhov is praising the play. He is presumably familiar with Gorky's style and thus compares this play to previous plays with this compliment.

16. **The correct answer is (B).** Red hair on a red-haired man cannot be corrected; it is a genetic trait that cannot be changed. Chekhov means that the "defect" in the play is natural and cannot be repaired.

17. **The correct answer is (D).** Even though Chekhov is being critical in lines 9–12, he makes the point that the play's problems are unavoidable. As a result, his criticism is more supportive than it is negative.

18. **The correct answer is (C).** The play's only defect, according to Chekhov, is "the conservatism of the form" (line 12), which undermines Gorky's new and original characters.

19. **The correct answer is (C).** Chekhov explains that "all that"—the play's unavoidable flaws—stem from the work's conservative structure, i.e., its traditional trappings.

20. **The correct answer is (B).** Chekhov seems concerned throughout with realism. This answer is the only one that makes sense in context.

21. **The correct answer is (B).** As stated in lines 39–41, Nil's modesty is "the element so characteristic of our decent working man."

22. **The correct answer is (D).** Lines 42–43 reveal Chekhov's concern.

23. **The correct answer is (A).** Chekhov is concerned that Elena "is not clear" (line 66); his suggestions attempt to correct that.

24. **The correct answer is (A).** "Both in life and on the stage," Chekhov considers characters such as Teterev unimportant. For this reason, he suggests that Teterev talk less.

25. **The correct answer is (E).** Choice (A) is covered in lines 26–29, choice (B) in lines 30–32, choice (C) in lines 50–54, and choice (D) in lines 59–63. Chekhov has ideas about the ending of the play, which has four acts, but never discusses the ending of the third act.

26. **The correct answer is (E).** Chekhov comments that Piotr "is good. Most likely you don't even suspect how good he is." His only suggestion is that Piotr should be portrayed by the actor Meierkhold.

Section 7

1. D	4. C	7. D	10. A	13. A
2. E	5. D	8. D	11. B	14. D
3. D	6. D	9. B	12. B	15. A

Note: A 🖩 following a math answer explanation indicates that a calculator could be helpful in solving that particular problem.

1. **The correct answer is (D).** Since both areas are equal, $\frac{1}{2}bh = \pi r^2$. Thus, knowing the base of the triangle and radius of the circle, $\frac{1}{2}(7)h = \pi(7)^2$, so $h = 14\pi$.

2. **The correct answer is (E).** Use your calculator to rewrite each number in decimal form:

$$\frac{9}{13} = 9 \div 13 = 0.69$$
$$\frac{13}{9} = 13 \div 9 = 1.44$$
$$70\% = \frac{70}{100} = 70 \div 100 = 0.7$$
$$\frac{1}{0.70} = 1 \div 0.70 = 1.43$$

   Compare the decimals to arrange the numbers in order from smallest to largest:

   $0.69 < 0.7 < 1.43 < 1.44$ so

   $$\frac{9}{13} < 70\% < \frac{1}{0.70} < \frac{13}{9}$$ 🖩

3. **The correct answer is (D).** The quadrilateral *PQRS* is a parallelogram as shown:

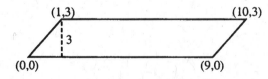

   It has a height of 3 and a base of 9. The area is, like that of a rectangle, *bh*, or 27.

4. **The correct answer is (C).** One simple way to solve this problem is to divide each side of the given equation by 4.

$$\frac{8x+4}{4} = \frac{64}{4}$$
$$2x + 1 = 16$$

5. **The correct answer is (D).** Since the center is at the origin, each coordinate point is the length of a leg of a triangle. The hypotenuse of each triangle is the radius of a new circle with its center at the origin. If the hypotenuse of the triangle is greater than 7, the points are outside the circle.

   (4,4): $h = \sqrt{4^2 + 4^2} = 5.7$, so (4,4) is inside the circle.

   (5,5): $h = \sqrt{5^2 + 5^2} = 7.07$, so (5,5) is outside the circle.

   (4,5): $h = \sqrt{4^2 + 5^2} = 6.4$, so (4,5) is inside the circle.

   (4,6): $h = \sqrt{4^2 + 6^2} = 7.2$, so 4,6) is outside the circle. 🖩

6. **The correct answer is (D).** The area of a square with side = 9 is 9 • 9 = 81. The surface area of a cube with edge = 3 is 3 • 3 • 6 = 9 • 6 = 54. The difference, therefore, is $81 - 54 = 27$. 🖩

7. **The correct answer is (D).**

   2 + 4 + 6 = 12 and 12 is evenly divisible by all three. 🖩

8. **The correct answer is (D).**

$$\frac{3(x^2-4)}{(x+2)} = \frac{3(x+2)(x-2)}{(x+2)}$$
$$= 3(x-2)$$
$$= 3x - 6$$ 🖩

9. **The correct answer is (B).** There are 5 • 2 = 10 different varieties of ice cream bars on the truck. Since the truck only runs four times a week, it would take a person 2 weeks + 2 days to purchase all the different varieties of ice cream bars. Therefore, the day would be the 16th of the month.

10. The correct answer is (A).

$$\frac{N!}{(N-2)} =$$

$$\frac{N(N-1)(N-2)(N-3)(N-4)\ldots\left[N-(N-1)\right]}{(N-2)(N-3)(N-4)\ldots\left[N-(N-1)\right]}$$

Dividing out common factors in the numerator and the denominator leaves only

$$\frac{N(N-1)}{1} = N(N-1) = N^2 - N$$

11. The correct answer is (B). This is more easily solved by using real numbers. If we assign a value of 6 to AB, then we can figure out that the perpendicular AD is $3\sqrt{3}$. The old perimeter was 18 and the new perimeter is $6 + 3 + 3\sqrt{3}$, or about 14.1. The fraction $\frac{14}{18}$ can be simplified to $\frac{7}{9}$, which is about 78%.

12. The correct answer is (B). If the circumference is 60 inches, since $C = 2\pi r$, substitute $C = 60$; therefore, $r = \frac{60}{2\pi}$.

13. The correct answer is (A). The radii of the pipe are 1.42 in. and 0.97 in. The thickness is their difference, or 0.45 in.

14. The correct answer is (D). The function will be undefined for any values of x that yield a denominator of 0. This will happen when $3x - 7 = 0$, that is, when $x = \frac{7}{3}$.

15. The correct answer is (A). The set $P \cap Q \cap R$ contains only the elements that are in all three sets. The element 5 is the only element in all three sets.

Section 8

1. D	5. E	9. B	13. B
2. D	6. A	10. E	14. B
3. A	7. D	11. C	15. D
4. C	8. C	12. E	16. E

1. **The correct answer is (D).** Choices (A) and (B) were probably easy to rule out, but choice (E) might have been more difficult. If you went back to Passage 1 and read the last two sentences, you would see that only choice (D) states the complete thought.

2. **The correct answer is (D).** The purpose is implied, not directly stated. While you might have settled on choice (B), it is only partially correct. The speaker is not refuting the English system in general terms but is explaining why it would not be appropriate for the United States.

3. **The correct answer is (A).** The other four choices are included in Passage 1 but not in Passage 2.

4. **The correct answer is (C).** Choice (B), *inflammatory*, means *to excite* or *incite to riot*, which is not borne out by the message either man presents.

5. **The correct answer is (E).** Stowe says as much in lines 6–9 and in paragraph 2.

6. **The correct answer is (A).** The book will "contain all the facts and documents" (lines 29–30), so it will not be fictional, choice (B). It will "contain, perhaps, an equal amount of matter" as the previous book (lines 27–29); in other words, it may be as long.

7. **The correct answer is (D).** Rereading this paragraph and the one before proves that Stowe is referring to the horrors of slavery, which she thought she knew, but now finds she "had not begun to measure."

8. **The correct answer is (C).** In this context, the word *exquisitely* means *enormously*, not its more conventional definitions—*expensively*, *lavishly*, or *ostentatiously*.

9. **The correct answer is (B).** "It seems to me that the book cannot but be felt . . . ." (lines 43–45). Stowe thinks that her readers will feel the pain she documents.

10. **The correct answer is (E).** Nowhere in the passage is it stated that Stowe feels that *Uncle Tom's Cabin* needs a sequel. But she does imply that a second book would support her original work (statement II) and that a presentation of more factual information will strengthen the reader's understanding (statement III).

11. **The correct answer is (C).** The passage vividly conveys the emotionalism with which Stowe approaches her writing.

12. **The correct answer is (E).** While there is some truth to choice (C), it is not implied in the passage. The entire passage concerns Stowe's deeply felt emotions concerning the evils of slavery.

13. **The correct answer is (B).** While all of the answers may have had something to do with slaves not escaping, only choice (B) is cited in the passage.

14. **The correct answer is (B).** The passage specifically states (lines 16–19) that Douglass's failed first attempt haunted him.

15. **The correct answer is (D).** Since this was his second attempt at escape, Douglass knew that he would be severely punished if he did not succeed.

16. **The correct answer is (E).** Although choice (D) has some appeal, it is obvious from the last sentence that "brave and persistent" is the best choice.

answers practice test 6

Section 9

1. E	5. D	9. D	13. B
2. B	6. E	10. A	14. D
3. C	7. B	11. E	15. A
4. E	8. E	12. C	

1. **The correct answer is (E).** As the sentence stands, there is a dangling participle (*recognizing*) so that the meaning conveyed is that the plumbing mishap recognized the expense of the repairs. A subject must be added in the main clause.

2. **The correct answer is (B).** The original includes the superfluous pronoun *it* and leaves *seatbelts* without a verb. Choices (D) and (E) do nothing to correct these problems. Choice (C) provides the verb needed to make a complete sentence, but it is awkward and wordy. Choice (B) is both correct and concise.

3. **The correct answer is (C).** When used as a conjunctive adverb, *however* is preceded by a semicolon and followed by a comma. In addition, a semicolon is used to join closely related independent clauses. Choice (B) is a comma splice, choice (E) is a fragment, and choice (D) changes the meaning of the original sentence.

4. **The correct answer is (E).** The correct expressions are *almost always* (not *most always*) and *different from* (not *different than*).

5. **The correct answer is (D).** The *victim* is the one who must be treated and rewarmed. Only choice (D) correctly places the subject next to the phrase that modifies it.

6. **The correct answer is (E).** The original sentence shifts needlessly from the imperative (*choose*) to the indicative mood (*you should make*). Choices (C) and (D) do the same. Choice (B) shifts subjects (from *you* to a *list*). Choice (E) is consistent in both subject and mood.

7. **The correct answer is (B).** The original sentence says, in effect, that the *traffic noise* is living in the city. Choice (B) provides the correct subject for the introductory phrase

and the rest of the sentence. Choice (C) uses *how* when logic calls for *that*. Choice (D) says that *her sleep* is living in the city. Choice (E) creates a series of introductory phrases with no main clause.

8. **The correct answer is (E).** There is a word missing in choice (A). The second clause (*will you . . . bicycle*), which is the object of *find out*, lacks a conjunction to link it to the main clause (*Elgin . . . out*). Only choice (E) provides this link in an indirect question.

9. **The correct answer is (D).** The verb is understood, so the phrase should read "as ingenuous as he (was) that first year."

10. **The correct answer is (A).** The sentence is correct.

11. **The correct answer is (E).** It is one student's question, so *he is* or *she is confused*, not *they are*.

12. **The correct answer is (C).** The sentence should be rephrased so that it does not seem as if *his hands* were *noticing*. Although choice (E) corrects the misplaced modifier, it creates a run-on sentence.

13. **The correct answer is (B).** The subject of the main clause is "conditions," a plural noun requiring a plural verb, "have been made." The subject of the subordinate clause is "strike," which requires a singular verb, "has been settled."

14. **The correct answer is (D).** A concept is not a place to be referred to as *where*. A concept is an idea, which is referred to by using such expressions as "according to which" or "by which."

15. **The correct answer is (A).** The sentence is correct.

COMPUTING YOUR SCORES

To get a sense of your progress in preparing for the SAT, you need to compute individual multiple-choice critical reading, math, and writing raw scores for this Practice Test. Keep in mind that these formulas have been simplified to give you a "quick and dirty" sense of where you are scoring, not a perfectly precise score.

To Compute Your Raw Scores

1 Enter the number of correct answers for each critical reading, mathematics, and multiple-choice writing section under Number of Questions Correct.

2 Enter the number of incorrect answers (not blanks) for each critical reading, math, and multiple-choice section under Number of Questions Incorrect.

3 Total the number correct and number incorrect.

4 Follow this formula: Take the total correct and subtract one quarter of the total incorrect. Round up in your favor to compute your raw score.

Critical Reading Section	Total Number of Questions	Number of Questions Correct	Number of Questions Incorrect
2	26		
6	26		
8	16		
Totals	68	Total Correct:	Total Incorrect:

Critical Reading Raw Score = Total Correct − ($\frac{1}{4}$ × Total Incorrect) = ___

Math Section	Total Number of Questions	Number of Questions Correct	Number of Questions Incorrect
3	20		
5	20		
7	15		
Totals	55	Total Correct:	Total Incorrect:

Math Raw Score = Total Correct − ($\frac{1}{4}$ × Total Incorrect) = ___

Multiple-Choice Writing Section	Total Number of Questions	Number of Questions Correct	Number of Questions Incorrect
4	35		
9	15		
Total	50	Total Correct:	Total Incorrect:

Multiple-Choice Writing Raw Score = Total Correct − ($\frac{1}{4}$ × Total Incorrect) = ___

CONVERSION SCALES

CRITICAL READING

Raw Score	Scaled Score	Raw Score	Scaled Score
68	800	30	480
65	760	25	440
60	710	20	410
55	670	15	370
50	620	10	340
45	590	5	290
40	550	0	230
35	520		

MATH

Raw Score	Scaled Score	Raw Score	Scaled Score
55	800	20	510
50	760	15	480
45	690	10	440
40	650	5	340
35	610	0	200
30	580		
25	550		

MULTIPLE-CHOICE WRITING

Raw Score	Scaled Score	Raw Score	Scaled Score
50	800	20	470
45	760	15	420
40	680	10	370
35	620	5	320
30	580	0	270
25	520		

SELF-EVALUATION CHARTS

Critical Reading: Raw Score

Excellent	60–68
Good	50–59
Average	30–49
Fair	20–29
Poor	0–19

Math: Raw Score

Excellent	50–55
Good	40–49
Average	20–39
Fair	10–19
Poor	0–9

APPENDIX

Parent's Guide to College Admission Testing

Parents' Guide to College Admission Testing

GETTING INVOLVED

The first step in creating a plan to help your teen prepare for college-admissions tests is to define your role. As a parent, you already play a variety of roles in raising your children, wearing different hats at different times. You may find yourself acting as mentor, chauffeur, cook, coach, mediator, or even prison warden. All of these roles require different time commitments and often even require you to acquire new skills.

When it comes to helping your teen tackle the SAT or ACT, you might feel confused about which role to take. Many parents find becoming involved with their teen's education a bit challenging. Teenagers can have a hard time accepting their parents as teachers. Sometimes, when parents try to teach their teen, their efforts lead to the three "Fs": *failure, friction,* and *frustration.* When these experiences arise, parents may conclude that they have no role to play in their child's education.

Of course, nothing could be further from the truth. In fact, there are many roles parents should choose to play in helping their teens prepare for college-admissions tests.

ROLES FOR PARENTS

You can play a variety of roles in helping your teen prepare for college-admissions tests. In guiding your teen, you may choose to be one, or any combination, of the following:

- Buyer
- Advocate
- Supporter
- Helper
- Organizer
- Manager
- Tutor

The Buyer

"Here's a check to buy the SAT books you want."

This parent feels that it is the teenager's job to prepare for college-admissions tests, and the parent's job is to offer financial support. The teenager is the main decision maker and is responsible for obtaining the necessary materials and services. This parental role is supportive and not too time-consuming, although it may present problems for parents who are on a tight budget.

NOTE

Educators and legislators recognize the importance of having parents involved in their children's education. Research shows that parents can successfully teach their teens, when they have been taught how to do it.

The Advocate

"How does your school help juniors prepare for the SAT or ACT?"

This parent believes that it is the school's job to prepare students for the test. The parent starts the ball rolling and requests information from school personnel about what services are available. The teenager may or may not be involved in this information-gathering process. Most parents feel comfortable in this role, as it requires little time and is accepted by both school personnel and teachers.

The Supporter

"I know it's a tough test. I see you're working hard and spending a lot of time studying for it."

This parent believes that the teenager has the major responsibility in preparing for the test. The teenager is the decision maker, and the parent offers suggestions and support. The parent is understanding, empathetic, and non-critical. This can be a comfortable parental role since it is non-threatening to the teenager, is positive, and requires a minimal amount of time.

The Helper

"I picked up this SAT practice book and made a list of some tutoring courses for you."

This parent believes that it is the parent's job to help the teenager with his plans, but that it is up to the teenager to make the final decisions. This parent only helps when asked and follows the teen's timetable when possible. This is a comfortable role since it is supportive, non-threatening, and not time-consuming. However, this role might pose problems for working parents who do not have flexible schedules.

The Organizer

"I've signed you up to take a test-prep course."

This parent feels that the teenager should not be responsible for the arrangements involved in test preparation. The parent assumes a major role in establishing a timetable, finding out about resources, arranging for services, and purchasing materials. The teenager's responsibility is to follow the parent's game plan. In short, the parent provides the framework so that the teenager can spend her time preparing effectively. This role is time-consuming and parent-directed.

The Manager

"After you study your vocabulary words for 30 minutes, you can use the car."

This parent believes that good intentions are not enough to make her child perform well on the SAT. She believes in the rule "work first, then play." Firm guidelines and consequences are established to keep the ball rolling. The degree to which the teenager is involved in planning and implementing this approach depends on a number of factors, such as the teenager's maturity and motivation.

Your comfort with this role is related to the extent to which you believe in the "work first, then play" philosophy. If you already ascribe to this rule in raising your children, extending it to SAT or ACT test preparation will be an easy task. Patience and willingness to check on study behavior are also important factors to consider when thinking about the role of manager.

The Tutor

"I'll explain the algebra problem to you."

Parents who take on the role of tutor believe that they can work effectively with their teenagers on academic subjects. These parents offer direct instruction in one or more of the SAT or ACT areas, such as vocabulary, reading comprehension, geometry, or science.

WHICH ROLE IS FOR YOU?

Defining your role requires two steps:

- Collecting information about yourself
- Using this information systematically, as you decide which role you want to take on and when

To collect information about yourself, take the following "Parent Survey."

TIP

Remember, no single role is superior to the other. Find roles that are best suited to you and your teenager's need.

PARENT SURVEY

Directions: Read each question and circle the answer that best describes you. You may find that you mark some questions low, others medium, and still others high.

	LOW	MEDIUM	HIGH
1. How much money available for test preparation, tutoring books, etc.?	Up to $25 for books	$25–$150 for books and tutoring	More than $150 for is courses, books, etc.
2. Do you question school personnel?	Never. I feel uncomfortable.	Sometimes, if it is important.	Usually. It's my right.
3. Do you make supportive statements about academic achievements?	Not usually. I don't want to spoil my child.	Sometimes, if grades are good.	Frequently, especially about trying hard.
4. What resources are available in your school or community?	I don't have the faintest idea!	I thought I saw an advertisement for an SAT course.	I know a tutor and saw an SAT book in the store.
5. How involved do you feel?	I don't know if I should be involved.	I'll do what I can if I'm asked.	This is important! I'll help whenever I can.
6. How much time are you willing to devote to SAT preparation?	1–3 hours total	1–2 hours per week	3 or more hours per week
7. How efficient is your decision making?	It's either too slow or too hasty.	Sometimes good, but it's a tiresome process.	Usually good. I consider options and select one.
8. Who should be the primary decision maker?	Not me. It's not my Job!	I'll make decisions sometimes.	Me. I have more experience.
9. How organized are you?	I lose papers, forget dates, and am often late.	I write schedules but forget to follow them.	A place for everything and everything in its place!
10. How comfortable are you with your teenager?	It's tough being around my child.	Some days are good, others aren't.	Minor problems, but we get along.
11. How firm or consistent are your limits?	No one listens to me. I nag and yell.	My children know the rules, but I forget to enforce them.	My children follow the rules.
12. Do you have reading and math skills?	Minimal skills; low confidence.	Some skills; average confidence.	Strong skills; high confidence.
13. How effective are you as your teenager's teacher?	We always end up fighting.	Sometimes it works, sometimes it doesn't.	It's not easy, but we work together.

Choosing Your Role by Interpreting Your Survey Responses

While there are no hard and fast rules to use in choosing a role, your answers to the survey questions will help you select your role in a systematic way. Using your survey responses, you can use the following guidelines to identify which roles to try first. Remember that any combination of roles is good. To help clarify:

- **The roles of buyer, advocate, and supporter** are appropriate if a majority of your answers fall in the low or medium columns. These roles demand the least amount of direct parent-as-teacher involvement, yet they are an important part of test preparation. Most parents can assume these roles.

- **The roles of helper, organizer, and manager** require that the majority of your answers fall in the medium or high columns. These roles involve more constant and direct interaction with your teen. Some parents can assume these roles.

- **The role of tutor** is the most demanding role and requires that at least eleven out of thirteen responses fall in the medium or high columns. There are few parents who can comfortably and successfully assume this role.

Depending on your time and resources, you may, for example, want to begin in the advocate and supporter roles, followed by that of a buyer. If necessary, you could find someone else to act as a manager and tutor. Or, alternatively, you might find yourself best suited to being an organizer, manager, helper, and supporter right away.

BECOMING ACTIVE

Parents entrust their most valuable assets—their children—to the schools. As an investor in your child's education, you have the same concerns as any other person investing in the future. Unfortunately, sometimes parents are made to feel that the school is the "expert." In some schools, parents are viewed as meddlers if they ask for, or insist upon, information about their children's progress. As a parent, you can, and should, be involved in your teen's education, even at the secondary level. Don't be afraid to pursue information on your teen's behalf—you need to be informed, ask questions, offer suggestions, and reject suggestions if they aren't the right solutions to the problems!

Originally published in a slightly different form in *Parent's Guide to the SAT & ACT* (Lawrenceville, NJ: Peterson's, 2005), 27–133. Reprinted by permission of the authors.

HOW TO APPROACH YOUR TEENAGER

For the first time, your teen may be striving for independence and questioning herself and the future. These changes may make your role as a parent additionally tough, and you may find it hard to help your teen prepare for college-admissions tests. The key to reaching your teen is to focus on where he is academically and personally.

GETTING INFORMATION FROM DIFFERENT SOURCES

To design your SAT or ACT preparation plan, you'll need to get up-to-date information about your teenager from several sources, including yourself, your teenager, and the school. Your child's guidance counselor is a primary source of information, since he can provide information from classroom teachers and across various subject areas.

You and Your Teen

The first source of information is you. Parents must neither overestimate nor underestimate the importance of their own information about their teenager. You can be most effective if you know which questions to ask and whom to ask. You need to know about your teenager's concerns, goals, attitudes, academics, work habits, general behavior, and special strengths and weaknesses.

To initiate this step, ask your teen to meet with you for an hour to discuss his college plans and how he feels about preparing for the SAT or ACT. You can begin by asking your teen for his opinions on matters concerning his education and future goals. In this first conversation, you can ask about colleges he's considering. As many colleges suggest that its applicants' test scores fall within a certain range, information about the college's requirements is important. The required scores may affect the amount of time and the kind of commitment required for SAT or ACT preparation.

You may also want to ask your teen to evaluate his study skills and the kind of study skills needed to prepare for the SAT or ACT. Some teenagers work effectively in groups. Others are uncomfortable or distracted when studying in a group. Students' work habits and interactions with other people also influence their attitudes toward college-admissions tests and toward their scores. Your teenager's reaction to tests in general is an important factor to take into consideration.

Don't feel rejected if your teen says, "I don't want to meet. I know what to do." Don't push it, just try again later. The timing may be right on the second go-around.

knowing your teen

The School

Another important source of information is the school. Guidance counselors, teachers, and others, such as coaches or band directors, can tell you about your teenager's attitudes and interactions with peers and adults outside the home. These attitudes may influence your teen's college selection and in turn lead you to the most appropriate type of preparation for the college-admissions tests.

Your teen's guidance counselor can review previous standardized test scores with you and discuss differences in performance between tests and grades. Reviewing standardized test scores and grades can help you establish realistic guidelines for SAT or ACT preparation.

Teachers and counselors can also describe specific weaknesses that might block an otherwise solid test performance. In addition, they can offer information about your child's work habits, such as whether homework is submitted on time or how well-organized her papers are.

Additional Options

Independent school counselors, or educational consultants, are another alternative to consider. These types of counselors are not affiliated with a school and work as private consultants. If you lack confidence in your teen's counselor or feel that the counselor is too busy to provide the extensive work necessary for appropriate college planning, you may want to work with an educational consultant.

A private consultant may work with students from all over the United States and foreign countries. This broader perspective can provide more diverse options for your child. Many independent counselors also have firsthand experience as college-admissions officers and therefore are aware of the kind of information that should be collected and ways of presenting such information to colleges.

WHAT TO ASK

The following is a list of questions you'll want to ask yourself, your teen, and school personnel or educational consultants.

Goals

- What career choices have been considered?
- Have specific colleges been identified?
- What is the range of SAT or ACT scores considered by those colleges?

Attitudes

- How positive are feelings toward the ability to succeed?
- What attitudes exist toward school and school personnel?
- Are current friends a good influence in terms of future plans?
- How helpful is the family in terms of school success?
- What attitudes exist toward the SAT or ACT?

Academics

- What have other standardized tests shown?
- Do standardized test scores accurately reflect skills or abilities?
- Do grades accurately reflect skills or abilities?
- What are the student's areas of strength?
- What are the student's areas of weakness?

Work Habits

- How effective are organizational and study skills?
- Are there preferred study procedures (e.g., groups or recorded lectures)?
- How effective are test-taking skills?
- Are there problems that might interfere with effective test preparation (e.g., job or extracurricular activities)?
- Are there problems that might interfere with effective test-taking (e.g., hates multiple choice, poor at long reading passages)?

Behavior

- To what degree does the teenager need or accept help?
- To what degree is the teenager a good decision maker?
- To what degree is the teenager a self-starter or self-manager?
- To what degree are limits or rules tested?
- How well does the teenager cope with stress or adversity?
- How good are relationships with school personnel?
- How good are relationships with other teenagers?
- How good are relationships with family members?
- With whom does the teenager talk about problems (e.g., brother or neighbor)?

Special Issues

- Are there special talents or strengths?
- Are there special or extraordinary problems?
- Have these issues been addressed previously?
- In what ways will these issues affect SAT or ACT preparation or test-taking?

SAT and/or ACT

- How do students in our school perform on the SAT or ACT?
- How did the teenager perform on other college-admissions tests?
- How do test scores compare with others in the class?
- How do test scores compare with others nationally?
- How have other students prepared for the SAT or ACT?
- What services do school personnel provide for SAT or ACT preparation?
- What remedial services are available within the school?
- What remedial or preparatory services are available within the community (e.g., tutors or courses)?

By asking these questions, you can really focus on your teenager. By answering these questions now, you'll reveal information gaps, identify consistencies or inconsistencies in opinions or behaviors, highlight strengths and weaknesses, and begin your systematic plan for helping your teen.

HOW TO USE THE INFORMATION

To get the most out of the information you have collected, pay particular attention to the following issues:

- **Consistency of answers provided by each of the sources**—for example, whether the counselor's answers conflict with your teenager's answers
- **Trends that emerge**—such as better work this year or more anxiety than last year
- **Gaps in information**—such as no previous standardized test scores available
- **Strengths and weaknesses**—such as being well organized or having poor reading comprehension

YOUR TEEN'S STRENGTHS

All teenagers have strengths. However, some teenagers' strengths are more obvious than others, and often, when teenagers are difficult, it's hard to think of them in a positive light. Your job as a parent includes:

- Identifying, highlighting, maintaining, and increasing existing strengths.
- Providing opportunities for new strengths to develop.

Strengths may be grouped into several broad categories—knowledge, work habits, attitude, behavior, and special. To help clarify:

- **Strengths in the knowledge area** include mastering basic skills, achieving good grades, and having a potential for learning.

- **Strengths in the area of work habits** include applying skills and knowledge in an organized and effective way and achieving desired goals.

- **Strengths in the area of attitude** include having clear goals, optimism, motivation, and self-confidence.

- **Strengths in the behavior category** refer to the teenager's ability to cope, follow rules, and get along with peers and adults.

- **Special strengths,** for example, include the teenager's talents in the areas of music, writing, or science.

Too frequently, both parents and teachers forget to accent the positive. They zero in on the weaknesses rather than on the strengths. To avoid this common mistake, review the information you have collected and list your teen's strengths and special talents in the following chart. We'll come back to filling in the problem areas later.

SOURCE		KNOWLEDGE	WORK HABITS	ATTITUDE	BEHAVOIR	SPECIAL
Parent	Strength					
	Problem					
Teenager	Strength					
	Problem					
School	Strength					
	Problem					

Remember to discuss these strengths with your teenager, especially if he does not recognize his own strengths or talents. Building your teen's confidence is important and will pay off enormously.

IDENTIFYING SPECIFIC PROBLEM AREAS

Several kinds of problems may become obvious as you collect information about your teenager. These problem areas may be grouped into the same five categories we used to identify strengths.

Knowledge Problems

Students with knowledge problems may make statements such as: "I'm not even sure about getting all the ratio and proportion problems right," or "I hate reading," or "I never do those vocabulary parts—I skip most of them."

Knowledge problems include:

- Lack of mastery of basic skills, such as arithmetic.
- Lack of understanding of rules and concepts in more advanced areas, such as geometry.
- Lack of experience, which leaves gaps in some areas covered on the SAT or ACT.
- Difficulties in one or more of the following: remembering previously learned material, analyzing material, or putting information together (e.g., as in a report).

Your teenager may have a knowledge problem in only one area, which may or may not have an effect on any other area. For example, Marcus, a 10th-grader, had a reading problem, and testing showed that he read two years below his present grade level. His computation skills were good, and he did well in algebra. However, word problems were his downfall. In this case, a knowledge problem in one area had an effect on another area.

Work-Habits Problems

Typical work-habits problems statements are: "I can't find my notes," or "I guess I left my books at school," or "I simply cannot do those sentence-completion things!"

Work-habits problems include:

- Poor study habits.
- Test anxiety.
- Ineffective test-taking skills.
- Lack of organization.

Teenagers with work-habits problems lack the skills necessary to study effectively or to apply the knowledge they have during a testing situation. These teenagers may work too slowly and be unable to complete portions of the test, or they may work too quickly and inadvertently skip questions and make careless errors.

Attitude Problems

Students with attitude problems may make statements such as: "It doesn't matter how much I study, I'll never be able to do it," or "I don't care—the SAT doesn't matter anyway."

Attitude problems involve:

- Unrealistic self-image and academic goals.
- Over- or under-estimation of the importance of the SAT or ACT.

On the one hand, teenagers may be overly optimistic in thinking that they are smart, do not need to prepare for the SAT or ACT, and can get into any college on the basis of grades alone. On the other hand, teenagers may have an overly negative view of their ability and therefore avoid school, worry about grades, panic on tests, and are difficult or quarrelsome.

Attitude problems can influence the degree to which teenagers are willing to spend time and energy preparing for the SAT or ACT.

Behavior Problems

Teenagers with behavior problems are likely to make statements such as: "I don't have to study just because you say so," or "I know I should study, but I just can't make myself do it," or "I keep getting headaches when I think about the SAT."

Behavior problems include:

- Poor self-control.
- Lack of responsible behavior.
- Inability to get along with peers, adults, or family.
- Inability or unwillingness to follow rules and maintain commitments in school and in the community.
- Drug and/or alcohol abuse.

Teenagers with behavior problems usually use ineffective ways of coping with stress, are overly dependent or rebellious, are unable to control anger, and are unwilling to face or discuss problems with adults.

Special Problems

Teenagers with special problems may make statements such as: "I've always had trouble with spelling and reading," or "I know I have physical problems, but I want to try to go to college," or "I can do those questions, I just need more time."

Special problems include:

- Specific learning disabilities.
- Severe physical, sensory, or emotional limitations.
- Dramatically different cultural backgrounds.

Other special problems include the language difficulties experienced by some bilingual students or a lack of culturally enriching experiences, which can hamper teenagers from disadvantaged backgrounds.

To begin designing an SAT or ACT plan, you need to review your teenager's problems. List these problems on the same chart where you have already listed the teenager's strengths. When discussing these problems with your teenager, remember to talk about his strengths as well.

HOW TO USE THE INFORMATION ABOUT YOUR TEEN

After collecting information about your teenager, you should summarize the information by reviewing the chart you completed. Remember that strengths, along with weaknesses, may exist in each area. Keep the following in mind as you evaluate and summarize the information you have gathered:

- The number of sources that agree or disagree
- The number of objective measures that agree or disagree, such as tests, grades, or reports
- The number of times you are aware of the strength or problem—for example, your teenager always studying or always complaining

WORKING WITH YOUR TEEN'S GUIDANCE COUNSELOR

Relative to college-admissions tests, the counselor's role is to help students understand the nature of these tests, the benefits of study and coaching, what test to take and when, and whether to retake a test in order to achieve a higher score.

The counselor can help you and your teen summarize information about how prepared your teen is for the SAT or ACT and can discuss strengths and weaknesses in light of current and past test results and grades. Making an appointment with your teen's guidance counselor now will enable you to make reasonable decisions about a course of action.

Originally published in a slightly different form in *Parent's Guide to the SAT & ACT* (Lawrenceville, NJ: Peterson's, 2005), 27–133. Reprinted by permission of the authors.

In addition to assessing knowledge of English, math, and other content areas, the SAT and ACT test how well your teen takes standardized tests. Part of becoming a successful test-taker involves developing effective work habits. Developing these habits now will save your teen lots of frustration, time, and energy and will inevitably improve her test scores.

MANAGING TIME

Consider the following example. John is a fairly good student and earns Bs and Cs in his high school courses. He is concerned about the SAT and wants to do well. During a practice SAT test, he plods through each section and spends extra time on some of the more difficult questions. He doesn't finish parts of the test. His practice SAT scores are unnecessarily low because he didn't have time to answer all of the questions he could have easily handled. John's test behavior indicates that he needs help in work habits, especially in learning to manage his time, or pace himself, during the test.

When people work in factories or offices, they are usually told how much time should be spent on different tasks. This process ensures productivity, allowing workers to know what is expected of them and helping them pace themselves so that they get the most done in the least amount of time. Similarly, your teen will also benefit from learning how to manage the time he has to take the SAT or ACT. Before taking the tests, he should know the following:

- How many questions are on each section of the test
- How much time is provided for each section
- Approximately how much time can be given to each question if he is to complete the test and if all of the questions are of equal difficulty
- The kinds of questions that he can't do and should skip until he has completed those questions he can definitely answer correctly

With test-taking, managing time means that your teen can predict what she has to do, how long it should take, how to pace herself to get the job done, and how to leave time to check her work. Although most testing centers have clocks, your teen should wear a watch during the test (and practice tests) to keep track of time and check her pacing.

effective work habits

GETTING ORGANIZED AND STICKING TO TASKS

Now consider the case of another test-taker, Vera. The following takes place in her parents' kitchen after dinner:

7:05 p.m.	"Mom, did you see my SAT practice book?"
7:10 p.m.	"Mom, I found some paper. Where are some pencils?"
7:15 p.m.	"Oh, I'd better call Nien to see if I have a ride tomorrow!"
7.20 p.m.	"What time is it?"
7:22 p.m.	"I need to get on the computer."
7:25 p.m.	"That's enough math! I think I'll do some vocabulary."
7:40 p.m.	"I hate vocabulary! I'll go back to math."

Vera displays several work-habits problems. One problem is that she hasn't recognized what she can't do during study time—for example, disrupting herself by making phone calls. Another problem is that Vera jumps from task to task, breaking her own concentration.

Good work habits entail being organized. Teenagers need to learn how to organize materials, list what has to be done, and specify how much time might be needed to complete each job. Study styles may differ, but teenagers must find the most effective ways to use their time and follow their own plans.

Students like Vera benefit from guidelines to follow during study time, such as:

- Spend at least 20–30 minutes on each activity, maintaining concentration, and building up skills.
- Stick to some basic study rules, including not avoiding work because it is too difficult or boring.
- Invoke the rule: "Work first and then play." For example, make phone calls only after work is completed.

Sticking to a task is an essential work habit. Unless she changes her habits, Vera will not reach the critical test-related goal: accurately completing the greatest number of problems she can within specific time limits. Vera is also operating under some misconceptions. She really believes that she is working hard and that her fatigue is a result of studying. She may also begin to think that she is not so bright as her friends because they are getting better results on practice tests. All of these potential problems can be resolved by changing her work habits.

IF IT WORKS, DON'T CHANGE IT

Another 10th-grader, Ralph, likes his comforts. He loads up on soda and chips before he settles down to work. The radio is an essential part of his lifestyle. When his mother and sisters pass by his room, they see him sprawled on his bed with a small light turned on and papers and books all over the floor. Sometimes he's sound asleep. Because he seems so casual, everybody stops by and talks to him.

Some parents might assume that the manner in which Ralph goes about studying is totally ineffective. It doesn't appear that any teenager could concentrate and maintain attention curled up in bed, with music blaring, people walking in and out, poor lighting, and a nap here and there. Most parents would be right. Ralph's parents had been concerned and were annoyed by his work habits.

However, Ralph earns high grades in school, and on the first SAT he took, he scored more than 600 on the Critical Reading, Writing, and Math sections. He has also shown his parents how his speed is increasing on certain practice SAT exercises. In this case, the parents have specific information and assurance that although his work habits appear inefficient, they happen to work for their teenager.

Your objective here is to check the effectiveness of your teenager's work habits. Consider what effect these habits have on classroom or college-admissions test performance. Remember to have your teen take a practice test under actual SAT or ACT conditions to see how his work habits hold up.

TAMING THE PROCRASTINATOR

Procrastination is a common problem for teens. Leslie is an 11th-grader having a conversation with her father, Mr. Rand.

Mr. Rand: "Did you start to study for the ACT?"

Leslie: "No, it's in two months."

Mr. Rand: "Shouldn't you start now?"

Leslie: "I wish you would stop nagging me. I can take care of myself."

Here's another scenario, between Mrs. Sanchez and her 11th-grader, Ricky:

Mrs. Sanchez: "I haven't seen that SAT book around. Are you studying in school?"

Ricky: "I started looking at it, but it's so long I'll never get through it."

Putting off work occurs when teenagers feel overwhelmed, don't know where to begin, feel pressured to get other things done, or are distracted by other things they would rather do. Parents who recognize this work-habits problem in their teenagers may have similar habits themselves.

Procrastination becomes a particular problem because:

- Time is limited; when time is limited, people feel pressure.
- There can be a penalty for delay—for example, when you miss the SAT or ACT because your check was mailed late.
- Avoiding work increases the load, rather than decreases it.

By taking into account the time available before the SAT or ACT and the preparation that has to be done, you can help your teenager create a sensible plan that reduces one seemingly overwhelming task to many smaller and more manageable ones. Predicting what has to be done, and doing those tasks one by one, gives teenagers control over feelings of being swamped and unable to cope.

A WORK-HABITS CHECKLIST

To help your teenager develop effective work habits, ask him questions regarding time management, materials, atmosphere, and space. You may want to use the following checklist.

Time Management

❑ Are there signals to others that this is a study time (e.g., a "Do Not Disturb" sign)?

❑ Are there rules set up for the study time (e.g., no phone calls or no visitors)?

❑ Is a time schedule agreed upon and posted?

❑ Are study breaks scheduled?

Materials

❑ Is a clock or kitchen timer available?

❑ Are supplies handy (e.g., pencils, eraser, computer)?

❑ Does the seating encourage attention and alert behavior (e.g., a chair and a desk rather than a bed)?

Atmosphere

❑ Is the lighting adequate?

❑ Is the noise level low?

❑ Is the area visually nondistracting?

❑ Is the area well-ventilated and does it have a moderate temperature?

Space

❑ Is there a special place designated (e.g., desk, room, or area)?

❑ Is this space away from the main traffic of the home?

❑ Is the space large enough to allow for writing?

❑ Is there space available for storing or filing materials?

HOW TO HELP YOUR TEEN WITH WORK HABITS

Teenagers have difficulty finding time to do homework or household chores, but they usually seem to have a lot of time to talk on the phone and meet with friends. Managing time comes down to establishing priorities. Here are some guidelines that you can use to help your teenager use her time more effectively:

- Set a realistic study schedule that doesn't interfere too much with normal activities.

- Divide the task into small and manageable parts—for example, instead of trying to memorize 2000 vocabulary words in two weeks, have your teen learn and use five new words a day, three times a week.

- Use what has just been learned whenever it is possible—for example, talk about, joke about, and use new or obscure vocabulary words.

- Find times that are best for concentration and, if possible, have your teen avoid studying at times when she is tired, hungry, or irritable.

- Plan a variety of study breaks, such as music or jogging, to revive concentration.

Using Study Groups

You may also want to encourage your teenager to get a group of friends together to practice taking the SAT or ACT, review test items, compare answers, and/or discuss the ways they used to solve the problems. Such a group can range in size from 2 to 6 students.

Consider this example: Ms. Franklin realized that her daughter, Barbara, liked to be with other teenagers and studied best in a group. If she waited for Barbara to begin studying independently, Ms. Franklin was afraid that Barbara would put off studying until it was too late.

Ms. Franklin asked her daughter if she would like to organize a study group. Ms. Franklin also volunteered to provide the house and find a tutor. Barbara's responsibilities were to call her friends and tell them which materials to buy, how much each session would cost, and where and when the group would meet. By doing this, Ms. Franklin provided a real service to a group of motivated students who needed some direction.

So, if you want to help set up a study group, you can:

- Make the initial arrangements.

- Provide the space for meetings.

- Set up a "study atmosphere" in your home.

- Help other parents to set up such groups.

More Tips on Organization

When reading about Ms. Franklin, you might think that she is very organized and efficient. Nope! In fact, she is usually disorganized and is a procrastinator herself. She rarely plans ahead, and there is a lot of confusion in her home when deadlines must be met. She and her husband even had to drive to several colleges to deliver Barbara's college applications so that they arrived on time.

Ms. Franklin's behavior shows that it really is possible for an otherwise hassled parent to become more organized and efficient for a short time just for the SAT or ACT. During this brief window, you can help your teen by doing the following:

- Save papers and announcements with dates and requirements for the SAT or ACT.

- Make copies of all correspondence, applications, checks, and bills and find one place to store or file these papers.

- Write the SAT and/or ACT date and your teenager's study-session schedule on your own calendar.

- Write notes to yourself so that you don't forget to do what you said you'd do, such as making phone calls or picking up materials.

Originally published in a slightly different form in *Parent's Guide to the SAT & ACT* (Lawrenceville, NJ: Peterson's, 2005), 27–133. Reprinted by permission of the authors.

WHY CREATE A PLAN?

It takes more than good intentions to do well on a college-admissions test. It takes time, organization, and hard work. A test-prep plan provides the means for converting good intentions into meaningful test preparation. An effective plan specifies:

- Goals
- Responsibilities of parent and teenager
- Available resources
- Schedules
- Budgets
- Instruction
- Possible problems or concerns

By clearly establishing who is responsible for what, a test-prep plan removes many sources of conflict between parent and teenager and allows each person to channel all of his efforts toward the goal of improving test scores.

CREATING TEST-PREP PLANS

Let's look at some step-by-step ways of creating test-prep plans and what to expect as you create a plan for your teen.

Make Time to Plan

Family life is hectic. Finding time to sit down and talk together is frequently a problem. Like a well-managed business, families with educational concerns and goals also need to have planning meetings. They need to find the time and place that will allow for discussion and working together.

Setting up a time to talk about a plan with your teen will work best if you approach her when she's most apt to be receptive. Try to avoid having the conversation when the teenager is busy or on her way out of the house. How you proceed is as important as what you do. A first step in developing a plan is to set goals.

List Goals

Goals help identify in a concrete way what you want to happen, such as your teen raising her verbal score by 40 to 60 points. Sometimes teenagers choose goals that are too general, such as doing geometry problems more accurately or completing the Critical Reading section more rapidly. Goals should be specific to the SAT or ACT even when they include study skills. For example, just having a goal of studying for 30 minutes a night does not guarantee improvement. The following list contains some sample goals.

For accuracy:	Increase the number of correct math and vocabulary test answers.
For speed:	Decrease the time needed to read comprehension exercises while maintaining an understanding of what is read.
For speed and accuracy:	Decrease the time needed to read comprehension exercises and increase understanding of what is read.
For quantity:	Increase the number of problems tried or completed.
For frequency:	Study vocabulary words and do essay writing practice exercises for about 30 minutes at least three times per week.
For duration:	Increase study sessions to 1 hour, adding additional practice math problems.

After outlining the goals, the next step in planning is to prepare a schedule.

Make a Schedule

A test-preparation schedule should include a timetable and weekly or daily activity lists. First make the timetable. You can use a regular calendar that covers the time between the current date and the date of the SAT or ACT. To make your timetable, write down all activities related to preparing for the test and the test date on the calendar.

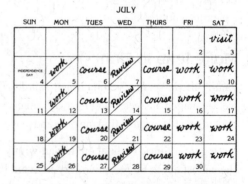

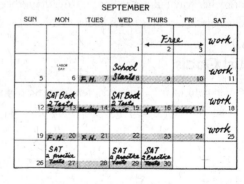

www.facebook.com/prep4sat

You should also keep weekly and/or daily lists to identify specific tasks, such as the type or number of practice exercises to be completed. Such scheduling spells out the tasks ahead of time, reduces unnecessary worrying, and allows for more realistic planning. Often, teenagers become overwhelmed by the thought of all that has to be done and end up doing nothing. Writing a list and assigning times to each task tends to make these jobs more doable and more realistic.

Talk About Costs

Although you want to do everything possible for your teen's college-admissions test preparation, cost is an important consideration. Most families' budgets are already strained without adding the expenses of materials, tutors, or commercial courses—especially since test preparation comes at a time when parents are trying to save up money for college tuition.

Regardless of who pays the bill—the parent, the teenager, or both—budgets should be discussed. The estimated costs of various alternatives should also be outlined. Any budget limits and expected responsibilities should be proposed. By discussing these issues up front, you clarify problems and provide a realistic basis for decision making.

Find Out About Resources

Your community may have a variety of resources to help teenagers prepare for college-admissions tests. However, it may take a little detective work to find them. For example, many religious groups sponsor young-adult activities. These groups usually know skilled people within the community who would be willing to help teenagers study for the SAT or ACT. In addition, parent or community groups may also be willing to sponsor special activities if they are aware of teenagers' needs.

Match Materials to Your Teen's Goals

You and your teen should now select which books, equipment, and/or specialized materials will be used. You should match these materials with your teenager's goals. Consider drawing on information from teachers or counselors, previous standardized tests, and test-prep books that analyze the SAT or ACT. Material can be purchased, borrowed, or shared by several teenagers.

Locate a Tutor

In finding a tutor, you should consider someone who has experience with the college-admissions tests. You may actually hire more than one tutor, since instruction may be provided by volunteers, peers, schoolteachers, or professional tutors. Discuss various tutoring options with your teen.

Find a Place to Practice and Study

Regardless of your plan's specifics, your teen needs a suitable place in which to study. Teenagers who register for courses or who receive tutoring have to practice test-taking at home too. It is important to select a quiet study place at home or at school for SAT or ACT homework assignments or for sessions with the tutor. It is also smart to turn off phones, the TV, and computers to reduce interruptions and distractions while your teen is preparing for the test.

Do a Subtle Sell Job

Doing a subtle sell job means helping your teenager realize that the long-term benefits of test preparation outweigh the short-term costs of studying. As you prepare to make a test-prep plan with your teen, you may want to use the following chart to guide your thinking about the plan's importance.

		COSTS (TIME, MONEY, ENERGY)	BENEFITS (SUPPORT, CHALLENGE, ACHIEVEMENT)
PARENTS	**SHORT-TERM**	"It takes me 20 minutes to drive to the tutor." "I've already spent $20 on books." "I'm tired of thinking and talking about the SAT. "I wasn't liked when I suggested an SAT course."	"I know I helped." "Her scores went up." "I feel good." "He knows we care."
	LONG-TERM	"I ought to have spent more time." "It's costing twice as much now." "I should have been firmer about SAT studying." "I wish I had been more aware."	"He did the best he could." "She got into three colleges." "Now I can relax." "She knows we all worked to help her." "
TEENAGERS	**SHORT-TERM**	"I'd rather be sleeping." "The SAT fee is so high!" "I'm tired of studying." "I don't feel like caring." "Suppose I don't do well?" "No one else is studying."	Studying takes time, but it's OK." "I stopped worrying when I started studying." "I'm learning how to take tests." "My math is actually improving. "I'm learning new words. "This is a first step toward being a lawyer
	LONG-TERM	"I didn't get into the college I wanted. I hope I can transfer later." "I could have done better." "I should have listened to my parents." "I wish I had tried harder."	"My scores were high and I won a scholarship." "I did the best I could." "I had a good choice of colleges." "My parents helped a lot."

TIP

Keep in mind that expertise is needed not only with the subject area but also with the SAT or ACT format and with effective test-taking techniques.

NOTE

A place to study doesn't have to be a separate room. Some teens work well as long as they have a desk and a quiet, well-lit space.

WRITE YOUR PLAN

As you create your plan and revise it, you and your teen should list specific responsibilities, as well as the expected and actual costs. Use the following outline to help you keep notes.

Describe the planning time:

_____

Identify goals:

_____

Set schedules and agendas:

_____

List possible materials, instructors, and/or locations:

_____

Identify resources:

_____

Assign responsibilities and roles:

_____

Specify costs and budgets:

Review and Revise Your Plan

After writing an initial plan, you should review it to make sure it's realistic. Remember that you can and should revise your plan as you go along. The following questions will help you and your teenager determine whether your plan is relevant, realistic, and useful.

Planning Time

❑ Has a specific time been selected?

❑ Has a quiet, comfortable place been chosen?

❑ Has all the necessary information been collected?

❑ Have costs and benefits been discussed?

❑ Have roles for both the parent and teenager been discussed?

Goals

❑ Have the teen's strengths been discussed?

❑ Have problems been identified and prioritized according to time and/or financial constraints?

❑ Have goals been discussed and written?

❑ Are the goals realistic?

❑ Are the goals listed in the order of their importance?

❑ Has a range of outcomes been considered (such as increasing scores by 25 to 50 points on the SAT writing section)?

Schedule

❑ Has a timetable that specifies all time commitments been designed?

❑ Does the schedule seem realistic in terms of goals and limitations?

❑ Have tutoring sessions been scheduled?

❑ Have study or practice sessions been scheduled?

❑ Have time limits been specified for those sessions?

Materials

❑ What materials are needed?

❑ How are materials matched with goals or problems?

❑ How will materials be used?

❑ Who is responsible for acquiring the materials?

Coaches and Instructors

❑ Who will provide the coaching or instruction?

❑ Does this person have the necessary skills?

❑ Are other teachers or tutors necessary?

Location

❑ Where will instruction occur?

❑ Has transportation been arranged?

❑ When studying at home, where will it be done?

❑ Will these places be available when needed?

Budget

❑ Have financial costs and resources been discussed?

❑ Have financial responsibilities been specified?

❑ If costs are a problem, have alternatives been considered and discussed?

❑ Are adjustments or alternatives necessary?

Resources

❑ Have the necessary or desired resources been identified?

❑ Who is responsible for selecting and contacting these resources?

❑ How will decisions be made about the usefulness of these resources?

Originally published in a slightly different form in *Parent's Guide to the SAT & ACT* (Lawrenceville, NJ: Peterson's, 2005), 27–133. Reprinted by permission of the authors.

ANTICIPATE POSSIBLE HURDLES

Some common problems that arise during the test-prep process include:

- The teenager hates the tutor.
- The instructor gets sick.
- The study group falls apart due to conflict.
- One of the parents loses a job, so money is no longer available for a commercial course.

More subtle problems can occur when:

- Teenagers set unrealistic goals and then feel tired, frustrated, and angry.
- Parents become worried that their teenager isn't making enough progress.
- Parents feel angry and disappointed when things don't work out exactly as planned.

When managing a plan, you must assume that problems will arise and that plans have to be changed to deal with these problems. Helping your teenager shift gears and learn how to make adjustments is vital preparation for the real world and a valuable skill for her to learn now.

WAYS TO TRACK PROGRESS

Here are some ways you can check on your teen's performance progress:

- Keep records for each study session.
- Keep track of the number of problems completed correctly.
- Keep track of how much time it takes to complete the work.
- Review the records to see if changes to the plan need to be made.
- Make sure your teen is focused on the specific SAT or ACT sections or questions that need special attention.

Teenagers can check on their progress in several ways. These methods include calendars, check-lists, charts, and graphs. The best method is the one that your teen will regularly use.

Timing Your Comments

You should comment on performance when the progress has occurred, not a week or two later. Teenagers usually do not want anyone to know that they are studying for the tests, so it's best to comment when no one else is around. You should also be especially sensitive to how your teenager will receive any comments about her work. Teenagers often view these helpful hints as criticism, even when they are offered in a positive way. You may find it easier to use notes or humor as a way of making a point that can be accepted by your teen. For example, Anne's mother wrote her the following note:

Dear Anne:

I see that you're keeping track of the number of problems you complete for the SAT. Looks like you're doing at least 2–3 more problems each time—HOORAY!

FIXING PROBLEMS

When teenagers are not progressing as anticipated, parents frequently jump to conclusions and think that the teenager has done something wrong. It may appear that the teenager is lazy. In fact, she may just be feeling overwhelmed, confused, and exhausted. When you become aware of problems, you may need to take a second look at the problem, looking for specific performance obstacles.

Rather than blaming your teenager, or labeling his behavior as right or wrong, you might consider behavior in terms of its being efficient or inefficient. To help you pinpoint what's going on, you may want to ask your teenager two questions:

- How is your study schedule working?
- Are you learning what you thought you would?

Your teen can give you the information to zero in on the specific problem. Some common problems teenagers face concern unrealistic goals, unsuitable materials, and inefficient organization.

Applying Solutions

Usually there is more than one solution for every identified problem. Here are some common SAT and ACT test-prep problems and a variety of possible solutions.

Problem:	The teen seems to give up because it appears to him that the material is too complicated.
Solution:	Divide the assignments into smaller parts or find a different tutor.
Problem:	Progress is slower than anticipated and not enough time is left to reach the original goal.
Solutions:	Lower the expectations about the scores. Rearrange the study schedule. Provide more intensive instruction. Take the test at a later date. Shoot for a later college-admissions date.
Problem:	The teenager is studying, but he does not remember anything the next day.

Solutions:	Change from group to individual tutoring.
	Change from reading the information to listening to some of the information.
	Practice aloud before doing the test exercises.
	Study in a different place.
	Check that the teaching materials are matched to the skills needed.
Problem:	The teenager is studying, but she seems to lose things and waste time.
Solution:	Give her information and techniques that will help her to become better organized.
Problem:	The teenager seems frantic and appears to be spending too much time studying.
Solution:	Provide some written material that will help him rank what has to be done in order of importance.

Review the goals, costs, and benefits, but keep in mind that the test is part of a larger picture.

Using Checklists to Manage Problems

It is important that teenagers try to manage their own problems. However, sometimes they lack the information they need to effectively deal with these problems. Use the following checklists to help your teenager learn how to manage her own problems.

Organizing Materials

Do You:

❑ Have papers and books that you haven't looked at for months?

❑ Waste time and break up your concentration looking for things you have misplaced?

❑ Lose test registration papers, exercise sheets, or materials?

❑ Have a study area that is a mess?

❑ Let things pile up because you don't know where to put them?

Then Try To:

❑ Schedule periodic clean-ups. Throw out the things you don't use.

❑ Find the necessary papers and materials before starting to study.

❑ Arrange your materials in a systematic manner, such as by using folders.

❑ Make a labeled file or box for different kinds of materials.

❑ Store your materials and supplies in an easy-to-spot place.

Organizing Time

Do You:

❑ Let assignments pile up because you can't decide what to do first?

❑ Forget regular school assignments that you can't study for as you had planned?

❑ Have a hard time sticking to your study schedule?

❑ Forget to do errands, like picking up materials or making phone calls?

❑ Find that your attention wanders when you begin to study?

Then Try To:

❑ Write down all your assignments—by the week or by the day—putting those that should be done first at the top of the list.

❑ Ask teachers for all future test or project dates and write them down on your calendar.

❑ See how long you can study and regularly increase this time in 5 – to 10-minute intervals.

❑ Write yourself notes and put them on your backpack or wallet. This looks funny but it works.

❑ Ask yourself, "At what time do I study best?" Change your study time if necessary.

Organizing Tasks

Do You:	*Then Try To:*
❏ Try to cram everything in?	❏ Be selective. Do only those tasks that are the most important.
❏ Feel anxious if you don't have every minute planned?	❏ Make sure that you allow time to relax and exercise.
❏ Feel uncomfortable if you need to change your schedule?	❏ Tell yourself, "Relax and be flexible. I have a schedule and I'll do the best I can."
❏ Feel overburdened by the responsibilities of test preparation?	❏ Get a study buddy you can call when you get discouraged.
❏ Want to study but don't, because someone asks you to do something else?	❏ Practice saying, "No. I'd really like to but I'm studying."
❏ Find the work difficult?	❏ Give yourself a pep talk and say, "This is hard, but it can be done."

MOTIVATING YOUR TEENAGER

Once you get the plan going, the next step is to keep it going. Studying for the test usually isn't fun. It is hard work and teenagers need encouragement to keep going.

Sometimes teenagers are motivated because they can immediately taste success. For example, Rico studied for a chemistry test and received an A. It is highly likely that he will study for the next test because he saw that his work paid off.

Checking on progress on the SAT or the ACT practice tests is important. Doing so gives your teenager the opportunity to realize that her work does pay off and progress is being made.

Sometimes parents need to boost motivation when they see signs of fatigue or signals that their teenager is being turned off to studying. If you are trying to find ways to encourage your teenager, consider the following:

- Make positive statements, such as "I know you're working hard."
- Provide extra treats, such as a special dinner or extra use of the car.
- Leave a small, silly gift, such as a huge pencil, key ring, etc.
- Organize some special event, such as going to the movies, a concert, out to eat, or to dinner with another family whose teenager is also taking the test.
- Do some chore for your teenager so that your teen can study.

Setting Up Rewards

Sometimes, you need to put into practice methodical and consistent ways to make sure that plans are followed. In other words, you may need to make sure that certain events occur after, and only

TIP

Regardless of the system of rewards, remember to be positive, low-key, and avoid negative or punishing situations. The goal is to encourage and support effective studying, not to control your teenager. By establishing realistic goals and rewards, you help your teenager do her best and show her that you really care.

after, a task is completed. The following examples show how you can build in rewards for work that was accomplished.

- Ron tends to be forgetful. For a month, he had not done the vocabulary exercises he agreed to do. He and his parents worked out a plan so that if a certain number of exercises were completed on Tuesday and Thursday nights, he could have the car on Fridays.

- Diana, on the other hand, did not want the car—she loved talking on the phone. Her family devised a plan that required her to work on her writing exercises for 30 minutes, three nights a week, before she could talk on the phone.

This final list of questions is provided to help you check on your teen's progress and iron out problems. When plans are well-managed, trouble spots are easily identified and changes can usually be made without anyone feeling that he has failed, especially the teenager.

Managing Your Plan: A Checklist

❑ Is progress being checked using charts, checklists, graphs, or other means?

❑ Do charts or graphs show any problems?

❑ What adjustments are necessary?

❑ Have alternative solutions been considered?

❑ Are any additional resources or checklists necessary?

❑ Has progress been made toward the goals?

Originally published in a slightly different form in *Parent's Guide to the SAT & ACT* (Lawrenceville, NJ: Peterson's, 2005), 27–133. Reprinted by permission of the authors.

· NOTES

NOTES